Disunion!

THE LITTLEFIELD HISTORY
OF THE CIVIL WAR ERA

Gary W. Gallagher and T. Michael Parrish, editors

Supported by the Littlefield Fund for Southern History, University of Texas Libraries

Elizabeth R. Varon

Disunion!

THE COMING OF THE
AMERICAN CIVIL WAR,
1789–1859

The University of North Carolina Press   CHAPEL HILL

© 2008 The University of North Carolina Press
All rights reserved

Designed by Courtney Leigh Baker
and set in Bodoni and Bulmer by Keystone Typesetting, Inc.
Manufactured in the United States of America

Library of Congress Cataloging-in-Publication Data
Varon, Elizabeth R., 1963–
Disunion! : the coming of the American Civil War, 1789–1859 / Elizabeth R. Varon.
p. cm. — (The Littlefield history of the Civil War era)
Includes bibliographical references and index.
ISBN 978-0-8078-3232-5 (cloth: alk. paper)
1. United States—Politics and government—1783–1865. 2. United States—Politics
and government—1783–1865—Sources. 3. Sectionalism (United States)—History.
4. Sectionalism (United States)—History—Sources. 5. United States—History—Civil War,
1861–1865—Causes. 6. Slavery—Political aspects—United States—History. 7. Antislavery
movements—United States—History. 8. Rhetoric—Political aspects—United States—History
I. Title.
E302.1.V37 2008
973.7′11—dc22

A Caravan book. For more information, visit www.caravanbooks.org

12 11 10 09 08   5 4 3 2 1

FOR MY FATHER

BENSION

Contents

Acknowledgments xi
Introduction 1
Prologue 17

PART I. 1789-1836

1

The Language of Terrifying Prophecy:
Disunion Debates in the Early Republic 31

2

We Claim Our Rights: The Advent of Abolitionism 55

3

Ruinous Tendencies: The Anti-Abolition Backlash 87

PART II. 1837-1850

4

The Idea Will Become Familiar:
Disunion in the Era of Mass Party Politics 127

5

Oh for a Man Who Is a *Man*: Debating Slavery's Expansion 165

6

That Is Revolution!: The Crisis of 1850 199

PART III. 1851–1859

7

Beneath the Iron Heel: Fugitive Slaves and Bleeding Kansas 235

8

To Consummate Its Boldest Designs:
The Slave Power Confronts the Republicans 273

9

War to the Knife: Images of the Coming Fight 305

EPILOGUE

The Rubicon Is Passed: The War and Beyond 337

Notes 349
Bibliography 401
Index 431

Illustrations

ETCHING: "The Hartford Convention or Leap No Leap,"
ca. 1814 38

ENGRAVING: William Lloyd Garrison, 1885 71

CARTOON: ".00001," 1831 88

LITHOGRAPH: "The Fugitive's Song," 1845 101

CARTOON: "Abolition Frowned Down," 1839 112

LITHOGRAPH: "Destruction by Fire of Pennsylvania Hall," 1838 135

CARTOON: "The Almighty Lever," 1840 142

LITHOGRAPH: Joseph Cinqué, "The Brave Congolese Chief,"
ca. 1839 156

CARTOON: "Anti Annexation Procession," 1844 170

CARTOON: "The Hurly-Burly Pot," 1850 218

LITHOGRAPH: "A Dream Caused by the Perusal of
Mrs. H. Beecher Stowe's Popular Work Uncle Tom's Cabin," ca. 1853 247

CARTOON: "Experiments on the Tight Rope," 1852 250

CARTOON: " 'Buck' Taking the 'Pot,' " 1856 276

Acknowledgments

As I wrote this book I benefited immeasurably from the sage advice of friends and colleagues. Keith Poulter was the first one to read the whole manuscript draft through—and his keen eye caught and corrected many infelicities of style and substance. Richard Newman and David Waldstreicher read the sections on the early republic and provided me with a wealth of insights and suggestions; they have helped me, as has my affiliation with the Society for Historians of the Early American Republic, appreciate just how crucial the "founding" decades are to understanding sectional tensions between North and South.

I owe my greatest editorial debt to Gary W. Gallagher and T. Michael Parrish, the Littlefield series editors, whose careful and generous attention to my manuscript modeled just how peer review, ideally, should work. Their comments, along with those of an anonymous "outside" reader, opened up new analytic vistas for me and charted a course for my revisions. I thank Stevie Champion for her thorough copyediting of the manuscript. And UNC Press editor-in-chief David Perry gracefully guided me through the publication process.

My colleagues at Temple University, too, shaped this book; working alongside them has made me a better and happier historian. I am especially grateful to two successive department chairs, Richard Immerman and Drew Isenberg, and to our former dean, Susan Herbst, for their support.

Thanks to the city of Philadelphia's matchless historical resources, it was a pleasure to research this book. I relied on the kind offices and expert assistance of the staffs of Temple's Paley Library and its Charles L. Blockson Afro-American Collection, the Historical Society of Pennsylvania, the Library Company of Philadelphia, the University of Pennsylvania's Van Pelt Library, the Civil War and Underground Railroad Museum, and the Friends' Historical Library of Swarthmore College. I had productive stints at the New York Public Library and the Wellesley College Rare Book Collection as well. And I thank Temple's reference librarian for history, David Murray, for introducing this former technophobe to the vast universe of electronic databases, and my research assistant, Valerie Buickerood, for helping me track down some key documents.

My husband, Will Hitchcock, and our children, Ben and Emma, have been so unfailingly delightful that I never lost heart, even when the challenges of writing this book seemed most daunting. They are each working day's sweet reward.

Will and my brother Jeremy helped me find the right words to frame this project, and I feel so fortunate that we have our own little family writers' circle. Our guiding spirit is my father Bension, to whom I dedicate this book. Since my mother Barbara passed away, his strength and joie de vivre have, more than ever, inspired and sustained me. He lives, as my family does, in the warm glow of my mother's love—and for me, she lives on in him. Thank you, Dad—for everything.

E.R.V.

WYNNEWOOD, PA.

Disunion!

Introduction

"Folly and wickedness are inherent proclivities of human nature." So began an editorial in the influential *Philadelphia North American*, published in January 1849, a time of bitter debates over whether slavery should extend into the Western territories the United States had claimed at the end of the Mexican War. Entitled "Union or Disunion—Life or Death," the editorial condemned proslavery Southerners who threatened to dissolve the Union if slavery's expansion were restricted. Disunion, the commentary warned, would bring "an almost immediate war, of the most deadly character" between the slave states and the free ones, a war "of treason on the one side, and of vengeance on the other." Civil war would soon give rise to a second kind of "mortal struggle": a "universal insurrection . . . of slaves against their masters" that would bathe the country in "flames and massacre." The prospect of such a descent into chaos, the editorial lamented, "makes the heart sick." Pleading for moderation and compromise, it concluded by saying of disunion: "Wo [*sic*] to the American, whether of the North or the South, who compels his countrymen to think such thoughts and dream such dreams."[1]

This book argues that "disunion" was once the most provocative and potent word in the political vocabulary of Americans. From the time of the Constitutional Convention in 1787 up to the Civil War, *disunion* conjured up the most profound anxieties of Americans as they considered the fate of their republic. This one word contained, and stimulated, their fears of extreme political factionalism, tyranny, regionalism, economic decline, foreign intervention, class conflict, gender disorder, racial strife, widespread violence and anarchy, and civil war, all of which could be interpreted as God's retributions for America's moral failings. Disunion connoted the dissolution of the republic—the failure of the Founders' efforts to establish a stable and lasting representative government. For many Americans in the North and the South, disunion was a nightmare, a tragic cataclysm that would reduce them to the kind of fear and misery that seemed to pervade the rest of the world. And yet, for many other Americans, disunion served as the main instrument by which they could achieve their political goals.

Can it be that such a word, so strange sounding and archaic to modern ears, had such a power over the imagination of antebellum Americans? This book makes the argument that it did, and indeed suggests that disunion—both the word and the varying meanings that nineteenth-century Americans assigned it—offers a new and hitherto hidden key to understanding the origins of the American Civil War. Disunion was, like freedom, slavery, democracy, and tyranny, a *keyword* of the nation's political vocabulary—a word that had no fixed "content," that captured complex ideas and values, and that served as a site for protracted moral, political, and economic conflicts in a deeply and multiply divided nation.[2] Debates over the meaning of disunion constituted a rhetorical mode that dominated antebellum politics and that gave sectional tensions an unmanageable cast. That is, disunion rhetoric shaped and limited Americans' political and moral imagination, ultimately discouraging a politics of compromise and lending an aura of inexorability to the cataclysmic confrontation of North and South.

Naturally, the argument that follows does not push to one side the long-standing, time-tested explanations for the origins of the Civil War, such as those concerning demographics, economics, ideology, culture, and least of all slavery. Rather, the analysis presented here offers a new way to look, literally, at the terms of the debate that pulled the Union apart. In what follows, we will analyze what the participants said, what they believed, and how they expressed their own passions, and agonies, as they set the Union on the road to war.

To place this new approach into some context, it is worth briefly recalling the ways that previous scholars have tried to explain the origins of the Civil War. The economic interpretation for the coming of the war was pioneered by Charles A. and Mary R. Beard, whose 1927 book *The Rise of American Civilization* argued that the because the economies of the dynamic industrializing North and the static agrarian South were incompatible, the two societies were on a collision course that led inexorably to war; issues such as banking, tariffs, and subsidies, not debates over the morality of slavery, divided the two sections. Arguing against the notion that armed conflict was inevitable, James G. Randall and Avery O. Craven, writing in the 1930s and 1940s, countered that irrational and irresponsible agitators in each section—abolitionists in the North and secessionists in the South—inflamed popular passions and prejudices and thus caused a "needless war." Slavery did divide the nation, but it should not have—the "peculiar institution" would have faded away naturally had blundering politicians not brought on its violent demise.[3]

This debate over whether the war was "irrepressible" or "repressible" has raged on in the modern day, with scholars aligned in two interpretive camps—the "fundamentalist" and the new "revisionist." Fundamentalists build on the work of W. E. B. Du Bois, the great black historian and champion of the "emancipationist" memory of the war. Taking issue with the Beards' approach and with the "blundering generation" school alike, Du Bois tirelessly insisted, in countless speeches, articles, and books, that slavery was the root cause and emancipation the noble purpose of the war. For Du Bois, the Civil War was not only a clash of economic systems but also a war of ideas and ideologies (systems of thought). With careful attention to both the economies and the ideologies of North and South, modern "fundamentalists" such as James M. McPherson, Eric Foner, Bertram Wyatt-Brown, Bruce Levine, John Ashworth, Brian Holden Reid, and Sean Wilentz have described the two sections as different and deeply antagonistic societies; all agree that slavery was the root cause of that antagonism. The North's commitment to capitalism and modernization, these scholars explain, was the context for abolitionism and for the free labor ideology of Abraham Lincoln's Republican Party. The South's commitment to staple production and slave labor was reflected in the region's distinctive cult of honor, its preoccupation with localism and states' rights, and its defense of social inequality.[4]

"Modern revisionists," for their part, have followed the lead of Kenneth Stampp and David M. Potter. Trying to recapture the contingencies, possibilities, and volatility of antebellum politics, Stampp and Potter emphasized the shared values of North and South and lamented the failure of political leaders to reach compromises that might have averted war. More recently, revisionists like Michael F. Holt, William E. Gienapp, William W. Freehling, and Joel H. Silbey have focused on those political debates *within* each section that do not fit neatly into a linear narrative of the slavery controversy. Northern voters, political historians have shown, were preoccupied with and motivated by issues such as nativism (anti-immigrant bias); slavery was not their overriding concern and did not explain their voting behavior. The Southern electorate, too, was deeply divided—on the basis of class, economic setting, and sub-region. The differences between the Upper South and the Deep South in particular make it treacherous to generalize broadly about the "fundamental" nature of Southern society.[5]

As Edward Ayers has put it, succinctly, "for the fundamentalists, slavery is front and center; for the revisionists, slavery is buried beneath layers of white ideology and politics." His own recent book—a careful comparison of a Pennsylvania county in the Shenandoah Valley with a nearby Virginia county—has straddled the line between fundamentalists and revisionists. On the one hand, Ayers demonstrates that the presence of slavery in the Virginia county rendered it fundamentally different, economically, socially, and politically, from the "free labor" Pennsylvania county. On the other hand, seeking to understand the war's origins on an "intimate scale," he emphasizes that average citizens did not see the war as irrepressible—up to the very end, they sought alternatives. Acknowledging the difficulty of breaking free of the fundamentalist/revisionist dichotomy, Ayers has called on historians to look anew for "catalysts" of sectionalism.[6] In other words, while scholars can agree that slavery, more than any other issue, divided North and South, there is still much to be said about why slavery proved so divisive and why sectional compromise ultimately proved elusive.

This book takes up Ayers's challenge. It aims both to provide a narrative synthesis of the best recent studies on antebellum America and to reframe the issue of Civil War causality. Inspired by scholars who have argued that language has a profound power to shape political reality, this book asks: Why could Americans not debate the fate of slavery without also conjuring up the notion of disunion?[7]

To answer this question, we must begin by recognizing the profound resonance of the concept of "Union" for Americans before the Civil War. For them, the word "Union" connoted "nation" and "country," and called to mind the geographic, linguistic, cultural, and historical bonds that held America's citizenry together. The Union was also the government, as it embodied the constitutional arrangement whereby individual states compacted with each other in a federal system. Most fundamentally, the Union was synonymous with the republic—America's unique experiment in self-rule "by the people." Although the Union existed on all these levels, it was for most Americans more, symbolically, than the sum of these parts: it had a transcendent, mystical quality as the object of their patriotic devotion and civic religion. No one in antebellum America did more to articulate these prevailing beliefs than clergyman and politician Edward Everett, of Massachusetts, who drew admiring audiences in North and South alike with his vast array of speeches on patriotic themes. A voice of conservative nationalism, Everett made a name for himself as the country's greatest orator by singing the praises of the Founders. The Union, he proclaimed again and again, was the "most auspicious mode" of "popular government" ever devised. It was "set up by Providence, as a great exemplar to the world, from which the most enlightened and best governed of the ancient nations have much to learn." Bound up in the Union were "all the feelings of ancestry, posterity, and fellow citizenship; all the charm, veneration, and love" that Americans felt for each other; and all the "delight, the enthusiasm, with which we seek out, after the lapse of generations and ages, the traces of our fathers' bravery and wisdom."[8]

The word "disunion" was so jarring because it suggested that the beloved Union might be contingent—and even fatally flawed. And yet disunion was pervasive in antebellum rhetoric among Northerners and Southerners alike. Disunion was invoked by Americans, across the political spectrum, in five registers: as a *prophecy* of national ruin, a *threat* of withdrawal from the federal compact, an *accusation* of treasonous plotting, a *process* of sectional alienation, and a *program* for regional independence. These five registers were distinct but overlapping, and while their uses changed and shifted over time, none of the five was ever fully drowned out by any of the others; predictions, accusations, and intimations of disunion were woven together in a kind of siren's song of civil war.

Because disunion had such a wide range of meanings, it is misleading to conflate it, as most scholarship on Civil War origins does, with another key word of the sectional conflict: "secession." Secession referred to a specific mechanism whereby states could leave the Union, and it reflected complex constitutional theories on the boundaries of state and federal power. Threats of secession flared up periodically at flash points of crisis—during the Hartford Convention in 1814, the nullification controversy in 1832–33, and the Nashville Convention in 1850, for example—but they issued from political leaders too isolated to translate them into viable programs. Only in the wake of John Brown's 1859 raid at Harpers Ferry were Southern nationalists able to convert calls for secession into a regional mandate—and to put the mechanism to the test.

While secession had a specific meaning, disunion by contrast was a sublimely adaptable concept and thus could be put to a stunning range of uses. What follows are illustrative definitions that introduce some key figures from the era and hint at how the rhetoric of disunion evolved.

DISUNION AS A PROPHECY

From the time of the Constitutional Convention, public debates over slavery featured prophecies of disunion. It must be emphasized that to prophesize disunion was not the same as to advocate it as a program. Indeed, such predictions typically came from those whose avowed goal was to preserve and redeem the Union. Self-styled political moderates, trying to define a pro-compromise "middle ground" in the slavery debates, warned that the nation faced ruin if extremists did not stop "agitating" the divisive issue. But opponents of slavery, too, prophesized that the nation faced ruin if it did not curb the political dominance of slaveholders and repent of the sin of human bondage. Defenders of slavery, for their part, predicted that the nation faced ruin if antislavery zealots disturbed the sectional balance of power and encouraged unrest among the slaves. In many of these variations, disunion was seen as the instrumentality wielded by an angry God to punish the unfaithful.

To predict disunion, at a time when Americans were steeped in biblical language and traditions, was to call to mind a distinct set of images: a prophet was, according to Western tradition, a "voice in the wilderness" seeking to "reassert the terms of the covenant to a people who had fallen away."[9] In antebellum American politics, prophecies of disunion were meant to alert the people that they had betrayed the promise that they would erect a shining "City on a Hill" as a moral beacon for the world, and had betrayed the constitutional covenant on which the security of the nation rested.

The language of prophecy was the language of metaphors—for it was the prophet's job to open the people's eyes to the overwhelming threat that faced them if they did not restore the covenant.[10] Disunion talk thus took the form of a startling range of images. Antebellum Americans likened disunion to a deformity, a disease, a monster, a storm, a sea, a whip, an arrow, a poison, a fire, a spell, and a curse. Those politicians who wielded the language of prophecy most effectively—Northerner Daniel Webster and Southerner Henry Clay—won reputations in the 1830s as great compromisers and mediators between the sections; both became national celebrities, widely respected for their oratorical skills and their patriotism. To these men, disunion could be avoided only if Americans were made, again and again, to imagine it in apocalyptic terms. For Webster, disunion was a "precipice" that looked out over a groaning "abyss" of civil war. Clay, too, favored this metaphor; he repeatedly asked Americans to "pause at the edge of the precipice, before the fearful and dangerous leap to be taken into the yawning abyss below, from which none who ever take it shall return in safety." As the antebellum era unfolded, Northern and Southern interpretations of the moral mandate of American society, and of the nature of the constitutional covenant, would sharply diverge—leaving Clay and Webster, in the eyes of their critics, forsaken martyrs who had sacrificed their reputations and integrity to the cause of compromise.[11]

DISUNION AS A THREAT

From the birth of the republic to the Civil War, disunion was frequently invoked as a threat, most often by Southerners seeking to preserve and extend slavery, but also eventually by radical abolitionists looking for a language in which to counter Southern menaces. These threats had their own distinct context in the cult of honor. In the absence of well-established political parties, the political combat of the early republic was highly personalized. Regional differences and distrust between North and South often translated into "honor disputes"—verbal assaults in which politicians questioned each others' manhood and "bullied and taunted" each other into submission. Threats of disunion were a key weapon in this sort of combat as a tactic of intimidation. Proslavery partisans repeatedly threatened disunion in an effort to establish their superior courage and to bully their opponents into making concessions. A few Northern advocates of slavery restriction responded in kind, claiming to prefer disunion to submission and hoping to use the threat to extract concessions from the slaveholding South. Those who introduced this congressional pattern of threat and counterthreat in the early republic were not seriously contemplating secession as a program, nor did they claim to speak on behalf of disunionist constituents. They sought to control the government, not to sever it. By invoking disunion as the prelude to civil war and then implying that such a war would be worth fighting, wielders of the threat practiced a kind of parliamentary maneuvering—they used fear as a political weapon. Northerners and Southerners who disapproved of this posturing worried that it would somehow prepare the public mind for the unraveling of the republic; they tried to silence the threats with the argument that disunion was the ultimate form of national dishonor.[12]

When Northern abolitionists launched their campaign for immediate emancipation in the 1830s, Southern threats multiplied and took on, especially among South Carolina nullifiers, ominous new forms. The master of such threats was the preening, relentless Robert Barnwell Rhett, who in a "clear, high-pitched voice" routinely "scorched" his listeners with fiery invective. More than anyone else, Rhett used disunion as a battle standard with which to rally defenders of slavery. "The whole world are in arms against your institutions," he told his fellow South Carolinians in 1833 as he urged the state to "nullify" the federal tariff and thereby resist the "tyranny" of a federal government hostile to the South's economic interests. Such posturing failed to win over most South Carolinians, let alone most white Southerners. But it did wring concessions from the North—in this case, a reduction of the tariff, brokered by "great compromisers" Henry Clay and Daniel Webster. In the 1840s Rhett began wielding threats not merely to secure tactical gains for slaveholders in their effort to assert power within national politics, but as a strategy for building a secessionist constituency, first in South Carolina and then throughout the region. Along with a vanguard of proslavery, states' rights fire-eaters, Rhett was determined to move disunion threats from the realm of pure rhetoric to the realm of stark realism.[13]

By the early 1840s, slaveholder threats had so often wrought compromises from Northern politicians and lawmakers that William Lloyd Garrison and his cadre of radical abolitionists declared themselves disunionists and threatened to foment disunionism in the North. At this point Garrison's followers— Northerners who demanded the immediate abolition of Southern slavery and spoke out on behalf of equal rights for whites and blacks—still constituted a small, beleaguered group on the fringes of political power; Garrison was under no illusion that any Northern state, even his own Massachusetts, would seriously consider secession. But Garrison was a passionate man, and he was passionately sick of watching the North accede to Southern demands. Thus his mantra of "no union with slaveholders" was a consciousness-raising tool. It was shorthand for a complicated argument that a truly moral Union had never existed—and that the sham Union, based on compromises with slavery, had to be forsaken before a true Union could ever exist.[14] This argument was a reaction not only to slaveholder threats, but also to accusations by Northerners targeting abolitionists like Garrison.

DISUNION AS AN ACCUSATION

From the time the immediatists took the stage in the 1830s, the primary obstacle facing them was the widespread charge that their antislavery program was inherently disunionist. This charge was the pretext for the violent suppression of abolitionist activity in the South; for abolition-disunion, slaveholders argued, would inevitably lead to slave rebellion. Abolitionists met with a furious backlash in the North as well. By forming interracial abolition societies and encouraging women to take a leading part in the antislavery movement, immediatists challenged the Northern social hierarchy. Lashing out against the racial and gender egalitarianism of radical antislavery societies, anti-abolitionists associated disunionism with the dreaded specters of racial equality and "woman's rights." Most important, anti-abolitionists contrasted the harmony and prosperity that awaited the Union, should abolition agitation cease, with the grim prospect of a bloody civil war brought on by immediatism and the attendant alienation of the South. Immediatists responded with a variety of interlocking arguments: that slavery, not abolition, was the root of sectional tensions; that Southern threats of disunion were not serious; and that the white South was not united in its support of slavery. But their critics did not relent: determined to associate abolition with treason, Northern anti-abolitionists persistently and willfully exaggerated the potency of Southern threats. They hoped that the image of an angry South turning its back on the Union would scare Northerners into rejecting both the emancipation of Southern slaves and the abolitionists' radical agenda for promoting social equality in the North.

While Garrisonians adopted in the early 1840s their own defiant disunionism, a new "political antislavery" movement in the North, intent on establishing a viable political party, promised that it would stand firm against Southern threats and against abolitionist extremism. In their own vocabulary of accusations, the activists who formed the core of the three successive antislavery parties—Liberty, Free-Soil, and Republican—placed the primary blame for the sectional crisis on the shoulders of the "Slave Power Conspiracy" of elite Southern masters and their malleable, subservient "doughface" allies among Northern Democrats. They charged that the small oligarchy of slaveholders who had dominated national politics and, increasingly, the three branches of the federal government, were determined to augment their power by spreading slavery into the Western territories—and that this affront to democracy would rob white Northerners of the right to establish the West as "free soil." The standard-bearer for this position was David Wilmot, a Pennsylvania Democrat who in 1846 repudiated his party's traditional alliance with the slaveholding interests of the South and offered to Congress his famous "proviso" that slavery should be barred from the Western territories acquired after the Mexican War. The proviso came with a stern rebuke to slaveholders for using the "cry of disunion" to appeal to people's fears and emotions. Although it failed to pass Congress, the proviso signaled the determination of the emerging Free-Soil coalition not to be "frightened into obedience," as Wilmot put it, by Southern intimidation.[15]

The Republicans took the stage in the mid-1850s promising not to interfere with slavery where it already existed; they wanted only to restrict its westward expansion. But no matter how hard the antislavery parties worked to establish their credentials as protectors of the Union against militant slaveholders, their opponents—the Democrats' conservative base—assailed them as disunionist. The use of disunion as an accusation among Northerners reached a crescendo in 1856, as the Democratic Party bludgeoned the Republicans with the charge that they were abolitionists in disguise; a Republican victory, it maintained, would bring national ruin. This strategy came from none other than the Democratic presidential candidate, James Buchanan of Pennsylvania. A "northern man with southern principles," Buchanan believed that the "Republicans must be, as they can be with justice, boldly assailed as disunionists and this charge must be reiterated again and again." This proved to be an efficacious tactic, in part because it tapped long-standing fears about the fate of the Union, and in part because the Republicans made themselves vulnerable, time and time again, by invoking disunion as a process.[16]

The notion that disunion was a process of sectional alienation took root, North and South, in the mid-1830s. The antislavery petition campaign of 1835–36—a grassroots effort that garnered the support of thousands of Northern citizens—furnished proslavery Southerners with the raw material to make, for the first time in the sectional debates, the case that disunion was a trend in public opinion. This was not the language of divine retribution or of impassioned honor but rather of a crude political science; to speak of disunion as a process was to regard the free labor North and slave labor South as political systems, and to reveal their internal dynamics. The most influential mouthpiece of this idea was John C. Calhoun of South Carolina. Calhoun was the mastermind of "nullification"—the notion that a state could void a federal law it regarded as unconstitutional, then appeal to a tribunal of the other states to amend the law, and finally, if the law were not amended, legally secede from the Union. He was also a leading proponent of the philosophy that slavery was a "positive good" for slaves and slaveholders alike. Thus Calhoun has earned a reputation as the godfather of secession. But Calhoun was no Robert Barnwell Rhett, given to extravagant threats. Calhoun regarded nullification as a means to "strengthen the Union, though not the federal government, by improving the chances that conflicts of sections or interests could be compromised or resolved peacefully." He invoked disunion as a way to systematically build a Southern proslavery consensus impervious to Northern interference. Thus he chose, during the height of the abolition petition campaign, to exaggerate the influence of the abolitionists; although they were not yet a controlling majority, he argued, abolitionists very soon would capture the hearts and minds of the North. This image of Northern solidarity was calculated to foster Southern solidarity. Calhoun again and again insisted that the sectional divergence need not sunder the Union—provided the South was strong enough to resist Northern interference and therefore to maintain the balance of power that the framers had intended.[17]

Antislavery forces, for their part, also regarded disunion as a process. In the 1830s, before they could lay claim to a Northern majority, they emphasized that sectional alienation was driven by Slave Power demands. By the late 1840s, political antislavery advocates could argue that Northern public opinion had coalesced around a Free-Soil agenda at odds with slaveholder designs on the West. That divergence need not sunder the Union, Free-Soilers like Wilmot explained, provided that the South yield to the growing Free-Soil electorate. If the alienation of North and South could not be reversed, it could still be forestalled and contained; compromise and sectional "repose" were still possible.

When Southern and Northern settlers came to blows over the Fugitive Slave Law and the Kansas Territory, however, the process of sectional alienation took on a fearful new cast. In the early 1850s, with Clay, Webster, and Calhoun all having passed from the scene, the two sections seemed not to be diverging but to be violently converging; images of warfare, of invasion, and even of annihilation suffused the public debates over slavery, and reached their apogee in New York Republican William Seward's 1858 "irrepressible conflict" speech. The politically ambitious Seward had a penchant for introducing memorable turns of phrase that instantly became part of the political vernacular. So it was with his notion of an "irrepressible conflict." The process of disunion, he argued, could not and regardless should not be reversed or contained. Yes, the South should yield to the Free-Soil majority— but because the very nature of slaveholding society was aggressive, it would and could not. Thus the irrepressible conflict was leading to a final reckoning, an epic clash in which Freedom would triumph over Slavery.

In invoking disunion as a process that would end in violent conflict, Seward and other commentators were not simply describing trends but interpreting them. Statistically and culturally, the North and South were actually, in many respects, becoming more similar in the 1850s. The South was modernizing, its cities growing and industries rapidly developing. Moreover, "intersectional migration, the exchange of information through newspapers and magazines, travel, and even kinship ties" were all potential sources of peaceful convergence between the sections. But because Southern boosters of modernization were increasingly determined to use slave labor as the basis of the region's industries, Northerners perceived in the new Southern economy the threat of competition rather than the promise of reconciliation.[18]

Militant Southern slaveholders such as Rhett, in trying to foster "Southern nationalism," capitalized at every turn on Northern disunion rhetoric. Honing arguments they had developed over the course of the 1850s, Southern extremists drew a distinction between Northern disunionism (which they equated with an unconstitutional assault on Southern rights) and their own disunionism (which they equated with the constitutional right of secession). In their view, Republicans like Seward, by advancing the process of disunion, were betraying their true desire: to force the South to secede and then to use secession as the pretext for a war of conquest in which emancipation would be imposed at bayonet point. John Brown's raid of 1859, a failed attempt to liberate Virginia's slaves that captured the imagination of many Northerners, was interpreted by Southern nationalists as the fruit of Seward's irrepressible conflict speech. They claimed, in other words, that Northern disunion caused Southern secession—that Northern abolitionist Republicans, in their uncompromising campaign to destroy the Southern way of life, had left the region's leaders no honorable resort but to secede. The heart of the secessionist argument was this: If the South were divided, weak and uncertain, Republicans would prosecute a war that brought all the horrors Americans had long associated with disunion—a war of chaos and massacre. But if the South were united and strong, it could control the outcome of disunion—it could quickly and decisively turn back the Northern invasion and build, in the form of a new nation, an impenetrable bulwark against future aggression.

As America lurched into the secession crisis, the Republican administration of Abraham Lincoln pledged to resist the Confederacy. Secession, Lincoln declared in his first inaugural address, was a rejection of the very principle of majority rule; it could produce only "anarchy" or "despotism." For Lincoln, whatever the secessionists might claim, disunion as a program was patently unconstitutional and a betrayal of the Founders' design. Southerners were the aggressors; they had chosen to bring the nation to the brink. If Confederates could banish fears that a disunion war would cause suffering and ruin, and imagine instead that such a war would bring swift victory to the righteous, then Northerners must do the same. The president had an "oath registered in Heaven," he intoned, to "preserve, protect and defend" the

Union. His message was unmistakable: the Union was perpetual, and the righteous would prevail.[19]

Lincoln was, of course, not only staking out a political position, but also expressing the hope that once the rebellion was defeated, the cacophonous and discordant debates over disunion would end forever. A prescient *Atlantic Monthly* editorial of August 1861, which sought to explain the origins of secession, captured this hope perfectly. Secessionists had "long meditated" the present conflict, the commentary intoned, and had steadily brought it to its "final consummation" by cannily making the "vocabulary of treason" the "vernacular of the country. . . . The danger of a dissolution of the Union . . . has so often been held up as a threat by one section, and so persistently used as a scarecrow by timid or profligate men in the other, that our ears have hardly ceased to be tormented" by disunion talk. Thus the linguistic stakes of the war were enormous. "It is time that this whole pernicious dialect should be exploded," the editorial concluded, "and the ideas which it represented be eradicated from the minds of intelligent men everywhere."[20]

THIS BOOK OFFERS a new perspective on Civil War causality by arguing that disunion was a far more pervasive concept than secession in antebellum politics, that debates over the meaning of disunion permeated the political cultures of both North and South and embittered each section against the other, and that those debates reached back to the very founding of the republic. What united the various kinds of disunion talk into what I have called a "rhetorical mode" was their shared tendency to create political "others"—an "us," defined as true Americans who upheld the principles of the Founders, and a "them," defined as traitors who betrayed those principles.

In arguing that disunion rhetoric—not just the threats, but the disavowals, condemnations, predictions, and expectations of disunion—worked at every stage to escalate sectional tensions, I have no wish to revive the tired, threadbare, "blundering generation" argument that blamed fanatical political leaders on both sides for starting a "needless war." The original proponents of that thesis suggested that there was a kind of equivalency between the extremism of radical abolitionists and that of proslavery secessionists. Indeed, some of them, echoing antebellum accusations of disunion, contended that abolitionists bore not only a share of the blame for the coming of war, but also the brunt of the blame. In this book, by contrast, radical abolitionists are not the villains of the sectional drama but the heroes. In 1878 the great black abolitionist Frederick Douglass wrote: "There was a right side and a wrong side in the late war, which no sentiment ought to cause us to forget, and while to-day we should have malice toward none, and charity toward all, it is no part of our duty to confound right with wrong."[21] What is true of the Civil War is true, too, of the antebellum war of words.

My purpose is to elucidate that war of words. In an effort to understand the most influential participants in that struggle, I focus not only on politicians such as Calhoun and Seward but also on a wide range of reformers, editors, writers, and commentators. The voices of fugitive slaves, of white Southern dissenters, of free black activists, of abolitionist women, and of other outsiders to the halls of power are integral to the history of sectionalism. Abolitionists like Garrison and Douglass occupy the central place in this book's narrative both because of the incisive and trenchant nature of their political analyses, and because their enemies worked relentlessly to keep them front and center in the slavery debates. Even when Garrison took his disunionist turn in the 1840s, and in a sense exiled himself to the margins of Northern politics, his proslavery enemies kept up the drumbeat of accusations that all antislavery supporters were disunionists. In other words, however hard immediatists tried to distinguish true abolitionism from gradual emancipation (with its emphasis on piecemeal, voluntary reform), and from Free-Soil political antislavery (with its faith in the electoral process), anti-abolitionists denied that there was a meaningful distinction between these varieties of opposition to slavery. To promote solidarity in their own ranks, defenders of slavery exaggerated the power and influence of radical abolitionists, even as the moderate Free-Soilers built a base of support in the North that far exceeded that of the immediatists.[22]

By the early 1830s—the pivotal moment at which immediate abolitionists clashed with proponents of the "positive good" defense of slavery—the discourse on disunion was a half-century old. If we view U.S. history in an international context, it was much older than that: Americans' disunion anxieties were shaped by Enlightenment writings on the inevitable decline of republics into tyranny, by the events of the English civil war and the French Revolution, and by the intrigues and strife of the European monarchies. Indeed, Americans' "sense of impending doom" reflected their fear, itself a legacy of the European Enlightenment, that "greed and lust for power . . .

were unquenchable in mortal men."[23] To say that Calhoun, Garrison, and the other opinion makers of the era inherited the discourse of disunion, and moved in its web, is not to deny their agency, but to better understand their choices. Defenders of slavery marshaled disunion, in all its guises, to justify the suppression of free speech and the perpetuation of human bondage. Opponents of slavery marshaled disunion, in all its guises, to defend democracy —and to promote imperfect visions, and irrepressible dreams, of freedom.

Did the antebellum discourse of disunion "cause" the Civil War? No. "Union and Disunion are but words—the *thing* is slavery," Douglass insisted in 1852, anguished at how the dread of national ruin cast a shadow over the prospect of abolition. Douglass emphasized that slavery was the root cause of sectional differences. He attempted to convince Northerners that the use of disunion for political advantage should not obscure the fact that a moral issue—slavery's sinfulness—was at the heart of the sectional crisis.[24] Disunion rhetoric did not make the war "inevitable." But it was more than a catalyst for political strife—it was an integral part of the course that strife took. Suffused as it was with images of treason, rebellion, retribution, and bloodshed, the discourse of disunion bred disillusionment with party politics; mistrust of compromise; and, in the 1850s, the expectation that only violent conflict would resolve the debate over slavery once and for all.

Prologue

The antislavery impulse was as old as the republic itself. So too were sectional tensions deriving from the diverging interests of the free labor North and the slaveholding South. By the eve of the American Revolution, slavery had existed in North America for more than 150 years; it was legal in every one of the thirteen colonies. But different patterns of settlement and different geographies distinguished the Northern colonies from the Southern ones and set them on different trajectories. Slavery was marginal to the economy of New England, which was "wedded to family and wage labor." It was pervasive in the middle colonies of New York, New Jersey, and Pennsylvania, but slave labor there was incorporated into a diverse economy; slaves worked in artisan shops, in the maritime industries, and on farms, alongside white and black indentured servants and wage workers. Slavery, in other words, was not the dominant form of labor in the North. The Southern colonies of Maryland, Virginia, the Carolinas, and Georgia, by contrast, were not merely societies with slaves but "slave societies," organized economically, socially, and politically around the principle and practice of human bondage. In 1760, 88 percent of the 325,806 slaves in the British mainland colonies lived in the South.[1]

Although the majority of white Southern families did not own slaves, the slaveholding minority, particularly the wealthy "planters" (those who owned twenty slaves or more and operated plantations), held the preponderance of power in the colonial South. In the deferential political culture of the region, wealth and, in plantation districts, slaveholding were the prerequisites for political leadership. The system of bondage defined black slaves as "chattels," pieces of property with few, tenuous rights. Slaves could not leave plantations without permission, could not buy or sell goods, could not have legally recognized marriages, could not claim authority over their own children. The separation, through sale, of slave families was commonplace;

so too was the rape of slave women by their masters. Slaves who defied their owners or the law were viciously punished—whipping, branding, and even mutilation were common penalties for misbehavior. The slave system, Anthony S. Parent forcefully argues, did not "emerge" as an "unplanned consequence of a scarce labor market." Rather, it was designed. In the period 1660 to 1740, a small class of ascendant planters in Virginia established the legal and ideological template for the development of slavery elsewhere in the colonies, and thereby "gave America its racial dilemma."[2]

The slave codes first established by seventeenth-century Virginia became the model for successive Southern states, and they reveal a great deal about slaveholders' anxieties and aims. Overturning traditions of English common law that stipulated that a child inherited the status of his father, the Southern slave codes provided that a child born to a slave mother would inherit his mother's status as a chattel—in this way, a master who coerced a female slave into sex stood to gain financially by his act, for any child born of it would be his slave. The slave codes not only rewarded masters for their coercion but also worked to prevent the growth of the free black population. Virginia and other colonies passed statutes that criminalized interracial sexual acts, but such laws were enforced selectively—the vast majority of those prosecuted under the Virginia law, for example, were white women who had had sexual relationships with black men; white men's interracial sexual misconduct went virtually unpunished. The system for policing sexuality was thus designed to "solidify the patriarchal stake of all white men in a slave system that offered the greatest benefits to large planters." Both wealthy planters and white men of lower status were guaranteed sexual access to black women and strict enforcement of the ban on interracial liaisons of white women.[3]

The system of law enforcement that developed in the South is documented by runaway notices that slaveholders ran in their newspapers: When a slave fled, the master typically printed a description of the fugitive and promised a reward for his or her capture and return. Thousands of these advertisements survive from the colonial era, and their descriptions of slaves with lashed backs, broken teeth, brand marks, cropped ears, and other deformities caused by deprivation or punishment testify to the conditions in which slaves lived. The work of tracking down fugitive slaves initially fell to private citizens and to sheriffs and militias. But by 1704 South Carolina had created a new category of law enforcement officials—slave patrollers—who tracked down fugitives, searched slave cabins for any sign of unrest, and broke up gatherings of slaves. Virginia and other Southern colonies followed suit. Eighteenth-century slave patrols drew on a broad cross section of white men, and patrol duty represented an opportunity for elite planters and men of modest means to collaborate across class boundaries. From the perspective of slaves, white patrollers were fearsome demons who embodied both white racial solidarity and white barbarity. Slave patrols' "indemnification and protection by courts of law allowed them to discipline, even brutalize, bondsmen with the legal imprimatur of Southern society."[4]

In addition to the laws and runaway notices they drafted, slaveholders have left behind "literary" sources, such as the diary of elite Virginia planter William Byrd II, that disclose the design of the slave system. Byrd's detailed account of his daily life remains one of the most revealing sources we have about the eighteenth-century Chesapeake Bay area. Byrd's diary shows that cruelty was routine in his household; in one particularly horrific episode, he recounts that, to punish his wife for whipping a slave named Prue without his permission, Byrd had another slave, named Anaka, whipped, "who had deserved it much more." Byrd also quarreled with his wife when she had a slave girl named Jenny "burned with a hot iron"—again, without his permission. Byrd's diary speaks both to the complicity of white plantation mistresses in the enforcement of the slave system and to the determination of planters to exert their supremacy over slaves and white women alike. In a 1736 letter, Byrd provided a pithy and chilling summation of his philosophy on the corporal punishment of slaves: "Foul Means must do, what fair will not."[5]

By the eve of the Revolution, then, nearly two centuries of law and custom had made slavery the foundation of the Southern economy and social order. Slaveholders did not, at this point, expend much energy in seeking to explain or justify their "peculiar institution." Rather, they rested secure in a long-standing set of assumptions that were not only dominant among Southern whites but widespread in the North, too. The first of those assumptions was that human society was, by God's design, hierarchical, with men of property and heads of households at the apex of the social pyramid. The second assumption was that both legal proscription and a certain amount of physical coercion were necessary for male patriarchs to enforce the submission of their dependents, be they wives, children, servants, or slaves; cruelty was, however lamentable, also necessary. The third assumption was that African slaves and their descendants were inferior; their lack of civilization rendered them unfit for freedom and suited them well for a life of dependence on whites, and for the backbreaking plantation labor that free white men could not be induced to perform. A fourth assumption was that slavery was not created by American slaveholders, but inherited by them from their English forebears. Thus slavery had the inevitability and sanctity of tradition.[6]

The ferment of the Revolutionary era posed a formidable challenge to these assumptions. "During the 1750s and early 1760s," David Waldstreicher explains, "Pennsylvania Quakers like John Woolman and Anthony Benezet had made significant headway against slavery on the grounds that the institution was inconsistent with Christian principles; by the late 1760s, however, Benezet broadened the argument to embrace contemporary politics." In other words, Benezet drew the analogy between British abrogation of the colonists' rights and the master's abrogation of the rights of slaves. This analogy was highly problematic for the emerging leaders of the Revolution, such as Benjamin Franklin, for it cast the aggrieved colonists as "hypocritical slave-drivers." Franklin himself devised a pragmatic solution. He redirected the analogy by training attention on British hypocrisy—reasoning that England was responsible for imposing slavery on the colonies, and that slavery was yet more "proof of British villainy." This view gained credence during the war, as British efforts to recruit American slaves, with the promise of freedom as an inducement, "only proved British corruption." The Declaration of Independence condemned the king for having incited "domestic insurrections" and enshrined the notion that slaves belonged with the "treasonous Tories" and therefore did not deserve citizenship or a place in the polity.[7]

But the analogy between American slavery and British tyranny, and the egalitarian implications of Thomas Jefferson's preamble to the Declaration, proved impossible to contain. Drawing on both the political philosophy of republicanism and the spiritual egalitarianism that undergirded the religious revivals of the First Great Awakening, free blacks such as the brilliant Boston poet Phillis Wheatley exposed the contradiction at the heart of the patriot cause: How could a country proclaim itself the beacon of freedom when it nurtured a system of human bondage? On the eve of the Revolution, slaves in Wheatley's native Massachusetts repeatedly petitioned the governor and house of representatives for emancipation, arguing that "we have in common with all other men a natural right to our freedoms." Free black militiamen staked a claim to these rights, fighting alongside white ones against the British in the opening engagements of the war, at Lexington and Concord. The upheavals of the war itself undermined slavery, as thousands of slaves fled their masters. With the British working to enlist such fugitives and the Continental army dangerously low in manpower, the Northern states recruited bondsmen as a way of complying with the federal draft. By war's end, more than five thousand blacks had rallied to the patriot cause as soldiers in the Continental army.[8]

In the wake of independence, Northern white leaders—confronting the erosion of slavery and the persistent pleas of free blacks for the redemption of their enslaved countrymen—adopted plans for emancipation. Not surprisingly, the abolition of slavery in the North proceeded most rapidly in those states least dependent on the institution. Slavery was liquidated quickly in northern New England but was only slowly dismantled, by formulas that gradually freed the slave population, in Connecticut, Rhode Island, Pennsylvania, and New York. The Pennsylvania law of 1780 decreed that slaves born after that date would win their freedom when they reached the age of twenty-eight, whereas those born before that date would remain forever in bondage; New York passed a similar law in 1799. A generation of "black founders," including free blacks Richard Allen of Philadelphia and William Hamilton of New York, promoted emancipation in their respective states—vigilance was required to ensure that masters actually released those legally eligible for freedom—and built the case for national emancipation. For example, Allen, the head of the African Methodist Episcopal Church, asked the nation's political leaders to follow the lead of George Washington, whose 1799 last will and testament decreed that his slaves would be emancipated when his wife Martha died. Slaves themselves, in places such as New York City, hastened the emancipation process and the demise of slavery by negotiating for their freedom, offering money or the promise of compliant service in exchange for "early" emancipation, before the law required it.[9]

In the tidewater areas of Maryland and Virginia, where generations of tobacco cultivation had eroded the soil, a transition was under way to plant fewer labor-intensive crops; thus masters there could serve both convenience and conscience by freeing their slaves. Washington's is the best-known such story, but the most remarkable is that of Richard Randolph. A young cousin of Jefferson's, Randolph took to heart the notion that "all men are endowed by their Creator with certain inalienable rights" and drafted a will in the early 1790s that not only liberated his bondspeople but also placed the blame for slavery squarely on the shoulders of his fellow Americans. His famous cousin's view that slavery was a "necessary evil" imposed on America by the British Randolph rejected as a "threadbare cover" for "the lust of power." Unlike contemporaries who freed slaves but insisted they emigrate from the South, Randolph set aside four hundred acres of his land for his former slaves to hold as their own property; free blacks did indeed establish a complex, resilient community—their own "Israel on the Appomattox"—on this bequest.[10]

According to the modern-day chronicler of the Israel Hill community, Melvin Ely, Randolph believed that slavery, with its power to corrupt all that touched it, had made "Tories" of the patriots themselves—they were traitors to their own cause. Randolph was unimpressed by the so-called wave of manumissions in the Upper South in this era. In Ely's words, "The 'wave,' though real, might better be called a substantial ripple when it is measured by the fraction of slaves who actually went free; Virginia remained by far the largest slaveholder among the states until bondage itself ended in 1865." The liberal burst of conscience on the part of some slaveholders, although it contributed to the growth of the free black population, did nothing to stem the advance of slavery. In fact, because the importation of slaves from Africa to the South continued unabated, and because so many Upper South masters preferred selling their slaves southward to manumitting them, slavery marched inexorably across the frontier and into the emerging "cotton kingdom" of the Deep South, leaving more blacks in bondage "at the end of the revolutionary age than at the beginning."[11]

SLAVERY, THE CONSTITUTION, AND DISUNION

Sectional antagonism shaped the Constitutional Convention of 1787. According to James Madison, the brilliant young nationalist from Virginia's planter class, the states differed "principally from the effects of their having or not having slaves"; the primary fault line lay between North and South. Sectionalism was inscribed in the actual blueprint of the new government, in the form of three provisions of the Constitution that were drafted in the name of compromise but became potent sources of controversy. The most important of these, the three-fifths compromise, stipulated that a state's tax burden and the size of its congressional and electoral college delegations would depend on the size of its population—namely, the number of free persons in the state plus "three fifths of all other persons." Here and elsewhere in the Constitution, the drafters consciously eschewed using the words "slave" or "slavery" in order to render the document acceptable to the North. Southern delegates had pressed to have slaves count as full persons when it came to tallying congressional representation; they regarded this as consistent with the fact that other dependent and subordinate groups—white women and children, and free blacks—were to count fully toward representation in the North and South alike. But the counting of Southern slaves as full persons struck some Northern delegates as patently hypocritical—if slaves were human enough to boost the representation of the Southern states, New Jersey's Gouverneur Morris declared, they should be treated as persons and not property in the South.[12]

The convention resolved this debate by resorting to the three-fifths formula. This compromise did not satisfy Morris. Although it gave the South *less* representation than its delegates demanded, the compromise fraction, according to Morris, still *exaggerated* Southern power—he deplored the notion that a Southern slaveholder would derive *any* votes in the Congress from the bodies he owned. Morris predicted that the three-fifths clause's real legacy would be to give slaveholders majority control over electoral politics. This interpretation would gain salience in the coming decades, though during the convention itself Morris's warning fell on deaf ears. Most Northern delegates accepted the three-fifths clause as a necessary compromise, insofar as slaves would count partially for both representation and taxation.[13]

The issue of the slave trade proved more divisive. Virginia and the states north of it wanted the African slave trade suppressed; by denouncing the commerce, Virginians could win points for compassion, knowing all the while that if foreign importations ceased, Virginia slaves would become more valuable. The delegations from the Carolinas and Georgia, by contrast, sought to have the slave trade protected. Establishing a pattern that would be endlessly repeated during the ensuing decades, South Carolinians took up the proslavery mantle and issued threats: delegates John Rutledge and Charles Cotesworth Pinckney said that South Carolina could not join the proposed Union if the slave trade were prohibited. These threats were experimental—a bid to see what concessions could be secured by uncompromising language. Neither man contemplated a separate Southern confederacy; indeed, both were committed Federalists who advocated and envisioned a strong national government dominated by Southern interests. Again the convention compromised, ruling that the slave trade would be guaranteed for another twenty years (following a motion by Pinckney to have the guarantee last until 1808, instead of 1800 as originally agreed upon in committee); after 1808 Congress could choose to renew or abolish the trade. Henry Weincek refers to the discomfort the convention's president, George Washington, must have felt as he watched the South Carolinians in action. Two years earlier Washington had confided to a friend that he could "foresee no evil greater than disunion," and now the "mere discussion of slavery" was poisoning the atmosphere. Washington followed the proceedings in silence, but his fellow Virginian, George Mason, gave voice to his fears. In a "moment of uncanny prescience," Mason railed against the "infernal traffic" of the slave trade and invoked disunion as divine retribution, warning that "as nations cannot be rewarded or punished in the next world, they must be in this. By an inevitable chain of causes and effects, Providence punishes national sins by national calamities."[14]

The last of the three major provisions on slavery sparked virtually no debate at the time of the convention. Worded vaguely so it could apply to apprentices as well as slaves, a clause requiring each state to extradite and deliver any fugitive from service to his or her master and state of origin passed with overwhelming support. Why was the North willing to concede so much? Northern supporters of the Constitution did not believe that the document defined slavery as constitutional; rather, at the time of the convention, the three slavery clauses "seemed to embody no ruling principle except compromise for the sake of union." Northern advocates of the Constitution naturally stressed its "antislavery potential" when speaking to their constituents, while Southern Federalists trumpeted its proslavery features in the South (Pinckney lauded the document to South Carolinians as unimpeachably proslavery). But the emphasis of Federalists, Northern and Southern, was on the equanimity and sanctity of the Constitution's compromises. It had to be, for Federalists were taken to task, during and after the convention, by those who maintained that the very formation of the Constitution was disunionist, as was the stipulation that only nine of thirteen states need ratify it to establish the Union. After all, the Constitution was dissolving the old Union of the

Articles of Confederation. Moreover, anti-Federalists such as James Winthrop of Massachusetts contended that centralization would lead to disunion, because an overbearing federal government would alienate the states. Federalists successfully countered this charge during the ratification debates by claiming that the old Union had already been undermined—the national government under the Articles of Confederation had not been strong enough to command the respect and compliance of the states, particularly with regard to raising revenue.[15]

Alexander Hamilton, of New York, an ardent nationalist whose political star was rising, addressed the issue of disunion by name in *The Federalist*, papers 6–8, enumerating potential sources of discord and division in a young republic. For Hamilton, Madison, and other Federalists, the disadvantages of disunion had been evident during the Confederation era and even during the Revolution itself. Shays' Rebellion of 1786, an armed uprising by backcountry farmers seeking debtors' relief, was the most dramatic example of how the financial legacy of the Revolution (economic recession and persistent tensions between procreditor merchants and landowners on the one hand and indebted artisans and farmers on the other) could threaten national stability. With the recent past in mind, Hamilton warned that disunion within and among the states could result from class conflict, from competition over the Western territories, from disagreements over commercial regulations or the handling of the national debt, and from debates over political apportionment. All of these varieties of disunion would make the country vulnerable to the machinations of foreign powers intent on stoking domestic rivalries and could result in "War between the states," with its attendant "violent destruction of life and property." Significantly, Hamilton also associated disunion with gender disorder—he introduced the topic with examples from European history of how female "bigotry," "petulancies," and "cabals" had fomented political discord within European monarchies. Naturally, the only "safeguard" against factionalism was, according to Hamilton, "a firm Union" designed on the federal principle. Only in "subordination to the general authority of the union" could states avoid becoming "jealous, clashing, tumultuous commonwealths."[16]

Even as they argued that a strong national government would be a bulwark against disunion, Federalists worked assiduously to reassure those, like George Mason, who feared that the individual states would lose all vestiges of sovereignty in the new arrangement; the increased power of the Senate, presidency, and federal judiciary could translate into policies, so anti-Federalists fretted, inimical to the economic and political interests of minorities—such as slaveholders. In urging fellow Virginians to ratify the document, Madison explained that the new Constitution would *both* empower the Union and permit the states to retain a significant measure of their authority and independence—it granted "few and defined" powers to the federal government, while those reserved to the states were "numerous and indefinite." Hamilton echoed Madison, as he encouraged citizens in his home state of New York to ratify the Constitution, in professing his respect for the rights of the thirteen individual states. This ambiguous, indirect language was, like the slavery compromises, an evasion—the Constitution failed to answer, directly and definitely, the question of just how far a state could go in defending its own sovereignty against that of the national government. Federalists could leave this question unresolved precisely because they understood that "even the most ardent believers in state sovereignty, thought of disunion as a calamity."[17]

Indeed, during Virginia's ratification debate, its leading anti-Federalists, including Mason, Patrick Henry, and Edmund Randolph, repeatedly assured their constituents that they "would not risk disunion to defeat the Constitution." Instead, once ratification was a fait accompli, they would pressure the Federalists to amend the new Constitution to include a Bill of Rights protecting basic liberties from government encroachment. Madison, leading the first federal Congress, understood that amendments to safeguard freedom of speech and assembly and other fundamental rights would satisfy anti-Federalists and thus lend further legitimacy to the new Union. Bringing the era of constitution making full circle, the Tenth Amendment, ratified in 1791, decreed that "the powers not delegated to the United States by the Constitution, nor prohibited by it to the States, are reserved to the States respectively, or to the people." By formalizing Madison's notion that the national government was one of "delegated," and therefore limited, powers, the amendment helped ensure widespread popular support for the new order—even though it left the exact line between state and federal jurisdiction theoretical and unclear.[18]

In essence, Federalists offered up, to use Rogan Kersh's recent formulation, the vision of a "sustainable union"—a Union made "more perfect because it could be preserved." In Madison's view, as parsed by Kersh, the new government would rest on the secure foundation of territorial unity, of bonds of affection among the people, and of the Federalist system, with its separation of powers and checks and balances. Unity, affection, and balance depended, in turn, on compromise—indeed, Kersh explains that "Union in the convention and ratifying debates served as a shorthand for compromise." In other words, Federalists, realizing how deeply the people feared disunion, reminded them again and again how close the confederation had come to collapse, and promised that the new government would be stronger.[19]

To effect ratification of and promote allegiance to the new order, Federalists elaborated a host of public rituals that celebrated the benefits of the Union. In their festivals, banquets, parades, toasts, and orations, Federalists defined the key elements of a nascent American nationalism: a providential sense of a distinct mission and destiny for the United States, a belief in the superiority of representative government led by a "natural aristocracy" of the virtuous, and a reverence for the military heroes of the Revolution and for the founding documents themselves. The Constitution, in this emerging nationalist ideology, was to be regarded as nothing less than a sacred document, the bedrock of an American civil religion.[20]

The Federalist view that compromise equaled union, and that a failure to compromise would bring disunion, was ascendant in the early days of the republic. But George Mason's warning—that no government could rest secure on immoral compromises—proved impossible to forget.

1789–1836

PART

1

The Language of Terrifying Prophecy

The era of constitution making bequeathed to the young nation not only a legacy of compromise and indecision on slavery, but also the beginnings of a discourse in which politicians summoned images of disunion to advance their own regional and partisan agendas. The early years of the republic witnessed periodic appeals to disunion; slavery was often, but not always, the principal source of contention. In 1790 Southern and Northern representatives in Congress clashed over the twin issues of where to locate the capital and whether Congress should assume the Revolutionary War debts of the states. Assumption was a key piece of the fiscal agenda of Secretary of the Treasury Alexander Hamilton, whose reputation for brilliance was matched by his reputation for arrogance. In Hamilton's view, the United States should aspire to be a manufacturing and commercial superpower, in the model of Great Britain; "Britain's funded debt" had fueled the "extraordinary growth of the British economy." Southerners in states, such as Virginia, that had already paid down their Revolutionary War debts saw Hamilton's plan as biased toward the North. Because Hamilton's assumption scheme would make the states "beholden to the federal government," and would create a large national debt that would need to be paid down by new federal taxes, it raised the specter of "consolidation": of aggrandizing the central government at the expense of local interests. The heavily indebted New England states, by contrast, eager for federal relief, viewed assumption as a "sine qua non of a continuance of the Union," according to Jefferson's memorandum on the controversy. With disunion threats on the lips of prominent Northerners and Southerners, Jefferson, Madison, and Hamilton reached a compromise whereby, in exchange for the passage of an assumption plan, Southerners won the promise that the national capital, after a temporary stint in Philadelphia, would be moved to a location on the Potomac, safely within slave country. The first of the "great compromises" between North and South, the measure did little to close the widening rift between Hamilton and the Virginians. Indeed, Jefferson later disowned the compromise, asserting that it "was unjust, in itself oppressive to the states, and was acquiesced in merely for a fear of disunion."[1]

In the midst of the assumption and residency controversy, the First Congress became embroiled in a bitter debate over slavery and the slave trade, sparked by an abolition petition presented to the lawmakers by the pioneering Quaker antislavery organization, the Pennsylvania Abolition Society (PAS). The petition, under the name of PAS president Benjamin Franklin, contended not only that slavery and the slave trade were incompatible with the new nation's charter, but also that Congress had the power and the obligation to terminate the slave trade prior to the end of the twenty-year waiting period stipulated in the Constitution. In response, irate representatives from the Deep South, led by William Loughton Smith of South Carolina (a pro-administration Federalist) and James Jackson of Georgia (a vocal critic of the Federalist administration), threatened disunion, reminding their Northern counterparts that they would never have agreed to enter the Union unless their property in slaves was guaranteed, and that the Southern states would never submit to an abolition scheme without civil war. Matthew Mason notes that these men and other such defenders of slavery in the early national era were not yet willing to assert, unequivocally, the morality of slavery. Their arguments on behalf of the institution were instead "experimental and directed mainly at fellow Southerners." The same might be said of their threats—their intimations of disunion, like their justifications of slavery, served to deny the *immorality* of slaveholding and to disparage slavery's opponents. At this moment in 1790, the experiment achieved the desired result: Madison intervened, in the spirit of compromise and indecision, to shepherd through a debate-ending resolution that denied Congress the authority to initiate gradual emancipation in the Southern states. But the strident tone of these early debates was nonetheless ominous—congressmen spoke a "language of honor" in which threats and accusations were wielded to make and break personal reputations, and to defend and promote regional interests. Certain Southern lawmakers were already cultivating a reputation for belligerence—capitalizing on the perception that "hot blooded" Southerners were more willing to resort to violence than their "cold blooded," cautious, puritanical Northern counterparts.[2]

As if playing out *The Federalist*'s warning about the many possible sources of disunion, Southerners and Northerners clashed repeatedly in the 1790s over aspects of Hamilton's program such as the apportionment of the Congress, the chartering of a national bank, and John Jay's 1795 treaty with Great Britain. Although slavery was the "most obvious difference" between North and South, it was not the explicit focus of these debates. As Sean Wilentz observes, "Northerners, some of whom were still squabbling about emancipation in their own states, did not perceive an antislavery agenda behind Hamilton's proposals." Southern farmers and planters viewed the Federalist position on each of these issues as a bid to increase the power of manufacturing interests at the expense of agrarian ones. In every instance, Southern intimations of disunion looked backward and forward. They tapped anxieties and resentments about the founding itself, particularly anti-Federalist fears that government consolidation would undermine state sovereignty. But disunion talk also served warning that a new opposition party was consolidating, with a strong base among Southern and Northern agrarians alike, and would challenge the Federalists for control of the national government.[3]

Disgust with the rising spirit of partisanship suffused George Washington's "Farewell Address" of 1796. To counter that spirit, Washington called on the American people to reassert their devotion to the Union. Only the Union, he said, could guarantee for the citizens of the new nation prosperity, security, and happiness; the country's leaders had a responsibility to act not as partisans but as stewards of a sacred trust. Washington deplored regional jealousies as well as partisan ones; he explicitly argued that the North and South were economically dependent on each other and could thrive only in partnership. In his view, "Local sentiments must be replaced by a sacred attachment to the Union and the Constitution."[4]

Although his speech quickly entered the annals of "sacred" American documents and contributed to the deification of Washington himself as the greatest single embodiment of the Union, it did little to stem the tide of partisanship or to discourage partisans, including Washington's own followers, from invoking disunion. For intimations of disunion could prove efficacious not only as threats but also as accusations. Thus the Federalist press, as the nation's "quasi-war" with France escalated in 1798, charged that Jefferson's new Democratic-Republican Party (commonly abbreviated as the Republicans, but not to be confused with Lincoln's Republican Party, which came on the scene in the 1850s) was in thrall to French Jacobin "anarchists." Such traitorous support of bloodthirsty revolutionaries, the Federalists alleged, was a threat to national security. Moreover, Federalists maintained that Republicans were fomenting uprisings among disgruntled farmers in both North and South and would stop "nothing short of DISUNION"— synonymous here with class warfare—in their campaign to bring down John Adams and Alexander Hamilton. Invoking the specter of the Union's downfall as a justification, the Adams administration used the Sedition Act, which criminalized dissent, to try to silence the Republican press.[5]

Republicans struck back in defense of free speech behind Jefferson's and Madison's Virginia and Kentucky resolutions. Drafted by Madison for the legislature of Virginia and by Jefferson for that of Kentucky, the resolutions— cast as a defense of the "true principles" of the Constitution and the Union— asserted that the federal government was a compact of the states, and that the Federalist abridgment of freedom of conscience and of the press was an unconstitutional assault on states' rights. Because the resolutions appealed to the states to take the "necessary and proper measures" to oppose such federal "consolidation," Jefferson's and Madison's words were later appropriated by nineteenth-century secessionists as a theory of disunion. But modern scholars have emphasized that the resolutions did not go so far as to assert the absolute sovereignty of the states; states' rights was a political means, not an end, for Jefferson and Madison. They sought, in the name of constitutional fidelity, to galvanize the opposition, both in the South and in the Mid-Atlantic, and to channel its energies toward the upcoming congressional elections and presidential contest—the "hint of disunion" would serve paradoxically to unify the Republicans. This tactic failed to pay off in the 1799 congressional elections but succeeded in forcing the hand of President Adams.

The "prospect of civil war" so "horrified" Adams that he forged a peace with France, "defusing the sectional crisis" and splitting his party—thus opening the way for the Democratic-Republican Party's ascendancy in 1800.[6]

Republicans kept up a drumbeat of disunion accusations as the 1800 elections approached, charging that Federalists were to blame for the bitter political divisions in the country and that Republicans alone could unify the nation. Integral to this Republican argument was the notion that Hamiltonians were in the thrall of the British, inviting Britain's corrupt influence to infiltrate the United States "through channels of exchange and credit." At their most strident, Republicans charged that the Federalist elite wanted to reinstate in America an English-style monarchy. Federalists countered with their own accusations. They brought sedition charges against journalists such as James Callendar on the grounds that the objective of the Republican press was to effect disunion. They held Republicans accountable for the planned slave uprising, Gabriel's Rebellion, that Virginia authorities had aborted in the summer of 1800. By talking so recklessly of "liberty and equality," so the Federalist accusation went, the Republicans had unwittingly emboldened the enslaved artisan Gabriel and his co-conspirators. (In fact, Gabriel had been inspired to think he might succeed by the very rumors of national ruin that overheated partisans on both sides were spreading during the election campaign.) They predicted that if he were elected, Jefferson's "infidel" regime would undermine American virtue and religion and bring civil war. The resort of politicians and editors to such language fostered a crisis mentality in the electorate. "With partisan animosity soaring and no end in sight," Joanne Freeman explains, "many assumed that they were engaged in a fight to the death that would destroy the Union."[7]

An electoral tie between Jefferson and his running mate, Aaron Burr of New York (who had skillfully built a Republican base to challenge Federalist dominance there), precipitated a constitutional crisis. With the Federalist Congress threatening machinations such as anointing the Federalist president pro tem of the Senate as the successor to Adams, Republicans, led by Governors James Monroe of Virginia and Thomas McKean of Pennsylvania, assumed a disunion posture again, threatening not to accede to any such Federalist "usurpation." Under the cloud of potential violence—realizing they must "take Mr. Jefferson" or "risk . . . a civil war," as one prominent Federalist put it—the House of Representatives finally broke the deadlock in

February 1801, and Federalists conceded Jefferson's victory. Republicans, having successfully used disunion talk as both threat and accusation, would now confront a Federalist opposition eager to perfect that art.[8]

THE WAR OF 1812

President Jefferson would find the extreme states' rights vanguard in his own party, the "Tertium Quids" (or "Old Republicans") led by John Randolph of Roanoke, willing to use intimations of disunion to counter any threat to slavery and to keep the Republican administration honest—loyal to the "principles of '98" as embodied in the Virginia and Kentucky resolutions. Randolph personally threatened disunion in 1807 to oppose Northern proposals that the interstate coastal slave trade be restricted even as the African trade was prohibited. Such posturing "could never attract much support in the South," William Cooper Jr. has written, "so long as southerners perceived governmental power being exercised by a party they identified as their own"; moreover, Randolph himself was a notorious eccentric who would "sometimes appear in Congress booted and spurred, flicking his riding whip." But the threats were nonetheless more than transparent pressure tactics—for Randolph, together with fellow Virginian John Taylor of Caroline County and Nathaniel Macon of North Carolina, led a group that began to weave from the Virginia and Kentucky resolutions and the Tenth Amendment an intricate philosophy of state sovereignty. The Old Republicans maintained unequivocally that the states were sovereign (indeed, Taylor, the political theorist in the group, called them "state-nations") and that the Union was a revocable compact, a treaty of sorts, between the states. In other words, the central government—they preferred the term "confederacy" to "nation"—was subordinate to the states. From this political philosophy, Randolph, Taylor, and Macon derived the right of secession: that is, each state could, if the government or other states tried to impose unwanted measures on it, secede, as a sovereign, from the confederacy. While Randolph and the leading Quids lacked an interest in "careful political planning," as Cooper has put it, they did hope to furnish successive generations of Southerners with a rationale for resisting any encroachment on the "agrarian independence" of the South.[9]

Randolph and the Old Republicans would have to bide their time, as mainstream Republicans focused during Jefferson's administration on stigmatizing Federalists as disunionists. Indignant that the Louisiana Purchase would open the way for the expansion of slavery and thus upset the political balance struck by the three-fifths compromise, a cadre of New England Federalists under Massachusetts senator Timothy Pickering explored, in 1803–4, the possibility of forming a New England confederacy and even allying with Quebec and Britain. Although this failed scheme "can hardly be called a plot since it never took concrete form," as Richard Buel Jr. points out, it nonetheless provided ammunition to Republicans in their campaign to tar their critics with treachery. So, too, did an ill-conceived scheme of Aaron Burr's: in 1806–7 he attempted to hatch his own "filibuster"—a private military expedition—to seize territory in the Southwest. Although the plan was stillborn, Republicans, who had abandoned and smeared Burr after the 1800 election imbroglio, cannily cast his machinations as profoundly dangerous—a grand conspiracy to destroy the Union—rather than as ineffectual. At this moment, and then again when Federalists objected to Jefferson's embargo of Britain and to Louisiana's statehood, Southern Republicans, in the name of nationalism, discredited their opponents as a "factious minority" that was inciting a rebellion against the government.[10]

Federalists persisted in trying to use disunion arguments to their own partisan advantage. When, under Jefferson's successor Madison, the economic standoff between the United States and Britain erupted into war in 1812, disaffected New England Federalists charged that Republicans were the tools of the French emperor Napoleon, and that the administration's purpose was to advance Southern and Western regional interests at the expense of the Northeast. Not only was New England's commerce undermined, but also its coastline was especially vulnerable to attack from the British military base in Halifax, Nova Scotia. Paradoxically, these New England Federalists did not see their defense of their own regional interests, even their threats of disunion, as sectional in nature, for they clung fiercely to the notion that they embodied the true principles of the Constitution and of the nation itself—that New England's founders, not Virginia's, had first planted the tree of liberty on America's shores.[11]

AS FEDERALIST "FIREBRANDS" such as John Lowell Jr. and Harrison Gray Otis of Massachusetts raised anew the possibility of New England's secession,

In this pictorial critique of the Hartford Convention, New England Federalists nerve themselves for the "dangerous leap" into the arms of England's King George III, while Timothy Pickering prays for their success. The image of the precipice soon became a ubiquitous metaphor for conveying the irrationality and self-destructiveness of disunion. (Courtesy of the Library of Congress)

Republicans in the North and South again counterattacked. Madison's vice president, Elbridge Gerry of Massachusetts, condemned the dissenters, charging that secession would be calamitous for his state and that the Federalists had fallen prey to "foreign influence." South Carolina's John C. Calhoun, discoursing on the difference between legitimate and illegitimate opposition, labeled the Federalist disunion talk as illegitimate—it was a "vicious" attempt to "deliver the country . . . to the mercy of the enemy." By the time of the Hartford (Connecticut) Convention in December 1814—a meeting that advertised itself as a constitutional convention of the aggrieved New England states—the dissenters were in retreat. The convention attracted a mere twenty-six delegates from three states who shied away from advocating secession; instead, they proposed constitutional amendments to curtail Congress's ability to "wage war, regulate commerce, and admit new states." This program, writes Buel, was "scarcely less subversive" than disunion and left New England Federalists, in the wake of a negotiated peace that ended the war, humiliated and divided. Southern opinion makers such as Thomas Ritchie, editor of the *Richmond Enquirer*, and even Quid leader John Randolph, delighted in branding the Hartford proposal as treasonous. The Missouri controversy of 1819 would provide the disgruntled Federalists an opportunity, according to Buel, for "refurbishing their morally tarnished credentials."[12]

THE MISSOURI DEBATES

The principle of compromise on slavery for the sake of union survived the birth of the first party system and the tumultuous transfer of power from Federalists to Republicans. It seemed to be at work in the Confederation Congress's passage of the Northwest Ordinance, which prohibited slavery in the territories north of the Ohio River, but made no such stipulation for the Southwest. And that principle governed the admission of new states in the early republic: paired admissions brought in one free state for each slave state, resulting in the addition of Indiana and Mississippi, then Illinois and Alabama, Maine and Missouri, and Arkansas and Michigan, to the roster of states.[13]

As the rancorous debates over the admission of Missouri demonstrate, however, extending the principle of compromise was a process fraught with difficulty. The Missouri debates were, first and foremost, arguments about just what the compromises of 1787 really meant—about what the Founders really intended. The admission of Missouri as a slave state was the culmination of a two-year legislative battle, sparked in 1819 by Representative James Tallmadge Jr., a New York lawyer just starting to make a name for himself in Congress. Tallmadge amended Missouri's statehood bill to provide that "the further introduction of slavery or involuntary servitude be prohibited" and that "all children born within the said State, after the admission thereof into the Union, shall be free at the age of twenty-five years." Tallmadge and his supporters had a genuine moral distaste for slavery, but their primary motivation was political: they were openly resentful of the fact that the three-fifths clause had translated into political supremacy for the South.[14]

By 1819 the North was already the more populous section, and thus Northern congressmen predominated in the House of Representatives. But the North's demographic edge did not translate into control over the federal government, for that edge was blunted by the constitutional compromises. The fact that the Founders had decided that each state, however large or small, would elect two senators meant that the South's power in the Senate was disproportionate to its population, and that maintaining a senatorial parity between North and South depended on bringing in equal numbers of free and slave states. The three-fifths clause inflated the South's representation in the House. Because the number of presidential electors assigned to each state was equal to the size of its congressional delegation (its senators and representatives), the South had a power over the election of presidents that was disproportionate to the size of the region's free population. However difficult it was to parse the numbers, the effect of this Southern edge was plain to see: the three-fifths clause gave Virginia the greatest number of electoral votes; since Jefferson's accession in 1801, a "Virginia dynasty" had ruled the White House. The War of 1812 had intensified the resentment of Northern Federalists, New Englanders in particular, against the "federal ratio." Opponents of the Virginia dynasty argued, Matthew Mason explains, that "were it not for the added power of slave representation, the Republicans would never have been able to enact commercial restrictions or initiate the war."[15]

Tallmadge's allies in the House and Senate made the case that it was constitutional for Congress to legislate the end of slavery in Missouri after its admission to statehood—to prescribe, that is, the details of its government. After all, as New York congressman John W. Taylor put it, hadn't Indiana and Illinois been bound to conform to the antislavery provisions of the Northwest Ordinance? Since Missouri lay on the same latitude as those states and had a similar geography, surely it too should be a free state. Southern opponents of this line of reasoning had a ready response: The Constitution guaranteed the Southern states sovereignty over slavery; Congress had no right to impose an antislavery proscription on a state. The Northwest Ordinance was irrelevant, as it had been passed under the Articles of Confederation, before the Constitution was ratified and took hold. The admission of Missouri should be governed instead by the 1803 treaty with France by which the United States acquired the Louisiana Purchase; according to that treaty, inhabitants of the new territories should have all the rights of other U.S. citizens, including the right to own slaves.[16]

A second line of argument made by restrictionists proved far thornier. They stipulated that Congress's power over slavery lay not only in the Northwest Ordinance precedent but in Congress's constitutional prerogative to require that each state's government was "republican in its form." Tallmadge backers mustered a wide array of supports for the case that slavery was incompatible with republicanism. One was that the Founders themselves believed slavery to be unrepublican. Antislavery lawmakers such as Representative Timothy Fuller, an earnest lawyer from Massachusetts, and Senator David L. Morril, a pious Congregationalist from New Hampshire, quoted none other than Thomas Jefferson: they cited his preamble to the Declaration of Independence ("all men are created equal") and very selectively culled his *Notes on the State of Virginia* (the passage in which Jefferson laments that slavery fosters "the most boisterous passions" and leads whites to exercise "unremitting despotism" over their slaves). Moreover, while the vast majority of the antislavery rhetoric in the Missouri debates focused on constitutional issues and on the Founders' intentions, Tallmadge supporters did, briefly but pointedly, probe the weak spots in their opponents' armor by evoking the sufferings of the slaves themselves. New Hampshire congressman Arthur Livermore, known for his sarcasm, was dead serious when he declared that "the sympathies of nature in slaves are disregarded; mothers and children are sold and separated; the children wring their little hands and expire in agonies of grief, while the bereft mothers commit suicide in despair."[17]

The principal Southern response to such charges was the "diffusion" argument. Most of the Southern representatives were willing to pay homage, at least rhetorically, to the notion that slavery was a "necessary evil"— meaning a system that had some inherent flaws but was too deeply rooted in the American landscape to be eradicated suddenly; the Founders had indeed hoped for and expected, so the "necessary evil" rationale ran, slavery's gradual demise. To admit Missouri as a slave state would promote such gradual emancipation. How? In the words of Senator John Elliot of Georgia: "Disperse this people [slaves], who would be so formidable when confined to narrow limits; suffer them to spread over an extensive country, and they would be lost amidst the great body of the white population which would surround them on every side. In this situation they might be gradually emancipated without endangering the safety of the State governments; and when emancipated, they could be supported on hire, at voluntary servitude, without greatly lessening the productive labor of the country." Diffusion would make slaves less of a security threat (a dispersed population was less likely to rebel) and an economic threat (scattered slaves could not compete with or displace white laborers) and therefore render whites willing to free them.[18]

But just as Northern representatives tentatively prodded the defenses of Southerners with the case for slavery's immorality, so too did some Southerners push back, tentatively articulating elements of what came to be known in the 1830s as the "positive good" defense of slavery. Senator Morril's antislavery reading of Jefferson's *Notes* was countered by North Carolina's Senator Nathaniel Macon, an Old Republican who believed that only a fellow Southerner could understand Jefferson: "What ought surely to be inferred from Mr. Jefferson's notes and life, is, that he thinks slavery is a curse, but thinks it a greater curse to emancipate in his native Virginia. His democracy, like that of his great countrymen who have been before mentioned, appears to be of the white family." Whatever its faults, then, slavery was not incompatible with republican government. The combative South Carolina senator William Loughton Smith, who had over his long career become ever more committed to upholding the morality of slaveholding, positioned himself as the most impassioned proslavery voice in the debates. He also took issue with Morril's invocation of Jefferson but made a much more strident reply. When Jefferson had written in his *Notes* that slavery gave rise to "boisterous passions," he was both wrong and untrue to himself; as he matured Jefferson disavowed such notions. According to Smith, the master had "no motive" for "boisterous hostility" to the slave. Rather, the relations between master and slave were "patriarchal," governed by mutual affection. But the ultimate proof of slavery's morality, Smith thundered, lay in the scriptures themselves: "Christ himself gave a sanction to slavery. He admonished them to be obedient to their masters. . . . Christ came to fulfill the law, not to destroy it."[19]

The Missouri debates gave rise to a "good deal of southern talk about disunion," as defenders of slavery extended their practice of wielding the image of civil war as a rhetorical weapon. The most oft-quoted example is from Georgian Thomas Cobb. Claiming to foresee a future that his opponents could not, he prophesized in the U.S. House of Representatives that the debates had "kindled a fire which all the waters of the ocean could not put out" and that the Union would be dissolved if antislavery forces persisted. Cobb's warning, like Smith's and Macon's defenses of slavery, was meant to uphold Southern "honor" against the "slanders" of the North. Cobb was not alone in favoring the metaphor of disunion as a potential conflagration. Virginia senator James Barbour, known for his dignity and moderation, charged James Tallmadge with igniting a spark that might engulf the nation. Northerners saw such "expressions of great warmth," as Tallmadge sneeringly called Cobb's prediction, as transparent efforts to intimidate slavery's critics into silence. Tallmadge retorted that "language of this sort has no effect on me; my purpose is fixed"; he would, rhetorically, take civil war over submission. He was echoed by Senator Walter Lowrie of Pennsylvania. A temperance advocate who founded the congressional prayer meeting, Lowrie was anything but temperate when he declared: "If the alternative be, as gentlemen broadly intimate, a dissolution of this Union, or the extension of slavery over this whole Western country, I, for one, will choose the former." Southerners opportunistically countered with dystopian images of what a civil war—brought on by the intransigence of the likes of Tallmadge and Lowrie—would look like. Senator Macon of North Carolina imagined "near relations plunging the bayonet into each other." Not to be outdone, Senator Freeman Walker of Georgia opined: "I behold the father armed against the son, and the son against the father. I perceive a brother's sword crimsoned with a brother's blood. I perceive our houses wrapt in flames, and our wives and infant children driven from their homes, forced to submit to the pelting of the pitiless storm." Accusations of disunion were intended to negate slavery restrictionists' claims that they were motivated by moral considerations and to cast them as power-hungry partisans. As Senator Smith of South Carolina put it, civil wars were "profuse in blood" and originated in the "jealousies and rivalries of wicked men."[20]

These images of fires and storms were, Senator Prentiss Mellen, a cautious Federalist jurist from Massachusetts, cogently noted, a familiar "language of terrifying prophecy." In a sense, proslavery Southern Republicans and antislavery Northern Federalists were resorting to a tried-and-true tactic—using disunion intimations, threats, and accusations to galvanize their own side and tarnish their opponents as treasonous. To be sure, such language did convince some commentators, politicians, and voters that the country was truly on the brink of disunion and that only a compromise between restrictionists and antirestrictionists could save it. Most notable among those was Hezekiah Niles, the influential editor of the Baltimore newspaper *Niles' Weekly Register*. Although he supported slavery restriction and gradual emancipation, Niles, shaken by the threats emanating from Northern and Southern delegates alike, regarded compromise as the "only manner in which the great question" could be "peaceably settled."[21]

But even as Niles quailed in the face of the "terrifying prophecies" of Congress, fearing that they might portend deep divisions in public opinion, many other commentators regarded the threats as transparent political ploys. William Plumer Jr., a restrictionist representing New Hampshire in the House, wrote his father about the dissolution menaces issuing from South Carolina's leaders, but reassured him that "this is all talk, intended to frighten us out of our purpose—& and is so understood." As the Philadelphia newspaper the *Union* put it in October 1820: "This canting about 'risks' and 'shaking the Union to its base,' is the old style all over again. Why are these gentlemen continually appealing to our fears?" Neither the "people of the north" nor the "people of the South," the paper pointedly noted, had "made any threats upon this subject." Disparaging the disunion posturing of Northern and Southern politicians alike, a correspondent to the *Carolina Centinel* in New Bern, North Carolina, trusted that the "prudence and wisdom of practical men" could avert a crisis. In similar language a New Orleans paper professed its faith that disunion sentiments were confined to politicians and that "the great mass of people [was] uncontaminated by them." In Washington, D.C., the *Daily National Intelligencer* regretted that the "excitement which existed in Congress" had found its way into some newspapers. But the paper was confident that such language did not reflect the majority opinion of either party or section of the country.[22]

The disunion rhetoric of the Missouri Compromise can be understood, then, as a kind of political gamesmanship or parliamentary maneuvering by Northern and Southern politicians at a moment of congressional crisis. Neither Tallmadge nor Cobb invoked disunion as a process or program, and neither man aimed, strategically, to foment a disunion movement among the public. Indeed, Southern antirestrictionists in Congress invoked disunion to tarnish Federalist opponents of slavery with the "stigma of the Hartford

Convention"—Federalists were again, so the charge went, pursuing a sectional agenda in defiance of the Constitution.[23]

Although the Missouri debates did not develop into a genuine secession crisis, they nonetheless significantly transformed the discourse of disunion. Because antirestriction Southerners regarded the Tallmadge amendment as an unprecedented bid by the federal government to abridge states' rights, the debates revived interest in the convoluted political theory of Old Republicans such as John Randolph of Roanoke and John Taylor of Caroline. Drawing on the Quid rhetoric of resistance to federal consolidation, the leading proslavery organs in the South, such as the *Richmond Enquirer*, articulated a "States Rights position that always implicitly concerned a state's right to protect slavery within its borders"; such arguments for the constitutionality of slavery, Eva Sheppard Wolf tells us, had the cumulative effect of casting the "States Rights position as particularly Southern." In other words, even as Southerners marshaled images of the Hartford Convention to attack their opponents, they invoked the language of state sovereignty in the name of self-defense.[24]

The Missouri controversy racialized the discourse of disunion by adding lurid word pictures of "servile war" to the "language of terrifying prophecy." Southerners attacked Tallmadge and his supporters for "endeavoring to excite a servile war." "You conduct us to an awful precipice, and hold us over it," Christopher Rankin of Mississippi intoned in the House. Alluding to the presence of African Americans, some of them slaves, as auditors in the Senate galleries over the course of the debate, Senator Edward Colston of Virginia charged that it was dangerous to call into doubt the "republican character of the slaveholding states" before a mixed audience. This accusation tapped deep-seated fears of slave rebellion, fears that had been stoked by the black revolution in St. Domingo (Haiti) in the 1790s and by the elaborate Gabriel conspiracy—the abortive slave uprising in Virginia inspired by the example of St. Domingo—in 1800. When Southerners like Senator Macon associated the antislavery agitation of Tallmadge and his followers with the "war of extermination" in Haiti, they were echoing the concerns of Thomas Jefferson, who had for years been "heralding the approach of an avenging angel"—warning that emancipation in the United States might resemble the "bloody process of St. Domingo."[25]

Tallmadge used the accusation to point up the inconsistency between the premises of the diffusion argument and the premises of the "positive good" brand of proslavery ideology. The diffusion argument—that it would be "safer" to emancipate slaves who were diffused over a wide area—was based on the notion that the slave system was insecure and vulnerable to violence. If slavery was "so fraught with such dire calamities," how could slaveholders like William Smith stipulate that the institution was benign and defend its morality? But Tallmadge proceeded to use the image of slave revolt for his own purposes. He painted a utopian picture of a thriving nation of freemen, then juxtaposed it with a dystopian picture of the "long vista of futurity" in a nation overrun by slavery—with discontented slaves holding a "dagger" at the "bosom" of the country. Slavery prepared the way for "dissolution"; it was the greatest source of both "individual danger" and "national weakness." Congressman Livermore likewise alluded to slave rebellion, asking: "Can we, sir, by mingling bond with free, black spirits with white, like Shakespeare's witches in *Macbeth*, form a more perfect union, and insure domestic tranquility?" The answer to this rhetorical question was, of course, no—the presence of slaves, ready to "draw the sword" against their masters, prevented the young nation from fulfilling the promises of the Constitution. Astute commentators on either side of the debate acknowledged that the advent of a vocabulary connecting state sovereignty with civil war and servile war was itself portentous. Senator Richard M. Johnson, of Kentucky, a frequent advocate of compromise, warned antislavery Northerners that if they persisted, they would "produce jargon" that might "eventuate in murder and devastation." The scholarly lawyer Senator James Burrill, of Rhode Island, for his part, rued "the magical force of certain words . . . to alarm prejudice."[26]

What was the end result of such congressional thrusts and parries? While the House, on the strength of bipartisan Northern votes, approved Tallmadge's proposal, the Senate rejected it. To break the impasse, Kentucky congressman Henry Clay brokered a compromise that not only paired Maine and Missouri as free and slave states but also, following the proposal of Senator Jesse B. Thomas of Illinois, demarcated the 36°30′ parallel as a line dividing slavery and freedom in any future Western territories. North of that line (awkwardly, the southern border of Missouri), slavery was to be "forever forbidden," but south of that line it could take root. The Senate passed the two proposals as a single bill, only to have the measure initially founder in the House. Thanks to Clay's parliamentary maneuvering and that of his hand-picked conference committee composed of members of both houses, the two bills were voted on separately. With unanimous Southern support and the breakaway votes of fourteen Northerners, the House admitted Missouri without restrictions on slavery, while a solid Northern bloc, with critical votes from the Border South, secured the 36°30′ compromise. President Monroe signed the Missouri bill into law on March 6, 1820. The fact that an overwhelming Northern majority and more than half of all Southern congressmen supported it gave the Missouri Compromise, as David Potter has put it, a "certain aura of sanctity."[27]

Historians still debate which side, North or South, prevailed in this exchange. The South won a clear victory in the sense that Missouri entered the Union as a slave state and the anti-Tallmadge position—that Congress might impose certain restrictions on territories but could not abridge the sovereignty of states by imposing antislavery measures after statehood—seemed to be vindicated. The South, however, made what looks in hindsight to be a huge concession in accepting the 36°30′ line, as some nine future free states would eventually be carved out of the Louisiana Purchase territory that lay above the line. Why was the South willing to concede so much? As John Ashworth has explained, some Southerners viewed the compromise not as an irrevocable "compact between the sections," but rather as "an ordinary, repealable legislative measure."[28]

More important still, Southerners accepted the compromise of 1820 because they were not yet ready to argue that slavery should be legal in all of the federal territories. The South itself was divided. The slaveholding border states of Kentucky, Delaware, and Maryland—the "least enslaved and most apologetic region of the South," as William Freehling has put it—favored the 36°30′ compromise. Support for the Thomas proviso was also strong in Louisiana, Mississippi, and Alabama because those frontier states wanted to attract slaveholding migrants from the "old centers of slave power," rather than having those migrants siphoned off to the other territories of the Louisiana Purchase. The delegations of Virginia, North Carolina, South Carolina, and Georgia, on the other hand, soundly rejected the 36°30′ line.[29]

But the rhetoric of Virginia's delegates reveal that even at the epicenter of the states' rights cause there was ambivalence and hesitancy. Senator James

Barbour stood strongly against the Tallmadge proposal but urged his fellow Virginians, in the name of sectional harmony, to accept the 36°30' compromise (the Thomas amendment). In an eleventh-hour about-face, he then voted against the compromise amendment when it came before the Senate, only to resume a conciliatory position when it became clear that the amendment had passed. Through all this posturing, Barbour was consistent about one thing—that the Missouri debate was not over moral issues. "It has been said that this is a question between slavery and freedom," Barbour intoned. Such a view was an "indefensible perversion." Virginia, he went on, had supported the suppression of the African slave trade and efforts to promote the colonization of freed American slaves in Africa. The American Colonization Society (ACS), which had been founded in 1816 with the blessing of elite slaveholders such as James Monroe and Henry Clay, represented another incarnation of the "diffusion" argument. By colonizing free blacks in Africa (the colony of Liberia was founded for this purpose) and thereby diffusing the black population in the United States, the ACS would facilitate the voluntary manumission of individual slaves by their masters and promote "gradual" emancipation. No, Barbour continued, the Missouri debate was not a moral one but rather a strictly constitutional one; he would leave it to philosophers and clergymen to determine whether slavery was a necessary evil or "ordained by God."[30]

No Virginian agonized more over the Missouri crisis than Thomas Jefferson, now a retired statesman. He privately lamented that the Missouri controversy was a "fire bell in the night" that filled him with "terror," as it seemed to be the "knell of the Union." Peter Onuf tells us that Jefferson interpreted the drawing of a line of separation between slave states and free ones as an ominous repudiation of his own cherished vision of America's future—an empire of states spreading across the continent, bound by shared interests, secure in their equality with one another, and free (unlike the colonies of the British Empire) from an overweening "metropolitan" power. The Missouri Compromise line, he feared, would make Americans "foreigners to each other" and embolden Northern neo-Federalists to impose a second-class citizenship on the South. In Jefferson's view, all the blame for this nightmarish scenario lay on the Northern side of the line—his hatred of Northern critics of slavery was now all consuming. The virulence of this hatred, Onuf observes, reveals how deeply complicit Jefferson was in betraying his own vision of a Union sustained by love. Jefferson so feared for the Union precisely because "he could not stop himself from imagining its destruction."[31]

THE UNFULFILLED UNION

As those whites immersed in the slavery debates of the early republic invoked, contemplated, and disparaged disunion, leaders and spokesmen among free African Americans in the North elaborated their own discourse of *Union*—the argument that they were, to quote modern-day scholar John Ernest, "the citizens of a nation imagined but not yet realized." This argument took a wide variety of forms. For example, the petition of Absalom Jones of Philadelphia, signed by seventy free blacks and submitted to Congress in 1799, inveighed against the slave trade and the Fugitive Slave Act of 1793 (particularly against the kidnapping and selling into slavery of free blacks) in the language of republicanism: blacks were, the memorialists insisted, entitled to "representation" along with "every other class of Citizens," according to the "declared design of the present Constitution." The Reverend Daniel Coker, a prominent black clergyman from Maryland, published in 1810 a fictive "Dialogue between a Virginian and an African Minister" that imagined a Union in which white leaders acted "benevolently on behalf of oppressed blacks." In 1813 James Forten, a successful Philadelphia sailmaker and Revolutionary War veteran, penned a "Series of Letters by a Man of Colour" to protest a Pennsylvania bill restricting black emigration to the state; he deplored the fact that Pennsylvania had abdicated its role as a beacon of tolerance and liberty, and he assailed the racist legislation of the Northern states as "characteristic of European despotism." These works reflect a distinctive African American prophetic tradition, rooted in evangelical religion, that "gave African Americans the Exodus narrative to counter the Anglo-Saxon city on a hill," as James A. Morone has put it—only black freedom would redeem the new nation from sin and fulfill its covenant with God.[32]

The growing popularity of the ACS among whites galvanized African American protest in the North. Free blacks resoundingly rejected the colonization scheme as a hypocritical and racist bid to deport them. The premise of colonization, they agreed, was the notion that blacks were biologically inferior to whites and could not assimilate—there was no hope that the two races could ever coexist in harmony.[33] The campaign against the ACS was orchestrated by James Forten. In a series of protest meetings that commenced in 1817 and led up to a national convention of free blacks in Philadelphia in 1830, Forten articulated a poignant critique of colonization. This critique was grounded in two principles: an idealistic reading of Jefferson's Declaration of Independence and a profound sense of connection to Southern slaves. Participants in the first meeting in 1817 passed a resolution that "we will never separate ourselves voluntarily from the slave population in this country; they are our brethren by the ties of consanguinity, of suffering, and of wrong; and we feel that there is more virtue in suffering privations with them, than fancied advantages for a season." Fired by the "strongest confidence in the justice of God," Forten tirelessly campaigned against colonization throughout the 1820s.[34]

VESEY'S REBELLION

The early republic's discourse of disunion came full circle with the trial and execution of free black carpenter Denmark Vesey of Charleston, South Carolina. Vesey and thirty-four other men were convicted of having planned a massive slave revolt—one in which black conspirators were to seize arsenals and guardhouses, set the city to the torch, commandeer sailing vessels, and flee to the black republic of Haiti. Outnumbered by their slaves and desperately dependent on them, South Carolina planters had long been obsessed with the nightmare of slave rebellion. South Carolina was the only state with a black majority; in its low-country plantation districts, slaves made up as much as 85 percent of the population. According to standard historical accounts, which drew on the "official report" of the court that sentenced Vesey to hang, Vesey was raised on the island of St. Thomas in the West Indies. He was sold to a planter on St. Domingo, only to be returned to his original master, a ship's captain, because he was afflicted by "epileptic fits." After serving this master for nearly two decades, Vesey bought his freedom in 1799, with money he won in a lottery, and set himself up as a successful carpenter in Charleston. Vesey's revolutionary zeal, so the conventional accounts go, derived from the distinctive Afro-Christianity practiced in Charleston's African Methodist Episcopal (AME) Church; from the example of St. Domingo; and from his knowledge that whites, during the Missouri controversy, were debating the future of slavery and that some were contemplating its demise. Vesey allegedly chose July 14, 1822—Bastille Day—as the moment of reckoning and contacted the Haitian republic for assistance. But the plot soon unraveled and met its doom when several blacks betrayed the plan to whites. The militia was able to crush the conspiracy in June 1822 before it became an open revolt; 131 blacks were arrested and at least 35 executed in a wave of retribution.[35]

Historians have hotly debated the extent of the conspiracy, with some giving credence to the notion that it involved hundreds and even thousands of blacks. Others, following the lead of historian Michael P. Johnson, argue that the "official record" of the Vesey case is a fabrication, based on coerced and contradictory testimony, and designed to justify the "legalized murder" of the rebels. Johnson contends that the sham trial actually "expanded the scope of the alleged conspiracy" by forcing so many fraudulent confessions and accusations. He concludes that the trial record "reveals more about the court and its supporters than about the Vesey insurrection conspiracy"; for example, whites read into black testimony the idea that the Missouri debates served as inspiration for the rebels. Vesey had not masterminded an elaborate revolt. Rather, he was scapegoated for openly subscribing to "heresies": "that blacks hated both slavery and whites, that slaves should be free, that blacks should be equal to whites."[36]

While the extent of the rebellion admits of no definitive answer, it is clear that whites in Charleston not only projected their fears onto the conspiracy, but also capitalized on it by invoking disunion as a warning and an accusation against the North. One commentator, in *Reflections, Occasioned by the Late Disturbances in Charleston*, opined that while the first cause of the plot was the "example of St. Domingo," the second was "the indiscreet zeal in favor of universal liberty, expressed by many of our fellow-citizens in the States north and east of Maryland; aided by the Black population of those States." This notion was drawn out by Baptist preacher Richard Furman, of Charleston, in his *Exposition of the Views of the Baptists, Relative to the Coloured Population of the United States*. An early articulation of the "positive good" defense of slavery, claiming that Christian masters were and should be humane to their slaves, Furman's essay blamed slave discontent on the baleful influence of false religion—the preachings of the AME Church, which had "intimate connection and intercourse with a similar body of men in a Northern city" (Philadelphia), and the "perversion of Scriptural doctrine" that had taken hold of some whites. Those whites, he warned, should nurture no delusions about the true impact of their alleged benevolence: Antislavery sentiment was a threat to the "peace and safety of the State" and was "the means of producing in our country, scenes of anarchy and blood."[37]

If Furman's proslavery reading of the Holy Book was, as he put it, "one of the best securities to the public, for the internal and domestic peace of the State," the legislature of South Carolina sought security of another kind when it passed, in direct contravention of federal treaties and statutes, the Negro Seaman's Act, which temporarily imprisoned all African American sailors who visited Charleston on the grounds that they were an insurrectionary influence. This was, it might be argued, the first of South Carolina's nullification acts. As Manisha Sinha points out, the Vesey plot was "discovered and put down by such future nullifiers as Robert J. Turnbull, Robert Y. Hayne, and James Hamilton, Jr." Turnbull, in declaring the Vesey conspiracy one of the "choicest fruits" of the Missouri Compromise, was not only foreshadowing the tariff nullification controversy, but also echoing the disunion rhetoric of Cobb, Macon, Walker, Smith, and other Southern politicians who had begun to build the case, in the 1819–21 congressional debates, that antislavery agitation would end in unimaginable scenes of bloodshed. In this formulation, "intemperate" and "indiscreet" Northern whites—driven by false benevolence or political ambition—were unwitting allies of slave rebels and unwitting agents of destruction. Although they did not directly incite slave rebellion or openly advocate or justify it, by raising the issue of slavery's demise, whites sent a dangerous signal to blacks. Only if they were made to confront the hideous specter of race war and civil war could antislavery whites be pressured to cease their agitation.[38]

Moreover, fears of slave rebellion were intimately linked to fears of European intervention. South Carolinian Whitemarsh Seabrook, future governor, nullifier, and, by 1850, secessionist, spelled out this connection in his 1825 pamphlet on the "future prospects of the slave-holding states." Suspicious of the growing antislavery movement in Britain, he worried that the English might "fan the flame of emancipation" to promote slave rebellion and "to sow among these States the seeds of disunion." Such intervention could well prepare the ground for conquest: "The despots of Europe know, that if judiciously encouraged, a disruption of our Union may reward their labors." Only a strong proslavery consensus could safeguard the South and the nation.[39]

The discourse of disunion in the early republic thus conjured pervasive fears about national survival and security—about the machinations of foreign powers, the divisiveness of political parties, the difficulty of maintaining an electoral balance of power between North and South, and the threat of slave rebellion. This focus on national security—this commitment of white Northern and Southern leaders to cast security as the paramount issue—was essential to the compromises and to the spirit of evasion that characterized the slavery debates of the era. It would take the advent of "modern" abolitionism to make the sinfulness of slavery the paramount issue. For "immediate" abolitionists would not ask whether the righteous Union could be safeguarded from the many sources of disunion. They would ask whether a righteous Union had ever existed at all.

We Claim Our Rights

THE ADVENT OF ABOLITIONISM

As America approached its fiftieth birthday, the "triumphal" 1824–25 tour of Revolutionary War hero the Marquis de Lafayette served as the occasion for a public outpouring of pride and optimism—and of praise for the inestimable benefits of the glorious Union. Albert Gallatin, former secretary of the treasury and U.S. minister to France, welcomed Lafayette to Uniontown, New York, with a speech proclaiming that America could now boast "a distinguished rank amongst the nations of the earth." The nation had "attained a height of prosperity unequalled, within so short a period, in the annals of mankind. Her villages are now populous cities; her ships cover the Ocean; new states have, as by magic, arisen out of the wilderness; her progress in manufactures, in arts, in internal improvements, latterly in science and literature, has kept apace with that of her wealth." Gallatin concluded that "the present generation has proved worthy of their fathers."[1]

Americans had much cause to wonder at their progress; "since the Revolution, the nation's population and territorial expanse had more than doubled," Eric Foner notes. But as Gallatin, a battle-scarred veteran of the partisan warfare of the early republic, knew all too well, Americans also had much cause for anxiety. His notion that the present generation had "proved worthy" was as much a wish as an assessment, for that generation was

55

experiencing a contentious political realignment. In the wake of the War of 1812, leaving the Federalist Party in shambles, the ruling Democratic-Republicans had split. So-called National Republicans, led by John Quincy Adams and Henry Clay, supported the "continuation of many old Federalist policies under Republican auspices and without the elitist tone of Federalist discourse." Clay elaborated plans for an "American System" of government-subsidized "internal improvements" (such as canals, turnpikes, and railroads) that, together with high protective tariffs on imports, would stimulate U.S. manufacturing and "encourage the virtues of hard work, thrift, sobriety, education, and self-control." For National Republicans, the issue of "protection" had a mystique that went beyond the revenues and productivity that tariffs would generate—they held that only commercial independence could insulate their new nation from the age-old conflicts of Europe's rival states.[2]

Repudiating this agenda as a betrayal of the "pure" agrarian principles of Jefferson (and believing that Adams and Clay "stole" the presidential election of 1824 by manipulating Congress), the other wing of the Republican Party rallied under Andrew Jackson, the renowned hero of the War of 1812, and began to call themselves "Democrats." The Jacksonians built a broad coalition of elements united by their opposition to the alleged aristocratic pretensions and corruption of the Adams administration. In Democratic campaign propaganda, Adams was fully complicit in the New England Federalists' disunionism—their attempts to "arouse the North against the South," as a New Hampshire Democratic pamphlet put it, by agitating the issue of "slave representation." Jackson's message—that he would champion the rights of the many against the privileges of the few—was carried to the country by an intricate new party machinery, designed by virtuoso politician Martin Van Buren of New York. The message resonated broadly, among groups as distinct as urban workers and artisans in the North who felt threatened by industrialization, and Southerners and Westerners who counted on Jackson, a famous "Indian fighter," to pursue the "removal" of Native Americans and thereby open up new lands for white farmers. Beneficiaries of a national trend toward democratization (the most important element of which was the removal of property qualifications for voting), Jackson and his vice president, John C. Calhoun of South Carolina, exacted their electoral revenge in 1828, winning 178 of 261 electoral votes.[3]

South Carolina's elite initially hoped that Jackson's election in 1828 would inaugurate a "Jeffersonian revival"—and that Jackson would strongly repudiate the neo-Federalist economic agenda of the National Republicans, symbolized by the high protective tariff on British imports that Adams had approved late in his administration. South Carolinians, who had superseded Virginians as the staunchest defenders of states' rights, declared the measure a "tariff of abominations," reasoning that it favored the interests of the industrializing Northern states over those of the staple-producing Southern states—if the British could not sell their manufactured goods in America, they would be less willing and able to purchase American exports such as cotton. As the South Carolinians saw it, the tariff exceeded Congress's limited constitutional mandate to raise revenue—and thus escalated a battle for the soul of Jefferson's once proud party.[4]

But relations between Jackson and Calhoun soon deteriorated, as the South Carolinian distrusted Jackson's political managers, especially Van Buren, and believed that the Northern wing of the Democratic Party was untrustworthy and was pressuring Jackson to take a "noncommittal middle ground" on the tariff. More was at stake for Calhoun than control of the party, for behind the tariff issue lay profound anxieties about the fate of slavery. Calhoun and other opponents of the tariff hoped both to preserve the balance between agrarian and manufacturing interests, and to serve notice they would not abide any direct federal intervention against the institution of slavery. Moreover, for Calhoun, neo-Federalism was a brooding threat not only in the tariff policy but also in the popularity of the American Colonization Society, which assiduously sought government support for its agenda of gradual emancipation.[5]

To answer the question of where the boundary lay between national and state sovereignty, Calhoun, in a ghost-written essay ("The South Carolina Exposition") published by the South Carolina legislature in 1828, articulated the doctrine of state interposition, or "nullification." Holding that the states were sovereign powers, that doctrine asserted that a single state, through a convention, could interpose to proclaim null and void within its territory any federal law that was inimical to its essential interests. If three-fourths of the other states, in a specially called federal convention, then upheld the constitutionality of the law, the nullifying state would be left with two legal recourses: to comply with the law or to secede from the Union. Although Calhoun considered interposition to be plainly derived from the Virginia and Kentucky resolutions, the doctrine went further than had either Jefferson or the Tertium Quids in the defense of states' rights. As Calhoun's modern biographer John Niven explained, Calhoun's stance "was not merely a static defense of the old order but a means of instilling a new vigor in the South's attitudes" so the "slave-plantation system would strengthen itself."[6]

Calhoun argued that his doctrine—with a tribunal of the states safeguarding the citizens against consolidation—was the means to reconcile states' rights and the Union. Indeed, since interposition would pass through a series of conventions at the state and federal levels, Calhoun's mechanism built in time for passions to abate and for compromise proposals to be hammered out. But the most ardent of his ideological lieutenants in South Carolina, like Robert Barnwell Rhett, had no patience for such a deliberate course. Instead, Rhett resorted to emotionally charged disunion rhetoric to drum up resistance to the tariff and to frighten the North into making concessions; he thundered at states' rights meetings in South Carolina that disunion "into a thousand fragments" was preferable to a "union of unlimited powers."[7]

Although this sort of Southern defiance seemed a bad omen for the antislavery cause, the year 1830 began with Pyrrhic victories. President Andrew Jackson, Calhoun's fellow Southern Democrat, resoundingly rejected his nullification scheme. The reasons were personal as well as political. Jackson naturally felt betrayed by Calhoun, whom he now saw as a cunning rival plotting to snatch away the presidency. Moreover, Jackson had been a moderate protectionist himself, on the grounds that the tariff could raise money for the national defense. Most important, Jackson and Calhoun had fundamentally different visions of the Union. For Jackson, who won the presidency as a champion of democracy and majority rule, "the Union was less a coercive institutional presence than the sustaining will for a common and glorious destiny," Major L. Wilson has written.[8]

Encomiums to the Union rang out in Congress, where National Republicans and Democrats closed ranks to isolate Calhoun's followers. The congressional debates over the tariff made a national hero of New England's Daniel Webster; his response to nullifier Robert Y. Hayne thoroughly discredited the South Carolinians. Hayne, hewing to the script of Calhoun rather than that of Rhett, had dissociated nullification from disunion. In fact, Hayne reversed the charge. He argued that the North, by criticizing slavery and pushing the hated tariff, was fomenting disunion, in keeping with the example New England had set during the Hartford Convention. Webster's masterful reply, on January 26 and 27, 1830, defended the sterling patriotism of New England and reminded Americans that South Carolina and Massachusetts had fought as one in the Revolution and had stood together in support of the Washington administration. Webster maintained forcefully that nullification was not a constitutional right—the Union was no mere league of sovereign states, but a nation, brought forth by the people, to guarantee them "high, exciting, gratifying prospects." Above all, Webster depicted disunion as the ultimate horror. "I have not accustomed myself to hang over the precipice of disunion, to see whether, with my short sight, I can fathom the depth of the abyss below," he said. He then proceeded to fathom disunion, to invoke the specter of "States dissevered, discordant, belligerent; on a land rent with civil feuds, or drenched, it may be, in fraternal blood!" The speech was hailed as one for the ages, and the appreciative Northern press followed Webster's lead in rebuking the nullifiers with dystopian visions of civil war; the *North American Review*, for example, opined that disunion would bring "an agonizing struggle of domestic parties . . . with the attendant train of rapine, assassination, judicial cruelty, and military execution." It concluded that "the act, by which one State severs itself from this union, entails a military despotism on that State, and probably on every other."[9]

Webster's speech was a powerful rebuke to the nullifiers, but it doubled as a rebuke to opponents of slavery. For the speech, by hailing "the Constitution as it is, and the Union as it is," sent the message that "Northerners and westerners were too busy and too well-off to worry about slavery," and that Southerners should "stop suspecting that [Northerners] would use federal powers to mount an attack on what was most assuredly a local matter." For now, the nullifiers were kept at bay by this reassurance and by two other checks: the prospect of a congressional adjustment of the tariff and the strength of proslavery Unionism in the South and in South Carolina itself. Believing the nullifiers to be isolated and out of step with public opinion, Southern politicians and newspaper editors rallied to denounce nullification as madness. As one North Carolina legislator put it: "Nullification is treason; and they who advocate it are traitors to our dearest rights." No one was more eloquent in such denunciations than Thomas S. Grimké, himself an elite Charlestonian. Grimké implored slaveowners to recognize that the Union had served and still served to protect slavery; nullification would bring disunion, which meant war and a future of "desolation and mourning." He prophesized that with the Union in shambles, "fanatics," domestic and foreign, would be able to do "ten times the mischief" against slavery than "they can do now."[10]

As the new decade dawned, slavery seemed to be protected by a powerful spell, in which images of the glorious Union were contrasted with hellish images of disunion. How could the spell be broken?

ENTER GARRISON

"The position of New England in 1829, was a most cheerless one for freedom . . . . Every body was, some way or other, actively or passively, sustaining slavery." Such was the opinion of Maria Weston Chapman, who would emerge as an abolitionist leader in the region in the 1830s. Her assessment of the political climate was widely shared by other Northern reformers, for there were many signs that since the Missouri Compromise, the North had grown more complacent toward and complicit in the Southern slave system. A majority of the white Northern electorate supported the ascendance of Jackson to the presidency; his administration was openly committed to extending the domain of slavery. The North had diverged from the agrarian South economically by developing a factory system, but the lifeblood of New England's textile industry was Southern cotton. The doctrine of white supremacy was strongly entrenched in the North, made manifest in a host of legal, political, and social disabilities imposed on the free black population there. Free blacks carried the burdens of citizenship (such as taxpaying) without full access to its benefits; public facilities such as schools were segregated; black men were, in most of the North, disfranchised; and white prejudice relegated blacks to a narrow band of occupations.[11]

According to Chapman, writing in 1839, what redeemed the North from its "utter ignorance" and saved it from careening recklessly down the road to perdition was the intervention of a deus ex machina—namely, abolitionist pioneer William Lloyd Garrison. Garrison, in founding his antislavery newspaper, the *Liberator*, in 1831 and establishing the American Anti-Slavery Society two years later, inaugurated a movement for immediate emancipation among Northern whites. He was the figurehead and lightning rod for "modern" immediatism.[12]

That Garrison, more than any other individual, wore the mantle of leader for the abolitionist movement in the 1830s is not in doubt; nor is it in doubt that he was a man of enormous courage and unshakable conviction who inspired the devotion of followers, like Chapman, from across the social spectrum. Yet the long shadow Garrison cast over the movement has served, in our time, as in his, to cloud our picture of immediatism and of Civil War causality. The first priority of modern scholarship on abolitionism was to account for the activism of Garrison and those like him—namely, white middle-class Northern men. In the 1970s historians generated a narrative of white men's embrace of immediatism, the essential elements of which are as follows: Inspired by the example of British abolitionists, fired by the spiritual "perfectionism" of the Second Great Awakening, eager to defend and extend the emerging wage labor system of the North, and anxious at the signs of increased slaveholder militancy, white men such as Garrison broke with other reform-minded Northerners, repudiated "gradual" solutions to the problem of slavery, and became abolitionists. The movement drew its numerical preponderance from the ranks of Northern white men (skilled wage earners and rising capitalists and professionals) and eventually splintered into a set of factions, each of which was led by white men—"Garrisonians," for example, broke from followers of Lewis Tappan and Theodore Weld. One acclaimed study of sectionalism goes so far as to describe the archetypal abolitionist thusly: "He was the quintessential northerner."[13]

This narrative has been considerably refined and amended in the past two decades by scholars, especially those working in the fields of African American and women's history, who have focused on the contributions of Northern free blacks, of white women, of black Southerners (especially fugitive slaves), and of dissident Southern whites to immediatism. This newer historiography has established that key elements of modern abolitionism—its strategies of grassroots activism, moral confrontation, and integration—were direct products of the mobilization of nonelites, particularly free blacks, male and female, and white women. These Northern nonelites drew inspiration both from the apostasy of white Southerners who broke ranks with the proslavery orthodoxy and, most important, from the resistance of those most courageous fighters against slavery—the slaves themselves. To define Northern white men as the "core" abolitionists is thus to obscure a central truth: What made immediatism revolutionary was the movement's success in crossing boundaries of race, gender, and region.[14]

Unlike the white majority, Northern free blacks did not regard the Missouri Compromise as a viable settlement of the issue of slavery. During the 1820s, African Americans used the printed word and the public meeting to formulate the defining doctrines of immediatism. Antislavery ferment was centered in three cities: Philadelphia, New York, and Boston, each of which was home to a welter of black reform (mutual-aid) societies that promoted racial uplift in the North and emancipation in the South—and continued to press the case against the colonization movement.[15] Finding that the impact of their protest meetings was undercut by the white press's refusal to publish fair accounts of these deliberations, prominent free blacks in New York rallied together to underwrite the establishment of their own newspaper, *Freedom's Journal*. Under the leadership of editor Samuel Cornish, a former minister, the paper refuted the colonizationist notion that blacks and whites could never coexist in harmony and mutual respect. Making a case that black Egyptians had been the cultural and scientific leaders of the ancient world, and that whatever deficiencies were evident in American blacks were the result of the environment of prejudice and deprivation in which they lived, Cornish argued that only equal treatment of blacks by whites would call forth the true capacities of a "now despised race."[16]

Cornish and his allies deplored the ways that slavery's defenders tried to conjoin abolition, rhetorically, with images of race war and civil war. Slaveholders who argued that black liberty would bring "ruin and infamy upon the nation" had succeeded in persuading whites, "from Maine to Mississippi," that "preservation will result from injustice and outrage—but danger from equity and mercy," Ohio abolitionists lamented in the pages of *Freedom's Journal*. They countered that "the experiment of our government, on the subject of equal rights, ought to put every idea of this nature to shame." If slaves were free and given the "stimulus of respectability and reward," they would exhibit the same "order and industry" as their white brethren, and a lasting peace would prevail.[17]

As Rogan Kersh notes, for pioneering black immediatists, disunion primarily connoted divisions among blacks—between slave and free, Northern and Southern, reform-minded and cautious—and "union" connoted the need for solidarity and concerted action. Calls for union reflected the fact that black reformers had to contend not only with the economic constraints on their communities but also with fear and even apathy. To woo converts to the cause of abolition, they had both to embolden Northern African Americans to risk potential reprisals from white employers, neighbors, and public authorities, and to persuade those blacks for whom Southern slavery seemed a distant prospect that it was an ever-present threat.[18]

The most powerful call to action and the most systematic attack on racial prejudice in this era came from the pen of David Walker, a Southerner by birth and upbringing. The scattered documentary record reveals little of his early life but suggests that his mother was a free black and his father was a slave; since, by law, a black child's status followed that of the mother, Walker was free. In both Wilmington, North Carolina, where he spent his youth, and in Charleston, South Carolina, where he journeyed as a young man, Walker was steeped in a culture of slave resistance. Slaves fought the regime of back-breaking labor, sadistic punishment, and physical deprivation by seeking solace in their own religious congregations; by running away and searching for refuge either in remote areas of the South, such as the Cape Fear swamps, or in the free states; and by plotting outright rebellions. Walker likely was aware that blacks' "revolutionary evangelicalism" had inspired the abortive slave revolts of Gabriel and Vesey; he surely knew that such acts of resistance were followed by periods of retaliation and repression. Not long after the Vesey rebellion, Walker made his way to the North and settled in Boston, where, by the mid-1820s, he had established himself as a successful businessman and leading activist. He served as an agent for *Freedom's Journal* and was instrumental in the founding of an ambitious black reform society, the Massachusetts General Colored Association.[19]

In 1829 Walker published his *Appeal to the Coloured Citizens of the World.* Declaring that "America is more our country than it is the whites—we have enriched it with our *blood and tears*," Walker's *Appeal* exposed the "colonizing trick" as a proslavery, racist gambit and echoed James Forten in asserting blacks' American citizenship. Stressing national complicity in slavery, Walker directed his righteous anger at the "White Christians of America" in the North and South alike. Most important, he explicitly rejected the notion that antislavery agitation was disunionist. Addressing the belief of whites that "if we were set free in America, we would involve the country in a civil war,"

Walker argued that that "assertion is altogether at variance with our feeling or design, for we ask them for nothing but the rights of man." If whites freed blacks and treated them with respect, "there will be no danger," he predicted, "for we will love and respect them, and protect our country." In Walker's formulation, emancipation would not threaten the Union but actuate it—by fulfilling the transcendent spirit of the Declaration of Independence and by permitting blacks to contribute fully to the prosperity and security of the nation.[20]

Walker juxtaposed his pleas and prayers for the formation of a moral Union with his own terrifying prophesies about what fate awaited the nation if it failed to repent. A few impassioned passages in the *Appeal*, in which Walker threatens that blacks might turn to violence as a last resort, earned him a long-standing and widespread reputation among whites as a menacing avenger. But in Walker's view, it was divine wrath—not intimations of black insurrection—that whites had most to fear. "God rules in the armies of Heaven," he proclaimed. "Does not the blood of our fathers and of us their children, cry aloud to the Lord of the Sabbath against you!!" White Christian Americans had to make a momentous choice: to "listen to the voice of the Holy Ghost" or to see their nation destroyed. For Walker, compromisers like Kentucky's archcolonizationist Henry Clay, who had brokered the Missouri deal, were not the saviors of the Union but the agents of its demise. "Is not God against him," Walker wrote of Clay, "for advocating the murderous cause of slavery?"[21]

What distinguished Walker's *Appeal* from other antislavery declarations by free blacks in this era was its author's Southern background and identity. Written in the cadences of the evangelical preachers Walker had heard as a young man, and designed to be distributed among and read aloud to illiterate blacks, the *Appeal* was animated by Walker's claim to authenticity: he knew Southern whites and Southern blacks intimately. "What I have written is what I have seen and heard myself." African Americans in the North embraced the *Appeal*; as one Connecticut minister recalled, crowds gathered around to hear it "read and re-read until [its] words were stamped in letters of fire upon our soul." Walker worked hard to establish a network of agents (black sailors were particularly useful, as they traveled to Southern ports) to take the *Appeal* to the South and succeeded in having it distributed in Richmond, Wilmington, Charleston, and Savannah, among other places. But once white authorities got wind of the *Appeal*'s inroads into the South, they acted quickly to suppress it. Southern legislatures passed laws restricting contact between free blacks and slaves and outlawing the teaching of blacks, free and slave, to read and write. Meanwhile, individual communities took measures to seize and destroy copies of the *Appeal* and to intimidate, harass, arrest, exile, fine, and even murder those suspected of disseminating it. In New Bern, North Carolina, in December 1830, sixty slaves were killed because of the suspicion that they had planned a revolt based on "Walker's inflammatory pamphlet." What most alarmed white Southerners about the *Appeal* was that it seemed to be evidence of a vast underground network that stretched from a "distant Northern city" into the heart of the South. The hostility that it generated was responsible for the resilient rumor that Walker, who died of consumption in 1830, had been murdered by an irate white Southern assassin.[22]

While Walker's *Appeal* raised the specter of a collaboration between Northern and Southern blacks, the writings and speeches of Maria Stewart (his coworker in the Massachusetts General Colored Association in Boston) suggested that women and men were collaborating politically as equals. From the start, African American women were integral to the free black campaign against prejudice and slavery. Indeed, they founded some of the first organizations committed to immediatism, such as the African American Female Intelligence Society of Boston led by Stewart. The Hartford native became an antislavery crusader after she embraced Christianity in 1831. Stewart was the first American woman to speak about political issues before "mixed" assemblages of men and women. Her speeches and published writings directly echoed Walker—"It is the blood of our fathers, and the tears of our brethren that have enriched your soils. AND WE CLAIM OUR RIGHTS," she announced in 1831. But by virtue of her gender, she embodied a radical claim, grounded in her reading of the Bible, that Walker had not made—that black women had the right to a political voice. In doing so, she confronted two widespread prejudices: the white view that African American women were not capable of true moral virtue and intellectual achievement, and the societywide notion (one so firmly held that it would survive into the twentieth century) that public speaking was inappropriate for women.[23]

The experiences of Walker and Stewart served notice that immediatism would challenge the status quo by breaching the lines that divided black from white, free from slave, North from South, public from private, and women's sphere from men's. But Northern cities were only one arena for the anti-slavery struggle. Nowhere was abolitionism's threat to traditional boundaries more dramatic than in the borderlands.

FIGHTING SLAVERY IN THE BORDERLANDS

"A lighted candle stood as a beacon which could be seen from across the river, and like the north star was the guide to the fleeing slave." This is how former slave John Parker described the home of John Rankin. The dwelling, preserved to this day as a National Historic Landmark, is located in Ripley, Ohio, on the banks of a narrow bend in the Ohio River, just across from neighboring Kentucky. Parker and Rankin, both natives of the South who had fled the region, were instrumental in making Ripley a depot on the Underground Railroad. The two men, in collaboration with antislavery neighbors in Ohio's Brown County, helped to spirit hundreds of slaves out of slaveholding Kentucky and into freedom.[24]

The story of Ripley's abolitionists provides a key link between the Revolutionary wave of manumissions in the Upper South and the emergence of Garrisonian abolitionism in the Northeast in the 1830s. In the late eighteenth and early nineteenth centuries a small but significant number of whites opposed to slavery left Virginia, Tennessee, the Carolinas, and Kentucky for Ohio and other free states. Such migrants from the South formed the core of Ripley's antislavery community and furnished it with its leader, the Reverend John Rankin. Born and raised in Tennessee, Rankin left the state in 1817 because of opposition to his antislavery preaching in the Presbyterian church where he was minister. He settled in Ripley, where by the mid-1820s he was helping fugitive slaves steer a course across the Ohio River, into free Ohio, and on to other free states such as Illinois and Indiana. Rankin also established himself as a pioneering author, publishing his immediatist manifesto, *Letters on American Slavery*, in 1826.[25]

Addressed to his brother Thomas, a slaveowner in Augusta County, Virginia, Rankin's *Letters* were a plea for empathy. To persuade Thomas to renounce slaveholding, Rankin asked him to put himself in the position of the slave. Rankin conjured up the image of a slave woman being whipped and asked Thomas to imagine that it was his wife undergoing this torture: "Tell me, dear brother, how could you have endured to see her tender frame beneath the lacerating whip? Would not such a scene shock the whole current of your nature . . . ?" This notion—that by searching their souls and confronting the question "How would *you* feel?" white men could fathom the pain of "black hearts"—would become a standard trope of immediatism in the 1830s. So, too, would another of Rankin's insights: that the presence of individual slave-holders who were relatively kind and conscientious could not redeem a *system* that was corrupt and corrupting. Noting, correctly, that slaveowners were le-gally entitled to punish disobedient slaves to the point of killing them, Rankin thundered: "Our system of slavery puts it completely in the power of the slaveholders to dismember their slaves, or even murder them at pleasure!"[26]

Significantly, Rankin fused the specter of divine wrath and that of slave rebellion. "If we refuse to do the Africans justice, we may expect the supreme Governor of the world to avenge their wrongs, and cause their own arm to make them free!" His solution was an abolitionist version of diffusion. If blacks were kept in bondage, their numbers would grow, as would their bitterness, and they would become "prepared for the day of battle." If they were liberated, they would "scatter over this Union—many of them will emigrate to Haiti and Africa"; so diffused and divested of causes for resent-ment, they would have "no inducements to do [whites] harm." For Rankin, as for Walker, the choice was momentous—emancipation or national ruin. Invoking what would become a stock image of disunion, Rankin warned: "The storm is gathering fast—dismal clouds already begin to darken our horizon. A few more years and the work of death will commence!"[27]

The violence of the slave system was evident in the response of proslavery Kentuckians to Rankin's work. Kentucky slaveholders resorted to a wide array of measures to close down the Ripley "line." They stepped up the work of slave "patrols" that sought to catch fugitives, made fraudulent claims that Ohioans had broken Kentucky's laws, tried to spark mob violence and blame it on the abolitionists, impersonated antislavery conductors to entrap un-suspecting blacks and whites, and attempted to intimidate the families and destroy the property of Rankin and his allies. In the words of Ann Hagedorn: "From the moment the Missouri Compromise was signed, what had begun as a moral dispute between neighbors who shared a river was evolving into a high-stakes, life-threatening duel that intensified throughout the 1820s. By the mid-1830s, it would prove to be nothing less than a war." Rankin refused to be driven from the field of battle, even by the $3,000 price that Kentucky put on his head, and continued to recruit fellow warriors into the 1850s. Most prominent among these was the aforementioned John Parker, who had been born into slavery in Virginia and sold, as a young child, to a doctor in Alabama; he was bought in turn by an elderly patient of the doctor who agreed to let Parker work to buy his own freedom. Parker moved to Ohio and began collaborating with Rankin in the late 1840s. A successful businessman (he established a foundry), Parker risked his livelihood and life by making numerous trips back across the Ohio River, into the maw of slavery, to help lead fellow blacks to freedom.[28]

Despite the courage of Rankin and Parker, and of the slaves whom they assisted, the chances of a successful escape to freedom were remote—even in the borderlands. For runaways faced the wrath not only of Kentucky slave catchers but of Ohio ones, too. The fugitive slave provisions of the Constitution had been made more stringent by a 1793 law, passed with the overwhelming support of Congress, that gave slaveholders and their agents the right to seize slaves in free states without arrest warrants; simply by testifying before a judge or magistrate that a slave was his, a master could legally establish his right to retrieve the slave. Moreover, the 1793 law made it illegal for anyone to give refuge to a fugitive slave or to interfere with the capture of one by slave catchers. Because of such measures, the Ohio River was a "formidable barrier." As John Hope Franklin and Loren Schweninger have related: "Authorities in counties along the river were on the lookout for those who might be trying to pass themselves off as hired hands or free persons. At certain jumping-off points and portage locations, sheriffs were particularly vigilant. . . . Indeed, there seemed to be no formula for success."[29]

Thus the "war" along the Kentucky-Ohio border was not, strictly speaking, a conflict between North and South, but rather a fight by proslavery white Northerners and Southerners for the security of the slave system and a fight by antislavery Northerners and Southerners for the salvation of the slaves.

NATIONALIZING THE CRUSADE:
GARRISON LAUNCHES THE *LIBERATOR*

"I am extremely happy to hear that you are about establishing a Paper in Boston. I hope your efforts may not be in vain; and may the 'Liberator' be the means of exposing, more and more, the odious system of Slavery, and of raising up friends to the oppressed and degraded People of colour." James Forten wrote these lines to his friend William Lloyd Garrison on December 31, 1830. The recent backlash against Walker's pamphlet had not shaken Forten's faith that the abolition cause was gathering momentum. He confided his hopes to Garrison: "Although the Southern States have enacted severe Laws against the Free People of Colour, they will find it impossible to go in opposition to the Spirit of the Times."[30]

As Garrison labored tirelessly to build an audience for his immediatist newspaper the *Liberator* in its inaugural year of 1831, he drew inspiration from the examples of Forten, Cornish, Walker, Stewart, and Rankin. His intellectual debts are plain to see in every issue: his attacks on colonization reprised those of Forten, Cornish, and other free blacks; his impassioned tones and apocalyptic rhetoric of sin and redemption echoed Walker; his realization that women would be vital agents in the immediatist crusade showed the influence of the activists in Stewart's milieu. Garrison openly acknowledged these debts—for example, he praised Rankin for his "early labors on behalf of the oppressed." The *Liberator* was designed, in other words, to bring the era's abolition ferment to the attention of the public, and to persuade readers that the movement's time had come. But for all his obvious debts, Garrison's fame—and infamy—soon eclipsed that of his co-workers in the cause. For Garrison, more than any other activist, saw in the agitation of this diverse group of immediatists the potential for a national movement. He envisioned a "mass action strategy," in which speaking tours by antislavery agents, petition drives, and the distribution of antislavery litera-ture would take place on a grand scale, and would connect the efforts of local, grassroots societies. Garrison believed that the first step in building a biracial abolition network was persuading white Northerners that they had a stake in the immediatist crusade. This he did by stressing, more than any previous writer had done, the complicity of the North in the system of bondage.[31]

Garrison's compassion was the product of his own troubled upbringing. Born in Newburyport, Massachusetts, in 1805 and abandoned by his father three years later, Garrison grew up poor and as a small boy was put to work to bring income into the family. He was ridiculed by the neighborhood children and thus came to identify with society's outcasts. The harshness of Gar-rison's early life was mitigated by his closeness to his mother, Maria Garrison, a devout Baptist who, in Garrison's words, was "sanctified by an ever-glowing piety." "His mother's was an active religion," biographer Henry Mayer has written, "an endless battle in which combat was conducted in volleys of words as well as deeds." She instilled in young William both a zeal for reform and a love of language. As a young man, Garrison made language his trade, working his way up the ranks of the newspaper business in New- buryport, Boston, and Bennington, Vermont, before joining Benjamin Lundy as coeditor of the *Genius of Universal Emancipation* in 1829.[32]

It was through the lens of these early influences that Garrison beheld and tried to make sense of the major trends of his day—the concomitant rise, in the North, of economic modernization and of religious revivalism. Every- where that the hallmarks of modernization were to be found—in proliferating cities and towns, with their "new" middle class of urban professionals and capitalists; in stunningly efficient factories, staffed by working-class wage earners, churning out goods such as textiles; along the networks of canals and railroads that transported such mass-produced goods to distant markets—so too did one find eager audiences for a new kind of evangelicalism. Popu- larized by itinerants like the charismatic Charles Finney, this religion was calculated to comfort and guide Northerners caught in a whirlwind of change. Finney's message was "perfectionism": Individuals could and should seek to be as perfect as God, and thus seize control of their own destinies and fortunes. Perfectionism found expression in a wide array of charitable (or "benevolent") causes embraced by antebellum Northerners, including cam- paigns to eradicate drunkenness and prostitution, to extend aid to impover- ished orphans and widows, and to distribute religious tracts to the poor. Garrison and the circle of immediatists he gathered around him were caught up in this spirit of reform and drew out its most radical and egalitarian implications. They sought "moral revolution" not "moral renovation," James Brewer Stewart explains, and "shattered religious orthodoxies time and again by improvising still more expansive ways of enacting God's will in everyday life."[33] If the new "free labor" economy produced such wealth and oppor- tunity, they asked, why shouldn't its benefits extend to blacks and to the South itself? If reformers should promote moral perfection, why shouldn't they seek to eradicate America's worst sin, that of slaveholding? These ques- tions formed the backdrop for the *Liberator*.

In his first editorial in the *Liberator*, Garrison declared that he found among Northerners "contempt more bitter, opposition more active, detraction

The serene and scholarly countenance of *Liberator* editor William Lloyd Garrison belied his fierce courage and devotion to the abolitionist cause. (Courtesy of the Library of Congress)

more relentless, prejudice more stubborn, and apathy more frozen, than among the slave owners themselves." This rhetorical flourish was in no way intended to exonerate slaveholders; rather, its purpose was to implicate, and provoke, white Northerners. Garrison pledged himself to "lift the standard of emancipation in the eyes of the nation" and to spare no one his wrath. "Let southern oppressors tremble—let their secret abettors tremble—let their northern apologists tremble—let all the enemies of the persecuted blacks tremble," he intoned. As Mayer has put it, Garrison "was determined to put a lurid cast upon the landscape of compromise and concession, to heat up the issue until the public felt ashamed of its connection to slavery and angry at granting political privileges to slaveholders."[34]

Such rhetoric marked Garrison's break from Quaker abolitionists who favored a course of moderation. With a theology that stressed the presence of God—the "Inner Light"—in all human beings, the Society of Friends had long been the most progressive Protestant sect. Quakers formed the core of the first association devoted to national emancipation, the Pennsylvania Abolition Society (PAS—founded in 1775); by the 1780s, after decades of effort to purge the sect of slaveholding, Quakers had pledged themselves to antislavery principles. Led by elite philanthropists, the PAS favored a strategy of petitioning the government against slavery, giving legal aid to African Americans (such as free blacks who had been fraudulently seized by slaveholders), and sending itinerant preachers into slave states like Delaware, Virginia, and North Carolina to plead with slaveholders to release their bondspeople.[35]

While Philadelphia was the center of Quaker life, the Friends established communities within slave states such as Maryland, Virginia, and North Carolina. The Quaker community in Loudoun County, Virginia, for example, dated back to the 1720s and was home to antislavery minister Samuel Janney, who was born there in 1801. In the 1820s Janney worked with other Virginia Quakers to found a benevolent society in Alexandria to rescue free blacks who were illegally captured by slave traders, wrote antislavery essays for the *Alexandria Gazette*, and coauthored a petition to Congress asking for the abolition of slavery in the District of Columbia. As Janney wrote in his memoir, the opposition to such work in Virginia was "not then so great as it became a few years later." Rather, slavery was "acknowledged to be an evil entailed on us by former generations." Although he had become a convert to immediatism, Janney adopted a public posture of moderation, claiming only to support gradual emancipation. "A calm, temperate, and yet decided bearing," he averred, "will have the most salutary influence in promoting the great cause of emancipation." While Janney used such public vehicles to advance the cause of emancipation, his community of Loudoun Quakers also clandestinely maintained a stop on the Underground Railroad at Edward's Ferry on the Potomac.[36]

Although antislavery Quakers had achieved some success in offering refuge and legal protection to blacks and in preaching the gospel of emancipation in the South, the scope of these efforts was limited by the reform style of the Friends. While they yearned for immediate emancipation, they "knew that even in their own religious society convincing people to do what was right had taken years of effort."[37] The ways that Garrison's rhetoric challenged the traditional Quaker approach are evident when we compare the *Liberator*'s editor with his journalistic mentor, Society of Friends and PAS member Benjamin Lundy. Lundy, who had traveled widely in the border states and Upper South as an antislavery itinerant, invited Garrison to become the coeditor of the *Genius of Universal Emancipation* in 1829. Among Lundy's many contributions to the antislavery cause was his hiring of a fellow Philadelphia Quaker, Margaret Chandler, to edit the "ladies" column in the *Genius*; a gifted writer, Chandler was a model for future female "Garrisonian" abolitionists. But Lundy's language was distinct from Garrison's. As Henry Mayer has observed: "Lundy shared Garrison's belief in the sinfulness of slavery, but the younger man's evangelical fervor and melodramatic style went against the Quaker grain. Lundy winced whenever Garrison referred to slaveholders as 'man-stealers.' "[38]

Both the emotional pitch and the high ambition of the *Liberator* distinguished it from earlier work by white abolitionists. And yet to focus on Garrison's determination to "heat up" the slavery issue is to miss another, equally important and innovative, part of his mission. Although the statement in his opening editorial, "I am in earnest—I will not equivocate—I will not excuse—I will not retreat a single inch—AND I WILL BE HEARD," is, to this day, the most quoted of all of his words, the bulk of the articles in the newspaper's first year of publication were devoted to a gentle mission: that of modeling for readers what true interracial friendship and collaboration looked like. Garrison filled the first volume of the *Liberator* with contributions—letters, articles, poems, and transcripts of meetings and speeches—by African Americans. The *Liberator* can be read as a series of conversations between Garrison and his black correspondents, conversations marked by a tone of grace and mutual admiration. Garrison hoped that he could persuade white readers to listen in on, and eventually to participate in, these conversations. By listening in, whites might be persuaded to abandon a prejudice that was the bedrock of the slavery system—namely, the notion that blacks were intellectually inferior. Garrison referred to his correspondents as "intelligent and highly respectable"; they referred to him as "esteemed friend."[39]

In forming and publicizing his friendships with blacks, no less than in his impassioned rhetoric, Garrison broke with the tradition of the PAS and moderate antislavery movement. At this stage the PAS did not yet welcome blacks as members, and Lundy, though he had some contacts among free blacks in Baltimore, did not forge the kind of friendships that Garrison enjoyed with reformers like James Forten. Garrison did not view white Northern men as his "core" constituents. Rather, he envisioned a biracial coalition of men and women working together as equals.[40]

The militancy of Garrison's empathy and the connection between the *Liberator*'s stern warnings to whites, on the one hand, and its mission of friendship to blacks, on the other, are evident in the coverage Garrison gave to David Walker's *Appeal*. Knowing well that blacks constituted the majority of his subscribers, and eager to prove to them that he was a true ally, Garrison featured numerous favorable notices about the *Appeal* in the first issues of the *Liberator*. He grappled with the thorniest aspect of the *Appeal*: namely, Walker's notion that violent resistance to slavery was for blacks a viable and justifiable last resort should peaceful reform fail. Garrison decried any calls to violence and upheld his nonresistant creed of "submission and peace." But he also pointedly noted that if a bloody insurrection took place in the South, slaveholders and their Northern allies would have no one to blame but them-selves: "If any people were ever justified in throwing off the yoke of their tyrants, the slaves are that people."[41]

Garrison, following the lead of *Freedom's Journal* and Walker's *Appeal*, thus tried to change the terms of disunion discourse. He insisted that it would take more, much more, than congressional compromises, or plans for the diffusion or restriction of slavery, to protect the nation from race war. Only true justice—immediate abolition and the offer of genuine equality to blacks—could secure the peace. For Garrison, there was no contradiction between his rhetoric of angry chastisement and that of Christian fellowship. He sought to persuade his readers, particularly white ones, that his anger was a righteous anger—that it sprang from love. For if whites could only see blacks, free and slave, as fellow Christians, as friends and potential friends, then whites, too, would become angry at the system of slavery, so angry that they could no longer close their hearts and avert their eyes.

NAT TURNER'S REBELLION

"The year 1831 seems to be big with great events," James Forten predicted in the pages of the *Liberator* nearly a month after the newspaper was founded. His words proved prophetic. On August 22 of that year, a slave preacher named Nat Turner led a dramatic if doomed revolt that would change the tra-jectory of the antislavery campaign and profoundly shape the white Southern-ers' response to immediatism. The stage for Nat Turner's Rebellion was Southampton County, Virginia, on the southeastern border of the state.

Southampton shared with its neighboring counties in North Carolina similarities not only in terrain but also in culture: these coastal border counties were the heart of a region, "running from north of Richmond south to Wilmington," in which blacks "had a tradition of fusing religion with resistance." David Walker had emerged from this very milieu.[42]

Turner was a Baptist preacher whose sermons at religious revivals had won him the admiration of others blacks in the region. Born into slavery, he had experienced the trauma of being repeatedly sold from one master to another; from a young age, Turner's striking intellect gave him the aura of one who had a special destiny. In the 1820s he began to experience visitations from a "Spirit" commanding him to lead his people into freedom. The solar eclipse of February 1831 he took to be a sign that the time for this rebellion was nearing; a second sign, "in the guise of a green-tinted sun," came on August 13. A little more than a week later Turner and his band of rebels began their bloody work: moving from farmhouse to farmhouse, they left about sixty whites dead—women and children among them—and others maimed and terrified in their wake. The Virginia militia and federal troops caught up with the insurgents and put down the outbreak on August 23, killing some and taking the rest into captivity. Turner managed to evade capture and hid out in the area for more than two months. Rumors of his whereabouts circulated in Virginia newspapers; the most plausible account seemed to be that he had sought refuge in the Great Dismal Swamp, a vast dense bog along the Virginia–North Carolina border, into which many fugitive slaves had disappeared. But on October 30, Turner's hiding place was discovered by a farmer in Southampton.[43]

Virginia papers rejoiced at the surrender of the "blood-stained monster." Less than two weeks later, on November 11, Turner was executed. The only record we have of his thoughts and motivations is the transcript of an interview conducted with Turner in prison while he awaited execution. The interviewer, lawyer Thomas R. Gray, shaped Turner's "confessions" to reflect his own prejudices. Gray published his interview and sold tens of thousands of copies. As readers of the *Confessions* dissected Turner's thoughts, the authorities literally dissected his body. Local doctors "skinned it and made grease of the flesh."[44]

The violence done to Turner's body was but a symbol of the horrifying backlash against blacks, free and slave, in the region. As soon as the insurrection came to light, furious whites in Virginia and nearby Southern states killed dozens of allegedly rebellious slaves. White violence was carried out in the name of revenge and of deterrence. A revealing account comes down to us in Harriet Jacobs's slave narrative. Published on the eve of the Civil War, after its author had escaped slavery and settled in the North, her chronicle reveals how this violent backlash reverberated in Edenton, North Carolina, where she grew up. The news of Turner's uprising "threw our town into great commotion," Jacobs recalled. The very atmosphere of panic gave the lie to slaveholders' claims that the institution was benign. "Strange that they should be so alarmed," Jacobs wrote, "when their slaves were so 'contented and happy.'" Whites in her town quickly formed vigilante posses to search the houses of blacks, free and slave, for "proof that they were plotting insurrection." The posses planted evidence to entrap blacks and then meted out sadistic punishments: "Every where men, women, and children were whipped till the blood stood in puddles at their feet."[45]

White hysteria was not restricted to slaveholders. In a trenchant insight into the social dynamics of a slave society, Jacobs observed that the backlash "was a grand opportunity for the low whites, who had no negroes of their own to scourge. They exulted in such a chance to exercise a little brief authority. . . . At night, they formed themselves into patrol bands, and went wherever they chose among the colored people, acting out their brutal will." For months after the rebellion, blacks lived in fear of further reprisals. As Jacobs remembered, "No two people that had the slightest tinge of color in their faces dared to be seen talking together." The reign of terror extended beyond Virginia and North Carolina and continued beyond the summer and fall of 1831. In January 1832, a correspondent to the *Liberator* revealed, a certain planter in Georgia had committed an act of "fiendish barbarity"—he had lashed and then burned alive a ten-year-old slave girl, blaming her, falsely, for an act of arson that had resulted in the destruction of his house. "We cannot help the poor victim," the correspondent lamented, "she must suffer, as the whites say, to make blacks fear and tremble, and to prevent a repetition of the massacres of Virginia."[46]

The failure of Nat Turner's Rebellion and the curtain of repression that descended on blacks in its wake illustrate why outright slave insurrections were so rare in the Old South—they were, as Eugene Genovese put it, "virtual suicide." The legal and extralegal means for detecting, deterring, and punishing rebellion were too strong. Whites across the social spectrum, nonslaveholder and master alike, were committed to maintaining the security of the system; on this issue, there were few fissures in the web of bondage that would-be rebels could exploit. The striking economic disparities in wealth between the average slaveholder and nonslaveholding farmer were counteracted by factors that bridged the divide of class. The two groups were linked by kinship networks; by evangelical Christianity; by economic interdependence (yeomen who lived in plantation districts generally raised some goods, such as cotton or livestock, for the market and did business with planters); by an ethos of noblesse oblige among the wealthy, whereby they extended aid and charity to poor citizens in times of crisis; and by a shared commitment to white supremacy. Tapping this shared racism, slaveholders when seeking office preached the gospel of *"Herrenvolk* democracy"—the notion that because black slaves constituted a permanent underclass, all white men shared a measure of equality as members of the master race. This doctrine was well suited to the Jacksonian era, as many Southern states removed property qualifications for voting and officeholding, and made formerly appointive offices elective. Moreover, based on evidence of upward mobility in the South, nonslaveholders could hope to move up the economic ladder into the ranks of slaveholders. Herrenvolk democracy played not only to the aspirations of nonslaveholders but also to their fear that "division and consequent weakness among whites on the slave question would invite rebellion by the blacks and aggression by abolitionists."[47]

Faced with desperate odds against successful rebellion, slaves in the Old South resorted to alternative means of resistance, including arson, poisoning, and acts of "silent sabotage" such as work slowdowns. The existence of a distinctive African American culture in the slave quarters was itself a form of resistance to masters' constant efforts to crush the spirit of their bondspeople and to prevent them from making common cause. Although Nat Turner had failed to free his people, he loomed large in slave culture, a recent study has shown, as a "legendary figure, famous for having outfoxed the white soldiers and bounty hunters who pursued him for more than two months before his capture." Among those Turner influenced, Catherine Clinton surmises, was Harriet Tubman, a legendary figure in her own right for her courageous work on the Underground Railroad in the 1850s. For Tubman, Turner's creed and legacy was "that freedom was something worth dying for." The image of

Turner as both trickster and martyr persisted well into the twentieth century. An ex-slave named Cornelia Carney told a white interviewer in 1938 that the true moral of the story of "Old Nat" was that blacks could "always out-smart de white folks."[48]

A demon in the eyes of proslavery Southern whites and a hero to Southern blacks, Turner represented, for William Lloyd Garrison, a grim vindication. In the September 3, 1831, issue of the *Liberator*, Garrison interpreted the Southampton insurrection as the fulfillment of his own prophecy. He had warned that terrible events would come to pass if the nation failed to re-pent its sins, and he was right. What had been "imagination" in his exhor-tations of January 1, 1831, was "now a bloody reality." The brutal back-lash against blacks he called "a dastardly triumph, well becoming a nation of oppressors." But while Garrison insisted that the North admit to its share of culpability, he rejected the charge that abolitionists themselves were some-how guilty of inciting rebellion. "The slaves need no incentive at our hands," he declared. They found incentive "in their emaciated bodies" and in "their ceaseless toil." What was the lesson of Nat Turner's Rebellion? That im-mediate abolition alone could save the United States from "the vengeance of Heaven."[49]

THE VIRGINIA SLAVERY DEBATES OF 1831–1832

Southern slaveholders and their allies resoundingly rejected Garrison's claim that the purpose of the *Liberator* was to "*prevent* rebellion." They deemed his words incendiary and incriminating. Whereas the Vesey scare had evoked vague Southern intimations of Northern culpability for slave discontent, the Turner insurrection brought forth a chorus of vitriolic, specific accusations. Newspapers such as the *Richmond Enquirer* and the *National Intelligencer* (the premier newspaper in Washington, D.C.) excoriated Garrison, declaring that his "diabolical" paper had spread the seeds of rebellion. Slaveholders passed laws that imposed penalties on anyone who distributed the *Libera-tor*. The legislature of Georgia went so far as to put a price on Garrison's head: Whoever arrested the offending editor and conveyed him South to stand trial for his treasonous language, would receive a reward of five thou-sand dollars.[50]

Based on private letters, published articles, and legal statutes, the belief that "abolitionist agitation" had caused Turner's Rebellion was common currency among elite Southern whites. Martha Jefferson Randolph, daughter of Thomas Jefferson, subscribed to this view in a letter of October 27, 1831; she singled out the writings of David Walker and Garrison for opprobrium. So too did Governor John Floyd of Virginia in a November 1831 letter to James Hamilton Jr., governor of South Carolina. Floyd began by offering the following thesis: "I am fully persuaded, the spirit of insubordination which has, and still manifests itself in Virginia, had its origin among, and eminated [*sic*] from, the Yankee population." He went on to trace the workings of Yankee influence. Northern preachers "were very assiduous in operating upon our population" and in making religion "the fashion of the times." They found a particularly willing audience among white Southern slaveholding women, Floyd opined, by appealing to their sentimentality and charitable natures. Such women "were persuaded that it was piety to teach negroes to read and write, to the end that they might read the *Scriptures*." The next step in the process of abolitionist infiltration was the enlistment of black Southern preachers in the cause of rebellion. The culmination of the process was the circulation of the "incendiary publications" of Walker and Garrison. All the while, Floyd lamented, Virginians rested in "apathetic security." But the spell of apathy had been broken—Floyd announced to Hamilton that he would propose to his legislature new laws that prohibited blacks from preaching and that would "drive from this State all free negroes" as a step preparatory to the gradual emancipation and removal from Virginia of all slaves.[51]

In its famous legislative session of 1831–32, the Virginia General Assembly did pass laws that banned slaves and free blacks from preaching or from attending religious gatherings unless supervised by whites. But Floyd's fantasy of the gradual removal of all blacks from Virginia proved far more controversial. If he had hoped to control the agenda of the winter legislative session, his hopes were quickly dashed—on December 14, 1831, Virginia Quakers submitted a petition to the General Assembly requesting that it abolish slavery in the commonwealth. The petition was referred to a special committee designated to rule on antislavery proposals. Although quick to dismiss the appeal of Quakers, the special committee had no choice but to consider the proposal of an insider. On January 11, 1832, delegate Thomas Jefferson Randolph—grandson of the sage of Monticello—presented a formula for "post-nati" emancipation, whereby all female slaves born in Virginia on or after July 4, 1840, would be freed at age eighteen and all male slaves born on or after July 4, 1840, would be freed at twenty-one. The slaves emancipated according to this formula would be given over to the state so they could be "colonized" in Africa. As Kenneth Greenberg has noted, this plan was "antiblack": it did not require the emancipation of a single slave, as masters were free to sell off slaves before they reached the age of "freedom." For Randolph, security was the issue. The alternative to gradual emancipation was to await the "inevitable"—the "dissolution of the Union" and a bitter border war, in which white and black invaders from the North would travel south "burning with enthusiasm" to liberate the slaves. When that moment comes, he warned white Virginians in his own terrifying prophecy, you "cannot save your wives and children from destruction."[52]

Randolph's approach found much favor, especially in the western portion of the state. A regional fault line defined Virginia's politics, dividing the lowland eastern counties from the western counties that lay astride the Blue Ridge Mountains. While the eastern economy was based on slave labor and plantation agriculture, western counties were characterized by small farms, few slaves, and close economic ties to the neighboring free states of Ohio and Pennsylvania. Western yeoman farmers had long resented the political dominance of the eastern planter elite. The eastern counties, with a disproportionately large number of representatives in the state legislature, had passed high taxes and restrictive property qualifications for voting, among other measures, over the objections of western men. Virginia's elite, in other words, had resisted the national trend toward political democratization. This recalcitrance stoked sectional animosity and revived the slavery debate within the state. "It was easterners' refusal to share power more equitably that drove westerners to oppose the basis of slaveholders' power—slavery—by 1832," Eva Sheppard Wolf explains. During the legislative debates, some western Virginians, such as James M'Dowell and Thomas Marshall, crafted an "incipient free-labor ideology." In their view, the labor of sturdy free white farmers was more morally virtuous and economically productive than that of slaves.[53]

Moreover, westerners wished to protect themselves against another Nat Turner. Randolph's plan, by insisting that freed slaves be deported, would keep the scourge of black rebellion out of western Virginia. The appeal of this proposal is demonstrated by gradualist petitions from the west, particularly the January 19, 1832, memorial signed by 215 women of Augusta County. The petitioners evoked the nightmare of their destruction at the hands of the "bloody monster" that lived at their "own hearths." They would rather do without slave labor than live with those hardships "we now endure in providing for and ruling the faithless beings who are subjected to us."[54]

The example of Mary Blackford of Fredericksburg reveals that some Southern slaveholders supported gradualism not out of antipathy to blacks but rather because they felt genuine guilt for the sin of slaveholding and genuine empathy for blacks. An avid supporter of the colonization movement and the matriarch of a slaveholding family, Blackford penned an unpublished journal, entitled "Notes Illustrative of the Wrongs of Slavery," that offers anecdotes about the horrors of slavery—not "isolated instances of wrong and oppression," she says, "but daily occurrences so common as scarcely to excite remark." In one such incident, from 1832, she tried in vain to intercede on behalf of a black woman whose son was about to be sold south by a slave trader. When Blackford's pleas that the mother be permitted to see her son one last time fell on deaf ears, Blackford fixed her eyes on the man guarding the slave jail and "warned him that such cruelty could not long go unpunished and reminded him of the affair at Southampton [Turner's Rebellion] which had just occurred." For Blackford, then, as for Garrison, Turner's revolt was a harbinger of the divine retribution that awaited slaveholders should they fail to repent. Just how many Southern slaveholders secretly felt this kind of guilt and remorse we have no way of knowing. But we do know that written expressions like Blackford's are rare and that, as the 1830s unfolded, Blackford felt herself isolated in an increasingly hostile proslavery environment.[55]

Despite the support of private citizens such as the Augusta petitioners and Mary Blackford, Randolph's proposal went down to defeat; a majority in the Virginia General Assembly declared it "inexpedient" to adopt any plan for the gradual emancipation of the slaves. Easterners, such as Alexander Knox, answered the gradualist arguments of westerners by reiterating that only in a slave society could whites achieve Herrenvolk democracy's vaunted equality. Paradoxically, they also raised the banner of "minority rights" (in this case, the right of the slaveholding minority of Virginians to control the destiny of the institution). Eastern delegates succeeded not only in thwarting emancipation schemes but also in indefinitely postponing the consideration of plans for the state-subsidized colonization of free blacks and manumitted slaves.[56]

Significantly, over the course of the debates, a few voices on each side resorted to threats of disunion. During the state's constitutional convention of 1829–30, planters had consolidated their dominance by arguing that "what gave eastern Virginia power within the state also gave Virginia power in Washington." If Virginia could overcome its sources of internal dissension— if westerners would cease their agitation and accept eastern leadership—the state would preserve its national primacy and the Union would be "perfected." In the last weeks of the 1832 slavery debates, some eastern planters opportunistically tapped the very fears of disunion they had stoked in 1829–30 by indulging in threats that *they* would divide the state—with disastrous implications for the Union—if westerners acted against slavery. A few westerners, too, called for separation, only to be roundly rebuked by the eastern press. The majority of convention delegates "abhorred the idea of division," and such talk faded along with Randolph's plan. But these debates illustrate that disunion threats and prophecies were marshaled as weapons in state politics, in battles among Southerners, as well as on the national stage.[57]

Historians have disagreed over just what this resolution to the 1831–32 debates meant for the fate of the South. For a long time, the dominant school of thought was that the General Assembly's inaction on emancipation and its new restrictions on black assemblies represented a turning point in the South's political history—the moment at which the old, defensive notion that slavery was a "necessary evil" gave way to a consensus among Southern whites that it was a "positive good." This interpretation has rested on a selective reading of Thomas Dew's highly influential *Review of the Debate in the Virginia Legislature of 1831 and 1832*, published in 1832. A professor at the College of William and Mary and a member of the Tidewater elite, Dew argued that state-sponsored and -directed gradual emancipation and colonization were "*totally* impracticable." He pointedly noted that slaves represented $94 million in Virginia alone, one-third of the state's total wealth; it would be impossible for the state to compensate slaveowners for a property loss of that magnitude. This emphasis on the South's enormous investment in slaves became a staple of proslavery ideology and never lost its force. By the eve of the Civil War, slaves accounted for $3 billion in capital, nearly 20 percent of the total wealth of the United States.[58]

Dew dismissed the gradualists' "language of terrifying prophecy" as irrational—he sought to banish the "appalling phantom" of "universal ruin and desolation" at the hands of slaves and to restore the "empire of reason." But he coolly invoked slave rebellion for his own purposes, noting that to raise the issue of gradual emancipation in response to Turner's uprising was well calculated to excite additional insurrections by slaves who were eager to accelerate the process of liberation. Dew tried to taint the gradualist schemes that the legislature had debated not only as irrational but also as sentimental. This he did by proclaiming that they appealed especially to white Southern women, whose "fine feelings" unchecked by rational calculation led them to "embrace with eagerness even the wildest and most destructive schemes of emancipation." Dew urged white women to realize that they were the special beneficiaries of slavery, as it released them from the burden of manual labor and made possible their "elevation" in society.[59]

According to Dew, to be rational was to be optimistic about the prospects of the South. He attacked the notion that slavery was morally wrong, asserting that the Bible did not contain a single passage that should bother the slave-holder's conscience; that slaves not only were well treated but also that they were the "happiest" of all Southerners; and that slavery, far from being inconsistent with republicanism, was the cause of the "equality" among Southern whites. Dew's defense of slavery, paradoxically, partook of the same kind of evangelical optimism that led Northern reformers to herald the dawning of a new age of moral progress and material prosperity. The rapid growth of slavery and of the cotton kingdom in the first decades of the nineteenth century were, for Dew, "incontrovertible evidence of divine pleasure" with the South. Culturally dominant in both North and South, evangelical moralism held that private virtues produced public rewards—according to Dew's version of this doctrine, and the profitability of slaveholding reflected the moral virtue of Southern slaveholders.[60]

Although Dew's rhetoric earned him a reputation as a progenitor of the "positive good" view of slavery, William Freehling has argued that neither he nor the other elite whites who opposed gradual emancipation in the 1831–32 debates were inaugurating an era of proslavery solidarity in Virginia. Freehling notes that Dew himself expressed the hope that Virginia would one day be free of blacks and of slavery, but Dew wanted economic change—not hysteria-driven political reform or sentimental benevolence—to be the engine of that transition. If Virginia could diversify and modernize its economy to attract white workers, it could drain away its black ones to the Deep South.

Dew thus shared Floyd's fantasy of a "whites-only" Virginia but disagreed about the means for achieving it. It is most important, then, according to Freehling, to understand that Dew was not arguing for the positive good of *perpetual* slavery—it would not be until the 1850s that Virginians rallied around that creed.[61]

Although Freehling is right to insist that we not project the proslavery doctrines of the 1850s back to the 1830s, it is just as important that we not conflate the "necessary evil" doctrine of the early republic with the defenses of slavery that emerged in the immediate aftermath of Turner's Rebellion. For in blaming Turner's Rebellion on "Yankee" immediatists, Southerners like Floyd and Dew were developing an ideological claim that had profound implications for the relations between the North and South. They were desperate to distinguish the gradualist fantasy of a South without blacks from the immediatist fantasy—a nightmare, in their view—of racial equality. There was no better way to do this than to make the argument—one that was functionally if not explicitly disunionist—that the boundaries between North and South needed to be fortified. To attribute slave discontent to the manipulation of Northern abolitionists was, of course, to deny the reality of the slaves' sufferings and the authenticity of their grievances. It was also to deny African Americans their identity as Southerners—blacks such as Walker and Turner who stood against the system had, by definition, renounced the South and become "Yankee" pawns. Moreover, Floyd and other Southern whites who grappled with Turner's Rebellion implicitly effaced the Southern backgrounds of antislavery men like John Rankin and Samuel Janney; Floyd insisted in his January 1831 letter to Governor Hamilton of South Carolina that it was *Yankee* preachers who had spread the gospel of discontent. Finally, both Floyd and Dew, in stating that white Southern women were especially vulnerable to antislavery appeals, were calling attention to immediatism's threat to traditional gender roles and warning whites, men as well as women, that what had once passed as piety might now be construed as radicalism. In other words, although Virginians like Floyd and Dew were not yet ready, in the early 1830s, to declare slavery a perpetual good, they were ready to define immediatism as a perpetual evil—as a doctrine utterly foreign to the body politic of the South.

Although it took on new political urgency and stridency, the Southern demonization of abolitionists in the wake of Nat Turner's Rebellion could not unify white Virginians across the state's regional fault line. Nor could it dispel the fear, evinced in the 1831–32 debates by some delegates, that the discussion of the issue of slavery by Virginians was itself potentially destructive. For proslavery spokesmen like easterner James Gholson, "Plans did not pose the danger; speech did"—to debate slavery out in the open was to embolden both slaves and the abolitionist "devils" who tried to incite them to "bloodshed." Abolitionist commentators, for their part, viewed the Virginia debate over gradual emancipation as dangerous not because it threatened to change the racial caste system but because it so signally failed to. Robert Purvis, one of the leaders of Philadelphia's black immediatists, warned in the wake of Turner's Rebellion that the slaveholding states would continue to "raise up Gabriels and Nats" as long as "slaveholders and their apologists" continued to blame slave discontent on "abstract and foreign causes." The "natural" cause of the "Southampton Tragedy" was clear—namely, that oppression begets rebellion. "Remove slavery, and the cause will cease," Purvis implored slaveholders, "and then you may lie down in peace."[62]

Ruinous Tendencies

THE ANTI-ABOLITION BACKLASH

"Who does not see that the American people are walking over a subterranean fire, the flames of which are fed by slavery?" These words, with their ominous ring, were written by abolitionist Lydia Maria Child as a commentary on the nullification crisis, the protracted clash between South Carolina and the federal government that lasted from 1828 until 1833. As we have seen, the ostensible cause of the crisis was Congress's passage, in 1828, of a "tariff of abominations" on European imports. In the first act of the crisis, President Andrew Jackson had condemned South Carolina's nullification scheme and hoped that a reduction in the tariff rate would ease tensions. But South Carolina states' rights men were singularly unimpressed by the tariff reform of 1832 (although it reset the tariff rate at its 1824 level), and in November of that year they held a Nullification Convention that enacted a veto of the hated measure and threatened secession if the U.S. government tried to enforce the nullified law. The South Carolina legislature voted to muster an army to protect the state against federal force. In December 1832 John C. Calhoun, the mastermind of nullification, resigned the vice presidency and took up the banner of state sovereignty in the U.S. Senate. Under pressure from extremists in his own state, Calhoun had made his stance of interposition public in his July 1831 "Fort Hill Address," and he now developed the doctrine in a

This 1831 anti-Jackson satire shows him beleaguered by infighting, as Van Buren and Calhoun compete over the ladder of "political preferment" while Webster and Clay look on. Webster remarks that Calhoun has "nullified the whole Concern," while Clay, given to dire prophecies of disunion, mutters "Famine! War! Pestilence!" (Courtesy of the Library of Congress)

host of speeches, letters, discourses, and other polemics. Interposition, he explained, provided a constitutional check on the "unrestrained will of a majority," by which he meant a numerical majority. The states, through Calhoun's mechanism of protest, could assert themselves as a "concurrent majority"—they could achieve consensus or compromise in consultation with each other. In other words, in Calhoun's view, the government was not designed to confer absolute power on a ruling majority based on a simple tally of votes. Instead, the government was designed to protect all of its constitutive interests—namely, the states. By "taking the sense of the community" (a favorite phrase of Calhoun's), the constitutional device of interposition would give "each interest or portion of the community" the right to defend itself against the others.[1]

Calhoun was at great pains, in his public and private writings, to distinguish nullification from secession. Secession was a separation of one state from its partners, whereas nullification set in motion a deliberative process among the states. Nullification could be "succeeded by secession," but that was a last resort; the purpose of nullification was to preserve the Union. The Union was the "means, if wisely used," Calhoun again and again reminded his followers, "not only of reconciling all diversities, but also the means and the only effectual one, of securing to us justice, peace and security, at home and abroad."[2]

With leading nullifiers such as Robert Barnwell Rhett, James Henry Hammond, and South Carolina governor James Hamilton Jr., rejecting such paeans to the Union in favor of militant rhetoric that promised martial resistance to federal "invasion," Calhoun's attempts to cast nullification as a patriotic doctrine rang false. President Jackson again took a defiant stance against his former partner—Jackson issued his own proclamation that nullified nullification, declaring it unconstitutional. Jackson believed that pro-nullification Southerners had been manipulated by designing leaders like Calhoun and Rhett. Addressing himself to South Carolinians, Jackson decried the "eloquent appeals to your passions, to your State pride, to your native courage, [and] to your sense of real injury" that "were used to prepare you for the period when the mask which concealed the hideous features of DISUNION should be taken off." Instead of looking with "horror" on the deformity of disunion, duped nullifiers now looked on it with "complacency." Jackson tried to restore their sense of horror, both by invoking the "bloody conflicts" that disunion would bring and by restoring its true definition: "Be not deceived by names," he warned—"Disunion, by armed force, is TREASON."[3]

This standoff set the stage for Senator Henry Clay, of Kentucky, the "golden-tongued" orator whose role in resolving the Missouri crisis of 1820 had already earned him a national reputation as the "Great Compromiser." He shepherded through Congress a reduced Compromise Tariff and a "force bill" that authorized President Jackson to use the might of the army and navy to enforce the law should South Carolina not back down. Clay used disunion rhetorically as the calamity to be disavowed by all reasonable men. "When a civil war shall be lighted up in the bosom of our own happy land, and armies are marching, and commanders are winning their victories, and fleets are in motion on our coast," he intoned in the Senate in February 1833, arguing on behalf of the Compromise Tariff, "tell me, if you can, tell me, if any human being can tell its duration. God alone knows where such a war would end." Such apocalyptic language served "Union" politicians in the Deep South as well, as they sought to taint nullification as treason. At a January 1833 meeting in Natchez, Mississippi, for example, Robert J. Walker, running for the Senate against a nullifier opponent, echoed Daniel Webster's 1830 reply to Robert Y. Hayne: America stood on "the precipice," and what lay below were "untried horrors." Tapping deep-seated associations between disunion and foreign intervention, Walker imagined that "disunion would be the signal for WAR—a war of conquest, in which the weak would fall under the power of the strong; and upon the ruins of this now happy Union might arise the darkest despotism that ever crushed the liberties of mankind." For as America lay prostrate, "exhausted and bleeding at every pore," the "sanguinary alliance" of European despots would send their "armies to our shores." To nullifiers, Walker warned: "Let us take the first step, and all may be lost forever." The notion that disunion would be the prelude to the imposition of a foreign monarchy was echoed in newspapers across the South.[4]

In March 1833 South Carolina grudgingly acceded to compromise and rescinded its nullification ordinance. Calhoun and South Carolina accepted the Compromise Tariff, although this measure lowered the tariff only incrementally, both because the leaders of the other Southern states overwhelmingly supported accepting this concession, and because Calhoun himself believed that the path of negotiation was an honorable one. For Clay and Calhoun, civil war was the shameful alternative to compromise, and it would result only if political leaders failed to fulfill their sacred trust of upholding the Constitution.[5]

Abolitionist Lydia Maria Child took a very different view, both of nullification and of political compromise, in her 1833 book *An Appeal in Favor of That Class of Americans Called Africans.* A literary trailblazer among women, Child transgressed the boundaries of her white New England Protestant milieu. She began her career writing novels and domestic advice books, only to be drawn into the antislavery campaign when she met William Lloyd Garrison in the late 1820s. The most analytically rigorous abolitionist text of its era, Child's *Appeal* argued that the "subterranean fire" that threatened America was the rising "*sectional* dislike" between the North and the South, and that the fire was stoked, not calmed, by political negotiations such as the Clay-Calhoun agreement of 1833. For the "system of compromises" did a grave injustice to a "third party, which is never heard or noticed, except for purposes of oppression"—the slaves themselves. By sacrificing their interests in the name of compromise, the U.S. government emboldened the "slaveholding power" to make further demands and threats, lulled the North into a deeper daze of complicity and submission, and hastened the fearful day when an unrepentant nation would face divine retribution. For Child, only an immediate renunciation of slavery could restore the honor of the United States and forestall civil strife and bloodshed; political compromise, by contrast, was both shameful and dangerous—it represented damnation, not salvation.[6]

The connection between South Carolina's taking offense at the tariff and its defense of slavery was plain for Child, and for any discerning observer, to see. Fear of slave rebellion was but one of the many bonds that held together South Carolina whites and made them the most cohesive ruling class in the region. Unlike in other Southern states, where plantation districts often clashed politically with areas where both slaves and plantations were scarce, in South Carolina "cotton mania" united the lowcountry and the upcountry. As William W. Freehling has put it, "no other southern elite faced so weak a pressure to compromise with nonslaveholding egalitarians."[7]

Both lowcountry and upcountry were firmly in the sway of "aristocrats," for South Carolina restricted membership in the legislature to men who could meet the most stringent property qualifications of any state in the nation. Those legislators, in turn, were given more authority than were assemblymen in any other state—they elected the governor, the judges, and the presidential electors for South Carolina. In other words, "no yeoman farmer ever cast a vote" for a presidential candidate; that prerogative was reserved for the wealthy. The South Carolina elite maintained its hegemony through careful and canny manipulation of political rituals and symbols. The nullifiers had won popular approbation by co-opting gatherings such as Fourth of July barbecues and militia musters and using them to preach a gendered message of racial unity. They stressed that the wealthy planter and the common farmer shared the special rights and responsibilities of "martial manhood." In the words of Stephanie McCurry, "As masters of dependents, even if only, or perhaps especially, of wives and children, every freeman was bound to defend his household, his property" against threats to his independence.[8]

South Carolina's ruling race was profoundly insecure about its waning national power. Falling cotton prices and westward migration threatened the state's economic well-being, and national political trends were alarming— white South Carolinians viewed the popular American Colonization Society as a threat to slavery, quailed at the news of Nat Turner's Rebellion, and condemned Virginia's recent deliberations over gradual emancipation as a terrible apostasy. Lydia Maria Child recognized the insidious dynamic that was at work: leaders such as Governor Hamilton and Senator Calhoun cast the very occurrence of the "remarkable debate in the Virginia legislature" as an "offence" chargeable to the "opinions and policy of the north." Nullifiers practiced the art of "Yankee baiting" and declared that any Southerner who opposed nullification was under the sway of Northern capitalists. South Carolina's leaders saw nullification as a way to consolidate their own power and to stem the antislavery tide.[9]

If South Carolina's assertion of states' rights was a veiled bid to protect slavery, why didn't Andrew Jackson and the other Southern states support it? One argument is that Jackson simply did not regard the tariff as a great economic burden to the South or as a threat to slavery; another, that he was keen that his Democratic Party retain strength in the West and North and not become an exclusively sectional party. Yet another is that because of his military background, Jackson would not tolerate insubordination in the ranks. A related explanation is that Jackson, who had risen from humble beginnings to achieve planter status, represented a different kind of Southern political culture than did Calhoun and his ilk. Jackson exemplified Herrenvolk democracy, the creed that black slavery made possible a rough equality among all white men, whereas Calhoun stood for "Old World republican-ism," which reserved power for the elite.[10]

Jackson's antinullifier stance, in other words, reflected the political culture of his home state of Tennessee. In contrast to South Carolina, Tennessee was characterized by three "grand divisions": mountainous eastern Tennessee, where slaves were scarce, was a realm of small-scale subsistence farming; western Tennessee was the state's cotton-producing "black belt"; and middle Tennessee had a hybrid economy. Tennessee farmers, most of whom prac-ticed "semi-subsistence, safety-first" farming, did not perceive the tariff as a major threat to the state's economy. Moreover, Tennessee politicians fa-vored egalitarian appeals to voters that promised to defend them against "the perceived assaults of demagogic politicians" like Calhoun. According to Jonathan M. Atkins, "Tennessee's solid support for Jackson during the Nul-lification Crisis proved most immediately influential in isolating South Caro-lina and compelling that state to accept compromise."[11]

Even in those states, such as Georgia, where there was substantial opposi-tion to the tariff, Jackson's popularity held, in part because Democrats there found ways to defend states' rights even as they rejected the "Tariff of Abomi-nations" and nullification alike. In Georgia, two Democratic factions squared off against each other during the nullification crisis. One, led by John Clark, claimed to stand, along with Jackson, for the "true" states' rights principle— that "the state and federal governments had separate and distinct powers and were sovereign within their respective spheres." This faction accused the other, led by George Troup and a handful of vocal nullifiers, of supporting an extreme, bastardized version of states' rights—one that "tolerated state de-fiance of federal laws" and would thus lead to disunion. The Clarkites, behind their rhetoric of states' rights Unionism, vanquished the Troupites in state elections. In the presidential election of 1832, both factions reunited in support of Jackson and in bitter opposition to the National Republican chal-lenger, Henry Clay. Although a number of prominent Democrats in Georgia and elsewhere in the South openly disapproved of Jackson's choice of New Yorker Martin Van Buren as his vice president and heir apparent, the South-ern electorate accepted Jackson's assurances that Van Buren could be trusted to advance the region's interests.[12]

As Michael Les Benedict has explained, the nullification crisis dramatized the conflict of *three* basic doctrines of constitutional interpretation. Those who had championed the tariff in the first place—National Republicans like Webster and Clay—interpreted the Constitution broadly and believed that it "delegated implied powers to the national government"; Article I, section 8, of the Constitution, which specified that Congress could "make all Laws which shall be necessary and proper" for executing its powers, undergirded this notion of "implied powers." Nullifiers, by contrast, insisted on the separate sovereignty of each state, believing that "the only cement that bound them together was the mutual regard, respect, and affection of their peoples." States' rights Democrats represented a middle ground between these two positions: they believed in a government of "delegated" powers rather than broad "implied" powers, but they "recoiled from the idea that the states should have the final say about the constitutionality of federal and state laws." They preferred, writes Benedict, to treat the "national and state governments as equally sovereign."[13]

Jackson successfully walked a fine line during the nullification crisis: his antinullification rhetoric was so unabashedly nationalistic that it pleased the likes of Webster, but his war against the "Monster Bank" rhetoric persuaded Southern voters that the president remained committed to states' rights. In July 1832, at the very moment the tariff was being adjusted downward, Jackson vetoed legislation that would have rechartered the Second Bank of the United States. A core component of Clay's "American System" for economic modernization, the bank held government deposits and regulated the money supply and credit system to provide capital for commercial development. Jacksonian Democrats, in what Michael F. Holt has called a "masterpiece of political propaganda aimed directly at voters," portrayed the bank as "an engine of aristocratic privilege that favored the rich at the expense of the poor"; such rhetoric implied that the bank's branch directors, including Daniel Webster, were profiting personally from the institution. While the average American did not understand the intricacies of national finance, Jacksonian antibank propaganda resonated in the South among voters who were eager to guard the legacy of Jeffersonian agrarianism against Clay and the "moneyed interest." The veto thus refurbished Jackson's credentials as a "strict constructionist" who would protect the states and people from federal "consolidation." And it set the stage for his overwhelming defeat of Clay in the 1832 presidential election.[14]

From her vantage point in 1833, Lydia Maria Child took no comfort in

Jackson's seeming defiance of South Carolina. She contrasted his proclamation against nullification with his subsequent "Message" to the nation in which he "maintained that the wealthy land holders, that is, the planters, are the *best* part of the population," conceded that high tariffs had been a burden to the South, recommended a "gradual withdrawing of protection from manufactures," and discouraged future appropriations for "internal improvements" that would modernize the economic infrastructure. This, for Child, was the real Jackson—a man committed to extending slavery and serving the interests of elite slaveholders. The ultimate proof of Jackson's commitment to slavery was his handling of an issue that had long been a passionate interest of Child's, namely the "Indian question." To her horror, Jackson had repudiated efforts to assimilate Native Americans in the Southeast and had instead endorsed their "removal" from their homelands to reservations in the West. Even as he had rejected South Carolina's invocation of state sovereignty, the president, in 1832, asserted the right of the state of Georgia to expel Cherokees forcibly from lands guaranteed them both by federal treaties and by the Supreme Court of the United States. In 1838, when Jackson's policy achieved its tragic culmination, thousands would die on the "trail of tears" to make way for white landowners to cultivate cotton.[15]

For Child, then, and for her fellow immediatists, the years 1831 to 1833 witnessed what Garrison called a "double rebellion" in the South—the uprising of slaves (Turner's band) against their masters and a "rebellion against the Government" by Southern whites, nullifiers and advocates of Indian removal alike. This "double rebellion" intensified the abolitionists' sense of urgency, and at the close of 1833 Garrison and his allies came together in Philadelphia to make their dream of a national immediatist campaign a reality. In its "Declaration of Sentiments," the fledgling American Anti-Slavery Society (AASS) straddled the line between moral absolutism and political pragmatism. The Garrison-penned "Declaration" gave voice to a kind of antislavery nullification doctrine: that "all those laws which are now in force, admitting the right of slavery, are . . . before God utterly null and void; being an audacious usurpation of the Divine prerogative." But it juxtaposed such unforgiving language with a pledge that abolitionists rejected the use of force and would instead rely on moral suasion to change the minds and hearts of the people. Moreover, the AASS declaration paid deference to the dominant interpretation of the Constitution—that Congress had "no right to interfere with any of the slave States"—and announced that immediatists would only press Congress to act where it did have jurisdiction. Abolitionists would petition for an end to "the domestic slave trade between the several States" and for the abolition of slavery in the District of Columbia and in other territories under Congress's control.[16]

BUILDING A COALITION

With their mandate thus laid out, abolitionists embarked on a period of intensive organizing. Agents such as Theodore Weld, Arthur and Lewis Tappan, and Gerrit Smith were dispatched to work the lecture circuit in the North; local societies proliferated; and an antislavery petition campaign took shape. As they took the stage, local societies, no less than the movement's national leaders, mixed caustic rebukes to slaveholders with appeals to empathy and Christian fellowship. The secretary of the New Haven Anti-Slavery Society, an immediatist organization founded in 1833, defined his group's purpose in this way: "We regard the system of Slavery as founded in wickedness, and tears, and blood, and as sustained by avarice and crime. We believe it ought immediately to be overthrown." He vowed that his society would form an "unbroken phalanx—unintimidated by calumny or threats" or by "the chimerical fears, & woful [sic] predictions of the results of emancipation." But he also promised, on a gentler note, that New Haven activists would promote justice and truth "in the spirit of Christ, and in love."[17]

Abolitionists dramatized the possibility of a new kind of Christian fellowship that crossed boundaries of gender, race, and region. Northern women, white and black, were core constituents of the movement, founding racially integrated organizations in Boston and Philadelphia that would serve as models for immediatist societies elsewhere in the North. These societies, in turn, furnished fund-raisers and orators for the movement, such as the indefatigable Abby Kelley, of Massachusetts, who eventually joined the "hardy group of lecturing agents [carrying] their message to the new towns along the Erie Canal, to the rich farm counties of Pennsylvania, and over the Alleghenies to Ohio and Michigan." Female abolitionists drew out the radical implications of the dominant doctrine of woman's place—the ideal of "separate spheres." Because of their natural piety and moral purity, so that doctrine held, women belonged in the domestic sphere of home and family; the hurly-burly public world of politics and business was the domain of men. With the approbation of men, antebellum women, particularly in the urban North, had extended their sphere by engaging in charitable work, justifying it as a special moral duty. Abolitionist women insisted that because slavery was primarily a moral problem, women had a paramount duty to oppose it, even if that meant crossing the boundary into the "male" sphere of politics.[18]

Immediatists such as Sarah Mapps Douglass, a free black Philadelphia Quaker, believed that the abolition cause was inextricably linked to the promotion of civil rights in the North—that blacks and whites must work together to fight racism everywhere they found it. She practiced what she preached. A teacher by profession, Douglass established a "female coloured school" in Philadelphia and enlisted the help of white abolitionists like Lucretia Mott to sustain it. Douglass also urged upon Northern free blacks an empathetic identification with Southern slaves by emphasizing, in her speeches and writings, the threat that slavery posed to the homes of free Northern women. Whereas the female petitioners of Augusta County, Virginia, had in 1832 evoked an image of homes menaced by slave rebellion, Douglass conjured up that same year an image of homes threatened by slave catchers. Speaking in Philadelphia, and thinking no doubt of the many ominous signs of slaveholder militance, Douglass confessed that while she had once imagined that slavery was a distant prospect, she now "beheld the oppressor lurking on the border of my own peaceful home!" She saw "his iron hand stretched forth" to seize her "as his prey." Garrison featured this speech in the *Liberator* and told Douglass that her eloquence had put a "new weapon" into his hands with which to fight slavery and prejudice.[19]

African American reformers again and again urged Northerners to identify with Southern slaves. For example, Elizabeth Wicks of the African Female Benevolent Society of Troy, New York, in an 1834 address to her fellow female activists, said: "Let our minds travel south and sympathize with the present state of the two millions of our brethren who are yet in bondage." Such appeals, which echoed the sentiments of James Forten and the preceding generation of black leaders, can and should be read as a commentary on the discourse of disunion. For even as the rift widened between white Northern critics and white Southern defenders of slavery, African Americans asserted that the interests and destinies of Northern blacks were inextricable from those of Southern ones. Disunion connoted for free blacks both the cutting off of slaves from their Northern allies and the disjuncture between America's transcendent ideals and its shameful realities. The promise of the Union, African American leaders stressed, would only be fulfilled if the Southern states followed the example of the Northern ones, by instituting emancipation. As free black activists commemorating emancipation in New York put it: " 'We hold these truths to be self-evident, that all men are born free and equal,' has been resounded from one end of the Union to the other by white Americans—May they speedily learn to practice what they so loudly proclaim."[20]

Antislavery white Southerners, although a statistically insignificant part of the immediatist coalition, loomed large as symbols for the movement. Three Southerners in particular—Angelina and Sarah Grimké of South Carolina and James Birney of Kentucky—represented the hope that slaveholders could be persuaded to repent and join the immediatist crusade. The Grimké sisters' religious convictions compelled them to forsake the elite slaveholding milieu in which they were raised. Their brother Thomas, it will be recalled, was a dominant voice against nullification; he had embraced colonization as the cure for sectional tensions. But the sisters instead followed the path blazed by Forten, Walker, Douglass, and Garrison. They settled in Philadelphia, where they joined another set of formidable siblings, Sara, Harriet, and Margaretta Forten (and Sarah Mapps Douglass and Lucretia Mott), in working for the Philadelphia Female Anti-Slavery Society. The Grimkés' status as Southern insiders made them valuable assets on the lecture circuit, where they could offer firsthand testimony about the cruelties of slavery. Moreover, "their own daily contact with blacks under the racist regime of slavery" attuned them to the prevalence of Northern racism, even within the antislavery ranks. As Carolyn Williams has noted: "Unlike many white abolitionists, the Grimké sisters regarded blacks as people rather than as abstract symbols of oppression and degradation." James Birney, for his part, had also willingly forsaken slavery and settled in the North, operating an abolitionist newspaper in Ohio and traveling the North as a lecturer before becoming executive secretary of the AASS. The editor of a paper in Essex County, Massachusetts, after reprinting a Birney speech of 1836, commented that anyone who was generally skeptical about abolitionism should take special note of Birney, "REMEMBERING THAT IT IS A RECENT SLAVEHOLDER WHO SPEAKS!"[21]

The most potent antislavery testimony of all came from fugitive slaves themselves, and their stories were featured in the speeches and publications of white immediatists like Lydia Maria Child. In the 1830s abolitionism tapped the power of published slave narratives. Works such as Charles Ball's *Slavery in the United States* and Moses Roper's *A Narrative of the Adventures and Escape of Moses Roper*, both published in 1837, provide searing indictments of the barbarity of slavery as well as trenchant analyses of the social dynamics of Southern society. Ball's narrative graphically depicts the tortures he suffered as a slave in Maryland and South Carolina. On one occasion he endured a whipping of ninety-six lashes, after which scalding pepper was poured directly onto the gashed, quivering flesh on his back. By the end of this ordeal, Ball's face was badly bruised as well, for "in the madness of my agony, I had not been able to refrain from beating my head violently against the [whipping] post." Ball positions himself, however, not just as a victim of slavery but as an authority on Southern society who has the duty to enlighten Northerners about it. No one who had not lived in the South "can fully understand the bonds that hold society together there, or appreciate the rules which prescribe the boundaries of the pretensions of the several orders of men who compose the body politic." Based on those rules, "every man who is able to procure a subsistence, without labor, regards himself a gentleman." But if the dream of rising into the ranks of gentlemen intoxicated nonslaveholders, it did not follow that the elite felt a genuine solidarity with and respect for striving nonelite whites. In fact, according to Ball, the planter class looked with disdain on common whites and did their best to keep them in ignorance. After escaping to the North, Ball realized that one of the most fundamental differences between the sections was that whites "are not nearly so well informed in the southern states, as they are in those lying farther north."[22]

Moses Roper's narrative, too, sought to lay bare the internal workings of Southern society. Describing how he accompanied his master to a political event in South Carolina, he notes that it was "at the time of the agitation of the Union and Nullifying party, which was expected to end in a general war. The Nullifying party had a grand dinner on the occasion, after which they gave their slaves all the refuse, for the purpose of bribing them to fight on the side of their party." The scene that ensued—drunken masters watching as slaves scrambled to get "bare bones and crumbs"—was in Roper's eyes both patently absurd and tragically telling. Roper juxtaposed it with a report that a few days later "a public auction was held for the sale of slaves, cattle, sugar, iron &c." by the leading men in his town. The first incident, no less than the second, Roper conveys, was intended to humiliate and dehumanize the slaves; masters demanded their loyalty but gave no loyalty in return. Roper, whose narrative was favorably reviewed in Garrison's *Liberator*, proved to be a popular speaker on the antislavery lecture circuit in the United States and Britain. Former slaves, then, used their writings and speeches to chart the gap between the rhetoric of slaveholder paternalism—with its claim that a system of mutual duties and obligations bound master and servant—and the realities of slave suffering.[23]

With the rise of Frederick Douglass (who no bore no relation to Sarah Mapps Douglass) to prominence as an orator in 1839-40, abolitionism found its greatest standard-bearer. Born in 1818 on the Eastern Shore of Maryland, Douglass was scarred, literally and figuratively, by a childhood spent in the grip of slavery. As a boy, he had fifteen of his kinfolk sold away from him to owners in the Deep South; he witnessed brutal punishments, such as the whipping of his elderly aunt with a "blood-clotted cowskin"; he experienced the daily trials of hunger, overwork, and exposure to the elements. A ray of light broke into this world of deprivation and brutality when a "kind and tender hearted" woman named Sophia Auld, the wife of his master Hugh Auld, taught him the rudiments of literacy. Enraged that his wife would put such a dangerous weapon into Douglass's hands, Auld forbade her to continue the lessons; soon Sophia's tenderheartedness dissipated, and she came to wear the cold countenance of the slaveholder. This experience—the corruption of Sophia Auld—persuaded Douglass that "slaveholding is learned behavior" and that it could be "unlearned" too.[24]

Sometime during the years 1830-31, while a slave in Baltimore, Douglass first heard of the abolitionist movement. As he recalls in his narrative, *abolition* "was always used in such connections as to make it an interesting word to me." If a slave "did any thing very wrong in the mind of a slaveholder, it was spoken of as the fruit of *abolition*." From then on, Douglass "always drew near when that word was spoken." The realization that "up there in the free North there was an 'argument' about slavery" strengthened his determination to escape. Years of planning and hoping came to fruition when, in 1838, Douglass managed to flee Baltimore disguised as a free black sailor. He made his way to New Bedford, Massachusetts, where he shortly gained prominence

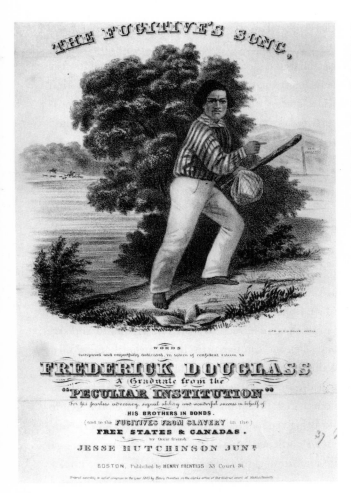

As this sheet music in honor of Frederick Douglass testifies, by the mid-1840s he had become an abolitionist icon—the most influential "graduate from the peculiar institution," according to the subtitle of the "Fugitive's Song." (Courtesy of the Library of Congress)

as a preacher in the African Methodist Episcopal Zion Church. On March 12, 1839, Douglass inaugurated his long career as an orator when he spoke out against colonization at a church meeting. Two months later, he addressed an integrated audience at an antislavery meeting attended by none other than William Lloyd Garrison; thus was born one of the most important partnerships in American political history. Hearing Douglass recount his story of a life in slavery, Garrison declared that "Patrick Henry, of revolutionary fame, never made a speech more eloquent in the cause of liberty" than the fugitive slave. Thousands of antislavery auditors who subsequently listened to Douglass's speeches on behalf of the AASS would draw the same conclusion.[25]

As a result of the tireless work of antislavery agents, membership in abolition societies reached 200,000 by 1840. Although this figure was but a small fraction of the 17 million inhabitants of the United States and abolitionists were still far afield of the mainstream, they had succeeded, during the period 1833 to 1840, in dramatically altering the course of American politics. According to David Grimsted, as white majorities in the North and South confronted the abolitionist campaign, two distinct "sectional systems of, and attitudes toward, social violence" took shape that would "mark and deepen all future North-South confrontations."[26]

THE SECTIONAL CRISIS OF 1835

Sectional tensions reached such a fever pitch in 1835 that commentators in the North and South declared that the Missouri controversy had been revived and had taken on a much more fearful aspect. That year saw forty-six proslavery riots and fifteen race riots. What precipitated these mob actions was the confluence of a series of slave insurrection scares in the South and the onset of a massive public relations campaign by the Northern abolitionist movement. In 1835 the AASS published over a million pieces of antislavery literature for distribution in the South as well as the North. Targeting slaveholders, abolitionists hoped that this information could effect the gentle moral suasion that would bring repentance. Insisting that slaves—not slaveholders—were the intended audience for AASS propaganda, supporters of slavery chose to cast the mail campaign as the "smoking gun" that linked abolitionism to the threat of slave insurrection. In the words of Postmaster General Amos Kendall, abolitionist literature was "calculated to operate on the passions of the colored men, and produce discontent, assassination, and servile war."[27]

Initially, Northern elites sought to reassure Southern ones of their opposition to abolitionism by chastising antislavery agitators in the press and by holding large, peaceful, pro-Southern meetings in Northern towns and cities. Anti-abolitionist rhetoric focused on the charge that abolition radicalism poisoned the relations between the sections and thus threatened the Union. Such accusations sent a chill through the antislavery ranks, as moderates no less than radicals felt themselves under attack. As Edwin Atlee of the Pennsylvania Abolition Society lamented, the patriots and philanthropists who dared to "reiterate the declaration 'that all men are created equal' " were denounced as "*incendiaries* and *fanatics*, the *enemies of their country*."[28]

But verbal attacks failed to appease the proslavery press and politicians of the South, who literally called for the blood of abolitionists, urging white Northerners to "teach the fanatics a lesson they can never forget." James Henry Hammond, a fiercely racist South Carolina politician, opined to a proslavery New York editor that abolitionists could be silenced only by "*Terror and Death*." Northerners were already rising to the bait. In September 1834, Connecticut anti-abolitionists destroyed the Cantebury school of Prudence Crandall, a white Garrisonian who had dared to offer education to African American girls. Crandall had been tried the previous summer for breaking a May 1833 state law that prohibited black students who lived outside the state from attending school in Connecticut without permission from local authorities. Although her case was dismissed by an appeals court on technicalities, it had sparked heated exchanges between the prosecution and the defense—both parties, significantly, invoked disunion as the inevitable consequence of defeat. On Crandall's behalf, lawyer William Ellsworth condemned the North's discriminatory black laws as "chains" that bound it to slavery and called slavery a "volcano" that would destroy the Union. The chief prosecutor, Andrew Judson, declared for his part that abolitionist agitation "will inevitably destroy the government itself." After her school was shut down, Crandall retreated from the reform field, but her mentor Garrison soldiered on, himself the subject of physical attacks. On October 21, 1834, for example, Garrison was mobbed in Boston, even as members of the New York Anti-Slavery Society were being assaulted in Utica, New York.[29]

However shocking to modern sensibilities, these Northern mob actions paled in comparison to Southern attacks on alleged abolitionists and insurrectionists. As Grimsted has stated, Southern riots were much more likely to be deadly, sadistic, and to go unpunished by the authorities than those in the North. Whereas Northern mob actions generally were exercises in intimidation and targeted property, Southern ones were punitive and targeted people. Four "abolitionists" were killed by mobs in South Carolina and Louisiana, and over forty alleged insurrectionists were murdered in Mississippi and Louisiana. An extension of the network of extralegal vigilantes who enforced the slave codes, Southern anti-abolition mobs represented a "tolerated, even a sanctioned mode of social control." Proslavery Southerners sought to justify violence by invoking the regional "cult of honor." To maintain their dominance over the nonslaveholding majority, elite slaveowners practiced rituals, such as dueling, that made conspicuous their personal courage, their willingness to use force, and the fact that they considered themselves above the law. This cult, no less than the principle of manly mastery that nullifiers had invoked to attract yeomen to their cause, served as a bond between elite and nonelite white men. According to defenders of Southern honor, abolitionists represented a threat not only to the security of Southern whites but also to their reputations.[30]

Even as distinct patterns of sectional violence were taking shape, so too were distinct stereotypes of abolitionists and their allies. An anti-abolition wood engraving, printed and circulated in the North, featured the heading "THE RESULTS OF ABOLITIONISM!" and depicted the edifice of a building under construction, with black craftsmen and a black employer exerting authority over white menial laborers. Such an image dramatized both the widespread fear that emancipation would bring an influx of former slaves to the North to compete for white men's jobs and the fear that abolitionism connoted not just social equality but black dominance. A second Northern anti-abolition lithograph, called "PRACTICAL AMALGAMATION," pictured the couch of a middle-class parlor on which a black man embraced a white woman and a white man kissed the hand of a black woman. Obviously, this image was intended to associate abolitionism with the social taboo of miscegenation. Northern newspapers such as the *New York Commercial Advertiser* hammered away at the abolitionists with charges that they were "traitors" who wanted to reduce white men "to the condition of mongrels"; if slaves were freed, they would of necessity "displace the whites."[31]

The Southern press, for its part, excelled in "verbal violence" and hyperbole. The image of abolitionists as insurrectionists predominated. A Georgia newspaper warned that the abolitionist mail campaign was calculated to "destroy the lives of our whole white population—men, women, and children, and lay waste the country." In Virginia, the *Norfolk and Portsmouth Herald* charged that abolitionist fliers would "excite sedition among the colored population of the South." Notably, moderate gradualists such as John Hampden Pleasants, editor of the *Richmond Whig*, changed their tune and adopted a posture of "outraged antiabolitionism." Pleasants thundered that the tariff controversy was "a light and trivial matter" compared to the antislavery mail campaign and that Garrison and company were "demons and fiends" intent on stirring "the slaves to rebellion."[32]

Although the anti-abolition tirades of Northerners and Southerners had different emphases, they were mutually reinforcing. Abolitionists tried to dispel Americans' fears of emancipation by imagining that if the nation strove for the ideal of social justice, it could achieve a new sort of moral rectitude and domestic tranquility. But this vision of Christian fellowship was condemned by anti-abolitionists as a dangerous perversion of the divinely ordained social order and as a threat to the nation's survival.

SLAVERY AND PARTISAN POLITICS

Such hyperbole could flourish because of the nature of antebellum political culture. All the major newspapers in the North and South were unabashedly partisan and favored either the Jacksonian Democrats or the emerging Whig Party. Press coverage had no pretense of neutrality and no aspirations to objectivity. Character aspersions, exaggeration, and fraudulent claims were standard fare in the coverage of electoral politics. This atmosphere reflected the Jacksonian era's establishment of mass political parties and extension of the franchise to unpropertied white men—the "partisan contagion," which in the early republic had been restricted to the elites who voted and held office, had by the 1830s "spread to the masses." Thanks to the advent of new print technologies and to the transportation revolution, newspapers could reach mass audiences and bring them a steady fare of political coverage. Partisan newspapers perfected a new "middling rhetoric" that both celebrated the highbrow oratorical styles of the great speakers, such as Clay and Webster, and offered editorials and commentaries laced with lowbrow slang and even vulgarity. Attacks on a man's honor had long been a staple of American politics, but now a new kind of aspersion came to the fore: the charge that a politician was a mere "party hack," lacking in principle and motivated only by ambition. Although Jacksonian speakers and editors were the first to make such overheated partisan appeals to the masses, the Whigs eventually followed suit.[33]

As the election campaign season of 1836 geared up, mob violence subsided and political energies were channeled into partisan rituals. But the spirit of sectional antagonism did not abate. Already in the presidential contest, soundness on the slavery issue was the main test by which white Southern men judged the contenders. Andrew Jackson's chosen successor was his vice president, New Yorker Martin Van Buren. Van Buren, who had risen to political influence in his home state in no small part because of alliances he formed with Virginians in the Monroe administration, was committed to maintaining the Democratic Party's standing as a bastion of Southern political dominance. Van Buren was well aware, as other leading free-state Democrats were, that Northerners were the "subservient wing" of the party and that they had to cater to Southern demands if they wanted to remain in power. Southerners held the majority of top governmental posts under Jackson and had disproportionate control over patronage appointments.[34]

But although Southern voters had regarded the Democratic Party as a vehicle for their views in 1828 and 1832, the party could not take Southern support for granted in 1836. The Whig Party, a new anti-Jackson coalition, had emerged in 1834, formed by disparate elements opposed to the "executive tyranny" of the Jackson administration. The majority wing was comprised of former National Republicans, such as John Quincy Adams and Henry Clay, who favored nationalizing the Northern market revolution through a program of government-sponsored economic development. They reviled "King Andrew" for the way he had escalated the "Bank War" in his second term (Jackson had unilaterally, without congressional approval, removed the federal government's deposits from the national bank before its charter ran out). The other, minority wing was made up of states' rights Southerners who had been alienated by Jackson's antinullification stance. While they generally rejected the National Republican economic agenda, many of these Southerners believed that Jackson, with the removal of the deposits, had gone too far— "By placing deposits in state banks chosen for their loyalty to the administration, Jackson had increased his patronage, his power to corrupt politics, and his capacity to yoke politicians to his will."[35]

Too divided to pick a single presidential candidate, the Whigs in 1836 offered three, including Southern slaveholder Hugh White. Southern Whigs claimed that Van Buren's record in office, especially his position during the tariff debate, was anti-Southern and even abolitionist. Democrats fired back that Van Buren would protect the rights of slaveholders and that the two Northern Whig candidates, William Henry Harrison of Ohio and Daniel Webster of Massachusetts, represented the real—Federalist and antislavery—

core of the party. To shore up his pro-Southern credentials, Van Buren endorsed the stance of Postmaster General Kendall, who encouraged Southern postmasters to destroy rather than distribute any abolitionist mailings that arrived in their offices. Van Buren also registered his opposition to abolition in the District of Columbia and sent letters to key Southern individuals and newspapers assuring them of his support for slavery and states' rights. The core Democratic argument on slavery in the election, directed at both Northern and Southern voters, was that "intersectional comity, achieved through the brotherhood of the national Democracy, offered the surest remedy for abolition agitation." In essence, Democrats lauded Van Buren's party loyalty and discipline—and promised that such loyalty and discipline were bonds that would keep the Union intact.[36]

Van Buren won the election, but by a margin that was too close for the Democrats' comfort. His inaugural address of March 4, 1837, declared optimistically that antislavery agitation had "signally failed" to "reach the stability of our institutions," and that the "masses of the people" remained devoted to the "bond of Union." The Whigs had done something that the former opposition party, the National Republicans, had never managed to do—that is, place "themselves securely on the southern political map." The first great contest between the two parties had, in the words of William J. Cooper Jr., "spotlighted the politics of slavery." In this overheated political climate, in which each party tried to taint the other as antislavery, the average white Southerner simply did not have access to what we might today consider a fair and balanced depiction of abolitionists. And to the severe disappointment of Garrison and his followers, politicians and the partisan press found, among the nation's foremost clergymen, staunch allies in their anti-abolitionism.[37]

CLERICAL ANTI-ABOLITIONISM IN THE NORTH AND SOUTH

No goal was more important to immediatists than that of enlisting the major Protestant denominations in the battle against slavery. But in the 1830s, that goal seemed to recede into the distance, as both Northern and Southern churches adopted positions that were hostile to abolitionists. As John R. McKivigan has pointed out, the Revolutionary era's "burst of antislavery vigor" in Northern churches "barely lasted out the [eighteenth] century."

Since the beginning of the new century, residual antislavery sentiment had been channeled into support for gradualist schemes such as colonization and into missionary work among slaves. Northern clergymen rationalized their toleration for slavery on the grounds that they needed slaveholder support to compete in the denominational scramble for converts and to pursue ameliorative programs in the South; clergymen also feared that abolitionism would divide congregations and introduce political controversy into a sphere in which it had no place. Most important, Northern ministers who condoned slaveholding, John Patrick Daly writes, did so "to protect and promote interests concomitant to slavery, namely biblical traditionalism, and social and theological authority." They perceived abolitionism not only as a threat to slavery but also to the very principle of social and ecclesiastical hierarchy. The focus of their anxiety was a small but growing cadre of ecclesiastical abolitionists—white ministers such as Luther Myrick and African American ones such as Samuel Ringgold Ward and Willis A. Hodges—who wedded their opposition to slavery with a determination to democratize and decentralize Protestant churches. Thus the immediatist controversy of the early 1830s split the Northern clergy into three camps—the majority of ministers, including such influential men as William Ellery Channing and Lyman Beecher, clung to gradualism, while minorities on either flank either supported outright abolition or actively promoted the proslavery position.[38]

Southern ministers rallied to the defense of slavery in the wake of the abolitionist mailing campaign of 1835. These clergymen assumed a leadership role in convening anti-abolitionist assemblies; "Presbyterian synods, Baptist associations, and Methodist conferences passed resolutions condemning abolitionist agitation." The South's burgeoning religious press also sounded the alarm against abolitionism, with journals—among them, the *Religious Herald, Southern Religious Telegraph, Virginia Conference Sentinel,* and *Southern Baptist and General Intelligencer*—accusing immediatists of perverting religion for their fanatical agenda. Well aware that politicians like Virginia's John Floyd suspected Southern ministers of lending aid and comfort to the antislavery cause, the region's clergymen tried to outdo each other in protestations of support for slavery. With a "striking unanimity," Southern clergymen decried Northern meddling with the South's institutions and feared that "abolitionism might lead to disunion."[39]

Southern clergymen sought to establish the righteousness of slavery by biblical exegesis that highlighted scriptural support for human bondage. As a resolution of the Synod of South Carolina put it, slavery had existed "from the days of those good old slaveholders and patriots, Abraham, Isaac, and Jacob." They believed they found a justification for black slavery in Genesis 9:25, interpreting the story of Noah's curse on Ham's descendants as a curse on Africans. Building on the proslavery template of Thomas Dew, clergymen also marshaled "providential facts" about life in the South. For proslavery ministers, as for Dew, the very spread of evangelical religion and slave labor in the South was a sign of divine favor. Ministers did not focus on defending slavery in the abstract but rather championed Christian slaveholding as it was practiced in the American South. Though conceding that some forms of slaveholding might be evil, they insisted that Southern slavery was not. Finally, Southern clergymen increasingly not only condemned abolitionists but also "stereotyped all northern religion on the basis of the biblical 'errors' of radicals"—they attributed to abolitionists a far greater influence than they actually had and charged them with leading Northerners down the path of heresy, away from the true religion. The "sectionalization" of religion—Southerners' tendency to associate the North with heresy—was intensified by the 1837 schism within the Presbyterian Church into a "New School" and an "Old School." The New School promoted a liberal Calvinism, with emphasis on man's agency to overcome sin and on interdenominational cooperation in benevolent projects. The Old School "defended Presbyterian orthodoxy," and in an effort to stem the reform tide, conservative Northerners reached out to slaveholding Southerners, attacking abolitionism as a variety of New School heresy. The Old School majority in the South characterized New School doctrines as "subversive" and "poisonous," as toxins that needed to be purged from the church. In the mid-1830s proslavery politicians, faced with a surging antislavery petition campaign, developed their own case for the ideological purification of the South.[40]

PETITIONING AND THE GAG RULE

In the aftermath of the 1835 postal campaign, sectional tensions found a new channel in debates over the "gag rule." From 1831 to 1836, Garrisonian abolitionists used petitions to Congress as vehicles for moral suasion, demanding that the lawmakers abolish slavery in the District of Columbia and federal territories. The trickle of petitions had swelled to a flood by 1835, thanks in part to a concerted effort by the antislavery press to call on Northern women to exercise their right of petition. As Susan Zaeske explains, "petitioning was seen as a pure expression of the moral conscience" and therefore as an appropriate political outlet for women. Female petitioners heeded the call, and thousands signed memorials that portrayed antislavery activism as a Christian duty. Despite their deferential cast, however, the petitions sparked controversy. As early as 1835, South Carolina's states' rights leaders, Representative James Henry Hammond and Senator John C. Calhoun, began giving "gag rule" orations, urging Congress to take a stance of "nonreception" of antislavery petitions and reject them outright. This uncompromising position was rejected by the lawmakers in favor of a more moderate one—namely, that antislavery petitions would be received and then immediately tabled, without being debated, printed, or referred to committee for consideration. Invoking a useful metaphor, William Lee Miller has noted that this rule allowed Congress to treat all antislavery petitions the "way that a sorting machine on an assembly line spits out misshapen parts." The architects of the modified gag rule were none other than presidential candidate Martin Van Buren and a former nullifier, Representative Henry L. Pinckney of South Carolina. Thanks to the strong support of Democrats in the North and South alike, their gag rule was enacted by the House of Representatives in the spring of 1836 and was repeatedly renewed until antislavery forces overturned it in 1844; in the Senate, an informal gag rule prevailed during this era to stifle debate on slavery.[41]

Supporters of the gag rule viewed antislavery petitions as attempts to vilify the South. The sheer volume of these memorials was alarming; by 1836 Congress had received over three hundred petitions containing over forty thousand signatures. Senator William C. Preston of South Carolina said that the "domineering insolence" of abolitionist "calumniators" had "impugn[ed] the honor" of the South. The end result of such meddling, which played on the fears aroused by Nat Turner's Rebellion and used appeals to martial manhood that he had honed during the nullification controversy, would be a servile war—"A War upon women and children. A war that spares no sex, respects no age, pities no suffering; that consigns our hearths and altars to flames and blood." Preston's colleague, Senator Alfred Cuthbert of Georgia, purported to expose the mechanism by which antislavery agitation would escalate into race war: abolitionists had "established a medium of intercourse with the slaves of the South, through which they were made to understand whatever is done in Congress." If Congress took one antislavery step, "could any one satisfy the slaves that that step would be the last?"[42]

The gag rule had the unanticipated consequence of ratcheting up the antislavery petition campaign. The 1836 resolution expired in July, at the end of the first session of the Twenty-fourth Congress. When the second session was under way in December, John Quincy Adams, the former president turned Massachusetts congressman who led the counterattack against the gag rule, had the "chance to present stacks of antislavery petitions" before a new gag could be imposed in mid-January 1837. Refusing to be deterred by the renewed rule, Adams tried a variety of parliamentary procedures to corner his colleagues into discussing abolition memorials and debating the gag resolution itself. In his most nervy stunt, he asked the Speaker of the House what he should do about a petition purporting to be from twenty-two slaves—What were the House rules on whether slaves had the right of petition? Southern representatives howled in fury, demanding that the petition be "committed to the flames" and that Adams be expelled or, at the very least, censured. Adams then delivered his coup de grace—he revealed that the slave petitioners were not abolitionists but were asking to remain in slavery (Adams suspected that they had been coerced to do so, and that the petition was really the work of slaveholders). Outraged that Adams had so mockingly turned the tables on them, the Southerners pressed for the passage of a resolution denying slaves the right of petition, and with ample support from their Northern colleagues, they succeeded. The Southern press meanwhile lambasted Adams as a "mad and mischievious" dotard who, by insulting Southern honor, was "recklessly sowing" the "seeds of disunion" in the public mind. There was a method in Adams's "madness." His slave petition gambit was not merely intended to raise the hackles of Southern congressmen and journalists. Rather, it was part of a deliberate strategy to cast the gag rule debate as a free speech issue. Adams repeatedly disavowed any sympathy for radical abolitionists and their aims; rather, he was defending their right—and the right of all Americans—to speak their minds.[43]

The gag rule controversy in Congress had an unmistakable partisan dimension, and it highlighted and exacerbated the sectional rift within the Whig Party. Northern Whigs, who constituted the nationalist/modernizing

ABOLITION FROWNED DOWN.

Here, South Carolina Whig Waddy Thompson "frowns down" upon abolition petitions, while John Quincy Adams lies prone in defeat on a stack on antislavery appeals and newspapers. This commentary on the gag rule captured divisions in the Whig Party, and suggested—erroneously—that slaves believed that abolition was beaten "down flat." In truth, Adams and his allies had not given up the fight. (Courtesy of the Library of Congress)

core of the party, "took a decidedly more antislavery stance than Northern Democrats," even as Southern Whigs were claiming to be more proslavery than Southern Democrats. Northern Whigs such as Adams and William Slade of Vermont introduced petitions before gag rules could be imposed during the congressional sessions of 1837 and 1838, then tried various methods to subvert the gags once they were reenacted. Their less daring colleagues stood behind them—Northern Whigs were "consistently more unified against the gag rule than were Democrats." Slade was the most zealous champion of antislavery petitioners; unlike Adams, he openly avowed his support for immediatism and his hostility to slavery. In December 1837 Slade used the occasion of presenting a petition to deliver an impassioned antislavery speech in which he argued that "'*all men*' of all colors, and all conditions, are, in respect to *rights*, 'equal'" and that the gag rule was "an arbitrary and unconstitutional infringement on the liberty of speech." This prompted some fifty or so Southern members of the House to storm out in anger. The result of this "memorable secession," as Rhett of South Carolina called it, was the drafting and passage of a new gag rule that tabled petitions relating to abolition not only in the states and District of Columbia, but also in the territories.[44]

What impact did the imposition of these successive gag rules have on rank-and-file abolitionists and on Northern public opinion? Senator Thomas Morris of Ohio observed that the gag rule had backfired, for abolition societies were proliferating in his home state, where citizens believed in "the right of the petitioners to be heard, although many disagreed as to the object of the petitioners." Abundant evidence confirms his impression that abolitionists were galvanized by the gag. When Congress convened in December 1838, it was greeted by abolition memorials signed by more than 400,000 Americans. Edward Magdol has established that the average number of signatures per petition to Congress rose steadily, from 32 in 1836 to 107 in 1840. Garrisonian agitators joined Northern Whig politicians in arguing that proslavery forces were infringing on the constitutional right of free speech. At the annual convention of the Rhode Island Anti-Slavery Society, for example, a delegate named S. Gould declared that just as the patriots of the Revolution had defied the British government to preserve their rights, so too must abolitionists defy the gag rule. Invoking the metaphor of slavery to dramatize the gag rule's threat to the rights of free citizens, Gould argued:

> In other lands the people do not rule. Who rules in America? THE PEOPLE. The matter, then, is to settle the question whether the people rule, or aristocrats rule among us. . . . [Proslavery politician Henry A.] Wise, of Virginia, may have his slaves, but we are not his slaves and never will be. . . . If we give up the right of petitioning, or cease to exercise it in this cause then we are indeed slaves. Let our representatives know that we are their masters. I despise the man who says our representatives will not mind our petitions. Suppose they will not. If they refuse, the next year will have a million of signatures to the petitions [*sic*], and the year after a million more.[45]

Gould's remarks demonstrate the growing currency of the notion that not only the South but also the national government was in the thrall of a "slave power conspiracy" comprised of planter "aristocrats" who followed the "dictates of their own selfish passions" and who were intent on extending their domain of influence into the North. The editor of the antislavery *Weekly Advocate*, after learning of the December 1837 gag resolution, drew the grim conclusion that "the actual slavery of one portion of a people must eventually lead to the virtual slavery of the other."[46]

African American abolitionists in the North, for their part, supported the free speech stand that John Quincy Adams and others were taking in Congress. But for free blacks, the gag rule was merely part of a broader attack on their precarious rights, on their virtual freedom, in the North. Free blacks focused their petition efforts on memorializing Northern legislatures to preserve and restore their rights. In February 1837, for instance, African American men and women of New York City petitioned that "persons of color arrested on a claim of being fugitive slaves" be given a trial by jury so the courts could protect blacks from fraudulent claims by slaveholders and their agents; the petitioners also asked that the right to vote, which New York had stripped from black men in 1822, be restored to them. For blacks, the gag rule represented not only the encroachments of the Southern Slave Power but also, more broadly, of white racism in both North and South.[47]

PETITIONING IN THE SOUTH

Even as the petition war unfolded in Washington, D.C., Southern free blacks were presenting their own state legislatures with memorials, a process that has largely escaped the notice of historians of sectionalism. Southern states moved, one by one, to restrict or outlaw the manumission of slaves by their masters. One restrictive device was the passage of laws that exiled manumitted slaves and thus prevented the growth of the free black population. Blacks fought back against these laws by petitioning Southern legislatures for exemptions from them; no less than the memorials of Northern free blacks against colonization, these Southern petitions asserted the citizenship of blacks and their deep connections to their kinfolk and to their home states. A Tennessee man named Stephen Lytle, for example, protested his threatened exile from Nashville on the grounds that "*there* are all his associations and feelings—his preferences are *there*—his attachments are *there*—he could not live and enjoy life *any where* else." A free black woman named Rebekah, of

Sullivan County, Tennessee, struck a similar chord when she represented to the legislature that she was "a native of this state—that she is far advanced in life—that all her children with the exception of one were sold into other states . . . —[and] that she now lives in the neighborhood of that remaining child and of her aged husband with whom she earnestly desires to pass the remnant of her days."[48]

Such petitions were usually declined; the best hope a petitioner had was to find some prominent whites in the community who were willing to lend their support. This was the strategy of Rachel Collins of Norfolk, Virginia. Collins stated in her 1836 petition that although she had long lived in Norfolk as a free person, that freedom was now threatened, as the authorities were rounding up free blacks and telling them they must leave the state. Collins pleaded her case by demonstrating that she had been a model citizen—not only was she law-abiding and tax-paying, but also she had tendered support to the Norfolk militia during the War of 1812, cooking for the soldiers, finding accommodations for them, and even nursing the sick. She asked that she be allowed to remain among those "who have known her in her days of usefulness and that she not be driven away in her Helplessness to beg her Bread amongst Strangers." Because she was able to obtain the signatures of the surviving members of the Norfolk Junior Volunteers, vouching for her patriotic service, Collins's request was deemed "reasonable" by the legislature and she was permitted to stay in Virginia.[49]

Southern free black petitions are important for historians of sectionalism because they challenge us to remember that abolitionism, contrary to the claims of its enemies, was not a doctrine foreign to the South and not a repudiation of the region. Free black petitioners wanted to preserve or extend their liberty and to maintain their identity as Southerners—as natives of Virginia, Tennessee, and other Southern states. Immediatism was at its heart a rejection of colonization, a rejection of the "diffusion" argument and of the fantasy of a "whites only" South. Black Southerners, through their petitions, articulated a core value of immediatism when they asserted their right to stay in the region; they implicitly developed the idea of a "moral union"—an interracial republic—that Rogan Kersh attributes to abolitionists, white and black, in the North.[50] The petitions also bespeak the political sophistication of their authors; they tried to exploit the contradictions in the reigning ideology of whites, who claimed that Southern blacks were dangerous even as they trumpeted slave loyalty to the master class. Petitioners reassured legislators of their loyalty in order to win favor.

The most remarkable instance of such political maneuvering was in a Fredericksburg, Virginia, petition of 1838. The petitioners were property-owning free black men, some of whom were descendants of Revolutionary soldiers, others of whom had aided the "efforts of their country" in the War of 1812. They were caught in a legal bind. An 1831 law prohibited free blacks from assembling at schoolhouses for the purpose of learning to read and write, and a recently passed law forbade free blacks from sending their children out of state for an education. The petitioners asked the General Assembly for special permission to authorize a school in Fredericksburg for free people of color. They cannily endorsed the recent law by noting that it had indeed been injurious to their children to send them to Northern schools, where they were exposed to the "risk of having their minds poisoned by doctrines alike inimical to the good order of society & distructive [*sic*] of their own interests." Wouldn't it be better, the petitioners implicitly argued, for free blacks to obtain a proper, legally sanctioned education in the South than to meet clandestinely or come under the sway of Northern abolitionists? An education, they reminded the legislators, was a prerequisite for "gaining an honest livelihood." This argument, though it failed to persuade the legislators, reveals that free blacks understood perfectly well the political climate. The petitions of Southern free blacks thus spoke in two registers. Their overt message was an anti-abolitionist one of loyalty and service and deference to the master class, but their covert message gave voice to a central tenet of the antislavery creed—that removal policies were immoral, that blacks had earned the right to live where they pleased, and that they should not be "diffused" from the lands of their birth.[51]

THE PROCESS OF DISUNION

If the gag rule backfired by prompting the proliferation of antislavery appeals, those abolition memorials had their own unanticipated consequence of in-ducing "ultras" like Calhoun to call for a closing of the Southern ranks. As the antislavery petition campaign escalated in 1836–37, it generated heated exchanges not only between Northern and Southern politicians and between Democrats and Whigs but also between Southerners. Calhoun inveighed against petitions by taking what he considered to be the high ground in making the broad assertion that slavery was a "positive good." Calhoun was one of a cadre of South Carolinians, such as former nullifier William Harper, who were at this moment extending the arguments of Thomas Dew and of proslavery ministers by building a case that "all human beings did not have identical rights but only the ones that attached to their social role." In their brand of proslavery nationalism, the South was the bulwark of American conservatism, safeguarding the traditional social order and Christian values against the destabilizing encroachments of radical egalitarianism.[52]

According to Calhoun, the slave was coddled and cared for, with "kind attention paid to him in sickness or infirmities of age." Invoking the comparative defense of slavery, he contrasted the harmonious social relations of the agrarian South with the political unrest and economic insecurity of the industrializing North. Abolitionism must be silenced, in other words, because it was wrong about slavery. Leading Southern Whigs agreed with Calhoun that abolitionist petitions were dangerous. In a pro–gag rule speech on the Senate floor, Henry Clay declared that abolitionists supported "amalgamation"—a "revolting admixture of the black element" with the white.[53]

But while they agreed that abolitionism was evil, not all preeminent Southerners were ready to accept Calhoun's "positive good" standard of faith. Senator William Cabell Rives, the leader of a faction of Virginia Democrats who would soon gravitate toward the Whigs, argued pointedly with Calhoun in February 1837, saying that although he staunchly opposed Northern interference with slavery, he nonetheless believed that slavery was a "misfortune and an evil in all circumstances." By defending slavery as a positive good, he said to Calhoun, you "shock the generous sentiments of human nature, you go counter to the common sense of mankind." Calhoun did not let this rebuff stand. He called Rives's position indefensible, charging that the timeworn "necessary evil" view of slavery was the "spring and well head from which all these streams of abolition proceeded." The debates about petitioning, to quote Freehling, called forth an intense "stridency about disloyalty" on the part of Calhoun and his allies.[54] This stridency was evident in the new rhetorical uses to which Southerners such as Calhoun and James Henry Hammond put the specter of disunion. Hammond, like Robert Barnwell Rhett, was an ardent nullifier who was given to making threats of disunion as he jockeyed for power among South Carolina's elite and tried to get out from under Calhoun's shadow. During the gag rule debates in the House, he vowed defiantly that he would not only "preach" but also "practice disunion" if Congress, some day, passed measures forcing emancipation on the South. But he also spoke of disunion in a more defensive, anxious register, not as a threat or a prediction of a distant calamity but as a *process* that was already well under way. Answering the claim that abolitionists were so "few in number" that they exerted "little influence," Hammond countered that antislavery petitions were proof that immediatism was spreading "with a rapidity almost beyond conception." Radicals like Garrison (whom Hammond condemned by name) were shrewdly bringing ignorant Northerners under their sway. Thus "every mail from the North brings fresh news of agitation; every breeze is tainted with it." He called on Southerners to mark abolition's "fearful progress" and "prepare to meet" the "approaching crisis." Anyone who failed to take "the highest and boldest ground" in the defense of slavery, Hammond bellowed, was a "traitor to the memory of those from whom he has inherited his rights."[55]

Calhoun, although less belligerent than his younger colleague, shared Hammond's sense of alarm at the trajectory of Northern public opinion. He, too, described the Union as dividing, with the free and slave states arrayed in a "deadly hatred" that "in the course of a few years" would separate them "into two nations." "A large portion of the Northern States" regarded slavery "to be a sin," Calhoun explained, and "would consider it as an obligation of conscience to abolish it if they should feel themselves in any degree responsible for its continuance." Although abolitionists had not yet fully succeeded in persuading the majority that immediate emancipation was an "obligation of conscience," they had already taken control "of the pulpit, of the schools, and, to a considerable extent, of the press." Therefore, it was only a matter of time—a short time, at that—before the North presented a united abolition front.[56]

Both men knew very well that the North was by no means solidly abolitionist; they collaborated with Northern Democrats in electing proslavery presidents and passing proslavery legislation. But they used the fiction of abolition solidarity to try to engineer proslavery solidarity—the idea of a united North could frighten white Southerners into closing ranks. In his Senate speech of February 6, 1837, Calhoun spoke directly to his fellow white Southerners, especially to men like Rives, when he declared that "all we want is concert, to lay aside all party differences, and unite with zeal and energy in repelling approaching dangers. Let there be concert of action, and we shall find ample means of security without resorting to secession or disunion." In other words, it would take a united South to prevail over the united North in the contest for control of the federal government.[57]

While Hammond and Calhoun were content to paint their images of disunion with broad strokes, their fellow South Carolinian, Senator Preston, offered a more nuanced rendering of the process of sectional alienation. Although overshadowed in modern historiography by Calhoun and Hammond, Preston was widely respected in his day for his powerful oratorical skills. A former nullifier who would cast his lot with the Whigs, Preston carefully cultivated an image of moderation. In a remarkable pro–gag rule speech delivered in the Senate on March 1, 1836, he pledged not to overestimate the strength of the abolitionists but rather to offer a dispassionate assessment of the "causes of [the] growth" of the movement. Abolition petitions, he intoned, did "not come as heretofore, singly and far apart, from the quiet routine of the Society of Friends, or the obscure vanity of some philanthropic club." Instead, they are "sent to us in vast numbers from soured and agitated communities, poured in upon us from the overflowing of public sentiment." What was the source of that sentiment? Preston credited the abolitionists with "zeal and energy" and identified a key source of their inspiration in British antislavery crusaders such as Thomas Clarkson and William Wilberforce, who had engineered the abolition of slavery in the West Indies in 1833. For Preston, the British example was highly instructive— Clarkson and Wilberforce had been part of a "neglected, despised" minority of reformers, but their own zeal and energy, combined with the apathy of slaveowning planters, had enabled them to win over the British public. Britain, in turn, exercised a "vast power" over the "public mind" of the northeastern United States.[58]

More ominous even than British influence was the abolitionists' skill at tapping the roots of American culture. Abolition sprang, Preston discerned, from evangelical religion and from revolutionary republicanism itself. "The cause of antislavery is made identical with religion, and men and women are exhorted by all they esteem holy . . . by all that can warm the heart or inflame the imagination, to join in the pious work of purging the sin of slavery from the land." Moreover, "all the sympathies of the American heart for liberty—

the word itself has a magic in it—achieved through war and revolution, are perverted into it." What faced the South was not merely the problem of gagging reckless fanatics but the challenge of harnessing on behalf of anti-abolition the powerful currents of religion and republicanism. While Calhoun appealed for Southern solidarity, Preston implored senators from free and slave states alike to counterpose their own "moral weight" and "patriotic feelings" against the appeals of abolitionists. "Erect yourself into a barrier between the opposing sections," he demanded. According to Preston, then, the process of disunion was indeed under way, but it was still in the power of reasonable men, Northern and Southern, to control and contain it. If the nation's leaders squandered the "blessed moments" left in which to dispel the clouds of sectional conflict, Preston feared, "a tempest surcharged with all the elements of devastation" would surely come.[59]

For us, the most chilling invocation of disunion in this era was Nathaniel Beverly Tucker's 1836 novel *The Partisan Leader*. Tucker was part of an academic "cabal," which included his fellow College of William and Mary professor Thomas Dew, of proslavery ideologues in Virginia. Alienated by the Jackson administration's antinullifier policies and opposed to Jackson's successor, Tucker, under a pseudonym, published *The Partisan Leader* as anti–Van Buren campaign propaganda. Set in the future, in 1849, the novel's premise is that the South has seceded and formed a new Confederacy to escape the oppression (particularly the high tariffs) of a Van Buren presidency. The book is more than a prophecy, for, as Tucker's characters debate whether Virginia, too, should secede and join the Confederacy, they rehearse the argument that disunion was an inexorable process. There had been a "steady tendency" on the part of the federal government to "increase the resources" of the North at the expense of the South; watching "northern cupidity and northern fanaticism" on the "march," the "southern States had been, at length, forced to see that the day for decisive action had arrived." In order to embrace secession, the main protagonist has first to unlearn what he had long been taught—that disunion was the "*maximum* of evil" and would bring "weakness, dissension, and the danger to liberty from the standing armies of distinct and rival powers." He finally comes to understand that the North itself was the source of such evil and that the imagined danger had come to pass—the North had furnished the "standing army" that was "fastened upon" the South.[60]

In his own day, Tucker's innovation was his effort to disarm disunion of its terrors—to imagine it, for Southerners, not as a fearful calamity, political lever, or last resort, but as a process that led to the successful establishment of an independent Confederacy. The Southern public was not yet receptive to this message; while the book had its admirers, most notably James Henry Hammond, it was a critical and commercial failure. But Tucker would one day earn the mantle of visionary. When it was reprinted in 1862, in wartime Richmond, *The Partisan Leader* was praised by real Confederates for having "substantially foretold the great leading features of the history of the twenty-five years."[61]

THE USES OF DISUNION IN THE NORTH

In the wake of the mail campaign and the imposition of the gag rule, the indictment that abolitionists were disunionists emerged as the principal one leveled against them in the North. Anti-abolitionists in Cincinnati charged that immediatism "by its effects" sought "the destruction and disunion of our happy government." In New York City, a new anti-abolition paper vowed to be "the uncompromising and watchful foe of ABOLITION, which is but another name for Disunion," and in Pottstown, Pennsylvania, another such paper declared immediatist doctrines "more dangerous to the harmony of the United States and to the permanency of our Union, than any that have yet been publicly advocated in this country." In Bristol, Rhode Island, an anti-abolition handbill predicted that immediatism would "*disunionize* the country—and lead to all the Bloody Horrors of a Civil War." In their own public addresses and newspapers, abolitionists repeatedly acknowledged that, as Joshua Leavitt, editor of the New York antislavery journal the *Emancipator*, put it, "no objection" to abolition was "more common, than an *alleged tendency to dissolve the Union.*"[62]

In the period 1835 to 1837 abolitionists elaborated a variety of responses to this charge. The first was to echo arguments that had been made by New York's James Tallmadge and the slavery restrictionists during the Missouri debates—namely, that slavery, not abolition, was the root cause of sectional tension. The managers of a Harrisburg, Pennsylvania, antislavery society, in acknowledging that they were "accused of acts which tend to a dissolution of the Union," retorted that "again, and again, we have seen the dissolution of the Union threatened, and mainly, as conceded by leading men of all parties, through the influence of Slavery. Scarcely is one crisis passed when another impends, and it is evident that this succession of dangerous excitements will never end but by the removal of its cause." According to this view, abolitionists, who sought to remove the root danger, were the true Unionists. In the words of Leavitt, "Slavery endangers the integrity of the Union, more than all other enemies; and unless soon destroyed, will be the destroyer of both us and it."[63]

A second kind of response to the charge of disunionism was to denigrate Southern threats of disunion as empty bluster. A letter to the *Emancipator* rejected the "great bugbear" that abolitionism "will provoke the South to dissolve the Union" as an "old story"—slaveholders had regularly made threats but would never dare follow them up. Slaveholders knew well, so this argument ran, that they would never survive outside of the Union. In addition to facing insurrection and internal disunion, a slaveholders' republic would be the "execration of the world" and have the "wrath of Heaven" hanging over it. Northerners should stop being "weak enough to be alarmed at [Southern] threats." As W. T. Allen, speaking to the Young Men's Anti-Slavery Society of New York put it, "The *dissolution of the Union* is the standing scare-crow to drive the North into the measures of the South." Like the notion that slavery was the root cause of disunion, the idea that proslavery disunionism was meaningless rhetorical brinkmanship found favor among moderate antislavery Northerners in Congress. New York's Representative Aaron Vanderpoel, during the gag rule debates in 1837, admitted that when he first entered the House, he had felt "holy horror when gentlemen presented to us the dreadful alternative of disunion!" But the scenario "no longer had the power to shake his nerves." For in Southern justifications of the gag rule, "threats of disunion had become as familiar here as household words." He would not allow himself to "be troubled with the apprehension of even the *possibility* of disunion." There was patriotism enough in the North and the South to ensure that "delusion and fanaticism would have only a brief and harmless career."[64]

Abolitionists denigrated not only Southern threats of disunion but also Northern accusations of it as familiar, even stale political tropes. William Ellery Channing, radicalized by the violent backlash against abolitionists and by the gag rule, responded philosophically to the charge that abolitionism had disunionist tendencies, noting that "almost all men see ruinous tendencies in whatever opposes their particular interests, or views." Alluding to the evolution of disunion discourse, he pointed out that "all the political parties which have convulsed our country, have seen tendencies to national destruction in the principles of their opponents." The very ubiquity of indictments of disunion rendered them meaningless: "Against whom has not this charge been hurled! What party among us has not been loaded with this reproach!" His message was that antislavery Northerners should not allow such morally and politically bankrupt accusations to silence them.[65]

A related argument in the antislavery press was that the South was not united against abolitionism, and that there was no realistic prospect of a proslavery disunion movement. Immediatist papers delighted in printing excerpts from border states and Upper South newspapers and politicians who took Unionist positions against the nullifiers. The *Pennsylvania Freeman*, for example, repeatedly featured evidence, drawn most often from Kentucky, that South Carolina's militants were isolated and disgraced. The paper printed the comments of a Kentucky Whig, Mr. Southgate, who mocked the "imperial" pretensions of the "immortals" of South Carolina and called them a "pack of bugaboos" singing a "stale and worn out ditty about the dissolution of the Union." An editorial in the *Louisville (Ky.) Journal*, condemning the "self-complacency, vanity, and vaporing of South Carolina politicians" as "laughable," was also published in the *Freeman* to illustrate "WHAT KENTUCKY THINKS OF SOUTH CAROLINA." Even Garrison's *Liberator* sometimes sang this refrain. Positing that "no argument has ever been urged against abolitionism with so much success as its alleged tendency to bring about the dissolution of the Union," Garrison in a September 1838 article countered with evidence from a recent dinner in honor of Daniel Webster, in which a featured speaker, Mr. Menitee, from Kentucky, had argued that his state, like Massachusetts, was devoted to the Union and rejected the revolutionary tendencies of South Carolina. "Kentucky, like Massachusetts," Menitee averred, "regards the overthrow of the Union as more frightful than all."[66]

In the wake of the mail campaign and gag rule, these arguments disavowing and denigrating disunion would come to coexist uneasily in abolitionist discourse with two new countervailing contentions—that disunion was, in some ways, already a reality, and, alternately, that nothing, including disunion, was worse than slavery. Garrison tentatively experimented with the first argument; although it did not become his mantra until the 1840s, by 1836 he was already testifying to the Massachusetts legislature, in answer to the charge that he was disunionist: "It is not true. We would save the Union, if it not be too late. But it would seem to us that the Union is already destroyed." Alluding to the proscription of free speech in the South, he continued: "*We have no Union. We, sir, cannot go through these States enjoying the privileges, which the Constitution of the Union professed to secure to all the citizens of this Republic. And why? Because, Sir, and only because, we are laboring to accomplish the very purposes, for which it is declared in the preamble to the Constitution, that the Union was formed . . . to establish justice, ensure domestic tranquility, and promote the general welfare!*" The second argument was developed by the Grimké sisters, who tried to nerve female antislavery converts for the prospect of social ostracism by counseling that their role was to act virtuously. "Duty is ours and events are God's," wrote Angelina in her 1836 "Appeal to the Christian Women of the South"— the consequences of moral actions were in God's hands. To inspire commitment to her cause, she played on fear; in language strikingly similar to Jackson's antinullification proclamation of 1832, Grimké wrote of unveiling the "monster of iniquity." But for her, the monster was slavery, not disunion. Only by unmasking slavery's "frightful features" could abolitionists shake Americans out of their "complacency." Acknowledging that slaveholders "seek to frighten us" with "fear of the consequences" of disunion, Grimké's Female Anti-Slavery Society of Philadelphia asked, during its October 14, 1836, meeting: "Can *any* consequences be worse than the consequences of Slavery itself?" As they understood it, the fate of the Union rested on the answer to that question.[67]

1837–1850

PART

2

The Idea Will Become Familiar

In 1837 a new litmus test for loyalty to slavery emerged as the issue of Texas annexation became a centerpiece of the antislavery petition campaign. The Republic of Texas had declared independence from Mexico in 1836; Texans overwhelmingly favored annexation to the United States. Abolitionists vehemently opposed the addition of Texas to the roster of states, and for good reason—the Lone Star Republic was a bastion of slavery. Texans had won their independence from Mexico with the help of militia companies raised in New Orleans, Mobile, Natchez, and other Southern locales. Newspapers such as the *New Orleans Picayune* had fostered sympathy for independence and spurred recruitment by casting Texans as "embattled, expatriated" Americans. Most important, Texans had earned the reputation as defenders of slavery—they had vehemently protested efforts by successive Mexican administrations to restrict and gradually dismantle the institution, winning concessions such as an 1828 decree that allowed Texans to register their slaves, in name only, as "indentured servants." Independence brought with it a swift affirmation of slavery. Texas's constitution established the legality of hereditary slavery, and its law code featured such measures as a statute that subjected both slaves and free blacks to whipping "not exceeding one hundred" lashes nor "less than twenty-five" for using abusive language toward whites. Massive Southern immigration to Texas after independence exponentially increased the slave population there from 5,000 in 1836 to 38,753 in 1840.[1]

Inspired by the impassioned treatise *The War in Texas*, written by antislavery editor and mentor to Garrison, Benjamin Lundy, abolitionists in 1837 flooded Congress with petitions, signed by more than two hundred thousand memorialists, against inviting Texas into the Union. Although hardly an abolitionist, the redoubtable congressman John Quincy Adams vocally supported the right of these petitioners to be heard. The House of Representatives responded by passing a new, more stringent gag rule (alluded to above) that prohibited discussing slavery in the territories. Immediatists had been ambivalent about invoking disunion as a process of sectional alienation— their rhetoric of Northern complicity and complacency emphasized the cultural affinities rather than antipathies of whites in the North and South. But the advent of the annexation issue pushed abolitionists to develop their own emerging interpretation of disunion as a process—one in which a "Slave Power Conspiracy" prosecuted a plan to consolidate its hold over the national government and spread the cotton kingdom. Lundy argued that the Southern bid to annex Texas was part of a "long premeditated crusade" to extend slavery, and that the crusade put North and South on a collision course. James Birney asserted in 1837 that Northerners could not accept annexation unless they were willing to "consent to become one great slaveholding nation." So Northerners should resist, even at the risk of alienating the South. He continued: "Annexation ought to persuade us to look forward to the dissolution of the Union as an event which will in all probability take place, and for which we ought to prepare." More than any one, John Quincy Adams led the charge in connecting the suppression of petitions to the bid for Texas—again and again he argued in Congress that both were part of a nefarious design. John C. Calhoun and James Henry Hammond had exaggerated the influence of abolitionists in order to close the Southern ranks; now Adams and his allies compiled evidence of slaveholder aggression and dominance to galvanize the North.[2]

To rebut such claims about the Slave Power Conspiracy, South Carolina's William Preston argued on the Senate floor that anti-annexation petitioners were "hostile to the institutions of the South, and purpose their destruction." He defended annexation as a simple bid on the part of the slave states to achieve parity with the North and maintain, as he pretentiously expressed it, an "equipoise" in the Senate chamber. For Preston, the Texas revolution was another chapter in the Missouri Compromise controversy. It was clear to him and other supporters of annexation that the "distribution of the Louisiana Purchase according to the Missouri Compromise had offered the free states greater opportunity for growth" than the slave states. Ironically, Preston presented bundles of petitions to the Senate, from climes as distant as Louisiana and Pennsylvania, to persuade his colleagues that "all parts of this Union" supported annexation.[3]

Unfortunately for Preston, many Southern leaders were not yet willing to accept annexation as a loyalty litmus test. Substantial opposition to annexation came from Preston's fellow proslavery Southern Whigs, who argued that if slavery expanded too quickly into the Southwestern frontier, the older slave states would fall prey to economic decline and marginality. The "equipoise" argument, in other words, cut both ways. So long as the principle of paired admissions of free and slave states prevailed, it was "child's play" for the South to control the Senate—all it needed was just one crossover vote from the Northern delegation. But trends in the House were more alarming and intractable. Ever since the U.S. victory in the War of 1812, the North had been attracting wave after wave of European immigrants, even as states like Virginia and South Carolina were depopulated by massive emigration to the frontier of the South and West. This had already resulted in the loss of congressional seats in the Old South and the steady consolidation of the North's dominance in the House. Behind the fear of losing electoral influence was a deeper fear— that as slaveholders and their slaves moved from East to West, the Old South's commitment to the peculiar institution would be attenuated, and slaveholders would "lose control of the land of Jefferson and Madison."[4]

Annexationists could not even count on the incoming Democratic administration to do their bidding. Newly elected President Van Buren shunned the project of annexation, as Michael Holt has put it, like a "leprous pariah." Preoccupied by the severe economic depression that fell over the nation in 1837, aware that the abolitionist anti-annexation campaign was gaining some traction among Northerners, and intent on ensuring that the Democrats had a strong base of support in both sections, Van Buren refrained even from recommending annexation to Congress. The stalemate would persist until a new president, John Tyler, took office in 1841.[5]

Even as the Van Buren administration assumed a holding pattern on the Texas question, debate raged in Congress over anti-annexation petitions. A centerpiece of these wrangles was a new stridency on the question of female loyalty. Proslavery politicians, alarmed that the gag rule had not deterred female petitioners and that women were now signing memorials on an issue (Texas annexation) that fell clearly into the male realm of electoral politics rather than religion and benevolence, issued a series of jarring chastisements to women. Representative Jesse A. Bynum of North Carolina declared in 1837 that it was a "portentous foreboding, an awful omen, when women were stepping into the political theatre, calling on men to act." To follow their exhortations was "supreme folly" and would result in "civil war, and one, too, that would drench the fairest fields of this great republic with brothers' blood." He called on Northern men, who in his mind had "little to do with getting up this excitement" over abolitionism and anti-annexation, to put it down. Two years later, Senator Henry Clay would invoke civil war as a tactic of intimidation when he cautioned that the "ink which [women] shed in subscribing with their fair hands abolition petitions may prove but the prelude to the shedding of the blood of their brethren." Some Northern politicians picked up this refrain. John Norvell, a Virginia-born Democrat representing Michigan, lamented that women had "seized the dagger of Abolitionism, to complete the work of death and desolation in the South."[6]

In response to these attacks, antislavery women and their male allies began to radicalize their rhetoric and elaborate justifications for female petitioning that cast it not simply as a moral duty but as a constitutional right. The most stirring defense of petitioning was a lengthy speech before the House of Representatives by John Quincy Adams in the summer of 1838. Adams reminded his audience of female heroism in the Old Testament and of female patriotic activism during the American Revolution. To the charge that women had no right to petition because they had no right to vote, Adams countered that it "was an injustice" that women did not possess the franchise. Adams also goaded his colleagues from South Carolina by making a reference to the Grimké sisters. He pointedly noted that a great number of antislavery signatures had been "obtained by the influence of two women of South Carolina, natives of that State" who were "well acquainted with the practical operations" of slavery. In response, Representative Pickens (not to be confused with Pinckney) of South Carolina disowned the Grimkés, proclaiming their

antislavery utterances a "tissue of prejudice and misrepresentation." Aspersions against their honor would not deter antislavery women, according to
Senator Thomas Morris, of Ohio, an antislavery Democrat who resented the
hold of the Slave Power Conspiracy over his party. "The liberty of the slave
seems to be committed to [woman's] charge, and who can doubt her final
triumph?"[7]

THE RADICALISM OF FEMALE ORATORY

Even as Southern and Northern anti-abolitionists in Congress conspired to
quash antislavery petitions, Northern clergymen worked to muzzle antislavery speakers—female ones, that is. Female oratory was widely associated with
the notorious Fanny Wright, an iconoclastic Scotswoman who had toured the
United States in the late 1820s giving theatrical speeches on behalf of radical
causes ranging from workingmen's rights, to the corruption of American
religion, to the amalgamation of the races and "free love" (sexuality outside
the confines of marriage). The Northern press branded Wright as a "bold
blasphemer and a voluptuous preacher of licentiousness." Only a "female
monster" would so overstep the bounds of modesty. Criticism of Wright
reveals that the age-old prohibition against female public speaking rested on
the notion that oratory was a form of exposure that carried with it, for women,
the taint of sexual impropriety.[8]

   Thus when Angelina and Sarah Grimké, exiles from South Carolina,
embarked on a speaking tour of New England in the spring of 1837, they
carried the burden not only of converting listeners to the antislavery creed
but also of dissociating female oratory from the dread doctrines of "Fanny
Wrightism." To earn a fair hearing from audiences drawn as much by curi-
osity as by sympathy, the Grimkés stressed their piety and their elite Southern
backgrounds—they justified antislavery activism as both a Christian duty and
a universal moral imperative. It soon came to light that the two sisters possessed not only social status and strategic savvy, but also genuine talent:
Angelina had a "musical, carrying voice and pleasing manner," and Sarah
used the "singsong speaking style" of Quaker ministers to sway her listeners.
The women, along with their male sponsors in the abolitionist movement,
were surprised to discover that their audiences were largely receptive. As the
Grimkés' reputations preceded them from town to town, they were "sur-

rounded by an electric atmosphere" that inspired them to greater and greater rhetorical heights.[9]

Alarmed by the progress of radicalism, Massachusetts clergymen issued a pastoral letter and delivered a series of sermons condemning the Grimké sisters. In speaking before "promiscuous assemblies" of men and women, they charged, the Grimkés had "perverted" the law of female subjection and displayed "boldness, arrogance, rudeness, [and] indelicacy." One religious journal went so far as to accuse them of "unfortunate hereditary insanity." Criticisms issued from the antislavery press, too. The New York–based *Colored American* charged that the Grimkés had crossed the line into Fanny Wrightism and "furnished a weapon to the . . . infidel"; editor Samuel Cornish urged African American women to avoid such immodesty. The most influential attack on the sisters came from Catharine Beecher, the beloved maven of Northern domesticity, who had become a national celebrity by celebrating the moral virtue and influence of women. Beecher's *Essay on Slavery and Abolitionism, with Reference to the Duty of American Females* (1837), accused abolitionist women of spawning hatred and resentment among Southerners, of undermining gradualist efforts to dismantle slavery, and of actually bringing the country, in what was becoming a ubiquitous image, to the "very verge of the precipice" of disunion. She drew her own dystopian picture of the "dismemberment" of the body politic—of a grim future in which "public credit staggers, . . . commerce furls her slackened sail, [and] when property all over the nation changes its owners and relations." She begged that the North and South stop provoking each other and urged women to play their divinely ordained role of peacemaker.[10]

Just as the gag rule had the unanticipated consequence of ratcheting up the petition campaign, such critiques of the Grimkés amplified rather than silenced their voices. The sisters, in a series of speeches and publications, the most important of which was Sarah's *Letters on the Equality of the Sexes*, honed their defense of women's political activism. Indeed, the abolitionist counterattack against the Massachusetts clergymen's pastoral letter was the opening salvo of the woman's rights movement. Garrison's newspaper served as a vehicle for the Grimkés' arguments and for the emerging analogy between the racist oppression of slaves and the sexist oppression of women. In the pages of the *Liberator*, Sarah Grimké refuted the biblical justifications for women's subordination. Jesus's Sermon on the Mount, she reminded readers, had defined the moral duties of his followers without making any distinction between men and women. In the Bible, one finds "nothing like the softness of woman, nor the sternness of man; but both are equally commanded to bring forth the fruits of the Spirit—Love, meekness, gentleness."[11]

In the eyes of Northern anti-abolition mobs, there was nothing of meekness and gentleness in the activism of antislavery women. Rather, the interracial cooperation of female abolitionist societies appeared to critics as the embodiment of social equality between the races; the nascent dialogue with these societies about the pernicious effects of sexism appeared to be a wholesale revolt against male authority. Moreover, the fact that American abolitionists, women included, had formed alliances with British abolitionists raised anew the specter of "foreign intervention" in U.S. affairs. These fears together proved dangerously volatile. In Boston in 1835, for instance, a mob broke up a meeting of the Boston Female Anti-Slavery Society that was to have featured a speech by visiting British abolitionist George Thompson. These rioters, like other Northern mobs that vented their fury against abolitionists, were led by men of authority and wealth—in this case, members of the Boston mercantile elite, and sympathetic newspaper editors, who wanted to protect their "trading and political connections with the South." They rallied artisans, clerks, apprentices, craftsmen, laborers, and other working-class men as "friends of the Union" to send an unmistakable message to the South: the North valued its ties to the South, and abolitionists were a radical fringe. The official position of leading Democrats and Whigs was to decry mob violence. But abolitionists believed that partisan paeans to law and order were a smokescreen—that "both political parties in the North were using a combination of high-toned resolutions and mob action" to do the bidding of slaveholders.[12]

Violence against antislavery women reached a crescendo in 1838. In May of that year, female abolitionists convened their second annual national convention, at Pennsylvania Hall in Philadelphia, only to find themselves surrounded by an enraged mob of ten thousand opponents. The "few policemen present," Margaret Hope Bacon has noted, "sided with the crowd and made no effort to restrain it." Angelina Grimké Weld (she had recently wed fellow activist Theodore Dwight Weld) and Abbey Kelley delivered their orations in the face of a seething crowd that had surged into the hall, hurling both verbal obscenities and actual stones and brickbats at the participants. Lucretia Mott adjourned the meeting before any one was injured. The mob that gathered the next morning was even more hostile and intimidating. But the women refused to give way; they conducted their business and, under Mott's direction, left the building in a solemn procession of pairs of white and black women linked arm-in-arm. The women "simply faced down the angry onlookers, relying on the moral force of their own courage and sense of right to protect them from attack." Miraculously, the tactic worked. But the mob, dead set on issuing an unmistakable warning, burned Pennsylvania Hall to the ground after the women had exited it.[13]

The torching of Pennsylvania Hall was especially chilling because it came just seven months after the most shocking mob attack on the antislavery movement: the murder of Elijah Lovejoy in November 1837. Lovejoy had persistently tried to establish an antislavery newspaper in Alton, Illinois, only to see his printing presses repeatedly destroyed by anti-abolition mobs. Seeking to protect his fourth printing press, he and his allies, with the endorsement of the town's mayor, obtained some pistols and steeled themselves to offer violent resistance to the next strike. When it came, Lovejoy never had a chance—he was gunned down before he could discharge his own weapon. On one level, the meaning of Lovejoy's murder was clear: abolitionists were risking their lives. The episode demonstrated how anti-abolition talk could materialize into a deadly reality and thus itself seemed a harbinger of disunion—of a descent into bloodshed. "We have long deluded ourselves with the belief, that there was too much intelligence and virtue in our land, for us to be in danger of general lawlessness or of civil war," a Boston newspaper editorialized, but the Lovejoy slaying had shown that the rule of law was "precarious" and "despotism" ascendant. The *Colored American* blamed the killing not on the "poor and ignorant wretches who consummate the work planned out by 'gentlemen of property and standing,'" but on the press, which had "kept alive by base misrepresentation, the worst passions of the human heart, and pointed at abolitionists as fit subjects for the assassin's dagger."[14]

On another level, however, the incident in Alton exposed fault lines within the antislavery movement. On one side, and in the minority, were activists, like the Grimkés, who staunchly opposed any resort to violence, even in self-defense, and who grieved that Lovejoy had ever armed himself. On the other side was a growing cadre of immediatists, including Wendell Phillips, Amos Phelps, and Lydia Maria Child, who embraced Lovejoy as a "martyr of God."

Destruction by Fire of Pennsylvania Hall,

The New Building of the *Abolition Society,* on the night of the 17th May,

Published by J. T. Bowen, 94 Walnut Street, and Sold by George and Cately, 95 Chesnut Street.

This 1838 image of Pennsylvania Hall engulfed in flames dramatized the ferocity of the anti-abolition backlash in the North. (Courtesy of the Library of Congress)

They not only defended his resort to arms as justifiable but also saw it as a precursor of a time when abolitionists would have to use violence against the slave system.[15]

The controversy over antislavery petitions, over women's public speaking, and over the use of force in the antislavery campaign all reveal that anxieties over gender roles and relations were central to the slavery debates in the North. What comprised a womanly public voice? What constituted a manly defense of principles? How best could men defend the honor of their women? These questions also preoccupied white Southerners, who elaborated their own distinctly sectional responses to them.

Southern opinion makers characterized women's public speaking before "mixed" audiences (of men and women) as a repugnant transgression, a "Yankee" heresy. So strong were the proscriptions of public opinion in the South that no woman tried to establish a reputation as an orator or go on a public speaking tour there. White Southern women were politically active, but within a clearly delineated field. As we have seen, in the early 1830s they exercised the right to petition state legislatures on behalf of the twin causes of gradual emancipation and colonization. By the mid-1830s, however, male proslavery leaders like Virginians John Tyler and James Garland condemned such petitioning as too close in spirit and intent to the dangerous practices of Northern female immediatists. Instead, Southern women were encouraged to channel their political energies into two safer channels—party politics and the literary defense of slavery. By the late 1830s, at the behest of the Whig Party, women were invited to assert public identities as partisans. Because Whigs were more supportive of the congeries of antebellum moral reform societies, and therefore more attuned to the efficacy of female activism, they urged women in the North and South to attend political rallies, to present banners and other tokens to men, and even to make comments at public events through male proxies. When Whigs ratcheted up their appeals to women in the 1840s, Democrats reluctantly followed suit.[16]

If party politics represented a point of convergence between Northern and Southern women, the field of literature showed signs of their divergence. White women in the South contributed essays and novels to the burgeoning genre of "plantation fiction." Painting a rosy picture of estates populated by kind and genteel masters and mistresses and contented, loyal slaves, authors such as Caroline Gilman and Caroline Lee Hentz suggested that the South was the repository of moral virtue and social stability. In some respects, the work of this first generation of Southern female novelists complemented the efforts of Southern men such as John Pendleton Kennedy, William Gilmore Simms, and Beverly Tucker, who put into literary form the proslavery polemics of Thomas Dew and Calhoun and Hammond. But female authors had a special agenda: they focused on the "resourcefulness" of plantation mistresses rather than the "heroism of the planter-cavalier," they asserted that planter women should serve as conservators of the region's values, and they laid claim to a "feminine" mission—that of easing sectional tensions and fostering mutual sympathy by offering a "realistic" portrait of slaveholders. Moreover, as Michael O'Brien points out, female authors like Gilman were "much more attentive to slaves" than their male counterparts, for it was impossible to depict the domestic sphere without portraying slave characters. To a great extent, the reading public accepted the representation of proslavery novelists as truth tellers. As William R. Taylor explained in his classic book *Cavalier and Yankee*, works of plantation fiction by men and women alike were wildly popular not only in the South but also in the North. Made anxious by the rapid pace of social, economic, and technological changes in their own region, many white Northerners took some psychic comfort in the image of the South as a pastoral paradise, at a safe remove from the strains of modernization.[17]

While literature was a sanctioned and popular field of public activity for women in both sections, however, Northern women's own genre of domestic fiction was already diverging from the Southern version, setting the stage for a full-blown literary war over slavery that Harriet Beecher Stowe's *Uncle Tom's Cabin* would provoke in the 1850s. Fiction by Northerners such as Catherine Sedgwick, Susan Warner, and E.D.E.N. Southworth was critical of the status quo, lamenting the dislocations (such as bankruptcies) caused by the rapid changes in the North and seeing them as signs of the corrosive and rampant materialism of men. Female authors featured assertive, independent heroines and provided a blueprint not for conserving existing values but for promoting moral regeneration. The "evangelical tone" of their writing "impelled many northern women to participate in reform activity" and to try to restructure the social order along "protofeminist lines."[18]

From the perspective of abolitionists, the incorporation of female authors and readers into a national literary dialogue on slavery and sectionalism posed a distinct challenge. How could the immediatist movement, which had won over only a small fraction of the Northern population, harness the reform energies of middle-class men and women, many of whom had fallen under the spell of plantation fiction? The abolitionists faced a formidable obstacle in the problem of disbelief—the majority of white Northerners simply did not believe that slavery was an inherently brutal, dehumanizing institution or that many slaveholders were systematically cruel. With their credibility under attack from the press, pulpit, legislative halls, and literary industry, three abolitionist leaders tried a new tack—they used the words of slaveholders themselves to expose the truth about Southern bondage.

AMERICAN SLAVERY AS IT IS

In 1838 Angelina Grimké Weld and her husband Theodore Dwight Weld, with the help of Sarah Grimké, undertook the massive project of collecting clippings from Southern newspapers—more than twenty thousand copies in all—to establish an unimpeachable record of the "actual condition of the slaves in the United States." They painstakingly arranged this "testimony from a thousand witnesses" under a series of thematic subheadings that described the tribulations of slaves: their suffering from hunger and exposure, the back-breaking toil that was extracted from them, the tortures to which they were submitted in the name of discipline, and the heartless, routine assault on the sanctity of their families. They then presented this evidence to the American public in a slender but explosive volume entitled *American Slavery as It Is.* The book is part legal brief, part sermon, part journalistic exposé, and part political treatise—its authors availed themselves of every rhetorical technique they could devise to frame and analyze their evidence. The introduction begins by asking the reader to imagine that he or she was "empanelled as a juror" to "bring in an honest verdict" on slavery. The reader's charge was to determine whether "slavery, as a condition for human beings, [was] good, bad, or indifferent." In the tone of courtroom prosecutors, the authors asserted that they would disprove, "by the testimony of a multitude of impartial witnesses," the popular fiction that slaves were well treated. They would "put slaveholders themselves through a course of cross-questioning which shall draw their condemnation out of their own mouths." Lest anyone doubt the authenticity of this testimony, the Grimkés and Weld deposited the newspaper clippings and other sources for their book at the New York City office of the American Anti-Slavery Society (AASS) to enable the skeptical and the curious to examine it firsthand.[19]

American Slavery as It Is delivers what it promises. Over the course of some two hundred pages, the authors lay out their indictment of slavery, drawing on the words of clergymen, judges, merchants, lawyers, physicians, professors, overseers, and drivers. Some of the testimony consists of observations by Northerners who had visited the South, or by Southerners, such as the Reverend John Rankin and the Grimkés themselves, who had joined the antislavery ranks. The authors also cite court records, highlighting such cases as *State v. Mann* (1830), in which the North Carolina Supreme Court ruled that slaveholders could not be prosecuted for assaulting their slaves. By far the most powerful sources are the runaway advertisements culled from Southern newspapers. Under the heading "BRANDINGS, MAIMINGS, GUN-SHOT WOUNDS, &c.," for example, are 119 quotations from representative newspapers—covering the Upper South and Deep South during 1837-38—spelling out in gruesome detail the mutilation of slaves. Anticipating the countercharge that slave injuries were the result of accidents, the Grimkés and Weld make it clear that slaves' scars revealed a pattern of systematic cruelty—they confront the reader with the inescapable fact that ear crop-pings, brandings, and lashed backs did not result from mere accidents. "De-scribing the work of their own hands," the authors note pointedly, slave-holders who penned the runaway advertisements showed a "commendable fidelity to truth."[20]

But *American Slavery as It Is* is more than a collage of horrors. In its final section, entitled "Objections Considered—Public Opinion," its authors probe the psychology of denial and offer cogent insights that have become staples of the modern-day historiography of slavery. This last section tries implicitly to answer two key questions: What were the sources of slave-holders' barbarity, and what explained Northerners willful blindness to it? The authors answer the first question with a proposition—namely, that slave-owners treated their bondspeople worse than they treated their horses and cattle. Why? Because the slaves' very humanity was a constant reproach and challenge to their owners. "It is impossible for *cattle* to excite in men such tempests of fury as men excite in each other," the Grimkés and Weld assert. "The greatest provocation to human nature is *opposition to its will*." To maintain their power, slaveholders had to crush not only the bodies but also the spirit of their slaves and make an example of anyone who defied them. Thus slaves were caught in a terrible trap—the more they asserted their humanity, the more inhumanity was visited upon them.[21]

As for Northern indifference to this suffering, the authors trace it to credu-lousness and hypocrisy. Northerners were constantly made dupes by South-ern slaveholders. Residents of the free states who traveled South, for instance, often reported that slaves had seemed happy, not realizing that their owners had kept the most shocking aspects of the system from these visitors' gaze and that the slaves, to protect themselves, dissembled when asked how they were treated. Most important, the Grimkés and Weld assert that to deny man's capacity for cruelty is to betray a shameful ignorance of human history and, in particular, of America's past. Citing the Salem witch trials, the persecution of religious dissenters such as Baptists and Quakers, the horrors of the transatlantic slave trade, and the recent mobbings of abolitionists in the North, the authors ask how one could acknowledge the existence of such cruelty but at the same time regard Southern slaveholders as incapable of systematic brutality? In its most powerful indictment of Northern hypocrisy, *American Slavery as It Is* reminds readers that the central article of faith of America's beloved doctrine of republicanism was that absolute power was, by definition, arbitrary in its exercise and corrupting in its influence. How could a nation founded to overthrow tyranny deny that slaveholders were tyrants?[22]

American Slavery as It Is was, by abolitionist standards, an instant success. Reported to have sold over one hundred thousand copies in the first year, it became a guide for antislavery activists; the book eventually served to inspire none other than Harriet Beecher Stowe. The volume was a fitting capstone to a decade of earnest agitation. But although abolitionists felt justifiable pride as the turbulent 1830s came to a close, in their concerted efforts to overcome Northern disbelief, they would find that the problem persisted in the new decade.

THE ELECTION OF 1840

The years 1840 to 1844 comprised the "zenith" of the two-party system, the heyday of competition between the established Whigs and Democrats. Voter turnout reached an unprecedented level (80 percent of the electorate voted in 1840), and economic issues dominated political campaigns, with the promodernization Whigs offering a clear alternative to the antimodernization Democrats. Partisan allegiances transcended sectional ones, and each party claimed to represent the nation. The Whigs' base of support was in the North, but their standard-bearer in Congress was Southerner Henry Clay; the Democrats were strongest in the South, but their leader was Northerner Martin Van Buren. Most important, the issue of slavery's territorial expansion did not yet out the economic debates over banking, tariffs, and the like, which were the parties' stock-in-trade.[23]

In the presidential campaign of 1840, the candidate of the Democrats was the incumbent, Van Buren. As president, he had tried to burnish his credentials as a defender of the Northern workingman and of the Southern slaveholder. He made legislation restricting the workday of government employees to ten hours and the creation of an "Independent Treasury" his signature economic issues. An extension of Andrew Jackson's "hard money" philosophy—which favored replacing paper or "soft" money with specie, or metal coins, in an effort to restrain the flow of credit and check rampant speculation—the independent or "subtreasury" would hold government deposits and thus control federal revenues. To preempt the charge that such an institution represented the very federal "consolidation" Democrats claimed to oppose, Van Buren and his administration cast the Independent Treasury as the vehicle of the "people" and banks as tools of the Northeastern Whig elite.[24]

Southern Democrats as well as Northern ones accepted this rationale—as a Richmond campaign paper put it, the "Sub-Treasury bill was passed in accordance with the will of the people, expressed at the polls." Even Calhoun, who had been drifting back into the Democratic fold, lined up behind Van Buren. To further shore up his Southern base, Van Buren continued to tout his record as a defender of slavery. He had opposed abolitionist efforts, for example, to win the freedom of the *Amistad* captives—Africans who had seized control of the schooner *Amistad*, on which they were being transported illegally from one Cuban port to another by Spanish slave traders. After the mutiny, the slave traders misled the rebels, who wanted to return home to Africa, about the ship's trajectory, navigating it into U.S. waters. The ship was captured by U.S. authorities off the coast of Long Island in June 1839, and the fate of the African mutineers lay in the hands of the American judicial system. Van Buren's administration tried a series of maneuvers to deny the *Amistad* rebels due process and favored returning them to Cuba—and Spanish jurisdiction—where they would face the harshest possible punishment.[25]

The Whig choice for president in 1840 was General William Henry Harrison. A renowned Indian fighter who as governor of the Indiana Territory and a U.S. senator from Ohio had fashioned himself a plain-spoken

THE ALMIGHTY LEVER

In this 1840 Whig cartoon, public opinion is a lever sliding the "Loco Foco" Democrats off
the precipice into the abyss of electoral defeat and poised to lift Harrison ("Tip") to victory.
(Courtesy of the Library of Congress)

Midwesterner (despite his elite upbringing in Tidewater Virginia), Harrison
had made a respectable showing in 1836 and was poised to co-opt Van
Buren's tactics and capitalize on his weaknesses. Harrison and the Whigs
tore a page from Van Buren's book of party discipline and voter mobilization
and launched the legendary "Log Cabin" campaign, offering an endless array
of public spectacles and slogans to arouse the enthusiasm of the electorate.
Although this "flummery, mummery, and hoopla" led some observers to
deride the Whigs for lack of substance, the party did have a cogent, and
potent, message for voters. The heart of that message was that the disastrous
economic policies of "Martin Van Ruin" were responsible for plunging the
country into a depression that had begun in 1837 and showed no signs of

abating. Whigs maintained that the subtreasury was an "odious" scheme calculated to "paralyse the efforts of the industrious classes of the community." They tarnished Van Buren with the same charge they had leveled against Andrew Jackson—that of executive tyranny. Van Buren's somewhat haughty, foppish personal style and fondness for luxury made him vulnerable to portrayal as "a dissipated, effete monarch." Is it any wonder, Whigs argued, that such a figure would adopt economic policies that favored the rich over the common man?[26]

Whigs offered promises not just of recovery but of progress, and they tailored those promises to sectional constituencies. When Daniel Webster, campaigning for Harrison, made a stop in Richmond in the fall of 1840, he avoided defining clear positions on divisive issues such as tariffs and banking. He knew that some Virginia Whigs, in the Clay school, favored developing Southern industry and diversifying the region's economy (and thus finding new outlets for slave labor), while others, the nullifier-defectors from the Democratic Party, had no patience for the "American System." Instead, Webster in his public pronouncements, including a speech to a throng of Whig "ladies," gave voice to the party's distinctive "political pietism"—the notion that the government, in the right hands, would promulgate "sound morals" and redeem the people from "falsehoods." This was a message that his Richmond sponsors could manipulate as they chose—to some, Webster seemed to be aligning the government with the "benevolent" reform societies that many Whigs, including urban Southerners, considered the answer to moral decay. To others, Webster seemed, by his visit to the state and his critique of Van Buren's unconstitutional "executive tyranny," to have come around to the "Virginia Standard" of "Strict Construction."[27]

As the Whiggish *New York World* put it in an analysis of the Log Cabin campaign: "In one quarter of the Union the Whigs represented their candidate as a friend, in another an enemy to a National Bank—here he was an abolitionist, there a slaveholder—in the East a champion of domestic industry, in the South a foe to the Tariff." Harrison did indeed try to finesse the slavery issue. In the South, Harrison supporters could trumpet his Virginia roots and the unimpeachable proslavery credentials of his running mate John Tyler, an elite Virginian and a representative of the states' rights wing of the Whig Party. To Northerners, Harrison could tout his support for colonization, which still commanded the support of many self-styled moderates on the slavery issue, and downplay Tyler's presence on the ticket. Southern Democrats scrambled to expose this duplicity and to indict Harrison as unsound on slavery. One campaign pamphlet, addressed to the Democrats of Alabama, claimed that the "notorious Garrison" exulted in the choice of Harrison as the "Whig Abolitionist" party's candidate.[28]

This was a specious claim. For even as Americans in the political mainstream were swept up in the excitement of the campaign, abolitionists were experiencing a schism over the issue of political action. In the face of the antiabolition onslaught in both North and South, Garrison and his followers had grown ever more alienated by and cynical about electoral politics. By 1839, Garrison was saying that abolitionists should repudiate the political process altogether and refrain from voting. At some distant time, he predicted in the *Liberator*, antislavery voters would possess the numerical strength to vote out the slaveholding interests and to change the laws. But first the movement had to effect a moral reformation of the people—and it could not do so by practicing the corrupt art of partisan campaigning. Rather, abolitionists should remain committed to the tactics of moral suasion and work to make the American people see that slavery was but the worst symptom of a terrible affliction. American culture, as Garrison saw it, was suffused with violence and coercion—the church, the state, the military, the prison system, the schools, and the political parties all used force to command the obedience of citizens. Following the lead of the Grimkés and other female reformers, Garrison went so far as to label the patriarchal family as coercive and to draw the analogy between the racist oppression of slaves and the sexist oppression of women.[29]

"We were too many and too popular, and it is well that our ranks have been winnowed out. God does not save by the many, but by the few," Garrison wrote of the 1840 schism. His stance of "nonresistance," with its call to reject rather than resist the political system and to embed antislavery pronouncements within a broader critique of American society, precipitated a split within the movement and the formation of two new antislavery organizations: the American and Foreign Anti-Slavery Society (AFASS) and the Liberty Party. The leading lights of both organizations believed that Garrison's extreme moral perfectionism "tended to tar all of abolition with its radicalism and thus frightened off many potential recruits." Lewis Tappan, leader of the AFASS, advocated a strategy of moderation, working within the churches and the "benevolent empire" of evangelical charities. Tappanites also bitterly opposed conflating the cause of abolition with that of woman's rights. In fact, it was the appointment of reformer Abbey Kelley to the business committee of the AASS at its annual convention in May 1840 that prompted Tappan, Amos Phelps, C. W. Denison, and others to walk out of the meeting and form the AFASS. Giving a woman like Kelley a leadership position in the movement, they held, was "contrary to the gospels and to their consciences." Tension over the "woman question" grew more acute when, in June 1840, female delegates who accompanied Garrison to the World Antislavery Convention in London, England, were refused permission to participate in its proceedings. Garrisonians were outraged. In the pages of the *Liberator*, Garrison thundered: "What *are* women, and who *are* slaves? Are not the rights of both identical? *Human* rights!—that is the great question which agitates the age."[30]

The second organization formed to provide an alternative to Garrison's "come-outer" radicals was a new political entity, the Liberty Party. Its leaders —James Birney, Gerrit Smith, William Goodell, Joshua Leavitt, and Alvan Stewart, among others—shared with the AFASS faction a distaste for Garrison's penchant to mix the antislavery question with controversial issues. such as woman's rights. But Liberty Party men were driven as much by frustration with the existing parties as they were by antipathy to Garrison. Both the tenor of electoral politics and the ongoing gag rule debacle furnished proof, as Birney and his cadre saw it, that abolitionists needed to "develop a more efficient political engine." Supporters of the new party feared that the duplicitous tactics of Democrats and Whigs were dangerously seductive. A writer using the pen name "Liberty" thus lamented to the *Colored American* that not only were Van Buren and the Democrats (whose *Amistad* machinations the writer exposed) pledged to keep slaves "forever bound," but also that Northern Whigs were unaware of John Tyler's true proslavery record. The Whig Party attempted to "keep [Tyler] back from the public gaze as much as possible, that the friends of freedom may not see the hideousness of the bear."[31]

If the state of the presidential campaign were not discouraging enough, the antislavery cause also had to contend with setbacks in Congress. On January 28, 1840, the House, on a motion by Whig representative William Cost Johnson of Maryland, made it a standing rule that no antislavery petition would "be received by the House, or entertained in any way whatever." This

Johnson gag was no mere resolution that would expire with each session, but a rule that would apply to all sessions of a given Congress. As William Lee Miller explains, "The onus would now be on Adams and his group to try to exclude that one rule from adoption, in the bundle of rather routinely adopted rules of the previous Congress, at the start of a Congress." This "undiluted" gag passed because of the support of Southern Whigs who wanted to prove their soundness on slavery in an election year and Northern Democrats who wanted to preserve their party's reputation for loyalty to the South. The rule's sponsor, Representative Johnson, positioned himself as a moderate who favored colonization and condemned the abolitionists for having "retarded" the "humane efforts" of the state of Maryland to send blacks back to Africa.[32]

Abolitionists naturally denounced the new rule as a travesty; in the pages of the *Pennsylvania Freeman*, Samuel Cornish wrote that "never before has an outrage so unblushingly profligate been perpetrated upon the Federal Constitution." But they knew well that the new gag rule, like its predecessors, would actually escalate the conflict between antislavery and anti-abolition forces. With John Quincy Adams ignoring its Whig sponsorship and assailing the rule as a Democratic trick, the Johnson gag sparked bitter debate in the House and Senate. In a presidential year, the opposing forces could not resist the temptation to make the new rule a partisan weapon. On February 13, 1840, the Senate floor was the scene of an "extraordinary debate" over whether the Whig Party was controlled by abolitionists. It began when Henry Clay presented an antislavery petition to his colleagues, along with an implicit critique of the gag rule that the House had just enacted—if there was not so much "harshness of language" used in condemning petitions, he had decided, there would have been "much less excitement" over the slavery question. Clay was immediately set upon by Calhoun, who made the familiar case that the right to petition was not unlimited, but who also took the opportunity to accuse Whigs like Clay of using the free speech issue "for the sake of victory at the elections." When Whig senator James Tallmadge of New York denied that his party was abolitionist, he was challenged by Senator Bedford Brown, a North Carolina Democrat, who dredged up old Senate votes to prove that the Democrats had consistently "sustained" the South while the Federalist/Whigs had taken the antislavery side. Connecticut's Senator Perry Smith, another Democrat, joined the chorus, alleging that the Northern

Whigs had the "benefit of Abolition votes." This left Clay, whose motion had started the fracas, to reassert his commitment to the "rights of the South" and mutter in exasperation that "he thought the day had been very unprofitably spent." The debate eventually fizzled out, and the Senate continued its "informal" gag rule practice of tabling abolition petitions. But such debates confirmed the view of commentators like "Liberty" that the Whig Party was not a reliable vehicle for abolition policies.[33]

After a series of false starts, "political antislavery" men met in Albany, New York, in April 1840 and nominated a ticket—James Birney for president and Thomas Earle, a Quaker and a Democrat, for vice president. The Liberty Party never became, Michael D. Pierson argues, a "modern, centralized political party" led by a large cadre of elected officials; instead, the party's "most effective apparatus proved to be its independently edited, partially subsidized newspapers." Organs such as the *Signal of Liberty* and *Free American* expounded the party's doctrine, the central tenet of which was that antislavery forces, if they acted in concert, were already strong enough, as Gerrit Smith put it, to "extort concessions" from Whigs and Democrats. If the numerical significance of the antislavery voting bloc could be demonstrated, the two established parties could be induced to compete for its support. To avoid the pitfalls of Garrison's approach, Liberty Party leaders vowed to focus exclusively on the slavery issue and to remain neutral on all others; the party also stood, at least initially, for adherence to traditional gender roles rather than for woman's rights.[34]

A key distinction between the approach of the Liberty Party and that of the Garrisonians was that the Liberty Party "made a special point of slavery's threat to the rights of *white* Americans." The Southern "Slave Power," they stressed, was comprised of a small oligarchy that, thanks to the shameful three-fifths compromise, wielded a disproportionate power within the federal government. This Slave Power was to blame for the economic depression that gripped the country, for it opposed the creation of financial institutions (such as a national bank) and fiscal policies (such as high tariffs) that would foster economic development and fund Northern industry, in particular; slavery drained away the economic vitality of the North. Though such an emphasis made the Liberty Party vulnerable to the charge that it had lost sight of the plight of blacks and watered down the antislavery message, from the start it received the support both of antislavery moderates who sought for the new party mass appeal in the North, and bona fide radicals, such as Gerrit Smith, who favored "aggressive action against slavery in the South." Liberty Party radicalism is exemplified in an 1842 speech that Smith gave at a party convention in New York. Inspired by evidence that slave escapes were on the rise, Smith urged white abolitionists to venture into the South to aid the Underground Railroad, and he encouraged slaves to assert their manhood and resist slavery by taking flight. This call for interracial cooperation in slave rescues was more "practically radical" than the Garrisonians' pacifist stance of non-resistance and "moral suasion."[35]

To the dismay of Smith, Birney, and their allies, the Liberty Party's mixed messages did not catch on with voters. In the 1840 presidential election the party garnered a mere 7,000 votes, and its showing in 1844—65,000 votes for Birney—was only modestly better. Harrison commanded 234 electoral votes to Van Buren's 60 and won 19 of the 26 states. In his lengthy inaugural address, Harrison articulated his mandate to preserve the "cordial, confiding, fraternal union." He warned, in words implicitly aimed at abolitionists, that any "attempt of those of one State to control the domestic institutions of another can only result in feelings of distrust and jealousy, the certain harbingers of disunion, violence, and civil war."[36]

Despite the new president's determination to keep the issue of slavery out of national politics, the early 1840s would provide no lull in the sectional crisis. Instead, Northerners and Southerners alike experienced these years as a time of sharply rising sectional tensions, of instability, uncertainty, and even chaos. Everywhere one looked—in the halls of Congress, courts of law, churches, and press rooms—new battles over slavery and disunion were being joined.

TYLER AND PARTY POLITICS

The Whig Party had precious little time to savor Harrison's victory in the 1840 presidential contest. His death from pneumonia on April 4, 1841, just one month after his inaugural address, resulted in the accession of his running mate, John Tyler. The nation held its breath to see whether Tyler would ally himself with the Clay-led group of Whig nationalists in Congress or defy them in the name of states' rights. The Democratic *Richmond Enquirer*, which had condemned the Harrison-Tyler ticket as an "abolition" slate and could barely muster a few respectful words on Harrison's demise ("It is wonderful, indeed, that more [presidents] have not perished in office," the paper editorialized), had low expectations that Tyler would champion Southern rights. The Whiggish *New York Tribune*, led by moderate antislavery editor Horace Greeley, was initially hopeful that Tyler would line up behind his party's prodevelopment economic policies. Both prognostications were confounded when Tyler, in August and September 1841, vetoed two key banking measures passed by the Whig Congress and thus thwarted Whig efforts to engineer an economic recovery. Clay's allies were appalled; the *Tribune* noted that the very exercise of the veto was "especially obnoxious to Whigs," who had earlier railed against President Andrew Jackson's abuse of the veto power. The fact that Tyler was an imperious slaveholder added insult to injury. The president exercised his veto power "contemptuously," Greeley wrote, and with "the authority of a master." Greeley took to referring to Tyler as the "deplorable Accidency." In September 1841 the Whigs literally read Tyler out of the party, leaving Clay as its acknowledged leader.[37]

Southern rights papers such as the *Richmond Enquirer* praised Tyler for his "moral courage." Though on the face of it, neither of the vetoed bills touched on the issue of slavery, states' rights Southerners saw Clay's measures, particularly his proposal for a national bank, as efforts, like the hated tariff, to benefit the Northeastern "monied aristocracy" at the expense of the agrarian South. In the eyes of Southern Democrats, Clay's program also represented an attempt by Congress to exceed its constitutionally mandated role and, in the words of Representative Robert Barnwell Rhett, "consolidate this Government"—namely, extend its power over the states. Moreover, Tyler "had been a committed expansionist for some time" and traded on this reputation by currying favor among Democrats who endorsed annexing Texas. While Democrats praised Tyler, they did not claim him as one of their own, preferring to take the position that the Whigs, as the price of their duplicity in 1840, were stuck with the traitor. The *Charleston Mercury* gloated that Whigs looked in vain for any sign that Tyler was in league with the Democrats and reminded its readers that the Whigs "are responsible—*they* vouched for [Tyler]—*they* placed him where he is." As the Democrats approached the 1844 presidential contest, three candidates—Calhoun, Van Buren, and newcomer James K. Polk—contended for leadership of the party, leaving Tyler out in the cold.[38]

Against the backdrop of the Whigs' White House woes, congressional debates over the gag rule and slavery intensified. In 1841 John Quincy Adams's efforts to rescind the Johnson gag were met with a new round of partisan mudslinging and of speeches on the widening rift between North and South. Representative Henry A. Wise of Virginia echoed William Preston's 1836 pro-gag peroration in invoking the example of Wilberforce and the British abolitionists; American abolitionists, too, by "keeping up agitation," would "gain their point, as certainly as that the solid marble would wear away by the constant running of the stream." They would not stop until "public sentiment was affected in the slaveholding states."[39]

In 1842 the discourse on disunion and on British influence took on new dimensions when Representative Adams essayed a daring new tactic to capture public attention. On January 24 he presented a petition from forty-six citizens of Haverhill, Massachusetts, "praying for a dissolution of the Union." Adams made it perfectly clear that he opposed the goals of the petitioners and that he presented the memorial both in deference to the rights of free speech and to seize an opportunity to defend the Union. His disclaimers were resoundingly rejected by anti-abolitionists, who rallied in support of a series of motions to censure him. The *Richmond Enquirer* charged that Adams's petition was no mere rhetorical ploy, but that he was cagily trying to lay the groundwork for actual disunion. "By degrees the idea will grow familiar, and the spirit of the people will be subdued," it predicted. The *Enquirer* also endorsed the view championed by the leading critic of Adams, Henry Wise. Wise fulminated in endless disquisitions on the floor of the House that Adams and the Northern Whigs were in league with the British government to effect its long-standing goal of breaking apart the Union; Adams's Whig faction was simply the old English Tory Party in disguise. Witness the proceedings of the recent annual World Antislavery Convention in London in 1841, Wise noted—there you would find American abolitionists inviting British agents to meddle with the domestic politics of the United States. This same "Anglo-American Abolition Dissolution party," Wise inelegantly added, was also fomenting opposition to the annexation of Texas. Representative Thomas Dickens Arnold of Tennessee expressed the feelings of many of his exasperated colleagues when he accused Wise of incendiary and unfounded accusations. He said that the Virginian's anti-British ramblings "sounded very much like the remnant of an old stump speech prepared for some obscure neighborhood where the people do not read much."[40]

The debate got even more bizarre when John Minor Botts, a Virginia Whig nationalist, rose to defend Adams. Botts was at pains to note that he opposed the antislavery movement. But he also opposed censuring Adams, both because the avowed purpose of Adams's gambit was to demonstrate the folly of disunion and because the old man's "dignity, and long service" entitled him to "so much kindness and forebearance." In a gutsy ploy worthy of Adams himself, Botts then charged two fellow Southerners—Representative Robert Barnwell Rhett and Secretary of the Navy Abel P. Upshur—with having advocated disunion. For consistency's sake, shouldn't they be branded with treason just as Adams was? Rhett and Upshur were symbols of the militant nullifier wing of the Southern rights movement. How could such militants have supported nullification and yet condemn Adams? The responses of Rhett and Upshur and their supporters are profoundly revealing. Rhett conceded that he had drafted some disunion resolutions in 1837, to be presented to his constituents, in response to William Slade's fiery antislavery speech in December of that year. But, Rhett argued, they were a rhetorical gambit to draw attention to the high stakes of the slavery debate; he knew the resolutions would never be voted on. In support of his colleague, Representative Thomas Marshall of Kentucky made the same distinction— Rhett's invocation of disunion, like that of the nullifiers, was a political lever, a parliamentary ploy. Adams, by contrast, had actually *proposed* disunion. Marshall accused the former president of going "a whole stone's cast beyond any thing the Southern nullifiers ever dreamed of," for Adams was actually suggesting that Congress had the power to dissolve the Union. Upshur took a different tack against Botts. He maintained that he had never been an unconditional advocate of immediate disunion, but he "would sooner see the Union dissolved, than witness the success of this very abolition movement." Botts wrote a series of letters to the friendly *Richmond Whig* claiming that Upshur's defense actually proved Botts's point. Botts's sense that he and Adams had won this round of the slavery debate was confirmed when, on February 7, 1842, the resolution to censure Adams was tabled and the matter dropped. The "censurers [had been] censured," proclaimed the *New York Tribune*.[41]

While Adams's parliamentary gambit was simply an effort to provoke another Southern overreaction and abridgment of free speech, Garrison and his followers began, in this same period, to embrace disunion. After the antislavery schism of 1840, Garrison gave full vent to his disgust with the political system and made calls for the "repeal of the Union" his editorial mantra. Calhoun and his ilk, we have seen, spoke of disunion in three registers—when invoked as a threat, it was a tool for extracting concessions from the North; when invoked as an accusation, it was a tool for branding abolitionists as treasonous and insurrectionary; and when invoked as a process of sectional divergence and alienation, it was meant to promote Southern solidarity. For Garrison, his biographer Henry Mayer has explained, "disunion began [in the late 1830s] as an angry change of attitude rather than a political remedy," a repudiation of any compromises wrought by "unholy alliances" of Northerners and Southern slaveowners. Many other immediatists, radicalized by the backlash against their campaign, experienced this "angry change of attitude" and drew out the argument that disunion was preferable to immoral compromises and cowardly submission. Addressing a convention of his fellow ministers in Worcester, Massachusetts, in January 1838, George Allen, a prominent immediatist clergyman, intoned: "If it has come to this, that the price of union is to be dumb when God calls for a voice . . . if we may not speak our minds against the most horrible atrocity with which earth is afflicted, let not the price be paid. . . . In such alternative let the Union expire, though the giving up of the ghost be with a nation's agony." A February 1839 article in the *Colored American* captured this growing spirit of defiance: "Far better that such dismemberment should take place, than that the 'freemen' of the North . . . should longer be held as convenient vassals of the South."[42]

By 1842, however, Garrison was using the lecture circuit to push disunion not only as a gesture of defiance but also as "a measure for adoption by various abolitionist bodies"—as a positive good, a process that human agency could and should expedite, not forestall. Although he "gained no group endorsements," Garrison believed that his hammering away at the disunion theme nonetheless brought political dividends: as Adams's victory in the House showed, antislavery forces could use disunionist language to counter Southern threats and expose Southern hypocrisy. At the heart of Garrison's disunion advocacy was his critique of the U.S. Constitution as a "covenant with death" and an "agreement with hell." Its protections for the slave trade, three-fifths compromise, and fugitive slave provisions were an attempt, "monstrous and impractical, to blend the light of heaven with the darkness of the bottomless pit." Garrison's attack on the Constitution had considerable shock value and served to distinguish his disunionism from the Southern states' rights version. Calhoun and Hammond viewed the Union as a compact embodied by the Constitution and premised on the protection of the property rights of slaveholders; they threatened to break the Union—as a last resort, so they said—in order to preserve those constitutional guarantees. But, they believed, whether or not political disunion ever became necessary, a cultural disunion was already under way, driven by the abolitionists' corrosive contempt for Southerners. In their reckoning, even if Southerners one day made good on their threats to withdraw from the Union, Northerners would bear the responsibility for the calamity, for Northerners had betrayed both the letter and the spirit of the original compact.[43]

Garrison's view was even more complicated, for he drew a distinction between the false Union—the "hollow mockery" created by the Constitution —and the true Union, a "glorious reality" that had never yet been achieved. The false Union, he repeated again and again, was not divinely ordained but rather "the work of men's hands": quoting the Bible, he declared that "it is only those things which are made, that can be shaken down." As Garrison saw it, slavery depended on the false Union for its survival—Northerners furnished Southern slaveholders with the markets for the slaves' produce, with the laws and slave-catching mobs that policed the boundaries of the system, with the votes to give slaveholders control of the federal government, and with the moral approbation to embolden slaveholders to spread their pernicious labor system. If this Northern support were withdrawn, slavery would be doomed. The spirit of the true Union, by contrast, was present in the preamble of the Declaration of Independence—it was the spirit of equality. A binding and valid compact between freedom and slavery was, for Garrison, a moral impossibility, and thus, in a sense, disunion already prevailed. With slaveholders campaigning aggressively to extend their domain and to curtail the rights of Northern citizens, it was inevitable and fitting that political disunion would flow from moral disunion. An 1842 antislavery meeting in Boston, presided over by Garrison, resolved that "the time is rapidly approaching when the American Union will be dissolved in form, as it now is in fact." In this formulation, disunion connoted not failure, shame, and anarchy but the necessary prelude to a national rebirth: the demise of the false, corrupt Union would prepare the way for the establishment of the true, righteous one. From the early 1840s on, then, disunion for Garrison connoted not only a threat and an accusation, but also a process by which Northerners were coming to see that only a total repudiation of the South could purge the nation of sin.[44]

This bracing political vision, Garrisonian abolitionists believed, was the only antidote to a new doctrine that gained support in antislavery circles in the years 1842 to 1844—the view that the Constitution was actually an antislavery document that empowered Congress not only to restrict the spread of slavery but also to dismantle it in the South. Advanced by Liberty Party men like Alvan Stewart, James Birney, and William Goodell, antislavery constitutionalism claimed that certain provisions of the Constitution and the Bill of Rights (such as the due process clause of the Fifth Amendment and the guarantee to each state of a "republican form of government") invalidated slavery, and that the egalitarian spirit of the Declaration of Independence— the true gauge of the Founders' intentions—had been incorporated into the Constitution. Garrison rejected this as wishful thinking. In his view, that the judicial system was more committed than ever to upholding the proslavery principles of the nation's shameful covenant.[45]

SLAVERY AND THE COURTS:
THE *AMISTAD, PRIGG,* AND *CREOLE* CASES

The issue of slavery's constitutionality had a special urgency in the early 1840s, thanks to a series of highly publicized judicial decisions. The first of these was the Supreme Court's ruling in the *Amistad* case. After the schooner's seizure by U.S. authorities in 1839, the African rebels aboard had been imprisoned in Connecticut to await trial on charges of piracy and murder. The Van Buren administration hoped to circumvent the American courts and return the *Amistad* rebels to the Spanish government, on the grounds that they were slaves belonging to Spanish masters and thus legally fell under Spanish jurisdiction; as intended, this interpretation found favor from Southern rights newspapers like the *Charleston Mercury* and *Richmond*

Enquirer. But abolitionists rallied to the cause of the Africans, prompting the *New York Herald,* an openly hostile paper, to marvel at their "immense exertions." Abolitionists were "raising subscriptions, collecting money, clothing and feeding [the Africans]; employing the most able counsel; riding over the country, by night and day, to get interpreters who can converse alike in their language and in English; [and] rummaging over musty records, old statutes, treaties and laws" in order to craft a case for their freedom. Antislavery papers, for their part, embraced the Africans as heroes. The *Colored American* declared that the rebel leader, Cinqué, had "placed himself side by side with Patrick Henry, John Hancock, Thomas Jefferson," and the other "fathers of the Revolution." The impressive way that the prisoners were learning English and embracing Christianity would be, the paper hoped, "a consuming fire to prejudice."[46]

The heart of the abolitionists' legal argument was that the *Amistad* blacks were not Cuban slaves who were being legally transported to another Spanish holding and thus the rightful possession of Spain. Rather, they were Africans, speaking a variety of African languages, who had been seized from their homelands and taken to Cuba in defiance of Spanish and U.S. treaties and statutes prohibiting the international slave trade. This view prevailed in the January 1840 ruling of district court judge Andrew T. Judson that the *Amistad* rebels be "freed under the rule of self-defense in international waters" and that the president return them to Africa. Van Buren's attorney general appealed the decision, setting the stage for a showdown in the Supreme Court.

None other than John Quincy Adams championed the cause of the Africans when the Court heard the case in February 1841. Calling the Declaration of Independence, a copy of which was on display in the courtroom, the only "law that reaches the case of my clients," Adams charged that the Van Buren administration had conspired to rob the *Amistad* mutineers of their fundamental natural rights. In some respects, Adams's bravura performance represented a high-water mark for the antislavery cause, for it was the culmination of a long collaboration between the various antislavery factions. Followers of Tappan, Garrison, Birney, and the growing Whig antislavery lobby in Congress saw in the *Amistad* case a special opportunity to win support for the movement. Henry Mayer has explained why: "As Africans who sought to return home, the captives struck a sympathetic chord with colonizationists; as

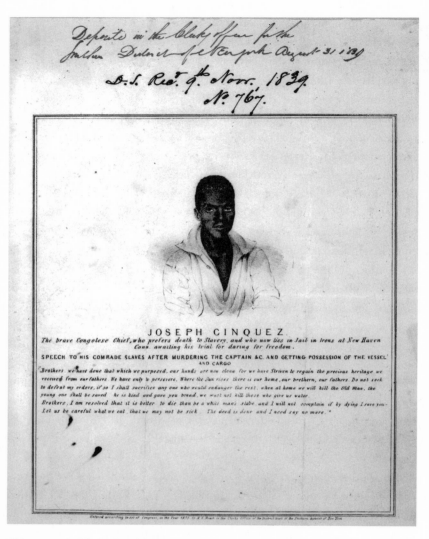

This portrayal of the leader of the *Amistad* rebellion, Cinqué (here "Cinquez"), quotes the speech he gave on behalf of his fellow Africans: "I am resolved that it is better to die than be a white man's slave." (Courtesy of the Library of Congress)

rebels against Hispano-Catholic tyranny on the high seas, they seemed more heroic and less threatening than mutinous plantation slaves in Protestant America; as orphans of the storm, they appealed to clergymen and missionaries; as curiosities who spoke an exotic language and had survived a despicable commerce, they made good copy for the newspapers." Adams's efforts brought a tangible victory for abolitionism. The Supreme Court, although dominated by a Southern proslavery majority, upheld Judge Judson's ruling that the Africans were not slaves and directed that they be freed. In November 1841 abolitionists secured their passage back to Africa.[47]

This victory brought into sharp relief affinities between Whiggery and abolitionism that the Log Cabin campaign and the Harrison-Tyler ticket had worked to obscure. While the so-called Cotton Whig commercial elite of Boston and New York, for the sake of intersectional trade and profits, had turned the "cultivation of Southern goodwill into a high art," they could not compete with the Democrats' "uniform eagerness to embrace Southern interests," James Brewer Stewart has observed—nor could they speak for the burgeoning Whig constituencies in the Northern "Bible belt" that spanned New England and the Midwest. In regions such as Ohio's Western Reserve (the home base of Joshua Giddings), Whigs steeped in evangelical reform culture were invariably drawn to certain of the abolitionists' arguments, especially those about slaveholder immorality and the natural rights and moral potential of blacks. Even though the party's official position was that Whigs "agreed to disagree" about slavery, Adams's dramatic gag rule and *Amistad* campaigns, as well as the growth of his antislavery coalition in Congress, marked the Whig Party as one that "produced and legitimized militant officeholders."[48]

There remained, however, a wide gulf between the antislavery Whiggery of Adams's congressional cadre and radical immediatism. Politicians such as Adams and Giddings retained their faith in the sanctity of the Constitution and the power of the federal government to effect moral uplift. As for Garrison and his followers, the *Amistad* decision did nothing to dissuade them that the Constitution and the judicial system that upheld it were fundamentally immoral and injurious to the Union. Justice Joseph Story's opinion in the case, after all, had ignored Adams's charge that the Van Buren administration was guilty of conspiring against the Africans and had rested on a narrow foundation—namely, that no one could sufficiently prove that the *Amistad* blacks were slaves. If it had been possible to prove that they were Cubans and not Africans, Story would have acceded to the administration's request that they be remanded into Spanish custody, however grim the consequences. There were no grounds for claiming that Story's decision endorsed Adams's interpretation of natural law. To make matters worse, the executive branch itself, under Tyler and each of his successors until Abraham Lincoln, rejected the Court's finding and recommended payment of reparations to Spain. This campaign was the hobbyhorse of proslavery politicians interested in the possible annexation of Cuba.[49]

Garrison's anticonstitutionalism only deepened as he witnessed the Court's —and Story's—handling of a new controversy. The case of *Prigg v. Pennsylvania*, taken up by the Supreme Court early in 1842, brought to an end a long period in which the federal government had remained aloof from the issue of fugitive slaves and their recapture. Constitutional provisions on fugitive slaves had been clarified by a 1793 federal law that held that a slaveowner, or his or her appointed agent, who had captured an alleged fugitive in a free state, could appear before a federal judge or local magistrate and provide "proof" of ownership, and thereby obtain permission (in the form of a certificate) to take the runaway back into slavery. Because the "proof" could consist of as little as an oral claim of ownership ("Yes, that is my slave"), the law "set aside normal legal process, such as the writ of habeas corpus and trial by jury." While the law imposed a financial penalty on anyone who interfered with the recapture of a fugitive, it did not specify a punishment for reenslaving a runaway without the proper certificate of proof. As a result, many Northern states regarded the law as an invitation to kidnap free blacks and thus passed "personal liberty laws" to protect them. In Pennsylvania, such a law passed in 1826 made it a felony to "carry away . . . any negro or mulatto" in order "by fraud or false pretences . . . [to make] him or her a slave or servant for life" (by 1843, ten Northern states had passed some kind of "personal liberty" measures). The *Prigg* case represented a clash between the federal law and the Pennsylvania law. Edward Prigg had been indicted by the state's supreme court for kidnapping, after he, in his capacity as the agent of a Maryland slaveowner, had taken the fugitive Margeret Moran back into slavery without first having obtained the proper certificate.[50]

Justice Story, chosen by Chief Justice Roger B. Taney to write the majority opinion, again delivered an ambiguous decision; if his *Amistad* verdict had been a Pyrrhic victory for abolitionists, in that it freed the captives but rejected Adams's interpretation of natural law, the *Prigg* judgment was a kind of Pyrrhic victory for slaveholders. On the face of it, Story's ruling was proslavery: in finding for Edward Prigg, he upheld the constitutionality of the 1793 Fugitive Slave Law, pronounced unconstitutional the 1826 Pennsylvania personal liberty law, and construed the Constitution's fugitive slave clauses to assert the "positive, unqualified right" of a slaveowner to recover his property.[51] These pronouncements naturally provoked the ire of radical abolitionists. In the *Liberator* of March 11, 1842, Garrison fumed that the decision "is not law. . . . It is to be spit upon, hooted at, trampled in the dust resolutely and openly." But precisely because the *Prigg* verdict sparked a "more determined opposition to the fugitive slave law itself," Donald E. Fehrenbacher points out, it "proved to be of dubious proslavery value." By vesting the power to legislate on fugitive slave recapture solely in the federal government, Story implied that states could wash their hands of the matter and permit their officials to stand aloof from the process. Exploiting this loophole, Massachusetts led the Northern states in passing a new kind of personal liberty law in 1843, one that prohibited state officials from assisting in the recapture of slaves, thus leaving slaveholders to rely on the small number of federal judges and marshals. Southern demands for more federal assistance in recapturing slaves would eventually lead to the Compromise of 1850—another effort to settle the issue that only escalated tensions. As for Story, a Massachusetts native whose personal distaste for slavery was well known, he could defend his *Amistad* and *Prigg* rulings as fully consistent with his centrist, nationalist outlook—that international slave trading should be prohibited but that domestic slavery, and the private property rights of slaveholders, should be preserved.[52]

The winter that brought forth the *Prigg* decision also witnessed a new congressional skirmish over slavery. This one was sparked by the *Creole* case. In November 1841 slaves aboard the *Creole*, bound from Newport News, Virginia, to New Orleans, mutinied and killed one of the slave traders. They demanded that the ship's crew take them to the British port of Nassau in the Bahamas; when they arrived there, the British authorities tried and executed those charged with the murder. But to the horror of American slaveholders, and over the objections of the U.S. government, the British emancipated the rest of the *Creole* slaves. The issue's potentially explosive implications both for domestic debates over slavery and for Anglo-American diplomacy became obvious when the owners of the freed slaves demanded compensation for their lost property. The Tyler administration took up their cause, with Secretary of State Daniel Webster issuing an angry protest to Great Britain claiming compensation "for the property loss on the ground that the ship's deck should have been considered an extension of American soil."[53]

Proslavery senators and congressmen rallied to support the executive branch's claim for compensation and called for "the punishment of the guilty." Senator Preston of South Carolina warned that the United States could ill afford to send the message that "the slaves on board the *Creole* acted in accordance with the decision of the Supreme Court in the case of the *Amistad*, and proved themselves worthy of their freedom." Calhoun was characteristically alarmist, arguing that if Britain denied the South's right to hold property in slaves, wasn't the next step to "extend the same rule to our cotton and other staples?" In a remarkable rhetorical question that reveals how well he understood the logic of the antislavery argument, Calhoun asked: "If we have no right to those whose labor produced them, what better right have we to the product of their labor?" Clay, for his part, rose above his feud with Webster and said it "was expressly desirable, that in all conflicts with a foreign power, whether actually existing or merely threatened, [the Congress] should present an unbroken phalanx."[54]

The antislavery lobby in the House begged to differ. It proceeded to endorse a series of resolutions by Ohio's Joshua Giddings that extended Adams's *Amistad* arguments about natural law. According to Giddings, when a ship belonging to citizens of a given state left the territories and waters of that state, the persons on board the ship "cease to be subject to the slave laws" of that state. Hence, once the *Creole* left Virginian waters, natural law superseded the slave codes of Virginia, and thus the slaves who revolted on the high seas were asserting their God-given freedom. Giddings's resolutions were resoundingly rejected by the House, but the matter did not rest there. Instead, John Minor Botts proposed to censure Giddings for fomenting "dissatisfaction, and division" within the United States at a time of delicate negotiations with Britain. (Those negotiations were protracted: more than a decade later, in 1855, the British government conceded that Bahamian officials should not have freed the *Creole* slaves and awarded American slaveowners $110,330 in compensation for their lost property.) The 1842 censure bid won by a vote of 125–69, and Giddings promptly tendered his resignation to the Speaker of the House.[55]

The victory over Giddings proved short-lived, as his constituents soon returned him to his vacated House seat. But for antislavery activists, the *Prigg* and *Creole* controversies together seemed to cloud the results of the *Amistad* case and to raise anew the specter of a federal government—in its executive, legislative, and judicial branches alike—committed not only to preserving slavery but even to extending its domain. The abolitionists' sense that America had arrived at a point of crisis in its race relations was given further credence by two incidents—the Philadelphia race riot in the summer of 1842 and the Latimer controversy in Boston that fall—that highlighted Northern complicity in the oppression of blacks. The Philadelphia riot, the fifth anti-black uprising in the city since 1834, erupted on August 1, 1842. Some 1,200 African Americans had gathered to march on behalf of the temperance cause and in commemoration of Britain's abolition of slavery in the West Indies. They were attacked by an irate mob of whites who burned down Smith's Hall on Lombard Street (where abolitionists had been meeting since Pennsylvania Hall was torched back in 1838), destroyed the Second African Presbyterian Church, and ransacked private residences in black neighborhoods, viciously beating countless individuals. An article in the *Liberator* described the scene: "Unoffending colored women were attacked in the streets, their furniture broken, destroyed or *stolen* . . . colored men and boys, having given no offence, except that of wearing the skin the Creator gave them . . . were beaten until their persecutors believed them to be dead."[56]

Prominent among these persecutors were recently arrived Irish immigrants who competed with blacks for the insufficient number of unskilled jobs in the city; the prejudice of white Protestants relegated Irish Catholics and blacks alike to the lowest economic rung. The rioters—both Irish and non-Irish—were fired by class resentments as well as racial antipathy; they targeted for destruction the homes of relatively affluent middle-class African Americans, while passing over the residences of working-class blacks. The very presence of a growing black middle class aroused concern among some whites of a "black threat" to white dominance. Together with the city police, state troops quelled the riot the next day, but not before blacks had been sent a chilling message. Robert Purvis, a leading African American abolitionist in the city, wrote in despair to his ally Henry C. Wright. "I know not where I should begin, nor how, or when to end in a detail of the wantonness, brutality and murderous spirit" of the mob; the "Press, Church, Magistrates, Clergymen and Devils are against us." He concluded, "I am sick—miserably sick—everything around me is as dark as the grave."[57]

A few months later, the tenuousness of freedom for blacks in the North was again dramatized in Boston, this time by a fugitive slave controversy. Early in October 1842 George Latimer, his wife Rebecca, and their young child had escaped from slavery in Norfolk, Virginia, and made their way to Boston. Their freedom was short-lived, as they were identified by a former associate of their master, James B. Gray; Gray posted a runaway advertisement and reward and made his way to Boston to reclaim his property. He soon had Latimer arrested, on trumped-up charges of larceny, and incarcerated in the Leverett Street jail, where he remained while Gray applied to the federal court for the requisite permission to return South with his three slaves. Remarkably, the judge in charge of the federal circuit in Boston at that time was none other than Joseph Story of the *Amistad* and *Prigg* decisions. Story proceeded to cement his reputation as a traitor to his own antislavery principles by ruling that Latimer was to remain in jail while Gray compiled the necessary proof of ownership. Abolitionists got wind of these machinations and agitated to make Latimer's a cause célèbre. Gray was reviled as a symbol of the long reach of the Slave Power. James W. C. Pennington, a former slave who had settled in Connecticut and established himself as a church pastor and leading black intellectual, decried the fact that Latimer was denied not only due process but also the benefit of clergy. "Ministers are not allowed to visit him on the subject of the salvation of his immortal soul!!," Pennington declared in a sermon in Hartford. "But where is this scene? In Virginia? No! But in Massachusetts!"[58]

Abolitionists held rallies outside the jail and lobbied the Massachusetts chief justice, Lemuel Shaw, to intervene. To the disgust of Garrison and his allies, Shaw demurred, claiming that the case rightly belonged in federal court. But the Garrisonians did not let up. On October 30 they held a mass meeting at Faneuil Hall. With Wendell Phillips's cursing of the Constitution ringing in their ears, and the looming prospect of another mass meeting and possibly mob action to free Latimer from jail, the sheriff and Latimer's owner retreated. Latimer was set free from jail, then manumitted by Gray, who claimed four hundred dollars from abolitionists as the price for this gesture.

The effect on the antislavery movement was electric. According to Henry Mayer, "the mass movement had never before secured so rapid an antislavery victory." But this victory, too, was clouded—for it ratcheted up tensions between the Garrisonian and Liberty Party wings of the abolitionist movement. Liberty men in Massachusetts had rallied around the case as enthusiastically as Garrisonians, forming a committee to sponsor meetings and demonstrations, and rushing to print *The Latimer Journal and North Star* to publicize the case. Garrison resented this competition and accused Libertyites of exploiting the case. The Libertyites, for their part, not only "bore Garrisonian anger with some magnanimity," but also, writes Bruce Laurie, "reaped a political dividend from the Latimer affair" by picking up enough seats in the fall 1842 state elections to hold the balance of power in a House equally divided between Whigs and Democrats. Moreover, Libertyites engineered the passage in 1843 of the personal liberty law mentioned above— dubbed the "Latimer Law"—that exploited the loophole in Story's *Prigg* decision. Those antislavery men who advocated participation in the political process felt that this success vindicated their stand that the antislavery movement had to change not only men's hearts but also the laws—and that only political engagement could achieve such legal reform. Indeed, Laurie argues, the Latimer Law symbolized the broad commitment of Liberty Party men and women in Massachusetts to fight segregation and other forms of racial discrimination in the Bay State.[59]

Garrisonians drew a different set of conclusions and emerged from the battles of 1841 and 1842 more committed than ever both to their critique of the Constitution and to tactics of civil disobedience. They believed that by pushing their case that the fugitive slave measures of the Constitution were illegitimate, they had set the stage for the public outcry over Latimer. Delivered at the height of the Latimer controversy, Pennington's sermon, entitled "Covenants Involving Moral Wrong Not Obligatory upon Man," captured the essence of the Garrisonian position: the Constitution was not "sovereign" over the people but a "creature of [their] will and power" and therefore could be amended and even rejected by them in accordance with the true principles of morality. Like Garrison, Pennington located those true principles in the Declaration of Independence, with its affirmation of human equality. The Latimer case was analyzed in song as well as sermon: an antislavery songbook compiled by black abolitionist William Wells Brown featured "The Bigot

Fire," with lyrics composed "on the occasion of George Latimer's Imprisonment in Leverett Street Jail, Boston." The first two stanzas present the views of a typical anti-abolition Northerner, who feared the consequences of alienating the South:

O, kindle not that bigot fire
'Twill bring disunion, fear and pain;
'Twill rouse at last the southerner's ire
And burst our starry land in twain.

Theirs is the high, the noble worth
The very soul of chivalry;
Rend not our blood-bought land apart,
For such a thing as slavery.

In the third stanza, an abolitionist's voice provides commentary on such conservative invocations of disunion:

This is the language of the North;
I shame to say it but 'tis true;
And anti-slavery calls it forth,
From some proud priests and laymen too.

The rest of the song is a pledge and a call to arms. New England's proud sons will not "bend forsooth to Southern rule . . . and be the base, the supple tool, of hell-begotten slavery." They would rather see the country "riven" into a "thousand fragments" than stoop before the "haughty" Slave Power. The last line promises to cast down on slaveowners "a curse so loud, so stern, so deep, / Shall start ye in your guilty sleep." As the public's attention turned to the issue of Texas and the coming presidential campaign, Garrisonians hoped that the moderate antislavery contingent would catch this ardent spirit of disunion and prove willing to defy the Slave Power.[60]

Oh for a Man Who Is a *Man*

When the fractious Twenty-seventh Congress came to a close, the antislavery lobby in the House (Adams, Slade, Giddings, and ten others) promulgated an address to the "people of the free states" on the subject of Texas annexation. The project of annexing Texas may have been on the political back-burner during the 1841–43 session, they warned, but it was "by no means abandoned." Rather, proslavery forces were steadily mounting an annexation campaign by which the "undue ascendancy of the Slave-holding power in the Government [would] be secured and riveted beyond all redemption." As proof, John Quincy Adams and his allies quoted from speeches and letters by Henry Wise, Thomas W. Gilmer, and others in which they professed that annexation was constitutional and was the perfect means to extend slavery. Sounding an alarm in tones conspicuously similar to proslavery appeals for vigilance against abolitionist encroachments, the antislavery lobby implored Northerners not to be lulled into a "false and dangerous security." Unless Northerners united, without distinction of party, the "nefarious project" of annexation would succeed; this would not only "result in a dissolution of the union," the authors of the address proclaimed, "but fully . . . justify it." The address found favor among moderates as well as hardcore abolitionists. Horace Greeley's antislavery Whig newspaper, the *New York Tribune* (which boasted a daily circulation of approximately ten thousand, making it the most popular newspaper in the country), commended the antislavery lobby for having exposed the "incessant plotting" of pro-annexation forces.[1]

The apprehensions of anti-annexationists were fully warranted. In the two years between March 1843, when antislavery Whigs issued this warning, and March 1845, when President Tyler signed the House and Senate's joint resolution of annexation, pro-annexation forces not only perfected their behind-the-scenes plotting, they also forcefully articulated and energetically publicized a new rationale for admitting Texas to the Union. Turning the disunion rhetoric of Adams and the other antislavery men against them, annexationists claimed that the admission of Texas would both promote domestic harmony between North and South, and safeguard the Union from threats from foreign powers, especially the empire-building nation-states of Europe. The annexation debates reveal that in the 1840s Americans' anxieties over internal sources of disunion were still closely linked to their anxieties over external threats.

President Tyler cherished annexation as a measure that could redeem his administration and enable him to build a loyal political constituency in the South. The presence of anti-annexationist Daniel Webster as secretary of state had hampered him. But once Webster, who had become disillusioned by Tyler's incessant overtures to the Democratic Party, quit the job in May 1843, Tyler was free to maneuver. He seized the opportunity to appoint a fellow annexationist, Secretary of the Navy Abel P. Upshur (the very man John Minor Botts had accused of advocating disunion) in Webster's place. Upshur belonged to the "annexation junto"—a cadre of ardent expansionists that included *New York Herald* editor James Gordon Bennett, editor John B. Jones of the administration organ the *Daily Madisonian*, and seasoned Maryland politico Duff Green. In 1841 Tyler had dispatched Green as an emissary to London, to move stealthily in diplomatic circles in search of "proof" that England had designs on Texas. This was the essence of the Tyler annexation strategy: to argue that Britain would promote abolition in Texas (by offering Texas loans and migrants and help in negotiating peace with Mexico) in order to undermine the South's cotton-producing capacity and establish the commercial supremacy of Britain's own cotton manufacturers in the East Indies. "Texas would be the decisive battleground" between the United States and Britain, the junto argued. If Britain succeeded in persuading Texans to abolish slavery and to reject U.S. annexation, Texas would become a haven for freed and fugitive slaves who would pose a constant threat to slavery in the rest of the South. Britain's ultimate goal was to exploit existing sectional tensions and promote enough discord in American politics that the Union itself would crumble. The only remedy was the "immediate annexation of Texas as a slave state." The president of the Lone Star Republic, Sam Houston, cagily manipulated these anxieties. He "allowed Americans to conclude that he was willing to negotiate slavery out of existence" in the hope that this would spur the United States to claim Texas.[2]

The rumors of British designs took on a new urgency in August 1843, when the British foreign secretary, Lord Aberdeen, claimed in Parliament that England was indeed committed to promoting abolition in Texas. Annexation thus rose, John Ashworth has written, "to the very top of the political agenda." There it remained during the bitterly contested presidential election campaign of 1844. When Upshur died in February 1844, Tyler replaced him with John C. Calhoun—a move that must have struck many Whigs as nightmarish. The experienced statesman completed an annexation treaty and submitted it to the Senate in April 1844, just as the presidential campaign was kicking into high gear. The Democratic standard-bearer at this time was ardent annexationist James K. Polk of Tennessee; the party had rejected Tyler and old stalwarts Calhoun and Martin Van Buren. With his rebellious heir apparent, Robert Barnwell Rhett, as campaign manager, Calhoun had run an abortive offensive to drum up support in the North. Van Buren had been tainted by his 1840 loss to William Henry Harrison, incessant criticism from the Calhounites, and his own equivocations on Texas. Rallying around Polk, Democratic newspapers in the South beat the annexation drum, claiming that the cause was "spreading like wildfire," and celebrated Calhoun's defiant April 18 letter to British envoy Richard Pakenham, in which the South Carolinian defended slavery as a positive good and unabashedly cast Texas as a stronghold for slavery.[3]

Calhoun's openly pro-Southern annexation propaganda sparked dissension in the Southern ranks. A handful of influential Northern and border state senators, including Thomas Hart Benton of Missouri and Silas Wright Jr. of New York, rejected Calhoun's sectionalist language and opposed the Tyler treaty. But Calhoun's was not the only approach, and annexationists were able to build momentum by arguing that the admission of Texas would benefit the North as well as the South. The pro-annexation resolutions of South Carolina's Barnwell district, for example, promised that Texas would both open up new domestic markets for Northern manufactured goods and "swell the amount of our exports," thereby increasing the revenue to the government and the overall wealth of the country. Annexationists argued that territorial acquisition would give wage earners in the North the opportunity to become landowners in the West and thus preserve Jefferson's dream of an agrarian republic. This message had a broad resonance in the North, appealing to the Democratic rank and file and bringing large numbers of new voters into the party fold. Democrats, Michael Morrison has explained, equated expansion and freedom: "Personal liberty, they would say, was incompatible with overcrowding, exhausted lands, and wage slavery." Moreover, annexationists cannily appealed to both chivalry and racism in casting Texas, metaphorically, as a "vulnerable European maiden" who needed to be saved from barbarous Mexican men by heroic—white—American ones. This was part of a broader strategy to align territorial expansion with the ideal of "martial manhood": the work of conquering and "civilizing" the West would, so this argument went, give American men the opportunity to display the "masculine qualities of strength, aggression, and even violence," and to prove the racial superiority of Anglo-Saxons to "primitive" peoples.[4]

The most important propaganda gambit by expansionists was their contention, articulated most forcefully by Senator Robert J. Walker of Mississippi, that annexation could be a boon to the gradual dismantling of slavery, as bondspeople transported to Texas "would eventually diffuse southward, into still richer tropics." According to William Freehling, the Walker thesis allowed Northern Democrats to deny the charge that they were lackeys of Southern interests and to pose instead as "heroes who would diffuse blacks farther from the North." Walker's widely distributed "letter" on annexation, a veritable "textbook" for expansionists, of course marshaled disunion as an accusation. Anti-annexationists, he charged, were in league with the very abolitionists whose fanaticism exposed the Union to slave insurrection and to foreign designs.[5]

While support for annexing Texas united Southern Democrats and most Northern ones, the Whigs, so Democrats charged, were conspiring to make Texas a sectional issue. The dissolution threat of Adams and the antislavery lobby back in 1843 had inspired small groups of citizens in Massachusetts,

Vermont, and elsewhere to threaten disunion should Texas be annexed. Southern annexationists vowed not to be intimidated by such posturing. Langdon Cheves, a former congressman and Speaker of the House, in an 1844 letter to the *Charleston Mercury* that was published as part of the pamphlet *Southern States Rights*, wrote of disunion: "Whence did the odious term originate? Not certainly at the South. It came in the chill blast of the North and East"—and it was the likes of John Quincy Adams who were "faithlessly perpetuating" the dread doctrine. "We shall certainly acquire Texas," the *Richmond Enquirer* crowed in June 1844, "and that, too, without disunion, without war, without a breach of faith, or violation of national honor, and in spite of the anti-American opposition of Mr. Clay, and the leading Whigs, on this vital question." That the South had a double standard was not lost on keen Northern commentators—G. W. Root, a free black correspondent to the Columbus, Ohio, antislavery paper the *Palladium of Liberty*, lamented that if a Northern man mentioned dissolution, the "whole South are up in arms against him," whereas Southerners themselves threatened disunion "at pleasure."[6]

Henry Clay won the Whig nomination for president and proceeded to mishandle the Texas issue grievously. In a widely publicized letter to the Washington, D.C., *National Intelligencer*, written while Clay was campaigning in Raleigh, North Carolina, he opposed annexation, arguing that the government should use its resources to develop and improve the territory it already had, not squander them on acquiring new territory. Such a view was fully consistent with Whig political philosophy—Whigs wanted to elevate America on the scale of moral worth and material prosperity, rather than expand it across the frontier. For them, Texas represented not a realm of economic opportunity but rather a primitive breeding ground for slavery, sectional tensions, licentiousness, and war. Clay, the "Great Compromiser," thus assailed annexation as a measure that would disturb the sectional balance by unduly promoting slaveholding interests, and disturb the diplomatic balance by drawing the United States into a bloody and costly war with Mexico. As he had before in times of political crisis, Clay invoked disunion as a prophecy: To fight a war for Texas would "sow the seeds of a dissolution of the Union."[7]

Early in the 1844 presidential campaign, it seemed that this position might prevail; in June, Whigs saw to it that Tyler's annexation treaty was rejected by

ANTI ANNEXATION PROCESSION.

Here, Clay's anti-annexation position is mocked, as he leads a procession that includes Hartford Convention disunionists and Garrison's "ABOLITION martyrs." (Courtesy of the Library of Congress)

the Senate. But over the course of the summer, the Democrats' relentless campaign for annexation began to drain away Whig confidence and solidarity. No one generated more rhetorical heat than Robert Barnwell Rhett, whose short-lived "Bluffton movement" served, paradoxically, to sharpen the rhetoric of disunion and galvanize Southern Democrats. According to Rhett, the rejection of annexation was inseparable from another act of broken faith— the tariff of 1842. Nullifiers had been promised, as part of the Compromise of 1833, that over the course of the decade Northern industries would outgrow the need for import taxes. But Henry Clay and other Whigs determined, as the old tariff's expiration date neared, that it was essential for the economy that it be renewed. The 1842 tariff passed by a slender margin, and President Tyler felt compelled to sign it because the government, running at a deep deficit, so clearly needed the revenue. Rhett and a small group of militant supporters linked the annexation and tariff issues "to the deep seated and growing animosity of the North to the South," and concluded that "pliant Clay [was] in the hands of abolition plotters." Rhett's fire-eaters pledged, in Bluffton, South Carolina, on July 31, 1844, that they would resist this latest Northern assault.[8]

Significantly, the speeches, resolutions, and toasts offered up at Bluffton revealed that Rhett and his acolytes had soured on nullification and were now weighing the merits of a different remedy—namely, secession. The fact that the Compromise of 1833 had been broken suggested to them that nullification was ultimately ineffectual. In theory, nullification's deliberate timetable, in which the nullifying state waited for the finding of the tribunal of its sister states, gave the opposition forces a chance to assert themselves. Immediate secession, without the intermediate step of nullification, was a much less complicated mechanism—a state convention need only vote for the measure. Given the stark choice between "resistance and submission," Rhett reasoned, South Carolina Unionists would have difficulty opposing secession without "branding themselves as disloyal to the state." As his modern biographer William C. Davis points out, Rhett did not yet imagine that secession would necessarily be a "permanent act, an end in itself." He merely saw it as a "stronger demonstration" than nullification of a "commitment to equal justice under the Constitution."[9]

Southern Democrats, including former champions of nullification Calhoun and James Hamilton, were not receptive to such impulsive talk at this key moment in the presidential campaign. The *Richmond Enquirer*, which had long prided itself on its states' rights record, solemnly informed the Bluffton agitators that they were "pursuing a course against which the democrats of Virginia are bound to protest," noting that "we have much greater confidence in Mr. Polk than they express." Hamilton, too, chastised Rhett, urging Southerners to "get up a momentum of public opinion" on behalf of Polk.[10]

The optimism of the Democrats was vindicated, for even as their party pressed the argument that expansion would benefit the whole nation, the Whig Party was imploding. Finding it impossible to sell their opposition to Texas to the Southern electorate, for which the prospect of cheap, fertile Western land was too enticing, Southern Whig politicians resorted to finessing the issue—taking a different line in the South than did their confederates in the North. They tried to interpret Clay's Raleigh letter as an endorsement of *eventual* annexation, rather than as an outright rejection of the measure.[11]

Just as that argument seemed to be gaining credence, however, Clay blundered by publishing his infamous Alabama letters. Addressed to newspaper editors in that Deep South state, Clay's letters recanted his former position and held instead that slavery's presence in Texas was no obstacle to annexation and that if it could be effected peacefully, he might support annexation if elected president. This turnabout made the Whigs extremely vulnerable—it was one thing for Southern Whigs to interpret Clay for their own constituents; it was quite another for Clay himself to openly embarrass antislavery Northern Whigs by publicly disavowing the position he had taken earlier. The prospect of slavery's westward expansion had intensified the antislavery sentiments of evangelical voters in the Northern "Bible belt," and Northern Whig leaders knew that this constituency—from which the Liberty Party threatened to wrest votes—was more essential than ever to their party's electoral success.[12]

Naturally, Democrats had a field day with Clay's gaff. Under pressure from Northern Whigs, Clay produced another letter, in September, reiterating his opposition to annexation. The net result was to give the impression that he had lost control of his own campaign. In the end, Polk emerged the victor, with Clay getting soundly defeated in the Deep South and barely prevailing in the Upper South. Polk won more votes in the North than Clay, primarily because of a surge of new voters, especially immigrant voters, into the Democratic Party, and also because anti-annexation Northerners turned off by Clay's waffling did turn to the Liberty Party, which was represented in the race, once again, by James Birney. In two states, New York and Michigan, Birney's vote tally, by taking away Whig ballots, did actually tip the balance toward the Democrats; Clay and Liberty votes together outnumbered Polk ballots in the North. The annexationists had won the battle, but not yet the war.[13]

CONGRESS DEBATES ANNEXATION

A tear in the fabric of Democratic solidarity seemed to be in evidence when, in the month after Polk's election, the House of Representatives finally rescinded the gag rule. On December 3, 1844, Adams's antigag resolution passed by a vote of 108 to 80. As the repeal of the twenty-first rule was being debated, Rhett and other proslavery militants had again menaced disunion to frighten Northern Democrats into line. Rhett was by now a master of invoking disunion as a threat, accusation, and process all in one breath. He argued that because of the "proceedings of [abolition] fanatics" there was in the South "a deep and growing disaffection to the Union"; if the North failed to uphold the gag, the South would know that "self-protection will be her only protection." The South would build its resources with "vigilance, energy, and courage. . . . In the Union or out of the Union, she can and will be free," Rhett portentously intoned. This time, however, such intimations of disunion did not work. Northern Democrats, a majority of whom had favored the previous gags, gave a majority to Adams. Why? To be sure, Northern Democrats felt betrayed by the choice of Polk over Martin Van Buren as the party's presidential candidate. But Northern Democrats were also very apprehensive about the advent of the Liberty Party and the prospect that it would unite with the Whigs. The final round of gag debates took place during the first session of the Twenty-eighth Congress, in January and February 1844 (the matter came to a decisive vote at the beginning of the second session in December). William C. McCauslen, an Ohio Democrat, believed that the Liberty Party "never would have existed" without the gag rule, as the party had exploited the free speech issue to gain followers; as he saw it, the Liberty Party was now the "hobby horse" on which Whigs and abolitionists alike were "speeding to political preferment." Democrats in favor of rescinding the rule complained that the purpose of the endless antislavery wrangling over the gag was to "divide and distract" the party and thus prevent it, with its sound majority in the House, from getting anything done. Representative Samuel Beardsley of New York asked, "What has the refusal to receive these petitions done but to create perpetual strife and denunciation?"[14]

President Tyler announced in his December 1844 annual message that he wanted annexationists in the House and Senate to rally support for a joint congressional resolution to acquire Texas. This was a way of offering up Calhoun's rejected treaty in a new guise. The joint resolution sparked nearly three months of acrimonious debate. The stakes were high—as the *Charleston Mercury* put it, Northern Democrats, having disappointed their Southern colleagues in rescinding the gag rule, had now to redeem themselves. This time, a strong party consensus prevailed. Democratic supporters of annexation interpreted the recent presidential election as a referendum in favor of Texas. Pennsylvania's Representative Charles J. Ingersoll, a staunch ally of the South, led the way, claiming pompously that the best argument for annexation was that "the public sentiment had come up to it, with extraordinary prompti-tude and distinctiveness of expression." Representative Robert Dale Owen, of Indiana, a onetime radical reformer, now promoted the Walker line that the "diffusion" of slaves would lead to "peaceful and gradual emancipation." To the delight of the *Charleston Mercury*, he gave a lurid pro-annexation speech in the House predicting that without U.S. protection, "our brethren of Texas, their wives and their little ones, [will be] butchered before our eyes"; appeal-ing to racial solidarity, he warned sternly against the threat of "Mexican barbarity." Democrats, Northern and Southern, continued to take palpable delight in posturing as Unionists and denouncing abolitionist threats of dis-union. Holding up a copy of the *Liberator*, Senator Levi Woodbury of New Hampshire declared it "the highest authority of the opponents of annexa-tion." Over the objections of his Whig colleagues, he then quoted some of Garrison's more inflammatory rhetoric and argued that such doctrines should be rebuked by "every friend of the constitution . . . for the sake of our Union." Representatives Rhett and Isaac Edward Holmes of South Carolina, among others, opportunistically condemned anti-annexationists as abolition disunionists.[15]

Northern Whigs—both immediatists and moderate gradualists on the slavery question—decried annexation as "monstrous beyond all expression," a plan "secretly and stealthily concocted" by Tyler. Warning that it was a war with Mexico that posed the greatest threat to the safety of the Union, Representative Jacob Collamer of Vermont spoke for many when he assailed the "inconsistency" of pro-annexation arguments. Out of one side of their mouths, Democrats claimed Texas was so feeble that it might fall into the arms of England for protection from Mexico; out of the other, they claimed that Texas was so strong that Mexico had no serious hope of reconquering it and therefore would not go to war with the United States over the territory. Even as they accused annexationists of playing on people's fears (of England, abolition, and Mexico), anti-annexation Whigs engaged in their own racist fearmongering. Representative Robert C. Winthrop, a Massachusetts conser-vative typical of the so-called Cotton Whigs (who wanted to preserve sec-tional harmony to keep Southern cotton flowing into New England textile mills), deplored the fact that annexation would mean "the introduction of a vast foreign nation into our boundaries—the naturalization of some thousands of Texans, as well as Mexicans—[and] the introduction of 25,000 thousand slaves into the Union." Whigs, he asserted, were content with the country as it already was.[16]

Most Southern Whigs toed the party line and remained committed to the anti-annexation position. They could justify it on a number of grounds: that a joint resolution was unconstitutional; that the lure of Texas would spell the demise of the Old South, as slaves and their masters would "desert her worn out soil" for the fertile fields of the Southwest; that no true Whig would support the traitor Tyler; and that Whig solidarity on the issue could prevent the Liberty Party from stealing antislavery votes from the Whig base. A small but aggressive cadre of Southern Whigs, however, certain that the annexation issue had decimated them in the recent election, broke ranks and joined the Democrats. A Southern Whig, Milton H. Brown of Tennessee, introduced the winning annexation plan in the House. It provided for the admission of the Republic of Texas as a single slave state, rather than as a territory, as Democrats had originally proposed—but stipulated that Texans could one day choose to split the state into as many as four additional slave states below the Missouri Compromise boundary. In the Senate, the prospects for the annexation bill looked bleak until Democrat Thomas Hart Benton amended it to encourage Polk to admit "only the small, populated eastern frontier" of Texas as a slave state and leave the rest as an unorganized territory that might in the future be designated as free soil. Polk gave his word that he would avail himself of this option. Such assurances prompted all of the Northern Democrats and even three Southern Whigs to vote for the annexation resolution and provide its margin of victory.[17]

In one of the great double crosses of American history, Tyler preempted president-elect Polk, and in the last act of his administration offered Texas admission to the Union, according to the Brown plan, as a single slave state. The offer was duly accepted in July 1845, and Texas entered the Union in December. Summing up the sentiments of many Whigs at this train of events, Henry Clay wrote to a friend "God Save the Commonwealth!" Clay knew as well as anyone that his anti-annexation position had been defeated not only because pro-Texas forces had mounted an effective propaganda campaign but also because they had aggressively stifled any dissent. The gag rule may have been history, but Southern society was more committed than ever to silencing antislavery voices. The struggles of Clay's distant cousin, Cassius Clay, dramatized the Southern abridgment of free speech. A native of Kentucky, Cassius Clay was influenced by the speeches and writings of William Lloyd Garrison while attending Yale University in New Haven, Connecticut. He returned to his home state a devout emancipationist, albeit one who favored a gradual dismantling of slavery (voluntary, compensated emancipation) rather than the radical Garrisonian position. A Whig and a supporter of Henry Clay's economic programs, Cassius Clay served several terms in the Kentucky legislature in the 1830s. But by 1840, the Kentucky electorate would no longer tolerate his antislavery stance, and he lost his seat. He served thereafter as an antislavery and anti-annexation spokesman and publisher, and as a thorn in the side of his cousin Henry. When Cassius published a letter during the 1844 campaign claiming that Henry was sympathetic to antislavery, Henry promptly denied the charge. Although disavowed by his cousin, Cassius Clay's brand of moderate antislavery was endorsed by Northern Whigs. Horace Greeley thought it a badge of honor that Cassius was too moderate for the Garrisonians or Liberty Party; he argued that Whigs should be proud to claim Cassius as one of their own.[18]

In 1845 Cassius Clay founded the newspaper the *True American*, in Lexington, Kentucky, to promote gradual emancipation and urge Kentuckians to "free themselves" of the "curse" of slavery. Proslavery forces rallied quickly to suppress it. The fine differences between Garrisonians, Liberty Party supporters, and Whiggish antislavery gradualists mattered not; in the eyes of the proslavery advocates, Cassius Clay was a radical. At an August meeting, citizens of Lexington, presided over by politician Thomas Marshall, passed resolutions that issued a stern warning to Clay. After positing that "the liberty of the press and the freedom of political discussion are essential elements of our social system," the resolutions proceeded to justify censorship. The principal charge laid at his feet was that Clay had been in frequent contact with Northern abolitionists. He had become "the agent of an incendiary sect . . . [and] acted as though he were in an enemy's country." His goal was to force upon Kentucky "principles fatal to her domestic repose"—to start a civil war in the state by rallying "the non-slaveholding laborers and the slaves to flock to his standard." Thus the meeting resolved that "no abolition press ought to be tolerated in Kentucky" and asked Clay to surrender his operation peaceably. If he did not, the press would be destroyed.[19]

The Lexington meeting's resolutions embodied the paradoxical position of proslavery censors. On the one hand, they portrayed antislavery doctrines as foreign to the South, as originating in a different country. On the other hand, they portrayed those doctrines as dangerously seductive, not only for slaves but also, potentially, for nonslaveholders. Determined not to run the risk that Clay might attract partisans, proslavery Kentuckians dismantled his press on August 18, 1845. Clay escaped with his life and in 1847, with the backing of Northern abolitionists, reestablished his newspaper under a new name, the *Examiner*, in Louisville, Kentucky—one of the South's leading cities and home to a large population of white workingmen who resented having to compete with slave labor. Emphasizing an economic critique of slavery's inefficiency, Clay and his allies reenergized Kentucky's antislavery gradualists. But this resurgence foundered on the shoals of violence; in 1849 Cassius Clay was attacked by a mob brandishing pistols, knives, and clubs, and was stabbed in the abdomen. In an atmosphere of lethal hostility, the state's gradualists suffered an irreversible setback, and Kentucky's indigenous antislavery movement "dramatically declined during the 1850s."[20]

THE CHURCH SCHISMS

At the height of the annexation controversy in the mid-1840s, the issue of slavery caused a rift in the Methodist and Baptist denominations. This ominous development—a "harbinger of disunion"—further fortified the South against the "foreign" influence of abolitionists. The Methodist split in 1844 had its roots in the growth of antislavery Methodism in the North. By the mid-1830s, abolitionism had attracted a small but determined vanguard of Methodist ministers. In the religious sphere, as in the political one, attempts to censor abolitionists had backfired. The Methodists' central organization, the General Conference, endorsed the rejection of antislavery petitions, only to find that such a position alienated many Northerners. Refusing to be silenced, antislavery ministers founded their own newspapers and organized conventions. The formation of the American and Foreign Anti-Slavery Society in 1840, the Tappan-led breakaway group from the Garrisonians, was a boon for evangelical abolitionists, as the organization worked hard to promote abolition in the churches. In 1843 Methodist abolitionists withdrew from the church and established the Wesleyan Methodist Connection. The following year, controversy exploded at the General Conference. As Mitchell Snay has noted, "Methodist leaders in the North, fearful of losing more members to the Wesleyans, took a stronger stance against slavery." They voted to divest Bishop James Osgood Andrew of his office because Andrew had, by virtue of his marriage and inheritance, become a slaveholder. Southern delegates, who were a minority at the conference, withdrew in protest. A year later they held their own conference in Louisville and formed the Methodist Episcopal Church, South.[21]

The Baptist schism, too, reflected the growth of abolition sentiment in the North. Like their Methodist counterparts, a vanguard of antislavery Baptists had campaigned hard to persuade Northerners "that slavery had no place in the church." When, in 1844, Northern Baptists who dominated the Home Missionary Society rejected a Southern request that a slaveholder named James Reeve be appointed a missionary to Native Americans, Southern Baptists took offense. They met in Augusta, Georgia, in May 1845 and formed the Southern Baptist Convention. Southern Methodists and Southern Baptists left their national churches because they believed the churches had exceeded their mandates. Southern ministers also understood that their acts of secession would remove from them "any last taint of sectional infidelity." Since the time of Nat Turner's Rebellion, it will be remembered, Southern politicians had regarded the region's clergymen as soft on slavery and susceptible to Northern moralizing. The schisms allowed Southern clergymen to confirm their loyalty to the South.[22]

While abolitionism was the catalyst to the denominational schisms, the schisms in turn were the catalyst to the development of proslavery thought. Northern and Southern ministers no longer sought compromises or exchanged ideas; the vast evangelical publishing empire was "now under sectional direction." John Daly observes that from the mid-1840s on, "proslavery arguments were increasingly directed toward other southerners rather than against the North." Proslavery evangelicals such as A. B. Longstreet, William Smith, Thornton Stringfellow, and Josiah Priest developed Thomas Dew's notion that the growth of the slave population and the extension of slavery across the frontier were providential signs of God's favor. They championed a version of biblical literalism that cast slavery as divinely ordained and slaves as childlike creatures who needed to be trained and restrained within a "beneficent patriarchate." Furthermore, Southern evangelicals contributed to the discourse on disunion by "advancing a conception of a union that was conditional on peace and harmony." Since the union of the churches had generated rancor, it was no longer viable and legitimate. Southerners defended the schisms as conservative bids to preserve the true doctrines of their churches, just as Calhoun, Hammond, and other states' rights spokesmen invoked secession as a last resort to preserve the state sovereignty guaranteed by the Constitution. The fact that the Southern churches not only used the last resort but thrived after the schisms—that the religious press blossomed, seminaries and other religious schools proliferated, and ministers commanded unprecedented support and respect—was perhaps the most ominous legacy of the split in the churches. For the presence of strong, independent Southern churches raised the prospect that other Southern institutions—cultural, educational, economic, and political—might also benefit from independence. The church schisms, in other words, advanced the argument that disunion was a process and furnished new evidence that that process might favor the South.[23]

Abolitionists did not reap as many dividends from the schisms as slavery's defenders did. Northern ecclesiastical leaders had denied slaveholders leadership positions, but such a stance fell far short of the kind of antislavery commitment that abolitionists wanted from the churches. Even after 1845, the Northern branches of the Methodist and Baptist churches in border states such as Maryland, Delaware, and Missouri continued to include thousands of slaveholders in their congregations. Neither denomination was willing to declare all slaveholding to be sinful. Moreover, Northern Methodists and Baptists collaborated with Southern ones in supporting so-called benevolent associations such as the American Colonization Society and interdenominational religious associations such as the American Bible Society. Thus Frederick Douglass lamented in his 1845 narrative that American Christianity was "bad, corrupt, and wicked." Just as Garrison contrasted the ideal Union with the corrupt one, Douglass maintained that the "pure, peaceable, and impartial Christianity of Christ" was a far cry from the religion that was practiced by most Northerners and Southerners. The most brutal of all slaveholders, in Douglass's view, were the ones who professed to be devout, for they were self-righteous in their cruelty. But he did not reserve his criticism for slave-holders. The religion of the South was, he argued, "by communion and fellowship, the religion of the north." Quoting Jeremiah 5:29, Douglass wrote: " 'Shall I not visit for these things? Saith the Lord. Shall not my soul be avenged on such a nation as this?' "[24]

Immediatists were more committed than ever to what Garrison called their "heaven-originated cause." The executive committee of the American Anti-Slavery Society resolved in 1844 that "allegiance to God" required that the "existing national compact should be instantly dissolved." In its 1845 annual report, the Massachusetts Anti-Slavery Society pledged itself to "peaceful but vigorous agitation for the Dissolution of the existing political Union which binds the Slave and the Free in one intolerable chain." More than ever, martial metaphors were intertwined with the society's claims to Christian pacifism. "The war which the American Anti-Slavery Society wages with the Government of this country," the Massachusetts report read, "is carried on in the invisible fields of thought, in the unseen regions of the mind, and is urged by the dint of the trenchant sword of the spirit."[25]

THE WILMOT PROVISO

"In a state of war every man of the one nation is at war with every individual of the hostile nation. . . . Can a law be sustained in this country, or a war be carried on successfully, against public opinion? Does not the Government rest upon the shoulders of the people?" Richard Brodhead, a Democratic representative from Pennsylvania, posed these fundamental questions on February 9, 1847, in the midst of fierce debates on the House floor during the second session of the Twenty-ninth Congress. The "hostile nation" to which he referred was Mexico, and the law was Congress's May 13, 1846, declaration of war; the answer to his first question was no and to the second, yes. Brodhead's rhetorical gambit was intended to stigmatize opponents of the war as unpatriotic—this war *was* sanctioned by popular opinion and by law; therefore even those at odds with the majority were honor bound to "submit" to its will and to rally around President Polk and the army.[26]

The origins of the war lay in Texas's annexation. Mexico had never conceded the independence of Texas, which it still regarded as a Mexican province. After Texas had accepted the U.S. offer of statehood in July 1845,

President Polk had dispatched an army under Zachary Taylor to occupy the disputed territory between the Nueces River and the Rio Grande. Since Mexico, over the course of its conflict with the Lone Star Republic, had considered the Nueces—not the Rio Grande—to mark its border with Texas, Polk's decision to send U.S. troops *beyond* the Nueces was seen by Mexico as an open provocation. Texas's official entrance into the Union in December 1845 escalated tensions. Diplomatic relations between the two countries broke down, and Mexico's new president, General Mariano Paredes, touting his country's military prowess, announced in January 1846 that he would restore Texas to Mexico. President Polk then ordered Taylor deeper into the disputed territory, right to the Rio Grande, across the river from the Mexican city of Matamoros. President Paredes directed troops to turn back what he considered an invasion, and in April and May 1846 a series of skirmishes between Mexican troops and Taylor's army inaugurated the Mexican War.[27]

Brodhead spoke in Congress for those Northerners who fervently believed that Mexico, through its designs on Texas, had provoked the war, and that American expansionism was justified by Robert Walker's "diffusion" argument about slavery's destiny. Brodhead regarded blacks as a "nuisance, whether slave or free" and preferred that they be directed away from the Northern states and toward the Western territories. He regarded abolitionists, who bitterly opposed the Mexican War, as disunionists. "The Union I hold to be of more value than the freedom of all the negroes that have ever lived in it," he said bluntly in the conclusion to his speech. "The constant talk about the dissolution of the Union" provoked by abolitionism "has a tendency to familiarize the public mind with the idea, and lead people to believe that such an event is possible."[28]

Even as he invoked the duties of patriotism, however, Brodhead was beset, he confessed to his colleagues, by "anxiety and perplexity." For the Polk administration found itself under attack from the right and the left. On the one hand, Calhoun had just broken ranks with those "All Mexico" expansionists who hoped that victory in the war would carve off large swaths of territory deep into Mexico. Calhoun favored the acquisition of sparsely settled regions above and west of the Rio Grande, but not of areas below it, teeming with "mongrelized" nonwhite Mexicans. "As Calhoun's racism grew stronger, his imperialism waned in proportion," Thomas Hietala has observed. That Calhoun was again critiquing a Democratic administration was not all that surprising. As far as he was concerned, the Democratic Party was always on probation; it had perpetually to prove itself worthy of his support. Much more alarming to the likes of Brodhead was the apostasy of a breakaway faction of Northern Democrats, led in the House of Representatives by Brodhead's fellow Pennsylvanian, David Wilmot. To the horror and disbelief of administration men, Wilmot had, on August 8, 1846, presented a proposal to ban slavery from any territories wrested from Mexico; this "Proviso" was a rider to a bill that would appropriate $2 million to indemnify Mexico for any territory the United States might acquire as part of a putative peace treaty. Wilmot's measure passed the House, only to falter in the Southern-dominated Senate. Although it never became federal policy, the Proviso subsequently garnered wide support in the North, including the endorsement of state legislatures. Wilmot's "firebrand," as Brodhead dubbed it, confounded the hopes of Polk supporters that they might unequivocally claim "public opinion" as their own—and plunged the country into a very different "state of war" than the likes of Brodhead had anticipated.[29]

Before Wilmot put forward his Proviso, prowar Democrats had hoped that debates over the faraway conflict would fall along familiar lines. Antislavery Whigs, Liberty Party men, and bona fide abolitionists—all of whom had opposed the annexation of Texas—argued, predictably, that President Polk had engineered the war with Mexico. In keeping with his long-cherished desire to augment the Slave Power, Polk had, they charged, deployed federal troops in the disputed territory between Texas and Mexico not for defensive purposes but to provoke Mexico to attack the United States. Thus Polk, whose real goal was the acquisition of upper California and New Mexico, had cast Mexico as the aggressor and the United States as the innocent victim.[30]

Although Polk's machinations were an "open secret" in Washington, D.C., prowar Democrats confidently trumpeted their version of events, in which the United States was the aggrieved party. In this war as in earlier ones, the nation could, as Brodhead put it, appeal with safety to the "God of righteous battles." Democrats counted on the drumbeat of war to drown out the doubters. After both houses of Congress enthusiastically passed Polk's war bill in May 1846, citizens around the country endorsed the measure in a series of prowar mass meetings. Later that month, the first reports of American success on the front, at Palo Alto and Resaca de la Palma, prompted a rush of volunteers into the army and seemed to augur a quick victory for the United

States. The penny press, which provided unprecedented coverage of the war, interpreted U.S. success on the battlefield as a vindication of the "American character." Even Northern Whigs seemed to be swept up in the martial ardor, seeing the war as a "nationalizing influence" to counter the racial, ethnic, and sectional tensions of the age.[31]

Prowar propaganda, Reginald Horsman has written, tapped two distinct strains of American nationalism. One was an idealistic tradition, stretching back to the Revolutionary era, in which America was cast as a "model republic" that could redeem the people of the world from tyranny; seen in this light, the Mexican War was a war of liberation that would bring the blessings of republican government to the Mexicans. The second strain, which had coalesced in the 1830s and 1840s and was advanced by a wide array of American writers in both North and South, was an ascendant "racial nationalism." Drawing on a long-standing tradition of British "Anglo-Saxonism" that claimed the Anglo-Saxon race had invented representative government, on a newer "romantic" racialism that sentimentalized the cultural distinctiveness and superiority of the "Caucasian" (Anglo-Saxon and Teutonic) peoples, and on a spate of pseudo "scientific" writings that purported to find biological evidence of white supremacy, "racial nationalism" cast Mexicans as an unassimilable "mixed" race "with considerable Indian and some black blood." The war would not redeem them, but it would hasten the day when they, like the American Indians, "would fade away."[32]

Both the idealistic and the racial strains of nationalism stoked a rampant spirit of militarism. As elaborated by journalists, politicians, military leaders, and other opinion makers, American militarism celebrated the virtues of the "citizen-soldier" and regarded the army's volunteers as heirs to the heroes of the Revolutionary War. As the U.S.-Mexican conflict progressed, a new crop of military heroes emerged, led by Zachary Taylor, to join George Washington in the nation's pantheon, and a class of young officers (Robert E. Lee, Ulysses S. Grant, Thomas Jackson, George McClellan, and William Tecumseh Sherman) earned military experience that would prepare them for their own ascendance as heroes of the Civil War. The U.S. Army was portrayed in the press both as an "instrument of Providence," advancing "God's cause" of democracy, and as an embodiment of Anglo-Saxon racial superiority, whose victories proved that Mexicans were of inferior stock.[33]

This uneasy mix of idealism and racialism was at the heart of "Manifest

Destiny," the doctrine, given its name by Democratic editor John L. O'Sullivan, that encapsulated the case for war. It was America's destiny, O'Sullivan asserted, to claim the continent. O'Sullivan was in the vanguard of the New York–based Young America movement, which attracted a rising generation of Democratic leaders and spokesmen (such as Stephen Douglas of Illinois) with rhetoric heralding the exceptional qualities of the vigorous American republic; in contrast to Europe's declining old states, the United States was "a young nation on the rise." While the Young America movement tapped a national spirit of optimism and "self-congratulation" that had been fed by Whig-sponsored advancements in technology, such as the advent of the steamboat and the railroad, Manifest Destiny was fundamentally a Democratic Party doctrine with deep resonance in the South. As Frederick Merk has explained, men like O'Sullivan believed the defense of states' rights to be integral to the case for national expansion, for the principle of local control over issues like slavery "permitted a spreading of the domain of the Union almost indefinitely without any danger that a central tyranny would emerge such as had disfigured the Roman and British empires."[34]

The Polk administration, marshaling this resurgent proslavery nationalism, imagined that the antiwar faction could swiftly be marginalized and tainted as unpatriotic, and that people would come to accept territorial expansion as the consequence of a just war rather than as the cause of an unjust one. But the Wilmot Proviso, coming just three months into the war, shattered this illusion. For it precipitated a break in the Democratic ranks and propelled Free-Soil Democrats from the North, such as David Wilmot himself, into an alliance with antislavery Whigs and abolitionists. Southerners, both Whig and Democratic, closed ranks against this emerging Free-Soil phalanx. Party discipline broke down, and the sectional fault line over slavery was laid bare.

Wilmot's actions have been painstakingly analyzed by historians, who have elaborated a many-faceted and persuasive explanation for why he and so many of his fellow Northern Democrats repudiated their long-standing practice of following the lead of the proslavery Southern wing of the party. Wilmot and his allies were still bitter over the way that Southerners in the party had renounced and marginalized former president Martin Van Buren for inconsistency on the slavery issue. Moreover, Van Burenite Democrats felt that Polk had repeatedly betrayed them—in the fraudulent manner in which he annexed Texas, in ceding part of Oregon (seen as a Free-Soil counterweight to Texas) to the British, in lowering the tariff at the behest of Southerners, and in shunning Van Buren men in forming his cabinet and exercising patronage. The Van Burenites believed that the "party had to come first"—and that Polk had rejected this philosophy by putting Southern interests over party loyalty. He had left Van Buren men no choice but to oppose him. The Proviso was thus a corrective to the Polk policy of bolstering the Slave Power—it would "limit the growth of the South's power in national politics." Northern Democrats were also motivated to support Wilmot by a "healthy respect for northern public opinion," writes Michael Holt; they were aware of the inroads of the abolitionist and Liberty Party movements and feared electoral repudiation should they seem to support a war for the extension of slavery. In other words, the Proviso would hold Polk accountable for the propaganda he had aimed at the Northern electorate—if the war was not a bid to gain slave states, then let him prove it.[35]

Wilmot and his supporters were committed to the idea that their own free labor system needed to expand into the West in order to thrive, and that honest hard-working Northern farmers and mechanics would find themselves degraded if they had to work alongside slaves. As Walt Whitman, a Northern Democrat and editor of the *Brooklyn Daily Eagle* during 1846–47, put it, slavery is "destructive to the dignity and independence of all who work, and to labor itself." Moreover, they feared that "industrialization and concentration" would increase in the North if men there could not migrate west. For many Northern whites, racism was a factor as well. Wilmot himself was no abolitionist and made it clear that he wanted Western lands to be free of both slaveholders and blacks. He repeatedly repudiated the popular diffusion argument that his party had used so effectively to win public support for Texas annexation. Slavery would not gradually wither away in the territories, Wilmot opined in unabashedly racist terms, because "slaves are like any other stock, of which merchandise is made. Widen the market for their sale, and you stimulate the production."[36]

Most important, Northern Democrats of Wilmot's ilk defended the Proviso as a "conservative document" that restored the "first principles" of the Founders, as embodied in the Northwest Ordinance—namely, that free territory would stay free. The crux of the issue was that Mexico had abolished slavery; therefore, the prizes of California and New Mexico were also free of the institution. Wilmot was at pains to note that he had supported the statehood of Texas, where slavery was already well ensconced. But he could not countenance introducing slavery into new territories where it did not exist. For all their attempts to align their position with that of their forebears, however, the sectional crisis of 1846–47 was fundamentally different from earlier sectional impasses. At the time of the Missouri debates, the territorial restriction of slavery had been a "means by which to reach compromise." But in 1846–47, as the heated congressional discourse over the Wilmot Proviso discloses, the viability of such territorial restriction was itself called into question.[37]

DEBATING THE PROVISO

While historians have a good fix on *why* Wilmot proposed his territorial restriction on slavery, there is much more to be said about *how* he and his allies chose to make their case. A central preoccupation of Provisoists, particularly of Northern Democrats but also of some Whigs, was to establish the manliness of the position of nonextension, and thereby to dissociate themselves from radical abolitionism and to neutralize a powerful weapon in the hands of Southern politicians. Proslavery anti-Proviso men moved quickly to lump Wilmot with Joshua Giddings and other abolitionists. Using time-tested language, Mississippi congressman Robert W. Roberts, in a speech on February 4, 1847, traced the Proviso to the "mawkish sensibilities" and "sickly, morbid philanthropy" of white Northerners. Similar charges were made in the Senate, where John Chipman, a Michigan Democrat, accused Proviso supporters of letting "sickly philanthropy" blind them to the duties of patriotism. Wilmot would not stand for it. Speaking on the House floor four days later, he chose not once but four times to disavow any special concern for slaves. He decried "squeamish sensitiveness upon the subject of slavery," or "morbid sympathy" or "morbid sensitiveness" for blacks. Speaker after speaker made similar disavowals. Democratic congressman John Petit of Indiana declared that "I am not one of those who have a sickly, fawning feeling for the blacks," and Representative James Dixon of Connecticut said that "the feeling which pervades the North, on the subject of slavery, is not one of sickly sentimentality."[38]

Such language was, of course, deeply gendered. Based on the dominant conventions of the day, which attributed to men and women different characters and "spheres" of influence, sentimentality was itself associated with femininity; women were creatures of the heart, while men were governed by reason. Anti-Proviso Democrat Charles Ingersoll tried to capitalize on this association by claiming that opposition to slavery's extension was "mere sentiment . . . without reason and without argument." This charge sparked a debate on the word "sentiment," in which Proviso supporters reappropriated it as a manly concept. The love of freedom was indeed a "sentiment," Representative Washington Hunt of New York retorted—one that had been defended "on many a battlefield." As for the words "morbid" and "sickly," which appeared again and again in the Proviso debates, they too had a distinct meaning in Victorian discourse, evocative as they were of women's purported fascination with death. The genre of sentimental fiction, of which antebellum women were the major producers and consumers, trafficked in melodrama and pathos and featured stories that cast suffering and death— particularly the deaths of mothers and infants—as acts of moral heroism and regeneration. When politicians used the terms "sickly" and "morbid" to tarnish abolitionists, they plainly meant to depict them as excessively emotional and seduced by maudlin, lurid exaggerations. Ironically, antislavery texts such as Grimké and Weld's *American Slavery as It Is*, though intended to enumerate the cold, hard facts, played into the stereotype—it was both weak and unhealthy, anti-abolitionists charged, to dwell so obsessively on evidence of the slaves' suffering.[39]

Wilmot and his supporters established the manliness of their position not only by distancing themselves from the ranks of male and female abolitionists, but also by disparaging the manhood and fertility of the South. The behavior of the executive branch, with its behind-the-scenes machinations, and of the Senate, which had delayed a vote on the Proviso in the hope that it would fade away, "had no stamp of manliness," Wilmot charged. "Why not meet this subject as men, and settle it upon a basis that all should understand?" But it was not only Southern leaders whose manhood Wilmot questioned. The effect of slavery on the nonslaveholding white laborer in the South, Wilmot opined in a popular trope, was that it "mars his manhood. It destroys his self-respect and dignity of character"; when charting the distance between himself and the "lordly planter," the Southern yeoman felt nothing but humiliation. Proviso supporters evoked images not only of Southern weakness but also of barrenness. The institution of slavery, of plantation agriculture, meant that the South wore "the aspect of decay." Staple crop production had left once proud states like Virginia "almost as barren" as the desert, argued Congressman Bradford R. Wood, a New York Democrat. In the words of Wilmot, slave labor exhausts the soil, and thus "sterility follows its path." Associating free labor with virility, Wilmot asserted that it had the power literally to regenerate the land. Such rhetoric tapped a powerful current in Northern culture—a distinctive Free-Soil interpretation of the agrarian ideal. This ideal celebrated the yeoman farmer as the denizen of a bucolic world of "small farms, neat schoolhouses, and village churches," where the values of "law, justice, order, industry, and temperance" prevailed. Such a world could not exist, slavery restrictionists argued, under the shadow of the plantation system.[40]

The concept of compromise was given a new, gendered reading by Proviso advocates. Those who supported Wilmot had to find a language with which to counter potent appeals by anti-Proviso Democrats to party solidarity—a solidarity that had united the Democratic brotherhood in North and South and translated, so often, into electoral supremacy for the party. This Wilmot and his allies did by casting further compromise with the South as an act of unmanly subservience and submission. The metaphor of enslavement was irresistible. According to Wilmot, if the North submitted to the South's demand for more slave territory, then Northern men were themselves "coward slaves" who "deserved to have the manacles fastened upon [their] own limbs." He was echoed by New York Democratic representative George O. Rathbun, who praised the "noble and manly" sentiments of Proviso supporters; any Northerner who would side with the South "must be a poor, miserable, degraded being, and fit only to be a slave." His fellow congressman Wood chose an equally compelling image when he likened compromise to sexual servitude. Any man who would "encircle himself in the arms of the South, let me say that an infamy awaits him deeper and blacker than the pit of perdition. . . . There is no highminded southern man but will look upon him with contempt. He may use him, but he will despise him." Whig congressman Columbus Delano of Ohio likewise evoked the images of both enslavement and prostitution when he warned that the executive branch would use patronage to buy support; "traitors are always marketable and always a cheap commodity," he said.[41]

Democratic newspapers in the North seized on this refrain. The *Cleveland Plain Dealer* was of the opinion that any "member of Congress from the West, who is found cuddling to the SLAVE POWER, for the sake of government favor, should be marked with the curse of Cain," while the *Sandusky Democratic Mirror* contended that any man who opposed the Wilmot Proviso should be "branded as the foulest traitor to the sacred cause of liberty." No Democratic journalist outdid Walt Whitman in associating support for the Proviso with manly strength and courage and opposition to it with cringing weakness. Whitman called upon his readers do their duty "as Christians, as men, and as Democrats" and endorse the restriction of slavery; the working-man, with his "rolled up sleeves" and "brawny chest," must lead the way. No one who was seduced by the "sophisms of Mr. Calhoun" or by the "far, very far lower influences of the darkest and meanest phrases of demagogism" practiced by anti-Proviso Northern Democrats deserved a place among the "respectable portion of our citizens."[42]

Wilmot and his supporters in the emerging Free-Soil coalition understood well that the key to defending their position was to steel themselves against what had been the most effective of all proslavery weapons—the rhetoric of disunion itself. Thus Wilmot repeatedly announced that he refused to be baited by such rhetoric and to be intimidated into making more compromises. "This cry of disunion is as idle as the nursery tale with which children are frightened into obedience," he said. Turning the charges of sentimentality against proslavery forces and associating them, deftly, with their mortal enemies the abolitionists, Wilmot argued that purveyors of disunion rhetoric were appealing to people's emotions. Reason, he countered, must prevail over fear. As another tactic, Proviso supporters openly rejected the Garrisonian uses of disunion as being counterproductive. John G. Palfrey, a Massachusetts clergyman and editor who opposed slavery but believed fervently in Anglo-Saxon superiority, wrote: "The Free States ought not to think of disunion, because it would separate them from their best auxiliaries . . . the non-slaveholding white men of the Southern States." He continued, "We want [their] help . . . and they want ours, to throw off the burden of this insufferable wrong." A third way of immunizing Free-Soilers against disunion threats was articulated by Congressman Dixon, an ardent opponent of expansion. He declared, in a statement that was both prophesy and veiled counterthreat, that if Southern fanaticism—"the frantic struggles of an infatuated slave power"—did someday instigate disunion and civil war, it was the white South that had the most to lose. Slavery would be destroyed in the "carnage and devastation" of such a war. Dixon did not advocate disunion. He wanted peace—and to end slavery by the "free consent of our southern brethren." But, whether by peaceful means or violent ones, he predicted, "liberty, though late, will come at last."[43]

This Free-Soil repudiation of both Southern and Garrisonian disunion was fully compatible with evocations of disunion as a process. Garrisonians, cloaked in the mantle of outsiders, and Liberty Party men, with their meager showing in the presidential elections, had difficulty making the case that antislavery principles were ascendant and that abolitionists would soon claim a Northern majority. Proviso supporters, by contrast, did evoke the North's gradual alienation from the Slave Power as a central theme and claimed that nonextension had majority support. As Ohio Whig Daniel Tilden reflected, the Texas controversy had awakened a "very deep antislavery feeling at the North"—and thus Northern politicians had to rally around the Proviso because "the people have taken this subject into their own hands." Dixon agreed that "public opinion has at last assumed a fixed and determined character." While Northern Whigs could fold this argument into their case against territorial acquisition and against Polk, Northern Democrats, historian Ashworth has written, "employed the traditional radical Democratic arguments against the 'aristocracy' [of bankers and manufacturers] and turned them against the slaveholders themselves." Seen this way, Free-Soilism was a doctrine with deep Democratic roots, and Provisoists were aligned, as Wilmot put it, with "those gallant and true men, who have fought the battle of popular rights against privilege and monopoly in all forms." The natural tendency of a free society, Democratic editor William Cullen Bryant elaborated, was toward social equality, whereas the tendency of slave society was toward aristocratic tyranny.[44]

The impulse to question the manliness of one's opponents, so prominent in the discourse on the Wilmot Proviso, had, of course, taken many forms during the slavery debates of the 1830s and 1840s. As Bertram Wyatt-Brown and others have shown, "inflammatory masculine rhetoric" was a key part of the arsenal of anti-abolitionists and immediatists alike. Southern slaveholders and Northern Democrats (such as *New York Herald* editor James Bennett) had routinely assailed the manhood of abolitionists, charging them with waging their campaign "from behind the whalebone and cotton padding of their female allies." Garrisonians had shot back by disparaging the false manhood of slaveholders, exposing their vaunted cult of honor as a cover for their violent and lascivious behavior toward slaves. True men, abolitionists argued, followed the dictates of their conscience and served as protectors of the weak and oppressed. True men, moreover, had the self-control to rebuff Southern attempts to bait them into violence. Joshua Giddings, for example, reacted to routine threats made against him in the halls of Congress "by scorning his attackers as morally stunted people who were to be pitied, not fought with, since they were literally beneath his contempt."[45]

The Proviso debates signaled an important shift in the use of gendered rhetoric. Before this moment, party allegiances had somewhat reined in the use of such attacks—Northern Democrats and Whigs knew that blanket caricatures, charges, and condemnations of Southern men would alienate their partisan brethren. But in the Proviso debates, the kid gloves came off, and the North and South pummeled each other, across party lines, with insults and accusations in the elemental language of gender aspersions.

SOUTHERN REACTIONS TO THE PROVISO

"Are they better men, wiser, purer, or greater? Have they accomplished more, fought more, or paid more proportionally for the Union than we of the South?" James Seddon of Virginia posed this question to the House as part of a diatribe against what he called the "arrogant assumption of superiority" by Northern Proviso supporters—their "pharisaical pretension that they are not as other men." Seddon was a dyspeptic, "cadaverous" man who fancied himself a Cavalier aristocrat (during the Civil War, his home was converted into the White House of the Confederacy). Turning the tables on them, he asked how it was that Northern men had become of such "delicate sensibility" that the "taint of a negro" in the Western territories was enough to unnerve them. Seddon's words elucidate why Southern Whigs and Democrats closed ranks against the Wilmot Proviso. They saw it in symbolic terms as a threat against their "manhood, their rights, their equality, and their political liberty." Southerners believed that the Proviso repudiated the spirit of compromise that had guided the founding generation and renewed the very struggle against tyranny that had produced the Revolution. David Wilmot's measure was, Congressman Franklin W. Bowden of Alabama said, "a daring move to banish a respectable minority from the common heritage of the nation."[46]

To counter that move, Southerners fell back on tried-and-true rhetorical gambits. They charged that the Proviso was the work of abolitionists who had been emboldened by the repeal of the gag rule. They evoked the specter of race war as the inevitable result of abolitionist intermeddling. In one of many examples, Mississippi's Congressman Roberts, who accused abolitionists of a "morbid" concern for slaves, warned Southern men in a morbid tone of his own that the "canting Abolitionist" planned to "murder [their] wives and children." In less melodramatic but no less biting terms, proslavery forces also conjured up images of promiscuity and illegitimacy. They charged that abolitionism had "its origins in infidelity"—it was a foreign doctrine, imported from across the Atlantic, and any American who embraced it was unfaithful to the United States. In the words of Georgia's Seaborn Jones, the Proviso was a bastard "child of many fathers," since Wilmot was only one among many Democratic leaders who could claim "paternity" over it. Democratic Provisoists were also characterized as faithless teases, who had been "incontinently infected" by abolitionism and "abandoned the South after tickling her for an indefinite period with flattering promises."[47]

The more astute Southern leaders realized that defenders of slavery had to do more than luridly assail the respectability of Free-Soil men—they had to stake out what they perceived to be the moral high ground. The brief moment in which proslavery Southerners could cloak themselves in the majoritarian mantle, on the grounds that Texas annexation and the Mexican War had popular support, had evaporated. Now Rhett and others had to retool the South's image as a beleaguered minority. They did this by restating the case for abolitionism's ascendancy in the North. No longer were antislavery measures the "insane ravings of associated fanatics" or the "invidious resolutions . . . of northern states," as Seddon put it—now the federal government itself, in the form of the pro-Wilmot majority in the House, conspired to rob the South of its rights. Rhett, for his part, thundered in a January 1847 speech that it was "not fanaticism, or a sense of right only" that drove the Free-Soilers; rather, they sought "political power" and "mastery" over the South. Such a power grab by the North was patently unconstitutional and an infringement of states' rights. Rhett conceded that he was stung by Northern charges of Southern "weakness" and "imbecility," and that he was well aware that "a taunt is often more potent than an argument." But, he sternly lectured his fellow Southern colleagues, "half of the sophistries in argument consist in the abuse of words. It is about sovereignty we are to reason."[48]

Rhett stated that neither Congress nor the federal government had sovereignty over the territories; such sovereignty lay in the states that held the territories as their common property. This standpoint echoed Calhoun's philosophy and position on the Proviso. Although Calhoun was ambivalent about acquiring too much territory from Mexico, he was certain that in whatever land the United States won, slavery should prevail. In his view, "Ours was a federal Constitution—the states were its constituents, not the people." It followed that Congress had no power whatsoever to proscribe or regulate slavery in the territories, nor could the residents of the territories themselves bar slavery—for to do so would be an unconstitutional infringement of the rights of the slave states. According to this reading of the Constitution, the slave codes of the Southern states had a legal aura that extended beyond the boundaries of those states and into the territories; Southern sovereignty, as Rhett's speech elaborated, "exists in all its plenitude over our territories; as much so, as within the limits of the States themselves."[49]

Although cloaked in constitutionalism and a reverence for tradition, this formulation was radical and defiant, historian Holt observes, as it "utterly flouted Northerners' hopes of blocking slavery extension" and closed the door on potential compromise and on a healing of the sectional rift that now divided each party. Significantly, the formulation was too radical for most of the Southern electorate. As the presidential election of 1848 approached, anti-Proviso Southerners lined up behind three alternative positions, each of which was calculated both to invalidate the Proviso and to offer grounds for reconciliation within each party. Southern Whigs rallied around the chimerical "No Territory" doctrine—the position that no territory at all should be acquired from Mexico. This was consistent with the Whigs' long-standing opposition to territorial expansion and had the additional merit of rendering the hated Wilmot Proviso irrelevant. Some Southern Democrats, including Polk, favored the extension of the Missouri Compromise line to the Pacific Coast, so that some of California could be safeguarded for slavery and the precedent of sectional compromise between North and South could be preserved. Most, however, favored the chameleonlike concept of "popular sovereignty." This doctrine, which left it to the settlers of a territory to determine whether to permit slavery, dovetailed with Calhoun's position in denying Congress jurisdiction over the territories. Derived by Democrats such as Lewis Cass of Michigan from the constitutional theory that a territory should exercise jurisdiction over its local, domestic institutions just as a state did, popular sovereignty promised Southerners "equal access" with Northerners to newly acquired land in the West. Moreover, Holt notes, Southerners could take heart from the fact that, in the past, "once slaveholders established a foothold in a territory, it always became a slave state when it entered the Union."[50]

Although Calhoun had not built a consensus for his constitutional position, he had nonetheless skillfully exploited the Proviso controversy. Whatever solution to the territorial impasse they favored, proslavery Southerners were united in the depths of their hatred for the Proviso, in their belligerent frame of mind, and in their righteous indignation. After tarring anti-annexationists as disunionists during the Texas debates, Southerners once again invoked disunion as a process and a threat. Augustus Baldwin Longstreet, in a book called *A Voice from the South*, consisting of fictional letters that "sister states" Massachusetts and Georgia sent to one another, argued that "prophecy has already become history": abolitionism had become "general at the North" and was growing ever more aggressive in its "lawless crusade." And in one of the many Southern speeches threatening disunion, Alabama congressman Henry Hilliard, a former professor and minister, warned: "The spirit will lingers in the South which produced our Revolution, a spirit which will contend for political rights to the very last." While the likes of Wilmot closed their ears to such threats, the disunion refrain was music to the ears of William Lloyd Garrison.[51]

ABOLITIONISTS AND THE PROVISO

"Within the last six months a most surprising change in public sentiment has undeniably taken place," Garrison wrote in March 1847, of Northern support for the Proviso. But the change hardly restored his faith in the political system. Rather, Garrison continued to relish the fact that his disunionism "terrifie[d] many," and that it put him and his followers "in constant collision with all the religious sects and political parties." To occupy disunion ground "requires a good deal of nerve," he boasted to his friend Richard Webb. Indeed, in the pages of the *Liberator*, Garrison seized on the Southern reaction to Wilmot's measure as further proof that the political system was not salvageable. To Calhoun's February 19, 1847, speech trumpeting his theory on state sovereignty and the constitutionality of slavery, Garrison responded: "Slave states are to be created indefinitely. . . . On this condition alone is the Union to be maintained. Mark that, ye idolators of the Union!" Although there was some confusion in the Garrisonian ranks about how to effect such disunion if immediatists had withdrawn from politics, the *Liberator* defended the doctrine as a moral stance—"a simple question of abstract right"—made all the more urgent by the corrupt nature of the Mexican War. For the "immoral Union" was now "bloodstained" by the brutal conduct of the U.S. Army in invading the "neighbor and sister Republic" of Mexico.[52]

Abolitionists were determined to focus the nation's attention on the repugnant nature of the war and its human costs. "The war that has been made on poor, helpless Mexico by this country is productive of evil, and nothing but evil," black abolitionist Thomas Van Rensellear wrote to a British antislavery journal in November 1847. It has cost "the lives of about 50,000 Americans by sword and pestilence" and had an even more tragic impact on Mexico— "Her peaceful villages and walled cities are battered down by our heavy artillery, and their helpless women and children slaughtered by the hundreds." Charles Sumner, of Massachusetts, an emerging leader of his state's antislavery "conscience" Whigs, tried, in a February 1847 speech in Boston, to counter the "support our troops" mentality by declaring that "the present war is offensive in essence. As such it loses all shadow of title to respect. The acts of courage and hardihood which in a just cause might excite regard, when performed in an unrighteous cause, have no quality that can command them to virtuous sympathy." The money wasted on the war, he lamented, was diverted from "colleges, hospitals, schools and churches."[53]

The abolitionists' image of the war as an exercise in atrocities was no morbid fantasy. Modern-day scholarship, most notably Paul Foos's book, *A Short, Offhand, Killing Affair*, has demonstrated that U.S. soldiers, embittered by the poor leadership, training, and supplies they received, did vent their anger on Mexican civilians in rioting, killing sprees, and vicious guerrilla warfare. These soldiers "decided at the company level to collect the wages of manifest destiny in the form of looting and racial atrocity." For abolitionists, the violence of the war was an extension of the violence of the Slave Power. James Russell Lowell's antiwar poems, published in 1847, had his character, the redoubtable New England Yankee Hosea Bigelow, so indict the war and its Southern advocates:

> Ez fer war, I call it murder,—
>> There you hev it plain an' flat;
> They may talk o' Freedom's airy
>> Tell they're pupple in the face,—
> It's a grand gret cemetary
>> Fer the Barthrights of our race;
> They just want this Californy
>> So's to lug new slave-states in
> To abuse ye, an' to scorn ye,
>> An' to plunder ye like sin.[54]

The unseemly conduct of the war justified not only Christian pacifism, but also "come-outerism"—a withdrawal from the political system and a withholding of support for the government. The most fabled act of individual opposition to the war was Henry David Thoreau's refusal to pay taxes to the U.S. government and his subsequent imprisonment, immortalized in his classic text *Civil Disobedience*, published in 1849. Steeped in a transcendental philosophy that held up the individual conscience as the ultimate moral arbiter, Thoreau rejected the idea that petitions, charities, and ballots could effect meaningful moral change—such were acts of complicity with a state whose "very Constitution is the evil." What Thoreau called for was manly resistance to the state itself—"Oh for a man who is a *man*, and as my neighbor says, has a bone in his back which you cannot pass your hand through! . . . How many men are there to a square thousand miles in this country? Hardly one." Thoreau's rhetoric in some sense echoed that of Wilmot's supporters, who cast the Free-Soil position as a bastion of courage and masculinity, and sought to transcend older, feminized forms of antislavery activism such as petitioning. Connecticut's Congressman Dixon, for example, had implored Proviso supporters to "resume the capacity of choice" that characterized true men and not be bound by "slavish" fidelity to old interpretations and alliances. But for Thoreau, the operative contrast was not between men and women or between men and slaves, but between men and machines. Most men, he believed, were automatons who served the state with their bodies, not their consciences. To all those who in their consciences opposed the war with Mexico, he advised "Let your life be a counter friction to stop the machine."[55]

Abolitionists' "come-outerism," as we have seen, was at the heart of their rhetoric of disunion. In the midst of the Proviso debates, they increasingly defended disunion not merely as a moral stance, but as a pragmatic one. Garrisonians made no secret of their hope that the Southern rejection of the Proviso would teach Northerners the "futility" of restricting slavery within the context of the Union. A September 10, 1847, essay in the *Liberator* argued that it was easier to dissolve the Union than to pass the Wilmot Proviso, "for the one can be done by the majority of the inhabitants of the free States, or of a portion of them; while the other cannot, though they were united as one man." In other words, the Senate would always do the bidding of the South.[56]

That Is Revolution!

THE CRISIS OF 1850

Garrisonian hope that the debates over the Mexican Cession would expose the futility of a national electoral system easily dominated by the South had to be deferred. With the House and Senate in turmoil over Wilmot's proposal, the fate of slavery in the territories "passed to the people, in a national presidential referendum." The Democratic nomination in 1848 went to Michigan senator Lewis Cass, who ran on a "popular sovereignty" platform. The genius of the doctrine was that it was so malleable. Northern Democrats who supported slavery restriction held that the people in a given territory could decide to ban slavery early in the territorial stage of government—as soon as there were five thousand residents—and therefore well before either slaveholders or slaves had a chance to ensconce themselves there. Proslavery Southern Democrats insisted that a territorial legislature could rule on slavery only after sixty thousand residents, enough for the territory to apply for statehood, had settled there. Under such an interpretation, slavery would have ample time to establish itself before popular sovereignty kicked in. Cass and his allies unabashedly claimed to support the former interpretation before Northern audiences and the latter when they addressed Southerners. The Whigs, as we have seen, coalesced briefly around the "No Territory" policy and its standard-bearer Henry Clay, restoring the alliance between the party's Northern and Southern branches in a "mechanical mixture," as one Southern critic called it, "without, I trust, the least possible chemical affinity." The mixture proved volatile. For the terms of the Treaty of Guadalupe Hidalgo, ratified by the Senate on March 10, 1848, invalidated the "No Territory" position and sent the Whigs casting about for a new position and a new leader.[1]

The treaty recognized the Rio Grande as the boundary of Texas and ceded New Mexico and California, almost 1.2 million square miles of territory, to the United States; in return, the U.S. government paid the Mexican government $15 million. As Richard Griswold Del Castillo has related, the treaty had a devastating effect on Mexico (the area it relinquished was nearly half of its national domain) and on the roughly 100,000 Mexican residents of the ceded areas. Relatively few of those residents chose the option of repatriation in Mexico, which was wracked by chronic political and economic turmoil. Of those who remained in the conquered territory, a small minority, in keeping with the treaty's provisions, chose to retain their Mexican citizenship, while the majority opted to become U.S. citizens. Opponents of the treaty in the Mexican Congress, such as Manuel Crescencio Rejón, predicted that American racism would consign all Mexicans in the cession to a future of dispossession and disfranchisement. He was right—the treaty's provisions protecting the rights of those who elected to remain citizens of Mexico were eventually superseded by local laws that imposed a second-class U.S. citizenship on Mexican Americans. The discovery of gold in California in 1848 and the ensuing competition in the gold fields between "native" miners and "foreigners" ratcheted up the xenophobia, and inaugurated outbreaks of vigilantism, with its "attendant lynchings, harassment, and abuse."[2]

The treaty's impact on party politics was seismic. Michael Holt explains: "Democrats could now run on a platform of peace, prosperity, and a successful war that along with Polk's Oregon Treaty of 1846 almost doubled the size of the United States. Simultaneously, Democrats could flay Whigs as unpatriotic naysayers who had opposed the war and territorial expansion." To salvage their hopes, Whigs fell back on a tried-and-true strategy, one that had worked in 1840 during the "Tippecanoe and Tyler, Too" campaign—they rallied behind a military hero whose lack of political convictions made him the ideal sectional shape shifter. This time it was a career army officer utterly innocent of politics and previous party allegiance, General Zachary Taylor, of

Louisiana, whose grand victories in the Mexican War made him a household name. Not only did his military garlands neutralize Democratic charges that Whigs were unpatriotic, but also Taylor proved just as adept as Cass at playing to his two distinct audiences. To Northerners, Taylorites argued that the general had promised "not to veto congressional legislation"—not to stand in the way, in other words, of slavery restrictionists in Congress. To Southerners, the Taylor campaign harped on the general's biography—surely an elite Southern planter could be counted on to oppose the Wilmot Proviso to the last.[3]

Whig William Seward interpreted the party's efforts to capture the Free-Soil constituency in the North as a sign of how "respectable" antislavery had become in politics, but Garrisonian abolitionists and Liberty Party supporters thought otherwise—they tracked the duplicitous machinations of the two major parties and were determined to expose them to the public. Frederick Douglass's newspaper, the *North Star*, declared it "ineffably disgusting" that the "South is going for Gen. Taylor on the avowed ground that he is opposed to the exclusion of slavery from California and New Mexico, [while] the North supports him for precisely the opposite reason." Northerners were so "completely the slaves of party" that they were unwilling to admit that their own candidate could do anything wrong. Douglass and his allies tried to shake voters out of their stupor with scathing portraits of the candidates. Cass was characterized in the *North Star* as "one of the most miserable demagogues alive. Gross in person—almost idiotic in visage . . . without one particle of frank manhood in his composition . . . and ready and eager to stoop to the dirtiest work of the slave power." Taylor, for his part, was "a human butcher, . . . expert at devising the most expeditious and effective modes of wholesale slaughter . . . a man-killing, town-destroying, blood-hound hunting slaveholder."[4]

Determined to woo those who shared their "ineffable disgust" with the partisan status quo, Free-Soilers held their own nominating convention in August 1848 in Buffalo, New York. Prominent antislavery Whigs such as Joshua Giddings were on hand, as were "Barnburner" Democrats (New York followers of Martin Van Buren, who was now ardently committed to slavery restriction), disaffected Liberty Party men and Clay Whigs, and African American leaders such as Frederick Douglass and Henry Bibb. The convention delegates chose Martin Van Buren as their standard-bearer for the presidential contest. The Northern press marveled at how quickly the new party had coalesced. As the *Philadelphia Evening Bulletin* put it, "Never before, in the history of the country, was the spectacle exhibited of a new party starting into life on the eve of a Presidential election . . . in robust health and vigor." The reason, the *Bulletin* suggested, was that "nine men out of ten north of the Potomac are opposed to the extension of slave territory." The Democratic press offered a different explanation—that the Free-Soil Party was not new at all, merely the latest incarnation of federalism and abolitionism, an unholy alliance with "philanthropy for its motto, and disunion for its object."[5]

Historians have debated the relationship of abolitionism to the Free-Soil movement. Free-Soilers' repudiation of disunion as an aim and their embrace of the Constitution as antislavery clearly distinguished their platform from the Garrisonian creed. Garrison cautioned his followers that while they might privately take heart from the ways that Free-Soilers were stoking Northern antipathy to the Slave Power, publicly they could "in no case ever [seem] to be satisfied with the new party"—they had to oppose it in order to push it toward rejection of the false Union. As for the party's stance on race relations, an old scholarly consensus that Free-Soilers dramatically diluted the moral message of abolitionism had given way to a case for Free-Soil progressivism. While the Free-Soil Party platform advocated the nonextension of slavery rather than its immediate abolition, and refrained from asserting the equality of blacks with whites, Free-Soilers were, Richard H. Sewell has maintained, "as much committed to uprooting slavery everywhere as the most dedicated Garrisonians. Their sense of outrage was less, their patience in the face of evil vastly greater. But their goal was the same." Over the course of the 1848 campaign, Free-Soilers repeatedly ignored the dictates of expediency— of playing to the racial bigotry of white Northerners—and instead argued against the prevailing "spirit of caste" in the language of natural rights. A Free-Soil meeting in Philadelphia, for example, condemned the South for abridging the right to education. The participants resolved that "a just recognition of the rights of others is implied in the just perception of our own—that universal intelligence is the best security of social order, as well as personal freedom; and that no institution, therefore, can be congenial to a Republic, which arrogates an exclusive title to personal rights in favor of a single class of men, or which repels education and finds safety in ignorance." Free-Soilers rallied around the Wilmot Proviso, historian Sewell wrote, not only to guarantee that white Northern men could spread the free labor system into the West, but also because the Proviso "represented an effective antidote to the poisonous notion that slavery was a positive good, a blessing to be spread far and wide."[6]

That antidote was made much more potent by the infusion of undiluted moral rhetoric—of condemnations that detailed slavery's horrors—enunciated by Free-Soil women. The male leaders of the party focused on defending the constitutionality of nonextension; they left to women the work of indicting the sexual assault, incest, torture, and murder that were commonplace in bondage. Such a rhetorical division of labor, of course, inoculated Free-Soil men against the charge that they had "morbid" and "sickly" sympathies for slaves. Jane Grey Swisshelm, editor of the *Pittsburgh Saturday Visitor*, and Clarina I. H. Nichols, of the *Brattleboro Wyndham County Democrat*, proved especially fearless in condemning the sinfulness of Southern slaveholders and detailing the variety of their "criminal violations of Christian principle." In so doing, these women "fashioned an antislavery rhetoric that focused on the lives of slaves and the need for immediate abolition."[7]

A cadre of the most progressive Free-Soil men and women was helpful to the nascent woman's rights movement and participated in its inaugural convention at Seneca Falls, New York, in the summer of 1848. The Seneca Falls area of upstate New York was a hotbed of Free-Soil sentiment where many voters had forsaken the old, established parties to join the new antislavery party. Men and women from Free-Soil families, together with Hicksite Quaker abolitionists, temperance advocates, and dissident Methodists, comprised a local network of activists who mobilized behind the woman's rights banner; their experience in charitable, reform, and antislavery organizations "predisposed them to accept radical pronouncements and challenging proposals." Their leader was Elizabeth Cady Stanton, a veteran crusader for married women's property rights and abolition who, as Kathryn Kish Sklar puts it, elaborated her "own independent combination of Garrisonian and non-Garrisonian politics." The idea for the Seneca Falls convention grew out of Stanton's disappointment with the discriminatory treatment of female delegates at the 1840 World Anti-Slavery Convention in London. She and other female delegates, including the venerable Quaker Lucretia Mott, were not allowed to deliberate alongside the male delegates but were instead directed to sit behind a curtain in the gallery. Stanton and Mott vowed to hold a meeting of their own to redress such inequities, and in 1848 their pledge became a reality.[8]

Although Stanton had learned organizational tactics and the language of radical discontent from the immediatist movement, she broke with Garrisonians over the issue of withdrawing from electoral politics. She wrote to a fellow female abolitionist that she could not embrace the "doctrine of no human government" and that she was "in favor of political action, & the organization of a third party as the most efficient way of calling forth & directing action." She and her husband Henry Stanton supported first the Liberty Party and then the Free-Soil Party. Stanton's conviction that the vote was the single most important tool for reforming society animated her "Declaration of Sentiments," the manifesto of the Seneca Falls meeting. Patterned on the Declaration of Independence, "Sentiments" charges "Man" with "having deprived [Woman] of this first right of a citizen, the elective franchise, thereby leaving her without representation in the halls of legislation." While the manifesto also called for women's property rights, for economic and educational opportunities, for an end to the sexual double standard that demanded purity of women but not of men, and for the psychological independence of women from men's crippling claim of female inferiority, the bid for the vote was by far the most controversial resolution of the convention. In demanding the franchise, after all, women were asking not just for protection from exploitation but for an active agency in the work of governing and for full access to the public sphere. The suffrage resolution passed thanks to "eloquent appeals" by Stanton and Frederick Douglass. Once they had won the day, there was no looking back. "Resolutions on the 'elective franchise' would become standard fare in future women's rights conventions, and pass with little debate."[9]

The tensions inherent in Stanton's blend of Garrisonian and Free-Soil politics are revealed by the Seneca Falls convention's evasion of the issue of race. The "Declaration of Sentiments" did not acknowledge the unique plight of enslaved African American women or in any way conjure up the horrors of slavery. No African American women attended the meeting (Frederick Douglass was the sole black delegate). As Sklar observes, Stanton wanted to "raise a big tent" that welcomed white men and women from a variety of reform movements, not only from the immediatist ranks; inflammatory attacks on racial prejudice, she reckoned, might scare more moderate reformers away. African American women found their own outlet for woman's rights advocacy through their participation in the Negro Convention movement; an 1848 convention in Cleveland, at the behest of Frederick Douglass, featured a female speaker and passed a resolution in favor of "the equality of the sexes." Along with Douglass, abolitionist Sojourner Truth assumed the mantle of liaison and conscience keeper, in crossing the boundary between the white women's movement and black reform circles—and in forcefully reminding white men and women that racism and sexism were interwined. But differences persisted, with Garrisonians (who "probably [were] the majority" within the movement) arguing that woman's rights conventions must forcibly condemn slavery, while Free-Soilers like Swisshelm insisted that since there were many Americans who wanted to elevate women but "hate [blacks] most sovereignly," the two issues should remain separate.[10]

Proslavery Southerners, just as they lumped Free-Soilers with abolitionists, believed the nascent woman's rights movement in the North to be just another species of Garrisonian radicalism. The Seneca Falls convention, in other words, was interpreted in the South as one more symbol of the growing cultural divergence between the two sections. Although woman's rights activists constituted only a tiny percentage of the Northern population, their very existence spoke volumes—a woman's rights convention in the conservative South was literally unthinkable, and the movement claimed no support whatsoever south of the Mason-Dixon Line. Southern newspapers derided woman's rights conventions, calling their participants "cackling geese" whose deliberations were "one continuous scene of uproar and confusion." Indeed, Southern anxiety about Northern "Fanny Wrightism" increased men's scrutiny of Southern women's own political participation—women were still encouraged to express their partisanship through publishing and through male proxies, but their opportunities for public speaking were sharply curtailed. Slavery's defenders considered antebellum feminism to be a direct attack on Southern culture, and in some respects it was. For while feminists charged both Northern and Southern men with systematic gender discrimination, they reserved special opprobrium for the cult of chivalry that Southern men claimed to uphold. As Nancy Isenberg has explained, Garrisonian women and Free-Soil women alike indicted the cult of chivalry for "making brute power—the 'law of physical might'—the basis of political rights." The militaristic hero worship stoked by the conflict with Mexico relegated women to the margins of political life, as victims in need of protection or even as the spoils of war.[11]

ORGANIZING THE HOUSE

The election in 1848 of Whig candidate Zachary Taylor, who won eight slave states and almost prevailed in Democratic bastions such as Alabama and Mississippi, seemed to Garrisonians to be a resounding victory for the cult of chivalry, especially Southern chivalry. The war hero had trounced his opponents (Free-Soil candidate Van Buren, though his ticket won five times more votes than the Liberty ticket had in 1844, did not win a single Northern state) without articulating a clear or consistent vision about how to break the sectional impasse. But the Democratic leadership cherished no illusions that Taylor would do the South's bidding, and they branded him a traitor to the region even before he took office. The *New York Herald* predicted that while the Free-Soil Party was "on the way to its tomb," the "free soil principle, or the restriction upon the extension of slavery, has prevailed to an extraordinary extent in both the old parties of the free States." Disgusted at this point with the equivocations of both the Democrats and the Whigs, Calhoun in January 1849 convened a caucus of Southern congressmen to declare their opposition to the plan, afoot among their antislavery Northern colleagues, to abolish the slave trade in the District of Columbia. The meeting provided Calhoun with the occasion to deliver his "Southern Address," which "rehearsed a long litany of supposed northern aggressions against slaveholders' rights." The speech was so intemperate that fewer than half of the Southerners in Congress signed it. Whereas Calhoun's gag rule perorations had looked grimly forward to a time when antislavery forces could claim a Northern majority, he now grimly declared that "the great body of the North is united against our peculiar institution." He conjured up dystopian images of the not-distant day when a sufficient number of Northern states would be willing to pass an emancipation amendment to the Constitution. Emancipation would give rise to the "prostration of the white race"—whites would "change condition" with blacks, thus suffering "a degradation greater than has ever yet fallen to the lot of a free and enlightened people." Whites would have to relinquish the homes of their ancestors, abandoning their "country to our former slaves," and the South would become the "permanent abode of disorder, anarchy, poverty, misery, and wretchedness."[12]

Joel Silbey argues that Calhoun's caucus of Southern congressmen and his address to them, although failing to forge the coalition he had hoped for, nonetheless markedly "raised the intensity" of the sectional struggle. For "southerners' distemper . . . now moved from rhetorical flourishes to something more concrete." The real purpose of the Southern caucus was to send a stark message to Taylor on the eve of his ascendance. As the Washington, D.C., *National Era* (the organ of Tappan's American and Foreign Anti-Slavery Society) put it, Calhoun and the "dissolution gentry" wanted "to present such a front in the South, to accumulate such a pressure of Southern influence, as might overawe Northern members and the new Administration; and thereby prevent any efficient action against the extension of slavery." Calhoun was playing a nervy game for "party-effect"—he would keep the Democrats in line and cow the Whigs. Although most Southern Whigs stayed away from the caucus, it nonetheless served them notice that the "Democrats planned to hammer them as untrustworthy on slavery extension." Southern Whigs responded with the by-now-familiar argument that the Calhounites were disunionists, and that, as the *Richmond Whig* asserted, "nothing so much as Disunion would secure the destruction of Southern institutions."[13]

Free-Soilers relished the fact that the "northern tier of slave states" continued to resist "Calhounism." But Free-Soilers also claimed that Calhoun's game was more hazardous now than it had been in the past, for the North itself was "unyielding." "The people of the free states are united," the *National Era* editorialized, "in their resolve to maintain freedom in free territory" and would not be cowed into compromise. The newspaper's editor, veteran antislavery journalist Gamaliel Bailey, was representative of many slavery restrictionists in the way that he tacked back and forth between two rhetorical positions. His standard practice was to disparage Southern threats of disunion as empty bluffs. But at times, when Calhoun and his ilk were being especially "obstructionist," Bailey could not resist the impulse to "denigrat[e] the value of the Union," insisting in exasperation that he would rather have the North dissolve "the federal connection" than have it submit to the Slave Power.[14]

Zachary Taylor refused to be "overawed" by Calhoun's theatrics. After his inauguration in March 1849, Taylor set to work on a plan whereby California and New Mexico would skip the territorial stage and apply for statehood while Congress was in recess between March and December 1849. The new president thus denied Texas's claim, which had been supported by Polk, that its own border (and therefore the institution of slavery) extended deep into New Mexico. When the Thirty-first Congress convened, he would encourage it to admit California as a free state and to accept New Mexico under whatever terms, free or slave, its citizens preferred according to popular sovereignty. The plan reflected Taylor's staunch belief, as a seasoned slaveholder, that plantation agriculture was unsuited to the terrain of the Southwest; his desire to establish law and order in California, then in the throes of the raucous gold rush; and his conviction that the Wilmot Proviso itself was the source of the sectional impasse. By taking the matter of slavery extension out of the hands of Congress, he would suppress debate over the Proviso and mollify the Southerners who loathed it. But before he had a chance to present Congress with his fait accompli of two new applications for statehood, the Proviso once more reared its head in the midst of bitter debates about who would serve as Speaker of the House. The Democrats, who commanded a slim majority in the House with 112 representatives, proposed Georgia's Howell Cobb, an elite slaveholder and ardent Unionist who had cautioned moderation and condemned Calhoun's "Southern Address." Whigs, with 105 delegates, again favored Robert C. Winthrop (who had been Speaker of the Thirtieth Congress), himself a member of the Massachusetts elite and a voice for compromise. The Free-Soil Party, potential spoilers with 13 representatives, endorsed David Wilmot as a symbolic gesture. Each of the candidates took a rhetorical beating over the course of eight days of intense, acerbic deliberations and countless failed ballots. On December 12, debate reached a seeming nadir when Indiana Democrat William Brown, whose prospects had risen as Cobb's fell, revealed that he had struck a deal with the Free-Soil Party and promised to promote the Proviso. Under scorching criticism from Southerners, he withdrew his candidacy. But the worst was yet to come.[15]

On December 13, the House floor was the scene of an unprecedented exchange on the subject of disunion. William Duer, a New York Whig, made a plea that the Whigs and the Democrats compromise; he vowed, in a thinly veiled strike at Southern Democrats, that he would support anyone who was not a disunionist. To this, Thomas Bayly of Virginia took exception, shooting back that there were "no Disunionists in this House." Duer then upped the ante by pointing to Congressman Richard K. Meade of Virginia and labeling him a disunionist. Meade denied the charge, Duer called him a liar, and the House exploded in a babble of threats and accusations. The incident carried over tensions and ill feelings from the Thirtieth Congress, specifically from heated debates over the fate of slavery in the District of Columbia. Those debates had been sparked by the capture, in the spring of 1848, of seventy-six slaves from Washington, D.C., who were trying to escape up the Chesapeake Bay, aboard the schooner *Pearl*, to Pennsylvania. Joshua Giddings and John Palfrey in the House and John Parker Hale of New Hampshire in the Senate had championed the cause of the slaves and used the occasion to argue, in vain, for the abolition of slavery and the slave trade in the nation's capital. Their efforts had met with a new round of disunion gasconade from Southerners like Bayly and had set the stage for Calhoun's 1849 "Southern Address."[16]

Duer's charge against Meade was not the first time such a personal allegation had been made—John Minor Botts had accused Rhett and Upshur of disunionism, and had defended John Quincy Adams against the charge, back in 1842. But whereas that contest had quickly played itself out in the press, with the Southerners disavowing that they purposely sought sectional separation, the Duer-Meade exchange escalated into a prolonged "debate upon the contingencies and probabilities of disunion," as one exasperated witness put it. In a brash move that shocked even his fellow Southern Democrats, Georgian Robert Toombs stood before the House and sternly avowed that he, for one, *was* a disunionist. If the North sought to "drive us from the territories of California and New Mexico, purchased by the common blood and treasure of the whole people, and to abolish slavery in this district, thereby attempting to fix a national degradation" upon the South, he thundered, then "*I am for disunion*." Toombs's inflammatory speech was met by "loud bursts of applause" from his fellow Southerners, then echoed by his friend Alexander Stephens, who said that he "never expected to live to see the day when, upon this floor, he should be called upon to discuss the question of the union of these states." But called upon he was, declaring that he too believed that Northern aggression should be met with disunion.[17]

To Northern charges that this was just more bluster, Southerners retorted that the discourse on disunion had entered a new phase. Congressman William F. Colcock opined that "South Carolina abstractions"—the old doctrine of nullification—had "now assumed the form and pressure of solid truth" and were finding favor among its "gallant sisters, Georgia, Alabama, Mississippi, and Virginia." Henry Hilliard of Alabama likewise made the case that public opinion in the South demanded that its representatives make a "manly, truthful, bold declaration" of their willingness to dissolve the Union to protect Southern rights. In other words, a vanguard among the defenders of slavery and states' rights was moving unmistakably toward the embrace of disunion as a *program*. The end result was another improbable parliamentary coup for the South. In light of these threats by his fellow Southerners, Democrat Cobb looked more and more like a viable compromise candidate and managed to eke out a victory as the new Speaker. "Thus did the southern minority overcome a substantial northern preponderance within the chamber," writes Michael Holt; that triumph dramatically decreased the chances that Taylor's plans would prevail and, indeed, "decisively influenced the attempt to resolve the territorial crisis."[18]

Senator Salmon P. Chase, writing the prominent antislavery lawyer Edwin Stanton from Washington, D.C., the day after the Duer-Meade exchange, said the South's machinations were transparent: the slaveholders "resort freely to menaces of disunion" because they "are bent on having everything their way." After making a name for himself as an antislavery lawyer and a crusader for black civil rights in Ohio, Chase was sent to the U.S. Senate as a Free-Soiler in 1849 by a coalition of Free-Soilers and Democrats in the Ohio legislature. As Sean Wilentz explains, Chase joined senators such as Hale, who had converted to the Free-Soil Party, and William Seward of New York, a Whig "of established antislavery convictions." Thus, "more than ever," Congress featured "northern members whose political careers were . . . linked to agitation over slavery." For Chase, this fact promised deliverance from the South's "menaces": If only the anti-extensionists would unite, the North could finally call the South's bluff and "all the Southern fume would pass off in smoke."[19]

THE COMPROMISE OF 1850

With the House organized, President Taylor could formally promulgate his plan for resolving the sectional crisis. The congressional reaction to his Christmas Eve annual message reflected predictable partisan and sectional positions. On the extreme left of the political spectrum, Free-Soilers castigated Taylor for his willingness to accept the principle of popular sovereignty in New Mexico; on the extreme right, Calhounites, along with Whigs Toombs and Stephens, fumed about the admission of California as a free state and invoked disunion both as a process and a threat.

The intemperate January 1850 speech of North Carolina Whig Thomas Lanier Clingman sheds light on how and why disunion appeals were now making some inroads in the Upper South. Clingman represented western mountain districts of his state, where nonslaveholding farmers predominated and middle-class business and professional men constituted the political elite. These westerners had traditionally supported the Whig Party for economic reasons, particularly its commitment to state-subsidized "internal improvements" such as railroads. Both Whigs and Democrats had appealed to these voters in a language that promised to protect minority interests against "government tyranny." In 1845 Clingman, who had opposed the annexation of Texas and the gag rule, lost his bid for Congress to an opponent who tarnished him as "soft" on slavery and states rights. An ambitious man, Clingman reentered the electoral fray in 1847 determined to match Calhoun as a champion of Southern rights. He won a seat in the House. On January 22, 1850, he gave a speech in Congress that "placed him firmly and irrevocably in the 'ultra' camp" and signaled his alienation from his fellow North Carolina Whigs. Opposing a free California, he predicted that if slavery were hemmed in, the "condition of the South would . . . become that of St. Domingo." This was an argument, John C. Inscoe has noted, tailored to the fears of Clingman's nonslaveholding constituents—it raised the specter of black slaves overrunning the yeoman's South. Looking back, Clingman reflected that the "events of the past few years" were "rapidly weakening" the South's commitment to the Union. "Seeing that there appeared to be a settled purpose in the North to put them to the wall, many of our people, regarding a dissolution of the Union as the inevitable result of this aggression, have looked forward to the consequence of such a state of things." And well they should—if disunion came, he promised, the South would thrive economically and undertake modernization independently, at its own pace. Thus Clingman, in an appeal to his region's middle class, "stressed the idea of creating a 'new' South while protecting the 'Old.' "[20]

In the middle of the political spectrum, among those who disparaged such talk of disunion, partisan calculations prevailed. Northern Whigs fully supported Taylor's plan, while moderate Southern Whigs, torn between their sectional loyalty to slavery and their partisan commitment to fellow Southern Whig Taylor, were diffident. Northern Democrats approved the admission of California but chided the president for hypocritically co-opting their own doctrine of popular sovereignty and for lacking a strategy to deal with the rest of the Mexican Cession. Southern Democrats, on the other hand, overwhelmingly rejected Taylor's plan; their conviction that Taylor was treacherous only deepened in January, when he delivered two "special messages" that implied he might accept congressional passage of the Wilmot Proviso if his own alternative were not embraced by the lawmakers.[21]

What doomed Taylor's plan was not only the divisive nature of its provisions for California and New Mexico's expedited statehood, but also its conspicuous evasions on the other "Union-splitting issues" at the heart of the sectional stalemate, such as the slave trade and fugitive slave questions. Democratic organs like the *New York Herald* ventured that Taylor's evasions had disunionist tendencies—they "left the question open to the agitators of both ends of the Union to work upon, to excite and endanger the peace and happiness of the country." At the "point of disunion," the *Herald* speculated, Taylor would opportunistically swoop in and position himself as a "moderator" who would save the country from the very agitation he had knowingly fomented. With Congress deadlocked and Taylor's inadequate settlement a dead letter that could not command the requisite votes, aged Kentucky senator Henry Clay, already the legendary "Great Compromiser," once again offered a potential resolution to the crisis in the form of eight proposals that addressed each of the sources of sectional agitation. On January 29, 1850, he urged that California be admitted as a free state, that Texas yield to New Mexico the disputed terrain on their borders, that the federal government assume Texas's public debt from the pre-annexation period, that slave auctions be abolished in the District of Columbia but that slavery itself continue to prevail in the District, that Congress declare it had no power to interfere with the slave trade in the states, that the Fugitive Slave Law be strengthened to promote the recapture of slaves, and that Congress create territorial governments in the Mexican Cession with no conditions or restrictions on slavery, on the grounds that the climate there and the still-valid Mexican antislavery statutes would serve as preexisting barriers to slavery. The *New York*

Herald praised Clay as "chivalrous and patriotic" for deterring both sections from their "present fratricidal course."[22]

Despite the fact that Clay repudiated Northerners' hopes for abolition in the District of Columbia and the Wilmot Proviso in the territories—and that he endorsed the proslavery scheme, championed recently by Virginia senator James Mason, for a harsher Fugitive Slave Law—his legislative package was greeted by some Southern Democrats as a capitulation to the antislavery North. "As soon as Clay sat down on January 29," Michael Holt writes, nine Southern senators "jumped to their feet to protest that his supposed 'compromise' was outrageously unjust to the South." They not only rejected a free California, they also interpreted the Texas border adjustment and Clay's support for Mexico's antislavery statutes as an effort to curtail slavery. Moreover, they excoriated him for conceding too much in his opinion that abolition in the District of Columbia was "inexpedient" at the moment, rather than "flatly unconstitutional." Although it has long been a commonplace of historical scholarship that Clay's proposal was eventually reworked into the Compromise of 1850, Holt offers a corrective to this view; he painstakingly maps out the "tumultuous, exhausting, and agonizing eight-month struggle in the Congress to shape a more acceptable, or at least passable, compromise than the plan Clay had offered."[23] Those months of struggle, it should be noted, witnessed both a distinct shift toward the discussion of disunion as a process and as a program.

A little more than a week after Clay submitted his proposal, with senators already scrambling to rework it, the petition debate flared up again in the Senate. The result was a protracted exchange over disunion, one that reveals just how acutely Northern and Southern representatives had come to distrust each other. The spark in this case was the presentation, by New Hampshire's John Parker Hale, of a petition from inhabitants of Pennsylvania and Delaware for the "peaceful dissolution of the Union." Hale, who with John Quincy Adams had led the charge against the gag rule, was the leading antislavery voice in the Senate and a pillar of the new Free-Soil coalition. Would the petition be "laid upon the table" (dismissed without a hearing) or would it be received, printed, and possibly referred to committee? In presenting the memorial, Hale was clearly seeking to expose Southern hypocrisy. Predictably, his Southern colleagues assailed the petition as scurrilous, charged Hale with acting as a tool of the "ultra abolitionists," and asserted in no uncertain terms that Congress had no jurisdiction to dissolve the Union. Hale shot back that the "forcible dissolution of the Union had been threatened here time after time" by Southerners, and that a petition from some disgruntled North Carolinians, calling for disunion should slavery be endangered, had recently been received without incident. Although the debate eventually fizzled out, and the Senate adopted the practice of tabling rather than receiving and referring disunion petitions, Hale's gambit served the purpose of clarifying the difference between Northern and Southern invocations of disunion. Northern petitioners claimed to seek "peaceful" dissolution by congressional fiat, while Southerners asserted that disunion would inevitably produce a clash between contending forces and that—as Jefferson Davis of Mississippi explained to Hale—"if this Union is ever to be dissolved, it must be by the actions of the States and the people," not Congress.[24]

Significantly, although Hale and others had presented a smattering of disunion petitions from Northern constituents in preceding years, none since Adams's controversial Haverhill petition of 1842 had been "considered [so] alarming," as Hale put it, and had brought such calumny upon the head of its presenter. (Hale, like Adams, disavowed the content of the petition, and claimed only to be defending the principle of free speech.) In the wake of the Hale controversy, Garrisonians pressed their case for disunion even as they decried Clay's compromise proposal. For example, a Philadelphia memorial for "peaceful dissolution," signed by whites and blacks in late February 1850, listed the grievances of the free states, among which was Clay's proposed compromise itself—the hated measure would oblige Northerners to aid the South in slave catching.[25]

Some Northerners chose to marginalize disunion petitioners as harmlessly misguided. Democratic congressmen Graham N. Fitch of Indiana, in a February 14, 1850, speech in the House, ridiculed Southerners for their "ludicrous" sensitivity to threats from the North: "If [Southerners] would pause, if they would but wait to examine the disunion petitions laid before certain northern Legislatures, they would find many of the signers to be females. Do they design making war upon these?" But more often moderate Northerners condemned disunion petitions as profoundly dangerous. The *Washington Daily Union* excoriated Hale and Giddings for catering to the "morbid delusions" of "fanatics." "In helping to weaken the bonds of the Union by familiarizing the public mind to the idea of disunion," the paper charged, "they commit a substantial treason against their country." The *Philadelphia Public Ledger* also considered disunion treasonable and warned that a separation of North and South would "*Europeanise* this continent" by filling it with "national subdivision, wars, standing armies, aristocracy, dynasties, poverty, ignorance, degradation, incessant fraud of upper classes to retain exclusive privileges, and occasional and bloody struggles of lower classes for rights which they would not know how to recover, enjoy or maintain." The *Ledger* claimed to speak for the "immense majority" in "both sections" who "consider separation as the greatest evil which could befall this continent and the world."[26]

By referring to Europe's turmoil, the *Ledger* tapped deep-seated fears among Americans about the implications of Europe's failed revolutions of 1848, particularly about the fate of France. Although France's new revolutionary movement had initially been hailed in both North and South as a strike for republicanism against "aristocratic misrule," the revolution's descent into mob violence and its culmination in the election of a new despot, Napoleon Bonaparte, as president of the Second Republic, caused Americans to recoil in confusion. The confluence of the European revolutions and the territorial debates over slavery, Michael Morrison observes, precipitated an identity crisis for Americans—a crisis over the meanings and legacy of America's own Revolution. The Proviso debates had given rise to distinct sectional interpretations of the American Revolution, with antirestriction Southerners arguing that the struggle against Britain was fundamentally "a defense of minority rights in a constitutional government" and Northern restrictionists maintaining that it was a struggle by colonists to "defend their autonomy from the encroachments of a government hostile to their liberties and ambitions." Both sides positioned themselves as conservators of the true principles of 1776. These positive images of a conservative Revolution were now juxtaposed with negative images of Europe's own struggles; the picture of European revolutions gone wrong was a painful reminder of the ever-present threat to republics of declension, of radicalism that led to anarchy. Moderate and conservative commentators in North and South alike worried that the "incubus of European radicalism" was infecting American public life, and that both abolitionism and woman's rights were symptoms of "external contamination." Significantly, some progressive antislavery commentators read their own message in Europe's woes. Thus the *Friends' Intelligencer* of

Philadelphia editorialized that the fact that Europe was "convulsed with revolutions and reactions" proved that pacifism was the only means to preserve the "most perfect fabric of government that the world ever saw."[27]

John C. Calhoun took little comfort from this Northern backlash against Garrisonian disunionism, for he believed that neither Garrison nor his followers truly desired peaceful separation from the South. To Calhoun, the 1848 revolutions were still more proof that slavery was "the world's great conservative republican social force," the best bulwark against excessive democracy and "tyranny of the mob"—against the "radical spirit in Europe [that] now threatened America." On March 4, 1850, Virginia's James Mason, acting as proxy for the ailing Calhoun, delivered what would be Calhoun's last address to the Senate. In some respects, the speech struck familiar notes— Calhoun premised the South's right to extend slavery on his theory of state sovereignty, and he focused on disunion as a long-standing and "natural" process. Tracing this process back to the abolition agitation of 1835, he declared that, one by one, the cords that bound the Union together were fraying and snapping; the religious schisms were a case in point. But Calhoun was also at pains to parse for his allies the North's discordant evocations of Union and disunion. Northern professions of love for the Union he discounted as fraudulent, and Garrisonian resolutions for peaceful dissolution, as equally dishonest. What the North and the "Government"—now fully in the sway of antislavery forces—really wanted, Calhoun contended, was not to restore harmony with the South or to cast it off. The North's "real objects," he asserted, were "power and aggrandizement"—namely, to destroy slavery and the "historic compromise" that sustained the republic, and to control and claim the South. The North was already the more powerful section and would use force if necessary to compel the South to submit to its will. Thus the North alone had "the responsibility of saving the Union." If it did not repudiate the treacherous antislavery creed, the South would have to choose between subjugation and secession.[28]

Two days after Calhoun's speech, Salmon Chase wrote to a constituent back in Ohio, articulating the Free-Soil alternative both to disunion from the South and to the forceful subjugation of it. The constituent, L. S. Abbott, had sent Chase a petition urging a "peaceful separation of the Union." Chase gently rejected the petition, explaining that it was not "beneficial to the great cause." Chase understood that Abbott's main objective was "to let the

South see that you cannot be intimidated by threats of disunion." But the best way to do that, Chase advised, was to critique the "aggressions of the Slave Power" and petition for "the removal of slavery from the whole sphere of exclusive national jurisdiction, without regard to Southern menaces of dissolution." Disunionism, Chase elaborated, was defeatist—it "[took] for granted that slavery & slaveholding dominion are to be perpetual and perpetually extended"; therefore, separation was a necessary prelude to abolition. Wasn't it more productive, Chase implied, to assume that Free-Soil forces, by working within the political process, might actually triumph in restricting slavery's spread?[29]

WEBSTER'S APOSTASY

The dangers for Free-Soilers of guilt by association with Garrison were dramatized in Daniel Webster's memorable March 7, 1850, address to the Senate. Calhoun, with his profession that Northerners alone could save the Union, had thrown down a gauntlet; Webster now picked it up and used it to deliver a rhetorical slap in the face to the abolitionists. An imposing orator whose cultlike following dubbed him the "god-like Daniel," Webster was the third pillar of the "Great Triumvirate" of antebellum statesmen (only Clay and Calhoun rivaled him in renown). Thus the Congress and the nation listened intently when Webster took the Senate stage on March 7 to deliver his procompromise rebuttal to Calhoun. Like Calhoun, Webster traced a process of declension whereby the nation lost sight of the consensus on slavery that had been forged in the days of the early republic. But whereas Calhoun had identified the abolitionists' petition campaign as the crucial moment of sectional betrayal, Webster argued that both sections had fallen away from the path of righteousness. The South's drift toward the "positive good" view of slavery had begun with the cotton boom of the 1790s. As for the North, Webster believed, it bore a significant share of the blame for the eclipse of "necessary evil" gradualism. Why? Because Northern abolitionists, misled by "strange enthusiasms," had excited such a backlash in the South that moderate voices had been silenced (Webster regarded the abortive Virginia slavery debates of 1832 as a case in point).[30]

This blow from Webster was quickly followed by another. In assessing the grievances of the two sections, the Massachusetts senator endorsed the

THE HURLY-BURLY POT.

This procompromise lithograph from 1850 casts Wilmot, Garrison, Calhoun, and Greeley as Macbeth's witches, stirring the pot of radicalism "Till disunion come!" (Courtesy of the Library of Congress)

South's complaint that the North, in passing personal liberty laws, had reneged on its constitutional commitment to return fugitive slaves. "The South is right, and the North is wrong," Webster said bluntly. He ended the speech with a critique of the concept of "peaceable secession" that was every bit as much directed to Garrisonians as it was to Calhounites. Knowing that disunionists in both camps claimed that they were making a moral—not a political—stand, Webster declared peaceful disunion a "moral impossibility." To drive home his point that talk of secession was the work of fanatics in each section—not a sign that the declension had produced two fundamentally antagonistic societies—he posed a series of rhetorical questions: "A voluntary separation . . . . Why, what would be the result? Where is the line to be drawn? What States are to secede? What is to remain American? What am I to be?—an American no longer? Where is the flag of the Republic to remain?" To Calhoun's claim that the process of disunion was natural, Webster retorted: "There are natural causes that would keep and tie us together, and there are social and domestic relations which we could not break, if we would, and which we should not, if we could." When Calhoun interrupted the speech to assert that "the Union can be broken" and that "great moral causes will break it," Webster replied: "I know, sir, this Union can be broken up; every Government can be." But such "forcible severance" could never masquerade as a constitutional act of self-defense. Of Calhoun's secessionist specter, Webster declared "That is revolution—that is revolution!"[31]

Webster's speech was an appeal to the "pragmatic Northerners" who were his "main base of support back home," John C. Waugh writes. And it worked. Northerners rallied to offer a dazzling array of public gestures of support for Webster; businessmen in New York and Boston, who "hated the idea of commerce-disrupting disunion," were especially vocal in their approbation. The Democratic *Washington Daily Union*, which had praised Calhoun's speech for alerting the nation to its impending danger and to Northern responsibility for the sectional breach, now thanked Webster for moving to "heal the breach in that spirit of conciliation, on those principles of compromise on which the Constitution was made." Even Southern newspapers hailed Webster's moral courage and credited him with turning back the tide of sectionalism. The *Richmond Republican* declared that he stood "upon an eminence of intellectual statesmanship unapproached in the present age" (and that Garrisonians, by contrast, were "cockroaches navigating shingles"). Calhoun himself, Wilentz points out, "found much to praise in Webster's speech," as it showed a " 'yielding on the part of the North.' "[32]

While those who longed for an end to sectional agitation could conclude that the Great Triumvirate—with Calhoun, Clay, and Webster each playing his appointed role—had skillfully steered the country through another crisis, abolitionists, of course, were appalled by Webster's attack on them and his support for the fugitive slave plank in Clay's compromise. They marshaled their finest invective in response. Wendell Phillips, in a review of Webster's speech for Boston's *Liberator*, called it a "cold, tame, passionless political commodity" not worthy of a so-called statesman. Of the endless rebukes to Webster featured in the *Liberator*, none perhaps was so pointed as a piece called "A Few Words to the Godlike Daniel" by an anonymous "Lady." She condemned his speech's "utter baseness" and his lack of empathy for slaves, writing "O that thou wert for a while compelled to take lessons in a rice swamp or a sugar plantation!" Abolitionists convened a series of anti-Webster meetings. An assembly of "the nominally free colored citizens of Boston and vicinity" lamented that "slave-hunters were already infesting Boston, and other cities and towns in the North, as an immediate result of Mr. Webster's speech." The group passed a resolution reminding Bostonians that if the new Fugitive Slave Law were passed, "it is *our households* and *our children* which will be outraged by its atrocious violations of all legal provisions for the security of citizens, and even of the Constitution of the United States." As for Webster's legendary skill as an orator, the Reverend Samuel Ringgold Ward noted that beautiful diction was no substitute for moral integrity: "Beauty unchaste is beauty in disgrace."[33]

On the heels of Webster's speech came the offering of New York's William Seward, the most radical antislavery Whig in the Senate and a trusted adviser to President Taylor. Seward disdained the pronouncements of the Great Triumvirate and rejected the idea that California's admission to the Union should be contingent on compromises with the Slave Power. He based his opposition to the Fugitive Slave Law and his support for the Wilmot Proviso on an antislavery interpretation both of the Constitution and of the Founders' intentions. Slavery, he said, is "temporary, accidental, partial and incongruous," while freedom is "perpetual, organic, . . . and in harmony with the Constitution of the United States." The address is best known for Seward's provocative assertion that not only the nation's founding document but also "a higher law than the Constitution" bound Americans to oppose slavery and extend liberty. Congressmen, "as God's stewards," had a moral obligation to guarantee freedom in the Mexican Cession. In their attention to Seward's "higher law" doctrine, historians have overlooked what is perhaps the real heart of this famous speech: his extended meditation on what he called the "all-absorbing argument that the Union is in danger of being dissolved." Seward agreed with Webster that there was no possibility of peaceful dissolution; happen when it may, he said, disunion "will and must be revolution." But Seward, like Wilmot and Chase, rejected as unreasonable the notion that there were "omens of revolution" in the air. Turning Calhoun's rationale against him, Seward argued that Southern threats of disunion were to be distrusted, not only because they were a product of "high excitement" and "passions" but also because they were disingenuous—"uttered under the influence of a controlling interest to be secured, a paramount object to be gained," namely "power in the republic."[34]

Seward, again reversing Calhoun, argued that it was not the North but the South that had the primary responsibility for putting out the fires of sectionalism. The South could and should choose to ride the "tide of social progress," which would bring peaceful, gradual, and voluntary emancipation. The alternative was disunion and civil war—a course clearly against Southern self-interests, for it would result in "violent but complete and immediate emancipation." Southerners should not fear that peaceful change would proceed too fast, because, Seward explained, the Constitution, the political process, the Democratic Party itself, and "prejudices of caste and color" in the North all served to "break the force of emancipation." Seward's message to both proslavery forces and abolitionists was clear: that the ingenious "machinery" of the American government was itself the best safeguard against revolution. The electoral process conceived by the Founders was the "common arbiter" to which North and South equally were bound to submit. The ancient fear of disunion—of the "trial of faction"—obscured the strength of the U.S. government and political system. Since the time of George Washington, Seward lamented, Americans had a "profound distrust" of the Union's "perpetuity." Americans had come to "cherish that distrust, with pious reverence." He concluded: "It is time to shake off that fear, for fear is always weakness."[35]

Seward was echoed by Senators Hale and Chase in speeches that were equal parts idealistic evocations of sacred duties and expressions of scorn for Clay, Webster, and Calhoun. The Democratic press flatly refused to acknowledge the ways that these antislavery senators tried to distance themselves from Garrisonian disunionism. Democrats predictably fastened onto the "higher law" theory and deemed it heretical—the speech was a sign that Seward was just a disciple of the "New Messiah" Garrison, as the *Democratic Review* sneeringly put it. While antislavery forces had "begun with ludicrous vehemence to assert their love for the Union," the journal opined, the truth was that they were "ceaselessly attempting to deprive the South of the rights guaranteed by the Constitution, and to destroy the compromises in which alone [the Union's] vitality exists." Seward, Giddings, and their allies were trying to lead Northerners, in a process foretold by the "far-seeing" Calhoun, "to the abyss." Eager to refute the charge that Southern threats of disunion were revolutionary, states' rights Southerners in Congress, in the weeks after

Seward's speech, turned it against the North. Congressman Thomas H. Averett, a Virginia Democrat, starkly proclaimed: "I accuse the accusers. I charge them with fomenting all of this strife, and getting up and fostering revolution." Averett's purpose was to keep alive Calhoun's argument that the antislavery North had effected an unlawful "usurpation . . . of this Government" and was now using the government to "destroy the equal rights of the southern States."[36]

When Calhoun finally succumbed, on March 31, 1850, to bronchitis and old age, Clay and Webster eulogized him on the Senate floor as a great statesman whose devotion to the Union never wavered—and who favored, to the last, honorable compromise, not revolution. But Calhoun's ardent enemies, such as Senator Thomas Hart Benton, felt no compassion or relief. "There may be no vitality in his body, but there is in his doctrines," Benton feared. As for Calhoun's acolyte Robert Barnwell Rhett, he was eager to claim that Calhoun had not merely warned of disunion but, in the end, had wished for it. Rhett extolled his idol before the South Carolina Senate, asking rhetorically: "Had [Calhoun's] mighty spirit devised some way to save the Union, consistent with the liberties of the South? Or did he wish to utter there that word which all his lifetime he could not speak, although wrong and oppression tortured him—that word, which dying despair could alone wring from his aching heart—disunion!!"[37]

Calhoun's legacy hung in the balance as Clay and his colleagues debated the merits of combining the various elements of the Mexican Cession proposal into an omnibus bill. On May 8, a select committee under Clay's leadership presented to the Senate the reworked compromise, with three elements: the fugitive slave measure, a bill illegalizing slave auctions in the District of Columbia, and an omnibus bill on the Mexican Cession. The omnibus bill conceded a greater share of land to Texas, and therefore to slavery, than Clay's original border adjustment had, but it also specified, following Stephen Douglas's proposal, that settlers in the newly designated New Mexico and Utah territories could resolve the slavery issue through popular sovereignty. The omnibus was the brainchild of Mississippi's Senator Henry Foote, who sought to link the admission of a free California to the repudiation of the Wilmot Proviso in the rest of the Mexican Cession. But the repackaging of the compromise did not bring instant results. With Northern pro-Proviso Whigs and Southern Democrats (who favored extending the

Missouri Compromise line to the west) arrayed against Clay's new proposal, Congress was at an impasse. "For the salvation of the South as well as their own," William J. Cooper Jr. has observed, "the southern Democrats put their faith in a southern convention."[38]

THE FIRST SECESSION CRISIS

The states' rights vanguard had hoped that the Nashville Convention of June 1850 might unite Southern Whigs and Democrats and produce an ultimatum to the North; that hope was founded on the fact that prominent Southerners of both parties had teamed up in October 1849 to plan the convention in the name of Southern unity. The disunionists drummed up delegates with belligerent talk of teaching the North a lesson. A speech by Colonel S. W. Trotti in Barnwell, South Carolina, for example, vowed that the convention would bring together the "leading intellects" from all parts of the South to threaten the North with disunion and to make the North feel the Southern "capacity for not only sustaining ourselves, *but injuring them.*" The masterminds of the convention, including General E. C. Wilkinson of Mississippi, James Hammond of South Carolina, and Beverly Tucker of Virginia, calculated that Southern unity would translate into "Cooperative State Secession"—a scenario in which South Carolina would no longer stand isolated in its defiance of the federal government. They contrasted the grim fate of race war, which awaited the South if the Free-Soil movement prevailed, with the "magnificent future and glorious destiny of the Southern Confederacy."[39]

Long-standing advocates of the right of secession such as Hammond and Tucker were joined in conjuring up a Southern confederacy by zealous new converts to the Southern rights standard, most notably Edmund Ruffin of Virginia and William Lowndes Yancey of Alabama. Ruffin, a noted agriculturalist nurtured on the political philosophy of John Taylor and the Tertium Quids, had long been urged by his friend Hammond to join in the work of preparing the South for disunion. Ruffin had hesitated; as late as March 1850, he wrote in the *Richmond Enquirer* that he was no disunionist and that abolitionists were the "true and only disunionists" for denying the constitutionality of slavery. But by the summer of 1850, Ruffin had shaken off his doubts and "joined the crusade for Southern nationalism." He had come to believe, his biographer Betty L. Mitchell has explained, that an independent

Southern confederacy could successfully "seal itself off from outside enemies and thus guarantee its own permanent internal safety." Yancey, for his part, had throughout the 1840s espoused a proslavery nationalism and denounced the likes of Rhett for raising the specter of secession. But his political trajectory shifted during the Mexican War, and in 1848, in a kind of singlehanded secession, he dramatically bolted the Democratic Party's national convention on the grounds that popular sovereignty was too weak a platform and would fail to guarantee slaveholder access to the territories. Yancey grew more disillusioned during the 1850 debates; he was so disgusted by the loss of California that he, too, entered the Southern nationalist camp. By the time of the Nashville Convention, Yancey shared Rhett's conviction that with antislavery forces ascendant in the federal government, there was no longer a "middle ground between *submission* and *secession*."[40]

But forces defending the middle ground prevailed. Clay's reworked compromise proposal dashed the hopes of would-be secessionists, as the Great Compromiser's fellow Southern Whigs rallied around him and dissociated themselves from the Nashville initiative. "A Southron," writing in the *American Whig Review*, asserted that "secession and dissolution are the very worst of all evils"; disunion would "cast loose [the South] from the only bond that links us with the civilized and enlightened world." The writer had faith that Northerners would abide by the new compromise. In other words, Southern Whigs, for partisan advantage, could and did again cloak themselves in the mantle of Unionism—of "southern rights with peace"—and tarnish their Democratic opponents as disunionists. William G. Brownlow of Tennessee, in his paper the *Knoxville Whig*, tried to taint Southern disunionists with Northern radicalism, likening the Nashville meeting to the Hartford Convention. Whig congressman Edward Stanly of North Carolina went so far as to charge that for the convention to meet in Nashville—so near the final resting place of Andrew Jackson, the man who had stopped nullification dead in its tracks—was an "insult" to Jackson's memory and an "outrage upon the feelings of the people of this country." North Carolina, he insisted, would not let itself be bullied by the haughty South Carolinians into any such "wicked scheme."[41]

This kind of talk forced the Southern Democrats meeting in Nashville to disavow any intention to break up the Union and to claim instead that a united Southern front would preserve Southern rights *and* the Union; they cast the meeting, J. Mills Thornton has written, as "not secessionist but merely consultative." The delegates passed a platform advocating the extension of the old Missouri Compromise line (36°30′) across the Western territories. The negative public reaction to the convention in most of the South revealed that Rhett and the fire-eaters, in calling for a united front, had underestimated not only the enduring strength of partisan divisions but also the general mood of the region. The vast majority of the Southern electorate had a wait-and-see attitude and continued to hope for a congressional resolution of the sectional struggle. Only in South Carolina, Alabama, and Mississippi did disunion radicals such as Rhett have significant leverage. In the rest of the South, mainstream politicians could use these "fire-eaters" as foils, as "radical purveyors of doom." "As long as the [Clay] compromise remained before the Congress," according to Cooper, the likes of Rhett could "do little more than howl in the political wilderness."[42]

Even the Deep South state of Georgia, whose Toombs and Stephens had so dramatically broken ranks with their own Whig Party in opposing Taylor's plan, offered little public support to the Nashville movement. The Georgia electorate was simply worn out by the squabble over California. Moreover, they did not share the secessionists' sense of urgency. "Skeptical about the chances for transplanting slavery anyway," Anthony Gene Carey has stated, "voters found it difficult to believe that the creation of a free state on the Pacific coast threatened their firesides or justified loose, radical talk." Attuned to this reality, Georgia's own "great triumvirate" of Democrat Cobb and Whigs Stephens and Toombs positioned themselves as a procompromise bloc and condemned the Nashville delegates for trying to hijack the Democratic Party as a "secession vehicle." These Georgia leaders were every bit as committed to the slave system as were Calhoun and Rhett. But they styled themselves, at this crucial moment, as pragmatists, arguing that a Senate compromise would destroy the hated Wilmot Proviso and establish the principle of congressional noninterference with slavery in the territories.[43]

The most significant barrier to compromise, it turned out, was President Taylor himself, who stubbornly clung to his own unpopular plan. To the disgust of his fellow Southern Whigs like Toombs and Stephens, Taylor was particularly adamant about the Texas–New Mexico border issue and had empowered New Mexico's governor to resist with force should Texans make good on their recent threat to encroach on his territory. Taylor's death, on

July 9, 1850, from an intestinal ailment he had contracted during a July 4 ceremony, ushered in the last act in the compromise drama. He was succeeded by the vice president, New York Whig Millard Fillmore, who, embittered by Taylor's dismissive treatment of him and appalled to learn just how close Texas and New Mexico were to a shooting war over the boundary dispute, moved quickly to support the compromise. He disbanded Taylor's cabinet and replaced it with one composed of procompromise men, most notably Daniel Webster. Fillmore's influence could not forestall the demise of the omnibus bill, which went up in flames in late July. But it did set the stage for a new would-be savior of the Union—Illinois senator Stephen Douglas—to try a new approach. Always skeptical of the omnibus method, Douglas calculated that he could push through the Senate a series of individual measures, united by a common principle, namely popular sovereignty. Fillmore lent him decisive aid in emphasizing to Congress the acute nature of the Texas–New Mexico imbroglio and urging the lawmakers to defuse the situation immediately by drawing up a border acceptable to Texas. The new Texas boundary bill indemnified Texas to the tune of five million dollars for "surrendering its claims" to New Mexican terrain. Although most antislavery Whigs considered it an unwarranted concession to the Slave Power, the measure received enough Northern Whig votes to pass the Senate. They had, Holt explains, "bent before the pressure of Fillmore [and] Webster."[44]

With the North having yielded somewhat on this first bill, the way was cleared for the rapid passage of the other measures—the California statehood bill, the organization of New Mexico and Utah on the basis of popular sovereignty, the Fugitive Slave Act, and the bill ending the slave trade in the District of Columbia. By the end of September the House of Representatives had followed suit. The longest session in Congress's history had produced the "Compromise" of 1850. But according to William Freehling, the word "armistice" better describes the fruits of Congress's labor. A procompromise cadre of Northern Democrats, "especially those from the most southern North," had, once again, "swallowed their resentment and aided the slaveholders" in passing the Fugitive Slave Law. Northern opponents of the statute, such as Indiana congressman George W. Julian, wasted no time in declaring that it tainted the entire compromise as immoral. Commenting on the atmosphere of fear that Clingman and other Southern militants had created, Julian said that "the threat of disunion is the thunder with which, as usual, we are to be driven from our purpose, and frightened into uncomplaining silence." Julian held that Northerners would not submit and the flawed compromise would not bring sectional repose. "Harmony, permanent peace, cannot result from the triumph of wrong, unless the world is governed by demons," he affirmed in a September 1850 speech.[45]

As for the other elements of the compromise, Southern Whigs "from the most northern South" had provided the decisive margin in the passage of the Texas adjustment and popular sovereignty measures in the House. The vote on California statehood was particularly revealing: 64 percent of congressmen from slaveholding border states supported a free California, as did 27 percent of the representatives from the Middle South. Only 2 percent of Deep South statesmen, by contrast, voted for California statehood. In other words, moderates in the middle of the political spectrum had acceded to the compromise; antislavery "upper North" Whigs and Lower South Democrats had not.[46]

Such statistics were ominous, as were the immediate efforts by Southern rights Democrats in the Deep South to declare the compromise (especially Texas's loss of territory and a free California) a travesty that justified renewed threats of disunion. A second Nashville Convention met in November 1850, with fifty-nine delegates representing seven Southern states. The delegates failed to support a South Carolina proposal advocating cooperative secession but did pass measures asserting the constitutional right of secession. The governors of Georgia and Mississippi called for special conventions to debate secession. And anticompromise Southern rights parties vied with procompromise Union ones for the governor's chair and seats in state legislatures and Congress in elections in 1850 and 1851.[47]

Significantly, the Southern rights position was compromised in these political contests by the persistent unwillingness of some of slavery's most ardent champions to accept the mantle of "disunionist." Senator Jefferson Davis, who had represented Mississippi during the congressional debates, was among the leading Southern opponents of the compromise; in a series of speeches delivered in his home state in 1851, he denounced it as a fraud and a terrible defeat for the South. Davis defended the abstract right of secession, arguing that "if the colonies had a right to secede from the British . . . by the same reason a State had a right to secede from the federal government." But unlike Mississippi's fire-eating governor John A. Quitman, who believed that the moment for actual secession had arrived, Davis maintained that the current crisis did not yet warrant such a last resort. Instead, he clung steadfastly to the notion that he and his Southern rights compatriots were the true Unionists—defending "the Union that our fathers bled to establish"—and that abolitionists were the real disunionists. Rather than following the lead of Rhett and Tucker in conjuring up images of a glorious Southern confederacy, Davis chose to tap the public's fear of dissolution. Abolitionist aggression, he insisted, threatened to engulf the country in "all the horrors of civil war." Davis's choice of tactics illustrates how closely bound he and other Southern defenders of slavery remained to the national Democratic Party, which had long succeeded in using disunion as an accusation. Even in the Deep South, the mystique of the party, like that of the Union itself, remained strong.[48]

On the face of it, this "secession crisis" of 1850–51 soon fizzled out. Despite the maneuvering of men like Davis, Unionists in the Southern states managed to tarnish their anticompromise opponents as extremists whose rash insistence on immediate secession would bring the nation to the brink of war. The Unionist tendencies of the Southern electorate again prevailed. State elections in Georgia, Mississippi, and Alabama returned strong majorities for the Union parties, uniting Whigs and nonslaveholding Democrats against the self-styled "States Rights" vanguard. Toombs, Stephens, and Cobb continued to try to have it both ways—to posture as ardent defenders of Southern rights and to cast disunion, as Webster had done in his March speech, as "revolution."[49]

While these Unionists held the field, however, it is important to remember that they shared with their disunionist counterparts in the Deep South not only an unequivocal commitment to slavery but also the language of "masculinity and male honor." Thus the Georgia platform of December 1850, passed by a state convention in which Unionist delegates predominated, declared that the "preservation of our much loved Union" depended on the North's "faithful execution" of the measures in the 1850 compromise, especially the Fugitive Slave Law. As Christopher J. Olsen shows in his study of Mississippi politics, the Union Party in that state successfully defended the Compromise of 1850 as "honorable and just." To disunionist charges that Unionism was a "submissionist," and therefore feminine and servile, position, compromise supporters retorted that the states' rights wing was too "sensitive" and "touchy," quick to see an affront where there was none. Petulant fire-eaters threatened Mississippi with disgrace by making threats of secession that they were not prepared to back up. Deep South Unionists believed that only if the secessionists backed down could the South keep alive the charge that Northern radicals were the true disunionists and would bear full responsibility for any future national schism. As one Mississippi Unionist wrote: "If the constitution is violated by them [Northern radicals], they are the disunionists, and they should be stigmatized as such." The writer saw no merit, at this stage, in wearing the mantle of the revolutionary—he desired, as he wryly put it, to "matriculate" at some school other than that of "South Carolina *Rhett-oric*."[50]

Of course, the unmistakable corollary to this argument that the South should support an honorable compromise was that the South should at all costs reject a truly dishonorable one. Northern papers thus discerned an ominous turn in the very convening of the Nashville and Georgia meetings; although the conventions had not adopted a program of secession, they had served notice to the North to "make the union of the States dependent upon the perpetuity of certain acts of Congress." In other words, even the Unionist resolutions of the Deep South states contained an implicit threat: disunion was the price that the North would pay if it did not honor the compromise. The *National Era* editors, commenting on the Georgia platform, countered: "We have had enough of this miserable dictation and menace. It is the discipline of the plantation, and may do for slaves, but not freemen." According to that paper, it was, in light of the conventions, "grossly unjust" to compare "philanthropic Disunionists" like Garrison, who "rely alone on moral influence," with the "demagogues and politicians of the South," who actually "assembled to plot disunion." But the *National Era* could not refrain from issuing its own warning: although Northern statesmen and politicians had not yet "broached or countenanced" disunion, "a few more measures so atrocious as the Fugitive Slave Bill would turn their love of the Union into hate."[51]

Demoralized but not deterred, the Southern rights vanguard howled on, determined to turn the rhetoric of revolution to their own advantage. In Virginia, although Unionism prevailed, a small cadre of extremists based in the Tidewater and eastern Piedmont—including Beverly Tucker, James Seddon, and Richard K. Meade—had come to control the Democratic Party. They steadily built the case for disunion and found a new champion in Muscoe R. H. Garnett, whose 1850 pamphlet, *The Union, Past and Future:*

How It Works and How to Save It, was misnamed, for it defended the constitutionality of secession and upheld the "mystique of the doctrines of '98." These Virginians looked to Madison and Jefferson's Virginia and Kentucky resolutions as proof that secession had the blessing of the Founders themselves.[52]

While Virginia disunionists carefully navigated the shoals of public opinion in their state, South Carolina's extremists plunged recklessly forward. Speaking in Charleston in the wake of the first Nashville Convention, Robert Barnwell Rhett once again called on South Carolinians to withstand the trial of isolation for the sake of saving the South. To the charge that he was a traitor, he defiantly replied: "But let it be that I am a traitor. The word has no terrors for me. I am born of traitors—traitors in England, in the revolution, in the middle of the seventeenth century; traitors again in the revolution of 1720, when, under the lead of an ancestor, South Carolina was rescued from the capricious rule of the Lord Proprietors; and traitors again in the revolution of 1776. I have been born of traitors; but thank God! They have been traitors in the great cause of liberty." According to Rhett's modern-day biographer William C. Davis, this speech, although "sophomoric" and "overblown," was a turning point for Rhett. His past invocations of disunion had been cagily vague, leaving open the possibility that secession was simply the strongest lever to ensure sectional parity and harmony. But now he insisted that there was no hope of reforming the government, no other recourse than secession; there was no going back once the South left the Union. Rhett understood that he and his allies had now to press the case that disunion was a positive good—that it would bring "redemption and honor, liberty and prosperity to the South"—and that the benefits of revolution outweighed the risks. As a writer under the pseudonym "Georgia" warned the *American Whig Review* in December 1850, the Deep South states' rights vanguard was convinced that "disunion, aye, even war, is to be preferred to the horrible consequences of an interference with slavery."[53]

Rhett and his separate-state secessionists were outmaneuvered in the October 1851 state elections by an alliance of so-called cooperationists (who thought separate state secession, while justified, was "impractical") and a small cadre of unconditional Unionists. This was no victory for Unionism; South Carolina's cooperationists considered themselves "Resistance men"; in the words of the *Charleston Mercury*, they were determined not to "sink down to the level of the Georgia platform." They fought with separate-state secessionists not over how to preserve the Union but over how best to craft a disunion program. Cooperationists thought the revolution could wait—wait until Northern aggression so outraged the South that the slave states would rebel in concert. The majority of white South Carolinians endorsed this position.[54]

South Carolinians, of course, had no monopoly on the language of revolution. Abolitionists, too, would invoke the right of revolution in opposing what became the most divisive element of the 1850 armistice. The resolution of a meeting of Philadelphia African Americans, condemning the new Fugitive Slave Law, set the tone for the coming battle: "Resolved, That we endorse, to the full, the sentiment of the Revolutionary Patriot of Virginia, and should the awful alternative be presented to us, will act fully up to it—'Give me Liberty or give me Death.' "[55]

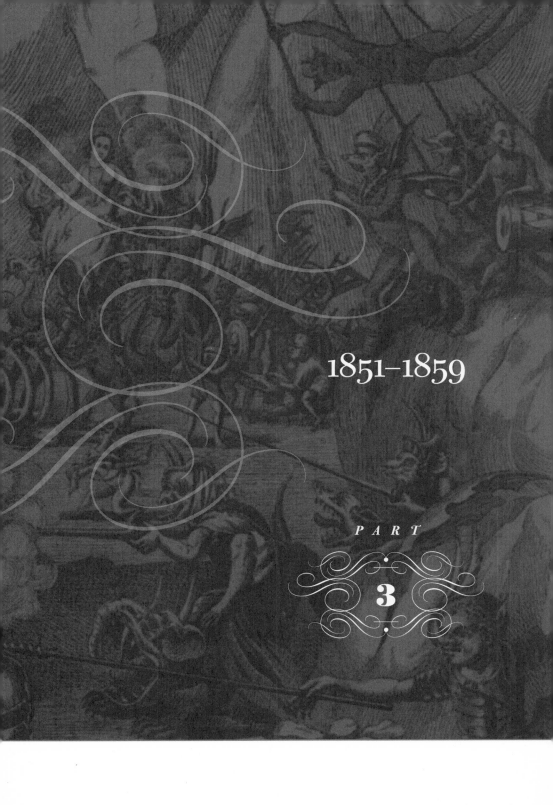

1851–1859

PART

3

Beneath the Iron Heel

The Fugitive Slave Act of 1850 legitimized and lent immediacy to an argu-ment that abolitionists had long been making—that Northerners were com-plicit in the slave system. Northern outrage at the law, in turn, legitimized a long-standing argument of the South's proslavery vanguard—that North-erners could not be trusted to keep their promises. Such a dialectic reflected the design of the bill's Southern sponsors. They knew well that its measures were "gratuitously provocative." The new fugitive slave policy created a class of federal commissioners who would act as judge and jury when claims for rendition of slaves were brought before them by slaveholders, their agents, or federal marshals, who were required by law to assist slaveholders. In such a case, a commissioner would hold a summary hearing (a slave in custody was not permitted to testify on his or her own behalf) and receive a fee of ten dollars if he found on behalf of the slaveowner and issued a certificate of removal to remand the fugitive into slavery; the commissioner would collect only five dollars if he found on behalf of the slave. A certificate of removal was literally the legal last word—under this law, the courts of the free states had no authority to overturn a finding by a federal commissioner. Moreover, the law increased penalties against anyone who dared to undertake extralegal action on behalf of a fugitive slave, threatening imprisonment as a penalty for such defiance. Perhaps the most galling feature of the Fugitive Slave Act for North-erners was that it made "private citizens liable to impressments as slave catchers": a federal commissioner and anyone he appointed to execute his warrants could create a *posse comitatus* of bystanders; if a Northerner refused such a summons, he could be imprisoned.[1]

The Southern militants who framed the legislation, such as James Mason of Virginia and Andrew Butler of South Carolina, fully expected that North-erners would resist compliance and that such resistance would "arouse south-ern indignation and hasten the achievement of Southern unity." But the proslavery vanguard could not have anticipated the myriad shapes that re-sistance would take. The Fugitive Slave Act, paradoxically, galvanized North-erners across the political spectrum even as it opened rifts in the antislavery ranks. The most dramatic acts of Northern defiance were a series of highly publicized slave rescues. The first of these took place in 1851, when African Americans in Boston rescued from custody a fugitive slave named Shadrach, who had been arrested on a warrant by the city's commissioner. Shadrach's successful flight to a safe haven in Canada infuriated Southern slaveholders and prompted President Fillmore to call for the prosecution of Shadrach's rescuers. Hard on the heels of this episode came the Christiana affair, in which a Maryland slaveowner named Edward Gorsuch led a posse to the home of William T. Parker, a free black farmer who lived in the Christiana area of rural Pennsylvania. Parker was suspected of harboring Gorsuch's runaway slaves. According to William Still, the leading nineteenth-century chronicler of the Underground Railroad, Parker had been warned by his antislavery network of the arrival of the posse and was ready to take it on. He refused to turn the fugitives over, sparking a melee in which Gorsuch was killed and his son wounded. Mainstream partisan newspapers in Pennsylvania outdid each other in condemning the resistance of Parker and his defenders as an "unwar-rantable outrage"—an "act of servile insurrection" and of "treason." Many local whites agreed and vented their hostility in a wave of terror directed against blacks. As the editor of the *Pennsylvania Freeman* related, the "col-ored people, though the great body of them had no connection with this affair, are hunted like partridges upon the mountains, by the relentless horde which has poured forth upon them, under the pretense of arresting the parties concerned in the fight." Eventually, a Philadelphia grand jury charged thirty-eight of the resisters with treason.[2]

It mattered little to slaveowners that such instances of resistance were rarely successful (from 1850 to 1853, "about seventy fugitives were returned to their owners by federal tribunals, whereas only about one-fifth of that number were released or rescued from custody"). Nor did they take comfort from the antiblack rhetoric of Northern newspapers or the vigilantism of antiblack mobs. Slaveowners fastened on the climate of hostility to the law, the refusal of states such as Massachusetts to strike their personal liberty laws from the books, and the fact that the vast majority of persons indicted for helping fugitives, such as the Shadrach and Christiana resisters, were found innocent by Northern courts. As Virginia's Senator Mason put it in the wake of the Shadrach episode, the law would be useless unless it was executed by the North with "alacrity, diligence, zeal and good faith." Mason saw the fugitive issue as potentially galvanizing for the Southern rights movement in slave states on the Northern border, as the prospect and probability of slave flight were highest there. Southerners now opportunistically cast antislavery Northerners as nullifiers; they predicted that Northern defiance of the Constitution would bring about "a state of things . . . compared with which revolution, with all its admitted horrors, would be trifling indeed," according to Alabama's Senator Jeremiah Clemens. Never to be outdone, Rhett warned that Northern defiance would "crush beneath it . . . all faith, brotherhood, and peace, until the whole fabric [of the Union] falls a vast pile of ruin and desolation." Such charges of Northern perfidy gained credence when Massachusetts antislavery senator Charles Sumner, in an impassioned speech on August 26, 1852, called for the repeal of the Fugitive Slave Law and likened resistance to the measure to the colonists' defiance of the hated Stamp Act. Southerners such as North Carolina's Senator George E. Badger, a Whig, charged not only that Sumner's speech would "stir up sedition," but also that it was "an assault on the memory of the dead."[3]

Especially ominous for proslavery Southerners in the early 1850s was the centrality of free blacks themselves to episodes of Northern resistance. The Fugitive Slave Law pushed many black abolitionists who had espoused Garrisonian nonviolence to justify the use of physical force as the only effective way to protect themselves and their communities. The law, by prohibiting blacks from testifying on their own behalf, was an invitation for slaveowners to kidnap free blacks; under the threat of false arrest, Northern blacks had no choice but to arm themselves. Former slave William Parker, of Pennsylvania, who had led the Christiana resistance, repeatedly clashed with kidnappers. In some confrontations "his band triumphed; in others it did not," Carol Wilson has written, but either way Parker and his allies "dealt slavery a double blow": they represented the universal right to self-defense and established that African Americans possessed the manhood and courage to stand up to their oppressors.[4]

The most notable convert to the doctrine of force was Frederick Douglass, who had reached the conclusion that "the law of God required the death of kidnappers." For Douglass, this reorientation was part of a broad tactical split with Garrison. At the May 1851 meeting of the American Anti-Slavery Society (AASS), Douglass repudiated the doctrine of disunion and announced that he would participate in the political process to advance an antislavery interpretation of the Constitution. His stance was in part a pragmatic effort to establish independence and secure financial backing for his new newspaper; Garrison had long withheld support from Douglass's journalistic endeavors. For Douglass, the break from his old mentor, like the embrace of violence as a justifiable means of resistance, was an attempt to defend black manliness against what he perceived as the paternalistic condescension of the Garrisonians. But Douglass also indicted the intellectual bankruptcy of disunion. Just as Garrison himself had long ago repudiated colonization when he realized that any scheme supported by slaveholders could not be genuinely antislavery, now Douglass condemned disunion as a doctrine calculated to serve the Slave Power. Precisely because the last best hope of slaveholders was to leave the Union, Douglass wrote, "I am, therefore, for bringing the slave States more completely under the power of the free States." The Constitution, he pointed out, began with "we the people," not with "we the white people"; it thus provided a "firm basis of opposition to slavery." To cry "no union with slaveholders," to insulate the South from the "presence of an advanced civilization," was an act of cowardice. Douglass's newspaper took approving note when other black abolitionists, such as Charles L. Remond, also abandoned Garrisonian disunion.[5]

The Fugitive Slave Law served as a catalyst not only of armed resistance but also of emigration. Freedom in the Northern states was so precarious for fugitives and free blacks that thousands sought refuge in Canada, while others promoted emigration to West Africa or the Caribbean. The leading advocate of black emigration was newspaper editor and physician Martin Delany.

Arguing against the Douglass view that emigration necessarily served the slaveholders' purpose of deporting free blacks, Delany made the case that, to effect their own redemption, blacks must establish their own nation in the Western Hemisphere: "That country is the best," he wrote, "in which our manhood can be best developed; and that is Central America and South America, and the West Indies." In his 1852 publication, *The Condition, Elevation, and Destiny of the Colored People of the United States, Politically Considered*, Delany railed against not only the political degradation that the law fastened upon all blacks but also the cultural paternalism practiced by even the most well-meaning whites. The antislavery movement permitted blacks to do "nothing but what our white brethren and friends say we must." Delany offered instead a vision in which "our Elevation is the work of our own hands," and in which a world of opportunity beyond the U.S. borders "bid[s] us come and be men and women, protected, secure, beloved and Free." According to Patrick Rael, Douglass and Delany both participated in a shift in Northern black protest culture from a rhetoric of "messianic deliverance" to one of "political revolution."[6]

In the wake of the Compromise of 1850, the South as well as the North witnessed a rise in black militancy. William Link's recent study of Virginia politics in the 1850s suggests that slaves themselves were aware of the "sea change in the national political atmosphere" and that they stepped up their acts of defiance accordingly. They challenged white authority by stealing, refusing to work, fighting with masters and overseers, and even by "engaging in murder, poisoning, or arson." Economic changes as well as political events contributed to this trend: in order to man the burgeoning industrial, commercial, and manufacturing sectors of the Virginia economy, slaveowners increasingly hired their slaves out to urban capitalists in cities such as Richmond. Ranked first in the nation in the tobacco-processing industry and second in flour milling, as well as boasting profitable iron, copper, and brass mills, Richmond exemplified the phenomenon of industrial slavery. By 1860, slaves accounted for 48 percent of the city's workingmen (whites constituted 44 percent and free blacks 8 percent). The preponderance of slave laborers was especially marked in tobacco manufacturing, where they made up between 80 and 90 percent of the workforce.[7]

The hiring-out system served masters by permitting them to translate "their excess slave labor into cash wages." But it also attenuated their authority and undermined their paternalistic fantasy that slavery was a benign "way of life" rather than a system for making profits. Link illustrates his contention that "resistance seemed more likely when slaves functioned outside the traditional master-slave relationship" by focusing on the controversial Jordan Hatcher case of 1852, which "coincided with an epidemic of slave challenges to white authority." Hatcher, a slave in Chesterfield County, Virginia, was hired out, by the widow who owned him, to work in a tobacco factory in Richmond. On February 25, 1852, he got into a brawl with the white factory overseer, who had attacked him with a cowhide strap for not working well enough. Hatcher defended himself against the rain of blows by striking the overseer on the head with a nearby iron poker. The wound proved fatal, and Hatcher, who had fled the scene, was apprehended, convicted of first-degree murder, and sentenced to hang.[8]

The case then took an unexpected turn when Virginia governor Joseph Johnson commuted Hatcher's sentence to sale and transportation. For Johnson, the decision was in some ways business as usual—he had "routinely approved" of sentences of sale and transportation in cases of slave crime, and some of the powerful business leaders of Richmond, supporters of the colonization cause, liked the idea of removal as punishment. But Johnson's action aroused expressions of public indignation, including a mob assault on the governor's mansion during which the crowd chanted that Johnson was a "damned old abolitionist." Even though Johnson reassured his followers that he believed a slave was never justified in resisting the authority of his master, there was a sense among Virginians that his undue leniency had contributed to a "uniform spirit of lawlessness" suffusing the slave system—that abolitionists were poised to infiltrate the South and stoke the fires of defiance.[9]

The political and economic atmosphere contributed to an increase in the flow of runaways from the South in the 1850s. The convergence of Northern resistance to the Fugitive Slave Act and of slaves' own increased militancy is dramatically illustrated by the case of Anthony Burns, a Virginia slave who was hired out to various Richmond employers. In 1854, while working on the city's docks, Burns hid aboard a northbound ship and escaped to Boston, where he soon melted into the city's free black population. But that freedom proved illusory. In 1855, Burns recounted the tale of his capture to a New York newspaper: "I kept my own counsel, and didn't tell anybody that I was a slave, but I strove for myself as I never had an opportunity to do before.

When I was going home one night I heard some one running behind me; presently a hand was put on my shoulder, and somebody said: 'Stop, stop; you are the fellow who broke into the silversmith's shop the other night.' I assured the man that it was a mistake, but almost before I could speak, I was lifted from off my feet by six or seven others, and it was no use to resist." Burns found himself in a courthouse where he was confronted by his former master. Boston abolitionists, black and white, soon rallied to Burns's defense. A meeting called at Faneuil Hall by the local antislavery Vigilance Committee attracted a crowd of five thousand (including many nonabolitionists), the "largest attendance anyone could remember." Leading abolitionists condemned the Fugitive Slave Law and the attack on Burns as an abrogation of states' rights. Theodore Parker began an impassioned speech by addressing his auditors as "Fellow-subjects of Virginia!" "Where are the Rights of Massachusetts?," he implored. "A fugitive slave bill Commissioner has got them all in his pocket. . . . Where are the laws of Massachusetts forbidding State edifices to be used as prisons for the incarceration of fugitives? They, too, are trampled under foot. 'Slavery is the finality.' "[10]

On May 26, 1854, one of Burns's jailers was killed in a failed attempt by abolitionists to rescue him. The mayor called out two companies of artillery to discourage further acts of defiance. By the time federal commissioner Edward G. Loring handed down his ruling in favor of Burns's master, tensions in the city were at a fever pitch. A brigade of Massachusetts militia and local police were required to run Burns through the gauntlet of a seething crowd of twenty thousand and deposit him on the ship that would remand him to Virginia. Burns was sold to a slave trader when he arrived in the Old Dominion, but Boston's black community did not forget or abandon him— rather, they purchased and freed him. As in the Shadrach and Christiana cases, the failure of Boston authorities to prosecute those who tried to rescue Burns was regarded by proslavery Southerners as a betrayal of the 1850 Compromise. Senator James C. Jones of Tennessee declared that "treason, rank, undisguised treason" stalked Boston and had it in the throes of a "wild and wicked infatuation." That 2,900 Massachusetts citizens had petitioned for the repeal of the Fugitive Slave Law in the wake of the Burns affair only proved to Jones that antislavery forces were bent on destroying the Union.[11]

The highly publicized slave rescues of the 1850s heightened slaveowners' fears of "emissaries in their midst" sent by the mysterious and elusive Underground Railroad. On the Ripley, Ohio, line, antislavery "conductors" such as John Parker had to "fine-tune their secrecy skills" in the wake of the 1850 law, as well as to contend with "a budding industry of con artists who told slaves they were part of the Underground Railroad and then turned them in for the reward." The state of Kentucky passed a series of laws, such as a measure appointing slave patrols to guard river crossings and make arrests without warrants, that were intended to supplement all of the extralegal deterrents to flight. But Ripley's stalwarts did not back down; Parker continued his excursions across the river, knowing full well that he might be reenslaved if he were caught, and the number of slave escapes continued to rise. Another former slave who dared to make such trips was Harriet Tubman, the symbolic leader of the Underground Railroad. A fugitive from Maryland who settled in Philadelphia, this "Moses of Her People" was long shrouded in legend, but recent scholarship has confirmed that she led dozens of daring raids into Maryland and Virginia, "eventually bringing hundreds out along liberty lines to freedom."[12]

Those liberty lines were anchored by stationmasters Thomas Garrett in Wilmington, Delaware, and William Still in Philadelphia. Garrett was the leader of a group of white middle-class Quaker abolitionists in Delaware—a slave state at this time—who helped to ferry some 2,500 slaves to freedom. The destination of most of these fugitives was Philadelphia, where Still's Vigilance Committee provided a temporary haven. Himself the son of slaves —his mother had escaped from slavery in Maryland—Still devoted his life to the twin goals of rescuing bondsmen and chronicling the remarkable history of the Underground Railroad. It is thanks to Still's meticulous, and surreptitious, prewar record keeping, and to his publication after the Civil War of his magisterial 800-page book *The Underground Railroad*, that we can reconstruct the stories of Tubman and the other members of Still's brave band. His interracial circle included white Quakers Lucretia Mott and Samuel Rhoads, leaders, respectively, of the woman's rights movement and the "free produce" movement, which boycotted all products of Southern slave labor; African American stalwart Robert Purvis, an influential officer and orator for both the Pennsylvania Abolition Society and the AASS; and Frances Ellen Watkins Harper, a Maryland native who used her prodigious gifts as writer and orator to speak out on behalf of abolition, the free produce movement, and woman's rights. As Harper traveled through the Northeast giving lectures, Still wrote, she "often came in contact with Underground Raid Road passengers, especially in Philadelphia." She gave them spiritual and material aid "with the same liberality as though they were her own near kin."[13]

Relying on these associates, Harriet Tubman established a "seasonal pattern of migration"—she would rescue a large party of slaves in the fall and take them through Wilmington and on to Philadelphia. As the Christiana incident of 1851 suggests, the border state of Pennsylvania was a primary hunting ground for slave catchers. Tubman's ultimate goal was to lead fugitives from this borderland through New York State and on into Canada, beyond the reaches of the Fugitive Slave Law. She generally spent a portion of the winter in Canada, then performed wage work in the North (as a domestic servant on Cape May, New Jersey, for example) during the spring and summer, all the while preparing to "plan and execute additional raids in the South" again in the fall. Biographer Catherine Clinton notes that Tubman "crafted her expeditions with extreme care"; for instance, she used "gospel music and spirituals to signal to fugitives hidden along the road." She drew inspiration from her faith—Garrett said of her: "I never met with any person of any color who had more confidence in the voice of God, as spoken direct to her soul."[14]

UNCLE TOM'S CABIN

Even as Tubman risked her life as a conductor, another Harriet established herself as a defender of fugitive slaves—only this one did not traverse the forbidding terrain of slavery but instead conjured it up. Harriet Beecher Stowe's wildly popular 1852 novel, *Uncle Tom's Cabin*, was written as a direct response to the Fugitive Slave Act. From an eminent family of New England reformers, Stowe began writing antislavery stories, sketches, and letters for publication in newspapers and journals in the 1830s. These were inspired by her family's long residence in Cincinnati, Ohio, just across the river from slaveholding Kentucky, where she beheld the "spectacle of bounty hunters carrying escaped slaves back into captivity" and the "fear and anger of freedmen." In those years she also learned of the heroic efforts of the Ripley, Ohio, line of the Underground Railroad. Although Harriet and her husband Calvin moved to Maine (where he joined the Bowdoin College faculty) in 1850, she keenly felt that the Fugitive Slave Act of that year represented the long arm of slavery reaching right into New England. Stowe registered her protest by writing *Uncle Tom's Cabin*, which initially appeared in forty serialized parts in an abolitionist newspaper in Washington, D.C.; it was published as a novel in 1852. The book sold a stunning three hundred thousand copies in the first year, putting her in company of the Victorian pantheon of writers alongside Jane Austen and Charles Dickens.[15]

Stowe's novel interweaves the "freedom narrative" of two slaves, George and Eliza, who successfully escape slavery, with the "bondage story" of Uncle Tom, a saintly and simple slave who is killed by the murderous Simon Legree. This story, together with slave narratives such as those of J. W. C. Pennington, "argued that slavery was best seen in the slave market," Walter Johnson has observed. Slaveowners had long cast the sale of their bondsmen as unfortunate incidents in which the market rudely broke the bonds of paternalism; they defended the purchase of slaves as an effort to "save" them from the horrific slave pens and auction blocks. But the slaves themselves understood implicitly that the slave pen—where a "human body was publicly stripped, examined, priced, and sold"—was not an aberration, but rather "stood for the whole of slavery." Thus Pennington wrote that "kind" masters were an impossibility, because the "chattel principle," which reduced human beings to commodities, had mastered all slaveowners. Stowe translated this theme into the language of sentimental fiction. Her seemingly sympathetic Kentucky slaveholder, Mr. Shelby, agrees to sell Eliza, her child, and Uncle Tom, and hands them over to a ruthless slave trader named Haley; Eliza flees this fate but Tom is sold to Legree. By placing the "family-separating trade . . . at the center of *Uncle Tom's Cabin*," she dramatized for readers the ways that all slaveowners were complicit in the "most brutal results of the system of slavery."[16]

Aimed at a readership of educated white women, whom Stowe hoped to mobilize against slavery, her story derives its emotional power from its portraits of mothers and children. At a time when high infant morality was a frightful prospect with which all parents had to contend (Stowe herself had lost her beloved eighteen-month-old son Charley to cholera), she asked her readers to imagine "what a poor slave mother may feel when her child is torn away from her." As her biographer Joan D. Hedrick has related, Stowe's stirring depiction of Eliza's frenzied flight from slave catchers, with her babe in her arms ("If it were *your* Harry, mother, or your Willie, that were going to be torn from you by a brutal trader," Stowe asks, "how fast could *you* walk?") and her loving portrait of the angelic child little Eva, who befriends Uncle Tom and blesses him on her deathbed, "tapped the overwrought feelings of white, middle-class parents" and enlisted them on behalf of abolition.[17]

Although Stowe trafficked in what one modern-day scholar has called "romantic racialism"—a tendency to replace negative stereotypes of African Americans with positive stereotypes such as the notion that the black race was naturally "affectionate," "assimiliative," and pious—most leading black abolitionists embraced her novel as a contribution to the cause of freedom. Frederick Douglass, for one, criticized Stowe for missteps such as having the characters George and Eliza leave for Liberia at the novel's end; nevertheless, he felt that on balance Stowe had done more good than harm and that she could be influenced to cast off the last vestiges of racism. That Stowe galvanized antislavery women is undeniable—in 1853, to give but the most dramatic example, half a million women in England, Ireland, and Scotland signed a massive petition advocating emancipation in the United States; this, in turn, encouraged American women to step up their petitioning. Acknowledging this contribution, Joshua Giddings declared on the floor of the House of Representatives that Stowe "had done more for the cause of freedom . . . than any savant, statesman, or politician of our land."[18]

To preempt the charge that she had encroached on the male domain of politics, Stowe cannily kept her distance from the nascent woman's rights movement in the North and presented herself as a paragon of female virtue and domesticity. Indeed, *Uncle Tom's Cabin* and Stowe's other works were not only a critique of the Southern family but also a celebration of idealized Northern families, in which women were "squarely in the home" yet were able to radiate moral virtue beyond its boundaries and to influence empathetic Northern men. She also refrained from formally affiliating with any of the various antislavery factions. She wanted her novel, Hedrick explains, to be "claimed by all."[19]

Although Stowe tried to position herself in the political mainstream of the free states, Northern anti-abolitionists and proslavery Southerners saw her as the very embodiment of radicalism, as an emissary of both abolitionism and woman's rights. Of Stowe and her ilk, a Cincinnati reviewer said: "It matters not what their avowed designs and intentions are . . . we know that revolution and disunion will be the result." Proslavery Southerners now redoubled their efforts to show, as one contributor to the Richmond journal the *Southern Literary Messenger* put it, that "it is to the institution of slavery that we [Southerners] owe our superiority in morals, politics, religion and obedience to the law." Stowe's book thus escalated the long-standing literary war over slavery. Southern critics declared that *Uncle Tom's Cabin* was "scandalous libel" and that Stowe had forfeited the "privilege of immunity" on the grounds of gender and "descended into the arena of civil dissension and political warfare." Her "labyrinths of misrepresentation," so proslavery ideologue G. W. Holmes railed, were an "effort to revive all the evils of civil discord—to resuscitate all the dangers of disunion." Stowe's popularity in England revived the Southern charge that abolitionists were intent on flattering the British into "interfer[ing] with our home affairs," wrote a correspondent to the *New Orleans Daily Picayune*. Southern critics also positioned Stowe firmly in the woman's rights camp as a traducer of the divinely ordained gender hierarchy. "When women despise the Bible," asked one Tennessee clergyman in a pointed attack on Stowe, "what next?"[20]

Even as they condemned Stowe, proslavery ideologues enlisted white Southern women to defend slavery and traditional gender roles. Louisa McCord, of South Carolina, who during this era was establishing herself as the preeminent female defender of slavery and of the South's conservative social order, published a scathing review of *Uncle Tom's Cabin* in the *Southern Quarterly Review*. Weaving images of disunion as a process and a prophecy, McCord insisted that even as the North was careening recklessly down its radical abolitionist path, the South was "developing to perfection" and "softening" the system of slavery (a system she described as a "providential caring for the weak"). Northern woman's rights and antislavery activists who sought to destabilize gender and race relations threatened to divert history from its "God-directed course." McCord warned them: "The natural order of things perverted, ill must follow. The magnitude of that ill, may heaven protect us from witnessing!"[21]

The most popular fictional proslavery response to *Uncle Tom's Cabin* was Mary Eastman's *Aunt Phillis's Cabin; or, Southern Life as It Is* (1852). Eastman offered readers both a panoply of archetypal "contented slaves," such as the irascible Aunt Phillis, and large doses of editorializing on slavery, in which she maintained that both the Bible and the Revolutionary forefathers had vouched for the institution. Eastman's characters espouse the old line that the

A. DREAM

Caused by the perusal of Mrs. H. Beecher Stowe's popular work Uncle Tom's Cabin.

Printed in Louisville, Kentucky, this critique of *Uncle Tom's Cabin* depicts the novel, for slavery's defenders, as a nightmare, in which a black man stands triumphant amid swirling scenes of hellish demons. (Courtesy of the Library of Congress)

separation of slave families was a "very uncommon" occurrence in the South and lay the blame for the country's fragile condition squarely on the shoulders of abolitionists. Her prescription for sectional harmony is mutual noninterference. This won her kudos in the Southern press and among conservative Northerners, who credited her with "stem[ming] the torrent which foamed around 'Uncle Tom.'" Antislavery papers naturally made light of the book. A notice in the *New York Independent* said of Eastman's portrait of slave life: "The pictures of the intense happiness of the slaves are so very charming, that one wonders why the inventors do not make haste to sell their children to the slave-traders."[22]

Although *Aunt Phillis's Cabin* and the flood of other "anti-Tom" stories and novels by Southern men and women generally purported to stem the tide of sectionalism, they nonetheless contributed to a nascent cultural Southern nationalism—a belief that Southern culture was distinct and that Southerners must achieve a cultural parity with the North as well as independence from it. With "millions of copies of *Uncle Tom's Cabin* . . . finding greedy purchasers," and with "preachers, periodicals and papers of every grade and degree" joining in the "general yell" against slavery, so the editor of the *Richmond Examiner* observed, Southerners needed more than ever to assert themselves.[23] Southern literature and criticism in this era bore the stamp of South Carolinian radicalism, for it advanced the cardinal Calhounian tenet that slave society was superior to free society. But even as the cultural program of Southern disunionists gained ground in the early 1850s, their political program foundered on the shoals of a Democratic resurgence.[24]

PARTY POLITICS AND THE ELECTION OF 1852

Both the Whig and the Democratic parties had emerged from the debates of 1850 and 1851 battered and divided. With Zachary Taylor's 1848 victory as their model, the Whigs in 1852 chose as their standard-bearer war hero General Winfield Scott, whose "campaign strategy [was] predicated on . . . maintaining a perfect silence on the issues of the day." This would permit the party to run distinct campaigns in the North and the South, pledging in the former not to abide by the Fugitive Slave Law and in the latter to uphold the finality of the 1850 Compromise. This time it did not work. Free-Soilers repudiated the Whigs. And nine Southern congressmen, including Alexander Stephens and Robert Toombs, certain that Scott would not stand by the compromise, "seceded" from the party's national convention in Baltimore in protest. In a desperate gambit, the Whigs appealed to a traditionally Democratic constituency, Catholic immigrants. This, too, failed. Immigrant voters had a longtime antipathy to the Whigs on the grounds that Whiggish Protestant reformers were antagonistic to immigrant cultures, and that Whigs in the past had opportunistically fused with anti-immigrant nativist parties, most successfully in Philadelphia. In the early 1840s such nativist parties had gained adherents by tapping into fear of "foreign infiltration" by "papist" Catholics, artisans' resentment at their displacement by immigrant factory workers, and the popular image of immigrant ghettos as dens of vice. The goal of nativists was not to restrict immigration but to lengthen the period of naturalization before an immigrant could become a citizen. The Democratic Party, by contrast, had assiduously wooed the vote of Irish Catholics, positioning itself as the defender of white workingmen against radical Protestant reformers who put the plight of black slaves above the duties of white solidarity. Themselves victims of an intense prejudice that relegated them to low-paying jobs and to slums, the Irish proved susceptible to such Democratic appeals. Now, in 1852, the Whigs asked immigrants to forget this history and align with them. Such pandering "galled nativist Whigs" and left immigrant voters, along with the Catholic press and clergy, cold.[25]

While the Whig Party struggled to find its footing, Democrats pulled off a stunning reunification. All over the South, William J. Cooper Jr. has written, "Southern Rights men furled their defeated banner and unfurled the old Democratic flag." Unionist coalitions that had defended the Compromise of 1850 proved to be ephemeral, victims of their own success—they had so persuasively argued that the compromise did no dishonor to the South that they facilitated the reentry of Southern Democrats into the party fold. The Democratic reunification was part opportunism—obviously the Whig Party was reeling and a genuine Democratic landslide was possible in the coming election. Democrats in the South effectively tarred Winfield Scott as a lackey of Northern antislavery Whigs led by William Henry Seward. "A vote for Scott now is a vote for Seward in '56," claimed one North Carolina paper in a popular refrain. Of the Democratic presidential nominee, Franklin Pierce of New Hampshire, Southerners said that he was "as reliable as Calhoun himself" on the issues of states' rights and slavery. A charismatic and easily manipulable man, who earned accolades as a general in the Mexican War, Pierce positioned himself as a "strict constructionist" who would vigorously enforce the Compromise of 1850, including the Fugitive Slave Law. His reputation for putting party loyalty above all else, as well as his belief in the "finality" of the compromise as a death knell to sectionalism itself, drew many Free-Soil Democrats back into the party. All told, "about half of the Free Soil rank and file drifted back to the two major parties or abstained from voting at all" in 1852. The Democrats reaped the bigger benefit—Pierce won the popular vote and 254 electoral votes to Scott's paltry 42. The Whigs won only two Southern states—Kentucky and Tennessee—where the Democratic

EXPERIMENTS ON THE TIGHT ROPE.

Here, Whig candidate Winfield Scott is portrayed as a fellow traveler with the likes of
Garrison, Wilmot, and Douglass, who try, in vain, to pull him into the president's chair.
(Courtesy of the Library of Congress)

Party was factionalized and the Whigs were still able to get traction from the
argument that the leading Southern Democrats were disunionists. In the
Deep South, by contrast, Whig votes fell off precipitously.[26]

For antislavery men and women who resisted the pull back into the two
major parties, the election campaign appeared as a hollow mockery. Frederick Douglass railed in his newspaper that the "Whig and Democratic parties
rely alone upon the Compromise and its kindred atrocities to keep them
together." Joshua Giddings, too, believed that the United States "was in the
midst of a revolution," as the "two great parties" were conspiring to "convert
this free Government into a slaveholding, a slave-breeding republic." Horace
Mann, in a stem-winding antislavery speech to Congress in August 1852, at
the height of the campaign, accused both major parties—by their invocations
of the "finality" of the compromise—of suppressing free speech, as in the

days of the gag rule. Their respective bans on "agitating" the slavery issue would forbid "genius from presenting Truth," as "that divine-hearted
woman," Harriet Beecher Stowe, had in *Uncle Tom's Cabin*, Mann lamented,
and silence moralists in the name of a "maniacal partisanship." He also
excoriated both parties for having once again capitulated to "that fraudulent
idea of 'danger to the Union'; that cry of 'wolf,' which the South always raises
when she has an object to accomplish; and which she will continue to raise,
on pretences more and more shadowy and evanescent, the more we have the
folly to heed it." Such capitulation had burdened the country with two
proslavery presidential candidates.[27]

Significantly, Mann chose to develop a theme that had surfaced in the
predictions of immediatists such as David Walker and in the speeches of
some Wilmot Proviso supporters—the theme of disunion as retributive justice. Invoking the prospect of slave resistance, Mann sternly warned the
South that it would pay the higher price should disunion come. "The knowledge of a north star is penetrating further and further into the southern
interior, and arousing new hearts to the effort of self-emancipation," he said.
"There are no motives more terrible than those that urge a bondsman to his
revenge. . . . In a civil or a servile war, the South will be in a more perilous
condition than if every kernel of gunpowder in all the magazines of an army,
just on the eve of battle, should suddenly become animated, and set itself on
fire." If the South wished to show the world the "natural retributions of
slavery," Mann thundered, all it had to do was "to dissolve this Union."
Although Douglass, Giddings, and Mann may have felt they were howling in
the wilderness, events in Kansas would soon make their conspiracy theories
seem prophetic.[28]

THE KANSAS-NEBRASKA ACT OF 1854

"In the year of our Lord eighteen hundred and fifty-four, the friends of
human chattelism . . . broke their plighted faith with their opponents, and
violated a compact which had been held sacred by the most eminent statesmen on both sides of the controversy for more than a third of a century." So
intoned George Thacher in an 1856 antislavery sermon delivered in Meriden,
Connecticut. Reflecting on the Kansas-Nebraska Act of 1854 and the civil
war it had set off in that territory, he grimly noted that the "friends of hu-

man chattelism" had "ventured on an extensive plan of rapine and murder, changed happy wives and children into maniac widows and homeless orphans, [and] spread desolation and fear and woe throughout that whole region." Thacher's sermon, entitled "No Fellowship with Slavery," updated Garrisonian disunionism, arguing that to side with those imposing slavery on Kansas was akin to "joining forces with Satan to fight against God."[29]

Thacher's melodramatic formulation reflected the outrage with which a growing antislavery coalition in the North greeted Illinois senator Stephen Douglas's 1854 measure to extend popular sovereignty to the new territories in the West. Chairman of the Senate Committee on Territories, Douglas championed both westward expansion and internal improvements—particularly a transcontinental railroad. But he faced the intransigence of Southern colleagues, who opposed organizing the enormous realm west of Iowa and Missouri (northern sections of the Louisiana Purchase) because the Missouri Compromise forbade slavery there, and thus any states carved out of that territory would be free. Determined to overcome this obstacle, Douglas colluded with Missouri senator David R. Atchison and the pliable President Pierce to draft a bill that created two new territories, Nebraska and Kansas, and repealed the Missouri Compromise on the grounds that it had been superseded by the Compromise of 1850. Atchison, who was fervently proslavery and had long vied with his nemesis, antislavery senator Thomas Hart Benton, for control of Missouri's Democrats, calculated that if slavery could not take root in the Kansas territory, Missouri would be girded to the north, east, and west by Free-Soilism and therefore vulnerable to abolitionist incursions and influence.[30]

While Douglas's proposed division of the territory seemed to imply that the northern section, Nebraska, would be Free-Soil and the southern one, Kansas, would be open to slavery, for Douglas, the animating principle of the bill was the unimpeachably Democratic doctrine of popular sovereignty. Douglas believed that the Compromise of 1850 had validated popular sovereignty and thus had nullified the Missouri Compromise; the 1820 measure's boundary line between slave and free territory abrogated the rights of citizens to self-government and so was unconstitutional, Douglas reasoned. In his view, popular sovereignty was rooted so deeply in the ideology of the dominant Democratic Party that it could serve as the basis for "sectional restoration" and simultaneously "revitalize the Democracy's heritage." The bill's supporters in Congress—the vast majority of Southern Whigs and Democrats and about half of all Northern Democrats—sang a similar tune. Congressman Hendrick B. Wright of Pennsylvania, to give one of many examples, defended the Kansas-Nebraska Act as perpetuating the struggle against centralized authority that the Revolutionary generation had inaugurated and that Andrew Jackson had so forcefully renewed with his veto of the Bank Bill. The Democrats, he claimed, stood for the principle that "Congress had no right to encroach on the power of the States and popular sovereignty."[31]

In assuming that popular sovereignty had a hypnotic appeal, Douglas made a terrible miscalculation. A substantial number of Northern Democrats, along with Northern Whigs and Free-Soilers, cast the "Nebraska bill," as Douglas's measure was dubbed, as the violation of a "sacred compact," namely the Missouri Compromise. In crafting this argument, they followed the lead of Free-Soiler Salmon P. Chase of Ohio and the other drafters of the "Appeal of the Independent Democrats," a January 1854 manifesto that has a well-earned reputation as "one of the most effective pieces of political propaganda in our history." Its principal authors—Chase and Joshua Giddings, with help from Charles Sumner and Gerrit Smith—were of course not Democrats, in the strict partisan sense, at all; they styled themselves "independent democrats" to signal their disgust with both major parties and to lay the groundwork for an anti-Nebraska political coalition. Their "Appeal" bristled with the rhetoric of disunion, warning that "imminent danger menaces . . . the Permanency of our Union." The source of the danger lay in the machinations of an aggressive "Slave Power Conspiracy" that had put "freedom on the defensive." In the "Appeal," this image of Southern aggression was tied to the argument, one that Chase had done more than any other Free-Soil politician to articulate, that the Constitution was an antislavery document—that the Founders, hoping for slavery's eventual demise, had explicitly made slavery a state institution, not a national one. Chase insisted that constitutional provisions such as the Fifth Amendment, which held that Congress could not deprive Americans of "life, liberty, or property" without due process of the law, empowered the federal government to abolish slavery in its own jurisdiction, namely the District of Columbia and the territories. This reading was echoed in the "Appeal's" contention that "the Union was formed to establish justice, and secure the blessings of liberty." Although Chase had developed his constitutional theory as far back as the early 1840s, it had a new salience in light of the Kansas-Nebraska Act. For now slavery restriction could be cast as a *defensive* measure and as a conservative one—an effort not to wage war on slavery where it already existed but to "defend free territory against the encroachments of slavery," not to impose new laws on the South but to preserve the sacred compact of the Missouri Compromise and do justice to the Founders' true intentions.[32]

While Chase's interpretation was a direct rejection of Garrison's notion of a proslavery Constitution, Garrison's view of disunion—that a nation that had betrayed its ideals could not and should not survive—was in fact echoed in the 1854 "Appeal." When it failed to uphold the promises of the Constitution, the "Appeal" read, the Union "will be worthless and when it becomes worthless it can not long endure." Garrison, we have seen, regarded the Declaration of Independence as an inscription of American ideals and the Constitution as a betrayal of them. Chase and his coauthors, by contrast, viewed the Constitution as a fulfillment of the Declaration's "fundamental maxim"—"EQUAL RIGHTS AND JUSTICE for all men."[33]

The "Appeal," which was widely circulated in the North, provided the template for the congressional debates that followed hard on the heels of its promulgation. Douglas and his backers were stung by the manifesto. They retorted that its authors were hypocrites—pro-Wilmot Northerners, who had refused to extend the Missouri Compromise line to Mexican Cession, were the ones who had made the 1820 compromise a dead letter. Southern supporters of the Nebraska bill countered the "Appeal" with a proslavery interpretation of the Founders' intentions, updated to fit the new crisis. Senator Andrew Butler of South Carolina cast the Founders as "hardy pragmatists" who would have spurned the "pseudo-philanthropy" of the abolitionists. Abolitionists, so Butler asserted, had never intended to honor the Missouri Compromise but rather saw in it the "seeds of agitation"—a pretext for the case that the North "had power to interfere with slavery." Significantly, Butler singled out women's political activism—symbolized by Stowe's novel and the woman's rights conventions that followed the Seneca Falls meeting— as the most loathsome spawn of the Northern "pseudo-philanthropy." Northern "isms," such as abolitionism and "strong-minded-womanism," were, he fumed, "the cankers of theoretical conceit, of impudent intrusion, and cheerless infidelity." Abolitionists were up to their old tricks of "inflaming, maddening, and distracting the public mind." Unless they were silenced, Butler predicted, the "results will be sectional alienation . . . civil strife, and, perhaps, servile insurrection." The *Richmond Enquirer*, which in the past had not hesitated to champion the "minority rights" of slaveholders, now opportunistically brushed aside the anti-Nebraska coalition as a treasonous "faction"—if its rebellion against the "will of the majority" succeeded, "disunion and civil tumult" would result.[34]

Antislavery forces shot back both with a narrow technical argument (that the Missouri Compromise applied only to the Louisiana Purchase) and with an expansive attack on slavery and a defense of free labor. Charles Sumner set the tone with a scathing February 21 speech that painted the Slave Power's repudiation of the Missouri Compromise as a sign of the country's decline and of the falling away from "the original Antislavery policy of our fathers." "Our Republic has swollen in population and power, but it has shrunk in character," he lamented. "It is not now what it was in the beginning, a Republic merely permitting, while it regretted Slavery . . . but a mighty Propagandist, openly favoring and vindicating it." A host of lesser lights took the congressional stage to make the case for the superiority of the free labor system. As Representative Richard Yates, an Illinois Whig, put it: "The effect of slave labor is always to cheapen, degrade, and exclude free labor." To introduce slavery into Kansas and Nebraska would "retard the prosperity" of those territories, for "slave labor converts the richest soil into barrenness," while "free labor causes fertility and vegetation to spring from the very rock." Anti-Nebraska congressmen also countered the charge, leveled by Butler and others, that abolitionist opponents of the Nebraska bill were "agitators" who were up to their old tricks of fomenting disunion. Illinois congressman Elihu B. Washburne, known to his colleagues as a crusader against corruption, tagged Kansas-Nebraska supporters as the real "agitators," who once again were attempting to use the specter of disunion to wring concessions from the North. "Let those who are sowing to the wind beware that they do not reap to the whirlwind," he cautioned, drawing from the Bible. Washburne followed with a familiar line from Shakespeare's *Macbeth*: "In repealing this Missouri Compromise, I tell gentlemen they do but 'teach bloody instructions which, being taught, return to plague the inventors.'"[35]

The Nebraska bill not only stoked congressional opposition but also galvanized the Northern clergy. In March 1854, Senator Edward Everett of Massachusetts presented a "mammoth memorial," signed by three thousand Northern clergymen, against the passage of the Kansas-Nebraska Bill. The petition called the measure "full of danger to the peace" and, echoing the prophecy of disunion as "retributive justice" that had been elaborated by Garrison and Horace Mann, warned that Congress had exposed the "beloved Union" to the "righteous judgments of the almighty." Antislavery immediatists such as Frederick Douglass contributed their own ominous tones to the anti–Kansas Act chorus. Douglass's paper fulminated that Senator Douglas "resolves to ride into power over hecatombs of the dissevered limbs, and bleeding hearts of the millions of his fellow countrymen . . . he writes 'NEBRASKA FOR SLAVERY' on his haggard brow, and with his vesture dipped in the blood of men, and women, and children, he sallies forth upon his murderous mission."[36]

Northern indignation at the Democratic Party for reopening the sectional Pandora's box gave rise not only to images of retribution but also to evidence of retribution, in the form of a stunning electoral setback for Democrats in the off-year elections of 1854. The opposition regained control of the House, and the vast majority of Northern Democrats who had voted for the Kansas-Nebraska Bill were turned out of office. Ominously for Democrats, two new parties appeared on the scene, each representing a fusion of Free-Soilers and anti-Nebraska Whigs and Democrats. As early as May 1854, anti-Nebraska representatives in Congress, inspired by Chase's "Appeal" and led by Israel Washburn of Maine, met and called for the establishment of a new party, dubbed the Republicans. Their fellow antislavery politicians, aided by stalwarts of the antislavery press, such as the *National Era* and the *New York Tribune*, tried to create Republican organizations at the state level. They were most successful in Wisconsin and Michigan, where embryonic Republican parties emerged in 1854, committed to stopping the expansion of slavery.[37]

From the start, the party was a "crazy-quilt coalition," as Michael Holt puts it. The coalition included wealthy manufacturers, merchants, and businessmen in commercial centers who wanted to protect the status quo and feared the economic effects of further sectional alienation; farmers, craftsmen, and wageworkers who believed that only a free labor economy offered upward mobility; and reform-minded antislavery elements who opposed the

Kansas-Nebraska measure out of moral considerations. Initially, these groups coalesced around their shared antipathy to the political dominance of the imperious Slave Power, as well as around a consensus that the economic progress of the North—measured in rates of population growth, immigration, industrialization, and urbanization that far exceeded those of the South— "epitomized the American spirit" of opportunity and self-improvement. The census of 1850, which had revealed that the free states' population growth was 20 percent greater than that of the slaves states during the 1840s, was as encouraging to Republicans as it was dispiriting to Southerners.[38]

In states such as New York, Illinois, and Massachusetts, however, efforts to get a Republican Party off the ground were stymied by persistent Whig opposition; by a lack of consensus on what policies, exactly, the party should stand for; and by the meteoric rise of the American, or Know-Nothing, Party. Initially, it was the American Party that most reaped the benefit of the North-ern electorate's disgust with the Kansas-Nebraska Bill and with politics-as-usual in Washington. The party, which began as a secretive, ritual-bound fraternal order (whose followers, when asked, claimed to "know nothing" of its doings), was committed primarily to a nativist, or anti-immigrant, plat-form. In myriad ways, it capitalized on a persistent strain of antipartyism in American culture—on voters' suspicion that the existing power structure was corrupt and unresponsive to the people's needs. The party tapped Northern voters' disillusionment with the Whigs, whose failed appeals to immigrants had alienated nativists. It took advantage of fears that Catholic immigrants, in particular, had weathered the nativist storms of the mid-1840s and were now poised to campaign aggressively for power and influence. President Pierce's appointment of a Catholic cabinet member, Postmaster James Campbell, and a speaking tour of the pope's representative, Archbishop Bedini, in early 1854 only stoked such fears. Many Northerners resented the fact that Irish Catho-lics constituted a loyal voting bloc for the Democrats. With such weighty measures as slavery's extension at issue, they considered it unseemly that immigrants might cast the crucial swing votes that gave Democrats the edge. The Know-Nothings advocated drastically extending the period of natural-ization required for citizenship and voting, from five years to twenty-one, and wanted to restrict officeholding to the native-born. The Know-Nothings also exploited voter discontent over local issues. Nativists in places such as Philadelphia and Boston had long simmered at Catholic criticism of the public school system and at Catholic lobbying for state-sponsored parochial schools. Thus they embraced the Know-Nothing demand that Catholic children be forced to attend public schools. Moreover, Whiggish Protestant reformers had long promoted temperance as part of a general campaign for moral virtue and a targeted campaign against the perceived vices of immigrant cultures; they saw " 'Rum and Romanism' as related forms of dependency," and embraced the Know-Nothings as the antiliquor party.[39]

But to attribute the party's success to its nativist platform and its ethnocultural appeal to Protestants is to misunderstand its significance fundamentally, Tyler Anbinder has argued. For crucial to its transformation from a "small-scale urban movement into a national power was the belief that the Know Nothings represented an anti-slavery alternative to the existing parties." The vast majority of Northern Know-Nothings, Anbinder has demonstrated, "opposed the extension of slavery and adamantly sought repeal of the Kansas-Nebraska Act." Such a view was consistent with their antipathy to the Democratic Party and their penchant for conspiracy theories—be they conspiracies of Catholic Papists or of the Slave Power.[40]

In the South and border states, by contrast, the American Party was built from the remnants of the Whig Party and tapped racism, nativism, class tensions, and a resilient strain of Unionism. In cities that attracted immigrants, such as St. Louis, New Orleans, and Baltimore, native-born white workers, through the vehicle of the American Party, waged political war against both the very poor (African American and immigrant workers) and the very rich (the plantation elite). They viewed Irish- and German-born newcomers as minions of the Democratic Party and believed that these immigrants used violence to suppress voting by the native-born. According to this variant on the Slave Power Conspiracy theory, wealthy planters colluded to use the immigrant vote to preserve their political stranglehold on the region. Know-Nothing politicians offered wage earners more than conspiracy theories—they provided practical help by creating municipal jobs and aiding workers' collective actions against their employers. This proved a combustible formula, as Know-Nothings who fashioned themselves the victims of mob violence proved ready and willing, in border cities, to initiate violence in order to maintain the party's hold on municipal offices, as a series of lethal riots in the mid-1850s attests. In Louisville, for example, Know-Nothing attacks on immigrant voters prompted the local Democratic paper to dub the American Party "a political Bruiseocracy."[41]

Fears of Northern radicalism were at the heart of Southern nativism. Know-Nothings who decried foreign influence in the South were expressing their profound anxiety that the immigrant North was a hotbed of radicalism and contagious social discord. At the same time, the political strife of Baltimore, New Orleans, and St. Louis became an ominous focal point for elite planter politicians, especially secessionists, because it illustrated for them the dangers of excessive democracy—of majority rule and of mobbism—and created a frightful "image for rural Southerners of what a future in the Union might hold." Paradoxically, even though it had a decidedly sectional cast, Southern Know-Nothingism advertised itself as a Unionist alternative to the inflammatory rhetoric of sectional extremists. In Virginia, for example, each member of the party was required to take the "third degree oath," a pledge not to vote for anyone in favor of disunion. According to Know-Nothings, such as Maryland pamphleteer Anna Ella Carroll, Northern abolitionists and Southern disunionists alike were to be condemned for needlessly fomenting sectional strife.[42]

Although the success of the Know-Nothing Party initially retarded the formation of an antislavery Republican Party that was viable on a national scale, the "very strength of Know-Nothingism," notes Michael Holt, "had one benefit for Republicans." For the Know-Nothings' 1854 victories sounded the death knell of the Whig Party. Divided into a Seward faction that wanted to shape the Whigs into an anti-Nebraska juggernaut and a Fillmore wing that mourned the days of compromise, the Whigs had lost the faith of voters. With the Whigs moribund, the way was now clear for party holdouts, including Abraham Lincoln and William Seward himself, to join the ranks of the fledgling Republican Party. Moreover, many disenchanted Whigs and Democrats used the Know-Nothing Party as a stepping stone—it served as a "screen—a dark wall," observed Joshua Giddings, "behind which members of old political organizations could escape unseen from party shackles" and, cloaked by the Know-Nothings' vaunted secrecy, safely await the establishment of the Republicans. What ultimately consigned the Know-Nothings to the status of a way station, however, was not the machinations of its supporters but rather events in far-off Kansas, where "popular sovereignty" was giving rise to chaos and bloodshed.[43]

In the spring of 1854, proslavery Missourians acted quickly to capitalize on their proximity to the Kansas Territory and establish a dominant presence there. Even as they crossed the state line to lay claim to homesteads, North-easterners organized their own migration movement under the auspices of the New England Emigrant Aid Company. The two sides were on a collision course, for they denied the legitimacy of each other's claim to the territory. Missourians, Nicole Etcheson explains, believed that their proximity to Kansas "legitimized and ensured their political dominance" there. Moreover, they feared that if Kansas were settled by Northern abolitionists, it would become a refuge for runaway slaves and threaten the "safety of slavery property in their state." Eastern migrants were, as Missourians saw them, the economic and social refuse of the free labor North, "paupers" who were the unwitting tools of conniving abolitionists.[44]

In reality, Midwesterners and emigrants from Mid-Atlantic states far out-numbered antislavery New Englanders in the ranks of Free-Soilers trekking to Kansas. These settlers did not favor racial equality but instead pursued the "free labor" dream of upward mobility and land ownership. They viewed slavery as an impediment to that dream and proslavery settlers as lackeys of the imperious Slave Power. Both sides were armed and spoiling for a fight by the time Andrew Reeder, the new territorial governor, arrived in Kansas in October 1854. Missouri senator David Rice Atchison had stoked proslavery belligerence in a series of meetings the previous summer in which he urged Missourians to use force, if necessary, to repel the abolitionist hordes. Reeder called for the election of a territorial delegate to Congress to take place on November 29, 1854. The proslavery candidate won easily, thanks to the "Border Ruffians" from Missouri who swarmed the polls on election day. The choosing of delegates to the territorial legislature, which occurred on March 30, 1855, was even more tumultuous, with Missourians again throng-ing the polling places, armed and marching to drumbeats in virtual battalions. Such martial posturing cast a chill over Free-Soilers, most of whom were too intimidated to vote. Proslavery forces resoundingly swept the field. When Reeder balked and ordered new elections in one-third of the districts, pro-slavery Missourians defiantly ignored the new voting results and arranged for Reeder's ouster. The proslavery legislature then proceeded to pass a series of deliberately provocative laws that made it a felony to criticize slavery, imposed the death penalty on anyone who aided runaway slaves, and prohibited antislavery men from holding office or serving as jurors. The legislature held itself aloof from the Democratic Party and declared itself a bastion of the "Pro-Slavery Party," warning that any faction seeking to challenge it would be considered "an ally of Abolitionism and Disunionism."[45]

Claiming that the proslavery Border Ruffians had violated the "solemn covenant" of popular sovereignty, Free-Soilers pronounced the March election fraudulent and professed, as Etcheson writes, a "sudden love of the Kansas-Nebraska Act." Free-Soilers then embarked on the dangerous journey of forming their own shadow government, one meant to reflect the fact that by the fall of 1855, they outnumbered proslavery settlers. Their constitutional convention, in Topeka in October 1855, represented a compromise between divergent groups of Free-Soil migrants: it outlawed slavery, as abolitionists wanted, but also excluded free blacks in deference to the majority of conservative, antiblack Free-Soilers. By January 1856 Free-Soilers had elected their own governor, Charles Robinson, an agent of the New England Emigrant Aid Company, and petitioned Congress that Kansas be admitted as a free state.[46]

As conflict in Kansas escalated in 1855, the Republican Party entered its "formative period." The congressional elections of that year returned a strong anti-Nebraska majority, with antislavery Know-Nothings outnumbered by Republicans, some of whom openly acknowledged that new party label and others who soon would. The American Party had proved too divided to capitalize on events in Kansas. At its first national council, in Philadelphia in June 1855, a coalition of conservative Northern and Southern Know-Nothings pushed through a platform plank supporting the Kansas-Nebraska Act. This prompted antislavery men, who constituted a majority of the Northern delegation, to withdraw from the meeting. The Philadelphia platform was "moist with the salivary contempt of all honest men," the *Boston Atlas* observed archly. Although this defection promised to shift the Know-Nothings' center of gravity to the South, the party soon experienced a telling setback there. The Virginia gubernatorial race pitted Know-Nothing candidate Thomas Flournoy against states' rights firebrand Henry A. Wise. A stirring public speaker whose oratorical intensity led some to suspect that he was "slightly deranged," Wise eviscerated his opponent by charging that Know-Nothings were lackeys of Northern abolitionists and that the party's penchant for secret meetings made it a breeding ground for slave rebellion. Wise even dusted off the old argument that American opponents of slavery were, in turn, minions of British abolitionists. Know-Nothing disclaimers that the party was enthusiastically proslavery failed to deflect Wise's charges, and the Democratic Party rode Wise's tirades to victory in May 1855.[47]

If Wise's victory pointed the way for Southern rights candidates to vanquish Know-Nothings in the years to come, another key gubernatorial race in 1855 served as a bellwether of Republican fortunes. With the American Party splintered, the Republicans moved quickly to claim disaffected Northerners. In Ohio, Republican candidate Salmon P. Chase won the governorship by cannily co-opting the Know-Nothing vote. This he did, James McPherson has explained, by rejecting "nativist *policies* while recognizing nativism as a cultural impulse." Chase made selective rhetorical gestures, depending on his audience, toward anti-Catholicism, but he did not endorse any of the nativist legislative measures that were anathema to immigrants, particularly the sizable population of German-born voters. With bolters from the American ticket providing a crucial margin, Chase was elected governor. His ascendance confirmed his belief that Northern Know-Nothings, already sincere advocates of the antislavery cause, could be persuaded that the only issue that mattered was the "vital issue of slavery." The potential for a successful fusion of Republicans and Know-Nothings gained more credence when the two parties combined, after a long struggle, to elect their candidate, Nathaniel P. Banks, Speaker of the House early in 1856.[48]

On the national scene, William Henry Seward, more than any other Republican, assumed the responsibility for weaving events in Kansas into a coherent Republican creed, one that would attract Know-Nothings and a wide array of other Free-Soilers and abolitionists. In two critical speeches he delivered during the 1855 canvass, in Albany and in Buffalo, Seward honed the argument that a "slave power conspiracy" menaced the North. An oligarchy of 350,000 slaveholders—scarcely more than 1 percent of the U.S. population—had imposed its proslavery agenda on 25 million nonslaveholding whites, Seward indignantly noted, offering as unassailable proof the laws that proslavery forces in Kansas had passed to proscribe free speech. Although he was no abolitionist, Seward said, his very speech would constitute treason in the eyes of proslavery Kansans, and the "reading and circulation of it in the Buffalo *Express* would be punished with death." Such laws, and the efforts by Southerners to enforce the Fugitive Slave Law, were "invasions of State [*sic*] rights" and revealed that slaveholders intended to extend their "tyranny" over nonslaveholding communities.[49]

Seward disavowed not only Garrisonianism but also the notion, pioneered by Liberty Party men such as Gerrit Smith, that the Constitution was so thoroughly antislavery that it empowered the federal government to enact abolition in the South. Instead, Seward, along with Sumner and other prominent Republicans during this formative period, embraced Salmon Chase's constitutional theory as the "basis of the Republican party's doctrine of nonextensionism." They conceded that the federal government was empowered only to restrict slavery's extension, not to abolish it where it already existed. This position reassured the Northern electorate that Republicans were not fanatical abolitionists intent on antagonizing the South. It also proved fully compatible with the genuinely antislavery sentiments of the most zealous Republican leaders. For they could and did regard nonextension as the "first practicable step" toward voluntary emancipation, in the words of Horace Greeley, influential editor of the *New York Tribune*.[50]

As they honed their attacks on the Slave Power, Republicans such as Seward, Chase, Greeley, and Sumner developed the theory that there was a "latent mass of antislavery feeling within the South" on the part of the nonslaveholding majority. Given the haughtiness of the slaveholder oligarchy, its stranglehold on political offices, and its selfish perpetuation of an economic system that degraded the free laborer and rendered the land barren, it was only natural that nonslaveholders should resent the slave regime. Based on their strong impression that the South's yeoman class increasingly despised rich and powerful slaveholders, Republicans were "convinced that once slavery was confined to the slave states and its extension forever prohibited," nonslaveholding Southerners would begin working for the gradual, voluntary dismantling of the institution on a state-by-state basis. If the party achieved success at the ballot box, antislaveholder sentiment in the South would blossom under the care of a Republican administration, which could use patronage to spread its principles. It is in light of such hopes, Eric Foner has stated, that we must interpret the Republican doctrine of nonextension.[51]

The most important of Seward's themes was that Republicans stood for Unionism and slaveholders for disunion. Echoing Free-Soilers who had defended the Wilmot Proviso in the mid-1840s, Seward cast disunion as a language of passion and Unionism as a language of reason. The Republican Party, he argued, could give guarantees of its faithfulness to the Declaration of Independence and the Constitution that slaveholders could never give: "We give the guaranties [*sic*] of peaceful, just, loyal lives, marked with a patience that has endured as long as they were tolerable, and without even a ruffling of the temper, not only the insults of slaveholders, but their menaces of disunion." Seward explicitly contrasted a Northern model of manhood—in which a true man calmly followed the "impartial counsel of [his] conscience" —with slaveholders' intemperance. They "argue only in threats" and made "perpetual appeals to the ignoble instinct of fear."[52]

Although ostensibly a repudiation of Southern disunion, Seward's formula served to dissociate the Republican Party from the disunion rhetoric of abolitionists as well. This was no mere rhetorical flourish, but a major priority for Republicans, for the very events that had stoked anti-Nebraska sentiment had also led to an upsurge of disunionism among radical Garrisonians, particularly African American ones. Black abolitionists such as William Wells Brown, Robert Purvis, and Uriah Boston made a series of potent disunion speeches in the mid-1850s. Brown, a former slave who, like Frederick Douglass, became an influential voice on the antislavery lecture circuit, argued before a meeting of the Pennsylvania Anti-Slavery Society in the fall of 1854 that disunion was not a proslavery program but rather a present-day reality, for the South was already a fortress that shut out men of conscience: "Go into the southern States an avowed enemy of slaveholding, and are you free?" Brown rejoiced that the "people of the North are beginning to be aroused, and the cry of 'disunion,' which they have heretofore hated so much to hear, is practically becoming their watchword." Uriah Boston, a New York activist, wrote two letters to *Frederick Douglass' Paper* in the fall of 1855 endorsing disunion and spelling out its likely results: it would weaken the Slave Power, release the North from having to do its bidding with regard to fugitive slaves, serve as a catalyst to increased slave flight, and eventually result in the abolition of slavery. In short, disunion would hurt the South more than it would hurt the North; if Northerners would only admit this and profess their desire for dissolution, Southerners would not make their customary threats anymore.[53]

Perhaps no one found a bigger audience for his disunionism than James S.

Pike of Maine, a Washington correspondent of Horace Greeley's wildly popular newspaper, the *New York Tribune*. Greeley was ambivalent about invoking disunion as a threat; he preferred to use it as an accusation. But in the name of free speech and the need to sell papers, he gave Pike free rein to contribute provocative disunion editorials. Since the Compromise of 1850, Pike had maintained that in a choice between disunion and slavery extension, disunion was the lesser of two evils. During the Kansas controversy, his pronouncements became more strident. He wrote in 1854 that he would rather belong to a "confederacy of twenty millions of Freemen" than a Union that included "conquest-seeking, slavery-extending" Southerners. "If this be treason," he declared, sounding eerily like Robert Barnwell Rhett, "make the most of it."[54]

Frederick Douglass, having repudiated Garrison's "no union with slaveholders," rejected Boston and Pike's position, too. Disunion, he countered, would not "weaken the South nor absolve the North of its complicity in the perpetuation of slavery"; nor would it promote slave escapes. Douglass, like Seward, was determined to portray advocacy of disunion as a malady that afflicted Southern slaveholders and had no place in the rhetoric of the non-slaveholding majority, which had both the Declaration of Independence and the Constitution on its side. When, in the fall of 1855, Governor Herschel Johnson of Georgia threatened disunion if Kansas were not admitted as a slave state, Douglass railed that Johnson was having "an annual attack of the Disunion fever," which made him "rave and tear, curse and swear" like a madman. Although he regarded disunion as a malignant disease, Douglass did not cast his lot with the Republican Party in its formative stage, choosing instead to affiliate with self-styled "Radical Abolitionists." Led by a remarkable interracial brotherhood—black activists Douglass and James McCune Smith and white activists Gerrit Smith and John Brown—the radical abolitionists convened their first meeting in Syracuse, New York, in June 1855, even as the American Party was imploding in Philadelphia. These radicals disavowed Garrisonian disunionism on the grounds that if the free states separated from the slave states, slaveholders "would be at perfect liberty to continue their oppression and torture of the black man." But while Seward's Republicans positioned themselves to the right of Garrisonians, as moderates, radical abolitionists positioned themselves to the left, as the one anti-slavery group committed to the view that the Constitution sanctioned abolition, the doctrine of Northern complicity, the repudiation of disunion, and the advocacy of violence as a legitimate tool against the Slave Power. The fate of the nation would be decided in Kansas, Douglass predicted, and radical abolitionists must not let the nonslaveholders of Kansas be trampled "beneath the iron heel of slavery."[55]

So far as Douglass could see, that "iron heel" bore the stamp of the Pierce administration. The Free-Soil shadow government of Kansas faced the opposition of President Pierce, who denounced the Topeka movement as treasonable and threatened military intervention to keep order. In fact, Pierce's position only emboldened proslavery forces, who provoked a series of violent clashes with Free-Soilers from November 1855 to May 1856, including an attack on an antislavery newspaper in Parkville. More than free speech was at stake. "With the essential frontier business of establishing land titles, validating timber claims, and settling water disputes subject only to the shotgun methods of frontier justice," Henry Mayer has noted, the territory turned into a "contested zone of sporadic violence." The escalating mayhem culminated in the sack of Lawrence on May 21, 1856. The trouble there dated back to November 1855, when some 1,500 Border Ruffians had marched on the town and faced off against 1,000 armed men determined to protect the Free-Soil bastion. Intervention from Governor Wilson Shannon persuaded the rival forces to stand down. But tempers flared again in the spring of 1856, when "the annual migration of settlers promised to increase the free-state majority." Emboldened by the decision of proslavery Judge Samuel Lecompte to indict members of the Topeka government for treason, proslavery forces carrying banners with the slogan "Southern Rights" fell upon Lawrence, destroying its newspaper offices and laying waste to stores and private residences, including the home of the free-state governor. In the eyes of antislavery Kansans such as Sara Robinson, whose home was pillaged and personal belongings were destroyed during the attack, the ruffianism of the proslavery forces gave the lie to Southern claims of chivalry. "O, southern honor! How her gloss has become dim, when her chief men, the self-constituted champions of southern institutions, attempt to gain their ends by stealing private correspondence, and pillaging a lady's drawers!'" she wrote in her published account of the incident, fostering Northern indignation at the ways that women and children had been victimized by proslavery mobs. Anti-Nebraska journals like the *Chicago Tribune* and the *New York Tribune*, which served as the mouthpieces of the emerging Republican Party, painted lurid and overblown pictures of the destruction wrought by the "Sack of Lawrence" to stoke antipathy to the Slave Power.[56]

About three days later, on May 24–25, antislavery zealot John Brown and seven of his followers entered the proslavery settlement of Pottawatomie in Kansas and hacked to death five unsuspecting settlers—nonslaveholding immigrants and poor Southern whites. A grim, volatile New Englander steeped in an unforgiving strain of Calvinism, Brown, wherever he settled in the Northeast and Midwest, was bedeviled both by economic failure and by the bitter conviction that he and all those around him, his family included, were mired in sin. Seeking redemption on the plains of Kansas, he assaulted the institution of slavery as an affront to the Christian value of personal freedom. But he took the doctrine of individual autonomy to a defiant extreme: although he condemned proslavery forces for their lawless abrogation of human rights, Brown himself was deeply contemptuous of society's rules and believed that he personally, by exacting violent retribution, could avenge the wrongs of the world. To quote historian James Oakes, Brown "distrusted any earthly government other than his own."[57]

In June 1855 Brown had participated in the inaugural convention of the radical political abolitionists in Syracuse, where he had taken up a collection to help arm free-state settlers in Kansas. During that meeting he had cast a spell over his fellow delegates with his vision of slavery as a "state of war" that necessitated armed resistance. According to John Stauffer, Brown "fashioned himself in the tradition of James Fenimore Cooper's Leatherstocking, a white man able to blur racial boundaries and cross fluidly from savagery to civilization and back." The proslavery press naturally rejected such a romantic view and characterized Brown and his men as bloodthirsty demons. Brown's supporters shuddered at the details of the Pottawatomie massacre but were determined to explain them, as Douglass put it, as a "terrible remedy for a terrible malady"; in a brutal environment, they reasoned, "one must become brutal or die." Unfortunately, Brown's violence had the effect of justifying the federal government's use of the U.S. Army against Free-Soil Kansans, whom it viewed as treasonous guerrillas. But even the army could not impose peace. By the summer of 1856, Kansas was engulfed in a full-scale guerrilla war.[58]

THE CANING OF CHARLES SUMNER

Brown's murderous spree in Kansas was sparked not only by his outrage at the proslavery assault on Lawrence but also by his indignation at a shocking turn of events in the nation's capital. On May 22, 1856, two days after Charles Sumner delivered an impassioned speech in the Senate entitled the "The Crime against Kansas," South Carolina congressman Preston Brooks entered the Senate chamber after the legislators had adjourned and the galleries had emptied, strode up to Sumner's desk, where the senator was quietly attending to some correspondence, and commenced striking Sumner with a gutta-percha cane, inflicting thirty-some blows that left him bleeding and unconscious. Brooks claimed to be defending his honor—for Sumner's speech had singled out for opprobrium Brooks's cousin, Senator Andrew Butler. The context for Sumner's two-day address was the ongoing heated debate on the Senate floor regarding the admission of Kansas as a state. Sumner was a leading voice in the anti-Nebraska coalition that favored admitting Kansas as a free state under the Topeka constitution, while Southern Democrats advocated admitting the state with its proslavery government seated in Lecompton. Both Brooks and Butler, speaking in the House and Senate respectively, had expressed their contempt for the Free-Soil faction in the territory and their conviction that the very destiny of the South hung in the balance—if Kansas became free, abolition would march across the West and even into slave states such as Arkansas and Texas.[59]

Sumner's speech bitterly mocked his Senate colleague in words calculated to raise his ire. For all his pretense of chivalry, Sumner declared, Butler had "chosen a mistress to whom he has made his vows, and who, though ugly to others, is chaste in his sight—I mean the harlot, slavery." Although Butler had accused free staters of abolition fanaticism, it was the South Carolinian who was the real fanatic, "the uncompromising, unblushing representative on this floor of a flagrant sectionalism, which now domineers over the Republic." Returning to the subject of Butler in his concluding remarks on May 20, Sumner said that the South Carolinian could "not open his mouth, but out there flies a blunder." Sumner thus portrayed his opponent as an incoherent, vain, hypocrite.[60]

While these personal attacks on their family name rankled Butler and his cousin Brooks, it was Sumner's broader arguments that rendered the speech inflammatory, ominous, and unforgettable. For Sumner masterfully used sexual imagery, anti-Catholic imagery, and the discourse of disunion in his "Crime against Kansas" address to consolidate the ranks of the fledgling Republican Party and capitalize on the decline of the Know-Nothings. Sumner described the depradations of proslavery forces as the "rape of a virgin Territory, compelling it to the hateful embrace of slavery." He contrasted the Christian virtue of the antislavery men and women of Kansas with the debauchery of the Border Ruffians, whom he described as "Hirelings, picked from the drunken spew and vomit of an uneasy civilization." In keeping with the efforts of Chase, Seward, and other party leaders to draw antislavery Know-Nothings into the Republican fold, Sumner peppered his speech with references to Protestant heroes who had withstood religious persecution. Thus he likened Pierce's complicity in the crime against Kansas with papal defense of the St. Bartholomew's Day Massacre of 1572, in which French Catholics slaughtered thousands of Protestants. Like Seward and Chase, Sumner made the case that "the Republican party of the Union is in no just sense sectional, but, more than any other party, national." He appealed to "the People," on the eve of the presidential election of 1856, to ensure that the "ballot-box of the Union" would redeem and rescue the antislavery citizens of Kansas. But, like Walker, Garrison, and Mann, he invoked disunion as retributive justice. Unless "happily averted by the triumph of Freedom," Sumner prophesized, the current conflict "will become war—fratricidal, parricidal war—with an accumulated wickedness beyond the wickedness of any war in human annals; justly provoking the avenging judgment of Providence."[61]

Congressional Democrats, Southern and Northern, moved quickly to brand Sumner's oration as, so Senator Lewis Cass put it, "the most unAmerican and unpatriotic speech that ever grated on the ears of the members of this high body." Disregarding Sumner's appeal to the ballot box as the ultimate arbiter of American political life, Stephen Douglas portrayed the Massachusetts senator as the head of an abolitionist conspiracy and warned that " 'Revolution' is becoming their watch-word. And why? Because disunion is the object." Senator Mason of Virginia went Douglas one better, charging that Sumner and others who were arrayed against the Union would go "as Cain did, with the curse upon their brow of fraternal homicide." It was with such sentiments ringing in his ears that Brooks mounted his assault on Sumner. Although Brooks was arrested after the incident and fined for a misdemeanor, the House did not have the two-thirds majority needed to expel him; he resigned, unrepentant, only to win reelection with "triumphant unanimity." Indeed, as Brooks put it in a letter to his brother, the fragments of the cane he used to beat Sumner were "begged for as *sacred relicts*" by adoring Southerners. Gleeful supporters sent Brooks hundreds of canes as gifts. And Southern newspapers hailed him, making the most of the incident's symbolism—Brooks had not met Sumner in a duel, the way he would have an honorable opponent; instead, he had beaten Sumner like a slave. In South Carolina, the *Edgefield Advertiser* lauded Brooks for giving Sumner "fifty stripes" and declared that "we feel that our Representative did exactly right." The *Richmond Enquirer* opined that all abolitionists should be so "lashed into obscurity" and took palpable pleasure at Brooks's report that Sumner had "bellowed like a bull-calf" beneath his blows. A Columbia, South Carolina, paper reported that "the ladies of the South" had vowed to send Brooks hickory sticks (since Andrew Jackson's day, a symbol of the Democratic Party) to "chastise Abolitionists" with, and that some Charleston gentlemen had given Brooks a cane with the inscription "Hit Him Again." Southern papers also accused Sumner, who claimed to be too badly hurt to return to the Senate, of "possuming"—feigning illness to keep alive the sympathy for him among "nigger-worshipping fanatics of the male gender, and weak-minded women and silly children," as the *Richmond Whig* put it.[62]

Antislavery Northerners interpreted the episode as a window into the Southern soul. The "logic of the Plantation, brute violence and might, has at last risen where it was inevitable it should rise to—the Senate of the United States," the *Albany Evening Journal* lamented. George S. Hilliard, of Massachusetts, speaking at a meeting at Faneuil Hall, condemned the cowardliness of the attack: "To approach a man imprisoned, tied hand and foot, so to speak, in an arm-chair and desk, and strike him over the head . . . is in my opinion the act of an assassin, and I say compared to such an act, the conduct of a man who meets me on the high road, and horsewhips me, or attempts to do so, soars to something like manliness and courage." Such rhetoric was calculated to expose the fraudulence of the so-called cult of Southern honor.

Northern "indignation" meetings passed resolutions that condemned the attack as yet one more effort by proslavery Southerners to suppress free speech. At a May 27, 1856, gathering at Union College in Schenectady, New York, students resolved that "as freemen we look upon this unprecedented outrage with horror; regarding it as a bold attempt to terrify the representatives of a free people in the exercise of their constitutional rights." Two weeks later, in Boston, African Americans resolved that the beating was a "dastardly attempt to crush out Free Speech."[63]

Even as the *Liberator* critiqued the Republican Party for advocating non-extension rather than immediatism, Garrison's paper praised Sumner for "the manly stand that he is maintaining in opposition to the Slave Power." At the end of May 1856, looking back on the "Sack of Lawrence" and the caning of Sumner, Garrison editorialized: "So eventful and startling a week as the past has not been known in American history since the formulation of that blood-stained Union which has legitimately resulted in this supremacy of the Slave Power." Surely now, "every true friend of freedom will lend all his energies, without hesitation or compromise," to the goal of disunion. "Who now needs any more persuasion on the subject?"[64]

To Consummate Its Boldest Designs

THE SLAVE POWER CONFRONTS THE REPUBLICANS

"The country is now passing through the most portentous crisis which it has encountered since the revolution," wrote Democrat Bedford Brown of Maryland to his party's candidate, James Buchanan, on the eve of the 1856 presidential election. From North to South, Buchanan received letters expressing fear for the Union's survival and counsel on what he needed to do to restore the sectional equilibrium. On the prospect of a Republican victory, a Philadelphia Democrat confided: "As an American, the bare possibility of the evils that might flow from the election of a sectional president cannot but alarm me." But this correspondent censured his own party for sectionalism, too, urging Buchanan to distance himself from the "intemperate language of some professed Democrats of the South." Many other Northern Democrats asked him to dispel the impression that their party served "the especial interest of the South and slavery." Southern constituents, for their part, also expressed fear for the fate of the Union—fear that Northern public sentiment would "sweep away" the "barriers" that protected slavery. R. H. Glass of Lynchburg, Virginia, warned Buchanan: "If you, and those who sustain you in this momentous crisis go down, the Union and the constitution will go down with you as sure as God rules in the Universe."[1]

With "Bleeding Kansas" and "Bleeding Sumner" dominating the headlines, the two major parties had geared up for the election of 1856 by holding nominating conventions in June. The Democrats met in Cincinnati on June 2 and passed over stalwarts Stephen Douglas and the incumbent Franklin Pierce in favor of Buchanan, a sixty-five-year-old bachelor (among the oldest men to run for president), with an impressive résumé of public service. A staunch Jacksonian and "doughface," Buchanan hailed from Pennsylvania, a state that boasted the second most electoral votes in the nation. That "Old Buck" was regarded as an officious bureaucrat served Democratic purposes, for his mandate was to uphold what Jean H. Baker calls the "clichés of mid-century conservatism": strict construction of the Constitution, the doctrine of state sovereignty, a commitment to reining in the power and spending of the federal government, and a belief that Northerners should cease "agitating" the slavery issue. Conveniently, Buchanan had been out of the country, serving as minister to Britain, during the Kansas-Nebraska agitation and thus could adopt the statesmanlike posture of someone who was above the fray.[2]

The Republicans, meeting about two weeks later in Philadelphia, passed over their own stalwarts such as Seward and Chase for a new face—that of John C. Frémont, a youthful adventurer who had already won public acclaim as an explorer of the Rocky Mountains and Far West. Frémont's romantic image was bolstered by his highly publicized elopement with the charismatic belle Jessie Benton—daughter of the powerful Democratic senator, Thomas Hart Benton of Missouri. Frémont stood on a Republican platform that spelled out the doctrine of nonextension, upheld the Missouri Compromise, arraigned the Pierce administration for the outrages in Kansas, called for the admission of Kansas as a free state, and dubbed slavery a "relic of barbarism." While Buchanan and Frémont faced off in the North, it was the American Party candidate, Millard Fillmore, who served as the alternative to Buchanan in the South. Representing a Whig–Know-Nothing coalition, Fillmore had little enthusiasm for nativism. As an architect of the Compromise of 1850, however, he was offered as a champion of Unionism; his party's platform condemned the Democrats for fomenting sectional strife and placing "Ultraists" in power.[3]

With their platforms and standard-bearers in place, the three parties embarked on a bitter and portentous campaign. In the Deep South, Democrats of both militant and moderate stripes predicted that a Frémont victory in the national election would justify disunion. Louisiana is a revealing example of how the political ground had shifted. The Whig Party had boasted a strong base in the state, as it attracted the support of sugar planters who favored high tariffs on imported sugar and of merchants in the commercial entrepôt of New Orleans. But "by 1856, the only one substantial issue [that] remained in Louisianians' minds" was "which party best protected the South and slavery." The Democrats had long been accustomed to branding the opposition party as unsound on slavery and as a tool of abolitionist disunionists. But now, for the "first time" in a presidential election campaign, threats supplanted such accusations—Louisiana Democrats openly warned that the state would secede should Frémont prevail. And that translated into a wide margin of victory for Buchanan.[4]

Outside of the Deep South, the Democrats' strategy was to paint their own party as the last truly national political institution in the country, to tarnish the "Black Republicans" (as Democrats derisively labeled their opponents) not just as sectional but as the tool of Garrisonian disunionists bent on overturning the social order, and to discredit the American Party as accomplices of the Republicans. Democratic campaign rhetoric hammered these themes home incessantly. The *Richmond Enquirer*, for instance, charged that "the Black Republicans in Congress are at open war with Government, and like their allies, the Garrisonian Abolitionists, are really at war with religion, female virtue, private property, and distinctions of race." The aim of that war was to reduce the South to a state of "despicable dependencies" and "spoliation and oppression." Democratic pamphlets and broadsides assailed John Frémont as the "candidate for the Presidency of [the] conjoined fanaticisms" of "free love. . . . woman's rights. . . . And disunion phrensy [*sic*]."[5]

Such rhetoric was by no means restricted to the South. In Pennsylvania, the *York Democratic Press*, to give one example, held up Buchanan as a man who represented "the whole American people" and who believed that "disunion is a word which ought not to be breathed among us, even in a whisper." But that paper, in more than a whisper, accused the Republicans of disunion —of "look[ing] forward to the day when the country may itself be torn into fragments and factions, in order that it may fall an unresisting prey to foreign and domestic foes." Sometimes, in a convenient elision, the Democratic press referred to the "Black Republican Know Nothing party," a coalition united, so Democrats alleged, by its determination to "overthrow . . . our glorious Union." In lockstep with Southern papers, the party organ, the *Democratic*

"*B U C K*" taking the "*P O T*".

This Democratic cartoon shows that Buchanan holds all the cards in the 1856 presidential contest and is determined to protect the "UNION SOUP." Fillmore stumbles blindly while hoisting a lantern (a nativist symbol), and Frémont trips over the "ROCK OF DISUNION" while clutching a spoon marked "ABOLITION." (Courtesy of the Library of Congress)

Review, based in New York, fumed that Republicans had "incorporate[d] in their disunion creed" the dread doctrines of "womans-rights-ism" and "socialism" and "whatever cause . . . a frenzied brain might find attraction in." The opposition, in other words, represented not only sectionalism but also infidelity to the divinely ordained social hierarchy.[6]

Some Northern Democrats tried to draw a moral and functional distinction between Southern and Northern invocations of disunion. When Calhoun had used the word, the *Democratic Review* opined, he had done so with "melancholy grandeur." But when abolitionists and Republicans spoke of disunion, they were geniuses of "evil-doing." Thus the younger generation of fire-eaters who "blurt[ed] out the filthy, execrable word" did so only because abolitionists who "deify niggers" had provoked them to, "pandering to a vicious craving after excitement." In short, while the South had "threatened" disunion, the "Frémont party desire it, they hail its advent as the dawn of a political millennium." And "that is "fiendishly malignant," the *Review* concluded. Democrats also tried to connect nativism to disunion by tracing the American Party's antipathy to foreigners back to the Federalist Alien and Sedition Acts and to the Hartford Convention. "All the schemes and plots and conspiracies, which have ever been gotten up to dissolve this Union," according to the *Review*, "have been the work of native-born New Englanders!" While such messages were calculated to attract Southerners and Northern doughfaces, Democrats reached out to moderate Northern voters with appeals to the sanctity of popular sovereignty as a doctrine that was neutral on the subject of slavery. Frémont Republicans, a Democratic pamphlet addressed to Connecticut voters declared, were guilty of wanting to take the future of slavery "out of the hands of the people" and put it into the hands of Congress—and guilty of wanting to "keep the civil war alive" in Kansas so they could use it as their "political stock in trade."[7]

Was it true that Republicans and Garrisonians were fellow travelers? Garrison himself was profoundly ambivalent about the new party, and that ambivalence pervaded the *Liberator*'s coverage of the 1856 campaign. On the one hand, the newspaper featured numerous articles lambasting the Republican Party for its idolatry of the Union. "The man who can lend his countenance to such a bastard Union," ran one article, "sinks his manhood, and becomes a prostitute." As the managers of the Pennsylvania Anti-Slavery Society succinctly put it: "The Republican party is a Union party; our party is . . . a Disunion party." "We speak not as politicians . . . [but] as the advocates of a moral principle," they explained. On the other hand, Garrison cautioned his followers to draw a sharp distinction between Republicans and their rivals. For although he disapproved of the Republican position on the Constitution and the Union, Garrison saw the party's very existence as the logical and inevitable outgrowth of immediatism, as a step toward the disunion he desired. Taking the "philosophical view," he described the party to immediatists as "the work of our own hands" and predicted that "in proportion to the growth of Disunionism will be the growth of Republicanism"—meaning that the party would be strongest in the places, like Massachusetts, where Garrisonianism had made the greatest progress. When Garrison's friend and follower Theodore Parker gravitated toward the Republicans and forswore disunionism, Garrison excused him with a handy bit of word play, arguing that Parker was not in favor of saving the Union that existed but the one "found in his liberty-loving imagination."[8]

Ironically, Garrison's complex relationship with the Republicans mirrored that of Frederick Douglass. Although Douglass had come to accept the doctrine of an antislavery Constitution, he favored the radical reading that empowered Congress to abolish and not merely to contain slavery; thus he condemned the Republicans for hewing to the anemic and ineffectual doctrine of nonextension. "Free soilism is lame, halt, and blind while it battles against the spread of slavery, and admits its right to exist anywhere," he wrote in 1855. But because he shared the Republicans' opposition to the Kansas-Nebraska Act and their commitment to political action, Douglass could not help but invest his hopes in the new party and wish for its success. In fact, by June 1856 Douglass had broken with Gerrit Smith and the radical abolitionists and officially endorsed the Republican Party. This was not a capricious about-face, but a move fully consistent with Douglass's earlier, hesitant embrace of the Liberty and Free-Soil parties. Douglass believed that political pragmatism in the here-and-now was totally compatible with high principles that looked to the future. He asked fellow radicals to accept the Republicans "not merely for what they are but for what we have good reason to believe they will become." Douglass was determined to shape the party; he would emerge again and again as a vociferous critic urging Republicans down a radical path. He was joined in this work by African American reformers in the black convention movement, such as Charles Henry Langston, of Ohio, who saw in the new party the potential realization of black dreams of a truly inclusive Union. "We are part of the American people," Langston averred at his state's annual convention in 1856, "and we and our posterity will forever be a constituent part of your population." By recognizing this fundamental fact, Langston reasoned, the Republican Party could do "great service in the cause of Freedom."[9]

Intent on inheriting the Whig voting bloc, co-opting the American Party, absorbing Free-Soilers, converting abolitionists, and even attracting moderate Democrats in the North, the architects of the Republican Party's 1856 campaign worked to tailor their message to these diverse constituencies. The party's leadership was itself divided into distinct camps—radicals, such as Sumner, Chase, and Seward, whose antislavery credentials even Garrison and Douglass could not question; conservatives, such as Senator Lyman Trumbull, of Illinois, a former Democrat whose opposition to slavery extension was grounded in his deep antipathy to blacks; and moderates, such as Abraham Lincoln, who had been "old-line" Whigs. They were, in the words of one of Lincoln's fellow Illinois Whigs, "opposed to extremes" and willing to be patient about slavery's demise provided "the union is safe [and] . . . the country is quiet and prosperous."[10]

Moderates and conservatives rejected the radicals' attempts to link abolition and free blacks' quest for racial equality in the North. For this reason, the Democrats' determination to define all Republicans as abolitionists flew in the face of a stark reality—that "at the center of northern politics there resided a broad group of whites whose opposition to slavery was balanced by support for various forms of discrimination against free blacks," as James Oakes cogently explains. The 1850s witnessed a deterioration in the status of Northern free blacks, marked by deepening segregation and disfranchisement, their displacement in the labor market by immigrants, and the revival of the colonization movement.[11]

With conservatives and moderates both willing to use racist rhetoric and to endorse the colonization of free blacks, Republicans, particularly when campaigning in the Midwest and Lower North, seemed eager to shed any association with abolitionism. Indeed, Republican pandering to white supremacy has led a school of modern historians to doubt the party's antislavery credentials and emphasize its status as an "anti-slave" and antiblack party—one that appealed to voters in places like Illinois, Indiana, Oregon, Kansas, and even the Northeast, with its pledges to preserve the country from the *"pestilential presence of the black man,"* to quote the *Hartford Courant*. While examples of such open race-baiting are relatively rare, Republicans did, routinely, disavow any "sentimental" sympathy for the suffering of slaves. Following the template established by David Wilmot and other Free-Soilers in the Proviso debates, moderate and conservative Republicans insisted that "the plight of the white man, not the black, concerned them."[12]

Nonetheless, as Eric Foner, Richard Sewell, William E. Gienapp, and Kenneth Stampp have shown, to portray the Republicans as "anti-slave" fails to put them in the context of their times and to draw an accurate contrast between them and the Democrats. As Stampp has argued, "Race was an issue on which the Republicans were always on the defensive, for the Democrats were quite successful in establishing themselves as preeminently the anti-Negro party." Republicans occasionally resorted to racist arguments as a matter of expediency, but they "exploited anti-black sentiment less than one might have expected," given the prevalence of racism in the North and West and the constant race-baiting of Democrats. Racist arguments were conspicuously absent from the Republican Party platform, which justified slavery nonextension "on moral grounds alone"; state platforms and conventions, too, eschewed racist rhetoric and instead condemned slavery as "a great evil and wrong."[13]

Generations of scholars have looked to Abraham Lincoln, who in the mid-1850s represented the moderate Republican outlook, as the test case with which to assess the party's racial attitudes. A consensus has emerged that Lincoln's support of colonization and disavowal of racial equality was, within the context of the time, compatible with his genuine, heartfelt loathing of slavery and desire that nonextension would lead to slavery's eventual demise. Daniel Walker Howe has provided the most cogent analysis of Lincoln's stance on slavery during the Kansas-Nebraska controversy. Lincoln, a native of Kentucky married to a fellow Kentuckian, Mary Todd, had come of age politically "under the spell of the great Kentucky Whig, Henry Clay." But the passing of Clay and his generation of compromisers, and the subsequent demise of the Whig Party, had inclined Lincoln, in his rebirth as a Republican, to gravitate toward the antislavery position of another former Whig, Joshua Giddings. In the wake of the Kansas-Nebraska Act, Lincoln "started catching up" with Giddings. Lincoln did not completely abandon the Upper South fantasies of gradualism and colonization. But "like Giddings, Lincoln reconciled his hatred for slavery with his dedication to legal tradition by concluding that the Founding Fathers had written a freedom-loving Constitution that corrupt successors were perverting into a proslavery instrument."[14]

Moderates such as Lincoln were strategic both in their concessions to racism and in their use of antislavery rhetoric, distancing themselves from abolitionists when it suited their purpose of converting skeptical, even hostile voters and invoking abolitionist themes when preaching to already converted groups of the party faithful. Lincoln in his speeches and writings eschewed the themes of slave suffering and of slavery's daily horrors, subjects that the electorate associated with radical abolitionism and with female writers like Stowe. He preferred to speak of the institution of slavery, and its historical, constitutional and political dimensions, rather than the plight of the slaves. Thus, in speeches he delivered in Bloomington, Springfield, and Peoria, Illinois, in 1854—as he was reviving his own political career in a bid for the state legislature and representing anti-Nebraska forces in a series of debates with his nemesis, Senator Stephen Douglas—Lincoln could say of slavery: "Let us return it to the position our fathers gave it; and there let it rest in peace." In an effort to attract unpersuaded voters, Lincoln repeatedly asserted that Thomas Jefferson was the true author of nonextension and that, thanks to the Northwest Ordinance, the Midwest was "now what Jefferson foresaw and intended—the happy home of teeming millions of free, white, prosperous people, and no slave amongst them." Lincoln advocated the restoration of the Missouri Compromise, which was a logical extension of the Northwest Ordinance, invoking the "high republican faith of our ancestors." Finally, he openly conciliated Southerners and Northern racists by disavowing any desire for the social equality and intermixing of the races; by conceding that "if we [Northerners] were situated as they [Southerners], we should feel and act as they do"; and by admitting that he knew of no "satisfactory way" to end slavery. Lincoln tepidly endorsed colonization and gradual emancipation but declined to judge Southerners for their "tardiness in this."[15]

When speaking before audiences of diehard antislavery Republicans, by contrast, as he did in his famous "lost address" to the Illinois State Republican Convention in Bloomington in 1856, Lincoln could present himself as a "soul maddened by the wrong" of human bondage, "fired by the moral enormities of slavery as well as its policy implications." Indeed, Lincoln's Bloomington speech was so stirring that it established him as the leader of the state Republican Party. Although his tone and emphasis varied, Lincoln's speeches of the mid-1850s were animated by three abiding themes: his belief that blacks were part of the family of humankind, referred to in Jefferson's preamble; his openly professed "hatred" of slavery; and his devotion to the Union. During the presidential campaign, this last theme became predominant in the fifty-some speeches Lincoln gave on behalf of his party.[16]

Lincoln had become convinced that the Republicans' first priority was to counter the pervasive charges that they were disunionists. "It is constantly objected . . . that [Republicans are] a sectional party, who by their sectionalism, endanger the National Union. This objection, more than all others, causes men, really opposed to slavery extension, to hesitate. Practically, it is the most difficult objection we have to meet," Lincoln wrote in his private notes. In 1854 he had reassured voters that "much as I hate slavery, I would consent to the extension of it rather than see the Union dissolved." By 1856, with the Republican coalition contending for electoral supremacy in the North, Lincoln took a different tack. In speeches at Galena, Illinois, and Kalamazoo, Michigan, he tried to expose charges of Republican disunionism as illogical. To those who predicted that a Republican victory would bring disunion, he pointed out that if the Republicans won, "we, the majority, being able constitutionally to do all we purpose, would have no desire to dissolve the Union." Lincoln repeated this winning formulation again and again, honing the argument that the Union *inhered in the majority* and that Republicans were committed to using constitutional means—namely, victory at the ballot box—to save it from the machinations of a disaffected minority. "A majority never will dissolve the Union. Can a minority do it?" he asked. Southern supporters of Buchanan "have five disunion men to one at the North." But this sectional oligarchy could not prevail over the nationalist majority. "We don't want to dissolve [the Union]," Lincoln said, rhetorically addressing those sectionalists. "And if you attempt it, we won't let you . . . . *We* 'won't' dissolve the Union, and *you* 'shan't.' "[17]

Susan-Mary Grant argues that Republican campaign rhetoric in 1856 articulated a distinctive Northern nationalism, "predicated on ideals that were perceived to be wholly antisouthern"—the Republican national platform was, in fact, a sectional one that exploited negative images of the South to promote Northern solidarity. And "nationality was not truly national when Lincoln spoke, but wholly northern." But such a viewpoint fails to take into account the centrality of the Republicans' belief in latent antislavery sentiment in the South; Lincoln's recognition of Northern complicity and responsibility for the spread of slavery; and his notion that sectionalism and disunion, by definition, were antidemocratic philosophies. In his 1856 speeches, he repeatedly reprised the familiar theme that "in intellectual and physical structure, our Southern brethren do not differ from us. They are, like us, subject to passions, and it is only their odious institution of slavery, that makes the breach between us." In Lincoln's view, "Our government rests in public opinion. Whoever can change public opinion can change the government." Southern slaveholders had been masterful manipulators of public opinion, appealing to "immense pecuniary interest" not only to maintain their dominance in the South but also to attract the "greedy eyes of Northern ambition." Republicans had an uphill battle, for they had only moral arguments with which to counter the passions of greed and self-interest. But the goal of that battle, Republicans asserted again and again, was to win over Northerners and thus lay the groundwork for winning over nonslaveholding Southerners, too. Disunionism, in Lincoln's eyes, was a repudiation of the very premise of representative government—disunion was a withdrawal from the national contest, whose ground rules the Constitution had clearly laid out, for public opinion.[18]

Lincoln's fellow architects of the 1856 campaign shared his view that Republicans had to "set forth the grounds . . . whereon conservative Unionism and radical Anti-Slavery . . . [could] meet and coincide," to use the words of Horace Greeley. The issue of free speech was the primary point of that convergence. The right to free speech—which Lincoln considered the bedrock of republican government—was the fundamental ground rule of the constitutional contest for public opinion, and Republicans made the Slave Power's abridgment of it a central campaign issue. The same tactics of intimidation and violence perfected by Preston Brooks and the Border Ruffians, Republicans reminded voters, were used by slaveholders to repress indigenous antislavery sentiment in the South. The efforts by Kentucky politician Cassius Clay and preacher John G. Fee to revive that state's gradual emancipation movement in the mid-1850s, for example, was met by slaveholder mob violence. Referring to the fate of John Underwood, a western Virginia Republican who had exiled himself from the South under threat of mob attacks, the *New York Times* lamented that "in Virginia, for the mere expression of opinion unfriendly to Slavery, citizens are compelled to flee to the Free States." Each of the Southern states had "large minorities," another editorial asserted, "which if they were permitted to speak, would gladly have joined the Republican Convention." But the "Oligarchy" demanded fealty to slavery and "commanded all men to think or speak otherwise at their peril." The right to free speech, the editorial implied, was not a sectional value but a national one—"There are some things which have no relation to place and geographical lines, except in the mousing expediency of hand-to-mouth politicians."[19]

Nowhere were Republicans more creative in merging Unionism and antislavery than in their manipulation of the images of "Frémont and Jessie," as their popular campaign slogan ran. John Frémont was born in Savannah, Georgia, and educated in Charleston, South Carolina. Foreshadowing his own elopement with Jessie, John's mother Anne Whiting, an elite Virginia matron, had left her loveless marriage to an aged wealthy planter to elope with John's father. Republican newspapers and campaign biographies opportunistically capitalized on John Frémont's Southern background. He was already associated in the public mind with California, having served as the new free state's governor and U.S. senator; his Southern roots could bolster the claim that he was truly national in stature. Frémont's Virginia heritage likened him to none other than George Washington, one campaign biography, published in Boston, asserted: "The same blood flowed in their veins. The domestic influences under which the mother of Frémont grew up, were derived from the same circle of family connections within which Washington was nurtured." The similarities between the two were a matter not only of character but also of policies: "Washington discerned the importance of connecting the Atlantic States with the interior, and labored to promote it. Following in the steps of the GREAT LEADER, the mind of Frémont has ever been engrossed with similar views and objects." Republican rhetoric also connected Frémont to Andrew Jackson, for Frémont had been in Charleston during the "time of [nullification's] greatest virulence" but had chosen to align with "General JACKSON, on the side of Freedom, Patriotism, Liberty and Union." "He never betrayed Freedom that he might rise by Slavery," an article in the *New York Times* concluded. "He never approved and counseled disunion and rebellion if he should be found in the minority."[20]

According to his campaign biographies, Frémont's heroic labors on behalf of the Union, as the famous "Pathfinder," converted him to the doctrine of nonextension. "Exploring the North American Continent, of which he has seen more than any other man," Frémont had "naturally become devoted to the cause of free labor." He had achieved success by playing by the rules of free society and abiding by the Constitution. In keeping with the Republicans' free labor creed, merchants, mechanics, shopkeepers, farmers, and laborers all belonged to the "productive classes" and shared an abiding interest in barring slavery from the territories, for human bondage by its very nature cast labor in disrepute and produced economic stagnation. Frémont, Republicans promised, would defend and promote not only free labor but also its essential corollary: the free institutions, such as common schools and churches, that fostered the virtue needed for economic success. Republican rhetoric encouraged Northerners to view their array of free institutions (including town meetings, debating clubs, postal facilities, newspapers, and colleges) as "sacred trusts" and emblems of opportunity.[21]

Jessie Benton Frémont's image proved every bit as malleable as John's. For conservative Republicans, Michael D. Pierson tells us, Jessie represented a "modern Helen of Troy whose beauty made her worthy of John's masculine heroics." As a "passive prize," this symbolic Jessie served to refute Democratic charges that the Republicans were Garrisonian gender radicals in disguise. Sometimes Republicans chose to cast her as a Southerner and John as a Northerner. That Jessie, over the objections of her overbearing slaveowning father, Senator Benton, had chosen Frémont suggested that the South might come to embrace the "economic and social promise of the North." For progressive Republicans, Jessie was a slave state convert to antislavery who, as a politician's daughter, was schooled in wielding domestic political influence and could do so for the cause of nonextension. According to a popular story, planted in the press by Jessie herself, when Southern ladies in California asked her to lobby for slavery's expansion, Jessie had refused them, saying that she would rather do her own work and be her own servant than see California become a slave state. Together, John and Jessie represented the persistence of latent antislavery sentiment among Southerners and the possibility that the Republican Party might one day claim Southern support on a large scale.[22]

With Jessie Frémont as a campaign centerpiece, the Republicans inspired an unprecedented degree of female rank-and-file activism. Republican women raised money to support free-state settlers in Kansas, attended rallies, hosted campaign events, and formed "Jessie Circles" to foster partisanship. At the same Kalamazoo event that featured Lincoln's famous 1856 speech, thirty-one ladies marched in procession, "dressed in white to represent the sister states, with a lone woman, representing Kansas, following sorrowfully behind, shrouded in mourning, deeply veiled, and bearing a rent and blackened flag." In a second procession, "13 horsewomen in the dress of old '76" rode by, "appropriately suggestive of the original states." These were intentionally national, not sectional, images—the women in each procession represented the country, not the North. The tableaux featuring thirty-two women, one of whom represented Kansas, became a fixture of the campaign and was presented by women in Wisconsin, Illinois, and elsewhere.[23]

The Frémonts' Southern and Western credentials enabled Republicans to make the most of another theme that united Unionism and antislavery: namely, the controversy over filibustering. Defined in this era as private military expeditions launched against nations with which the United States was formally at peace, filibusters had their heyday in the mid-1850s as part of the frenzy for national expansion and "manifest destiny." Significantly, the most notorious filibusters were Southern slaveholders, such as Tennessean William Walker, who invaded Nicaragua but failed to establish a proslavery regime there, and Mississippi fire-eater John Quitman, who mounted an unsuccessful campaign to take over Cuba. These men cultivated images as "southern crusaders" who would save slavery from Republican Party non-extension by creating a zone of U.S. slave territory in Central America. The praise of filibusters by slavery expansionists such as Robert Toombs, the sympathy for Walker expressed by the Democratic platform, and the endorsement by James Buchanan, while secretary of state, of diplomatic negotiations to acquire Cuba were enough to tarnish filibustering as another aggressive plot by the Slave Power Conspiracy. Republican campaign rhetoric contrasted Frémont's heroic and patriotic commitment to national expansion with the filibusters' extralegal machinations. According to a popular campaign song:

Border ruffians, filibusters
Will be swept by strong nor'westers
Bully Brooks and all such cattle
Fall lifeless by this ballot battle.

On this theme, moderate and conservative Republicans found themselves in full agreement with the likes of Garrison and Douglass, who missed no opportunity to condemn filibusters as minions and "scoundrels" of the Slave Power.[24]

In the end, the Republicans' hope of triumphing in the "ballot battle" fell short, although the party won eleven of sixteen free states. James Buchanan carried his home state of Pennsylvania and four other Northern states, along with every slaveholding state except Maryland. He obtained 45 percent of the total popular vote, with Frémont winning 33 percent and Fillmore the remaining 22 percent; this translated into 174 electoral votes for the Democrat, 115 for the Republican, and 8 for the American Party candidate. But could Buchanan and his party claim a mandate? The Republicans, based on encouraging trends that underlay the vote tally, declared themselves victorious in defeat. For they had benefited more than the Democrats from the high turnout on election day: 79 percent of the electorate had voted, with turnout in the North up 7 percent from the 1852 election—and "most of these new voters were Republicans." As Jean Baker points out, "Even in [Buchanan's] home state the combined Frémont-Fillmore vote was only a few hundred less than his, and he a favorite son." The Republican Party's own mandate was clear: over the next four years, it had to win over Fillmore's Northern voters as well as continue attracting new voters. That way it could capture the crucial battleground states of the Lower North—Pennsylvania, Illinois, and Indiana— where Fillmore's votes had cut into Frémont's support and thrown the victory to Buchanan. "All of us who did not vote for Mr. Buchanan, taken together, are a majority of four hundred thousand," Abraham Lincoln declared at a Republican banquet in Chicago in December 1856, rallying the troops for the coming contest. "Can we not come together, for the future[?] . . . Let past differences, as nothing be; and with steady eye on the real issue, let us reinaugurate the good old 'central issues' of the Republic. We *can* do it. The human heart *is* with us—God is with us. We shall again be able not to declare, that 'all States as States, are equal,' nor yet that 'all citizens as citizens are equal,' but to renew the broader, better declaration, including these and much more, that 'all *men* are created equal.' "[25]

BUCHANAN'S ELECTION AS A PYRRHIC VICTORY

In an article triumphantly entitled "The Verdict of the People," the *Democratic Review* predicted one month after Buchanan's election that "every scheme of disunion will soon perish from amongst us, and the old sentiment of fraternal amity be reestablished." By July 1857, the journal struck an altogether more cautionary note, warning that "although the flame of disunion . . . has since been trodden down and extinguished . . . nevertheless the materials for another conflagration lie around us; the fire still smoulders, though no longer blazing; and enemies are at work scattering fresh faggots over each latent spark, and secretly fanning the embers that are to burst forth with redoubled fury during the storm of the next Presidential contest." The enemies the *Review* named were, of course, abolitionists and Republicans. But the Democratic administration faced an equally potent threat from within, in the form of renewed Southern militancy. The meteoric rise of the Republican Party in the years 1854 to 1856 inspired a new wave of proslavery propaganda. The need for such propaganda was both political and military— slaveholders not only needed a bulwark against antislavery legislation, they also had to recruit and motivate the legions of settlers literally fighting for slavery in Kansas.[26]

The leader of the proslavery crusade in the mid-1850s was Virginian George Fitzhugh, a lawyer who fashioned a new career as a public intellectual. His screeds, *Sociology for the South; or, the Failure of Free Society* (1854) and *Cannibals All! or, Slaves without Masters* (1857), honed the comparative defense of slavery. While the Democratic Party line was to cast radical "isms" as the mad delusions of an insurgent minority of Northerners, Fitzhugh argued that abolitionism and woman's rights and socialism were diseases that afflicted all of "free society." Free society's purported devotion to liberty and equality was just a cover for the doctrine of "FREE COMPETITION"—another name for "Might makes right." Fitzhugh contrasted the heartlessness of the North, where workingmen, virtual slaves, were pitted against each other and against capitalists in a fierce struggle for survival with his South, where black slaves did the drudge work so white men and women would not have to. "We need never have white slaves in the South, because we have black ones," Fitzhugh intoned, realizing that by invoking white slavery, even to disclaim it, he impressed his readers with the grave stakes of the sectional contest. Defending the racial hierarchy as natural and divinely ordained, Fitzhugh contended that "the character of slavery is necessary to protect the white man, whilst it is more necessary for the government of the negro." Black inferiority meant that the race could never survive in a free society. Blacks were "weak, ignorant and dependent brethren."[27]

Purging proslavery ideology of any vestige of the "necessary evil" argument, Fitzhugh offered categorical declarations of slavery's rectitude. "The slaves are all well fed, well clad, have plenty of fuel, and are happy. They have no dread of the future—no fear of want," he proclaimed. "The children and the aged and infirm work not at all, and yet have all the comforts and necessaries of life provided for them." Moreover, "No man in the South, we are sure, ever bred slaves for sale." Fitzhugh even sought to dispel as "imaginary" the "cases of distress occasioned by the breaking up of families of Southern negroes"; he by pointed out that, thanks to the lure of settlement in the Southwest, "the breaking up of families of whites and blacks keeps equal pace"—that is, kinfolk were sometimes separated but only so families, white slaveowners and their black dependents, could seek opportunities in new states and territories. Fitzhugh's innovation, Michael O'Brien observes, was to repudiate any "cynicism about the brutality of the human condition" and to cloak the South's social system in a gauzy sentimentality that shared as much with the genre of women's fiction as it did with the detached polemics of Thomas Dew.[28]

Fitzhugh's purpose—to "inspire every white man with pride of rank and position"—was shared by a host of proslavery ideologues who published during the Republican Party's formative period. South Carolina lawyer William J. Grayson, for example, decried the treatment of free laborers in the North in his fifty-page poem, "The Hireling and the Slave," published in 1854. For the Northern wage worker:

No boon successful commerce yields
For him no harvest crowns the joyous fields
The streams of wealth that foster pomp and pride
No food no shelter for his wants provide
He fails to win, by toil intensely hard
the bare subsistence—labor's least reward.

The slave, by contrast:

Guarded from want, from beggary secure
He never feels what hireling crowds endure
Nor knows, like them, in hopeless want to crave
For wife and child, the comforts of the slave.

Such rhetoric struck slavery's opponents as ludicrously hypocritical—indeed, Lincoln wrote in his personal notes in 1854 that "although volume upon volume is written to prove slavery a very good thing, we never hear of the man who wishes to take the good of it, *by being a slave himself.*" But Republican expressions of antipathy only reinforced the determination of proslavery ideologues to go on the offensive.[29]

By the mid-1850s, the South's leading preachers and professors were churning out an endless stream of "positive good" propaganda. Educators such as Virginians William A. Smith of Randolph-Macon College and Albert T. Bledsoe of the University of Virginia tried to enlist young men coming of age in the 1850s in the promotion of slavery, insisting that the system had actually become more humane over the years and had attained a kind of moral perfection. As slaves, under the benign guidance of their Christian masters, became less "barbarous," lectured Smith, slavery became more gentle. In present-day Virginia, he declaimed in 1856, "the slaves are fat, sleek, cheerful, and long-lived: spending their leisure time in cheerful conversation, in sing-ing, or in those little personal offices which give elasticity to mind and body." Smith conceded the slaves' humanity while belaboring the case for their inferiority. Historian O'Brien says that those proslavery ideologues who "most granted the humanity of slaves" were also the "most racist." "A slave that is a thing and not a human does not, after all, need a race" to justify his subordination, O'Brien cogently notes. Bledsoe, taking aim in 1856 at anti-slavery speeches by the "Chases, the Sewards, and the Sumners," reprised the biblical defenses of slavery, amassed evidence purporting to show the dire consequences of emancipation in the British West Indies, and declared that "no fact is plainer than that the blacks have been elevated and improved by their servitude in this country."[30]

"We have, under our present Union, advanced in prosperity and greatness beyond all former example in the history of nations," Bledsoe asserted, but he warned that abolitionists threatened the Union's survival. Neither Fitzhugh nor Grayson nor Smith nor Bledsoe were aligned with the fire-eaters in the mid-1850s. These four men, along with many other influential defenders of slavery, styled themselves as committed Unionists. Yet by encouraging Southerners—particularly the young men who served as a captive audience at the region's colleges and universities—to define themselves in opposition to and in competition with Northern free society, these proslavery ideologues primed the pump for the genuine disunionists and contributed to their re-surgence in the wake of Buchanan's 1856 election. As William Blair has observed in a study of the Old Dominion, for defenders of slavery, pride in race and region were inseparable from state pride. Thus Fitzhugh and Bledsoe could find common ground with fire-eaters like Edmund Ruffin in their shared conviction that slavery had made Virginia great, and that the nonslaveholding "plain folk" had as much reason to be proud and protective of Virginia's glorious heritage as the planters did. Blair wrote that this state pride could cut both ways: it could contribute to "attachment to a Union that [Virginians] had founded," or it "could unite white Virginians against the North." Fire-eaters, determined to ensure that state allegiance was channeled into Southern nationalism, elaborated a rhetoric of wounded pride that encouraged all white Southerners—slaveholders and nonslaveholders alike—to see themselves as assailed and besieged by the North. Whereas Republicans had been eager to claim victory in defeat, the fire-eaters were intent on claiming defeat in victory—on proving that the Democratic Party would not and could not protect slavery within the Union.[31]

THE FIRE-EATERS AT MID-DECADE

The strong Republican showing in 1856 galvanized the fire-eaters. The fact that the Buchanan administration claimed the support of prominent defenders of slavery such as Secretary of the Treasury Howell Cobb of Georgia and House Speaker James L. Orr of South Carolina, and even co-opted (or so it briefly seemed) the militant William Yancey of Alabama, was cold comfort for unwavering fire-eaters. They disparaged the "dream" that Southerners could control the Buchanan administration and use it as a vehicle to extend slavery. Robert Barnwell Rhett renewed his work for secession, fashioning a new platform for himself with the purchase of the *Charleston Mercury* in 1857. His tactic was to "infiltrate" the Democratic Party, pledging his support for it and all the while working to cripple it as a national party. His speeches and editorials bolstered the case that secession was a "positive good," and that the conflict between the abolitionist North and the slaveholding South was irrepressible—the two fundamentally antagonistic societies could no longer be harmonized under one political system.[32]

The language of honor was spoken in ominous and belligerent cadences by Rhett and other leading secessionists, such as South Carolinian Lawrence M. Keitt, Louis T. Wigfall of Texas, Mississippi's John Quitman, J. B. De Bow of Louisiana, and Edmund Ruffin of Virginia. These men all built the case that the rise of the Republicans so dishonored the South that secession was inevitable. The Republican critique of the South, they argued, was a humiliating, degrading affront to their status "both as 'real' men and 'true' Christians." Republicanism was "much more than a threat to slavery"—it was an "intolerable slap in the face." In February 1857, believing that he had been insulted by Congressman Galusha Grow of Pennsylvania during debates over slavery in Kansas, Keitt physically attacked Grow (that "Black Republican puppy," according to Keitt) on the floor of the House of Representatives, sparking a "general melee in front of the speaker's podium in which dozens of congressmen fell upon each other." Keitt, who already had a reputation as a "gallant," now "earned the sobriquet 'Harry Hotspur of the South.' "[33]

The central argument of the fire-eaters was that the Republican contempt for the South would grow as Republican electoral power grew. Ruffin published a series of articles in the *Richmond Enquirer* in December 1856 explaining how the Republicans, sure to ride the North's population growth to victory in 1860, would then proceed to transform "all federal property into centers for abolitionist operations and havens for runaway slaves" as a step toward the congressional abolition of slavery and the subjugation of the South. As a lead article in February 1857, *De Bow's Review* featured a letter from an anonymous Washington correspondent warning that "sixteen millions . . . of people at the North, Northwest, and West, will stand marshaled in serried ranks around the ballot boxes to control the State and general elections in 1860." The inevitable Republican victory would have disastrous consequences that would exceed the "most exaggerated fears or extravagant fancies of the Southern mind"—the South would lie prostrate before the rapacious North as it imposed abolition, race and class war, and moral degradation on the region. More and more, newspapers that had postured as moderate now accepted this logic: the *New Orleans Crescent*, for example, despairing over the strong Republican showing in the North, confessed that it no longer had an "answer to the disunion pronunciamentos of the more impulsive among our Southern brethren"—it had to concede that a Republican triumph in 1860 would warrant secession.[34]

Increasingly, fire-eaters used agricultural and commercial conventions as forums for their secessionist views. Ruffin had long promoted agricultural reform and De Bow, commercial reform. These causes, which had appealed to progressive Southerners eager for the South to emulate Northern productivity, were now co-opted as the building blocks of economic and political independence for the region. At the Knoxville Commercial Convention of 1857, De Bow announced that the South's commercial infrastructure already was strong enough not only to separate from the North but also to "maintain the rank of a first rate power." Conventions provided extremists with a captive audience for their argument that the 1856 election had forever changed the stakes of the sectional conflict. Virginian James Lyons, president of the December 1856 Savannah Commercial Convention, said in his opening address that "the war is not yet ended, but only deferred, to be finished in the year 1860, when this war upon our institutions and upon our homes, and of course upon our liberties, is to be renewed." It was the work of the convention, he continued, to prepare the South to stand its ground in the coming contest.[35]

Agricultural and commercial conventions also promoted Southern education, in rhetoric more caustic and alarmist than that of the likes of William Smith and Albert Bledsoe. *De Bow's Review* featured a letter by an anonymous South Carolinian to C. K. Marshall, chairman of the "Committee on Home Education" appointed by the Savannah convention, calling for Southerners to shake off the "unpardonable apathy which has hitherto existed on the subject of education." The writer, like Lyons, used the metaphor of war: "We and others who have engaged in the war against Abolition teachers and Anti-Slavery Text Books" have shown that the "books from which our children imbibe their earliest lessons" must be written by those who can properly "expound and vindicate" Southern institutions. "Now, more than ever, every Southern man should feel that an important crisis . . . is impending."[36]

The potential of the proslavery argument and of disunionism to appeal to nonslaveholding "plain folk" was dramatized by the career of upcountry yeoman Joseph E. Brown of Georgia. Brown rose up the social ladder from a humble rural upbringing to establish himself as a lawyer and a slaveholding landowner. He emerged as a leading states' rights spokesman during the crisis of 1850–51 and would champion Southern nationalism in the crisis of 1860–61, all the while maintaining his reputation as a "man of the soil." When he was elected governor of Georgia in 1857, Brown was not yet an avowed fire-eating secessionist; indeed, his election demonstrated the vitality of the Democratic Party in his state and the waning fortunes of the Whig-American opposition. But Brown's campaign platform and his agenda as governor, which found favor in nonplantation districts from the hills of northern Georgia to the wiregrass region of southern Georgia, nonetheless served to popularize key elements of the secessionist creed. Even as he invoked tried-and-true principles of Jacksonian democracy, such as antipathy to bankers and other such moneyed elites, Brown made a case for Southern economic and educational independence. The promotion of regional railroads, he argued, would help Southerners to "rid themselves of Yankee middlemen in the transatlantic traffic in cotton," and the promotion of schools would build mutual respect between the sons of planters and of yeomen. Brown's political gospel encouraged pride in the "communalism and localism" of sturdy yeomen and fear that "abolition rule" would undermine the South's distinctive Herrenvolk democracy. The crux of his message was that, in the face of external threats from the North, racial solidarity among Southern whites should override class differences.[37]

The most provocative and revealing element of the fire-eaters' renewed campaign was their effort to reopen the African slave trade. The idea originated in the early 1850s among South Carolina extremists, such as newspaper editor Leonidas W. Spratt, who anxiously observed that while the slave economy in the Southwest was booming, the extension of the cotton kingdom was draining slaves away from the Old South, especially from South Carolina's rice plantations. In November 1856, the movement received official sanction when South Carolina governor James H. Adams endorsed it in his message to the state legislature. Adams advocated the slave trade on broad "expansionist and proslavery grounds": it would enable the South to keep pace with Northern growth (especially immigration) and expansion, and rebut the Northern accusation that slave trading was an immoral brand of piracy. Slave traders, as the radical proponents of this doctrine were known, soon used commercial conventions to press their case. The Savannah Commercial Convention of 1856 witnessed a lively debate on the issue, in which slave traders marshaled every major element of proslavery ideology. They condemned the "sickly sentimentality" of the trade's opponents; argued that if it had once been a blessing to bring the African "within sight of Christianity," it still was; and claimed that fresh imports would "counterpoise the influx of hireling labor from abroad to the Northern states." As William B. Goulden of Georgia put it, there was no moral difference "between buying a man in Virginia who was a slave there, and buying one in Africa who was a slave there." When opponents of the measure argued that it would be so controversial that it would create "prejudice [against] Mr. Buchanan's administration," Goulden dismissed their concern, saying that a great moral issue was at stake: "Now was the time to say to the North and to the whole world that [slaveholders] would have their right, their whole right, and nothing but their right."[38]

In the slave trade, fire-eaters had found an issue with deep emotional resonance for slaveholders. The fact that Northerners regarded slave trading as another manifestation of slavery's "moral turpitude" was, in the fire-eaters' reckoning, just another degrading, humiliating insult. It was Northerners' arrogant claims to moral superiority, more than anything else, that rendered the South unsafe, extremists maintained—and Buchanan's election had done nothing to chasten the North. By now, fire-eaters had perfected the art of howling in defeat every time the South achieved a seeming political victory. But that tactic proved needless when the U.S. Supreme Court handed down a decision that filled slaveholders with glee.

THE *DRED SCOTT* DECISION

"This innovating decision carries no moral force," declared the Hicksite *Friends' Intelligencer* of the Supreme Court's March 6, 1857, ruling in *Dred Scott v. Sandford*. "It is extralegal, gratuitous, unprecedented, and illegal." Propagating the "absurd assumption that the Constitution regards men of African descent as mere property," the *Dred Scott* ruling was merely the last in a series of proslavery "aggressions" designed to "introduce by law slavery into the free states, and fasten upon us a system which our education and humanity alike testify against." Worst of all, the editors of the *Intelligencer* concluded, "there is every reason to believe that this case got into the Supreme Court *collusively*."[39]

In interpreting the Court's *Dred Scott* findings as innovative, aggressive, and collusive, the Quaker newspaper, so long on the progressive margins of American political life, captured the essence of the Northern critique of the latest Slave Power victory. From the start, the stakes of Scott's case were high—it was nothing less than a referendum on the Missouri Compromise and on the right of Congress to exclude slavery from the territories. Back in 1846, in the midst of the Mexican War debates, Dred Scott—with the help of unlikely white allies drawn from among his former owners, the Blow family—had sued the woman, the widow Eliza Irene Sanford Emerson, who currently claimed to own him. Scott, who had been born into slavery in Virginia, had moved west with the Blows, only to be sold by them to army surgeon Dr. John Emerson. He sought his freedom on the grounds that Emerson had taken Scott with him to live in the free state of Illinois and in the free Wisconsin Territory. Scott and his lawyers held that such residence in a free state and a free territory rendered Scott free, even after he returned to the slave state of Missouri and was, after Dr. Emerson's death, claimed as property by Emerson's widow. (Scott's wife Harriet filed a parallel suit for her own freedom and that of the couple's children.)[40]

As Sean Wilentz observes, Scott had a strong argument, for Missouri courts had long made it a practice to rule for plaintiffs in such cases. Indeed, Scott initially prevailed in the St. Louis district court, only to find its decision overturned on appeal by the Missouri Supreme Court in 1852. Chief Justice William Scott, a proslavery Democrat, left no doubt as to his own assessment of the high stakes involved. Invoking disunion, he argued that to free Scott was to fall under the spell of a "dark and fell spirit in relation to slavery," a spirit that aimed at "the overthrow and destruction of our government"—in other words, since times had changed, the 1852 decision had to be overturned. A federal district court upheld the Missouri court's ruling in 1854. Fortunately for Scott, his supporters succeeding in enlisting the aid, on a pro bono basis, of Free-Soil politician and lawyer Montgomery Blair, who in turn brought an appeal to the U.S. Supreme Court against the widow Emerson's brother, John Sanford, who in the meantime had asserted that he was the true owner of the Scott family. The Court heard the case early in 1856, reconsidered the evidence during the 1856–57 term, and rendered a decision shortly after Buchanan's accession to the presidency. Of the Court's nine justices, seven had been appointed by proslavery Southern presidents, and five of those seven were from slave states and presently owned or had owned slaves. Their spokesman and leader was none other than the chief justice, Roger Brooke Taney of Maryland.[41]

The decision handed down by Taney on March 6 was innovative in ways that were deeply gratifying to his Southern backers and disturbing to the Northern public. This was by design. Taney, fervently proslavery, considered himself a defender of the Union. He calculated that if his decision mollified angry slaveholders and placed slavery beyond the reach of Congress and abolitionists, then sectional tensions would abate. The Court could have found against Scott simply by upholding the 1851 precedent of *Strader v. Graham*, which had accorded to individual states the right to determine whether a slave who had resided in a free state was thus rendered free. Instead, Taney delivered a series of blows to the hopes of antislavery forces. The first was the ruling that because Dred Scott was African American, he was not a citizen of the United States and therefore could not legally bring suit against John Sanford in a federal court. As the two dissenting justices, John McLean and Benjamin Curtis noted, and as modern-day legal scholars and historians have confirmed, this decision was based on a willful misreading of the Constitution and of state laws at the time the Constitution was drafted. Taney projected the pseudoscientific racism of the late antebellum "positive good" defense of slavery back into the past and held that the founding generation had never imagined that blacks, slave or free, should be considered citizens. The legislation of the states in the early republic had "stigmatized" all blacks with "enduring marks of inferiority and degradation"; no subsequent laws could remove the stigma. To make such a case, Taney had to disregard evidence that free African American men in the early republic possessed many legal rights that established their citizenship. As Justice Curtis noted in his dissent: "In five of the thirteen original states, colored persons then possessed the elective franchise, and were among those by whom the Constitution was ordained and established." For Curtis, the status of blacks in the early republic proved beyond doubt that "color was not a necessary qualification of citizenship" under the Constitution. And no subsequent legislation by the states could alter this fact.[42]

Taney's ruling was not only innovative in its denial of citizenship to blacks, but it was also aggressive in its stance on the territorial controversy. Taney could have cast the majority's finding on citizenship as the last word; if Scott was not a citizen, the Court had no jurisdiction to hear his case or to consider the other issues that the case raised. But Taney chose instead to offer a dictum on the status of the territories, one again based on a willful and selective misreading of the Constitution and of American history; it was, as legal historian Stuart Streichler has put it, "one of the most prominent examples of judicial overreaching in the Supreme Court's history." Consigning the Missouri Compromise to the ashes, Taney declared that the Wisconsin Territory had never been free, for Congress had never possessed the power to exclude slavery from that or any other territory. The territories clause of the Constitution, empowering Congress to make rules and regulations for U.S. properties, "applied only to those territories the United States owned in 1787"; this reading aligned Taney with the fringe of proslavery militants. Moreover, Taney gave a militant proslavery spin to the Fifth Amendment, arguing that its due process and just compensation clauses protected the right of slaveholders to take their slaves anywhere into the territories. This clearly repudiated the possibility that settlers might ban slavery through "popular sovereignty" and raised the specter that no free state or territory could constitutionally ban slavery from its borders. Taney summed up his position by concluding that "the right of property in a slave is distinctly and expressly affirmed in the Constitution."[43]

In his dissent, Justice Curtis countered Taney point by point, addressing both the issue of the Founders' original intentions and that of congressional practice and precedent. Referring to the Constitutional Convention debates and the Federalist Papers, Curtis asserted that the Founders absolutely expected to apply the territories clause to property acquired after 1787. Indeed, they entertained a "confident expectation"—one soon borne out by events—that North Carolina, Georgia, and Virginia would soon cede their claims to western territory and thereby enable Congress to admit new states. He then enumerated the federal laws that regulated slavery in the territories that became slaves states (such as Tennessee and Louisiana) and those that became free states (such as Indiana and Illinois). The key to Curtis's dissent, his biographer Stuart Streichler explains, was his view that Congress's "practical construction" of the law—its repeated regulation of slavery in the territories "through a long series of years"—decisively settled the issue. Relying on judicial and congressional precedent, Curtis argued that antislavery laws in the free states and territories were valid and thus could change the status of slaves who were brought into such domains of liberty.[44]

Both the fact that Curtis dissented and the way that he dissented from the majority opinion served notice of the explosive potential of the *Dred Scott* decision. For Curtis was no antislavery Republican, but rather a conservative Whig from Massachusetts. He had been appointed to the bench by President Fillmore precisely because he strongly upheld the Fugitive Slave Act of 1850. Curtis's judicial philosophy had been shaped by his deep fears of disunion;

he had worried that if Northerners resisted the Fugitive Slave Law, they would bring the country to "the brink of a precipice." Taney's judicial overreaching outraged Curtis's conservative Whiggish conviction that Congress had the constitutional power to regulate slavery in the territories. The *Dred Scott* decision compelled him to make an argument that was "neutral in form" but not "neutral in effect": as Streichler writes, by putting faith in Congress's legislative discretion in the territories, Curtis "left the fate of slavery . . . to the political process." Given the rapid rise of the Republicans and their growing presence in Congress, this was not a "neutral" argument.[45]

Antislavery moderates saw the merits of Curtis's posture of neutrality and used his dissent as the blueprint for their own protests, favoring it over the more political and partisan dissent of Justice McLean, a Republican with political ambitions. Some Northern state legislatures drew on Curtis's language to pass resolutions that condemned the *Dred Scott* judgment as an infringement on states' rights and sovereignty. Ironically, a special joint committee of the New York legislature closed its report on the Supreme Court decision "with a states' rights quotation from the Virginia and Kentucky resolutions of 1798." While antislavery Northerners could use the dissents to form the basis of their case that the Taney ruling was an act of judicial innovation and of political aggression, they looked to the world of partisan politics for proof that the decision was an act of collusion.[46]

They found damning evidence in the very timing of the decision. Horace Greeley led the way in charging that Buchanan and Taney delayed the ruling until March "in order not to flagrantly alarm and exasperate the Free States on the eve of an important Presidential election." Buchanan had set the stage for Taney's finding in asserting during his inaugural address that it was up to the Supreme Court to determine the constitutionality of popular sovereignty. The new president's promise to "cheerfully submit" to the wisdom of the Court, along with the whispered words he exchanged with Taney before the chief justice administered the oath of office, all seemed to Greeley and administration critics to be signs of an unholy alliance between the executive and judicial branches. In fact, although Republicans did not know the details, their suspicions were justified: Buchanan had followed the Court's deliberations carefully and, as president-elect, had pressured Justice Robert Grier, a fellow Pennsylvanian, to throw his support behind the proslavery Taney clique. When Buchanan on inauguration day urged Americans to follow the

Court's lead on the question of slavery in the territories, he knew full well that Taney was about to issue a proslavery ruling in the case of *Dred Scott*.[47]

Antislavery forces saw clear evidence of collusion in the ardent affirmation that Taney's decision won from Southern proslavery forces and from Buchanan's Northern supporters. Papers such as the *Richmond Enquirer* and *New Orleans Picayune* praised the finding as a great victory for the South and as a blow against Northern sectionalists. Again defenders of slavery hurled disunion as an accusation against the North. An editorial in the *Milledgeville Federal Union* (a Democratic paper in Georgia) stated that the antislavery "enemies of the South" had now to choose between allying with the "Union men of the country, in sustaining the determination of the Supreme Court," or fomenting "treasonable" disunion. The *Washington Daily Union*, the organ of the Buchanan administration, took the same tack in endorsing the Court's ruling; it editorialized on March 12 that the *Scott* decision was a rebuke to those "whose livelihood is to create sectional animosity . . . and [that] the wounds they have made before will become healed." On the same day, the *New York Herald* warned that to oppose the ruling was "treason" and would reduce the opposition to the "same impotent and debasing level as the abolition disunionists of the Garrison and Parker fraternity." The *Philadelphia Public Ledger* urged readers to support the decision with the lament: "If the Supreme Court cannot be trusted, in what branch of our institutions can we confide? To assail this decision as dishonest, is virtually to pronounce republicanism a failure."[48]

The growing antislavery coalition asked this same question and answered that the federal government had indeed broken faith with the people. Garrisonian abolitionists and Republicans continued to disagree over the extent to which blacks should be granted citizenship; radical abolitionists assailed the racism of the *Dred Scott* ruling, while Republicans, determined to dispel Democratic accusations that they favored racial equality, focused their anger on the second part of Taney's decision—namely, his repudiation of the Missouri Compromise and of any slavery restriction. They continued to disagree on whether the Constitution was a proslavery perversion of the Declaration of Independence, as Garrison held, or a potential weapon against slavery, as Seward, Chase, Douglass, and other political antislavery advocates believed (and as Curtis and McLean had suggested in their dissents). But in the language of Slave Power aggression and collusion, Garrisonians and Republi-

cans found a point of convergence. The Supreme Court's judgment acceler-
ated the process by which Garrisonians moved shifted their emphasis from
the complicity of Northerners to the culpability of the Slave Power. At the
same time, the decision undercut the Republicans' confidence in the political
process, tempered their predictions that appeals to the "ingenious machinery
of government" and to the ballot box would inevitably bring them to power,
and impelled them to fortify the boundary between North and South.[49]

Back in January 1857, on the eve of Buchanan's accession, the Garrisonians had held a Massachusetts "State Disunion Convention" in the city of
Worcester. The meeting was ridiculed as ludicrous by Republican and Democratic papers alike—the work of "lunatics and idiots," as one commentator
put it—and has been derided, when not overlooked altogether, by modern-
day historians. Kenneth Stampp has written that the Worcester meeting "did
nothing but harm to the abolition movement." Yet the gathering deserves
serious consideration, as its rhetoric discloses a subtle shift in the Garrisonians' strategy. Garrison and his fellow conveners paid homage to John
Quincy Adams's Haverhill petition of 1842. That petition, although signed by
a mere thirty supporters, had thrown Congress and the South into "convul-
sions," Garrison asserted. "To the slaveholders, it was as the voice of God,
saying, 'Your covenant with death shall be annulled.'" Although Adams's
petition had served as a terrifying prophecy, Garrison's followers now invoked disunion in an altogether more determined register. They emphasized
that their purpose was not so much to effect disunion as to prepare the
Northern public for the inevitable and soon-to-come moment at which the
South would provoke it. Referring to well-known incidents such as the caning
of Sumner and the tragic 1856 case of Margaret Garner, a fugitive slave from
Kentucky who had killed her two-year-old daughter rather than let her be
taken from her hiding place in Ohio back into slavery, Garrisonians pledged
that "for another such outrage, we can create a public opinion ready to say
'Thus far, and no farther.'"[50]

With Southern slaveholders determined to take Buchanan "into their
keeping, and use him for their purposes," New England abolitionist Parker
Pillsbury noted, Slave Power collusion was the "form in which Disunion will
come." He continued, "We must educate the national conscience up to the
point of demanding rigid duty on such occasions." Wendell Phillips elaborated on this theme. To the rhetorical question of how he as an abolitionist

proposed to dissolve the Union, Phillips responded: "I expect to have it dissolved for me" by Southern aggression. He, too, declared that the true purpose of Garrisonian disunion was to "familiarize the public ear to the word Disunion," to "disarm" it of its "terrors," and so to prepare the North for the next slaveholder-instigated crisis. The essence of the Garrisonian position was summed up in the convention's resolution that "the sooner the separation takes place, the more peaceful it will be; but that peace or war is a *secondary consideration*, in view of our present perils."[51]

In light of the rhetoric of "thus far, and no farther," abolitionists interpreted the *Dred Scott* decision as an opportunity. In an open letter to the "antislavery men and women of the north," Phillips, Garrison, and other disunionists declared that "if the Dred Scott case be an abstraction, it is one of those abstractions whose practical consequences convulse the world." They observed with satisfaction that "it is evident that the mass of republican voters, in many states, are becoming more radically antislavery"—and concluded that abolitionist talk of disunion was increasingly providing the context in which the electorate interpreted political events; disunion talk was serving to "create a united and determined North." As Henry C. Wright wrote to the *Liberator* in March 1857: "The South has done it. . . . Now let the North go to work, and consolidate themselves into one mighty bulwark of defense." In the face of the latest Slave Power aggressions, the *Liberator* contrasted the "all-prevailing competence, intelligence and happiness" of the North with the "dark, dreary, hopeless" South. Garrisonians called on Northerners to defend themselves against the federal government itself—against, as Robert Purvis put it in the wake of *Dred Scott*, "one of the basest, meanest, most atrocious despotisms that ever saw the face of the sun." But they increasingly distinguished between the corrupt government and the Northern public. For example, Charles Lenox Remond, in a stirring speech on the "contemptible" Taney decision, defended disunion as "the only means of saving the American people" from the "American Government."[52]

Although they did not endorse disunion, Northern mainstream newspapers repeatedly echoed the abolitionist analysis, charging that the Supreme Court's ruling alienated Northerners from the government and that all free men must defend themselves from this Slave Power encroachment. According to the *New York Evening Post*, the decision was the work of a "conspiracy" of the most "treasonable character" between the Court and the "leading members of the new administration"; thus the Court had lost the "confidence of the people." The *Chicago Tribune* also condemned the "grand conspiracy against Freedom" and predicted that it would be "denounced by common consent." The *New York Times* declared: "This decision revolutionizes the Federal Government, and changes entirely the relation which Slavery has hitherto held towards it. Slavery is no longer local; it is national." It believed that the decision would do more to stimulate the growth of an abolition party than "has been done by any other event since the Declaration of Independence." Greeley's *New York Tribune*, for its part, condemned the "spirit of federalism which pervades the dominant party" and promised that Northerners would defend their "States rights and State sovereignty. The *Albany Evening Journal* decried the conspiracy's efforts to make "state laws bend to Federal demands."[53]

In Wisconsin, the *Columbus Republican Journal* crystallized the prevailing sentiment in that party: the *Dred Scott* decision was the work of a "band of tyrants" who "cannot be reached thro' the ballot box." The paper acknowledged that anyone who dared defy the ruling would be "ridiculed" as a "disunionist." But it urged defiance on the grounds that "our states rights have been invaded by the court"—and surely would be again. The image of invasion was invoked in state resolutions as well as in press coverage of the decision. A joint committee of the New York state legislature, for instance, expressed "apprehension that some future decision of the Pro-Slavery majority of the Supreme Court will authorize a slave-driver, as threatened by the devotees of Slavery, to call the roll of his manacled gang at the foot of the monument on Bunker Hill."[54]

The convergence between the Garrisonian and mainstream antislavery interpretations of the sectional conflict is evident in Frederick Douglass's speech on *Dred Scott*. Delivered at the May 1857 annual meeting of the American Anti-Slavery Society, the address disavowed the Garrisonian position on the Constitution and on disunion. Like Curtis in his dissent, Douglass argued that the Founders had granted citizenship to blacks and that they had hoped for slavery's eventual demise. But he also spoke, as Garrisonians and Republicans did, of the Slave Power's "poisoning, corrupting, and perverting the institutions of the country," and he too warned that "the white man's liberty has been marked out for the same grave with the black man's." The "ballot box is desecrated [and] God's law set at naught," Douglass concluded. The only hope for national redemption lay in the "overthrow" of slavery, "sooner or later, by fair means or foul means, in quiet or in tumult, in peace or in blood." Such language of militant resistance to the Slave Power had been heard in the wake of the Fugitive Slave Law and the Kansas-Nebraska Act. But this was different. The fact that *Dred Scott* was an "abstraction," as Garrison had put it—a radical reinterpretation of the nation's laws and its history, and a denial that there "is yet an inch of truly Free Soil in the nation"—gave the ruling a terrifying boundlessness. Douglass captured this when he imputed to Taney a desire to "change the essential nature of things—making evil good, good evil." Resistance to the Fugitive Slave Law played out in localized incidents; resistance to the Kansas-Nebraska Act played out on the far-off frontier. The *Dred Scott* decision, by contrast, threatened to dissolve the very boundary between the North and the South. Chief Justice Taney was trying, Douglass averred in a striking image, to "pluck the silvery star of liberty from our Northern sky."[55]

Taney's ruling, then, with its taint of innovation, aggression, and collusion, translated for the antislavery coalition into a palpable fear: the fear of invasion by slaveholders. To focus on the threat of invasion was to forge common ground among Northerners. The Republican Party, faced with the troubling implications of *Dred Scott*, for its position on racial equality and for its cherished doctrine of nonextension, chose to "portray itself as the sectional defender of the free states against a slave-power conspiracy to nationalize the institution." This suited abolitionists just fine. For if Northerners came to realize that the threat of invasion was the "fearful price" the North "paid for the Union"—that invasion was "no vain threat" but rather "just retribution," as Henry Wright asserted in a speech replete with images of Northern laborers enslaved to Southern masters and their wives and daughters prey to slaveholder "passions"—then maybe the North would finally reckon the price too high.[56]

War to the Knife

IMAGES OF THE COMING FIGHT

The antislavery consensus that the *Dred Scott* decision was a link in a chain of portentous events—by which the Slave Power escalated its claims that the Constitution protected slavery in perpetuity—soon found affirmation in Kansas. Railing against the proslavery Lecompton constitution that had been forced on Kansans, Congressman John Bingham, a prominent Ohio Republican, declared in a January 25, 1858, speech that the Lecompton government and the *Dred Scott* ruling embodied the same "precise principle" and the same "stupendous lie": that "one class of men have no rights which another are bound to respect." The Kansas and Supreme Court ruses alike, Bingham insisted, were the workings of a "base conspiracy" to perpetuate "the wild and guilty fantasy of property in man."[1]

When Bingham delivered his speech to Congress in January 1858, the Lecompton controversy had been steadily escalating for a year. Back in January 1857 the proslavery legislature of Kansas, in defiance of territorial governor John W. Geary, had called for a constitutional convention to be held that September in Lecompton. Free staters boycotted the election of delegates to the convention, to the frustration of Geary's replacement, Robert J. Walker of Mississippi. President Buchanan, hoping that Walker could uphold popular sovereignty to pacify Kansas, had handpicked him after Geary resigned in a huff. Walker, who had justified Texas annexation with his "diffusion" argument (that westward expansion would diffuse the slave population to the Southwest and eventually into Latin America) in the mid-1840s, revived that rationale now, only to meet with "instant outrage" from Southern Democrats. As William Freehling succinctly puts it: "1857 was not 1844. Now, Southerners prospered. Now, they needed more slaves, not a safety valve for excess slaves."[2]

Popular sovereignty was conspicuously absent during the convention itself, as the free-state boycott had left proslavery delegates in charge. With Walker hoping to salvage credibility (and the chance that Kansas might enter the Union as a Democratic state) by having the new constitution submitted for popular ratification, and with the convention in the hands of "antisubmission" forces, the stage was set for another showdown. On October 5, 1857, during the constitutional convention's recess, Kansans voted to create a territorial legislature. Despite the fact that free staters had heeded Walker this time and turned out to cast ballots, voting fraud resulted in an ostensible proslavery victory. Walker invalidated the false returns and declared a victory for the free staters, and they, in turn, demanded that the illegitimate constitutional convention be aborted. But the convention resumed its deliberations, declared the rights of slaveowners to be "inviolable," and fashioned a cynical response to Buchanan and Walker's calls for a ratification vote: a referendum would be held on December 21, 1857, in which voters could support "the Constitution with slavery" or the "Constitution with no Slavery." There was no true free-state option, Nicole Etcheson explains. A vote for "no slavery" only prohibited "future importations of slaves, not the holding of slaves already in Kansas, and no future amendment could affect the right to existing property in slaves."[3]

To the horror of Walker, Buchanan accepted this "partial submission," and, invoking the *Dred Scott* precedent on the inviolable property rights of slaveowners, made public his support for the Lecompton constitution in his December 8, 1857, annual message. The president had been forewarned by Stephen Douglas, who had met with him on December 3, that many Northern Democrats, following Douglas's lead, would view the Lecompton constitution as a travesty of popular sovereignty. But Buchanan banked on the Democratic majority in both houses of Congress—both the president pro tempore of the Senate and the Speaker of the House were slaveholding

Southerners—and persisted in his fantasy that free staters might be induced to lend sanction to partial submission by weighing in at the polls in December. Free staters truculently avoided this trap: they once again refused to participate in what they justly regarded as a rigged election, and the December 21 "referendum" resulted in a resounding proslavery victory. The new free-state territorial legislature countered with its own January 4, 1858, referendum—this one duly boycotted by proslavery men—that overwhelmingly rejected the Lecompton constitution. It would now fall to Congress to decide which referendum—the Lecompton vote, endorsed by Buchanan, or the Topeka vote, embraced by Republicans as a reflection of the true will of Kansans—to endorse.[4]

For the leading fire-eaters, or the "Disunion Party," as the Northern press now routinely called them, the Lecompton question posed a dilemma. Should they, capitalizing on Buchanan's initial show of support, pose now as nationalists and renew the charge, wielded so assiduously by the Democratic Party, that the Free-Soil forces were the true disunionists? Or should they stoke sectional solidarity and hold Buchanan's feet to the fire by threatening disunion if a proslavery Kansas was rejected by Congress? The fire-eaters' determination to have it both ways gave rise to streams of discordant rhetoric in Congress and the Southern press. At moments in the Lecompton debates, Robert Toombs, James Mason, Lawrence Keitt, L. Q. C. Lamar, and others stood for law and order and Democratic orthodoxy. They blamed the discord in Kansas entirely on the abolitionists, claiming that the antislavery conspiracy in Congress, which could trace its unholy history back to Federalist machinations in the Missouri controversy, was working to "use a popular fanaticism in their own section of the country in order to seize the government of the whole." Opposition to admitting Kansas as a slave state was, Lamar declared, "an offshoot of that damnable policy which has been preying upon the vitals of the South for the last forty years—that of buying peace from the turbulent and fanatical at the expense of the quiet and orderly." Moreover, fire-eaters heaped scorn on those Democrats—most notably Stephen Douglas, Governor Henry A. Wise of Virginia, and former territorial governor Frederick P. Stanton of Tennessee—who had broken ranks with the Buchanan administration. Keitt excoriated Douglas Democrats for hypocrisy, declaring that their "swords flash no longer against the Black Republican Saracens" but now were turned on their own doctrine of popular sovereignty. Southern Democratic newspapers called out the traitors with the lament, "How the mighty are fallen." The *Texas State Gazette*, for example, observed of Douglas that "once the favorite of the South for the Presidency," he was now "branded as a traitor from Washington to New Orleans. The false god was destroyed by his own worshippers." Governor Wise, as the most prominent Southern leader to take an uncompromising anti-Lecompton stance, cemented his reputation as "one of the shiftiest politicians in the South."[5]

For these Southerners to posture as good Democrats was to indulge the fantasy that, as Manisha Sinha tells us, the "controversy would 'blow over' and purge the Democratic Party of unsound northerners," thereby fulfilling the hope that "Buchanan's victory [had] secured the sectional dominance of the slave South." But this fantasy coexisted uneasily with a second one—that Northern treachery and betrayal would not purify the Democratic Party but instead destroy it, leaving slaveholders no recourse but secession and independence. In service to this vision, fire-eaters in Congress leavened their perorations with allusions to and threats of disunion. Lamar warned the North: "You may reject [Kansas's Lecompton] application, if you will; but it will be at your own peril." Toombs stated that he had calculated the value of the Union and that "its value to the South is less than to any other portion of the Republic." Keitt opined in a March 1858 speech that the South had been "made firmer" by its resistance to the North's fanatical campaign, and that events pointed "to a dissolution" of the Union. The leading fire-eater newspapers, such as the *New Orleans Delta*, *Charleston Mercury*, *The South* (Richmond), and *Mobile Register*, encouraged the view that Lecompton was the "test struggle" of the viability of slavery within the Union and offered up a string of disunionist ultimatums to the North.[6]

More than any other fire-eater, James Henry Hammond of South Carolina tried to harmonize the dissonant strains of Southern rhetoric in his "mudsill" speech to the Senate on March 4, 1858. Cautiously hopeful that the present controversy would inaugurate an "unchallenged reign of Southern slaveholders" in the Democratic Party, Hammond argued that the South's economic might and social stability gave the North no choice but to yield to Southern dominance. "Cotton is King," he declared, and the North could not survive without it. Moreover, the South possessed the best "frame of society . . . in the world," for slaves' status as the "mudsill" of Southern society exempted Southern whites from exploitation. Hammond wedded the image of Southern strength within the Union to the prospect of Southern independence from it by casting Northerners as the agents of disunion—as invaders of the South. He accused them of having made ideological assaults on Southern "hearthstones" for years, warning that any escalation of the war of words into physical combat would be suicidal. For the South, if forced to fight a "defensive war," could muster "a larger army than any Power of the earth can send against her." This was no metaphorical army, of editors and ministers and politicians and novelists, but "an army of soldiers—men brought up on horseback, with guns in their hands." In Hammond's formula, the same economic and social might that made the South the natural and rightful ruler of the Union would guarantee its victory in a "defensive" war and a glorious future as an independent nation.[7]

Hammond's allusion to invasion was a direct reply to the March 3 speech of William Seward. Seward implicitly addressed the Republicans' dilemma: Should they suggest that some sort of political repose—in which Republican electoral success restored the sectional peace and equilibrium desired by the Founders—was possible? Or should they cast the struggle over slavery in the territories as one that ultimately lay beyond political resolution, in the complete and irrevocable domination of the country either by free or by slave states? Seward tried to have it both ways. Condemning the Lecompton constitution as a product of "tyranny" and "stupendous imbecility," he accused supporters of a proslavery Kansas of agitating the issue "only to divide the Union." He pledged that, by contrast, the free states would not "menace the Republic" but would choose instead "an easy and simple remedy, namely, to take the Government out of unjust and unfaithful hands, and commit it to those who will be just and faithful." But after this by now familiar reference to the Republicans' political prospects, Seward ended his speech on a decidedly belligerent note. Observing that "free labor has at last apprehended its rights," he employed the language of invasion, casting the North as invader. Free labor, he warned slaveholders, "has driven you back in California and Kansas; it will invade you soon in Delaware, Maryland, Virginia, Missouri, and Texas. It will meet you in Arizona, in Central America, and even in Cuba." How could he reconcile this image with the long-standing abolitionist claim that the Slave Power was the aggressor? He did so by arguing that whereas those Southerners bent on nationalizing slavery wielded the weapons of "tyranny," the Northern "invasion" by contrast would be "not merely harmless, but beneficent," if the South would only yield: yield to the tide of history, which was sweeping away slavery across the globe; yield to the host of statistics that proved the superiority of the free labor system; and yield to the better judgment of Northern men.[8]

That Seward's speech, with its images of repose and invasion, was interpreted in wildly divergent ways is illustrated by two letters found in his unpublished correspondence. One, addressed to his wife Frances by a Massachusetts clergyman, praised the speech for the "grandeur of its moral sentiment." Another, written to Seward by a Mississippi Democrat, informed the senator that he was regarded in the South "as the most dangerous enemy of our peace and our existence as states in the American Union" and warned him that "yours will be the most prominent name on the most melancholy pages of our history."[9]

Other congressional Republicans, too, awkwardly juxtaposed images of sectional quietude with images of Northern domination. Anson Burlingame of Vermont, in a March 31, 1858, speech to the House, promised that once Lecompton was defeated, "Kansas will be saved, and the whole country repose in good will, and peace dwell in all our borders." But, on behalf of Republicans, he alerted Southern disunionists that "we shall beat you like a threshing-floor . . . we are to-day filling all the land with the portents of your general doom." Also in the House, Eli Thayer of Massachusetts condemned Southerners for time and time again invoking a "false deity." "The sulphurous God is disunion," and Southerners had threatened it to perpetuate their hold on the government. The North had acceded to years of Southern dominance, but now it was the South's turn to yield. In the name of the "Christian Republic," Thayer disavowed "aggressive" language and aims. He nonetheless foreclosed the possibility that the political pendulum would ever again swing the slaveholders' way—their "political power is forever doomed." In the Senate, Henry Wilson dissected Hammond's speech theme by theme, rebuking the South Carolinian for his "language of scorn and contempt" and empty boasts of Southern superiority. Wilson countered, in a reference to Republican hopes of inroads among nonslaveholders, that the "ballot-box is stronger than any army with banners." But he also called for the "utter annihilation of the oligarchic Democracy," noting that it was destiny that Northern "merchants, manufactures and capitalists grasp the globe." These congressional speeches were echoed in "anti-Lecompton meetings" across the North. A May 1858 assembly in Buffalo, New York, assailed the "Disunion Party" for demanding the "absolute and unconditional surrender of the national government into the hands of the aggressive and intolerant slave-power"; it looked forward to the time when Republicans would "crush this Disunion Oligarchy" and "wrest" the government from it.[10]

Republicans, most prominently Seward and Wilson, drew ammunition in the Lecompton debates from an unexpected source: the recently published antislavery diatribe, *The Impending Crisis of the South and How to Meet It*, by Hinton Rowan Helper. Helper was an alienated North Carolinian, of the sturdy nonslaveholding yeomen class, who blamed slaveholders and slavery for his own personal struggles, and who channeled his anger into a scheme for gradual, compensated emancipation and colonization. During the Civil War and Reconstruction, Helper would reveal himself to be a virulent racist who fantasized about a world purged of nonwhites. But in his prewar writings, his views on race were conflicted; at times he invoked the language of natural rights and at times that of "scientific" racism. This ambiguity distinguished him from most of the South's opinion makers. "In the context of the 1850s South," biographer David Brown notes, Helper's "attitude towards blacks was considerably less hostile than that of the vast majority of his peers." One thing was perfectly clear: Helper's principle argument in *The Impending Crisis* was that the system of slavery harmed whites.[11]

What Helper provided the Free-Soil movement in 1858 was both a Southern spokesman and, as Horace Greeley reckoned, a "heavy artillery of statistics" with "rolling volleys and dashing charges of argument and rhetoric." His *Impending Crisis* deftly incorporated statistics (many of which were inaccurate) into the rhetoric of invasion. Disavowing the "sickly sentimentality" of female antislavery authors, Helper set out to prove that slavery had retarded the South's economic progress in every quantifiable measure of productivity (agricultural and manufacturing), and had relegated the South to a humiliating colonial dependency on the North. Of his statistics, he said: "Those unique, mysterious little Arabic sentinels on the watch-towers of political economy . . . have allied themselves to the powers of freedom, and are hemming in and combating the institution [of slavery] with the most signal success." The main victims of slavery were nonslaveholding whites— "It makes us poor; poverty makes us ignorant; ignorance makes us wretched; wretchedness makes us wicked, and wickedness leads to the devil!!," Helper wrote, in a typical "dashing charge of argument." As the Lecompton debates heated up, Helper's book won plaudits from the antislavery press. A July 1857 column of the *National Era* declared the *Impending Crisis* the "Greatest Anti-Slavery Book Ever Published" and featured ringing endorsements from Seward, Joshua Giddings, Cassius Clay, Theodore Parker, and other anti-slavery stalwarts.[12]

Helper finessed the issue of who were the invaders and who were the invaded through a judicious use of metaphors. Of abolitionists, he proclaimed: "It is against slavery on the whole, and against slaveholders as a body, that we wage an exterminating war." And to nonslaveholders: "You must either be for us or against us—anti-slavery or pro-slavery; it is impossible for you to occupy a neutral ground." Helper retained the image of the Slave Power as aggressor by likening the encroachments of slavery onto free soil to a disease, or to a predatory beast, ravaging its victim. Thus he warned that "not content with eating out the vitals of the South, slavery, true to the character which it has acquired for insatiety [*sic*] and rapine, is beginning to make rapid encroachments on new territory."[13]

Some Northern reviewers worried that Helper's intemperate language would alienate the border state and Upper South constituents he needed most to reach. They had a point—while metaphors of invasion suited both Republicans and fire-eaters, they grated on the ears of moderate anti-Lecompton men. Their leader, Stephen Douglas, shocked at how Buchanan had cravenly bowed to the demands of Southern extremists, was determined to salvage the image and electoral prospects of his party. He and his fellow anti-Lecompton Democrats, including Henry Wise of Virginia and Frederick P. Stanton of Tennessee, positioned themselves as spokesmen for the "only conservative party that can preserve the Union." They asserted that Democrats must unite around the true meaning of popular sovereignty—for that doctrine embodied the essential principle of free government—and expose the Lecompton constitution as a mockery, an abrogation rather than an expression of the popular will. Most important, they repeatedly implored their colleagues to recognize that congressional endorsement of Lecompton would increase the power of the abolitionists and Republicans, and that antislavery forces would tap resentment against Lecompton and ride it to victory in the next presidential election.[14]

Meanwhile, Southerners representing the moderate, Whiggish, gradualist strain of proslavery sentiment—John J. Crittenden of Kentucky, John Bell of Tennessee, and Henry Winter Davis of Maryland, among others—themselves stepped forward as would-be saviors of the Union. While Republicans on occasion opportunistically claimed that such men's opposition to Lecompton had "nationalized" the party by giving it credibility in the Upper South, the truth was that Crittenden and his allies served up a rhetoric of peace and compromise, and dealt out rebukes to fire-eaters and abolitionists alike. Crittenden, in his March 17 speech to the Senate, agreed with Buchanan that the Free-Soilers in Kansas had at times been "disreputable, disorderly and seditious"; there was plenty of blame to go around on both sides, he said. But the fact remained that the majority of voters wanted a free state, and there was, he insisted, "nothing to be gained" for the South by imposing slavery on the prairie state; by climate and geography, Kansas was destined to be free soil. Crittenden derided extremists on both sides for falling away from the example of harmony set by the Founders, and he had a pointed rejoinder for Hammond. If it was true that "each of [the] sections would, by itself, make a mighty country . . . what a magnificent country is made when we put it all together?" To Toombs and others who questioned his fealty to the South, Crittenden responded, "I want to see the South always right." In other words, the region should not squander moral capital for so little political gain. Such sentiments were echoed by John Bell, who rebuked Seward for his "oracular" prediction that "there will never be quiet on the slavery question" until the South yields. "No conquering general in a cooler manner, or with an air of greater authority, ever dictated to vanquished foes the terms on which they could have peace." At the same time, Bell took the likes of Hammond and Toombs to task for their blinding "passion for victory"—a malady that caused their reason to be "taken captive."[15]

In the end, Crittenden proposed a compromise whereby the Lecompton constitution would be resubmitted to the voters of Kansas. The administration would agree to a new vote only on the condition that the referendum contain a face-saving measure—according to the English Bill (named for its sponsor, William H. English of Indiana), part of the Lecompton package that Kansans would vote up or down was a drastically reduced land grant. (The Lecomptonites had requested a whopping 23 million acres of public land on Kansas's admission to statehood; Congress now offered them a much more traditional package of approximately 4 million acres.) Moreover, if they rejected Lecompton and the reduced land grant, Kansans would have to defer statehood for two years and would be unable to reapply until the territory's population reached 93,000. No one did more to explain to the public just how this saved face for the South than Jefferson Davis, who, after representing Mississippi's States' Rights Party in 1850–51, had recently positioned himself as a champion of the Buchanan administration and of the Democratic Party as a "shield for the South." The English Bill meant, he wrote in a widely published letter, that Kansans' ratification vote was not a referendum on slavery but on the reduced land grant; if they rejected the land grant, "they had a right to do so." And, of course, to reject the land grant was to delay Kansas's statehood—and the impact its free-state congressional delegation might have on the balance of power.[16]

In August 1858, when it came time to vote, the Free-Soil majority at last unequivocally asserted itself and resoundingly rejected the chance for immediate statehood under the Lecompton constitution. In the midst of renewed violence, a Republican Party took root in Kansas and drafted a new constitution there in 1859. To the dismay of both pro- and anti-Buchanan moderates, the demise of the Lecompton constitution only stoked the fire-eaters' "passion for victory." The secessionist vanguard had prepared for this scenario— men like Hammond now abandoned their fleeting fantasy of dominating a Democratic Party purged of unsound Northerners, and argued that events in Kansas demonstrated the bankruptcy of the Democratic Party and the need for Southern independence. In May 1858 William Yancey presided over a "Southern Commercial Convention" in Montgomery, Alabama. The conference was a platform for Nicaragua's would-be liberator William Walker (as the head of a "new filibustering element in the Convention," scoffed a *New York Times* correspondent) and for advocates of reopening the African slave trade. It was also a forum for Deep South disunionists to exert pressure on their wavering Upper South counterparts. When Roger Pryor, representing Virginia's fire-eater contingent, expressed opposition to renewing the African slave trade, Yancey accused him of hypocrisy—for if it was morally legitimate to hold slaves, surely it was equally so to buy and sell them. When Pryor equivocated on the issue of disunion, saying that he still required both "a case of oppression and tyranny sufficient to justify" it and a "united South" as preconditions, Yancey replied that, "unlike the gentleman from Virginia," he was for disunion now. Why? Because the "coalition between Crittenden,

Seward and Douglas," by blocking Lecompton in Congress, had betrayed the South. The "Union of our fathers has already been dissolved by oppression and fraud," Yancey declared. He would shed every drop of blood in his heart in defense of Southern rights. Chastised thus, Pryor tried to redeem himself with the pledge that Virginia would not wait for a united South; when the time came, it would "vindicate her rights and redress her wrongs."[17]

Even as the leading fire-eaters pressed their advantage, the Republicans faced the challenge of "shor[ing] up the party against slippage toward Douglas Democracy," as Richard Carwardine puts it—of pressing the case that Northern Democratic opposition to Lecompton notwithstanding, the Democratic Party was still unquestionably a proslavery party. Its champion in this work would be the Illinois candidate for the Senate, Abraham Lincoln.[18]

THE LINCOLN-DOUGLAS DEBATES

According to Lincoln scholar Harold Holzer, the Lincoln-Douglas debates, the now-legendary oratorical showdown staged in seven Illinois towns from August to October 1858, turned on one central "crucible of contention": whether slavery was, as Lincoln claimed, "a wrong which the nation's founders had earmarked for extinction," or, as Douglas held, an issue "always best left to local areas to decide." In his landmark edition of the debates, featuring opposition accounts of the two candidates' speeches (Democratic newspaper transcriptions of Lincoln's speeches and Republican ones of Douglas's), Holzer stresses that Lincoln and Douglas had few new ideas to offer in their arguments. Instead, they were reprising and refining positions they had first taken up in 1854, in the first stages of the Kansas-Nebraska controversy.[19]

Although Holzer's characterization of the two senatorial candidates' positions on slavery is apt, he is less successful in elucidating the centrality of a second crucible in the debates between Lincoln and Douglas—namely, the issue of disunion. For Holzer, Lincoln's memorable "House Divided" speech to the Republican state convention on June 16, 1858, inaugurating his senatorial bid, was the "most radical statement of his career." Having asserted in that speech that the "government cannot endure, permanently, half *slave* and half *free*," Lincoln was "compelled to defend his dire prophecy" for the duration of the Douglas debates and parry, again and again, Douglas's charge that Lincoln, like all antislavery Republicans, was a disunionist.[20]

The problem with Holzer's reading of the debates is that it does not capture what a striking departure Lincoln's June speech, and his subsequent exchanges with Douglas, was from the Lecompton congressional debates of 1857–58. Conspicuously absent from Lincoln's rhetoric were Free-Soil legions on the march, promising to overrun and redeem the South. From the "House Divided" speech on, Lincoln portrayed the free labor system as on the defensive: "Either the *opponents* of slavery, will arrest the further spread of it, and place it where the public mind shall rest in the belief that it is in course of ultimate extinction," he said in June, "or its *advocates* will push it forward, till it shall become alike lawful in *all* the States, *old* as well as *new—North* as well as *South*." His use of the metaphor of extinction, rather than of invasion, was purposeful, and in his debates with Douglas he speculated that slavery would end, in "God's own time," deliberately—that it would not be "brought to ultimate extinction in less than a hundred years." Lincoln held that America's leaders could align themselves with God's plan by returning to the attitudes and policies of the Founders, who had understood that it was the country's destiny one day to become completely free.[21]

Lincoln was at pains to establish himself as a moderate by contrasting his own vision of a peaceful and gradual evolution toward freedom with that of the Slave Power Conspiracy's urgent design for dominance. His "House Divided" speech was intended not as a dire prophecy of disunion but as a pledge that Republicans would resolve the slavery controversy *within* the Union—that the "nature of the Union, not its existence, was the issue," according to Lincoln scholar John Channing Briggs. "I do not expect the house to *fall*," Lincoln had said at the Springfield convention, "but I *do* expect it will cease to be divided." Such "meticulously controlled" rhetoric served to distance Lincoln from Seward and congressional Republicans who had recently indulged in images of Northern military conquest. Lincoln was trying, paradoxically, to tap old themes in order to give a new face to the Republican Party. His 1858 speeches in Illinois, relative to the Lecompton speeches of Seward and other Republicans, deemphasized the struggle between North and South and reemphasized the struggle between Republicans and Democrats. His goal was to align Douglas firmly with the "advocates" of slavery. Significantly, when Lincoln alluded to the Slave Power Conspiracy, he singled out Pierce, Buchanan, and Taney (two Northerners and a Marylander), rather than the Deep South fire-eaters, as its ringleaders. Douglas, in posturing as neutral on the slavery issue, was deeply complicit in the conspiracy, for he was part of a "cooperative effort to create a public indifference to the expansion of slavery." The real purpose of the Kansas-Nebraska Act was to mold public opinion, "not to *care* whether slavery is voted *down* or *up*." Such indifference would permit Taney and the Supreme Court to take the next step in nationalizing slavery—to rule that the Constitution "does not permit a *state* to exclude slavery from its limits." Then every master could do with "one thousand slaves" what Dred Scott's master did with one. Lincoln eschewed "clash of civilizations" rhetoric and instead expressed his faith in a political remedy: the way to reverse the ominous tendency of events was to throw the "present political dynasty" out of office.[22]

Douglas, for his part, painted Lincoln as a radical abolitionist. When he wasn't accusing Lincoln of favoring race equality and race mixing, he harped relentlessly on the "House Divided" speech as proof that voters faced a choice between a "sectional party on the one side and a national party on the other." Again and again he accused Lincoln of "inviting a warfare between the North and South, to be carried on with ruthless vengeance." Douglas's proposed political remedy was to "restore peace and quiet to the country by leaving each State to mind its own business." He pledged that the Democrats would "pursue no course of conduct" to give the South "just cause for the dissolution of the Union."[23]

As Lincoln aligned Douglas with Taney and Buchanan, Douglas explicitly aligned Lincoln with Seward (and with Salmon Chase, Joshua Giddings, and Frederick Douglass); by "abolitionizing" the old Whig party, these men had destroyed the only viable national opponent to the Democrats. This strategy hinged on a willful deafness to the differences between Lincoln's rhetoric and Seward's, differences that were amplified when Seward delivered his momentous "irrepressible conflict" speech in Rochester, New York, on October 25, 1858, ten days after the last Lincoln-Douglas debate.

THE IRREPRESSIBLE CONFLICT

Like Lincoln, William Seward hammered home the fact that the Democratic Party was pledged to "execute all the designs of the slaveholders." Those designs he spelled out in dystopian detail: slaveholders would use the principle of *Dred Scott* to carry slavery into all the territories, they would annex foreign slaveholding states in Central and Latin America, they would repeal the 1808 prohibition of the slave trade, and then, with the free states thoroughly "demoralized," they would impose slavery on the North. But for Seward the contest at hand was not fundamentally between two parties or even two ideas but between two antagonistic "political systems"—Free Labor and Slave Power—long destined for an irrepressible, epic "collision." The Founders, he said, had seen the collision coming and, recognizing that the "two systems could not endure within the Union," had "expected that within a short time slavery would disappear forever."[24]

In a counterpoint to Lincoln's deliberate timetable for slavery's demise, Seward believed that the Founders regarded one hundred years as a "short period" and that they had anticipated, counting forward from the Revolution, that slavery would end in the nineteenth century. The nation could not restore the Founders' vision by resorting to compromise—but only by hastening the collision, already overdue, that the Founders had anticipated. Not only did he reject Lincoln's gradualism, he refused in this speech to give the public any reassurances about the possibility of peace, any claims that the "house would not fall." Rather, he offered martial imagery—of "gathering together the forces with which to recover back again all the fields and all the castles which have been lost, and to confound and overthrow, by one decisive blow, the betrayers of the constitution."[25]

Seward's speech exposed anew the contradiction at the heart of Republican doctrine, a contradiction that Lincoln's measured rhetoric and Seward's earlier, more temperate speeches had obscured. As recently as his March 3 speech on Lecompton, Seward had invoked the possibility of a simple political remedy—of the South yielding the government peacefully to the victorious Republican Party. But such a fantasy of repose was fundamentally incompatible with Seward's own analysis of the nature of slavery. The "slave system," he asserted in his "irrepressible conflict" speech, was one of "constant danger, distrust, suspicion, and watchfulness." It was the nature of slaveowners to "secure all political power." They could not do otherwise. In other words, although the Slave Power *should* yield, should peacefully acquiesce to the majority, Seward contended that it would not and, in some profound sense, could not—it represented principles antithetical to freedom, democracy, compromise, and repose. Moreover, it was the nature of free labor society to "prosper and flourish," and to "bring into the highest possible activity all the physical, moral, and social energies of the whole state." Compromise between the two antagonistic systems was, Seward argued, not only undesirable but fundamentally impossible.[26]

In conceptualizing disunion as a cataclysmic collision, rather than as a breach that could be closed by compromise or concession, Seward gave a new visibility to ideas that had been nurtured by groups on the margins of mainstream politics. As we have seen, radical abolitionists had long maintained that slavery and freedom were fundamentally irreconcilable, and many political abolitionists had taken up the refrain.[27] Robert Barnwell Rhett and the most militant fire-eaters claimed by the mid-1850s that compromise and concession were no longer remotely possible. Seward was not the first antebellum opinion maker to cast the sectional conflict as irrepressible, but he was the first major Northern politician, and presumptive presidential nominee of his party, to do so. What was so striking, substantively, in the Rochester speech was the picture Seward painted of the culmination of the process of disunion. This time, he did not promise a peaceful and beneficent, metaphorical "invasion," but instead a violent conquest, with the free labor forces on the offensive, winning back the territory they had lost and conceded.

What were Seward's intentions? Did he really want to be perceived, at this crucial juncture in his political career, as a radical? The modern-day scholarly consensus, repeated in works by Eric Foner, William Gienapp, Donald Fehrenbacher, and Doris Kearns Goodwin, among others, is that Seward's rashness got the best of him. His "rhetorical flourishes" made him "appear more extreme than he really was"; he "never comprehended fully the power of his words," nor did he anticipate that his speech would "cause a political uproar."[28]

But it might be said that the discourse of disunion itself got the best of Seward—that it proved, for him, irresistible. Visions of sectional repose and equilibrium, achieved at the ballot box, had been the Republicans' chosen answer to Southern prophecies and accusations of disunion. But how were Republicans to answer Slave Power threats? For so long, slaveholders' menaces of disunion had been inchoate and isolated. Again and again Republican leaders had met such warnings by saying to Southern militants, in effect, "You wouldn't dare!" But now, as disunion threats materialized into a regional program, and as images of revolution and invasion swirled in the political atmosphere, a different answer was required, one that would uphold

Northern honor and promise victory in the coming struggle. William Lloyd Garrison and John Quincy Adams had long ago accepted that only threats could answer threats, and now Seward did too. In his irrepressible conflict speech, he said to the Slave Power, in effect, "We dare you!" If disunion was to be the instrument of Southern independence, it would also be the instrument of Northern triumph—the prelude to Freedom's final eclipse of Slavery. "I know, and all the world knows," Seward concluded the address, "that revolutions never go backward."[29]

Seward's Rochester speech and Lincoln's exchanges with Douglas were reprinted by newspapers and read by hundreds of thousands of Americans, and the November congressional election results suggested that the Republicans' mixed messages resonated with Northern voters. The radical antislavery core in the Northeast could uphold Seward's version of Republican dogma, and black abolitionists in particular, Patrick Rael has observed, could easily fold Seward's secular vision of deliverance into the older, religious language of divine redemption. At the same time, those Northerners who rejected Seward's radicalism could embrace the pragmatic and moderate position articulated by Lincoln. Moreover, Republicans across the political spectrum blamed Buchanan for the national economic depression that began in 1857; for Republicans, the panic of 1857, like the Lecompton "swindle," was emblematic of the rampant corruption of Buchanan's administration. Again and again, the charge went, Buchanan pandered to Southern aristocrats (by lowering tariffs, for example) to the detriment of the common good. Claiming to represent not only free labor but also the triumph of "honesty" over "depravity," Republicans made inroads in the Midwest—in Michigan, Ohio, Indiana, and Wisconsin—and picked up eighteen seats in the House of Representatives.[30]

Lincoln lost to Douglas, as state legislators in Illinois chose senators, and the Democrats captured more legislative seats than the Republicans. But historians agree that Lincoln "would have been elected to the Senate that year in a head-to-head popular vote, under twentieth century rules," and that Lincoln's speeches boosted Republican totals in the sites of the debates with Douglas. Moreover, Douglas's victory was a blow to the Buchanan administration and its supporters, as it vindicated the anti-Lecompton position and primed Douglas to seek nomination as the party's presidential candidate in 1860.[31]

While Lincoln's surprising showing enhanced his status and prospects in the North, it did little to displace Seward as the face of the Republican Party. Northern Democratic papers attributed Republican gains not to a "regular, well organized, homogeneous party" with a coherent message but rather to a motley "opposition" united only by the "common impulse of hatred." Seward had allegedly stoked this hatred with his insistence that one section must "drive the other to the wall, and force it to surrender." What Seward advocated, his Northern critics charged, was nothing less than a "war of extermination . . . in which neither side is to get, or to give, quarter." Seward's defenders, in journals such as the *National Era*, claimed that his talk of an irrepressible conflict had been taken out of context, and that he did not "contemplate a plan of action but merely a scheme of natural development"— his words were "a speculation, not a project." But Democrats summarily rejected that interpretation. Fire-eaters especially flourished the speech as "the avowal of a distinct design on the part of the Republicans to wage fierce and unrelenting and bloody war upon Slavery wherever it exists." As Eric Walther, the leading historian of Southern nationalists, notes, James Henry Hammond hailed Seward's speech as nothing less than "glorious." "We have got them dead," he wrote to a friend, by which he meant that if Seward or another Republican were elected in 1860, the South could now justify disunion as a defensive measure against the North's plans for armed intervention to eliminate slavery.[32]

The effect of the speech in galvanizing fire-eaters was dramatic. Take the case of Jefferson Davis. Clinging to the notion that the English Bill was an honorable resolution to the Lecompton debacle and to fantasies of emerging as the leader of a resurgent Democratic Party, Davis, even as Lincoln and Douglas were crisscrossing Illinois, went on a heralded speaking tour of New England from July to October 1858, in which he trafficked in platitudes about how, if each section simply minded its own business, the balance of power could be restored and maintained. While Northern Democratic papers praised Davis's patriotism, Southern ones lambasted his hypocrisy, and political rivals such as Mississippi's Albert Gallatin Brown jockeyed to claim Davis's discarded mantle as a supreme protector of the South. Alarmed by these attacks, Davis sang a different tune when he returned home to Mississippi, trying to refurbish his reputation with what the *New York Times* called a "fire eating, union dissolving speech" delivered to the state legislature. Invoking the Rochester speech, Davis singled out Seward as the "arch-enemy of the South" and called on Mississippi to make "warlike prepara-tions" for the coming fight. (Of Davis's abrupt about-face, the *National Era* observed that "there must be, in the atmosphere of Mississippi, some quality which sets the brain on fire.")[33]

Meanwhile, the League of United Southerners, the brainchild of Yancey of Alabama and Edmund Ruffin of Virginia, established chapters around the South dedicated to the proposition that the election of a Republican in 1860 would justify and indeed necessitate disunion. In his private diary, Ruffin lamented in the summer of 1858 that while "nearly all the leading and promi-nent men of the South" agreed with the fire-eaters "in general opinion," too many were still loathe, lest they run ahead of the Southern electorate, to make "*public* avowals of disunion sentiments." The specter of a Republican victory in 1860 and evidence of grassroots support for the "League," Ruffin calcu-lated, would break Southern politicians of their timidity. As the December 10, 1858, manifesto of the Montgomery League chapter put it, the Republicans, "with Seward at their head, declare a war of extermination—a war to the knife—upon slavery in the States; and their policy has been accepted by the North." Affirming Seward's notion that compromise was "fatal" and that the two sections were fast nearing the "vortex of ruin," the league pledged its readiness "to embark our fortunes on the open sea of disunion, and trusting to the justness of our cause, leave the issue to Heaven."[34]

Increasingly, fire-eaters spoke on the national stage not only of disunion but also of the specific mechanism by which the South would, as they saw it, defend itself from Northern aggression—namely, secession. In the opening months of 1859, the "slavery propagandists [fell] back again on Congress," the *New York Times* observed, where they pushed for the annexation of slaveholding Cuba and for federal legislation safeguarding slavery in the terri-tories, while clashing with Northern representatives over tariffs, the Home-stead Act, and the transcontinental railroad. Each issue provided occasions for sectional grandstanding. In a Senate speech in January 6 on the railroad bill (ostensibly advocating a Southern route for the Pacific Railroad), Geor-gia's Alfred Iverson stated boldly that "the election of a Northern President, upon a sectional and anti-slavery issue, will be considered cause enough to justify secession." Calling Seward's "irrepressible conflict" formulation a declaration of "war to the knife," Iverson threatened that if Seward or any other man endorsing the Rochester speech were elected president, more than one Southern state would take "immediate steps towards separation." Iverson made it clear that he was not merely predicting but actually advocating such a course. Significantly, even as he excoriated Seward, Iverson invoked the same logic of expansion—whereby the free labor system would inexorably grow more powerful—that the New York senator had. Compromise was impossible, Iverson believed, because the "Republican party cannot stand still; if it does, it dies. To live and reign, it must go on." The party would not rest until it had achieved one or the other of its twin goals: abolition or disunion.[35]

The Northern press noted that Iverson's was the "first disunion speech" in the newly constructed Senate chamber; its coverage of the speech ran the gamut from mockery of Iverson's feigned "mournful gravity" to accusations that it was Iverson who endorsed the doctrine of "war to the knife." Northern politicians answered Iverson in a series of speeches that were intended as damage control but came across, to Iverson's ilk, as new provocations. In the Congress, Lyman Trumbull, Israel Washburn Jr., and Henry Wilson sought to marginalize Iverson and his "very strange language" by reassuring the public that Seward and the Republicans intended no aggression against the rights of the South and that the party's purpose was to "restore peace and harmony" to the country. But these men did not and could not reject the logic of expansion. Trumbull, quoting Iverson's statement that the Republican Party "must go on," conceded: "Sir, I believe that. It cannot stand still. It is a party of progress, of power." The most celebrated answer to Iverson came from Texas senator Sam Houston, a national hero and former president of the Republic of Texas. Deploring the dominant place that the word "disunion" had come to occupy in the "vocabulary of American politics," Houston called secession "madness" and "revolution." He lambasted Iverson for having the nerve to claim that secessionists "speak for the South"—and countered, "I answer for part of the South." The South that Houston represented was the South of unconditional Unionists, a group that historians can define only in hindsight. Such Unionists rejected secession absolutely and stayed true to this position, as Houston himself did, even after the Confederacy came to life. The Northern press hailed Houston's chastisement of Iverson as a sign that secession still found little favor in the South. But such assessments failed to account for the inroads secessionists were making among the *conditional* Unionists in the South—that is, those who regarded secession as a last resort.[36]

Secessionists' principal organizations continued to be their "League" and their annual "Southern Convention." *De Bow's Review* printed the most recent manifesto of the League of United Southerners in March 1859; it showed how far the secessionists had come. In their minds, disunionists were no longer voices in the wilderness. "No prophet's ken is needed to foresee the terrible events of the future which will follow, as certain as the night follows the day, unless this fatal compromise policy is abandoned henceforth and forever," the league's "address" began. It was self-evident that the Republican Party was driven by a "lust of dominion" and would impose emancipation on the South. At such a time of crisis, the South could no longer "safely build her castles on the shifting sands of party." She must "rely on herself." At the Southern Convention's May 1859 meeting in Vicksburg, Mississippi, Yancey, J. B. De Bow, and Leonidas W. Spratt, editor of the secessionist *Charleston Standard*, pressed this interpretation on their fellow delegates, along with the notion that the reopening of the slave trade was the only way to defend slavery's moral rectitude and to ensure Southern prosperity. Spratt, the leading advocate of the slave trade, declared that the "contest is impending and inevitable"; echoing Iverson, he said that if a single state were to lead the way in secession, others were sure to follow. As for the slave trade, if slavery were to survive, it must "start from its repose, it must take the moral strength of an aggressive attitude."[37]

Spratt was countered in the convention by former U.S. senator and Mississippi governor Henry S. Foote, a Unionist who had triumphed over his disunionist nemesis, fire-eater John A. Quitman, in the state's "first secession crisis" of 1850–51. Foote rejected the notion of single-state secession as well as the bid to reopen the African slave trade, on the grounds that both policies played right into the hands of the evil William Seward. Seward's oft-repeated charge that the "South is aggressive" had "done more to sow the seeds of unkindness in the minds of the patriotic men of the North than anything else." Southerners should stick to the old Calhoun position that "all they wanted was to be let alone." Foote's impassioned speech, like Houston's, was hailed by the Northern press as a setback for the secessionists. But the numbers told a different story—for the first time, in May 1859, Spratt won a resolution, which passed by a vote of 40 to 19, that state and federal laws prohibiting the African slave trade "ought to be repealed." (Foote himself upheld the Union and opposed secession until after the firing on Fort Sumter;

although he then served in the Confederate Congress, he was an implacable foe of the Jefferson Davis administration.)[38]

Secessionists proved canny—realizing that the slave trade remained a divisive issue, they increasingly focused on two themes. The first was the demand that, in keeping with the *Dred Scott* decision, Congress protect the rights of Southerners to take their slaves into the territories by passing a federal code that would legalize slavery once and for all. The corollary to this demand was the proposition, with Yancey as its leading spokesman, that if Douglas Democrats refused to safeguard slavery in the upcoming national party convention in Charleston in 1860, then states' rights men should secede from the convention; this secession would be the prelude to state secession from the Union. The second theme, in keeping with Hammond's "Cotton is King" speech, was the bright prospects of a putative Southern Confederacy. De Bow led the way here, with endless statistics purporting to prove that a "confederacy of the Southern States would become one of the most powerful nations on the face of the earth." In the light of such statistics, a *De Bow's* contributor, Alfred A. Smith, declared, "Then we do glory in the name of *disunionists!*"[39]

Northern newspapers tried to refute the argument about the Confederacy's bright prospects, but conceded that secessionists were, more and more, finding a receptive audience in the South. As a Georgia correspondent to the *New York Observer* put it, in a June 1859 article on the "true state of public opinion" in the South, there were three major parties there: the disunion party, the quasi-Union party, and the Union party. In his opinion, the quasi-Union party, consisting of "old school" states' rights men who upheld the Union on the condition that it preserve Southern rights, was numerically predominant. Second in popularity was the Union party, full of "respectable" men who thought the Union was "the great paramount good"; this party, despite the fact that it represented "many of the wealthiest men of the South," was losing members "as we recede from revolutionary times and associations." The disunion party, according to the anonymous "Georgian," was numerically the smallest but possessed certain distinct advantages and momentum: it was "compact, zealous, and determined," and it was attracting the "educated young men of the South." This assessment was remarkably accurate. Recent scholarship has shown that there was a strong generational component to secessionists' appeals. Young white men, eager to achieve wealth and glory, took to heart the promise that secession would guarantee them access to slaves and to land, even as well-established older planters, especially in long-settled areas of the tidewater and coastal South, clung to the Union that had brought them prosperity and influence.[40]

It was the quasi-Union party that was the most volatile, as the correspondent, himself a part of "that class," noted. For despite their abiding love for the Union, its adherents stood ready to "strike for independence" if abolitionists persisted in their "mad and dangerous schemes." Less than a week after the *Observer* printed this warning, abolitionist John Brown rented the Kennedy farm, in Maryland, about five miles from the crossroads town of Harpers Ferry. It was intended as the temporary headquarters for his army of emancipation.[41]

JOHN BROWN'S RAID

Recent years have seen a flowering of scholarship on Brown, much of it animated by the question of whether he was a "freedom fighter" or a "terrorist." A middle position has emerged that Brown embodied the conflicting "forces of light and darkness that grappled for the republic's soul"—and that his Harpers Ferry raid, with its spirit of "universal freedom," was the "light" to the darkness of his Pottawatomie massacre.[42]

Brown's Virginia raid was the culmination of his long-cherished vision of using the Allegheny Mountains as a base of operations from which to launch emancipatory raids in the South. Having educated himself about the historical precedents for such a strategy, Brown was inspired both by guerrilla resistance to Napoleon in Europe and by slave and Indian resistance in the Americas; indeed, he hoped to create his own "maroon" stronghold, of blacks and whites, in the mountains. It is unclear exactly when Brown identified Harpers Ferry as his target, but biographer David S. Reynolds believes that he may have chosen the Virginia town as early as 1850. In many ways it was a logical choice. Positioned where the Potomac and Shenandoah rivers met, Harpers Ferry was the site of a federal arsenal stocked with weapons and ammunition; Brown imagined these in the hands of his band of liberators. Moreover, it sat in Jefferson County—home to strong communities of free blacks and white Quakers who had long aided fugitive slaves on the route of the Underground Railroad known as the "Great Black Way." According to new research by Hannah Geffert and Jean Libby, Brown had learned about the Appalachian fugitive slave routes from African American associates such as Frederick Douglass, Willis Hodges, and Henry Highland Garnet, whom he had met during his travels in the east from 1847 to 1855.[43]

Even when Brown was fighting in Kansas in 1855 and 1856, Reynolds writes, Harpers Ferry was "never far from his mind." Concrete plans for the raid took shape when Brown returned to the East in late 1856. For the next three years (1857–59) he focused on raising money and advocates among abolitionists intellectuals, especially in Boston. He successfully consolidated the support of the "secret six"—Gerrit Smith, George L. Stearns, Franklin B. Sanborn, Samuel Gridley Howe, Theodore Parker, and Thomas Wentworth Higginson—the inner circle of prominent white abolitionists to whom he confided his Southern strategy. Smith was Brown's most assiduous backer, and Higginson was his most radical one—he had fought for the freedom of Anthony Burns in 1854 and had headed up the Worcester Disunion Convention of 1857. Brown also worked to expand his network of black supporters. In May 1858 he sponsored, with Martin Delany (a native of Jefferson County), an interracial convention in Chatham, Canada. It was at this convention that Brown promulgated his most controversial and revealing blueprint for radical change—his "Provisional Constitution and Ordinances for the People of the United States."[44]

The Provisional Constitution began with a preamble that called slavery an "unprovoked, and unjustifiable war" and a "violation of those self-evident truths set forth in our Declaration of Independence." It continued with a series of "articles" establishing the different branches and administrative functions of government. This grandiose vision has been easy for scholars to mock; one recent article offering a "psychological examination" of Brown asserts that the document was written in a manic state, in which the author's sense of reason was unraveling. But read in the context of its times, Reynolds and others counter, Brown's constitution is eminently reasonable, even heroic. It is an extension of both Garrison's condemnation of the U.S. Constitution and Seward's "higher law" argument. At the same time, it transcends the work of Brown's white antislavery contemporaries by envisioning a truly multicultural, inclusive society, in which, to quote Reynolds, "all ethnic groups or women could assume leading roles"; in fact, the Chatham convention elected blacks to offices in the new government.[45]

His constitution also reveals how Brown struggled with the issue of disunion. At the urging of the black delegates at the convention, Brown abandoned the idea of creating a new "state" within the nation and opted instead to create a "new sovereign nation." Yet he saw this act of separation as a means to save the Union, not to destroy it—article forty-six says that the constitution's provisions "look to no dissolution of the Union, but simply to Amendment and Repeal." Brown believed he was defending the Union from slavery. This high-wire act reveals the influence of Frederick Douglass—Brown shared Douglass's conviction that Garrisonian disunion would amount to abandoning Southern blacks, when abolitionists should be reaching out to them. Despite this shared philosophy, however, Douglass declined to endorse Brown's Harpers Ferry plan on the grounds that to attack a federal arsenal was to attack the national government and such a bold plan could never succeed.[46]

DAYS OF RECKONING

After renting the Maryland farm in July 1859, Brown concentrated on gathering recruits and supplies. By mid-October he had a loyal band of twenty-one "soldiers" (sixteen of them white, five black) in his service; he chose Sunday, October 16, for the attack. At first, his men succeeded—they cut the telegraph wires, seized the arsenal, armed an estimated twenty-five to fifty local black men, and took white hostages. But then Brown made a fatal miscalculation. Instead of a strategic retreat into the mountains, where he could have planned further raids, he chose to hunker down at the Harpers Ferry armory, in the hope that more locals would flock to his banner or that he could use the hostages as leverage for an escape. In other words, Reynolds writes, Brown abandoned his own plans for guerrilla warfare and "opted for a macho fight to the death." Brown and his warriors held out against the irate townsmen who surrounded the armory but then were overwhelmed by the state militias of Virginia and Maryland, and by the U.S. Marines, under Brevet Colonel Robert E. Lee, whom President Buchanan had sent to the scene. On October 18 the marines captured Brown and four others. Ten of Brown's men were killed or mortally wounded; the remaining seven of the original twenty-one escaped (two of whom were recaptured). Brown, immobilized and in intense pain from severe wounds incurred in the fighting, was conveyed to the jail in Charles Town, Virginia, on October 19; his trial began on October 25. By

November 2 he was convicted of treason and sentenced to the gallows. One month later, on December 2, 1859, he was executed.[47]

Brown went to his death stoically, maintaining in his last days that he was more valuable to the abolitionist cause dead than alive. In his brilliantly crafted letters from jail (widely disseminated in newspapers such as the *New York Tribune*) and in his testimony in court, Brown forged a legacy as a martyr. He "invested his own trial and execution with cosmic meaning" by likening himself to Jesus on the Cross. Soon antislavery intellectuals (most notably Ralph Waldo Emerson, Henry David Thoreau, Horace Greeley, William Lloyd Garrison, Frederick Douglass, John Greanleaf Whittier, Walt Whitman, and Herman Melville), enthralled by Brown's courage, came forward to sanctify him. As Thoreau put it: "Christ was crucified . . . Captain Brown was hung. These are the two ends of a chain." Brown had "earned immortality." Most important for his legacy was the way that Brown himself spoke in the prophetic mode of the final reckoning. On the day of his execution, he gave one of his guards a note with the following prophecy: "I John Brown am now quite *certain* that the crimes of this *guilty land: will* never be purged away; but with Blood. I had *as I now think: vainly* flattered myself that without *very much* bloodshed; it might be done." Such language is a far cry from his call, in the Provisional Constitution, for "amendment and repeal" of the political status quo. Brown, in his last moments, and for himself, resolved the dilemma that had plagued slavery's opponents—whether to herald a political remedy to the sectional controversy or to foretell an epic clash of civilizations. In the end, Brown chose war. Ever since, his champions and critics alike have cast him as a portent—a "meteor," as Whitman put it—of disunion.[48]

The Harpers Ferry raid, together with antislavery approbation for Brown's heroic martyrdom, effected a sea change in white Southern public opinion. To the delight of the fire-eaters, many formerly moderate Southern politicians and editors flocked to the secession standard, and newspaper after newspaper claimed, as the *Richmond Enquirer* did, that "the Harpers Ferry invasion has advanced the cause of disunion more than any other event." The raid profoundly shook the faith of white Southerners—even those who clung to the Union—that the North could be trusted. Communities all over the South raised companies of armed men for defense against further insurrectionary attacks, and they passed resolutions warning the North against further provocations. A public meeting in Virginia's Augusta County—a Shenandoah Valley setting in which moderate Unionists predominated—captured the prevailing mood in the South with the resolution: "Thus far have you gone, but you shall go no farther!" Unconditional Unionists in the South understood all too well the perilous shift in public opinion. Elizabeth Van Lew, of Richmond, a keen political observer who would one day lead a Union spy ring in her native city, lamented: "There is no denying that our people were in a palpable state of war from the time of the John Brown raid."[49]

In the context of the discourse of disunion, what is most striking about public reactions is the extent to which both Northerner and Southerners—across the political spectrum—viewed the raid through the prism of Seward's "irrepressible conflict" speech. In the immediate aftermath of the attack, "secret six" member Higginson wrote that "twenty years ago John Brown made up his mind that there was an irrepressible conflict between freedom and slavery, and that in that conflict he must take his share." Brown was a prophet who saw "what the rest of us are only beginning to see, even now—that slavery must be met, first or last, on its own ground." While Higginson invoked Seward in praise of Brown, Southern commentators claimed that Brown's evil scheme was the direct outgrowth of Seward's disunionist philosophy. Not only in hotbeds of Deep South secessionism such as Charleston, but also in towns with strong Unionist traditions, such as Richmond, Nashville, Wilmington (North Carolina), and Milledgeville (Georgia), Democratic newspapers unanimously declared that Brown's raid was the "result of Sewardism" and the "commencement of what Seward spoke of as the 'irrepressible conflict.'" Southern disunionists and Unionists alike held Seward personally responsible for Harpers Ferry. According to the *Raleigh Register*, his Rochester speech was "calculated, if not designed, to incite the treasonable plot"—and thus the sectional conflict had entered an ominous new phase. "As long as such men as Garrison, Phillips, & Co., raved, ranted and blasphemed, and did nothing else," the editorial asserted, "conservative men" might dismiss them in contempt. "But when we see Senators of the United States" encouraging "cool and deliberate plans for making actual war upon half the Union," then the crisis was truly at hand. Seen as an extension of Republican policy, the raid deepened Southern foreboding of the election of

1860. "If, in our present position of power and unitedness, we have the raid of John Brown . . . what will be the measures of insurrection and incendiarism, which must follow our notorious and abject prostration to Abolition rule at Washington[?]," the *Charleston Mercury* asked, tapping into pervasive fear among white Southerners that the election of a Republican like William Seward would bring spiraling antislavery violence.[50]

Seward's culpability for the Harpers Ferry raid was trumpeted in formal state resolutions, such as the Tennessee legislature's declaration that Brown's raid was the "natural fruit of this treasonable 'irrepressible conflict' doctrine put forth by this great head of the Black Republican party." It was also proclaimed in the federal capital, where the Thirty-sixth Congress, convening in December 1859, fell into unprecedented acrimony. Southern Democrats "deadlocked" the House in opposition to the Republican candidate for Speaker, John Sherman of Ohio; they successfully tarnished him, based on his endorsement of Helper's book, as an antislavery militant in the Seward mold. "Men talked of disunion in plainer terms than ever before," David Potter has written—and as Congressman Roger Pryor's anti-Sherman speech on December 29 illustrates, Southern disunion talk continued to be a torturous welter of accusations and threats. Pryor imputed to Seward the treasonous doctrine that "the Union, like the womb of Rebecca, is torn by two associate but irreconcilable elements . . . that this controversy is inevitable and incurable, and must go on with increasing fury until one or the other principle be vanquished or exterminated." When Representative Robert McKnight of Pennsylvania countered that John C. Calhoun's 1849 manifesto was the first articulation of the irrepressible conflict notion, Pryor was at first indignant. Southerners, he asserted, believed not only that the rights of the South were compatible with the interests of the North, but also that "the resources of one section are exactly responsive to the deficiencies of the other. . . . We plant and produce, they fetch and fabricate." But, significantly, Pryor was unable to reject Seward's logic fully. He went on to say that there *was* an "irrepressible conflict"—not between slave labor and free labor systems but between the interests of the South and the Union on the one hand and the schemes of the Republican Party on the other. By the end of his speech Pryor's accusation had devolved into a warning: referring to the "explosion at Harper's Ferry," he intoned that "eight million freemen, educated to the use of arms" would not

be subjugated by "conscience-stricken traitors." They were ready, if necessary, "to organize a confederacy of our own resources, and to rear a government which shall survive the lapse of ages."[51]

While Southern Democrats grappled openly and awkwardly with the challenge of disparaging Northern disunionism as treason and at the same time
heralded Southern secession as a positive good, Northern Democrats, free of
this dilemma, portrayed disunion as an evil from which no good could come.
From Concord, New Hampshire, to Cincinnati, Ohio, to Springfield, Illinois, Democratic editors seized the opportunity to prove once and for all
that the Republican Party was intent on disunion. Brown had made a "practical application of the 'irrepressible conflict' doctrine," wrote one; another
opined that the Harpers Ferry raid was the "natural consequence . . . of the
doctrine of 'irrepressible conflict' which [Republicans] are now urged to
make the sum and substance of their faith." Not surprisingly, the Democratic
Illinois State Register in Springfield took both Seward and Lincoln to task,
the one for his Rochester speech and the other for his "House Divided"
address. The national journal, the *Democratic Review*, which had done more
than any other party organ to tarnish the Republicans as disunionists, thundered that "the manifesto of Gov. Seward at Rochester, anticipates the riot at
Harper's Ferry as inevitably as night follows day." But eager to tarnish all of
the possible Republican contenders in the upcoming 1860 election, the *Review* implicated Lincoln, too. Together Lincoln and Seward had devised a
program—the *Review* claimed, using what was becoming a ubiquitous phrase
—of "war to the knife against Southern institutions." Such editorial expressions found public affirmation in the series of anti-Republican "Union" meetings that took place around the North. For example, at a December 8, 1859,
meeting in Boston—home to many of John Brown's most ardent supporters
and apologists—prominent New England Democrat Caleb Cushing charged
that abolitionists and Republicans shared the blame for Brown's Union-
destroying treachery.[52]

How did Republicans react to these charges? Lincoln and Seward quickly
condemned Brown's raid and joined their fellows in a concerted effort to
shore up the party's Unionist credentials and image. Republican spokesmen
attempted to turn the tables on their accusers by offering their own interpretation of the origin and the lesson of Harpers Ferry. They contended that
Brown's violent scheme was an outgrowth of the lawlessness, vigilantism, and

"filibustering" that proslavery forces had perpetrated in Kansas—and that Brown's failure and execution constituted a "warning to traitors" (Southern disunionists as well as radical abolitionists) that treason would be punished by death. In preparation for the election, Republicans worked to brand the Democratic Party itself as secessionist. In a January 25, 1860, speech that parsed for voters "who are the political disunionists, and on what grounds," Senator Henry Wilson of Massachusetts quoted at length the secession threats of Keitt, Mason, Toombs, Butler, and other leading Southern politicians as proof that disunionists were at the helm of the "sectionalized, slavery-extending Democracy." In the House, Representative Edward McPherson took the same tack. "If there be meaning in language and sincerity in men," he said, then "the master spirits of the Democratic Party in Congress are covered with the scrofulous taint of disunion." On behalf of his own party, McPherson promised that "the cardinal doctrine of my political faith is THE MAINTENANCE OF THE UNION OF THE STATES." Massachusetts representative Henry L. Dawes, in one of the most eloquent speeches on the subject, forcefully reminded his colleagues that the disunion prophecies and threats of Southerners served a single nefarious purpose—to convert the nation to the "dogma" that slavery was a "boon and a blessing." "Whether it be the political seer . . . bidden to read, magnified and horrified in his magic lantern, the painted words 'THIS IS THE BEGINNING OF THE END,'" or the "gorgon head of disunion, which rises upon this floor and threatens treason till timid conservatism quakes and quails," the effect and purpose were the same: "The conversion of the nation is to be achieved by the irresistible agency of terror."[53]

Republicans searched for ways to reassure the Northern public that in contrast with the fear-mongering Democrats, the Republican Party's "core was wrapped in a comforting concern with maintaining order." Lincoln's speech of February 27, 1860, at Cooper Union, in New York City, was the centerpiece of this effort. Appreciated now, thanks to Harold Holzer's recent study, as the "speech that made Lincoln president," the address was orchestrated by Seward's opponents within the Republican Party. Lincoln was carefully introduced to East Coast voters as a hero from the West, fresh from his David-versus-Goliath contest with Stephen Douglas—and as a moderate alternative to the controversial Seward. Lincoln's goal in the address was nothing less than to "separate himself from both Seward's negative fatalism and John Brown's dangerous radicalism." Thus he eschewed any references to the "house divided" and honed his strategy of citing the Founding Fathers as the unimpeachable authorities on the fate of slavery in the territories. Armed with detailed accounts of their votes, he set out to prove that the vast majority of the Founders—36 out of 39, by Lincoln's calculations—believed that the federal government could and should restrict slavery's expansion. He sought, as Holzer writes, "to convert the founders themselves to Republicans." Next, in a section ostensibly directed to Southern voters but really designed to win over Northern ones, Lincoln sought to expose the hypocrisy of those Southerners who wielded disunion as both accusation and threat. To say that Northern disunion caused Southern secession was akin, Lincoln noted in a memorable image, to a highwayman holding a pistol to the ear of a victim and threatening "Stand and deliver, or I shall kill you, and then you will be a murderer!" For the sake of the Union, Northerners had to resist such extortion.[54]

Having enshrined the Founders' gradualism as the means to reestablish sectional harmony, Lincoln then, in the last section of his speech, to rally voters for the coming electoral battle, explained why such harmony was elusive. Militant Southern slaveholders and their Northern Democratic allies would never accept that the North simply leave slavery alone—rather, they would continue to demand, more and more aggressively, that the North concede the rightness of slavery and desist from condemning the institution as wrong. This concession the North would not and could not make. Lincoln did not, as Seward had, conjure up the coming collision as the long-awaited chance for the North to vanquish its foe. But, as Holzer reminds us, at Cooper Union Lincoln did speak of wrong and right, and of duty: Northerners had a moral duty not to make the sort of compromises that perpetuated slavery. "Neither let us be slandered from our duty by false accusations against us, nor frightened from it by menaces of destruction to the Government," he concluded, in direct reference to Southern uses of disunion as a charge and a warning. "LET US HAVE FAITH THAT RIGHT MAKES MIGHT, AND IN THAT FAITH, LET US, TO THE END, DARE TO DO OUR DUTY AS WE UNDERSTAND IT."[55]

The address received exhaustive coverage by the New York press and was soon widely disseminated throughout the North. For Republicans like *New York Post* editor William Cullen Bryant, Lincoln had "vindicated" the Republicans, aligning them with the Founders rather than with Seward and Brown. Significantly, a few days later Seward, in a speech on the Senate floor, seemed to recant his Rochester doctrine, choosing instead to hail the Founders' wisdom and to cast Republicans as the Union party.[56]

Could such Republican professions banish the specter of John Brown? No—and writing two decades after the start of the Civil War, Frederick Douglass sought to explain why. In Douglass's formulation, Brown did not *embody* the "irrepressible conflict" doctrine—rather, he *transcended* it. The Harpers Ferry raid brought antebellum politics—and its tangled practices of demand and concession, advance and retreat—to an abrupt end. "The irrepressible conflict was one of words, votes and compromises. When John Brown stretched forth his arm the sky was cleared. The time for compromises was gone, the armed hosts of freedom stood face to face over the chasm of a broken Union, and the clash of arms was at hand."[57]

The Rubicon Is Passed

THE WAR AND BEYOND

"The question of Union or Disunion is dead and buried," declared an article
that ran in the *Staunton Vindicator* in March 1861, during Virginia's secession convention. Led by South Carolina and the Deep South states, dissolution had already taken place, and now Virginia faced a stark choice between
joining its "sister States" or "subordination of our section to Black Republican and abolition aggression and outrage." Secessionists promised those
white Southerners who embraced the Confederacy, among many other boun-
ties, linguistic clarity—an end to the long, harrowing debates over the causes
and imagined consequences of disunion, and a new emphasis on the justness
of secession, the need for martial vindication, and the bright prospects of the
Southern nation.[1]

This book has argued that from the very founding of the United States, the
"question of Union or Disunion" was inseparable from the issue of slavery's
destiny. The central premise of American political culture, in the North and
South alike, was that the republic was fragile—beset by external and internal
enemies, and in perpetual danger of moral decline. Americans proved endlessly creative in tapping deep anxieties about the republic's survival as a
rhetorical weapon in their political combat. By the time immediatists took the
stage, Americans with rival political agendas had already, for nearly half a

337

century, honed the art of casting their opponents as traitors bent on destroying the Union.

On one level, the story I have told is the story of how Americans came to regard slavery as the most potent of all sources of disunion. But I have also tried to show that slavery as a political issue did not *displace* other disunion anxieties—it *encompassed* them. For Southern slaveholders, the end of slavery represented a congeries of dangers: race war and civil war, most prominently, but also class and gender disorder, foreign intervention, moral decline, and economic decay. For antislavery Northerners, it was the "Slave Power" that embodied all of these various dangers to the nation.

From the start, defenders of slavery used prophecies, threats, and accusations of disunion to stigmatize opponents of slavery as treasonous. In the 1830s, in response to the rise of immediatism, proslavery ideologues popularized the idea that disunion was an inexorable process of sectional alienation, and that the South needed guarantees of protection against the increasingly hostile North. By the late 1840s, a cadre of disunion strategists had taken the field, led by Robert Barnwell Rhett, to argue that such guarantees were no longer possible now that abolitionists controlled Northern politics. In the region's newspapers, colleges, commercial conventions, literature, and other public forums, these strategists built the case that disunion need not be a fearful prospect, provided that the South was prepared for it—unified, prosperous, righteous, and defiant. Only if the white South were divided and "submissive" would "Black Republicans" be able to fulfill their own disunion dream of destroying the slave regime.

Northerners, no less than Southerners, used the rhetoric of disunion to grapple with the problem of slavery. Anti-abolitionists, fearful of the prospect of racial equality, stigmatized all opponents of slavery as agitators who would bring national ruin. Antislavery forces, notwithstanding the profound tactical and philosophical differences in their ranks, elaborated their own rhetoric of disunion as a process—a process that revealed the incompatibility of freedom and slavery and the superiority of the free labor system to the slave labor one. In the mid-1850s, Republicans took up the challenge of convincing Northerners that the Slave Power, in suppressing the fundamental rights of free speech and majority rule, sought to weaken the North and even impose slavery there. Northerners could no longer allow themselves to be manipulated by Southern threats of secession into giving up ground—for the prospect of subjugation was even more frightful than that of separation.

John Brown's raid vindicated Southern secessionists' fear of a Northern invasion, and Southern reactions to the raid vindicated Republicans in their argument that the Slave Power was more intent on domination than ever. The Harpers Ferry incident thus opened the last chapter in the history of the Civil War's origins—the "secession crisis" of 1859 to 1861. When he asserted that the Harpers Ferry clash had closed the "time for compromises," Frederick Douglass had in mind a cascade of events—the schism of militant Southern states' rights Democrats from the national party; the bitter presidential election campaign that pitted Abraham Lincoln against Stephen Douglas in the North and fire-eater John Cabell Breckinridge against Unionist John Bell in the South; the election, on the strength of Northern votes, of Lincoln; the secession, led by South Carolina, of the Deep South states; the formation of the Confederacy; the Confederate firing on Fort Sumter in South Carolina; and the entry of Virginia and three other Upper South states into the new slaveholders' government. These events have merited countless books of their own and will receive a new, detailed interpretation in the subsequent volumes of the Littlefield series. What follows here are some of the ways that disunion rhetoric conditioned the secession crisis and persisted into war, and beyond.

SOUTHERNERS DREW ON a wide range of disunion images in their responses to the Republican victory in 1860. As Charles B. Dew shows, when the Deep South secessionists who formed the Confederacy after Lincoln's election urged the Upper South to join the new nation, they focused on the perils of remaining in an abolitionized Union, conjuring up specters of slave insurrection, race competition, and race mixing. This dystopian litany had been pressed into service repeatedly during the antebellum decades by proslavery forces seeking political leverage and protection *within* the Union—now it served to prove that the Union was irredeemably corrupt.[2]

Southern Unionists, their ranks thinning, continued to warn that disunion itself was a "deep, dark vortex" that would destroy the South. Drawing graphic and familiar pictures of the horrors of civil war, they argued that when war came, those who "have property to defend and interest at stake, will find themselves surrounded by enemies on every hand, [and] it will be too late to avert the awful ruin." Leading Southern Unionists also continued to blame the crisis on Northern and Southern radicals alike. John Minor Botts, a longtime standard-bearer of Virginia Whigs, argued, in a speech entitled "Union or Disunion," that "South Carolina is a very extreme State— Massachusetts is another. . . . I do not think it just to take either as reflecting fairly the conservative sentiment of either section of the country."[3]

During the debates over secession held by state conventions in the South, Unionists were outmaneuvred politically by fire-eaters. Many Upper South Unionists in particular seemed complacent or even paralyzed, lulled into a false sense of security by the familiarity of secessionist threats—after all, the old arguments that compromise was still possible and that sectional war was the ultimate calamity had defused Southern disunionism so many times before. Even the most ardent Unionists, alert to the precipitous shift in public opinion toward separation, failed to appreciate that the old arguments had lost their salience. Botts, for example, tried to align secessionists historically with the "philosophy" of Benedict Arnold, of Aaron Burr, and of the Federalists of the Hartford Convention; he reminded Virginians that these Northern disunionists were now universally held "in terms of scorn and ignominy." But secessionists made emotionally resonant counterarguments—that Botts and his ilk were the stooges of the very abolitionists who dishonored the South, and that, as De Bow's Review intoned, "war is not the only, nor is it the greatest evil to which a people can be subjected. War is preferable to dishonor." The language of honor was readily translated into the language of Christian duty. With the "atheistic" Lincoln now "clad in the black garments of discord and schism," explained New Orleans secessionist the Reverend B. M. Palmer, a war was no longer the most woeful of human tragedies but instead the South's chance for a "baptism by fire."[4]

Northerners, too, mobilized a wide range of disunion images during the secession crisis. Northern Democrats yearning for compromise, like Southern Unionists, continued to condemn "Abolitionist-Republicans" as treasonous disunionists. "What has brought us to the verge of this precipice?," asked the Reverend Henry J. Van Dyke, on behalf of conservative Northerners, in a sermon delivered in December 1860. How was it that "disunion— that used to be whispered in corners—stalks forth in open daylight, and is recognized as a necessity by multitudes of thinking men in all sections of the land?" His answer was that disunion was "begotten of Abolitionism" and had been "rocked in its cradle and fed with its poisoned milk." This was a familiar refrain. As one conservative Boston paper succinctly put it, the "secession movement may be justly attributed to the Abolitionists of the Northern cities." Opponents of the Republicans conjured up the "impending horrors" of civil war. If Republicans did not desist from their treasonable abolitionism, New England Democrat Caleb Cushing warned, war would come and bring with it "economic and political chaos."[5]

To Horace Greeley, whose *New York Tribune* was still the most widely read newspaper in the North, such yearning for compromise and fear of a final reckoning was pathetic. Although the *Tribune* had in the past articulated a "good riddance to the slave South" sort of disunionism, in the winter of 1860–61 it took a firm stance for the Union and against secession. In an acid article entitled "Disunion by the Unionists," published on December 6, 1860, Greeley, fully anticipating the secession of South Carolina and the Deep South, assailed the hypocrisy of Northern Democrats. For those men who had so long claimed the mantle of Unionist and had so often accused Republicans of seeking to drive the South away now timidly objected to any effort to resist or coerce the secessionists. Reveling in the irony of this situation, Greeley painstakingly traced the history of the word "disunion" from Aaron Burr, to the Hartford Convention, to the nullification crisis, to John Quincy Adams's Haverhill petition. He noted that " 'Abolition is Disunion' has been the most potent weapon wielded by the defenders of the 'peculiar institution.' " For Greeley, the success of Southern secessionism was a vindication, as it proved once and for all that Southern fire-eaters, not antislavery Northerners, were the ones who practiced and perfected treason. For Republicans, as for Confederates, secession promised linguistic clarity: "The Rubicon is passed," Greeley wrote, "the argument ended: there remains only the choice between a prompt acquiescence in the secession of the Slave States and a resort to the Trial by Battle."[6]

These defiant resolutions were echoed by men and women all over the North. Especially revealing are the comments of Frances Seward, William's wife. As Doris Kearns Goodwin's recent book on Lincoln's cabinet shows, Frances was an astute political analyst. When William Seward, by now feeling a keen personal responsibility for the crisis and eager to parlay his new appointment as secretary of state into a grand Union-saving gesture, made a conciliatory procompromise speech on January 10, 1861, Frances chastised him. "No one can dread war more than I do," she wrote him. "For 16 years I have prayed earnestly that our son might be spared the misfortune of raising his hand against his fellow man—yet I could not to day assent to the perpetuation or extension of slavery to prevent war." Frances Seward, like so many Republicans, had come to accept the position that the women of the Philadelphia Anti-Slavery Society had articulated twenty-five years earlier when they asked: "Can *any* consequences be worse than the consequences of Slavery itself?"[7]

For the great champions of abolition, secession represented not only the perfidy and guilt of the Slave Power, it also proved that slavery, more than any other danger, had all along been the greatest threat to the survival of the nation. In May 1861 Douglass wrote in his newspaper: "At last our proud Republic is overtaken. Our National Sin has found us out. . . . No distant monarch, offended at our freedom and prosperity, has plotted our destruction; no envious tyrant has prepared for our necks his oppressive yoke. Slavery has done it all." Those still in bondage in the South shared this interpretive framework of sin and redemption; many slaves viewed the secession crisis through the lens of biblical allegories. The eleventh chapter of Daniel, for example, seemed to portend the Civil War: it warned that the "king of the north shall come, and cast up a mount, and take the most fenced cities: and the arms of the south shall not withstand." William Roane, of Richmond, a slave in the household of the Unionist Van Lew family, was sure of the Confederates' fate: "You will see. . . . They shall fall down slain. That is the fulfillment of prophecy."[8]

William Lloyd Garrison, who clung to the old platform of peaceful disunion well into the secession crisis, took a prowar stance after Fort Sumter's fall. His circle of white immediatists now recognized that the question was no longer whether to accept or reject armed conflict, but rather "how to direct it toward the noblest possible ends." Thus they embraced a new mission—to persuade the Northern public that "immediate, unconditional emancipation was the only way either to justify or win the war." Abolitionist dreams and prophecies of disunion had come to pass, Wendell Phillips observed, in a February 1861 speech on the "lessons of the hour." But disunion was never an end in itself—just the means for a new republic to take root. "Let us," he implored his listeners, "*plant* a Union whose life survives the ages."[9]

The onset of war, then, seemed to many observers to herald the end of disunion talk—of the predictions, threats, and accusations that had been a staple of antebellum political culture and that had undergirded and undermined the great compromises of the era. In surprising and revealing ways, however, disunion talk persisted in the language of the opposition within each section.

In the South, what formed this opposition talk varied with the political geography of the region. In Confederate strongholds such as Richmond and Atlanta, unconditional Unionists were driven underground, sharing their hopes for a Northern triumph clandestinely "inside the small band of die-hards who remained after the winnowing of the secession crisis." In both cities, Unionist undergrounds consisting of elite whites, yeomen, and African American slaves collaborated to aid Union prisoners and gather military intelligence for the Federals. In the bitterly contested areas of the South not dominated by the secessionist planter class, critics of the Confederacy openly challenged the Davis administration. In North Carolina, a peace movement called the "Order of the Heroes of America" took shape in the western part of the state; its champions charged that, having caused a needless war, the secessionists who populated the government now sought to needlessly prolong it. In the 1863 elections to the Confederate Congress, "Conservative" party candidates in North Carolina, from the old Whig elite, outpolled the secessionist elite by tapping the disaffection of yeomen farmers and working-men with "military despotism." This voting pattern "represented a desire on the part of many Confederates to 'turn instinctively to those old leaders, who foretold their present situation, for counsel and instruction.'" By contrast, in East Tennessee opposition to secession and to the Davis administration took the form of bitter and brutal guerrilla warfare. Yeomen there had long resented the planter class, and, fired by the conviction that the oppressive Davis regime was imposing a kind of slavery on poor nonslaveholders, loyalists mounted a violent campaign to throw off Confederate rule. Their literary champion was devout Unionist William Brownlow, who published a book—a best seller in the North—detailing the atrocities of Confederates against Southern Unionists; in his view, disunion was a "wasteful disease" that had brought anarchy, lawlessness, and suffering to the South.[10]

Between these appeals to ballots and to bullets lay a broad spectrum of resistance. In the last two years of the war, strikes, bread riots, and desertion rocked the Confederacy. The active support of white Southern Unionists for the Federal cause, coupled with the defeatism, desertion, recalcitrance, and, in some places, insurgency of disillusioned Confederates, took a major toll on the Confederate military. Evidence of disillusionment does not demonstrate the weakness of Southern nationalism but rather its complexity—the difficulty of weaving elements of local, state, Southern, Confederate, and American identity into a new form of national allegiance. Even many ardent Confederates struggled to harmonize conflicting loyalties, and thereby to sustain their faith in the "Cause" in the face of terrible setbacks and sacrifices.[11]

Writing on the Confederate "psyche," the great military historian Russell Weigley observes that "always there was a psychological rift deep inside Southern purposes." Southerners had been "nurtured from birth in the civic religion of United States nationalism." They could not "shake off their nurturing so abruptly as secession and the creation of the Confederacy demanded." That rift, one that Confederate ideology was unable fully to close, derived, it might be said, from deep ambivalence about disunion itself. For white Southerners across the political spectrum had been nurtured in the use of disunion as a dark accusation—defenders of slavery had for decades hurled curses at abolitionists for conspiring to undo the republic. If it was not so easy to shake off the old faith in the Union, neither was it easy for white Southerners to shake off their fear that disunion, so long dreaded, would bring in its wake a long train of tragedies.[12]

In the North, too, disunion rhetoric persisted in debates over emancipation as a Union war aim. Abolitionists tirelessly lobbied the Lincoln administration to recognize that slavery must die if slaveholders were to be defeated. As Philip A. Bell, editor of the *Pacific Appeal* put it, disunion was like the poisonous upas tree—slavery was the trunk of the tree and secession its branches—and if the Lincoln administration merely cut off the branches while leaving the trunk intact, the tree would "branch forth again and diffuse its malignant and pestiferous poison over the land." In an 1863 speech Frederick Douglass declared: "We are fighting for something incomparably better than the old Union. We are fighting for unity . . . in which there shall be no North, no South, no East, no West, no black, no white, but a solidarity of the nation, making every slave free and every free man a voter." Democratic opponents countered with the accusation that Republicans had a "bitter, open and vindictive hostility" to the Union, and that emancipation as a war aim was just another manifestation of abolition disunionism. Having brought on the war, radical "Black Republicans" were now intent on using it to revolutionize the South and even to impose racial equality on the North. It was disunionist, these critics charged, to oppose an honorable negotiated peace that would restore the Union and the antebellum status quo; the radicals were willfully and unnecessarily prolonging the war. An 1863 broadside against the "great disunion conspiracy of Massachusetts" traced the history of Bay State radicalism by referencing the Hartford Convention, the Haverhill petition, and the disunion petitions submitted by Senator John Parker Hale in 1850. The broadside asked, "Why make this an Abolition war, instead of a war for restoring and preserving our glorious Union?" Such accusations reached a crescendo during the presidential election campaign of 1864, with Peace Democrats under George B. McClellan running on a platform of "the Union as it was."[13]

Significantly, some Confederate newspapers revealed the "psychological rift" at the heart of Southern nationalism by joining Northern Democrats in accusing Republicans of disunion. The Confederate *Richmond Daily Dispatch*, for example, covered the speeches and resolutions of Democratic peace meetings in the North to prove that the Republican Party had been "conceived and brought forth in disunion," and that its leaders were reaping the "bloody harvest" of "John Quincy Adams and Joshua R. Giddings . . . Senator Hale . . . and Mr. Seward," and other Northerners who had sowed the "seeds of dissolution."[14]

Republicans, for their part, successfully branded McClellan supporters as abettors of the secessionists, and with the Union army riding a wave of victories, Lincoln was resoundingly reelected in 1864. But this crucial victory and the North's final triumph at Appomattox silenced Democratic charges of Republican disunionism only temporarily. Significantly, disunion accusations resurfaced after the war in debates over radical Reconstruction. Radical Republicans stressed that Confederate defeat had not ended the struggle to kill slavery and restore the Union. "Slavery is not abolished until the black man has the ballot," Frederick Douglass insisted in a May 10, 1865, speech entitled "The Need for Continuing Anti-Slavery Work." In the wake of the passage of the Thirteenth Amendment, Douglass defined the new challenge facing the champions of freedom. The war had, he reiterated, provided a "highly instructive disclosure . . . of the true source of danger to republican government." That danger was not simply slavery but slavery's root cause—inequality. "No republic is safe that tolerates a privileged class, or denies to any of its citizens equal right and equal means to maintain them," Douglass explained. Inequality was the "deadly upas, root and branch, leaf and fibre, body and sap, [that] must be utterly destroyed."[15]

Northern conservatives countered in the time-tested language of disunion aspersions. By insisting on black suffrage and protections for black civil rights, radical Republicans, so it was charged, wanted to return the country to war. As an 1865 article in the *Valley Spirit* of Chambersburg, Pennsylvania, put it: "The radicals should beware, for the moment they start the disunion programme, based on negro suffrage, that moment will seal their fate as the originators of disunion, war, and all the ills under which the nation has so long suffered." Such language was echoed in the South. According to Virginia's *Staunton Spectator* in 1866, "Those who oppose the Union as it existed before the war . . . [and] create distrust, dissension and discord . . . are, by whatever name they may be called, disunionists."[16]

Only in the late nineteenth century did such talk of disunion fade away. In the ascendant dialect of the "Lost Cause"—in which Confederate and Union soldiers alike nobly embodied the universal principles of courage, and in which slavery's centrality to the war was forgotten—the "national sin," as Douglass had called it, was wiped clean. For the white Northerners and Southerners who embraced reconciliation, the time for accusations was over. But for African Americans and their white allies in the struggle for justice, although the word "disunion" had lost its currency, a spirit of disunion—a widening gulf between blacks and whites—continued to threaten the republic. The reconciliation of white Northerners and Southerners had come at the expense of black hopes for equal rights and opportunities. In 1883, twenty years after the Emancipation Proclamation, with the pall of disfranchisement, lynching, and one-party Democratic rule hanging over the South, Douglass observed that "what Abraham Lincoln said in respect of the United States is as true of the colored people as of the relations of those States. They cannot remain half slave and half free. You must give them all or take from them all. Until this half-and-half condition is ended, there will be just ground of complaint. You will have an aggrieved class, and this discussion will go on."[17]

Susie King Taylor, who had escaped slavery during the war and worked heroically for the Union cause, stepped forward to represent this aggrieved class in a memoir published in 1902. Looking out over a dystopian landscape in which blacks were "burned, tortured, and denied a fair trial for any imaginary wrong conceived in the brain of a negro-hating white man," Taylor drew the same conclusion that Garrison and the other abolitionist-disunionists had drawn before the war: that there was in reality no Union to be found on American soil. "They say, 'One flag, one nation, one country indivisible.' Is this true? Can we say this truthfully, when one race is allowed to burn, hang, and inflict the most horrible torture weekly, monthly, on another? No, we cannot sing, 'My country, 'tis of thee, Sweet land of Liberty'! It is hollow mockery." In the new century, a true Union would have to be imagined, and fought for, all over again.[18]

Notes

INTRODUCTION

1. *North American* (Philadelphia), as quoted in *National Era* (Washington, D.C.), January 18, 1849. On the politics of the *North American*, see Russell F. Weigley, ed., *Philadelphia: A 300-Year History* (New York: Norton, 1982), 300, 388, 404.

2. On the role of keywords in history, see Raymond Williams, *Keywords: A Vocabulary of Culture and Society* (New York: Oxford University Press, 1976), and Daniel T. Rodgers, *Contested Truths: Keywords in American Politics since Independence* (New York: Basic Books, 1987). For a model study, see Eric Foner, *The Story of American Freedom: The Reality and the Mythic Ideal* (New York: Pan Macmillan, 2000).

3. Charles Beard and Mary Beard, *The Rise of American Civilization* (New York: Macmillan, 1927). For the most influential expressions of the "blundering generation" thesis, see James G. Randall, "The Blundering Generation," *Mississippi Historical Review* 27 (June 1940): 3–28, and Avery O. Craven, *The Repressible Conflict, 1830–1861* (Baton Rouge: Louisiana State University Press, 1939), and *The Coming of the Civil War* (New York: Charles Scribner's Sons, 1942).

4. W. E. B. Du Bois, *Black Reconstruction: An Essay toward a History of the Part Which Black Folk Played in the Attempt to Reconstruct Democracy in America, 1860–1880* (New York: Russell and Russell, 1935); David W. Blight, *Race and Reunion: The Civil War in American Memory* (Cambridge: Belknap of Harvard University Press, 2001); James M. McPherson, *Battle Cry of Freedom: The Civil War Era* (New York: Oxford University Press, 1988); Eric Foner, *Free Soil, Free Labor, Free Men: The Ideology of the Republican Party before the Civil War* (New York: Oxford University Press, 1970); Bertram Wyatt-Brown, *Southern Honor: Ethics and Behavior in the Old South* (New York: Oxford University Press, 1982); Bruce Levine, *Half Slave and Half Free: The Roots of the Civil War* (New York: Hill and Wang, 1992); John Ashworth, *Slavery, Capitalism, and Politics in the Antebellum Republic*, vol. 1: *Commerce and Compromise, 1820–1850* (Cambridge,

U.K.: Cambridge University Press, 1995); Brian Holden Reid, *The Origins of the American Civil War* (London: Longman, 1996); Sean Wilentz, *The Rise of American Democracy* (New York: Norton, 2005). For an excellent overview of the historiography on Civil War origins, see Edward L. Ayers, *What Caused the Civil War: Reflections on the South and Southern History* (New York: Norton, 2005), esp. 112–25 and 132–42.

5. Kenneth Stampp, *And the War Came: The North and the Secession Crisis, 1860–61* (Baton Rouge: Louisiana State University Press, 1950); David M. Potter, *The Impending Crisis, 1848–1861* (New York: Harper and Row, 1976); Michael F. Holt, *The Political Crisis of the 1850s* (New York: Wiley, 1978); William E. Gienapp, *The Origins of the Republican Party, 1852–1856* (New York: Oxford University Press, 1986); William W. Freehling, *The Road to Disunion*, vol. 1: *Secessionists at Bay, 1776–1854* (New York: Oxford University Press, 1990) and *The Road to Disunion*, vol. 2: *Secessionists Triumphant, 1854–1861* (New York: Oxford University Press, 2007); Joel H. Silbey, *Storm over Texas: The Annexation Controversy and the Road to Civil War* (New York: Oxford University Press, 2005); James L. Huston, "Interpreting the Causation Sequence: The Meaning of the Events Leading to the Civil War," *Reviews in American History* 34 (September 2006): 324–31. For two recent studies that emphasize the contingency of events and the role of individual politicians in causing the war, see Michael F. Holt, *The Fate of Their Country: Politicians, Slavery Extension, and the Coming of the Civil War* (New York: Hill and Wang, 2004), and Nelson D. Lankford, *Cry Havoc! The Crooked Road to Civil War, 1861* (New York: Viking, 2007).

6. Ayers, *What Caused the Civil War*, 133, 138, and *In the Presence of Mine Enemies: War in the Heart of America, 1859–1863* (New York: Norton, 2003).

7. On the importance of language in the "making of political reality" in the early republic, see David Waldstreicher, *In the Midst of Perpetual Fetes: The Making of American Nationalism, 1776–1820* (Chapel Hill: University of North Carolina Press, 1997), esp. 221–30, and Andrew W. Robertson, "'Look on This Picture . . . And on This!' Nationalism, Localism, and Partisan Images of Otherness in the United States, 1787–1820," *American Historical Review* 85 (December 1980): 1119–49. For recent work on antebellum political rhetoric, see Kenneth Cmiel, *Democratic Eloquence: The Fight over Popular Speech in Nineteenth-Century America* (New York: William Morrow, 1990), and Andrew W. Robertson, *The Language of Democracy: Political Rhetoric in the United States and Britain, 1790–1900* (Charlottesville: University of Virginia Press, 2005). See also Michael A. Morrison, *Slavery and the American West: The Eclipse of Manifest Destiny and the Coming of the Civil War* (Chapel Hill: University of North

Carolina Press, 1997). Morrison shows how the values of the American Revolution, "understood in terms of independence, freedom, and self-government," were invoked by antislavery Northerners and proslavery Southerners alike to support antagonistic stances on the issue of territorial expansion; from the time of the Wilmot Proviso, each side built the case that the other was betraying the Revolution's ideals and the nation's common heritage. For the classic exposition of discourse analysis in history, see Michel Foucault, *The History of Sexuality*, vol. 1 (New York: Pantheon, 1978). For an excellent illustration of how Foucault's insights can help us understand antebellum America, see Lori D. Ginzberg, *Untidy Origins: A Story of Woman's Rights in Antebellum New York* (Chapel Hill: University of North Carolina Press, 2005).

8. Edward Everett, *Orations and Speeches, on Various Occasions* (Boston: American Stationers' Co., 1836), 186–87, 199, and *An Oration Delivered at Cambridge on the Fiftieth Anniversary of the Declaration of Independence of the United States of America* (Boston: Cummings, Hilliard and Co., 1826), 32. On Everett, see Paul A. Varg, *Edward Everett: The Intellectual in the Turmoil of Politics* (Selinsgrove, Pa.: Susquehanna University Press, 1992).

9. James Darsey, *The Prophetic Tradition and Radical Rhetoric in America* (New York: New York University Press, 1997), 16–26.

10. Ibid., 30–31.

11. Daniel Webster, "Second Reply to Hayne," in Robert C. Byrd, ed., *The Senate, 1789–1989*, vol. 3, *Classic Speeches, 1830–1993* (Washington, D.C.: Government Printing Office, 1994). See also Harry Watson's introductory essay in Harry L. Watson, *Andrew Jackson vs. Henry Clay: Democracy and Development in Antebellum America* (Boston: Bedford/St. Martin's, 1998), 114–15, and two of the documents included in that book: Henry Clay, "On the American System," 198, and Clay, "On the Compromise Tariff," 209–13.

12. On "honor disputes," see Joanne B. Freeman, *Affairs of Honor: National Politics in the New Republic* (New Haven: Yale University Press, 2001), 169–73, 229, 243, 273.

13. William C. Davis, *Rhett: The Turbulent Life and Times of a Fire-Eater* (Columbia: University of South Carolina Press, 2001), 199–200; Wilentz, *Rise of American Democracy*, 388 (Rhett quotation). Eric H. Walther devotes a chapter to Rhett in his book on the leading proponents of secession: *The Fire-eaters* (Baton Rouge: Louisiana State University Press, 1992).

14. Garrison's disunionism is analyzed in Henry Mayer, *All on Fire: William Lloyd Garrison and the Abolition of Slavery* (Boston: St. Martin's Press, 1998).

15. *Congressional Globe*, 30th Cong., 1st sess., Appendix, 1076–80.

16. Jean H. Baker, *James Buchanan* (New York: Henry Holt, 2004), 56–74 (Buchanan quoted on 71).

17. Lacy K. Ford Jr., *Origins of Southern Radicalism: The South Carolina Upcountry, 1800–1860* (New York: Oxford University Press, 1988), 135.

18. Jonathan Daniel Wells, *The Origins of the Southern Middle Class, 1800–1861* (Chapel Hill: University of North Carolina Press, 2004), 1–19, 208–9 (quotation, 17); Edward Pessen, "How Different from Each Other Were the Antebellum North and South?," *American Historical Review* 85 (December 1980): 1119–49.

19. William E. Gienapp, ed., *This Fiery Trial: The Speeches and Writings of Abraham Lincoln* (New York: Oxford University Press, 2002), 88–97; James Oakes, *The Radical and the Republican: Frederick Douglass, Abraham Lincoln, and the Triumph of Antislavery Politics* (New York: Norton, 2007), 141. On how Northern popular culture offered "calls to battle" laced with images of a "triumphant, holy Unionism" in the early days of the war, see Alice Fahs, *The Imagined Civil War: Popular Literature of the North and South, 1861–1865* (Chapel Hill: University of North Carolina Press, 2001), 61–79.

20. "Where Will the Rebellion Leave Us?," *Atlantic Monthly* 46 (August 1861): 236–42.

21. Frederick Douglass, "There Was a Right Side in the Late War," in Philip Foner, ed., *Frederick Douglass: Selected Speeches and Writings* (Chicago: Lawrence Hill Books, 1999), 632.

22. The tendency of many antebellum Americans to conflate the different forms of opposition to slavery complicates the historian's quest for clarity. Generally, in this text, "antislavery" is used as an adjective that can describe gradualists and Free-Soilers and Garrisonians alike, whereas "abolitionist" refers specifically to radical immediatism. In other words, all abolitionists were antislavery, but not all those who opposed slavery were abolitionists.

23. Carol Berkin, *A Brilliant Solution: Inventing the American Constitution* (New York: Harcourt, 2002), 6–9.

24. *Frederick Douglass' Paper* (Rochester, N.Y.), July 16, 1852.

PROLOGUE

1. Ira Berlin, *Many Thousands Gone: The First Two Centuries of Slavery in North America* (Cambridge: Belknap Press of Harvard University Press, 1998), 179–88, 229.

2. Anthony S. Parent, *Foul Means: The Formation of a Slave Society in Virginia, 1660–1740* (Chapel Hill: University of North Carolina Press, 2003).

3. Kathleen M. Brown, *Good Wives, Nasty Wenches, and Anxious Patriarchs: Gender, Race, and Power in Colonial Virginia* (Chapel Hill: University of North Carolina Press, 1996), 198–211 (quotation, 198); Peter W. Bardaglio, *Reconstructing the Household: Families, Sex, and the Law in the Nineteenth-Century South* (Chapel Hill: University of North Carolina Press, 1995), 48–55.

4. Latham Windley, comp., *Runaway Slave Advertisements: A Documentary History from the 1730s to 1790*, vol. 1 (Westport, Conn.: Greenwood Press, 1983); Sally E. Hadden, *Slave Patrols: Law and Violence in Virginia and the Carolinas* (Cambridge: Harvard University Press, 2001), 21, 32, 103 (quotation).

5. Louis B. Wright and Marion Tinling, eds., *The Secret Diary of William Byrd of Westover, 1709–1712* (Richmond: Dietz Press, 1941), 205, 533; Parent, *Foul Means*, xvi. See also Philip D. Morgan, *Slave Counterpoint: Black Culture in the Eighteenth-Century Chesapeake and Lowcountry* (Chapel Hill: University of North Carolina Press, 1998), 271.

6. Mary Beth Norton, *Founding Mothers and Fathers: Gendered Power and the Forming of American Society* (New York: Vintage, 1997); Kathleen M. Brown, *Good Wives*; Morgan, *Slave Counterpoint*.

7. David Waldstreicher, *Runaway America: Benjamin Franklin, Slavery, and the American Revolution* (New York: Hill and Wang, 2004), 193, 213–14.

8. Berlin, *Many Thousands Gone*, 228–33; James Oliver Horton and Lois E. Horton, *Slavery and the Making of America* (New York: Oxford University Press, 2005), 52–64 (Massachusetts petition quotation on 52).

9. On emancipation in the North, see Berlin, *Many Thousands Gone*, and Joan Pope Melish, *Disowning Slavery: Gradual Emancipation and "Race" in New England* (Ithaca, N.Y.: Cornell University Press, 1998); Shane White, *Somewhat More Independent: The End of Slavery in New York City, 1770–1810* (Athens: University of Georgia Press, 1991); Leslie M. Harris, *In the Shadow of Slavery: African-Americans in New York City, 1626–1863* (Chicago: University of Chicago Press, 2003); and Gary B. Nash and Jean R. Soderland, *Freedom by Degrees: Emancipation in Pennsylvania and Its Aftermath* (New York: Oxford University Press, 1991). On the "black founders," see Richard Newman, "Protest in Black and White: The Formation and Transformation of an African American Political Community during the Early Republic," in Jeffrey L. Pasley, Andrew W. Robertson, and David Waldstreicher, eds., *Beyond the Founders: New Approaches to the Political History of the Early American Republic* (Chapel Hill: University of North Carolina Press, 2004), 180–206.

10. Melvin Patrick Ely, *Israel on the Appomattox: A Southern Experiment in Black Freedom* (New York: Knopf, 2004), 23–35. On Washington, see Henry Weincek,

An Imperfect God: George Washington, His Slaves, and the Creation of America (New York: Farrar, Straus and Giroux, 2003).

11. Ely, *Israel on the Appomattox*, 23–35 (quotation, 35); Berlin, *Many Thousands Gone*, 219–27 (quotation, 223). See also Eva Sheppard Wolf, *Race and Liberty in the New Nation: Emancipation in Virginia from the Revolution to Nat Turner's Rebellion* (Baton Rouge: Louisiana State University Press, 2006). Wolf finds not only that the number of people emancipated in post–Revolutionary Virginia was smaller than traditional estimates suggest, but also that manumissions motivated by antislavery principles gave way by the early 1800s to manumissions based on "personal and singular reasons," such as the desire to reward certain slaves for "loyal service and upright behavior" (64–65).

12. Madison quoted in William J. Cooper Jr. and Thomas E. Terrill, *The American South: A History* (New York: Knopf, 1990), 102. On the three-fifths compromise, see, e.g., Leonard L. Richards, *The Slave Power: The Free North and Southern Domination, 1780–1860* (Baton Rouge: Louisiana State University Press, 2000), 33–39, and Garry Wills, *"Negro President": Jefferson and the Slave Power* (Boston: Houghton Mifflin, 2003), 49–58.

13. Berkin, *A Brilliant Solution*, 113–14; Wills, *"Negro President,"* 50.

14. Berkin, *A Brilliant Solution*, 256–58; Jeff Broadwater, *George Mason: Forgotten Founder* (Chapel Hill: University of North Carolina Press, 2006), 192–94; Weincek, *An Imperfect God*, 265–70 (Mason quoted on 269).

15. Donald E. Fehrenbacher, *The Dred Scott Case: Its Significance in American Law and Politics* (New York: Oxford University Press, 1978), 26 (quotation); Kenneth M. Stampp, "The Concept of a Perpetual Union," *The Imperiled Union: Essays on the Background of the Civil War* (New York: Oxford University Press, 1980), 5–9; William J. Cooper Jr., *Liberty and Slavery: Southern Politics to 1860* (New York: Knopf, 1983), 60–67; Rogan Kersh, *Dreams of a More Perfect Union* (Ithaca, N.Y.: Cornell University Press, 2001), 63–69.

16. Kersh, *Dreams of a More Perfect Union*, 63–69; Clinton Rossiter, ed., *The Federalist Papers: Alexander Hamilton, James Madison, John Jay* (New York: Mentor, 1999), 48–66; Darren Staloff, *Hamilton, Adams, Jefferson: The Politics of Enlightenment and the American Founding* (New York: Hill and Wang, 2005), 310.

17. Stampp, "The Concept of a Perpetual Union," 16–17 (quotations); Daniel A. Farber, "Completing the Work of the Framers: Lincoln's Constitutional Legacy," *Journal of the Abraham Lincoln Association* 27 (Winter 2006): 1–10.

18. Broadwater, *George Mason*, 217–36 (quotation, 225). On the Tenth Amendment's implications for theories of states' rights and sovereignty, see Michael Les Bene-

dict, "Abraham Lincoln and Federalism," *Journal of the Abraham Lincoln Association* 10 (1988–89): 4–8.

19. Kersh, *Dreams of a More Perfect Union*, 59; Rossiter, *The Federalist Papers*, 66–71. On Federalist invocations of disunion, see also Peter B. Knupfer, *The Union As It Is: Constitutional Unionism and Sectional Compromise, 1787–1861* (Chapel Hill: University of North Carolina Press, 1991), 40.

20. Waldstreicher, *In the Midst of Perpetual Fetes.*

CHAPTER 1

1. Wilentz, *Rise of American Democracy*, 44–45 (first quotation); Freeman, *Affairs of Honor*, 22–27 (second quotation, 22); Thomas Jefferson, "Memorandum on the Compromise of 1790," in Lance Banning, ed., *Liberty and Order: The First American Party Struggle* (Indianapolis: Liberty Fund, 2004), 64.

2. *Annals of the Congress of the United States*, 1st Cong., 2nd sess., 1236–44; Joseph Ellis, *Founding Brothers: The Revolutionary Generation* (New York: Vintage, 2002), 81–117; Matthew Mason, *Slavery and Politics in the Early American Republic* (Chapel Hill: University of North Carolina Press, 2006), 22–23; Freeman, *Affairs of Honor*, 20–21, 168–69.

3. Richard Beeman, Stephen Botein, and Edward C. Carter III, eds., *Beyond Confederation: Origins of the Constitution and American National Identity* (Chapel Hill: University of North Carolina Press, 1987), 252–54; Staloff, *Hamilton, Adams, Jefferson*, 328; Wilentz, *Rise of American Democracy*, 46.

4. Matthew Spalding and Patrick J. Garrity, *A Sacred Union of Citizens: George Washington's Farewell Address and the American Character* (Lanham, Md.: Rowman and Littlefield, 1996), 63–67, 85 (quotation). See also Paul C. Nagel, *This Sacred Trust: American Nationality, 1798–1898* (New York: Oxford University Press, 1971), xiii–27, and Wilbur Zelinsky, *Nation into State: The Shifting Symbolic Foundations of American Nationalism* (Chapel Hill: University of North Carolina Press, 1988), 34.

5. Seth Cotlar, "The Federalists' Transatlantic Cultural Offensive of 1798 and the Moderation of American Democratic Discourse," in Pasley, Robertson, and Waldstreicher, *Beyond the Founders*, 274–302; Susan Dunn, *Jefferson's Second Revolution: The Election Crisis of 1800 and the Triumph of Republicanism* (Boston: Houghton Mifflin, 2004), 100–103, 111; Staloff, *Hamilton, Adams, Jefferson*, 329–31; Wilentz, *Rise of American Democracy*, 84 (quotation).

6. "Virginia Resolution: 1798" and "Kentucky Resolution: 1799," Avalon Project at

Yale Law School (www.yale.edu/laweb/avalon); Dunn, *Jefferson's Second Revolu-tion*, 100–103, 111, 236–39; John Niven, *John C. Calhoun and the Price of Union: A Biography* (Baton Rouge: Louisiana State University Press, 1988), 160–62; Staloff, *Hamilton, Adams, Jefferson*, 329–31 (quotations).

7. Staloff, *Hamilton, Adams, Jefferson*, 329–31; Peter S. Onuf, *Jefferson's Empire: The Language of American Nationhood* (Charlottesville: University Press of Vir-ginia, 2000), 89 (quotation), 99; Dunn, *Jefferson's Second Revolution*, 142–43, 168–69; Wilentz, *Rise of American Democracy*, 88–89; Wills, *"Negro President,"* 83–85; Catherine Allgor, *A Perfect Union: Dolley Madison and the Creation of the American Nation* (New York: Henry Holt, 2005), 65; Freeman, *Affairs of Honor*, 229–30. On Gabriel's Rebellion, see Douglas Egerton, *Gabriel's Rebellion: The Virginia Slave Conspiracies of 1800 and 1802* (Chapel Hill: University of North Carolina Press, 1993), and James Sidbury, *Ploughshares into Swords: Race, Re-bellion, and Identity in Gabriel's Virginia, 1730–1810* (New York: Cambridge University Press, 1997).

8. Dunn, *Jefferson's Second Revolution*, 142–43, 168–69; Wills, *"Negro President,"* 83–85; Staloff, *Hamilton, Adams, Jefferson*, 329–31 (quotations).

9. Cooper, *Liberty and Slavery*, 106–7, 109, 129 (quotations); Adam L. Tate, *Con-servatism and Southern Intellectuals, 1789–1861: Liberty, Tradition, and the Good Society* (Columbia: University of Missouri Press, 2005), 30–36; Benedict, "Abraham Lincoln and Federalism," 4–6.

10. Dunn, *Jefferson's Second Revolution*, 238–39; David Brion Davis and Stephen Mintz, eds., *The Boisterous Sea of Liberty: A Documentary History of America from Discovery through the Civil War* (New York: Oxford University Press, 1998), 294; Steven Deyle, *Carry Me Back: The Domestic Slave Trade in American Life* (New York: Oxford University Press, 2005), 22–23; Richard Buel Jr., *Amer-ica on the Brink: How the Political Struggle over the War of 1812 Almost Destroyed the Young Republic* (New York: Palgrave Macmillan, 2005), 23 (quotation), 113; Nancy Isenberg, "The 'Little Emperor': Aaron Burr, Dandyism, and the Sexual Politics of Treason," in Pasley, Robertson, and Waldstreicher, *Beyond the Found-ers*, 129–58; and Nancy Isenberg, *Fallen Founder: The Life of Aaron Burr* (New York: Viking, 2007), 282, 299, 300–307, 365.

11. Buel, *America on the Brink*, 146, 159; Waldstreicher, *In the Midst of Perpetual Fetes*, 254–62.

12. Davis and Mintz, *Boisterous Sea of Liberty*, 310; Buel, *America on the Brink*, 174, 195–98, 235 (Calhoun quoted on 196); Donald E. Fehrenbacher, *Sectional Crisis and Southern Constitutionalism* (Baton Rouge: Louisiana State University Press, 1995), 123; Mason, *Slavery and Politics*, 73.

13. Fehrenbacher, *Dred Scott Case*, 23–26, 80–81; Richards, *Slave Power*, 75–77.

14. *Annals of Congress*, 15th Cong., 2nd sess., 1170; Freehling, *Road to Disunion*, 1:153; Yoshwanda L. Trotter, "James Tallmadge," in John A. Garraty and Mark C. Carnes, eds., *American National Biography*, 24 vols. (New York: Oxford University Press, 1999), 21:280–81 (hereafter cited as *ANB*).

15. Freehling, *Road to Disunion*, 1:146–47; Mason, *Slavery and Politics*, 51.

16. *Annals of Congress*, 15th Cong., 2nd sess., 1170–79, 1187.

17. Ibid., 1181, 1191; *Annals of Congress*, 16th Cong., 1st sess., 149–50; Eve Kornfeld, *Margaret Fuller: A Brief Biography with Documents* (Boston: Bedford Books, 1997), 9; Donald B. Cole, "David Morril," in *ANB* 15:880; E. V. Moffet, "Arthur Livermore," in Dumas Malone, ed., *Dictionary of American Biography*, 23 vols. (New York: Charles Scribner's Sons, 1933), 6:304 (hereafter cited as *DAB*).

18. *Annals of Congress*, 16th Cong., 1st sess., 133. On the diffusion argument, see Freehling, *Road to Disunion*, 1:151–52.

19. *Annals of Congress*, 16th Cong., 1st sess., 229, 269–70; Mitchell Snay, "Nathaniel Macon," in *ANB* 14:283–84; Patrick G. Williams, "William Smith," in *ANB* 20:307–9. Historians continue to fiercely debate Jefferson's stance on slavery. See Paul Finkelman, "Jefferson and Slavery: 'Treason against the Hopes of Humanity,'" in Peter Onuf, ed., *Jeffersonian Legacies* (Charlottesville: University of Virginia Press, 1993), 181–224; Wills, *"Negro President"*; and Joseph J. Ellis, *American Sphinx: The Character of Thomas Jefferson* (New York: Vintage, 1998).

20. Fehrenbacher, *Sectional Crisis*, 22–23 (quotation); *Annals of Congress*, 15th Cong., 2nd sess., 1203–5, 1435–37, and 16th Cong., 1st sess., 107, 175, 209, 385; James H. Peeling, "Walter Lowrie," in *DAB*, 6:476.

21. *Annals of Congress*, 16th Cong., 1st sess., 177; David M. Gold, "Prentiss Mellen," in *ANB* 15:268–69; *Niles' Weekly Register* (Baltimore), March 11, 1820; Knupfer, *Union As It Is*, 97–98.

22. Everett Somerville Brown, ed., *The Missouri Compromise and Presidential Politics, 1820–1825: From the Letters of William Plumer, Jr.* (St. Louis: Missouri Historical Society, 1926), 12; *Union, United States Gazette and True American* (Philadelphia), October 19, 1820; *Carolina Centinel* (New Bern, N.C.), February 26, 1820; *City of Washington Gazette*, May 23, 1820; *Daily National Intelligencer* (Washington, D.C.), October 28, 1820.

23. Mason, *Slavery and Politics*, 193.

24. Cooper, *Liberty and Slavery*, 142–43; Tate, *Conservatism and Southern Intellectuals*, 75–76; Mason, *Slavery and Politics*, 183–85; Wolf, *Race and Liberty*, 172–76.

25. *Annals of Congress*, 15th Cong., 2nd sess., 1180, and 16th Cong., 1st sess., 227;

Adam Rothman, *Slave Country: American Expansion and the Origins of the Deep South* (Cambridge: Harvard University Press, 2005), 211–13 (Rankin quoted on 212); Scot French, *The Rebellious Slave: Nat Turner in American Memory* (Boston: Houghton Mifflin, 2004), 19–20.

26. *Annals of Congress*, 16th Cong., 1st sess., 213, 253–55, 359, and 15th Cong., 2nd sess., 1192; Edgar J. McManus, "Richard M. Johnson," in *ANB* 12:118–20; Frank Edward Ross, "James Burrill," in *DAB* 2:325–26.

27. Wilentz, *Rise of American Democracy*, 232–33; Fehrenbacher, *Dred Scott Case*, 110–15; Freehling, *Road to Disunion*, 1:152–53; Potter, *Impending Crisis*, 56. A second congressional compromise was reached in 1821 to admit Missouri, over the objections of restrictionists, with a constitution that not only safeguarded slavery but also prohibited free blacks from emigrating to the state. Mason, *Slavery and Politics*, 177.

28. Ashworth, *Slavery, Capitalism*, 70.

29. Fehrenbacher, *Sectional Crisis*, 19–20; Freehling, *Road to Disunion*, 1:154; Rothman, *Slave Country*, 214–15.

30. *Annals of Congress*, 16th Cong., 1st sess., 315; Charles Lowery, *James Barbour: A Jeffersonian Republican* (University: University of Alabama Press, 1984), 114–27; Dunn, *Jefferson's Second Revolution*, 277.

31. Onuf, *Jefferson's Empire*, 113–46 (quotations, 113–14).

32. John Ernest, *Liberation Historiography: African American Writers and the Challenge of History, 1794–1861* (Chapel Hill: University of North Carolina Press, 2004), 79; "Petition of Absalom Jones and Others," in Raymond W. Smock, ed., *Landmark Documents on the U.S. Congress* (Washington, D.C.: Congressional Quarterly Press, 1999); Daniel Coker, "A Dialogue between a Virginian and an African Minister," and James Forten, "Series of Letters by a Man of Colour," in Richard Newman, Patrick Rael, and Phillip Lapansky, eds., *Pamphlets of Protest: An Anthology of Early African American Protest Literature* (New York: Routledge, 2001), 10 (quotation), 52–73 (Forten quotation on 69); James A. Morone, *Hellfire Nation: The Politics of Sin in American History* (New Haven, Conn.: Yale University Press, 2003), 133.

33. As a counterpoint to the scholarly consensus that free blacks in the North rejected colonization as deportation, Eric Burin shows that Southern blacks who were manumitted "selected from several unpalatable, volatile scenarios" and tried to negotiate the best terms they could. For example, the frequency of "conjunctive emancipations," whereby different slaveholders manumitted various members of one black family, suggests that slaves sometimes succeeded in persuading masters to respect their kinship bonds. Slaveholders increasingly

feared that ACS operations conceded the slaves' right to freedom and gave them some leverage for obtaining education and property (as preparation for Liberia); these fears led to the passage of antimanumission codes in the Southern states. In the face of this backlash, antislavery gradualists in the North, who had argued that colonization was the only scheme that could avert civil war, retreated from their policy of encouraging Southern manumissions. Thus in Burin's telling, the ACS story is one of unintended consequences—the actions of freed blacks and their white detractors demonstrate that the ACS had a destabilizing effect on slavery and on sectional relations. Eric Burin, *Slavery and the Peculiar Solution: A History of the American Colonization Society* (Gainesville: University Press of Florida, 2005).

34. Ray Allen Billington, ed., *The Journal of Charlotte Forten* (New York: Norton, 1953), 16; David Brion Davis, ed., *Antebellum American Culture: An Interpretive Anthology* (Lexington, Mass.: Heath, 1979), 284–85 (first quotation); Julie Winch, *A Gentleman of Color: The Life of James Forten* (New York: Oxford University Press, 2002), 236 (second quotation).

35. Edward A. Pearson, ed., *Designs against Charleston: The Trial Record of the Denmark Vesey Conspiracy of 1822* (Chapel Hill: University of North Carolina Press, 1999); Peter P. Hinks, *To Awaken My Afflicted Brethren: David Walker and the Problem of Antebellum Slave Resistance* (University Park: Pennsylvania State University Press, 1997); William W. Freehling, *Prelude to Civil War: The Nullification Controversy in South Carolina, 1816–1836* (New York: Oxford University Press, 1992) and *Road to Disunion*, 1:220–22; Stephanie McCurry, *Masters of Small Worlds: Yeoman Households, Gender Relations, and the Political Culture of the Antebellum South Carolina Low Country* (New York: Oxford University Press, 1995), 256–60.

36. Michael P. Johnson, "Denmark Vesey and His Co-Conspirators," *William & Mary Quarterly* 58 (October 2001): 915–76.

37. Archates [pseudo.], *Reflections, Occasioned by the Late Disturbances in Charleston* (Charleston: A. E. Miller, 1822), 6–7; Richard Furman, *Exposition of the Views of the Baptists, Relative to the Coloured Population of the United States in Communication to the Governor of South Carolina* (Charleston: A. E. Miller, 1823).

38. Manisha Sinha, *The Counterrevolution of Slavery: Politics and Ideology in Antebellum South Carolina* (Chapel Hill: University of North Carolina Press, 2000), 15; Horton and Horton, *Slavery and the Making of America*, 95; Fehrenbacher, *Sectional Crisis*, 129.

39. Whitemarsh Seabrook, *Concise View of the Critical Situation, and Future Pros-

pects of the Slave-Holding States, in Relation to their Coloured Population (Charleston: A. E. Miller, 1825), 20.

CHAPTER 2

1. Albert Gallatin, Speech Welcoming Lafayette to Uniontown, May 27, 1825, Supplement to Gallatin Papers, Microfilm Collection, Paley Library, Temple University, Philadelphia.
2. Eric Foner, *Story of American Freedom*, 47; Watson, *Andrew Jackson vs. Henry Clay*, 21–23, 83 (quotations); Clyde N. Wilson, ed., *The Essential Calhoun* (New Brunswick, N.J.: Transaction Publishers, 2000), xxiii–xxv; Nicholas Onuf and Peter Onuf, *Nations, Markets and War: Modern History and the American Civil War* (Charlottesville: University Press of Virginia, 2006), 243–46.
3. Watson, *Andrew Jackson vs. Henry Clay*, 67–71; "Proceedings and Address of the New Hampshire Republican State Convention of Delegates Friendly to the Election of Andrew Jackson," in Joel H. Silbey, ed., *The American Party Battle: Election Campaign Pamphlets, 1828–1876*, vol. 1 (Cambridge: Harvard University Press, 1999), 67, 77 (quotations); Wilentz, *Rise of American Democracy*, 310.
4. Freehling, *Road to Disunion*, 1:260.
5. Watson, *Andrew Jackson vs. Henry Clay*, 89; Clyde N. Wilson, *Essential Calhoun*, xxiv (quotation); John C. Calhoun to Virgil Maxcy, September 11, 1830, in Clyde N. Wilson, ed., *The Papers of John C. Calhoun*, vol. 11, *1829–1832* (Columbia: University of South Carolina Press, 1978), 227–29.
6. Michael O'Brien, *Conjectures of Order: Intellectual Life and the American South, 1810–1860*, vol. 2 (Chapel Hill: University of North Carolina Press, 2004), 825–27; Niven, *John C. Calhoun*, 162.
7. William C. Davis, *Rhett*, 45; Niven, *John C. Calhoun*, 160–62; Walther, *Fire-eaters*, 122–23 (Rhett quotation).
8. Watson, *Andrew Jackson vs. Henry Clay*, 86; Major L. Wilson, *Space, Time and Freedom: The Quest for Nationality and the Irrepressible Conflict, 1815–1861* (Westport, Conn.: Greenwood Press, 1974), 7.
9. *Register of Debates in Congress*, 21st Cong., 1st sess., 43–80 (Webster quotation on 80); "Debate in the Senate of the United States," *North American Review* 31 (October 1830): 533–34; Benedict, "Abraham Lincoln and Federalism," 11–12.
10. Mayer, *All on Fire*, 105–6 (quotations); *Salem Gazette* (Mass.), January 21, 1831; Larry Ceplair, ed., *The Public Years of Sarah and Angelina Grimké* (New York: Columbia University Press, 1989), 12–13; Thomas S. Grimké, *Oration on the*

Absolute Necessity of Union, and the Folly and Madness of Disunion, Delivered
Fourth of July, 1809 and Speech of Thomas S. Grimké, Delivered in December,
1828, on the Constitutionality of the Tariff and on the True Nature of State
Sovereignty (Charleston: W. Riley, 1829), 79–97.

11. Maria Weston Chapman, *Right and Wrong in Massachusetts* (Boston: Dow and
Jackson's Anti-Slavery Press, 1839), 3; Martin H. Blatt and David Roediger, eds.,
The Meaning of Slavery in the North (New York: Garland Publishing, 1998). In
1830 the total free black population in the United States was 319,599, with
137,529 free blacks living in the North, 151,877 in the Upper South, and 30,193 in
the Lower South. Ira Berlin, *Slaves without Masters: The Free Negro in the*
Antebellum South (New York: New Press, 1974), 136.

12. Chapman, *Right and Wrong*, 3.

13. Aileen S. Kraditor, *Means and Ends in American Abolitionism: Garrison and His*
Critics on Strategy and Tactics, 1834–1850 (New York: Pantheon Books, 1969);
Ronald Walters, *The Antislavery Appeal: American Abolitionism after 1830* (Bal-
timore: Johns Hopkins University Press, 1976); James Brewer Stewart, *Holy*
Warriors: The Abolitionists and American Slavery (New York: Hill and Wang,
1976); Lewis Perry, *Radical Abolitionists: Anarchy and the Government of God in*
Antislavery Thought (Ithaca, N.Y.: Cornell University Press, 1973); Richard H.
Sewell, *Ballots for Freedom: Antislavery Politics in the United States, 1837–1860*
(New York: Oxford University Press, 1976); Lawrence J. Friedman, *Gregarious*
Saints: Self and Community in American Abolitionism, 1830–1870 (New York:
Cambridge University Press, 1982); Edward Magdol, *The Antislavery Rank and*
File: A Social Profile of the Abolitionists' Constituency (Westport, Conn.: Green-
wood Press, 1986); Ashworth, *Slavery, Capitalism*, 191 (quotation).

14. For works that provide a more inclusive history of abolitionism, see, e.g., Jean
Fagan Yellin and John C. Van Horne, eds., *The Abolitionist Sisterhood: Women's*
Political Culture in Antebellum America (Ithaca, N.Y.: Cornell University Press,
1994); Stanley Harrold, *The Abolitionists and the South, 1831–1861* (Lexington:
University Press of Kentucky, 1995); Julie Roy Jeffrey, *The Great Silent Army*
of Abolitionism: Ordinary Women in the Antislavery Movement (Chapel Hill:
University of North Carolina Press, 1998); Mia Bay, *The White Image in the Black*
Mind: African-American Ideas about White People, 1830–1925 (New York: Ox-
ford University Press, 2000); John Stauffer, *The Black Hearts of Men: Radical*
Abolitionists and the Transformation of Race (Cambridge: Harvard University
Press, 2002); Richard S. Newman, *The Transformation of American Abolition-*
ism: Fighting Slavery in the Early Republic (Chapel Hill: University of North

Carolina Press, 2002); Susan Zaeske, *Signatures of Citizenship: Petitioning, Antislavery, and Women's Political Identity* (Chapel Hill: University of North Carolina Press, 2003); and Timothy Patrick McCarthy and John Stauffer, eds., *Prophets of Protest: Reconsidering the History of American Abolitionism* (New York: New Press, 2006).

15. Bay, *White Image in the Black Mind*, 22–30.

16. Ibid., 25–26; Jane H. Pease and William H. Pease, *They Who Would Be Free: Blacks' Search for Freedom, 1830–1861* (New York: Atheneum, 1974), 24–25. Struggling for subscribers, both *Freedom's Journal* and a successor paper founded by Cornish, *Rights of All*, had folded by 1829.

17. *Freedom's Journal* (New York), December 7, 1827.

18. Kersh, *Dreams of a More Perfect Union*, 156–57.

19. Peter P. Hinks, ed., introduction to David Walker, *David Walker's Appeal* (University Park: Pennsylvania State University Press, 2000); Hinks, *To Awaken My Afflicted Brethren*.

20. As Northern and Southern politicians had during the Missouri debates, Walker confronted the legacy of Jefferson. It is revealing that his interpretation of that legacy was, in some respects, closer to the one offered by proslavery politicians than to the idealistic appropriation of Jefferson's words made by slavery's opponents. For Walker, as for proslavery politicians, the *real* Jefferson was an inveterate defender of slavery and white supremacy. But whereas those politicians had endorsed Jefferson's defense of slavery, Walker decried it. The passages in Jefferson's *Notes on the State of Virginia* claiming that blacks were a biologically inferior species "injured us more," Walker wrote, than "any thing that has ever been advanced against us." Walker, *David Walker's Appeal*, 29–30, 67, 69; Hinks, *To Awaken My Afflicted Brethren*, 108–12; Patrick Rael, *Black Identity and Black Protest in the Antebellum North* (Chapel Hill: University of North Carolina Press, 2002).

21. Walker, *David Walker's Appeal*, 50–53.

22. Ibid., xliv, 79; Hinks, *To Awaken My Afflicted Brethren*, 236–47; *Liberator* (Boston), February 12, 1831.

23. Kathryn Kish Sklar, ed., *Women's Rights Emerges within the Antislavery Movement, 1830–1870: A Brief History with Documents* (Boston: Bedford/St. Martin's, 2000), 78–83 (Stewart quotation on 80). See also Marilyn Richardson, ed., *Maria Stewart: America's First Black Woman Political Writer: Essays and Speeches* (Bloomington: Indiana University Press, 1987).

24. Stuart Seely Sprague, ed., *His Promised Land: The Autobiography of John P. Parker, former Slave and Conductor on the Underground Railroad* (New York:

Norton, 1996), 86; Ann Hagedorn, *Beyond the River: The Untold Story of the Heroes of the Underground Railroad* (New York: Simon and Schuster, 2004).

25. Hagedorn, *Beyond the River*.

26. John Rankin, *Letters on American Slavery* (1826; reprint, Boston: Garrison and Knapp, 1833), 19–20, 28, 59; Stauffer, *Black Hearts*, 18.

27. Rankin, *Letters on American Slavery*, 106–9.

28. Hagedorn, *Beyond the River*, 56.

29. John Hope Franklin and Loren Schweninger, *Runaway Slaves: Rebels on the Plantation* (New York: Oxford University Press, 1999), 116–17.

30. James Forten to William Lloyd Garrison, December 31, 1830, in Black Abolitionist Papers, Microfilm Collection, Clapp Library, Wellesley College, Wellesley, Mass.

31. Garrison quoted in Hagedorn, *Beyond the River*, 121.

32. Mayer, *All on Fire*, 13; William E. Cain, ed., *William Lloyd Garrison and the Fight against Slavery: Selections from the Liberator* (Boston: Bedford/St. Martin's, 1995), 4.

33. James Brewer Stewart, "Reconsidering the Abolitionists in an Age of Fundamentalist Politics," *Journal of the Early Republic* 26 (Spring 2006): 4–9.

34. *Liberator*, January 1, 1831; Mayer, *All on Fire*, 124.

35. Newman, *Transformation*, 16–17. The extent of the PAS's reputation is demonstrated in an 1826 letter from a resident of Bibb County, Georgia (he withheld his name) to the society. The Georgian tells the heartrending story of an African American youth, free by birth, who was kidnapped by slaveholders as a child in Philadelphia and then sold into slavery, first in Maryland and later in Georgia. The writer of the letter provided the PAS with the name of the youth's father, who was still in Philadelphia, as well as the name of a trustworthy white doctor in Bibb County who was willing to intercede on the youth's behalf. As a next step in trying to restore this Georgia slave to freedom, the writer planned to send letters, so he informed the PAS, to other "quakers in your town" (Philadelphia). [Anonymous] to PAS, July 25, 1826, Pennsylvania Abolition Society Letters, Loose Correspondence, Historical Society of Pennsylvania, Philadelphia (hereafter cited as HSP).

36. Brenda E. Stevenson, *Life in Black and White: Family and Community in the Slave South* (New York: Oxford University Press, 1996), 16–17, 278–79, 252–53; Samuel Janney, *Memoirs of Samuel S. Janney: Late of Lincoln, Loudoun County, Va.* (Philadelphia: Friends' Book Association, 1881), 29.

37. As Garrison's star rose, Quakers divided over tactics. On one end of the antislavery spectrum were those orthodox Friends who continued to work with the

ACS. On the other were radical Hicksites. Named for Elias Hicks, who had broken away from the established Quaker leadership in a schism within the Philadelphia Yearly Meeting in 1827, the Hicksites were more "democratically inclined" than their Orthodox counterparts and gravitated toward Garrison's grassroots movement. The PAS represented a sort of middle ground, an institutional link between the extremes. Traditionalists, Quaker historian Christopher Densmore has written, favored "quiet testimony, anti-slavery but without denouncing the slave-owners," while radicals practiced "unceasing activism," condemning slaveowners and criticizing those Friends who, for fear of worldly entanglements, stood aloof from the antislavery struggle. Christopher Densmore, " 'Let Us Make Their Case Our Own': The Anti-Slavery Work of the Society of Friends in Philadelphia, 1754–1863," manuscript lent to author.

38. Newman, *Transformation*, 134–35; Ceplair, *Public Years of Sarah and Angelina Grimké*, 14; Mayer, *All on Fire*, 73–74.

39. *Liberator*, January 22, 1831. As Henry Louis Gates has explained in his essay on Revolutionary-era black poet Phillis Wheatley, white disparagement of blacks' capabilities had long turned on the specious claim that blacks could not write with sophistication. It was such prejudice that Wheatley battled to overcome and that led Thomas Jefferson, in his *Notes on the State of Virginia*, to dismiss her as an inferior mind. Henry Louis Gates Jr., *The Trials of Phillis Wheatley: America's First Black Poet and Her Encounters with the Founding Fathers* (New York: Basic Civitas Books, 2003).

40. *Liberator*, January 22, 1831.

41. Mayer, *All on Fire*, 115; Louis P. Masur, *1831: Year of Eclipse* (New York: Hill and Wang, 2001), 29 (Garrison quotation).

42. *Liberator*, January 22, 1831; Hinks, *To Awaken My Afflicted Brethren*, 160.

43. Masur, *1831*, 15–21.

44. Ibid.; Kenneth S. Greenberg, ed., *The Confessions of Nat Turner and Related Documents* (Boston: Bedford/St. Martin's, 1996), 1–19 (quotation, 19).

45. Harriet Jacobs, *Incidents in the Life of a Slave Girl*, ed. Jean Fagan Yellin (Cambridge: Harvard University Press, 2000), 64.

46. Ibid.; *Liberator*, February 11, 1832.

47. Eugene D. Genovese, *Roll, Jordan, Roll: The World the Slaves Made* (New York: Vintage, 1972); Charles C. Bolton, "Planters, Plain Folk, and Poor Whites in the Old South," in Lacy K. Ford, ed., *A Companion to the Civil War and Reconstruction* (Malden, Mass.: Blackwell, 2005), 82–90; Bruce Levine, *Half Slave and Half Free*, 37–39; Peter Kolchin, *American Slavery, 1619–1877* (New York: Hill

and Wang, 1993), 180–81; Steven A. Channing, *Crisis of Fear: Secession in South Carolina* (New York: Norton, 1970), 35 (quotation).

48. Catherine Clinton, *Harriet Tubman: The Road to Freedom* (Little, Brown, 2004), 42–43; French, *Rebellious Slave*, 205 (Carney quotation).

49. *Liberator*, September 3, 1831.

50. Mayer, *All on Fire*, 122–23.

51. Martha Jefferson Randolph to Joseph Coolidge Jr., October 27, 1831, Edgehill-Randolph Papers, Alderman Library, University of Virginia, Charlottesville; John Floyd to James Hamilton Jr., November 19, 1831, in Kenneth S. Greenberg, *Confessions of Nat Turner*, 101–11.

52. Kenneth S. Greenberg, *Confessions of Nat Turner*, 22–24; Freehling, *Road to Disunion*, 1:182; Masur, *1831*, 62 (Randolph quotation).

53. Wolf, *Race and Liberty*, 183, 227–29.

54. Freehling, *Road to Disunion*, 1:187; Elizabeth R. Varon, *We Mean to Be Counted: White Women and Politics in Antebellum Virginia* (Chapel Hill: University of North Carolina Press, 1998), 50–51.

55. Varon, *We Mean to Be Counted*, 54–56.

56. Wolf, *Race and Liberty*, 221–33.

57. O'Brien, *Conjectures of Order*, 813–14; Christopher Curtis, " 'Can These Be the Sons of Their Fathers?': The Defense of Slavery in Virginia" (M.A. thesis, Virginia Polytechnic Institute, 1997); *Richmond Whig*, February 16, 1832; Wolf, *Race and Liberty*, 229.

58. James L. Huston, *Calculating the Value of the Union: Slavery, Property Rights, and the Economic Origins of the Civil War* (Chapel Hill: University of North Carolina Press, 2003), 24–27.

59. Thomas Roderick Dew, "The Abolition of Negro Slavery," in Kenneth S. Greenberg, *Confessions of Nat Turner*, 115–17; Varon, *We Mean to Be Counted*, 58; Freehling, *Road to Disunion*, 1:190–91.

60. John Patrick Daly, *When Slavery Was Called Freedom: Evangelicalism, Proslavery, and the Causes of the Civil War* (Lexington: University Press of Kentucky, 2002), 15, 33–54.

61. Freehling, *Road to Disunion*, 1:189–91.

62. Wolf, *Race and Liberty*, 210–11, 223–24, 229; Louis P. Masur, "Nat Turner and Sectional Crisis," in Kenneth S. Greenberg, ed., *Nat Turner: A Slave Rebellion in History and Memory* (New York: Oxford University Press, 2003), 156; Margaret Hope Bacon, *But One Race: The Life of Robert Purvis* (Albany: State University of New York Press, 2007), 32–33 (Purvis quotation).

CHAPTER 3

1. Lydia Maria Child, *An Appeal in Favor of That Class of Americans Called Africans*, ed. Carlyn L. Karcher (1883; reprint, Amherst: University of Massachusetts Press, 1996), 111–15; Freehling, *Road to Disunion*, 1:275–76; Calhoun, "Fort Hill Address" and "A Disquisition on Government," in Clyde N. Wilson, *Essential Calhoun*, 20–30, 275–76.

2. John C. Calhoun to James Hamilton Jr., August 28, 1832, in Clyde N. Wilson, *Papers of John C. Calhoun*, 630–32; Calhoun, "Fort Hill Address," in Clyde N. Wilson, *Essential Calhoun*, 370.

3. McCurry, *Masters of Small Worlds*, 256–71; Andrew Jackson, "Proclamation regarding Nullification," in James D. Richardson, comp., *A Compilation of the Messages and Papers of the Presidents, 1789–1897*, 10 vols. (Washington, D.C.: Government Printing Office, 1897), 2:640–56.

4. Henry Clay, "On the Compromise Tariff," in Watson, *Andrew Jackson vs. Henry Clay*, 209–13; "Nullification and Secession," *Continental Monthly* 3 (February 1863): 179–80 (Walker quotation); *Richmond Enquirer*, January 8, 1833; *Newbern (N.C.) Spectator*, as quoted in *Rhode-Island American and Gazette* (Providence), April 27, 1832.

5. Freehling, *Road to Disunion*, 1:284; Michael F. Holt, *The Rise and Fall of the American Whig Party: Jacksonian Politics and the Onset of the Civil War* (New York: Oxford University Press, 1999), 20.

6. Child, *An Appeal*, 111–15.

7. Freehling, *Road to Disunion*, 1:220–22.

8. Ibid.; McCurry, *Masters of Small Worlds*, 256–60.

9. Freehling, *Road to Disunion*, 1:273–75; Child, *An Appeal*, 98 (quotation); Jane H. Pease and William H. Pease, *The Web of Progress: Private Values and Public Styles in Boston and Charleston, 1828–1843* (New York: Oxford University Press, 1985), 74. In 1833 and 1834 leading nullifiers went so far as to demand that state officials take a "test oath" swearing that their primary allegiance was to South Carolina. This proved too militant for public opinion in the state, and a compromise was reached that allowed oath takers to pledge their fealty to both the state and the Constitution. John Barnwell, *Love of Order: South Carolina's First Secession Crisis* (Chapel Hill: University of North Carolina Press, 1982), 33.

10. Freehling, *Road to Disunion*, 1:220.

11. Jonathan M. Atkins, *Parties, Politics, and the Sectional Conflict in Tennessee, 1832–1861* (Knoxville: University of Tennessee Press, 1997), xiv, 14, 28.

12. Anthony Gene Carey, *Parties, Slavery, and the Union in Antebellum Georgia*

(Athens: University of Georgia Press, 1997), 25–27; William J. Cooper Jr., *The South and the Politics of Slavery, 1828–1856* (Baton Rouge: Louisiana State University Press, 1978), 22.

13. Benedict, "Abraham Lincoln and Federalism," 1–18.

14. Holt, *Rise and Fall of the American Whig Party*, 16.

15. Child, *An Appeal*, 115; Theda Perdue and Michael D. Green, eds., *Cherokee Removal: A Brief History with Documents* (Boston: Bedford/St. Martin's, 1995).

16. Cain, *William Lloyd Garrison*, 90–91.

17. Robert B. Hall to the Secretaries of the Pennsylvania Abolition Society (PAS), June 17, 1833, PAS Papers, Correspondence, HSP.

18. Dorothy Sterling, *Ahead of Her Time: Abby Kelley and the Politics of Antislavery* (New York: Norton, 1991), 1 (quotation); Yellin and Van Horne, *Abolitionist Sisterhood*; Jeffrey, *Great Silent Army of Abolitionism*; Debra Gold Hansen, *Strained Sisterhood: Gender and Class in the Boston Female Anti-Slavery Society* (Amherst: University of Massachusetts Press, 1993).

19. Lucretia Mott et al. to the Penn. Abolition Society, June 29, 1836, PAS Papers, Correspondence, HSP; C. Peter Ripley, ed., *Witness for Freedom: African American Voices on Race, Slavery, and Emancipation* (Chapel Hill: University of North Carolina Press, 1993), 96–98; *Liberator*, July 21, 1832.

20. Elizabeth Wicks, "Address Delivered before the African Female Benevolent Society of Troy," in Newman, Rael, and Lapansky, *Pamphlets of Protest*, 116; *Freedom's Journal*, July 20, 1827.

21. Carolyn Williams, "The Female Antislavery Movement: Fighting against Racial Prejudice and Promoting Women's Rights in Antebellum America," in Yellin and Van Horne, *Abolitionist Sisterhood*, 67; Sewell, *Ballots for Freedom*, 72; Newman, *Transformation*, 167 (Birney quotation).

22. Charles Ball, *Slavery in the United States: A Narrative of the Life and Adventures of Charles Ball* (New York: John S. Taylor, 1837), 288–91, 360.

23. Moses Roper, *Narrative of My Escape from Slavery* (1837; reprint, Mineola, N.Y.: Dover, 2003), 26–27; *Liberator*, March 30, 1838.

24. Newman, *Transformation*, 126; Frederick Douglass, *Narrative of the Life of Frederick Douglass: An American Slave, Written by Himself*, ed. David W. Blight (Boston: Bedford/St. Martin's, 2003), 8, 45, 63–64.

25. Frederick Douglass, *Narrative*, 8, 69–70; William S. McFeely, *Frederick Douglass* (New York: Norton, 1991), 83–84.

26. Cain, *William Lloyd Garrison*, 13–14; David Grimsted, *American Mobbing, 1828–1861: Toward Civil War* (New York: Oxford University Press, 1998), 13.

27. Grimsted, *American Mobbing*, 4, 12–18; Emma Jones Lapansky, "The World the Agitators Made: The Counterculture of Agitation in Urban Philadelphia," in Yellin and Van Horne, *Abolitionist Sisterhood*, 202; Amos Kendall, *Report of the Postmaster General*, 1835, in *Congressional Globe*, 24th Cong., 1st sess., Appendix, 9.

28. Edwin P. Atlee to the Conference of Abolitionists to Assemble in the City of New York, October 23, 1833, PAS Papers, Miscellaneous Correspondence, HSP.

29. Grimsted, *American Mobbing*, 13–22 (Hammond quoted on 22); Anne Farrow, Joel Lang, and Jenifer Frank, *Complicity: How the North Promoted, Prolonged, and Profited from Slavery* (New York: Ballantine, 2005), 160–63 (Ellsworth and Judson quoted on 161).

30. Grimsted, *American Mobbing*, 13–22. See also Wyatt-Brown, *Southern Honor*; Steven M. Stowe, *Intimacy and Power in the Old South: Ritual in the Lives of the Planters* (Baltimore: Johns Hopkins University Press, 1987); and Kenneth S. Greenberg, *Honor and Slavery: Lies, Duels, Noses, Masks, Dressing as a Woman, Gifts, Strangers, Humanitarianism, Death, Slave Rebellions, the Proslavery Argument, Baseball, Hunting, and Gambling in the Old South* (Princeton: Princeton University Press, 1996).

31. Phillip Lapansky, "Graphic Discord: Abolitionist and Antiabolitonist Images," in Yellin and Van Horne, *Abolitionist Sisterhood*, 224–27; William Jay, *An Inquiry into the Character and Tendency of the American Colonization, and American Anti-Slavery Societies* (New York: Leavitt, Lord and Co., 1835), 142, 168.

32. Grimstead, *American Mobbing*, 29–32 (first quotation); Carey, *Parties, Slavery*, 36 (second quotation); Daniel Crofts, *Old Southampton: Politics and Society in a Virginia County, 1834–1869* (Charlottesville: University Press of Virginia, 1992), 117–19, 218 (last quotations).

33. Cmiel, *Democratic Eloquence*, 60–61; Glenn C. Altschuler and Stuart Blumin, *Rude Republic: Americans and Their Politics in the Nineteenth Century* (Princeton: Princeton University Press, 2000), 109; Andrew W. Robertson, "Voting Rites and Voting Acts: Electioneering Ritual, 1790–1820," in Pasley, Robertson, and Waldstreicher, *Beyond the Founders*, 67.

34. Richards, *Slave Power*, 92, 111–12, 121.

35. Holt, *Rise and Fall of the American Whig Party*, 24.

36. Cooper, *South and the Politics of Slavery*, 53–83; Carey, *Parties, Slavery*, 37 (quotation); Wilentz, *Rise of American Democracy*, 450.

37. Carey, *Parties, Slavery*, 36–37; Crofts, *Old Southampton*, 118–19; Grimsted, *American Mobbing*, 25–32; Van Buren, "First Inaugural," in James D. Richard-

son, *Messages and Papers of the Presidents*, 2:1535–37; Cooper, *South and the Politics of Slavery*, 96.

38. John R. McKivigan, *The War against Proslavery Religion: Abolitionism and the Northern Churches, 1830–1865* (Ithaca, N.Y.: Cornell University Press, 1984), 25–31; Daly, *When Slavery Was Called Freedom*, 38; Douglas M. Strong, *Perfectionist Politics: Abolitionism and the Religious Tensions of American Democracy* (Syracuse, N.Y.: Syracuse University Press, 1999), 44–63.

39. Mitchell Snay, *Gospel of Disunion: Religion and Separatism in the Antebellum South* (New York: Cambridge University Press, 1993), 33–37, 47 (quotation).

40. Edward R. Crowther, *Southern Evangelicals and the Coming of the Civil War* (Lewiston, N.Y.: Edwin Mellen Press, 2000), 70–75; Daly, *When Slavery Was Called Freedom*, 61; Snay, *Gospel of Disunion*, 116–26.

41. Zaeske, *Signatures of Citizenship*, 3, 47–48; Freehling, *Road to Disunion*, 1:323–36; Holt, *Rise and Fall of the American Whig Party*, 155; William Lee Miller, *Arguing about Slavery: John Quincy Adams and the Great Battle in the United States Congress* (New York: Knopf, 1996), 220.

42. William Bassett, *Letter to a Member of the Society of Friends, in Reply to Objections against Joining Antislavery Societies* (Boston: Isaac Knapp, 1837), 12, 21; *Register of Debates*, 24th Cong., 1st sess., 79–80, and 2nd sess., 714–15.

43. Zaeske, *Signatures of Citizenship*, 78–81; Miller, *Arguing about Slavery*, 230–36; *Richmond Enquirer*, February 9, 1837.

44. Miller, *Arguing about Slavery*, 279–82; *Speech of Mr. Slade, of Vt., on the Abolition of Slavery* (Washington, D.C.: N.p., 1837), 3–9.

45. *Register of Debates*, 24th Cong., 2nd sess., 710; Zaeske, *Signatures of Citizenship*, 119; Miller, *Arguing about Slavery*, 307; Magdol, *Antislavery Rank and File*; *Philanthropist* (Cincinnati), December 2, 1836.

46. *Weekly Advocate* (New York), January 21, 1837.

47. *Weekly Advocate Extra* (New York), February 22, 1837; *Colored American* (New York), July 8, 1837.

48. Loren Schweninger, ed., *The Southern Debate over Slavery*, vol. 1: *Petitions to Southern Legislatures, 1778–1864* (Urbana: University of Illinois Press, 2001), 139–41, 162–63.

49. Petition of Rachel Collins, December 9, 1836, Legislative Petitions to the General Assembly, Norfolk Borough, Library of Virginia, Richmond.

50. Kersh, *Dreams of a More Perfect Union*, 155–60.

51. Schweninger, *Southern Debate over Slavery*, 165–66.

52. O'Brien, *Conjectures of Order*, 946–52; McCurry, *Masters of Small Worlds*, 212

(quotation); Larry E. Tise, *Proslavery: A History of the Defense of Slavery in America, 1701–1840* (Athens: University of Georgia Press, 1987), 343.

53. John C. Calhoun, "Speech in the U.S. Senate," in Paul Finkelman, *Defending Slavery: Proslavery Thought in the Old South* (Boston: Bedford/St. Martin's, 2003), 54–60; *Congressional Globe*, 25th Cong., 3rd sess., 358–59.

54. *Register of Debates*, 24th Cong., 2nd sess., 718–22; Freehling, *Road to Disunion*, 1:298.

55. *Congressional Globe*, 24th Cong., 1st sess., Appendix, 611–15; David F. Ericson, *The Debate over Slavery: Antislavery and Proslavery Liberalism in Antebellum America* (New York: New York University Press, 2000), 125–28. On Hammond, see Drew Gilpin Faust, *James Henry Hammond and the Old South: A Design for Mastery* (Baton Rouge: Louisiana State University Press, 1982), esp. 172–74.

56. Faust, *James Henry Hammond*, 174; Calhoun, "Speech in the U.S. Senate," in Finkelman, *Defending Slavery*, 58–60.

57. Calhoun, "Speech in the U.S. Senate," in Finkelman, *Defending Slavery*, 58–60.

58. *Congressional Globe*, 24th Cong., 1st sess., Appendix, 220–23.

59. Ibid.

60. Holt, *Rise and Fall of the American Whig Party*, 128; Judge [Nathaniel] Beverly Tucker, *The Partisan Leader: A Novel, and an Apocalypse of the Origin and Struggles of the Southern Confederacy*, ed. Thomas Ware (1836; reprint, Richmond: West and Johnson, 1862), 22–24, 96–97, 135–36.

61. Walther, *Fire-eaters*, 40–42; Tucker, *Partisan Leader*, iii (quotation).

62. *National Enquirer* (Philadelphia), October 15, November 19, 1836, June 10, 1837; *Pennsylvania Freeman* (Philadelphia), July 4, 1839; *Emancipator* (New York), November 9, 1837.

63. *National Enquirer*, May 13, 1837; *Emancipator*, November 9, 1837.

64. *Emancipator*, May 5, 26, 1836; *Congressional Globe*, 24th Cong., 2nd sess., Appendix, 189–91.

65. *National Enquirer*, December 31, 1836.

66. *Pennsylvania Freeman*, May 31, October 11, 1838; *Liberator*, September 14, 1838.

67. Massachusetts Anti-Slavery Society, *An Account of the Interview Which Took Place on the Fourth & Eighth of March, between a Committee of the Massachusetts Anti-Slavery Society, and a Committee of the Legislature* (Boston: Massachusetts Anti-Slavery Society, 1836); Angelina Emily Grimké, "Appeal to the Christian Women of the South," in Ceplair, *Public Years of Sarah and Angelina Grimké*, 58, 70; *National Enquirer*, October 15, 1836.

CHAPTER 4

1. Richard Bruce Winders, *Crisis in the Southwest: The United States, Mexico, and the Struggle over Texas* (Wilmington, Del.: Scholarly Resources, 2002), 26, 64, 79–81; Mark M. Carroll, *Homesteads Ungovernable: Families, Sex, Race, and the Law in Frontier Texas, 1823–1860* (Austin: University of Texas Press, 2001), 33, 54–59.

2. Lundy quoted in Silbey, *Storm over Texas*, 117; Birney quoted in *National Enquirer*, July 20, 1837.

3. *Congressional Globe*, 25th Cong., 2nd sess., Appendix, 555–58; Winders, *Crisis in the Southwest*, 78–79; *Register of Debates*, 24th Cong., 1st sess., 1414–16.

4. Richards, *Slave Power*, 88, 101–5.

5. Morrison, *Slavery and the American West*, 24–26; Holt, *Rise and Fall of the American Whig Party*, 168–69.

6. *Register of Debates*, 24th Cong., 2nd sess., 1330–37; *Congressional Globe*, 25th Cong., 3rd sess., Appendix, 359, and 2nd sess., Appendix, 20–21.

7. John Quincy Adams, *Speech of John Quincy Adams, of Massachusetts, upon the Right of the People, Men and Women, to Petition* (Washington, D.C.: Gales and Seaton, 1838), 78; Zaeske, *Signatures of Citizenship*, 136–43; *Congressional Globe*, 25th Cong., 3rd sess., Appendix, 173. On Morris, see Jonathan H. Earle, *Jacksonian Antislavery and the Politics of Free Soil, 1824–1854* (Chapel Hill: University of North Carolina Press, 2004).

8. Kimberly K. Smith, *The Dominion of Voice: Riot, Reason, and Romance in Antebellum Politics* (Lawrence: University Press of Kansas, 1999), 89–92 (quotation, 91).

9. Stephen Howard Browne, *Angelina Grimké: Rhetoric, Identity, and the Radical Imagination* (East Lansing: Michigan State University Press, 1999), 115; Sterling, *Ahead of Her Time*, 39–41 (quotations, 40).

10. Boston Female Anti-Slavery Society, *Right and Wrong in Boston: Annual Report of the Boston Female Anti-Slavery Society* (Boston: Isaac Knapp, 1837), 48–50, 52–59; *Liberator*, October 6, 1837; Barbara Cutter, *Domestic Devils, Battlefield Angels: The Radicalism of American Womanhood, 1830–1865* (DeKalb: Northern Illinois University Press, 2003), 114–15 (*Colored American* quotation); Catharine E. Beecher, *An Essay on Slavery and Abolition, with Reference to the Duty of American Females* (Philadelphia: Henry Perkins, 1837).

11. Boston Female Anti-Slavery Society, *Right and Wrong*, 48–50, 52–59; Cutter, *Domestic Devils*, 114–15; *Liberator*, October 6, 1837.

12. Mayer, *All on Fire*, 196–203 (quotations, 198); Morone, *Hellfire Nation*, 184; Grimsted, *American Mobbing*, 18–19, 46–47. See also Leonard L. Richards, *"Gentlemen of Property and Standing": Abolition Mobs in Jacksonian America* (New York: Oxford University Press, 1970).

13. Margaret Hope Bacon, "By Moral Force Alone: The Antislavery Women and Nonresistance," in Yellin and Van Horne, *Abolitionist Sisterhood*, 285–87.

14. *Colored American*, November 25, 1837, January 13, 1838.

15. Friedman, *Gregarious Saints*, 199–202.

16. Varon, *We Mean to Be Counted*.

17. Ibid.; Elizabeth Moss, *Domestic Novelists in the Old South: Defenders of Southern Culture* (Baton Rouge: Louisiana State University Press, 1992), 18–23; O'Brien, *Conjectures of Order*, 766–70; William R. Taylor, *Cavalier and Yankee: The Old South and American National Character* (New York; G. Braziller, 1957), 95–141.

18. Moss, *Domestic Novelists*, 18–19; Cutter, *Domestic Devils*, 143–44 (quotation).

19. Angelina Grimké and Theodore Dwight Weld, *American Slavery as It Is: Testimony of a Thousand Witnesses* (1839; reprint, Arno Press, 1988), 1–10; Miller, *Arguing about Slavery*, 323–33.

20. Grimké and Weld, *American Slavery*, 77–82, 143; Mark V. Tushnet, *Slave Law in the American South: State v. Mann in History and Literature* (Lawrence: University Press of Kansas, 2003).

21. Grimké and Weld, *American Slavery*, 110–12.

22. Ibid., 112–16.

23. For a view of the years 1840–44 as the "high point of party stability and cohesion," see, e.g., Ashworth, *Slavery, Capitalism*, 381–414.

24. Wilentz, *Rise of American Democracy*, 436–40, 499; Holt, *Rise and Fall of the American Whig Party*, 95–111.

25. *Crisis* (Richmond), September 23, 1840; Cooper, *South and the Politics of Slavery*, 103; Howard Jones, *Mutiny on the Amistad: The Saga of a Slave Revolt and Its Impact on American Abolition, Law and Diplomacy* (New York: Oxford University Press, 1997), 49–50.

26. Holt, *Rise and Fall of the American Whig Party*, 105–11; "Defeat of the Sub-Treasury Bill," *American Monthly Magazine* (July 1838): 1.

27. Varon, *We Mean to Be Counted*, 78–80; *Daily National Intelligencer*, October 9, 10, 12, 1840; *Richmond Whig*, October 3, 9, 1840; *Crisis*, October 14, 1840. On promodernization Southern Whigs, see Larry K. Menna, "Southern Whiggery and Economic Development: The Meaning of Slavery within a National Context," in Blatt and Roediger, *Meaning of Slavery in the North*, 55–76. On Whig "political pietism," see James Brewer Stewart, "Abolitionists, Insurgents, and

Third Parties: Sectionalism and Partisan Politics in Northern Whiggery, 1836–1844," in Alan M. Kraut, ed., *Crusaders and Compromisers: Essays on the Relationship of the Antislavery Struggle to the Antebellum Party System* (Westport, Conn.: Greenwood Press, 1983), 25–43, and Richard J. Carwardine, *Evangelicals and Politics in Antebellum America* (New Haven: Yale University Press, 1993). On the Whig definition of progress, see Major L. Wilson, *Space, Time and Freedom*, 4.

28. *New York World*, as quoted in *Charleston Mercury*, October 4, 1841; "To the Democratic Republican Party of Alabama" (n.p., 1840), in Silbey, *American Party Battle*, 1:174.

29. Cain, *William Lloyd Garrison*, 28–29, 106.

30. Sewell, *Ballots for Freedom*, 27; Cain, *William Lloyd Garrison*, 28–29, 106, 158 (quotations); *Liberator*, July 28, 1840.

31. Sewell, *Ballots for Freedom*, 10 (quotation); *Colored American*, September 26, October 10, 1840.

32. Miller, *Arguing about Slavery*, 370–72; *Congressional Globe*, 26th Cong., 1st sess., 150.

33. *Pennsylvania Freeman*, February 27, 1840; *Congressional Globe*, 26th Cong., 1st sess., 188–95.

34. Michael D. Pierson, *Free Hearts, Free Homes: Gender and American Antislavery Politics* (Chapel Hill: University of North Carolina Press, 2003), 25–28; Sewell, *Ballots for Freedom*, 71–72, 85 (Smith quotation).

35. Sewell, *Ballots for Freedom*, 101–2; Stanley Harrold, *The Rise of Aggressive Abolitionism* (Lexington: University Press of Kentucky, 2004), 108–9, 115–16; 321–23 (quotations); John L. Thomas, ed., *Slavery Attacked: The Abolitionist Crusade* (New York: Prentice Hall, 1965), 74. See also Bruce Laurie, *Beyond Garrison: Antislavery and Social Reform* (New York: Cambridge University Press, 2005).

36. William Henry Harrison, "Inaugural Address," in James D. Richardson, *Messages and Papers of the Presidents*, 4:6–20.

37. *Richmond Enquirer*, April 6, 1841; *New York Tribune*, September 13, 1841, March 3, May 11, 1843; Holt, *Rise and Fall of the American Whig Party*, 139.

38. *Richmond Enquirer*, August 20, 1841; Silbey, *Storm over Texas*, 31; *Charleston Mercury*, September 18, October 1, 1841.

39. *Congressional Globe*, 27th Cong., 1st sess., 51.

40. *Richmond Enquirer*, January 29, February 3, 5, 8, 1842; *Richmond Whig*, February 4, 1842.

41. *New York Tribune*, February 4, 10, 1842; *Richmond Enquirer*, February 12, 1842; *Richmond Whig*, January 31, February 4, 10, 12, 25, 1842.

42. Mayer, *All on Fire*, 314; George Allen, *Mr. Allen's Speech before the Convention of Ministers* (Boston: Isaac Knapp, 1838), 44–45; *Colored American*, February 2, 1839.

43. Mayer, *All on Fire*, 313–17.

44. William Lloyd Garrison to Elizabeth Pease, July 2, 1842, and Garrison to Richard D. Webb, February 28, March 1, 1845, in Walther M. Merrill, ed., *The Letters of William Lloyd Garrison*, vol. 3: *No Union with Slaveholders, 1841–1849* (Cambridge: Belknap Press of Harvard University Press, 1973), 89, 127–29, 288; Garrison to James Miller McKim, October 14, 1856, in Louis Ruchames, ed., *The Letters of William Lloyd Garrison*, vol. 4: *From Disunion to the Brink of War, 1850–1860* (Cambridge: Belknap Press of Harvard University Press, 1975), 409; *National Anti-Slavery Standard* (New York), February 17, 1842; Cain, *William Lloyd Garrison*, 113–14; Mayer, *All on Fire*, 326–27.

45. Pierson, *Free Hearts*, 49–50.

46. *New York Herald*, September 9, 1839; *Colored American*, March 27, May 22, 1841.

47. Jones, *Mutiny on the Amistad*, 175–90; Mayer, *All on Fire*, 307–9 (quotation, 308).

48. Stewart, "Abolitionists, Insurgents," 28, 30–33, and "Reconsidering the Abolitionists," 10–14.

49. Howe, *Political Culture of the American Whigs*, 175 (quotation); Jones, *Mutiny on the Amistad*, 192–93; Mayer, *All on Fire*, 309–10; Fehrenbacher, *Dred Scott Case*, 39.

50. Fehrenbacher, *Dred Scott Case*, 40–47 (quotation, 41), and *Slaveholding Republic*, 219–25; *Prigg v. Pennsylvania*, Supreme Court of the United States (1842), 41 U.S. 539. For a checklist of Northern personal liberty laws, see the appendix to Thomas D. Morris, *Free Men All: The Personal Liberty Laws of the North, 1780–1861* (Baltimore: Johns Hopkins University Press, 1974).

51. Jones, *Mutiny on the Amistad*, 193–94; Fehrenbacher, *Slaveholding Republic*, 220, and *Dred Scott Case*, 42–45.

52. *Liberator*, March 11, 1842; Fehrenbacher, *Slaveholding Republic*, 221–22.

53. Mayer, *All on Fire*, 312–13.

54. *Congressional Globe*, 27th Cong., 2nd sess., 115–16, 203–4; *Charleston Mercury*, January 18, 1842.

55. Miller, *Arguing about Slavery*, 444–54; Howard Jones, "The Peculiar Institution and National Honor: The Case of the *Creole* Slave Revolt," *Civil War History* 21 (March 1975): 28–50.

56. Emma Jones Lapansky, " 'Since They Got Those Separate Churches': Afro-

Americans and Racism in Jacksonian Philadelphia," *American Quarterly* 32 (Spring 1980): 54–78; *Liberator*, August 19, 1842.

57. Emma Jones Lapansky, " 'Since They Got Those Separate Churches' "; Robert Purvis to Henry C. Wright, August 22, 1842, Black Abolitionist Papers, Microfilm Collection.

58. Mayer, *All on Fire*, 316–20; James W. C. Pennington, *Covenants Involving Moral Wrong Not Obligatory upon Man* (Hartford: John C. Wells, 1842), 11.

59. Mayer, *All on Fire*, 316–20; Laurie, *Beyond Garrison*, 76–80, 124.

60. Pennington, *Covenants*, 7; William Wells Brown, *Anti-Slavery Harp: A Collection of Songs for Anti-Slavery Meetings* (Boston: Bela Marsh, 1849), 40–41; Mayer, *All on Fire*, 321.

CHAPTER 5

1. *New York Tribune*, May 16, 1843; Lorman A. Ratner and Dwight C. Teeter Jr., *Fanatics and Fire-Eaters: Newspapers and the Coming of the Civil War* (Champaign: University of Illinois Press, 2003), 12.

2. Thomas R. Hietala, *Manifest Design: American Exceptionalism and Empire* (Ithaca, N.Y.: Cornell University Press, 1985), 15–25 (quotation, 17); Freehling, *Road to Disunion*, 1:392–93; Walther, *Fire-eaters*, 129–30; Silbey, *Storm over Texas*, 58–59; Ashworth, *Slavery, Capitalism*, 420 (quotation).

3. Ashworth, *Slavery, Capitalism*, 421; *Richmond Enquirer*, May 24, 1844; Silbey, *Storm over Texas*, 39–40.

4. Silbey, *Storm over Texas*, 44–46; *Richmond Enquirer*, April 20, 26, June 14, 21, 1844; Morrison, *Slavery and the American West*, 15–17; Amy S. Greenberg, *Manifest Manhood and the Antebellum American Empire* (New York: Cambridge University Press, 2005), 12–13, 23.

5. Freehling, *Road to Disunion*, 1:418–20; Hietala, *Manifest Design*, 50.

6. Morrison, *Slavery and the American West*, 15–17; *Southern States Rights* (Charleston: Walker and Burke, 1844); *Richmond Enquirer*, April 20, 26, June 14, 21, 1844; *Palladium of Liberty* (Columbus, Ohio), June 12, 1844.

7. Morrison, *Slavery and the American West*, 22; Robert V. Remini, *Henry Clay: Statesman for the Union* (New York: Norton, 1991), 630–39; Gary J. Kornblith, "Rethinking the Coming of the Civil War: A Counterfactual Exercise," *Journal of American History* 90 (June 2003): 76–105 (Clay quotation).

8. Holt, *Rise and Fall of the American Whig Party*, 146–48, 178; Remini, *Henry Clay*, 605–6; *Niles' National Register* (Baltimore), August 17, 1844.

9. *Niles' National Register*, August 17, 1844; William C. Davis, *Rhett*, 207.

10. *Niles' National Register*, August 17, 1844 (*Richmond Enquirer* quotation), August 24, 1844 (Hamilton quotation).

11. Remini, *Henry Clay*, 630–39; Kornblith, "Rethinking the Coming of the Civil War," 76–105.

12. Freehling, *Road to Disunion*, 1:437–38; Holt, *Rise and Fall of the American Whig Party*, 178–83; Stewart, "Reconsidering the Abolitionists," 11–12, and "Abolitionists, Insurgents," 35.

13. Remini, *Henry Clay*, 660; Freehling, *Road to Disunion*, 1:437–38; Holt, *Rise and Fall of the American Whig Party*, 196–97.

14. Miller, *Arguing about Slavery*, 476–80; Zaeske, *Signatures of Citizenship*, 266; *Congressional Globe*, 28th Cong., 1st sess., Appendix, 32, 172–73, 175.

15. *Congressional Globe*, 28th Cong., 2nd sess., 299; *Charleston Mercury*, January 7, 8, 15, February 6, 1845; Hietala, *Manifest Design*, 47.

16. *Congressional Globe*, 28th Cong., 2nd sess., 94, 181; Thomas H. O'Connor, "Slavery in the North," in Blatt and Roediger, *Meaning of Slavery in the North*, 47.

17. Freehling, *Road to Disunion*, 1:440–47; Morrison, *Slavery and the American West*, 22–24; Holt, *Rise and Fall of the American Whig Party*, 220–22, and *Fate of Their Country*, 14–16.

18. Remini, *Henry Clay*, 661–62, 676–78 (Henry Clay quotation, 676); *New York Tribune*, January 22, 1844; Holt, *Fate of Their Country*, 14–16.

19. Remini, *Henry Clay*, 678; *Louisville Daily Democrat* (Ky.), August 23, 1845.

20. Harold D. Tallant, *Evil Necessity: Slavery and Political Culture in Antebellum Kentucky* (Lexington: University Press of Kentucky, 2003), 128–32.

21. Snay, *Gospel of Disunion*, 126–31, 136; Crowther, *Southern Evangelicals*, 94; John R. McKivigan, "The Northern Churches and the Moral Problem of Slavery," in Martin H. Blatt and David Roediger, eds., *The Meaning of Slavery in the North* (New York: Garland Publishing, 1998), 86.

22. Snay, *Gospel of Disunion*, 126–31, 136; Crowther, *Southern Evangelicals*, 94; McKivigan, "The Northern Churches," 86.

23. Daly, *When Slavery Was Called Freedom*, 78–79; Snay, *Gospel of Disunion*, 144–49 (quotation, 147); Crowther, *Southern Evangelicals*, 78; Elizabeth Fox-Genovese and Eugene D. Genovese, *The Mind of the Master Class: History and Faith in the Southern Slaveholders' World View* (New York: Cambridge University Press, 2005), 478–79.

24. McKivigan, "The Northern Churches," 86–87; Frederick Douglass, *Narrative*, 122–23.

25. William Lloyd Garrison to Thomas Clarkson, August 19, 1845, Garrison Papers, Microfilm Collection, Paley Library, Temple University; Massachusetts Anti-Slavery Society, *Thirteenth Annual Report Presented to the Massachusetts Anti-Slavery Society* (Boston: Andrews, Prentiss and Studley, 1845); American Anti-Slavery Society, *Disunion: Address of the American Anti-Slavery Society; and F. Jackson's Letter on the Pro-Slavery Character of the Constitution* (New York: AASS, 1845).

26. *Congressional Globe*, 29th Cong., 2nd sess., Appendix, 328–32; Hietala, *Manifest Design*, 168.

27. Robert W. Johannsen, *To the Halls of the Montezumas: The Mexican War in the American Imagination* (New York: Oxford University Press, 1985), 7–12; Richard Griswold Del Castillo, *The Treaty of Guadalupe Hidalgo: A Legacy of Conflict* (Norman: University of Oklahoma Press, 1990), 4–14; William H. Goetzmann, *When the Eagle Screamed: The Romantic Horizon in American Diplomacy, 1800–1860* (New York: Wiley, 1966), 55–61.

28. *Congressional Globe*, 29th Cong., 2nd sess., Appendix, 328–32; Hietala, *Manifest Design*, 168.

29. *Congressional Globe*, 29th Cong., 2nd sess., Appendix, 328–32; Hietala, *Manifest Design*, 117–18, 162–63; Freehling, *Road to Disunion*, 1:457.

30. Morrison, *Slavery and the American West*, 40; Holt, *Fate of Their Country*, 14–18.

31. Johannsen, *To the Halls of the Montezumas*, 25–29.

32. Reginald Horsman, *Race and Manifest Destiny: The Origins of American Racial Anglo-Saxonism* (Cambridge: Harvard University Press, 1981), esp. 232–48 (quotations, 210, 243).

33. Ibid., 218–25; Johannsen, *To the Halls of the Montezumas*, 21, 39, 49 (quotations), 51, 57, 114.

34. Robert E. May, *Manifest Destiny's Underworld: Filibustering in Antebellum America* (Chapel Hill: University of North Carolina Press, 2002), 112; Sam W. Haynes, *James K. Polk and the Expansionist Impulse* (New York: Longman, 1997), 87–93; Frederick Merk with Lois Bannister Merk, *Manifest Destiny and Mission in American History* (Cambridge: Harvard University Press, 1963), 26–27 (quotation), 35, 54–55, 59.

35. Silbey, *Storm over Texas*, 119; Holt, *Fate of Their Country*, 19–28 (quotations, 23, 28); Freehling, *Road to Disunion*, 1:459; Bruce Levine, *Half Slave and Half Free*, 178.

36. Walt Whitman, "American Workingmen, versus Slavery," in Mason I. Lowance Jr., ed., *A House Divided: The Antebellum Slavery Debates in America, 1776–1865*

(Princeton: Princeton University Press, 2003), 199; Hietala, *Manifest Design*, 122; *Congressional Globe*, 30th Cong., 1st sess., Appendix, 1076–80. On Whitman's political evolution, see David S. Reynolds, afterword to *Walt Whitman's Leaves of Grass: 150th Anniversary Edition* (New York: Oxford University Press, 2005), 88–89. Reynolds argues that Whitman's 1855 masterpiece reflects his moderate position on slavery and his ardent Unionism: "Whitman's solution to the problem of impending disunion was to launch a loving poetic persona who embraced both North and South."

37. Morrison, *Slavery and the American West*, 42–53.

38. *Congressional Globe*, 29th Cong., 2nd sess., Appendix, 150–53, 315–17, 323, 334; *Congressional Globe*, 29th Cong., 2nd sess., 180–82.

39. *Congressional Globe*, 29th Cong., 2nd sess., Appendix, 364–66; Jane P. Tompkins, "Sentimental Power: *Uncle Tom's Cabin* and the Politics of Literary History," in Elizabeth Ammons, ed., *Uncle Tom's Cabin: A Norton Critical Edition* (New York: Norton, 1994), 503–11; Anne Douglass, *The Feminization of American Culture* (New York: Knopf, 1977), 200–26.

40. *Congressional Globe*, 29th Cong., 2nd sess., Appendix, 315–19, 343–45, and 30th Cong., 1st sess., Appendix, 1076–80; Henry Nash Smith, *The Virgin Land: The American West as Symbol and Myth* (Cambridge: Harvard University Press, 1950), 140, 152.

41. *Congressional Globe*, 29th Cong., 2nd sess., Appendix, 177–80, 313–17, 278–82, 343–45.

42. *New Orleans Bee*, September 16, October 15, 1846 (*Plain Dealer* and *Democratic Mirror* quotations); *Brooklyn Daily Eagle*, April 22, September 1, 1847.

43. *Congressional Globe*, 30th Cong., 1st sess., Appendix, 1076–80; John G. Palfrey, *Papers on the Slave Power* (Boston: Merrill, Cobb and Co., 1846); Robert L. Gale, "John Palfrey," in *ANB* 16:932–34; *Congressional Globe*, 29th Cong., 2nd sess., Appendix, 334.

44. *Congressional Globe*, 29th Cong., 2nd sess., Appendix, 170–72, 315, 334; Ashworth, *Slavery, Capitalism*, 445–47.

45. Abolitionists, to use recent scholarly terminology, countered the ideal of "martial manhood" with appeals to "restrained manhood." See Bertram Wyatt-Brown, *Yankee Saints and Southern Sinners* (Baton Rouge: Louisiana State University Press, 1985); Kristin Hoganson, "Garrisonian Abolitionists and the Rhetoric of Gender, 1850–1860," *American Quarterly* 45 (December 1993): 582–87; Amy S. Greenberg, *Manifest Manhood*, 10–11; David G. Pugh, *Sons of Liberty: The Masculine Mind in Nineteenth-Century America* (Westport, Conn.: Greenwood Press, 1983), 28–31; Michael Kimmel, *Manhood in America: A Cultural History*

(New York: Free Press, 1995), 72–74; Donald Yacavone, "Abolitionists and the 'Language of Fraternal Love,'" in Mark C. Carnes and Clyde Griffen, eds., *Meanings for Manhood* (Chicago: University of Chicago Press, 1990), 85–95; James Brewer Stewart, "Joshua Giddings, Antislavery Violence, and Congressional Politics of Honor," in John McKivigan and Stanley Harrold, eds., *Antislavery Violence: Sectional, Racial, and Cultural Conflict in Antebellum America* (Knoxville: University of Tennessee Press, 1999), 185 (quotation).

46. *Congressional Globe*, 29th Cong., 2nd sess., Appendix, 76–79, 136; Leonard Schlup, "James Alexander Seddon," in *ANB* 19:575–77; Holt, *Fate of Their Country*, 33; Morrison, *Slavery and the American West*, 60–61.

47. *Congressional Globe*, 29th Cong., 2nd sess., Appendix, 116–18, 134, 170, 361; *New Orleans Bee*, February 25, 1847.

48. *Congressional Globe*, 29th Cong., 2nd sess., Appendix, 79, 244–47.

49. Ibid.; *Liberator*, February 26, 1847; *New Orleans Bee*, February 26, 1847; Holt, *Fate of Their Country*, 35–38; Bruce Levine, *Half Slave and Half Free*, 181; Arthur Bestor, "The American Civil War as a Constitutional Crisis," *American Historical Review* 69 (January 1964): 350–51.

50. Holt, *Fate of Their Country*, 35–38 (quotations, 35–36); Bestor, "American Civil War as a Constitutional Crisis," 347; Freehling, *Road to Disunion*, 1:457.

51. Potter, *Impending Crisis*, 68; Cooper, *South and the Politics of Slavery*, 234–42; Augustus Baldwin Longstreet, *A Voice from the South* (Baltimore: Western Continent Press, 1847); *Congressional Globe*, 29th Cong., 2nd sess., Appendix, 254–58; Paul M. Pruit, "Henry Hilliard," in *ANB* 10:815–17.

52. William Lloyd Garrison to Richard D. Webb, March 1, 1845, in Merrill, *Letters of William Lloyd Garrison*, 470–73; *Liberator*, October 8, 1846, January 1, 8, February 26, 1847.

53. Thomas Van Rensellear to Editor, *Monthly Illustrations of American Slavery*, November 28, 1847, in C. Peter Ripley, ed., *The Black Abolitionist Papers* vol. 4: *The United States, 1847–1858* (Chapel Hill: University of North Carolina Press, 1991), 16–17; Charles Sumner, *Works of Charles Sumner*, vol. 1 (Boston: Lee and Shepard, 1870), 377–80.

54. Paul Foos, *A Short, Offhand, Killing Affair: Soldiers and Social Conflict during the Mexican-American War* (Chapel Hill: University of North Carolina Press, 2002), 6; Johannsen, *To the Halls of the Montezumas*, 218 (Lowell quotation).

55. *Congressional Globe*, 29th Cong., 2nd sess., Appendix, 334; Henry David Thoreau, *Civil Disobedience and Other Essays* (1849; reprint, Mineola, N.Y.: Dover, 1993).

56. *Liberator*, September 10, 1847.

CHAPTER 6

1. Freehling, *Road to Disunion*, 1:475 (quotation); Holt, *Fate of Their Country*, 36; *Congressional Globe*, 30th Cong., 1st sess., Appendix, 379.

2. Del Castillo, *Treaty of Guadalupe Hidalgo*, 47–51, 67–68.

3. Holt, *Fate of Their Country*, 41–43.

4. Eric Foner, *Politics and Ideology in the Age of the Civil War* (New York: Oxford University Press, 1980), 44; *North Star* (Rochester, N.Y.), July 14, 28, October 6, 20, 1848.

5. *Philadelphia Evening Bulletin*, September 21, 1848; "The Election," *United States Magazine and Democratic Review* 23 (October 1848): 289 (hereafter cited as *Democratic Review*).

6. William Lloyd Garrison to Edmund Quincy, August 10, 1848, in Merrill, *Letters of William Lloyd Garrison*, 581–82; Sewell, *Ballots for Freedom*, 156–61, 189–91; *North Star*, September 15, 1848.

7. Pierson, *Free Hearts*, 52–61 (quotation, 61); Nancy Isenberg, *Sex and Citizenship in Antebellum America* (Chapel Hill: University of North Carolina Press, 1998), 142–47.

8. Sklar, *Women's Rights Emerges*, 54–55; Judith Wellman, "The Seneca Falls Women's Rights Convention: A Study of Social Networks," *Journal of Women's History* 3 (Spring 1991): 9–37; Alison M. Parker, "The Case for Reform Antecedents for the Woman's Rights Movement," in Jean H. Baker, ed., *Votes for Women: The Struggle for Suffrage Revisited* (New York: Oxford University Press, 2002), 34–36.

9. Sklar, *Women's Rights*, 55–60 (Stanton quoted on 55).

10. Ibid., 61, 183–85, 191–92 (Swisshelm quoted on 192).

11. Varon, *We Mean to Be Counted*, 99–102; Isenberg, *Sex and Citizenship*, 144–47.

12. *New York Herald*, as quoted in *Philadelphia Evening Bulletin*, October 28, 1848; Holt, *Fate of Their Country*, 51–55; John C. Calhoun, "Southern Address," in Richard K. Cralle, ed., *The Works of John C. Calhoun*, vol. 6 (Columbia, S.C.: A. S. Johnston, 1851), 290–313; *National Era*, January 4, 11, 1849.

13. Silbey, *Storm over Texas*, 144–46; Holt, *Fate of Their Country*, 51–55; *National Era*, May 31, January 4, 11, 1849; *North Star*, June 27, 1849 (*Richmond Whig* quotation).

14. *National Era*, May 31, January 4, 11, 1849; Stanley Harrold, *Gamaliel Bailey and the Antislavery Union* (Kent, Ohio: Kent State University Press, 1986), 130–32.

15. John C. Waugh, *On the Brink of Civil War: The Compromise of 1850 and How*

It Changed the Course of American History (Wilmington, Del.: Scholarly Resources, 2003), 38–48; Holt, *Fate of Their Country*, 51, 56–58. On the centrality of the border dispute to the crisis, see Mark J. Stegmaier, *Texas, New Mexico, and the Compromise of 1850: Boundary Dispute and Sectional Crisis* (Kent, Ohio: Kent State University Press, 1996).

16. Josephine F. Pacheco, *Pearl: A Failed Slave Escape on the Potomac* (Chapel Hill: University of North Carolina Press, 2005), 173–75, 195; Waugh, *On the Brink*, 48–52; *Congressional Globe*, 31st Cong., 1st sess., 27–35.

17. Waugh, *On the Brink*, 48–52; *Congressional Globe*, 31st Cong., 1st sess., 27–35.

18. *Congressional Globe*, 31st Cong., 1st sess., 27–35; Holt, *Rise and Fall of the American Whig Party*, 472.

19. Salmon P. Chase to Edwin Stanton, December 14, 1849, Chase Papers, HSP; Wilentz, *Rise of American Democracy*, 631.

20. *Speech of T. L. Clingman, of North Carolina, in Defense of the South against the Aggressive Movement of the North* (Washington, D.C.: Gideon and Co., 1850); John C. Inscoe, *Mountain Masters, Slavery, and the Sectional Crisis in Western North Carolina* (Knoxville: University of Tennessee Press, 1989), 7, 185–91.

21. Holt, *Fate of Their Country*, 58–67; Waugh, *On the Brink*, 52–55.

22. Waugh, *On the Brink*, 74–75; *New York Herald*, February 1, 4, 8, 1850; *Daily National Intelligencer*, January 29, 1850.

23. Holt, *Fate of Their Country*, 70–71.

24. *Congressional Globe*, 31st Cong., 1st sess., 319–23, and Appendix, 138–41.

25. *Congressional Globe*, 31st Cong., 1st sess., 319–23, and Appendix, 138–41; *Liberator*, February 22, March 1, 1850.

26. *Congressional Globe*, 31st Cong., 1st sess., Appendix, 138–41; *Washington Daily Union*, March 2, 1850; *Philadelphia Public Ledger*, February 20, 25, 1850.

27. Michael A. Morrison, "American Reaction to European Revolutions, 1848–1852: Sectionalism, Memory, and the Revolutionary Heritage," *Civil War History* 49 (June 2003): 114–22 (quotations, 119); Fox-Genovese and Genovese, *Mind of the Master Class*, 41–68; *Friends' Intelligencer* (Philadelphia), March 16, 1850.

28. Fox-Genovese and Genovese, *Mind of the Master Class*, 53, 68 (quotation); *Congressional Globe*, 31st Cong., 1st sess., 451–55.

29. Salmon P. Chase to L. S. Abbott, March 6, 1850, Chase Papers, HSP.

30. *Congressional Globe*, 31st Cong., 1st sess., 481–84.

31. Ibid.

32. Waugh, *On the Brink*, 106; *Washington Daily Union*, March 6, 12, 1850; *Liberator*, March 22, April 5, 19, 1850; Wilentz, *Rise of American Democracy*, 641.

33. *Liberator*, March 22, April 5, 19, 1850.

34. William Seward, "Freedom in the New Territories," in George E. Baker, ed., *The Works of William H. Seward*, vol. 1 (New York: Redfield, 1853), 74–93.

35. Ibid., 88–90.

36. "Political Miscellany," *Democratic Review* 26 (March 1850): 279; "Abolition vs. Christianity and the Union," *Democratic Review* 27 (July 1850): 5–7; *Congressional Globe*, 31st Cong., 1st sess., Appendix, 393.

37. Cooper, *South and the Politics of Slavery*, 291–97; J. Mills Thornton III, *Politics and Power in a Slave Society: Alabama, 1800–1860* (Baton Rouge: Louisiana State University Press, 1978), 186–89; Walther, *Fire-eaters*, 141 (Rhett quotation).

38. Holt, *Fate of Their Country*, 72–73; Cooper, *South and the Politics of Slavery*, 291.

39. *Congressional Globe*, 31st Cong., 1st sess., Appendix, 693–95 (Trotti quoted in John Crowell speech); Freehling, *Road to Disunion*, 1:481–85; Thelma Jennings, *The Nashville Convention: Southern Movement for Unity, 1848–1850* (Memphis: Memphis State University Press, 1980).

40. Betty L. Mitchell, *Edmund Ruffin: A Biography* (Bloomington: Indiana University Press, 1981), 59–73 (quotations, 70, 72–73); Wilentz, *Rise of American Democracy*, 615–16; Eric H. Walther, *William Lowndes Yancey and the Coming of the Civil War* (Chapel Hill: University of North Carolina Press, 2006), 73, 131–32.

41. A Southron [pseud.], "The True Issue between Parties in the South: Union or Disunion," *American Whig Review* 12 (December 1850): 587–602; Atkins, *Parties, Politics*, 165; *Congressional Globe*, 31st Cong., 1st sess., Appendix, 344.

42. Thornton, *Politics and Power*, 186–89; Cooper, *South and the Politics of Slavery*, 291–97.

43. Carey, *Parties, Slavery*, 161–65.

44. Waugh, *On the Brink*, 177–81; Holt, *Fate of Their Country*, 79–80.

45. Freehling, *Road to Disunion*, 1:508–10; George W. Julian, *Speeches on Political Questions* (New York: Hurd and Houghton, 1872), 26, 47.

46. Freehling, *Road to Disunion*, 1:508–10.

47. Jennings, *Nashville Convention*; Holt, *Fate of Their Country*, 82–85.

48. William J. Cooper Jr., *Jefferson Davis: American* (New York: Vintage, 2001), 221–38; Jefferson Davis, "Speech at Fayette, July 11, 1851," in Lynda Lasswell Crist, ed., *The Papers of Jefferson Davis*, vol. 4, *1849–1852* (Baton Rouge: Louisiana State University Press, 1983), 201, 211.

49. Carey, *Parties, Slavery*, 161–65.

50. Ibid., 168–72; Christopher J. Olsen, *Political Culture and Secession in Missis-*

sippi: Masculinity, Honor, and the Antiparty Tradition, 1830–1860 (New York: Oxford University Press, 2000), 49–51; A Southron [pseud.], "The True Issue."

51. *National Era*, December 5, 1850.

52. William G. Shade, *Democratizing the Old Dominion: Virginia and the Second Party System, 1824–1861* (Charlottesville: University Press of Virginia, 1996), 225, 257–59; William A. Link, *Roots of Secession: Slavery and Politics in Antebellum Virginia* (Chapel Hill: University of North Carolina Press, 2003), 140–41.

53. *Liberator*, August 9, 1850; William C. Davis, *Rhett*, 208, 278; Walther, *Fire-eaters*, 144; Georgia [pseud.], "Plain Words for the North," *American Whig Review* 12 (December 1850): 555–56.

54. Freehling, *Road to Disunion*, 1:475, 530–31; *Charleston Mercury*, as quoted in the *New York Times*, October 23, 1851; Ford, *Origins of Southern Radicalism*, 198–209; Barnwell, *Love of Order*, 157–59.

55. *Pennsylvania Freeman*, October 31, 1850.

CHAPTER 7

1. Fehrenbacher, *Slaveholding Republic*, 231–33.

2. Ibid., 232 (quotation); Clinton, *Harriet Tubman*, 57; William Still, *The Underground Railroad* (1871; reprint, Chicago: Johnson Publishing Co., Inc., 1970), 361–65.

3. Fehrenbacher, *Slaveholding Republic*, 234–35 (quotation); Freehling, *Road to Disunion*, 2:63–64; *Congressional Globe*, 31st Cong., 2nd sess., Appendix, 295, 304, 320, and 32nd Cong., 1st sess., Appendix, 1102–17.

4. Carol Wilson, "Active Vigilance Is the Price of Liberty: Black Self-Defense against Fugitive Slave Recapture and Kidnapping of Free Blacks," in John R. McKivigan and Stanley Harrold, eds., *Antislavery Violence: Sectional, Racial, and Cultural Conflict in Antebellum America* (Knoxville: University of Tennessee Press, 1999), 120–21.

5. Mayer, *All on Fire*, 428–31; Philip Foner, ed., *Frederick Douglass on Slavery and the Civil War: Selections from His Writings* (Mineola, N.Y.: Dover, 2003), 39–41; *Frederick Douglass' Paper*, October 30, 1851.

6. Delaney, excerpts from *The Condition, Elevation and Destiny*, in Deirdre Mullane, ed., *Crossing the Danger Water: Three Hundred Years of African-American Writing* (New York: Anchor, 1993), 124–27; Ripley, *Witness for Freedom*, 195–96. On black nationalism, see Rael, *Black Identity and Black Protest* and "Black Theodicy: African Americans and Nationalism in the Antebellum North," *North Star: A Journal of African American Religious History* 3 (Spring 2000): 9–12.

7. Link, *Roots of Secession*, 6–8, 37–38; Midori Takagi, *"Rearing Wolves to Our Own Destruction": Slavery in Richmond, Virginia, 1782–1865* (Charlottesville: University Press of Virginia, 1999), 72–78.

8. Link, *Roots of Secession*, 80–81.

9. Ibid., 97–100.

10. Ibid., 110; *Liberator*, March 9, 1855; Albert J. Von Frank, *The Trials of Anthony Burns: Freedom and Slavery in Emerson's Boston* (Cambridge: Harvard University Press, 1998), 59 (Parker quotation).

11. Link, *Roots of Secession*, 110; *Congressional Globe*, 33rd Cong., 1st sess., Appendix, 1037–39.

12. Hagedorn, *Beyond the River*, 242–52; Clinton, *Harriet Tubman*, 81–91.

13. Still, *Underground Railroad*.

14. Hagedorn, *Beyond the River*, 242–52; Clinton, *Harriet Tubman*, 81–91.

15. Joan D. Hedrick, *Harriet Beecher Stowe: A Life* (New York: Oxford University Press, 1994), 211–15.

16. Walter Johnson, *Soul by Soul: Life Inside the Antebellum Slave Market* (Cambridge: Harvard University Press, 1999), 218–19 (Pennington quoted on 218).

17. Hedrick, *Harriet Beecher Stowe*, 192–93.

18. *Frederick Douglass' Paper* (Rochester, N.Y.), January 7, 1853. On romantic racialism, see George M. Frederickson, *The Black Image in the White Mind: The Debate on Afro-American Character and Destiny, 1817–1914* (New York: Harper and Row, 1971).

19. Robert S. Levine, *"Uncle Tom's Cabin* in *Frederick Douglass' Paper*: An Analysis of Reception," in Ammons, *Uncle Tom's Cabin*, 523–41; Pierson, *Free Hearts*, 78–80; Hedrick, *Harriet Beecher Stowe*, 236.

20. A. Woodward, *A Review of Uncle Tom's Cabin; or, An Essay on Slavery* (Cincinnati: Applegate and Co., 1853), 12; Varon, *We Mean to Be Counted*, 108; *New Orleans Daily Picayune*, June 7, 26, 1853; George Frederick Holmes, "Uncle Tom's Cabin," *Southern Literary Messenger* 18 (December 1852): 721–31.

21. Louisa S. McCord, "Uncle Tom's Cabin," *Southern Quarterly Review* 23 (January 1853): 109, 118–19. For background on McCord, see Elizabeth Fox-Genovese, *Within the Plantation Household: Black and White Women of the Old South* (Chapel Hill: University of North Carolina Press, 1988), 281–89.

22. Varon, *We Mean to Be Counted*, 108–11; *New York Independent*, October 28, 1852.

23. *Richmond Examiner*, December 6, 1853. While Stowe's novel was the most controversial Northern literary intervention in the slavery debates, the most con-

founding was Herman Melville's 1851 masterpiece, *Moby-Dick*. Modern-day scholars have read the book as an allegory of disunion—or, rather, as a series of alternate allegories. In one reading of the book, Ahab, the ship's captain, who is "monomaniacal" in his pursuit of the white whale, stands for none other than John C. Calhoun, obsessive in his pursuit of states' rights. In another interpretation, Ahab is William Lloyd Garrison, obsessive in his abolitionist zeal. And in a third, Ahab is Daniel Webster, who has sold his soul by supporting the Fugitive Slave Law. Ahab's ship, the *Pequod*, might represent the Union, the "ship of state" foundering on the shoals of fanaticism. Or perhaps the *Pequod* is a "ship of fools," and the white whale, Moby-Dick, symbolizes the Union—thus the sinking of the *Pequod* "[saves] the Union from its monomaniacal enemies." What is clear, according to Michael Paul Rogin, is that for Melville, "Ahab embodied all the dangers facing America in 1850"—he is the quintessential fanatic. Detractors of the novel, writing in the 1850s, saw Melville himself as a fanatic, motivated by "morbid self-esteem" and "licentiousness." Ahab's "ravings, and the ravings of some of the tributary characters, and the ravings of Mr. Melville himself," the *Southern Quarterly Review* observed in 1852, "are such as would justify a writ *de lunatico* against all the parties." Andrew Delbanco, *Melville: His World and Work* (New York: Knopf, 2005), 163–66; Michael Paul Rogin, *Subversive Genealogy: The Politics and Art of Herman Melville* (New York: Knopf, 1983), 107–8, 124, 134, 142–44; "Moby Dick; or, the Whale," *Democratic Review* 30 (January 1852): 93–94; *Southern Quarterly Review* 5 (January 1852): 262.

24. On Southern nationalism, see John McCardell, *The Idea of a Southern Nation: Southern Nationalists and Southern Nationalism, 1830–1860* (New York: Norton, 1979); Sinha, *Counterrevolution of Slavery*, 123.

25. Gienapp, *Origins of the Republican Party*, 16–27 (quotations, 17, 25); Wilentz, *Rise of American Democracy*, 663; Noel Ignatiev, *How the Irish Became White* (New York: Routledge, 1995); *New York Times*, July 7, 1852.

26. Cooper, *South and the Politics of Slavery*, 318–44 (quotations, 319, 334); Atkins, *Parties, Politics*, 175–83; Reid, *Origins of the American Civil War*, 131–33; Eric H. Walther, *The Shattering of the Union: America in the 1850s* (Wilmington, Del.: Scholarly Resources, 2004), 17–19 (quotation, 19); *Raleigh (N.C.) Standard*, as quoted in *Frederick Douglass' Paper*, July 23, 1852; Holt, *Rise and Fall of the American Whig Party*, 754–58.

27. *Frederick Douglass' Paper*, May 13, 1852; *Congressional Globe*, 32nd Cong., 1st sess., Appendix, 738–42, 1071–81.

28. *Congressional Globe*, 32nd Cong., 1st sess., Appendix, 738–42, 1071–81.

29. George Thacher, *"No Fellowship with Slavery": A Sermon Delivered June 29, 1856* (Meriden, Conn.: L. R. Webb, 1856).

30. Wilentz, *Rise of American Democracy*, 671–72.

31. Morrison, *Slavery and the American West*, 142–51 (first quotation, 146); Bestor, "American Civil War as a Constitutional Crisis," 348; Nicole Etcheson, *Bleeding Kansas: Contested Liberty in the Civil War Era* (Lawrence: University Press of Kansas, 2004), 9–15; *Congressional Globe*, 33rd Cong., 1st sess., Appendix, 459.

32. Eric Foner, *Free Soil*, 76, 94–95; "Appeal of the Independent Democrats," in T. Lloyd Benson, *The Caning of Senator Sumner* (Belmont, Calif.: Wadsworth/ Thomson Learning, 2004), 34–35.

33. "Appeal of the Independent Democrats," 34–45.

34. "Senator Andrew Butler's Speech on the Nebraska Bill, 24–25 February 1854," in Benson, *Caning of Senator Sumner*, 49–53; *Richmond Enquirer*, May 15, 1854.

35. *Congressional Globe*, 33rd Cong., 1st sess., Appendix, 447, 462–63; John Y. Simon, "Elihu B. Washburne," in *ANB* 22:750–51; Shakespeare, *Macbeth*, Act I, Scene VII.

36. *Frederick Douglass' Paper*, February 17, March 24, 1854.

37. Gienapp, *Origins of the Republican Party*, 240–41; Eric Foner, *Free Soil*, 127; Benson, *Caning of Senator Sumner*, 84–85.

38. Michael F. Holt, "Making and Mobilizing the Republican Party," in Robert F. Engs and Randall M. Miller, eds., *The Birth of the Grand Old Party: The Republicans' First Generation* (Philadelphia: University of Pennsylvania Press, 2002), 35; Bruce Levine, *Half Slave and Half Free*, 193–94; Pierson, *Free Hearts*, 115 (last quotation); James M. McPherson, *Battle Cry of Freedom*, 91.

39. Gienapp, *Origins of the Republican Party*, 91; Tyler Anbinder, *Nativism and Slavery: The Northern Know Nothings and the Politics of the 1850s* (New York: Oxford University Press, 1992); Mark Voss-Hubbard, *Beyond Party: Cultures of Antipartisanship in Northern Politics before the Civil War* (Baltimore: Johns Hopkins University Press, 2002); Benson, *Caning of Senator Sumner*, 84–85.

40. Anbinder, *Nativism and Slavery*, 44–45; Cooper, *South and the Politics of Slavery*, 368.

41. Frank Towers, *The Urban South and the Coming of the Civil War* (Charlottesville: University of Virginia Press, 2004).

42. Towers, *Urban South*, 15–21; Grimsted, *American Mobbing*, 229–32; Link, *Roots of Secession*, 123–25; Varon, *We Mean to Be Counted*, 97; Janet L. Coryell, *Neither Heroine nor Fool: Anna Ella Carroll of Maryland* (Kent, Ohio: Kent State University Press, 1990), 23.

43. Holt, "Making and Mobilizing the Republican Party," 37; Anbinder, *Nativism and Slavery*, 50 (Giddings quotation).

44. Etcheson, *Bleeding Kansas*, 29–39.

45. Ibid., 56–64 (quotation, 63); Gienapp, *Origins of the Republican Party*, 170–71; Benson, *Caning of Senator Sumner*, 94–95.

46. Etcheson, *Bleeding Kansas*, 65; Stauffer, *Black Hearts*, 196–97; Walther, *Shattering of the Union*, 67–69.

47. James M. McPherson, *Battle Cry of Freedom*, 141–44; Link, *Roots of Secession*, 132–34; Freehling, *Road to Disunion*, 2:92; *Boston Atlas*, as quoted in *Frederick Douglass' Paper*, June 29, 1855.

48. James M. McPherson, *Battle Cry of Freedom*, 140–44.

49. William Henry Seward, *The Dangers of Extending Slavery, and, The Contest and the Crisis* (Washington, D.C.: Buell and Blanchard, 1856), 15–16.

50. Ibid.; Blight, *Frederick Douglass's Civil War*, 31–32; Eric Foner, *Free Soil*, 118 (Greeley quotation).

51. Eric Foner, *Free Soil*, 119.

52. Seward, *Dangers of Extending Slavery*, 14.

53. "Speech by William Wells Brown," and "Uriah Boston to Frederick Douglass, Aug.–Sept. 1855," in Ripley, *Black Abolitionist Papers*, 4:249, 304–9.

54. Robert C. Williams, *Horace Greeley: Champion of American Freedom* (New York: New York University Press, 2006), 215 (Pike quotation).

55. "Uriah Boston to Frederick Douglass, Aug.–Sept. 1855," in Ripley, *Black Abolitionist Papers*, 4:309; *Frederick Douglass' Paper*, April 27, May 25, July 27, November 23, 1855; Stauffer, *Black Hearts*, 22–23.

56. Mayer, *All on Fire*, 446; Kristen A. Tegtmeier, "The Ladies of Lawrence are Arming!: The Gendered Nature of Sectional Violence in Early Kansas," in McKivigan and Harrold, *Antislavery Violence*, 223 (Robinson quotation); James M. McPherson, *Battle Cry of Freedom*, 148–49; Gienapp, *Origins of the Republican Party*, 298.

57. Bruce Levine, *Half Slave and Half Free*, 197–98; Oakes, *The Radical and the Republican*, 96–97.

58. Stauffer, *Black Hearts*, 27, 198–201 (quotations, 196, 198); Etcheson, *Bleeding Kansas*, 111–18 (quotation, 118).

59. James M. McPherson, *Battle Cry of Freedom*, 148–49.

60. Sumner, "The Crime against Kansas," in Benson, *Caning of Senator Sumner*, 99.

61. Ibid., 97–98, 104, 108, 155.

62. Benson, *Caning of Senator Sumner*, 122, 125, 129, 134, 173, 205 (newspaper quotations); *Liberator*, June 13, 1856.

63. Benson, *Caning of Senator Sumner*, 171, 179, 183; *Liberator*, May 30, 1856.

64. *Liberator*, May 30, 1856.

CHAPTER 8

1. Bedford Brown to James Buchanan, September 21, 1856, E. H. M. to Buchanan, September 21, 1856, Nathaniel Niles to Buchanan, September 20, 1856, and R. H. Glass to Buchanan, September 18, 1856, Buchanan Papers, HSP.

2. Jean H. Baker, *James Buchanan*, 56–74.

3. *The Tribune Almanac and Political Register for 1857* (New York: Greeley and McElrath, 1857); Walther, *Shattering of the Union*, 104–7.

4. Kenneth M. Stampp, *America in 1857: A Nation on the Brink* (New York: Oxford University Press, 1990), 8–9; John M. Sacher, *A Perfect War of Politics: Parties, Politicians, and Democracy in Louisiana, 1824–1861* (Baton Rouge: Louisiana State University Press, 2003), xiii, 253–63.

5. *Richmond Enquirer*, June 9, 1856; Link, *Roots of Secession*, 161–62; *Infidelity and Abolitionism: An Open Letter to the Friends of Religion, Morality, and the American Union* (N.p., 1856).

6. *York Democratic Press* (Pa.), June 24, September 2, 1856; "Reasons Why All Should Vote for James Buchanan," newspaper clipping, John Geary Scrapbook, vol. 4: 1852–57, Geary Family Papers, HSP; "The Disruption of Parties, Here and in Great Britain," *Democratic Review* 35 (March 1855): 157.

7. S. W. C., "Seward-Republicanism," *Democratic Review* 37 (January 1856): 25; J. G., "The Union—The Dangers Which Beset It," *Democratic Review* 37 (February 1856): 95; S. W. C., "Public Opinion," *Democratic Review* 37 (March 1856): 235; S. W. C., "Wisdom & Folly," *Democratic Review* 37 (July 1856): 572–73; *The Extension of Slavery: The Official Acts of Both Parties in Relation to This Question* (N.p., [1857?]).

8. *Liberator*, April 11, June 20, November 7, 1856.

9. Blight, *Frederick Douglass's Civil War*, 49–52 (Douglass quotation, 50); Frederick J. Blue, *No Taint of Compromise: Crusaders in Antislavery Politics* (Baton Rouge: Louisiana State University Press, 2005), 77 (Langston quotation).

10. Charles Ballance, quoted in Eric Foner, *Free Soil*, 209.

11. Oakes, *The Radical and the Republican*, 117; Laurie, *Beyond Garrison*, 266–68; Burin, *Slavery and the Peculiar Solution*, 93.

12. For an overview of these debates, see Stampp, "Race, Slavery and the Republican Party," *Imperiled Union*, 118–22, and Gienapp, *Origins of the Republican Party* (quotations, 354–55).

13. Stampp, "Race, Slavery and the Republican Party," *Imperiled Union*, 118–22; Gienapp, *Origins of the Republican Party*, 355.

14. Daniel Walker Howe, *The Political Culture of the American Whigs* (Chicago: University of Chicago Press, 1979), 272–80.

15. Phillip Shaw Paludan, "Lincoln and Negro Slavery: I Haven't Got Time for the Pain," *Journal of the Abraham Lincoln Association* 27 (Summer 2006): 1–23; Roy P. Basler, ed., *The Collected Works of Abraham Lincoln*, vol. 2: *1848–58* (New Brunswick: Rutgers University Press, 1953), 230–82 (quotations, 249, 255, 275–76 ["Speech at Peoria, Illinois, Oct. 16, 1854"]).

16. Richard J. Carwardine, *Lincoln: Profiles in Power* (London: Pearson Education Limited, 2003), 25–26, 65–66 (quotation, 65).

17. Basler, *Collected Works of Abraham Lincoln*, 349–50 ("Fragment on Sectionalism," ca. July 23, 1856), 270 ("Speech at Peoria, Illinois, Oct. 16, 1854"), 364–66 ("Speech at Kalamazoo, Michigan, Aug. 27, 1856"), 355 ("Speech at Galena, Illinois, July 23, 1856").

18. Susan Mary-Grant, *North over South: Northern Nationalism and American Identity in the Antebellum Era* (Lawrence: University Press of Kansas, 2000), 150–52; Basler, *Collected Works of Abraham Lincoln*, 362 ("Speech at Kalamazoo"), 385 ("Speech at Republican Banquet, Chicago, Illinois, Dec. 10, 1856"), 350–51 ("Fragment on Sectionalism"); Carwardine, *Lincoln*, 46.

19. Horace Greeley, *Recollections of a Busy Life* (New York: J. B. Ford and Co., 1868), 293; Freehling, *Road to Disunion*, 2:231; *New York Times*, August 25, October 21, 1856.

20. *New York Times*, October 21, 1856; Charles Wentworth Upham, *Life Explorations and Public Services of John Charles Frémont* (Boston: Ticknor and Fields, 1856), 348–55.

21. Upham, *Life Explorations*, 348–55; Gienapp, *Origins of the Republican Party*, 355–56; Earl J. Hess, *Liberty, Virtue, and Progress: Northerners and Their War for the Union* (New York: Fordham University Press, 1997), 10–12.

22. Pierson, *Free Hearts*, 130–33.

23. Thomas Starr, annotator, *Lincoln's Kalamazoo Address against Extending Slavery* (Detroit: Fine Book Circle, 1941), 21–22.

24. May, *Manifest Destiny's Underworld*, 59 (campaign song), 269–76; Amy S. Greenberg, *Manifest Manhood*, 135–69.

25. Jean H. Baker, *James Buchanan*, 72–73; Holt, *Fate of Their Country*, 118–19; Basler, *Collected Works of Abraham Lincoln*, 385.

26. S. W. C., "The Verdict of the People," *Democratic Review* 38 (December 1856): 348; "The Review under Its New Management," *Democratic Review* 40 (July 1857): 3.

27. Melba Jensen, "George Fitzhugh and the Economic Analysis of Slavery," in Mason I. Lowance Jr., ed., *A House Divided: The Antebellum Slavery Debates in America, 1776–1865* (Princeton: Princeton University Press, 2003), 129–41 (Fitzhugh quotation on 134–35).

28. Jensen, "George Fitzhugh," 129–41; O'Brien, *Conjectures of Order*, 976–80.

29. William J. Grayson, "The Hireling and the Slave," in Finkelman, *Defending Slavery*, 173–87; Basler, *Collected Works of Abraham Lincoln*, 222 ("Fragment on Slavery," July 1, [1854?]).

30. William A. Smith, *Lectures on the Philosophy and Practice of Slavery* (Nashville: Stevenson and Evans, 1856), 219, 291; O'Brien, *Conjectures of Order*, 964; Albert Taylor Bledsoe, *An Essay on Liberty and Slavery* (1856; reprint, Freeport, N.Y.: Books for Libraries Press, 1971), 298–300.

31. Bledsoe, *Essay on Liberty and Slavery*, 298–300; Peter S. Carmichael, *The Last Generation: Young Virginians in Peace, War, and Reunion* (Chapel Hill: University of North Carolina Press, 2005), 108–10; Link, *Roots of Secession*, 168; William Blair, *Virginia's Private War: Feeding Body and Soul in the Confederacy, 1861–1865* (New York: Oxford University Press, 1998), 29–30.

32. Walther, *Fire-eaters*, 144–47; *National Era*, November 20, December 18, 1856.

33. Olsen, *Political Culture*, 181–85; Stephen W. Berry II, *All That Makes a Man: Love and Ambition in the Civil War South* (New York: Oxford University Press, 2003), 47–49.

34. Walther, *Fire-eaters*, 179, 213–15 (Ruffin quoted on 252–53); Thornton, *Politics and Power*, 368–71; Sinha, *Counterrevolution of Slavery*, 188–90; Carey, *Parties, Slavery*, 205; "Southern Convention at Savannah," *De Bow's Review* 22 (February 1857): 121; *New Orleans Crescent*, as quoted in *National Era*, November 27, 1856.

35. Walther, *Fire-eaters*, 215; "Southern Convention at Savannah," *De Bow's Review* 22 (January 1857): 86–87.

36. Walther, *Fire-eaters*, 215; "Education at the South," *De Bow's Review* 21 (December 1856): 650–52.

37. Carey, *Parties, Slavery*, 208; Stampp, *America in 1857*, 186; Steven Hahn, *The Roots of Southern Populism: Yeoman Farmers and the Transformation of the Georgia Upcountry, 1850–1890* (New York: Oxford University, 1983), 86–87; Mark V. Wetherington, *Plain Folk's Fight: The Civil War and Reconstruction in Piney Woods Georgia* (Chapel Hill: University of North Carolina Press, 2005), 57–66 (quotations, 58, 61); *New York Times*, November 9, 1858.

38. Sinha, *Counterrevolution of Slavery*; Freehling, *Road to Disunion*, 2:22–23, 168, 172–73; "Southern Convention at Savannah," *De Bow's Review* 22 (February 1857): 219–24.

39. *Friends' Intelligencer*, March 28, 1857.

40. Paul Finkelman, *Dred Scott v. Sandford: A Brief History with Documents* (Boston: Bedford/St. Martin's, 1997), 1–22.

41. Wilentz, *Rise of American Democracy*, 709–10; Finkelman, *Dred Scott*, 22–31 (William Scott quoted on 22).

42. Freehling, *Road to Disunion*, 2:110; Finkelman, *Dred Scott*, 66 (Taney quotation), 112 (Curtis quotation); Stuart Streichler, *Justice Curtis in the Civil War Era: At the Crossroads of American Constitutionalism* (Charlottesville: University of Virginia Press, 2005), 129. Recently Austin Allen has argued that although the *Dred Scott* decision was innovative in its reliance on the doctrine of black inferiority, in another important sense the ruling "sat squarely within the general drift of Supreme Court doctrine since the mid-1820s." For Taney and the majority upheld the position that "states could not make people federal citizens by recognizing them as state citizens," emphasizing the "division of governing authority" between the states and the federal government. "A state's power to create new citizens stopped at its borders and conferred no legal standing within any other state"; likewise, only the federal government could confer federal citizenship. The majority in *Dred Scott* coupled this argument with the contention that free blacks and slaves alike, because of their inherent inferiority, lacked the will to consent to either state or federal citizenship. Austin Allen, "The Political Economy of Blackness: Citizenship, Corporations, and Race in Dred Scott," *Civil War History* 50 (September 2004): 229–60.

43. Finkelman, *Dred Scott*, 38–40; Streichler, *Justice Curtis*, 137–38, 143 (Taney quoted on 137).

44. Finkelman, *Dred Scott*, 120–22; Streichler, *Justice Curtis*, 139–40; Fehrenbacher, *Dred Scott Case*, 412.

45. Streichler, *Justice Curtis*, 145.

46. Fehrenbacher, *Dred Scott Case*, 433.

47. Finkelman, *Dred Scott*, 144 (Greeley quotation); Jean H. Baker, *James Buchanan*, 83–84; Wilentz, *Rise of American Democracy*, 707–8.

48. Finkelman, *Dred Scott*, 128–36 (quotation, 136); *Milledgeville Federal Union* (Georgia), March 31, 1857; *New York Herald*, March 12, 1857; *Philadelphia Public Ledger*, March 10, 1857.

49. Fehrenbacher, *Dred Scott Case*, 429–37.

50. *Liberator*, February 6, 13, 20, 1857; *New York Times*, January 20, 1857; Stampp, *America in 1857*, 128; Ruchames, *Letters of William Lloyd Garrison*, 419.

51. *Liberator*, February 6, 13, 20, 1857.

52. William Lloyd Garrison, "To the Antislavery Men and Women of the North," in

Ruchames, *Letters of William Lloyd Garrison*, 454–55; *Liberator*, March 18, 27, June 19, 1857; Ripley, *Black Abolitionist Papers*, 4:364 (Remond quotation).

53. Finkelman, *Dred Scott*, 146–62 (newspaper quotations); *Albany Evening Journal* (New York), March 7, 1857.

54. *Columbus Republican Journal* (Wisconsin), March 31, 1857; *The Case of Dred Scott in the United States Supreme Court* (New York: Greeley and McElrath, 1857), 102.

55. William Lloyd Garrison, "To the Antislavery Men and Women of the North," in Ruchames, *Letters of William Lloyd Garrison*, 454–55; Frederick Douglass, "The *Dred Scott* Decision," in Finkelman, *Dred Scott*, 169–82.

56. Mayer, *All on Fire*, 473; *Liberator*, March 28, 1857 (Wright quotation).

CHAPTER 9

1. John A. Bingham, *The Lecompton Conspiracy* (Washington, D.C.: Buell and Blanchard, 1858), 7–8.

2. Etcheson, *Bleeding Kansas*, 140–47; Freehling, *Road to Disunion*, 2:128–29.

3. Craig M. Simpson, *A Good Southerner: The Life of Henry A. Wise of Virginia* (Chapel Hill: University of North Carolina Press, 1985), 161; Etcheson, *Bleeding Kansas*, 148–57 (quotations, 153, 156).

4. Etcheson, *Bleeding Kansas*, 157–68; Walther, *Shattering of the Union*, 139–44.

5. *Congressional Globe*, 35th Cong., 1st sess., Appendix, 51–53, 62, 78, 125–26; Lawrence Massillon Keitt, *Admission of Kansas: Speech of Hon. Lawrence M. Keitt, of South Carolina, in the House of Representatives, March 9, 1858* (N.p.: Washington, D.C., 1858), 7; *Texas State Gazette* (Austin), May 15, 1858; Simpson, *Good Southerner*, 172.

6. Sinha, *Counterrevolution of Slavery*, 192; *Congressional Globe*, 35th Cong., 1st sess., Appendix, 51–53, 62, 125–26; Keitt, *Admission of Kansas*, 7; Berry, *All That Makes a Man*, 47–49; *New York Times*, January 6, 1857; Stampp, *America in 1857*, 121, 315.

7. Sinha, *Counterrevolution of Slavery*, 192; James Henry Hammond, "The Mudsill Speech," in Finkelman, *Defending Slavery*, 80–88.

8. *Congressional Globe*, 35th Cong., 1st sess., 939–45.

9. William R. G. Mellen to Frances Adeline Miller Seward, May 11, 1858, and S. Morris to William Seward, May 17, 1858, Seward Papers, Correspondence, May–December 1858, Microfilm Collection, Paley Library, Temple University.

10. Anson Burlingame, *An Appeal to Patriots against Disunion and Fraud* (Washington, D.C.: Buell and Blanchard, 1858), 6–8; *National Era*, April 15, 1858;

Congressional Globe, 35th Cong., 1st sess., Appendix, 168–74; *Proceedings of the Union Anti-Lecompton Mass Meeting of the Citizens of Erie County, N.Y.* (Buffalo, N.Y.: Commercial Advertiser Steam Press, 1858), 11–15.

11. David Brown, *Southern Outcast: Hinton Rowan Helper and the Impending Crisis of the South* (Baton Rouge: Louisiana State University Press, 2006), 111–15.

12. Hinton Helper, *The Impending Crisis of the South and How to Meet It*, ed. George Frederickson (1857; reprint, Cambridge: Belknap Press of Harvard University Press, 1968), x (Greeley quotation), 26, 32; *National Era*, July 23, 1857.

13. Helper, *Impending Crisis*, 111, 120–21, 139.

14. Potter, *Impending Crisis*, 394; *New York Evangelist*, August 6, 1857; *Congressional Globe*, 35th Cong., 1st sess., Apprndix, 196; Frederick Perry Stanton, *The Frauds in Kansas Illustrated* (Washington, D.C.: Buell and Blanchard, 1858), 15, and *Democratic Protests against the Lecompton Fraud* (N.p., 1858), 6–7; *Letters to the Great Democratic Anti-Lecompton Meeting* (Washington, D.C.: Lemuel Towers, 1858), 12 (quotation).

15. *Proceedings of the Union Anti-Lecompton Mass Meeting*, 13; *Congressional Globe*, 35th Cong., 1st sess., Appendix, 131–38, 518–24.

16. Cooper, *Jefferson Davis*, 295, 305–7; *New York Times*, May 26, 1858.

17. Jean H. Baker, *James Buchanan*, 104–6; Walther, *Shattering of the Union*, 144–45; Sinha, *Counterrevolution of Slavery*, 192–93; James M. McPherson, *Battle Cry*, 168–69; *New York Times*, May 19, 26, 1858; "Southern Convention at Montgomery, Alabama," *De Bow's Review* 24 (May 1858): 424–38. Kansas would enter the Union, in January 1861, as a free state.

18. Carwardine, *Lincoln*, 74–75.

19. Harold Holzer, ed., introduction to *The Lincoln-Douglas Debates: The First Complete, Unexpurgated Text* (New York: Harpercollins, 1993), 21–23.

20. Ibid.

21. Gienapp, *This Fiery Trial*, 43–44; Holzer, *Lincoln-Douglas Debates*, 157–58, 227–28.

22. Carwardine, *Lincoln*, 77; John Channing Briggs, *Lincoln's Speeches Reconsidered* (Baltimore: Johns Hopkins University Press, 2005), 169; Gienapp, *This Fiery Trial*, 48–50.

23. Holzer, *Lincoln-Douglas Debates*, 141–55 (quotations, 149, 153, 155). When Lincoln pressed Douglas to answer the question of whether the people of a territory could ever exclude slavery prior to the formation of a state constitution, Douglas responded with his "Freeport Doctrine"—the notion that since slavery depended on the enforcement of slave codes, by refraining to pass such laws a legislature could keep the institution out.

24. William Henry Seward, "The Irrepressible Conflict, Rochester, October 25, 1858," in George E. Baker, ed., *Works of William H. Seward*, vol. 4 (Boston: Houghton Mifflin, 1887), 289–302.

25. Ibid.

26. Ibid.; *Liberator*, November 5, 1858.

27. Eric Foner, *Free Soil*, 69–70.

28. Ibid., 70; Fehrenbacher, *Slaveholding Republic*, 298; Gienapp, as quoted in Doris Kearns Goodwin, *Team of Rivals: The Political Genius of Abraham Lincoln* (New York: Simon and Schuster, 2005), 192.

29. Seward, "Irrepressible Conflict."

30. James M. McPherson, *Battle Cry of Freedom*, 189–93; Rael, "Black Theodicy," 7; Mark W. Summers, *The Plundering Generation: Corruption and the Crisis of the Union, 1849–1861* (New York: Oxford University Press, 1987), 256, 281.

31. Holzer, *Lincoln-Douglas Debates*, 1; Walther, *Shattering of the Union*, 158–59; Potter, *Impending Crisis*, 355.

32. *Albany Atlas & Argus*, *Hartford Times*, and *New Haven Register*, as quoted in *Pittsfield Sun* (Mass.), November 11, December 9, 1858; *National Era*, December 16, 1858; Walther, *Shattering of the Union*, 159 (Hammond quotation).

33. *Liberator*, December 3, 1858; Cooper, *Jefferson Davis*, 314–16; *New York Times*, November 24, 1858; *National Era*, December 2, 1858, July 14, 1859.

34. William Kauffman Scarborough, ed., *The Diary of Edmund Ruffin*, vol. 1: *Toward Independence, October 1856–April 1861* (Baton Rouge: Louisiana State University Press, 1972), 222–24; Walther, *Shattering of the Union*, 148–49; *Liberator*, December 31, 1858.

35. *New York Times*, May 18, 1859; Walther, *Shattering of the Union*, 165; *Congressional Globe*, 35th Cong., 2nd sess., 242–43.

36. *National Era*, January 13, 20, 1859; *New York Times*, January 8, 13, 1859; *Congressional Globe*, 35th Cong., 2nd sess., 264–66, 299–302, 307–8, 333, 352; *Farmer's Cabinet* (Amherst, N.H.), January 19, 1859.

37. "Address of the Southern League," *De Bow's Review* 26 (March 1859): 346–47; "Southern Convention at Vicksburg, Pt. 2," *De Bow's Review* 26 (August 1859): 205–20; *National Era*, May 26, 1859; *New York Times*, May 19, 1859.

38. "Address of the Southern League," 346–47; "Southern Convention at Vicksburg, Pt. 2," 205–20; Cooper, *Jefferson Davis*, 500.

39. Potter, *Impending Crisis*, 402–4; *Farmer's Cabinet*, July 27, 1859; Alfred A. Smith, "A Southern Confederacy," *De Bow's Review* 26 (May 1859): 571.

40. *New York Observer*, June 30, 1859. On the generational argument, see Berry, *All That Makes a Man*, and Carmichael, *Last Generation*.

41. *New York Observer*, June 30, 1859.

42. John Stauffer and Zoe Trodd, eds., *Meteor of War: The John Brown Story* (Maplecrest, N.Y.: Brandywine Press, 2004); David S. Reynolds, *John Brown, Abolitionist: The Man Who Killed Slavery, Sparked the Civil War, and Seeded Civil Rights* (New York: Knopf, 2005); McCarthy and Stauffer, *Prophets of Protest*; Scott John Hammond, "John Brown as Founder: America's Violent Confrontation with Its First Principles," in Peggy A. Russo and Paul Finkelman, eds., *Terrible Swift Sword: The Legacy of John Brown* (Athens: Ohio University Press, 2005), 63 (quotations).

43. Reynolds, *John Brown*, 106–13; Hannah Geffert (with Jean Libby), "Regional Black Involvement in John Brown's Raid on Harper's Ferry," in McCarthy and Stauffer, *Prophets of Protest*, 166–68.

44. Reynolds, *John Brown*, 13; Potter, *Impending Crisis*, 364; Stauffer and Trodd, *Meteor of War*, 101.

45. John Brown, "Provisional Constitution," in Stauffer and Trodd, *Meteor of War*, 110–19; Kenneth R. Carroll, "A Psychological Examination of John Brown," in Russo and Finkelman, *Terrible Swift Sword*, 127–28; Reynolds, *John Brown*, 250–52.

46. Stauffer and Trodd, *Meteor of War*, 109–10, 119; Reynolds, *John Brown*, 253–54; Geffert, "Regional Black Involvement," 166–68.

47. Reynolds, *John Brown*, 310; Paul Finkelman, "John Brown and His Raid," in Finkelman, ed., *His Soul Goes Marching On: Responses to John Brown and the Harper's Ferry Raid* (Charlottesville: University Press of Virginia, 1995), 7–8.

48. Eyal Naveh, "John Brown and the Legacy of Martyrdom," in Russo and Finkelman, *Terrible Swift Sword*, 83 (quotation); Stauffer and Trodd, *Meteor of War*, 135, 232–51 (Thoreau quotation, 232, and Whitman quotation, 248); Reynolds, *John Brown*, 395 (John Brown quotation).

49. Charles Joyner, " 'Guilty of Holiest Crime': The Passion of John Brown," in Finkelman, *His Soul Goes Marching On*, 305 (*Enquirer* quotation); Ayers, *In the Presence of Mine Enemies*, 37 (Augusta Unionists' quotation); Varon, *We Mean to Be Counted*, 140 (Van Lew quotation).

50. Stauffer and Trodd, *Meteor of War*, 187 (Higginson quotation). On connections between Brown and Seward, see, e.g., *Charleston Mercury*, November 24, 1859; *Richmond Enquirer*, October 25, 1859; *Raleigh Register and North Carolina Gazette*, November 2, 1859; *Milledgeville Federal Union*, November 1, 1859; *Nashville Union and American*, October 21, 1859; *Wilmington Daily Herald* (North Carolina), December 5, 1859. On the election of 1860, see *Charleston*

Mercury, October 11, 1860, in Kenneth M. Stampp, ed., *The Causes of the Civil War* (New York: Simon and Schuster, 1991), 151.

51. Peter Wallenstein, "Incendiaries All: Southern Politics and the Harpers Ferry Raid," in Finkelman, *His Soul Goes Marching On*, 166 (quotation); Potter, *Impending Crisis*, 389; Roger A. Pryor, *Speech of Hon. Roger A. Pryor of Virginia, on the Principles and Policy of the Black Republican Party* (Washington, D.C.: Congressional Globe Office, 1859), 11–14. On the speakership controversy, see also David Brown, *Southern Outcast*, 166–71.

52. *New Hampshire Patriot* (Concord), October 26, 1859; *Cincinnati Enquirer*, October 19, 1859; *Springfield State Register* (Illinois), October 20, 1859; "Logical Results of Republicanism," *Democratic Review* 43 (October 1859): 201–17; John M. Belohavek, *Broken Glass: Caleb Cushing and the Shattering of the Union* (Kent, Ohio: Kent State University Press, 2005), 300–302. William Seward served as governor of New York from 1838 to 1842.

53. Peter Knupfer, "A Crisis in Conservatism: Northern Unionism and the Harpers Ferry Raid," in Finkelman, *His Soul Goes Marching On*, 134–36; *Liberator*, February 3, 1860; Edward McPherson, *Disorganization and Disunion: Speech of Hon. Edward McPherson of Pennsylvania: Delivered in the House of Representatives, Feb. 24, 1860* (Washington, D.C.: Buell and Blanchard, 1860); Henry L. Dawes, *The New Dogma of the South—"Slavery a Blessing"* (N.p.: Washington, D.C., 1860).

54. Knupfer, "Crisis in Conservatism," 134–36; Harold Holzer, *Lincoln at Cooper Union: The Speech That Made Abraham Lincoln President* (New York: Simon and Schuster, 2004), 117, 128–29, 136–37 (Lincoln quoted on 137).

55. Holzer, *Lincoln at Cooper Union*, 140–43 (Lincoln quoted on 143).

56. Ibid., 157, 167.

57. Frederick Douglass, "John Brown: An Address at the Fourteenth Anniversary of Storer College," in Trodd and Stauffer, *Meteor of War*, 210.

EPILOGUE

1. *Staunton Vindicator* (Virginia), March 22, 1860.

2. Charles B. Dew, *Apostles of Disunion: Southern Secession Commissioners and the Causes of the Civil War* (Charlottesville: University of Virginia Press, 2002); Potter, *Impending Crisis*, 500–502.

3. *Christian Banner* (Fredericksburg), as quoted in *Christian Observer*, September 27, 1860; Potter, *Impending Crisis*, 472–73; Link, *Roots of Secession*, 230–31; Thomas Dyer, *Secret Yankees: The Union Circle in Confederate Atlanta* (Bal-

timore: Johns Hopkins University Press, 1999), 30–31, 44–48; John Minor Botts, *Union or Disunion: The Union Cannot and Shall Not be Dissolved* ([Lynchburg?]: 1860), 23; Ayers, *In the Presence of Mine Enemies*, 137.

4. Botts, *Union or Disunion*, 2, 8, 11; Link, *Roots of Secession*, 240–41; A. Roane, "The South: In the Union or Out of It," *De Bow's Review* 29 (October 1860): 448–65; B. M. Palmer, *The South: Her Peril, Her Duty* (New Orleans: N.p., 1860), 10–11.

5. Henry J. Van Dyke, *The Character and Influence of Abolitionism* (New York: George F. Nesbitt and Co., 1860), 27; *Boston (Catholic) Pilot*, as quoted in the *Liberator*, December 21, 1860; Belohavek, *Broken Glass*, 304–5 (Cushing quotation). See also C. L. Ward, *The Evils of Disunion: An Address Delivered at Smithfield, Bradford Co., Penn'a., July 4, 1861* (Towanda, Pa.: Argus Office, 1861).

6. Robert C. Williams, *Horace Greeley*, 217; *New York Independent*, December 6, 1860; Potter, *Impending Crisis*, 525–27. A few days after Greeley's editorial, *New York Times* founder and editor Henry J. Raymond expressed similar sentiments in a published letter to fire-eater William Yancey. For Raymond, secession was treason, and disunion meant war. The South was to blame for the "irrepressible conflict," he wrote, for slaveholders had insisting on forsaking the original Constitution and making a new one. And now they must face the consequences: Northerners did not seek the war, but they would fight it and "crush" the Southern "revolution." Henry J. Raymond, *Disunion and Slavery: A Series of Letters to Hon. W. L. Yancey, of Alabama, by Henry J. Raymond, of New York* (New York: N.p. 1860), 20, 27, 36.

7. Frances Seward quoted in Goodwin, *Team of Rivals*, 301–3.

8. Philip Foner, *Frederick Douglass: Selected Speeches*, 450; Ervin L. Jordan Jr., "Afro-Virginians' Attitudes on Secession and Civil War, 1861," in William C. Davis and James I. Robertson, eds., *Virginia at War, 1861* (Lexington: University Press of Kentucky, 2005), 89–90; Elizabeth R. Varon, *Southern Lady, Yankee Spy: The True Story of Elizabeth Van Lew, a Union Agent in the Heart of the Confederacy* (New York: Oxford University Press, 2003), 50 (Roane quotation).

9. John D'Entremont, *Southern Emancipator: Moncure Conway, The American Years, 1832–1865* (New York: Oxford University Press, 1987), 150–53; Wendell Phillips, *Disunion: Two Discourses at Music Hall, January 20th, and February 17th, 1861* (Boston: Robert F. Walcutt, 1861), 9–16.

10. Dyer, *Secret Yankees*, 51–52 (first quotation); Varon, *Southern Lady*; Richard E. Beringer et al., *The Elements of Confederate Defeat: Nationalism, War Aims, and Religion* (Athens: University of Georgia Press, 1989), 132–33 (second quotation);

Noel C. Fisher, *War at Every Door: Partisan Politics and Guerrilla Violence in East Tennessee, 1860–69* (Chapel Hill: University of North Carolina Press, 1997), 114–24; David Williams, *A People's History of the Civil War: Struggling for the Meaning of Freedom* (New York: New Press, 2005), 57; James M. McPherson, *Battle Cry of Freedom*, 693–96; Stephen V. Ash, ed., *Secessionists and Other Scoundrels: Selections from Parson Brownlow's Book* (Baton Rouge: Louisiana State University Press, 1999), 41–43 (third quotation). Southern opposition to the Confederacy ranged across a wide spectrum of beliefs. At one end were antislavery unconditional Unionists, such as John Minor Botts and Elizabeth Van Lew in Richmond and James A. Stewart in Atlanta, who adopted the perspective that emancipation was the key to Union victory and that the war would bring redemption to the South in the form of radical social change. Then there were those Southern Unionists, among them slaveholders, who feared radical change and who hoped that the war would somehow preserve their property and restore their political prominence, while undermining that of the secessionists. Unionist yeomen farmers who resented the master class constituted another complex interest group; they were ambivalent about emancipation—many accepted it to the extent that it was a punitive measure against secessionist planters, but most did not favor any change in the racial caste system. As the war's toll in death and destruction mounted, disillusioned Confederates added their own voices to the chorus of opposition to the Davis administration. The Confederate draft, from which the wealthy could exempt themselves, along with taxation, impressment, and the imposition of martial law, exacerbated class tensions and persuaded countless white Southerners that disunion had brought despotism. Some of the disillusioned joined the ranks of outright Unionists, while others protested Confederate policies in the hope of either reforming the Confederacy and reversing its fortunes or pressuring the government into a negotiated peace.

11. For the argument that Southern Unionism, dissent, and disillusionment were decisive factors in the Confederate defeat, see, e.g., William W. Freehling, *The South vs. the South: How Anti-Confederate Southerners Shaped the Course of the Civil War* (New York: Oxford University Press, 2001), and Armstead L. Robinson, *Bitter Fruits of Bondage: The Demise of Slavery and the Collapse of the Confederacy, 1861–1865* (Charlottesville: University of Virginia Press, 2005). Gary Gallagher, by contrast, stresses the resilience of Confederate patriotism in *The Confederate War: How Popular Will, Nationalism, and Military Strategy Could Not Stave Off Defeat* (Cambridge: Harvard University Press, 1997). For studies that emphasize the complexity of Southern nationalism, see, e.g., Blair, *Virginia's Private War*; Wetherington, *Plain Folk's Fight*; and Anne Sarah

Rubin, *A Shattered Nation: The Rise and Fall of the Confederacy, 1861–1868* (Chapel Hill: University of North Carolina Press, 2005). For insights into the struggle of one prominent Confederate to cast off old loyalties and assume new ones, see Joan E. Cashin, *First Lady of the Confederacy: Varina Davis's Civil War* (Cambridge, Mass.: Belknap Press, 2006).

12. Russell F. Weigley, *A Great Civil War: A Military and Political History, 1861–1865* (Bloomington: Indiana University Press, 2000), xxvii.

13. Ripley, *Witness for Freedom*, 229 (Bell quotation); Frederick Douglass, "The Mission of the War," in Philip Foner, *Frederick Douglass: Selected Speeches*, 553–62; "Democratic Party of Pennsylvania, Resolutions 1862," in Vaux Family Papers, HSP; *Valley Spirit* (Chambersburg, Pa.), December 17, 1862; *Startling Record! The Great Disunion Conspiracy of Massachusetts!!* (N.p., 1863). On the election of 1864, see John C. Waugh, *Reelecting Lincoln: The Battle for the 1864 Presidency* (New York: Crown, 1997).

14. *Richmond Daily Dispatch*, April 18, 1864.

15. Douglass, "The Need for Continuing Anti-Slavery Work," in Philip Foner, *Frederick Douglass: Selected Speeches*, 578, 594.

16. *Valley Spirit*, August 2, 1865; *Staunton Spectator* (Virginia), February 6, 1866.

17. Blight, *Race and Reunion*; Douglass, "The United States Cannot Remain Half-Slave and Half-Free," in Philip Foner, *Frederick Douglass: Selected Speeches*, 661.

18. Susie King Taylor, *Reminiscences of My Life in Camp with the 33rd United States Colored Troops, Late 1st S.C. Volunteers* (Boston: Published by the Author, 1902), 61–62.

Bibliography

PRIMARY SOURCES

Manuscript and Archival Sources

Black Abolitionist Papers, Microfilm Collection, Clapp Library, Wellesley College, Wellesley, Massachusetts

James Buchanan Papers, Historical Society of Pennsylvania, Philadelphia

Salmon P. Chase Papers, Historical Society of Pennsylvania, Philadelphia

Edgehill-Randolph Papers, Alderman Library, University of Virginia, Charlottesville

Albert Gallatin Papers, Microfilm Collection, Paley Library, Temple University, Philadelphia

William Lloyd Garrison Papers, Abolition and Emancipation Collection, Microfilm Collection, Paley Library, Temple University, Philadelphia

Geary Family Papers, Historical Society of Pennsylvania, Philadelphia

Legislative Petitions to the General Assembly, Norfolk Borough, Library of Virginia, Richmond

Pennsylvania Abolition Society Papers, Historical Society of Pennsylvania, Philadelphia

William H. Seward Papers, Microfilm Collection, Paley Library, Temple University, Philadelphia

Vaux Family Papers, Historical Society of Pennsylvania, Philadelphia

Official Papers

Annals of the Congress of the United States. 1st Congress–16th Congress (1789–1820).

Byrd, Robert C., ed. *The Senate, 1789–1989.* Vol. 3: *Classic Speeches, 1830–1993.* Washington, D.C.: Government Printing Office, 1994.

Congressional Globe. 23rd Congress–36th Congress (1835–61).

Prigg v. Pennsylvania, Supreme Court of the United States (1842), 41 U.S. 539.

Register of Debates in Congress. 18th Congress–25th Congress (1824–37).

Richardson, James D., comp. *A Compilation of the Messages and Papers of the Presidents, 1789–1897.* 10 vols. Washington, D.C.: Government Printing Office, 1897.

Smock, Raymond W., ed. *Landmark Documents on the U.S. Congress.* Washington, D.C.: Congressional Quarterly Press, 1999.

Newspapers

Albany Evening Journal (New York)

Brooklyn Daily Eagle

Carolina Centinel (New Bern, N.C.)

Charleston Mercury

Chicago Tribune

Cincinnati Daily Enquirer

City of Washington Gazette

Colored American (New York)

Columbus Republican Journal (Wisconsin) (www.furman.edu/~benson/docs/)

Crisis (Richmond)

Daily National Intelligencer (Washington, D.C.)

Emancipator (New York)

Farmer's Cabinet (Amherst, N.H.) (Early American Newspapers, ser. 1, 1690–1876)

Frederick Douglass' Paper (Rochester, N.Y.)

Freedom's Journal (New York)

Friends' Intelligencer (Philadelphia)

Illinois State Register (Springfield) (www.furman.edu/~benson/docs/)

Liberator (Boston)

Louisville Daily Democrat (Kentucky)

Milledgeville Federal Union (Georgia) (www.furman.edu/~benson/docs/)

Nashville Union and American

National Anti-Slavery Standard (New York)

National Enquirer (Philadelphia)

National Era (Washington, D.C.)

New Hampshire Patriot (Concord) (www.furman.edu/~benson/docs/)

New Orleans Bee

New Orleans Crescent

New Orleans Daily Picayune

New York Evangelist

New York Evening Post

New York Herald

New York Independent

New York Observer

New York Tribune

New York World

Niles' Weekly Register (Baltimore)

North Star (Rochester, N.Y.)

Palladium of Liberty (Columbus, Ohio)

Pennsylvania Freeman (Philadelphia)

Philadelphia Evening Bulletin

Philadelphia Public Ledger

Philanthropist (Cincinnati)

Pittsfield Sun (Massachusetts) (Early American Newspapers, ser. 1, 1690–1876)

Raleigh Register and North Carolina Gazette

Rhode-Island American and Gazette (Providence)

Richmond Daily Dispatch

Richmond Enquirer

Richmond Whig

Salem Gazette (Massachusetts)

Springfield State Register (Illinois)

Staunton Spectator (Virginia)

Staunton Vindicator (Virginia)

Texas State Gazette (Austin)

Union, United States Gazette and True American (Philadelphia)

Valley Spirit (Chambersburg, Pa.)

Washington Daily Union (Washington, D.C.)

Weekly Advocate (New York)

Weekly Advocate Extra (New York)

Wilmington Daily Herald (North Carolina) (www.furman.edu/~benson/docs/)

York Democratic Press (Pennsylvania)

Magazines, Weekly Journals, and Periodicals

American Monthly Magazine (New York)

American Whig Review (New York)

Atlantic Monthly (Boston)

Continental Monthly (New York and Boston)

De Bow's Review (New Orleans and Charleston)

Harper's Weekly (New York)

North American Review (Boston)

Southern Literary Messenger (Richmond)

Southern Quarterly Review (New Orleans and Charleston)

United States Magazine and Democratic Review (New York)

LETTERS, DIARIES, REMINISCENCES, AUTOBIOGRAPHIES, PAMPHLETS, SPEECHES, PETITIONS, DOCUMENT COLLECTIONS, AND ANTHOLOGIES

Adams, John Quincy. *Speech of John Quincy Adams, of Massachusetts, upon the Right of the People, Men and Women, to Petition.* Washington, D.C.: Gales and Seaton, 1838.

Allen, George. *Mr. Allen's Speech before the Convention of Ministers.* Boston: Isaac Knapp, 1838.

American Anti-Slavery Society. *Disunion: Address of the American Anti-Slavery Society; and F. Jackson's Letter on the Pro-Slavery Character of the Constitution.* New York: American Anti-Slavery Society, 1845.

Archates [pseud.]. *Reflections, Occasioned by the Late Disturbances in Charleston.* Charleston: A. E. Miller, 1822.

Ash, Stephen V., ed. *Secessionists and Other Scoundrels: Selections from Parson Brownlow's Book.* Baton Rouge: Louisiana State University Press, 1999.

Baker, George E., ed. *The Works of William H. Seward*. Vol. 1. New York: Redfield, 1853.

———. *The Works of William H. Seward*. Vol. 4. Boston: Houghton Mifflin, 1887.

Ball, Charles. *Slavery in the United States: A Narrative of the Life and Adventures of Charles Ball*. New York: John S. Taylor, 1837.

Banning, Lance, ed. *Liberty and Order: The First American Party Struggle*. Indianapolis: Liberty Fund, 2004.

Basler, Roy P., ed. *The Collected Works of Abraham Lincoln*. Vol. 2: *1848–58*. New Brunswick: Rutgers University Press, 1953.

Bassett, William. *Letter to a Member of the Society of Friends, in Reply to Objections against Joining Antislavery Societies*. Boston: Isaac Knapp, 1837.

Beecher, Catharine E. *An Essay on Slavery and Abolition, with Reference to the Duty of American Females*. Philadelphia: Henry Perkins, 1837.

Billington, Ray Allen, ed. *The Journal of Charlotte Forten*. New York: Norton, 1953.

Bingham, John A. *The Lecompton Conspiracy*. Washington, D.C.: Buell and Blanchard, 1858.

Bledsoe, Albert Taylor. *An Essay on Liberty and Slavery*. 1856. Reprint, Freeport, N.Y.: Books for Libraries Press, 1971.

Boston Female Anti-Slavery Society. *Right and Wrong in Boston: Annual Report of the Boston Female Anti-Slavery Society*. Boston: Isaac Knapp, 1837.

Botts, John Minor. *Union or Disunion: The Union Cannot and Shall Not Be Dissolved*. [Lynchburg?], Va.: 1860.

Brown, Everett Somerville, ed. *The Missouri Compromise and Presidential Politics, 1820–1825: From the Letters of William Plumer, Jr.* St. Louis: Missouri Historical Society, 1926.

Brown, William Wells. *Anti-Slavery Harp: A Collection of Songs for Anti-Slavery Meetings*. Boston: Bela Marsh, 1849.

Burlingame, Anson. *An Appeal to Patriots against Disunion and Fraud*. Washington, D.C.: Buell and Blanchard, 1858.

Cain, William E., ed. *William Lloyd Garrison and the Fight against Slavery: Selections from the Liberator*. Boston: Bedford/St. Martin's, 1995.

The Case of Dred Scott in the United States Supreme Court. New York: Greeley and McElrath, 1857.

Ceplair, Larry, ed. *The Public Years of Sarah and Angelina Grimké: Selected Writings, 1835–1839*. New York: Columbia University Press, 1989.

Chapman, Maria Weston. *Right and Wrong in Massachusetts*. Boston: Dow and Jackson's Anti-Slavery Press, 1839.

Child, Lydia Maria. *An Appeal in Favor of That Class of Americans Called Africans*. Edited by Carlyn L. Karcher. 1833. Reprint, Amherst: University of Massachusetts Press, 1996.

Clingman, T. L. *Speech of T. L. Clingman, of North Carolina, in Defense of the South against the Aggressive Movement of the North*. Washington, D.C.: Gideon and Co., 1850.

Cobb, Joseph B. *Leisure Labors; or, Miscellanies Historical, Literary, and Political*. New York: D. Appleton, 1858.

Cralle, Richard K., ed. *The Works of John C. Calhoun*. Vol. 6. Columbia, S.C.: A. S. Johnston, 1851.

Crist, Lynda Laswell, ed. *The Papers of Jefferson Davis*. Vol. 4: *1849–1852*. Baton Rouge: Louisiana State University Press, 1983.

Davis, David Brion, ed. *Antebellum American Culture: An Interpretive Anthology*. Lexington, Mass.: Heath, 1979.

Davis, David Brion, and Stephen Mintz, eds. *The Boisterous Sea of Liberty: A Documentary History of America from Discovery through the Civil War*. New York: Oxford University Press, 1998.

Dawes, Henry L. *The New Dogma of the South—"Slavery a Blessing."* N.p.: Washington, D.C., 1860.

Dew, Thomas Roderick. "The Abolition of Negro Slavery." In *Confessions of Nat Turner and Related Documents*, edited by Kenneth S. Greenberg, 112–31. Boston: Bedford/St. Martin's, 1996.

Douglass, Frederick. *Narrative of the Life of Frederick Douglass: An American Slave, Written by Himself*. Edited by David W. Blight. Boston: Bedford/St. Martin's, 2003.

The Extension of Slavery: The Official Acts of Both Parties in Relation to This Question. N.p., [1857?].

Everett, Edward. *An Oration Delivered at Cambridge on the Fiftieth Anniversary of the Declaration of Independence of the United States of America*. Boston: Cummings, Hilliard and Co., 1826.

———. *Orations and Speeches, on Various Occasions*. Boston: American Stationers' Co., 1836.

Faust, Drew, ed. *The Ideology of Slavery: Proslavery Thought in the American South, 1830–1860*. Baton Rouge: Louisiana State University Press, 1981.

Foner, Philip, ed. *Frederick Douglass on Slavery and the Civil War: Selections from His Writings*. Mineola, N.Y.: Dover, 2003.

———, ed. *Frederick Douglass: Selected Speeches and Writings*. Chicago: Lawrence Hill Books, 1999.

Furman, Richard. *Exposition of the Views of the Baptists, Relative to the Coloured Population of the United States in Communication to the Governor of South Carolina*. Charleston: A. E. Miller, 1823.

Gienapp, William E., ed. *This Fiery Trial: The Speeches and Writings of Abraham Lincoln*. New York: Oxford University Press, 2002.

Greeley, Horace. *Recollections of a Busy Life*. New York: J. B. Ford and Co., 1868.

Greenberg, Kenneth S., ed. *The Confessions of Nat Turner and Related Documents*. Boston: Bedford/St. Martin's, 1996.

——, ed. *Nat Turner: A Slave Rebellion in History and Memory*. New York: Oxford University Press, 2003.

Grimké, Angelina Emily. "Appeal to the Christian Women of the South." In *The Public Years of Sarah and Angelina Grimké*, edited by Larry Ceplair. New York: Columbia University Press, 1989.

Grimké, Angelina, and Theodore Dwight Weld. *American Slavery as It Is: Testimony of a Thousand Witnesses*. 1839. Reprint, New York: Arno Press, 1988.

Grimké, Thomas S. *Oration on the Absolute Necessity of Union, and the Folly and Madness of Disunion, Delivered Fourth of July, 1809 and Speech of Thomas S. Grimké, Delivered in December, 1828, on the Constitutionality of the Tariff and on the True Nature of State Sovereignty*. Charleston: W. Riley, 1829.

Helper, Hinton. *The Impending Crisis of the South and How to Meet It*. Edited by George Frederickson. 1857. Reprint, Cambridge: Belknap Press of Harvard University Press, 1968.

Holzer, Harold, ed. *The Lincoln-Douglas Debates: The First Complete, Unexpurgated Text*. New York: Harpercollins, 1993.

Infidelity and Abolitionism: An Open Letter to the Friends of Religion, Morality, and the American Union. N.p., 1856.

Jacobs, Harriet. *Incidents in the Life of a Slave Girl*. Edited by Jean Fagan Yellin. Cambridge: Harvard University Press, 2000.

Janney, Samuel. *Memoirs of Samuel S. Janney: Late of Lincoln, Loudoun County, Va.* Philadelphia: Friends' Book Association, 1881.

Jay, William. *An Inquiry into the Character and Tendency of the American Colonization, and American Anti-Slavery Societies*. New York: Leavitt, Lord and Co., 1835.

Julian, George W. *Speeches on Political Questions*. New York: Hurd and Houghton, 1872.

Keitt, Lawrence Massillon. *Admission of Kansas: Speech of Hon. Lawrence M. Keitt, of South Carolina, in the House of Representatives, March 9, 1858*. N.p.: Washington, D.C., 1858.

Letters to the Great Democratic Anti-Lecompton Meeting. Washington, D.C.: Lemuel
   Towers, 1858.

Longstreet, Augustus Baldwin. *A Voice from the South*. Baltimore: Western
   Continent Press, 1847.

Lowance, Mason I., ed., Jr. *A House Divided: The Antebellum Slavery Debates in
   America, 1776–1865*. Princeton: Princeton University Press, 2003.

McPherson, Edward. *Disorganization and Disunion: Speech of Hon. Edward
   McPherson of Pennsylvania: Delivered in the House of Representatives, Feb. 24,
   1860*. Washington, D.C.: Buell and Blanchard, 1860.

Massachusetts Anti-Slavery Society. *An Account of the Interview Which Took Place
   on the Fourth & Eighth of March, between a Committee of the Massachusetts Anti-
   Slavery Society, and a Committee of the Legislature*. Boston: Massachusetts Anti-
   Slavery Society, 1836.

——. *Thirteenth Annual Report Presented to the Massachusetts Anti-Slavery Society*.
   Boston: Andrews, Prentiss and Studley, 1845.

Merrill, Walther M., ed. *The Letters of William Lloyd Garrison*. Vol. 3: *No Union
   with Slaveholders, 1841–1849*. Cambridge: Belknap Press of Harvard University
   Press, 1973.

Mullane, Deirdre, ed. *Crossing the Danger Water: Three Hundred Years of African-
   American Writing*. New York: Anchor, 1993.

Newman, Richard, Patrick Rael, and Phillip Lapansky, eds. *Pamphlets of Protest: An
   Anthology of Early African American Protest Literature*. New York: Routledge,
   2001.

Palfrey, John G. *Papers on the Slave Power*. Boston: Merrill, Cobb and Co., 1846.

Palmer, B. M. *The South: Her Peril, Her Duty*. New Orleans: N.p., 1860.

Pearson, Edward A., ed. *Designs against Charleston: The Trial Record of the
   Denmark Vesey Conspiracy of 1822*. Chapel Hill: University of North Carolina
   Press, 1999.

Peissner, Elias. *The American Question in Its National Aspect: Being Also an
   Incidental Reply to Mr. H. R. Helper's "Compendium of the Impending Crisis of
   the South."* New York: H. H. Lloyd and Co., 1861.

Pennington, James W. C. *Covenants Involving Moral Wrong Not Obligatory upon
   Man*. Hartford: John C. Wells, 1842.

Perdue, Theda, and Michael D. Green, eds. *Cherokee Removal: A Brief History with
   Documents*. Boston: Bedford/St. Martin's, 1995.

Phillips, Wendell. *Disunion: Two Discourses at Music Hall, January 20th, and
   February 17th, 1861*. Boston: Robert F. Walcutt, 1861.

*Proceedings of the Union Anti-Lecompton Mass Meeting of the Citizens of Erie
   County, N.Y.* Buffalo, N.Y.: Commercial Advertiser Steam Press, 1858.

Pryor, Roger A. *Speech of Hon. Roger A. Pryor of Virginia, on the Principles and Policy of the Black Republican Party*. Washington, D.C.: Congressional Globe Office, 1859.

Rankin, John. *Letters on American Slavery*. 1826. Reprint, Boston: Garrison and Knapp, 1833.

Raymond, Henry J. *Disunion and Slavery: A Series of Letters to Hon. W. L. Yancey, of Alabama, by Henry J. Raymond, of New York*. New York: N.p., 1861.

Reynolds, David S., ed. *Walt Whitman's Leaves of Grass: 150th Anniversary Edition*. New York: Oxford University Press, 2005.

Richardson, Marilyn, ed. *Maria Stewart: America's First Black Woman Political Writer: Essays and Speeches*. Bloomington: Indiana University Press, 1987.

Ripley, C. Peter, ed. *Witness for Freedom: African American Voices on Race, Slavery, and Emancipation*. Chapel Hill: University of North Carolina Press, 1993.

Ripley, C. Peter, et al., eds. *The Black Abolitionist Papers*. Vols. 1–5. Chapel Hill: University of North Carolina Press, 1985–91.

Roper, Moses. *Narrative of My Escape from Slavery*. 1837. Reprint, Mineola, N.Y.: Dover, 2003.

Rossiter, Clinton, ed. *The Federalist Papers: Alexander Hamilton, James Madison, John Jay*. New York: Mentor, 1999.

Ruchames, Louis, ed. *The Letters of William Lloyd Garrison*. Vol. 4: *From Disunion to the Brink of War, 1850–1860*. Cambridge: Belknap Press of Harvard University Press, 1975.

Scarborough, William Kauffman, ed. *The Diary of Edmund Ruffin*. Vol. 1: *Toward Independence, October 1856–April, 1861*. Baton Rouge: Louisiana State University Press, 1972.

Schweninger, Loren, ed. *The Southern Debate over Slavery*. Vol. 1: *Petitions to Southern Legislatures, 1778–1864*. Urbana: University of Illinois Press, 2001.

Seabrook, Whitemarsh. *Concise View of the Critical Situation, and Future Prospects of the Slave-Holding States, in Relation to Their Coloured Population*. Charleston: A. E. Miller, 1825.

Seward, William H. *The Dangers of Extending Slavery, and, The Contest and the Crisis: Two Speeches of William H. Seward*. Washington, D.C.: Buell and Blanchard, 1856.

Silbey, Joel H., ed. *The American Party Battle: Election Campaign Pamphlets, 1828–1876*. Vol. 1. Cambridge: Harvard University Press, 1999.

Smith, William A. D. D. *Lectures on the Philosophy and Practice of Slavery*. Nashville: Stevenson and Evans, 1856.

Southern States Rights. Charleston: Walker and Burke, 1844.

Speech of Mr. Slade, of Vt., on the Abolition of Slavery. Washington, D.C.: N.p., 1837.

Sprague, Stuart Seely, ed. *His Promised Land: The Autobiography of John P. Parker, Former Slave and Conductor on the Underground Railroad*. New York: Norton, 1996.

Stanton, Frederick Perry. *Democratic Protests against the Lecompton Fraud*. N.p.: Washington, D.C., 1858.

——. *The Frauds in Kansas Illustrated*. Washington, D.C.: Buell and Blanchard, 1858.

Starr, Thomas, annotator. *Lincoln's Kalamazoo Address against Extending Slavery*. Detroit: Fine Book Circle, 1941.

Startling Record! The Great Disunion Conspiracy of Massachusetts!! N.p., 1863.

Stauffer, John, and Zoe Trodd, eds. *Meteor of War: The John Brown Story*. Maplecrest, N.Y.: Brandywine Press, 2004.

Still, William. *The Underground Railroad*. 1872. Reprint, Chicago: Johnson Publishing Co., Inc., 1970.

Sumner, Charles. *Works of Charles Sumner*. Vol. 1. Boston: Lee and Shepard, 1870.

Taylor, Susie King. *Reminiscences of My Life in Camp with the 33rd United States Colored Troops, Late 1st S.C. Volunteers*. Boston: Published by the Author, 1902.

Thacher, George. *"No Fellowship with Slavery": A Sermon Delivered June 29, 1856*. Meriden, Conn.: L. R. Webb, 1856.

Thomas, John L., ed. *Slavery Attacked: The Abolitionist Crusade*. New York: Prentice Hall, 1965.

Thoreau, Henry David. *Civil Disobedience and Other Essays*. 1849. Reprint, Mineola, N.Y.: Dover, 1993.

The Tribune Almanac and Political Register for 1857. New York: Greeley and McElrath, 1857.

Tucker, Judge [Nathaniel] Beverly. *The Partisan Leader: A Novel, and an Apocalypse of the Origin and Struggles of the Southern Confederacy*. Edited by Thomas Ware. 1836. Reprint, Richmond: West and Johnson, 1862.

Upham, Charles Wentworth. *Life Explorations and Public Services of John Charles Frémont*. Boston: Ticknor and Fields, 1856.

Van Dyke, Henry J. *The Character and Influence of Abolitionism*. New York: George F. Nesbitt and Co., 1860.

Walker, David. *David Walker's Appeal to the Coloured Citizens of the World*. Edited by Peter P. Hinks. University Park: Pennsylvania State University Press, 2000.

Ward, C. L. *The Evils of Disunion: An Address Delivered at Smithfield, Bradford Co., Penn'a., July 4, 1861*. Towanda, Pa.: Argus Office, 1861.

Whitman, Walt. "American Workingmen, versus Slavery." In *A House Divided: The Antebellum Slavery Debates in America, 1776–1865,* edited by Mason I. Lowance Jr. Princeton: Princeton University Press, 2003.

Wilson, Clyde N., ed. *The Essential Calhoun.* New Brunswick, N.J.: Transaction Publishers, 2000.

———. *The Papers of John C. Calhoun.* Vol. 11: *1829–1832.* Columbia: University of South Carolina Press, 1978.

Windley, Latham, comp. *Runaway Slave Advertisements: A Documentary History from the 1730s to 1790.* Vol. 1. Westport, Conn.: Greenwood Press, 1983.

Woodward, A. *A Review of Uncle Tom's Cabin; or, An Essay on Slavery.* Cincinnati: Applegate and Co., 1853.

Wright, Louis B., and Marion Tinling, eds. *The Secret Diary of William Byrd of Westover, 1709–1712.* Richmond: Dietz Press, 1941.

SECONDARY SOURCES

Allen, Austin. "The Political Economy of Blackness: Citizenship, Corporations, and Race in Dred Scott." *Civil War History* 50 (September 2004): 229–60.

Allgor, Catherine. *A Perfect Union: Dolley Madison and the Creation of the American Nation.* New York: Henry Holt, 2005.

Altschuler, Glenn C., and Stuart Blumin. *Rude Republic: Americans and Their Politics in the Nineteenth Century.* Princeton: Princeton University Press, 2000.

Anbinder, Tyler. *Nativism and Slavery: The Northern Know Nothings and the Politics of the 1850s.* New York: Oxford University Press, 1992.

Ashworth, John. *Slavery, Capitalism, and Politics in the Antebellum Republic.* Vol. 1: *Commerce and Compromise, 1820–1850.* Cambridge, U.K.: Cambridge University Press, 1995.

Atkins, Jonathan M. *Parties, Politics, and the Sectional Conflict in Tennessee, 1832–1861.* Knoxville: University of Tennessee Press, 1997.

Ayers, Edward L. *In the Presence of Mine Enemies: War in the Heart of America, 1859–1863.* New York: Norton, 2003.

———. *What Caused the Civil War: Reflections on the South and Southern History.* New York: Norton, 2005.

Bacon, Margaret Hope. *But One Race: The Life of Robert Purvis.* Albany: State University of New York Press, 2007.

———. "By Moral Force Alone: The Antislavery Women and Nonresistance." In *The Abolitionist Sisterhood: Women's Political Culture in Antebellum America,* edited by Jean Fagan Yellin and John C. Van Horne, 275–300. Ithaca, N.Y.: Cornell University Press, 1994.

Baker, Jean H. *James Buchanan*. New York: Henry Holt, 2004.

Bardaglio, Peter W. *Reconstructing the Household: Families, Sex, and the Law in the Nineteenth-Century South*. Chapel Hill: University of North Carolina Press, 1995.

Barnwell, John. *Love of Order: South Carolina's First Secession Crisis*. Chapel Hill: University of North Carolina Press, 1982.

Bay, Mia. *The White Image in the Black Mind: African-American Ideas about White People, 1830–1925*. New York: Oxford University Press, 2000.

Beard, Charles, and Mary Beard. *The Rise of American Civilization*. New York: Macmillan, 1927.

Beeman, Richard, Stephen Botein, and Edward C. Carter III, eds. *Beyond Confederation: Origins of the Constitution and American National Identity*. Chapel Hill: University of North Carolina Press, 1987.

Belohavek, John M. *Broken Glass: Caleb Cushing and the Shattering of the Union*. Kent, Ohio: Kent State University Press, 2005.

Benedict, Michael Les. "Abraham Lincoln and Federalism." *Journal of the Abraham Lincoln Association* 10 (1988–89): 1–46.

Benson, T. Lloyd. *The Caning of Senator Sumner*. Belmont, Calif.: Wadsworth/Thomson Learning, 2004.

Beringer, Richard E., et al. *The Elements of Confederate Defeat: Nationalism, War Aims, and Religion*. Athens: University of Georgia Press, 1989.

Berkin, Carol. *A Brilliant Solution: Inventing the American Constitution*. New York: Harcourt, 2002.

Berlin, Ira. *Many Thousands Gone: The First Two Centuries of Slavery in North America*. Cambridge: Belknap Press of Harvard University Press, 1998.

——. *Slaves without Masters: The Free Negro in the Antebellum South*. New York: New Press, 1974.

Berry, Stephen W., II. *All That Makes a Man: Love and Ambition in the Civil War South*. New York: Oxford University Press, 2003.

Bestor, Arthur. "The American Civil War as a Constitutional Crisis." *American Historical Review* 69 (January 1964): 327–52.

Blair, William. *Virginia's Private War: Feeding Body and Soul in the Confederacy, 1861–1865*. New York: Oxford University Press, 1998.

Blatt, Martin H., and David Roediger, eds. *The Meaning of Slavery in the North*. New York: Garland Publishing, 1998.

Blight, David W. *Race and Reunion: The Civil War in American Memory*. Cambridge: Belknap Press of Harvard University Press, 2001.

Blue, Frederick J. *No Taint of Compromise: Crusaders in Antislavery Politics*. Baton Rouge: Louisiana State University Press, 2005.

Bolton, Charles C. "Planters, Plain Folk, and Poor Whites in the Old South." In *A Companion to the Civil War and Reconstruction*, edited by Lacy K. Ford, 75–93. Malden, Mass.: Blackwell, 2005.

Briggs, John Channing. *Lincoln's Speeches Reconsidered*. Baltimore: Johns Hopkins University Press, 2005.

Broadwater, Jeff. *George Mason: Forgotten Founder*. Chapel Hill: University of North Carolina Press, 2006.

Brown, David. *Southern Outcast: Hinton Rowan Helper and the Impending Crisis of the South*. Baton Rouge: Louisiana State University Press, 2006.

Brown, Kathleen M. *Good Wives, Nasty Wenches, and Anxious Patriarchs: Gender, Race, and Power in Colonial Virginia*. Chapel Hill: University of North Carolina Press, 1996.

Browne, Stephen Howard. *Angelina Grimké: Rhetoric, Identity, and the Radical Imagination*. East Lansing: Michigan State University Press, 1999.

Buel, Richard, Jr. *America on the Brink: How the Political Struggle over the War of 1812 Almost Destroyed the Young Republic*. New York: Palgrave Macmillan, 2005.

Burin, Eric. *Slavery and the Peculiar Solution: A History of the American Colonization Society*. Gainesville: University Press of Florida, 2005.

Carey, Anthony Gene. *Parties, Slavery, and the Union in Antebellum Georgia*. Athens: University of Georgia Press, 1997.

Carmichael, Peter S. *The Last Generation: Young Virginians in Peace, War, and Reunion*. Chapel Hill: University of North Carolina Press, 2005.

Carroll, Kenneth R. "A Psychological Examination of John Brown." In *Terrible Swift Sword: The Legacy of John Brown*, edited by Peggy A. Russo and Paul Finkelman, 118–40. Athens: Ohio University Press, 2005.

Carroll, Mark M. *Homesteads Ungovernable: Families, Sex, Race, and the Law in Frontier Texas, 1823–1860*. Austin: University of Texas Press, 2001.

Carwardine, Richard J. *Evangelicals and Politics in Antebellum America*. New Haven: Yale University Press, 1993.

——. *Lincoln: Profiles in Power*. London: Pearson Education Ltd., 2003.

Cashin, Joan E. *First Lady of the Confederacy: Varina Davis's Civil War*. Cambridge, Mass.: Belknap Press, 2006.

Channing, Steven A. *Crisis of Fear: Secession in South Carolina*. New York: Norton, 1970.

Clinton, Catherine. *Harriet Tubman: The Road to Freedom*. Little, Brown, 2004.

Cmiel, Kenneth. *Democratic Eloquence: The Fight over Popular Speech in Nineteenth-Century America*. New York: William Morrow, 1990.

Cooper, William J., Jr. *Jefferson Davis: American*. New York: Knopf, 2000.

——. *Liberty and Slavery: Southern Politics to 1860*. New York: Knopf, 1983.

——. *The South and the Politics of Slavery, 1828–1856*. Baton Rouge: Louisiana State University Press, 1978.

Cooper, William J., Jr., and Thomas E. Terrill. *The American South: A History*. New York: Knopf, 1990.

Coryell, Janet L. *Neither Heroine nor Fool: Anna Ella Carroll of Maryland*. Kent, Ohio: Kent State University Press, 1990.

Cotlar, Seth. "The Federalists' Transatlantic Cultural Offensive of 1798 and the Moderation of American Democratic Discourse." In *Beyond the Founders: New Approaches to the Political History of the Early American Republic*, edited by Jeffrey L. Pasley, Andrew W. Robertson, and David Waldstreicher, 274–302. Chapel Hill: University of North Carolina Press, 2004.

Craven, Avery O. *The Coming of the Civil War*. New York: Charles Scribner's Sons, 1942.

——. *The Repressible Conflict, 1830–1861*. Baton Rouge: Louisiana State University Press, 1939.

Crofts, Daniel. *Old Southampton: Politics and Society in a Virginia County, 1834–1869*. Charlottesville: University Press of Virginia, 1992.

Crowther, Edward R. *Southern Evangelicals and the Coming of the Civil War*. Lewiston, N.Y.: Edwin Mellen Press, 2000.

Curtis, Christopher. "'Can These Be the Sons of Their Fathers?': The Defense of Slavery in Virginia." M.A. thesis, Virginia Polytechnic Institute, 1997.

Cutter, Barbara. *Domestic Devils, Battlefield Angels: The Radicalism of American Womanhood, 1830–1865*. DeKalb: Northern Illinois University Press, 2003.

Daly, John Patrick. *When Slavery Was Called Freedom: Evangelicalism, Proslavery, and the Causes of the Civil War*. Lexington: University Press of Kentucky, 2002.

Darsey, James. *The Prophetic Tradition and Radical Rhetoric in America*. New York: New York University Press, 1997.

Davis, William C. *Rhett: The Turbulent Life and Times of a Fire-Eater*. Columbia: University of South Carolina Press, 2001.

Delbanco, Andrew. *Melville: His World and Work*. New York: Knopf, 2005.

Del Castillo, Richard Griswold. *The Treaty of Guadalupe Hidalgo: A Legacy of Conflict*. Norman: University of Oklahoma Press, 1990.

Densmore, Christopher. " 'Let Us Make Their Case Our Own': The Anti-Slavery Work of the Society of Friends in Philadelphia, 1754–1863." Manuscript lent to author.

D'Entremont, John. *Southern Emancipator: Moncure Conway, The American Years, 1832–1865*. New York: Oxford University Press, 1987.

Dew, Charles B. *Apostles of Disunion: Southern Secession Commissioners and the Causes of the Civil War*. Charlottesville: University of Virginia Press, 2002.

Deyle, Steven. *Carry Me Back: The Domestic Slave Trade in American Life*. New York: Oxford University Press, 2005.

Douglass, Anne. *The Feminization of American Culture*. New York: Knopf, 1977.

Du Bois, W. E. B. *Black Reconstruction: An Essay toward a History of the Part Which Black Folk Played in the Attempt to Reconstruct Democracy in America, 1860–1880*. New York: Russell and Russell, 1935.

Dunn, Susan. *Jefferson's Second Revolution: The Election Crisis of 1800 and the Triumph of Republicanism*. Boston: Houghton Mifflin, 2004.

Dyer, Thomas. *Secret Yankees: The Union Circle in Confederate Atlanta*. Baltimore: Johns Hopkins University Press, 1999.

Earle, Jonathan H. *Jacksonian Antislavery and the Politics of Free Soil, 1824–1854*. Chapel Hill: University of North Carolina Press, 2004.

Egerton, Douglas. *Gabriel's Rebellion: The Virginia Slave Conspiracies of 1800 and 1802*. Chapel Hill: University of North Carolina Press, 1993.

Ellis, Joseph. *American Sphinx: The Character of Thomas Jefferson*. New York: Vintage, 1998.

———. *Founding Brothers: The Revolutionary Generation*. New York: Vintage, 2002.

Ely, Melvin Patrick. *Israel on the Appomattox: A Southern Experiment in Black Freedom*. New York: Knopf, 2004.

Ericson, David F. *The Debate over Slavery: Antislavery and Proslavery Liberalism in Antebellum America*. New York: New York University Press, 2000.

Ernest, John. *Liberation Historiography: African American Writers and the Challenge of History, 1794–1861*. Chapel Hill: University of North Carolina Press, 2004.

Etcheson, Nicole. *Bleeding Kansas: Contested Liberty in the Civil War Era*. Lawrence: University Press of Kansas, 2004.

Fahs, Alice. *The Imagined Civil War: Popular Literature of the North and South, 1861–1865*. Chapel Hill: University of North Carolina Press, 2001.

Farber, Daniel A. "Completing the Work of the Framers: Lincoln's Constitutional Legacy." *Journal of the Abraham Lincoln Association* 27 (Winter 2006): 1–10.

Farrow, Anne, Joel Lang, and Jenifer Frank. *Complicity: How the North Promoted, Prolonged, and Profited from Slavery*. New York: Ballantine, 2005.

Faust, Drew Gilpin. *James Henry Hammond and the Old South: A Design for Mastery*. Baton Rouge: Louisiana State University Press, 1982.

Fehrenbacher, Donald E. *The Dred Scott Case: Its Significance in American Law and Politic*. New York: Oxford University Press, 1978.

———. *Sectional Crisis and Southern Constitutionalism*. Baton Rouge: Louisiana State University Press, 1995.

———. *The Slaveholding Republic: An Account of the United States Government's Relations to Slavery*. New York: Oxford University Press, 2002.

Finkelman, Paul. *Defending Slavery: Proslavery Thought in the Old South: A Brief History with Documents*. Boston: Bedford/St. Martin's, 2003.

———. *Dred Scott v. Sandford: A Brief History with Documents*. Boston: Bedford/St. Martin's, 1997.

———. "Jefferson and Slavery: 'Treason against the Hopes of Humanity.' " In *Jeffersonian Legacies*, edited by Peter Onuf, 181–224. Charlottesville: University of Virginia Press, 1993.

———. "John Brown and His Raid." In *His Soul Goes Marching On: Responses to John Brown and the Harpers Ferry Raid*, edited by Paul Finkelman, 3–9. Charlottesville: University Press of Virginia, 1995.

Fisher, Noel C. *War at Every Door: Partisan Politics and Guerrilla Violence in East Tennessee, 1860–1869*. Chapel Hill: University of North Carolina Press, 1997.

Foner, Eric. *Free Soil, Free Labor, Free Men: The Ideology of the Republican Party before the Civil War*. New York: Oxford University Press, 1970.

———. *Politics and Ideology in the Age of the Civil War*. New York: Oxford University Press, 1980.

———. *The Story of American Freedom: The Reality and the Mythic Ideal*. New York: Pan Macmillan, 2000.

Foos, Paul. *A Short, Offhand, Killing Affair: Soldiers and Social Conflict during the Mexican-American War*. Chapel Hill: University of North Carolina Press, 2002.

Ford, Lacy K. *Origins of Southern Radicalism: The South Carolina Upcountry, 1800–1860*. New York: Oxford University Press, 1988.

Foucault, Michel. *The History of Sexuality*. Vol. 1. New York: Pantheon Books, 1978.

Fox-Genovese, Elizabeth. *Within the Plantation Household: Black and White Women of the Old South*. Chapel Hill: University of North Carolina Press, 1988.

Fox-Genovese, Elizabeth, and Eugene D. Genovese. *The Mind of the Master Class: History and Faith in the Southern Slaveholders' World View*. New York: Cambridge University Press, 2005.

Franklin, John Hope, and Loren Schweninger. *Runaway Slaves: Rebels on the Plantation*. New York: Oxford University Press, 1999.

Frederickson, George M. *The Black Image in the White Mind: The Debate on Afro-American Character and Destiny, 1817–1914*. New York: Harper and Row, 1971.

Freehling, William W. *Prelude to Civil War: The Nullification Controversy in South Carolina, 1816–1836*. New York: Oxford University Press, 1992.

———. *The Road to Disunion*. Vol. 1: *Secessionists at Bay, 1776–1854*. New York: Oxford University Press, 1990.

———. *The Road to Disunion*. Vol. 2: *Secessionists Triumphant, 1854–1861*. New York: Oxford University Press, 2007.

———. *The South vs. the South: How Anti-Confederate Southerners Shaped the Course of the Civil War*. New York: Oxford University Press, 2001.

Freeman, Joanne B. *Affairs of Honor: National Politics in the New Republic*. New Haven: Yale University Press, 2001.

French, Scot. *The Rebellious Slave: Nat Turner in American Memory*. Boston: Houghton Mifflin, 2004.

Friedman, Lawrence J. *Gregarious Saints: Self and Community in American Abolitionism, 1830–1870*. New York: Cambridge University Press, 1982.

Gallagher, Gary W. *The Confederate War: How Popular Will, Nationalism, and Military Strategy Could Not Stave Off Defeat*. Cambridge: Harvard University Press, 1997.

Garraty, John A., and Mark C. Carnes, eds. *American National Biography*. 24 vols. New York: Oxford University Press, 1999.

Gates, Henry Louis, Jr. *The Trials of Phillis Wheatley: America's First Black Poet and Her Encounters with the Founding Fathers*. New York: Basic Civitas Books, 2003.

Geffert, Hannah, with Jean Libby. "Regional Black Involvement in John Brown's Raid on Harper's Ferry." In *Prophets of Protests: Reconsidering the History of American Abolitionism*, edited by Timothy Patrick McCarthy and John Stauffer, 165–79. New York: New Press, 2006.

Genovese, Eugene D. *Roll, Jordan, Roll: The World the Slaves Made*. New York: Vintage, 1972.

Gienapp, William E. *The Origins of the Republican Party, 1852–1856*. New York: Oxford University Press, 1986.

Ginzberg, Lori D. *Untidy Origins: A Story of Woman's Rights in Antebellum New York*. Chapel Hill: University of North Carolina Press, 2005.

Goetzmann, William H. *When the Eagle Screamed: The Romantic Horizon in American Diplomacy, 1800–1860*. New York: Wiley, 1966.

Goodwin, Doris Kearns. *Team of Rivals: The Political Genius of Abraham Lincoln*. New York: Simon and Schuster, 2005.

Grant, Susan-Mary. *North over South: Northern Nationalism and American Identity in the Antebellum Era*. Lawrence: University Press of Kansas, 2000.

Greenberg, Amy S. *Manifest Manhood and the Antebellum American Empire*. Cambridge: Cambridge University Press, 2005.

Greenberg, Kenneth S. *Honor and Slavery: Lies, Duels, Noses, Masks, Dressing as a Woman, Gifts, Strangers, Humanitarianism, Death, Slave Rebellions, the Proslavery Argument, Baseball, Hunting, and Gambling in the Old South*. Princeton: Princeton University Press, 1996.

Grimsted, David. *American Mobbing, 1828–1861: Toward Civil War*. New York: Oxford University Press, 1998.

Hadden, Sally E. *Slave Patrols: Law and Violence in Virginia and the Carolinas*. Cambridge: Harvard University Press, 2001.

Hagedorn, Ann. *Beyond the River: The Untold Story of the Heroes of the Underground Railroad*. New York: Simon and Schuster, 2004.

Hahn, Steven. *The Roots of Southern Populism: Yeoman Farmers and the Transformation of the Georgia Upcountry, 1850–1890*. New York: Oxford University Press, 1983.

Hammond, Scott John. "John Brown as Founder: America's Violent Confrontation with Its First Principles." In *Terrible Swift Sword: The Legacy of John Brown*, edited by Peggy A. Russo and Paul Finkelman, 61–76. Athens: Ohio University Press, 2005.

Hansen, Debra Gold. *Strained Sisterhood: Gender and Class in the Boston Female Anti-Slavery Society*. Amherst: University of Massachusetts Press, 1993.

Harris, Leslie M. *In the Shadow of Slavery: African-Americans in New York City, 1626–1863*. Chicago: University of Chicago Press, 2003.

Harrold, Stanley. *The Abolitionists and the South, 1831–1861*. Lexington: University Press of Kentucky, 1995.

———. *Gamaliel Bailey and the Antislavery Union*. Kent, Ohio: Kent State University Press, 1986.

———. *The Rise of Aggressive Abolitionism*. Lexington: University Press of Kentucky, 2004.

Haynes, Sam W. *James K. Polk and the Expansionist Impulse*. New York: Longman, 1997.

Hedrick, Joan D. *Harriet Beecher Stowe: A Life*. New York: Oxford University Press, 1994.

Hess, Earl J. *Liberty, Virtue, and Progress: Northerners and Their War for the Union*. New York: Fordham University Press, 1997.

Hietala, Thomas R. *Manifest Design: American Exceptionalism and Empire*. Ithaca, N.Y.: Cornell University Press, 1985.

Hinks, Peter P. *To Awaken My Afflicted Brethren: David Walker and the Problem of Antebellum Slave Resistance*. University Park: Pennsylvania State University Press, 1997.

Hoganson, Kristin. "Garrisonian Abolitionists and the Rhetoric of Gender, 1850–1860." *American Quarterly* 45 (December 1993): 558–95.

Holt, Michael F. *The Fate of Their Country: Politicians, Slavery Extension, and the Coming of the Civil War*. New York: Hill and Wang, 2004.

———. "Making and Mobilizing the Republican Party." In *The Birth of the Grand Old Party: The Republicans' First Generation*, edited by Robert F. Engs and Randall M. Miller, 29–59. Philadelphia: University of Pennsylvania Press, 2002.

———. *The Political Crisis of the 1850s*. New York: Wiley, 1978.

———. *The Rise and Fall of the American Whig Party: Jacksonian Politics and the Onset of the Civil War*. New York: Oxford University Press, 1999.

Holzer, Harold. *Lincoln at Cooper Union: The Speech That Made Abraham Lincoln President*. New York: Simon and Schuster, 2004.

Horsman, Reginald. *Race and Manifest Destiny: The Origins of American Racial Anglo-Saxonism*. Cambridge: Harvard University Press, 1981.

Horton, James Oliver, and Lois E. Horton. *Slavery and the Making of America*. New York: Oxford University Press, 2005.

Howe, Daniel Walker. *The Political Culture of the American Whigs*. Chicago: University of Chicago Press, 1979.

Huston, James L. *Calculating the Value of the Union: Slavery, Property Rights, and the Economic Origins of the Civil War*. Chapel Hill: University of North Carolina Press, 2003.

———. "Interpreting the Causation Sequence: The Meaning of the Events Leading to the Civil War." *Reviews in American History* 34 (September 2006): 324–31.

Ignatiev, Noel. *How the Irish Became White*. New York: Routledge, 1995.

Inscoe, John C. *Mountain Masters, Slavery, and the Sectional Crisis in Western North Carolina*. Knoxville: University of Tennessee Press, 1989.

Isenberg, Nancy. *Fallen Founder: The Life of Aaron Burr*. New York: Viking, 2007.

——. "The 'Little Emperor': Aaron Burr, Dandyism, and the Sexual Politics of Treason." In *Beyond the Founders: New Approaches to the Political History of the Early American Republic*, edited by Jeffrey L. Pasley, Andrew W. Robertson, and David Waldstreicher, 129–58. Chapel Hill: University of North Carolina Press, 2004.

——. *Sex and Citizenship in Antebellum America*. Chapel Hill: University of North Carolina Press, 1998.

Jeffrey, Julie Roy. *The Great Silent Army of Abolitionism: Ordinary Women in the Antislavery Movement*. Chapel Hill: University of North Carolina Press, 1998.

Jennings, Thelma. *The Nashville Convention: Southern Movement for Unity, 1848–1850*. Memphis: Memphis State University Press, 1980.

Jensen, Melba. "George Fitzhugh and the Economic Analysis of Slavery." In *A House Divided: The Antebellum Slavery Debates in America, 1776–1865*, edited by Mason I. Lowance Jr., 128–41. Princeton: Princeton University Press, 2003.

Johannsen, Robert W. *To the Halls of the Montezumas: The Mexican War in the American Imagination*. New York: Oxford University Press, 1985.

Johnson, Michael P. "Denmark Vesey and His Co-Conspirators." *William and Mary Quarterly* 58 (October 2001): 915–76.

Johnson, Walter. *Soul by Soul: Life Inside the Antebellum Slave Market*. Cambridge: Harvard University Press, 1999.

Jones, Howard. *Mutiny on the Amistad: The Saga of a Slave Revolt and Its Impact on American Abolition, Law and Diplomacy*. New York: Oxford University Press, 1997.

——. "The Peculiar Institution and National Honor: The Case of the *Creole* Slave Revolt." *Civil War History* 21 (March 1975): 28–50.

Jordan, Ervin L., Jr. "Afro-Virginians' Attitudes on Secession and Civil War, 1861." In *Virginia at War, 1861*, edited by William C. Davis and James I. Robertson, 89–112. Lexington: University Press of Kentucky, 2005.

Joyner, Charles. " 'Guilty of Holiest Crime': The Passion of John Brown." In *His Soul Goes Marching On: Responses to John Brown and the Harpers Ferry Raid*, edited by Paul Finkelman, 296–334. Charlottesville: University Press of Virginia, 1995.

Kersh, Rogan. *Dreams of a More Perfect Union*. Ithaca, N.Y.: Cornell University Press, 2001.

Kimmel, Michael. *Manhood in America: A Cultural History*. New York: Free Press, 1995.

Knupfer, Peter. "A Crisis in Conservatism: Northern Unionism and the Harpers Ferry Raid." In *His Soul Goes Marching On: Responses to John Brown and the Harpers Ferry Raid*, edited by Paul Finkelman, 119–48. Charlottesville: University Press of Virginia, 1995.

——. *The Union As It Is: Constitutional Unionism and Sectional Compromise, 1787–1861*. Chapel Hill: University of North Carolina Press, 1991.

Kolchin, Peter. *American Slavery, 1619–1877*. New York: Hill and Wang, 1993.

Kornblith, Gary J. "Rethinking the Coming of the Civil War: A Counterfactual Exercise." *Journal of American History* 90 (June 2003): 76–105.

Kornfeld, Eve. *Margaret Fuller: A Brief Biography with Documents*. Boston: Bedford Books, 1997.

Kraditor, Aileen S. *Means and Ends in American Abolitionism: Garrison and His Critics on Strategy and Tactics, 1834–1850*. New York: Pantheon Books, 1969.

Lankford, Nelson D. *Cry Havoc! The Crooked Road to Civil War, 1861*. New York: Viking, 2007.

Lapansky, Emma Jones. "'Since They Got Those Separate Churches': Afro-Americans and Racism in Jacksonian Philadelphia." *American Quarterly* 32 (Spring 1980): 54–78.

——. "The World the Agitators Made: The Counterculture of Agitation in Urban Philadelphia." In *The Abolitionist Sisterhood: Women's Political Culture in Antebellum America*, edited by Jean Fagan Yellin and John C. Van Horne, 91–100. Ithaca, N.Y.: Cornell University Press, 1994.

Lapansky, Phillip. "Graphic Discord: Abolitionist and Antiabolitonist Images." In *The Abolitionist Sisterhood: Women's Political Culture in Antebellum America*, edited by Jean Fagan Yellin and John C. Van Horne, 201–30. Ithaca, N.Y.: Cornell University Press, 1994.

Laurie, Bruce. *Beyond Garrison: Antislavery and Social Reform*. New York: Cambridge University Press, 2005.

Levine, Bruce. *Half Slave and Half Free: The Roots of the Civil War*. New York: Hill and Wang, 1992.

Levine, Robert S. "Uncle Tom's Cabin in Frederick Douglass's Paper: An Analysis of Reception." In *Uncle Tom's Cabin: A Norton Critical Edition*, edited by Elizabeth Ammons, 523–42. New York: Norton, 1994.

Link, William A. *Roots of Secession: Slavery and Politics in Antebellum Virginia*. Chapel Hill: University of North Carolina Press, 2003.

Lowery, Charles. *James Barbour: A Jeffersonian Republican*. University: University of Alabama Press, 1984.

Magdol, Edward. *The Antislavery Rank and File: A Social Profile of the Abolitionists' Constituency*. Westport, Conn.: Greenwood Press, 1986.

Malone, Dumas, ed. *Dictionary of American Biography*. 23 vols. New York: Charles Scribner's Sons, 1933.

Mason, Matthew. *Slavery and Politics in the Early American Republic*. Chapel Hill: University of North Carolina Press, 2006.

Masur, Louis P. *1831: Year of Eclipse*. New York: Hill and Wang, 2001.

———. "Nat Turner and Sectional Crisis." In *Nat Turner: A Slave Rebellion in History and Memory*, edited by Kenneth S. Greenberg, 148–61. New York: Oxford University Press, 2003.

May, Robert E. *Manifest Destiny's Underworld: Filibustering in Antebellum America*. Chapel Hill: University of North Carolina Press, 2002.

Mayer, Henry. *All on Fire: William Lloyd Garrison and the Abolition of Slavery*. Boston: St. Martin's Press, 1998.

McCardell, John. *The Idea of a Southern Nation: Southern Nationalists and Southern Nationalism, 1830–1860*. New York: Norton, 1979.

McCarthy, Timothy Patrick, and John Stauffer, eds. *Prophets of Protest: Reconsidering the History of American Abolitionism*. New York: New Press, 2006.

McCurry, Stephanie. *Masters of Small Worlds: Yeoman Households, Gender Relations, and the Political Culture of the Antebellum South Carolina Low Country*. New York: Oxford University Press, 1995.

McFeely, William S. *Frederick Douglass*. New York: Norton, 1991.

McKivigan, John R. "The Northern Churches and the Moral Problem of Slavery." In *The Meaning of Slavery in the North*, edited by Martin H. Blatt and David Roediger, 77–94. New York: Garland Publishing, 1998.

———. *The War against Proslavery Religion: Abolitionism and the Northern Churches, 1830–1865*. Ithaca, N.Y.: Cornell University Press, 1984.

McPherson, James M. *Battle Cry of Freedom: The Civil War Era*. New York: Oxford University Press, 1988.

Melish, Joan Pope. *Disowning Slavery: Gradual Emancipation and "Race" in New England*. Ithaca, N.Y.: Cornell University Press, 1998.

Menna, Larry K. "Southern Whiggery and Economic Development: The Meaning of Slavery within a National Context." In *The Meaning of Slavery in the North*, edited by Martin H. Blatt and Davis Roediger, 55–76. New York: Garland, 1998.

Merk, Frederick, with Lois Bannister Merk. *Manifest Destiny and Mission in American History*. Cambridge: Harvard University Press, 1963.

Miller, William Lee. *Arguing about Slavery: John Quincy Adams and the Great Battle in the United States Congress*. New York: Knopf, 1996.

Mitchell, Betty L. *Edmund Ruffin: A Biography*. Bloomington: Indiana University Press, 1981.

Morgan, Philip D. *Slave Counterpoint: Black Culture in the Eighteenth-Century Chesapeake and Lowcountry*. Chapel Hill: University of North Carolina Press, 1998.

Morone, James A. *Hellfire Nation: The Politics of Sin in American History*. New Haven, Conn.: Yale University Press, 2003.

Morris, Thomas D. *Free Men All: The Personal Liberty Laws of the North, 1780–1861*. Baltimore: Johns Hopkins University Press, 1974.

Morrison, Michael A. "American Reaction to European Revolutions, 1848–1852: Sectionalism, Memory, and the Revolutionary Heritage." *Civil War History* 49 (June 2003): 111–32.

———. *Slavery and the American West: The Eclipse of Manifest Destiny and the Coming of the Civil War*. Chapel Hill: University of North Carolina Press, 1997.

Moss, Elizabeth. *Domestic Novelists in the Old South: Defenders of Southern Culture*. Baton Rouge: Louisiana State University Press, 1992.

Nagel, Paul C. *This Sacred Trust: American Nationality, 1798–1898*. New York: Oxford University Press, 1971.

Nash, Gary B., and Jean R. Soderland. *Freedom by Degrees: Emancipation in Pennsylvania and Its Aftermath*. New York: Oxford University Press, 1991.

Naveh, Eyal. "John Brown and the Legacy of Martyrdom." In *Terrible Swift Sword: The Legacy of John Brown*, edited by Peggy A. Russo and Paul Finkelman, 77–90. Athens: Ohio University Press, 2005.

Newman, Richard S. "Protest in Black and White: The Formation and Transformation of an African American Political Community during the Early Republic." In *Beyond the Founders: New Approaches to the Political History of the Early American Republic*, edited by Jeffrey L. Pasley, Andrew W. Robertson, and David Waldstreicher, 180–206. Chapel Hill: University of North Carolina Press, 2004.

———. *The Transformation of American Abolitionism: Fighting Slavery in the Early Republic*. Chapel Hill: University of North Carolina Press, 2002.

Niven, John. *John C. Calhoun and the Price of Union: A Biography*. Baton Rouge: Louisiana State University Press, 1988.

Norton, Mary Beth. *Founding Mothers and Fathers: Gendered Power and the Forming of American Society*. New York: Vintage, 1997.

Oakes, James. *The Radical and the Republican: Frederick Douglass, Abraham Lincoln, and the Triumph of Antislavery Politics.* New York: Norton, 2007.

O'Brien, Michael. *Conjectures of Order; Intellectual Life and the American South, 1810–1860.* Vol. 2. Chapel Hill: University of North Carolina Press, 2004.

O'Connor, Thomas H. "Slavery in the North." In *The Meaning of Slavery in the North,* edited by David Roediger and Martin H. Blatt, 45–54. New York: Garland, 1998.

Olsen, Christopher J. *Political Culture and Secession in Mississippi: Masculinity, Honor, and the Antiparty Tradition, 1830–1860.* New York: Oxford University Press, 2000.

Onuf, Nicholas, and Peter Onuf. *Nations, Markets and War: Modern History and the American Civil War.* Charlottesville: University Press of Virginia, 2006.

Onuf, Peter S. *Jefferson's Empire: The Language of American Nationhood.* Charlottesville: University Press of Virginia, 2000.

Pacheco, Josephine F. *Pearl: A Failed Slave Escape on the Potomac.* Chapel Hill: University of North Carolina Press, 2005.

Paludan, Phillip Shaw. "Lincoln and Negro Slavery: I Haven't Got Time for the Pain." *Journal of the Abraham Lincoln Association* 27 (Summer 2006): 1–23.

Parent, Anthony S. *Foul Means: The Formation of a Slave Society in Virginia, 1660–1740.* Chapel Hill: University of North Carolina Press, 2003.

Parker, Alison M. "The Case for Reform Antecedents for the Woman's Rights Movement." In *Votes for Women: The Struggle for Suffrage Revisited,* edited by Jean H. Baker, 21–41. New York: Oxford University Press, 2002.

Pease, Jane H., and William H. Pease. *They Who Would Be Free: Blacks' Search for Freedom, 1830–1861.* New York: Atheneum, 1974.

——. *The Web of Progress: Private Values and Public Styles in Boston and Charleston, 1828–1843.* New York: Oxford University Press, 1985.

Perry, Lewis. *Radical Abolitionists: Anarchy and the Government of God in Antislavery Thought.* Ithaca, N.Y.: Cornell University Press, 1973.

Pessen, Edward. "How Different from Each Other Were the Antebellum North and South?" *American Historical Review* 85 (December 1980): 1119–49.

Pierson, Michael D. *Free Hearts, Free Homes: Gender and American Antislavery Politics.* Chapel Hill: University of North Carolina Press, 2003.

Potter, David M. *The Impending Crisis, 1848–1861.* New York: Harper and Row, 1976.

Pugh, David G. *Sons of Liberty: The Masculine Mind in Nineteenth-Century America.* Westport, Conn.: Greenwood Press, 1983.

Rael, Patrick. *Black Identity and Black Protest in the Antebellum North*. Chapel Hill: University of North Carolina Press, 2002.

———. "Black Theodicy: African Americans and Nationalism in the Antebellum North." *The North Star: A Journal of African American Religious History* 3 (Spring 2000): 1–24.

Randall, James G. "The Blundering Generation." *Mississippi Historical Review* 27 (June 1940): 3–28.

Ratner, Lorman A., and Dwight C. Teeter Jr. *Fanatics and Fire-Eaters: Newspapers and the Coming of the Civil War*. Champaign: University of Illinois Press, 2003.

Reid, Brian Holden. *The Origins of the American Civil War*. London: Longman, 1996.

Remini, Robert V. *Henry Clay: Statesman for the Union*. New York: Norton, 1991.

Reynolds, David S. *John Brown, Abolitionist: The Man Who Killed Slavery, Sparked the Civil War, and Seeded Civil Rights*. New York: Knopf, 2005.

Richards, Leonard L. *"Gentlemen of Property and Standing": Abolition Mobs in Jacksonian America*. New York: Oxford University Press, 1970.

———. *The Slave Power: The Free North and Southern Domination, 1780–1860*. Baton Rouge: Louisiana State University Press, 2000.

Robertson, Andrew W. *The Language of Democracy: Political Rhetoric in the United States and Britain, 1790–1900*. Charlottesville: University of Virginia Press, 2005.

———. " 'Look on This Picture . . . And on This!' Nationalism, Localism, and Partisan Images of Otherness in the United States, 1787–1820." *American Historical Review* 85 (December 1980): 1119–49.

———. "Voting Rites and Voting Acts: Electioneering Ritual, 1790–1820." In *Beyond the Founders: New Approaches to the Political History of the Early American Republic*, edited by Jeffrey L. Pasley, Andrew W. Robertson, and David Waldstreicher, 57–78. Chapel Hill: University of North Carolina Press, 2004.

Robinson, Armstead L. *Bitter Fruits of Bondage: The Demise of Slavery and the Collapse of the Confederacy, 1861–1865*. Charlottesville: University of Virginia Press, 2005.

Rodgers, Daniel T. *Contested Truths: Keywords in American Politics since Independence*. New York: Basic Books, 1987.

Rogin, Michael Paul. *Subversive Genealogy: The Politics and Art of Herman Melville*. New York: Knopf, 1983.

Rothman, Adam. *Slave Country: American Expansion and the Origins of the Deep South*. Cambridge: Harvard University Press, 2005.

Rubin, Anne Sarah. *A Shattered Nation: The Rise and Fall of the Confederacy, 1861–1868*. Chapel Hill: University of North Carolina Press, 2005.

Sacher, John M. *A Perfect War of Politics: Parties, Politicians, and Democracy in Louisiana, 1824–1861*. Baton Rouge: Louisiana State University Press, 2003.

Sewell, Richard H. *Ballots for Freedom: Antislavery Politics in the United States, 1837–1860*. New York: Oxford University Press, 1976.

Shade, William G. *Democratizing the Old Dominion: Virginia and the Second Party System, 1824–1861*. Charlottesville: University Press of Virginia, 1996.

Sidbury, James. *Ploughshares into Swords: Race, Rebellion, and Identity in Gabriel's Virginia, 1730–1810*. New York: Cambridge University Press, 1997.

Silbey, Joel. *Storm over Texas: The Annexation Controversy and the Road to Civil War*. New York: Oxford University Press, 2005.

Simpson, Craig M. *A Good Southerner: The Life of Henry A. Wise of Virginia*. Chapel Hill: University of North Carolina Press, 1985.

Sinha, Manisha. *The Counterrevolution of Slavery: Politics and Ideology in Antebellum South Carolina*. Chapel Hill: University of North Carolina Press, 2000.

Sklar, Kathryn Kish. *Women's Rights Emerges within the Antislavery Movement, 1830–1870: A Brief History with Documents*. Boston: Bedford/St. Martin's, 2000.

Smith, Henry Nash. *The Virgin Land: The American West as Symbol and Myth*. Cambridge: Harvard University Press, 1950.

Smith, Kimberly K. *The Dominion of Voice: Riot, Reason, and Romance in Antebellum Politics*. Lawrence: University Press of Kansas, 1999.

Snay, Mitchell. *Gospel of Disunion: Religion and Separatism in the Antebellum South*. New York: Cambridge University Press, 1993.

Spalding, Matthew, and Patrick J. Garrity. *A Sacred Union of Citizens: George Washington's Farewell Address and the American Character*. Lanham, Md.: Rowman and Littlefield, 1996.

Staloff, Darren. *Hamilton, Adams, Jefferson: The Politics of Enlightenment and the American Founding*. New York: Hill and Wang, 2005.

Stampp, Kenneth M. *America in 1857: A Nation on the Brink*. New York: Oxford University Press, 1990.

———. *And the War Came: The North and the Secession Crisis, 1860–61*. Baton Rouge: Louisiana State University Press, 1950.

———. *The Imperiled Union: Essays on the Background of the Civil War*. New York: Oxford University Press, 1980.

———, ed. *The Causes of the Civil War*. New York: Simon and Schuster, 1991.

Stauffer, John. *The Black Hearts of Men: Radical Abolitionists and the Transformation of Race*. Cambridge: Harvard University Press, 2002.

Stegmaier, Mark J. *Texas, New Mexico, and the Compromise of 1850: Boundary Dispute and Sectional Crisis*. Kent, Ohio: Kent State University Press, 1996.

Sterling, Dorothy. *Ahead of Her Time: Abby Kelley and the Politics of Antislavery*. New York: Norton, 1991.

Stevenson, Brenda E. *Life in Black and White: Family and Community in the Slave South*. New York: Oxford University Press, 1996.

Stewart, James Brewer. "Abolitionists, Insurgents, and Third Parties: Sectionalism and Partisan Politics in Northern Whiggery, 1836–1844." In *Crusaders and Compromisers: Essays on the Relationship of the Antislavery Struggle to the Antebellum Party System*, edited by Alan M. Kraut, 25–43. Westport, Conn.: Greenwood Press, 1983.

———. *Holy Warriors: The Abolitionists and American Slavery*. New York: Hill and Wang, 1976.

———. "Joshua Giddings, Antislavery Violence, and Congressional Politics of Honor." In *Antislavery Violence: Sectional, Racial, and Cultural Conflict in Antebellum America*, edited by John R. McKivigan and Stanley Harrold, 167–92. Knoxville: University of Tennessee Press, 1999.

———. "Reconsidering the Abolitionists in an Age of Fundamentalist Politics." *Journal of the Early Republic* 26 (Spring 2006): 1–24.

Stowe, Steven M. *Intimacy and Power in the Old South: Ritual in the Lives of the Planters*. Baltimore: Johns Hopkins University Press, 1987.

Streichler, Stuart. *Justice Curtis in the Civil War Era: At the Crossroads of American Constitutionalism*. Charlottesville: University of Virginia Press, 2005.

Strong, Douglas M. *Perfectionist Politics: Abolitionism and the Religious Tensions of American Democracy*. Syracuse, N.Y.: Syracuse University Press, 1999.

Summers, Mark W. *The Plundering Generation: Corruption and the Crisis of the Union, 1849–1861*. New York: Oxford University Press, 1987.

Takagi, Midori. *"Rearing Wolves to Our Own Destruction": Slavery in Richmond, Virginia, 1782–1865*. Charlottesville: University Press of Virginia, 1999.

Tallant, Harold D. *Evil Necessity: Slavery and Political Culture in Antebellum Kentucky*. Lexington: University Press of Kentucky, 2003.

Tate, Adam L. *Conservatism and Southern Intellectuals, 1789–1861: Liberty, Tradition, and the Good Society*. Columbia: University of Missouri Press, 2005.

Taylor, William R. *Cavalier and Yankee: The Old South and American National Character*. New York; G. Braziller, 1957.

Tegtmeier, Kristen A. "The Ladies of Lawrence Are Arming!: The Gendered Nature of Sectional Violence in Early Kansas." In *Antislavery Violence: Sectional, Racial, and Cultural Conflict in Antebellum America*, edited by John R. McKivigan and Stanley Harrold, 215–35. Knoxville: University of Tennessee Press, 1999.

Thornton, J. Mills, III. *Politics and Power in a Slave Society: Alabama, 1800–1860.* Baton Rouge: Louisiana State University Press, 1978.

Tise, Larry E. *Proslavery: A History of the Defense of Slavery in America, 1701–1840.* Athens: University of Georgia Press, 1987.

Tompkins, Jane P. "Sentimental Power: *Uncle Tom's Cabin* and the Politics of Literary History." In *Uncle Tom's Cabin: A Norton Critical*, edited by Elizabeth Ammons, 501–22. New York: Norton, 1977.

Towers, Frank. *The Urban South and the Coming of the Civil War.* Charlottesville: University of Virginia Press, 2004.

Tushnet, Mark V. *Slave Law in the American South: State v. Mann in History and Literature.* Lawrence: University Press of Kansas, 2003.

Varg, Paul A. *Edward Everett: The Intellectual in the Turmoil of Politics.* Selinsgrove, Pa.: Susquehanna University Press, 1992.

Varon, Elizabeth R. *Southern Lady, Yankee Spy: The True Story of Elizabeth Van Lew, a Union Agent in the Heart of the Confederacy.* New York: Oxford University Press, 2003.

———. *We Mean to Be Counted: White Women and Politics in Antebellum Virginia.* Chapel Hill: University of North Carolina Press, 1998.

Von Frank, Albert J. *The Trials of Anthony Burns: Freedom and Slavery in Emerson's Boston.* Cambridge: Harvard University Press, 1998.

Voss-Hubbard, Mark. *Beyond Party: Cultures of Antipartisanship in Northern Politics before the Civil War.* Baltimore: Johns Hopkins University Press, 2002.

Waldstreicher, David. *In the Midst of Perpetual Fetes: The Making of American Nationalism, 1776–1820.* Chapel Hill: University of North Carolina Press, 1997.

———. *Runaway America: Benjamin Franklin, Slavery, and the American Revolution.* New York: Hill and Wang, 2004.

Wallenstein, Peter. "Incendiaries All: Southern Politics and the Harpers Ferry Raid." In *His Soul Goes Marching On: Responses to John Brown and the Harpers Ferry Raid*, edited by Paul Finkelman, 149–73. Charlottesville: University Press of Virginia, 1995.

Walters, Ronald. *The Antislavery Appeal: American Abolitionism after 1830.* Baltimore: Johns Hopkins University Press, 1976.

Walther, Eric H. *The Fire-eaters*. Baton Rouge: Louisiana State University Press, 1992.

——. *The Shattering of the Union: America in the 1850s*. Wilmington, Del.: Scholarly Resources, 2004.

——. *William Lowndes Yancey and the Coming of the Civil War*. Chapel Hill: University of North Carolina Press, 2006.

Watson, Harry L. *Andrew Jackson vs. Henry Clay: Democracy and Development in Antebellum America*. Boston: Bedford/St. Martin's, 1998.

Waugh, John C. *On the Brink of Civil War: The Compromise of 1850 and How It Changed the Course of American History*. Wilmington, Del.: Scholarly Resources, 2003.

——. *Reelecting Lincoln: The Battle for the 1864 Presidency*. New York: Crown, 1997.

Weigley, Russell F. *A Great Civil War: A Military and Political History, 1861–1865*. Bloomington: Indiana University Press, 2000.

——, ed. *Philadelphia: A 300-Year History*. New York: Norton, 1982.

Weincek, Henry. *An Imperfect God: George Washington, His Slaves, and the Creation of America*. New York: Farrar, Straus and Giroux, 2003.

Wellman, Judith. "The Seneca Falls Women's Rights Convention: A Study of Social Networks." *Journal of Women's History* 3 (Spring 1991): 9–37.

Wells, Jonathan Daniel. *The Origins of the Southern Middle Class, 1800–1861*. Chapel Hill: University of North Carolina Press, 1988.

Wetherington, Mark V. *Plain Folk's Fight: The Civil War and Reconstruction in Piney Woods Georgia*. Chapel Hill: University of North Carolina Press, 2005.

White, Shane. *Somewhat More Independent: The End of Slavery in New York City, 1770–1810*. Athens: University of Georgia Press, 1991.

Wilentz, Sean. *The Rise of American Democracy*. New York: Norton, 2005.

Williams, Carolyn. "The Female Antislavery Movement: Fighting against Racial Prejudice and Promoting Women's Rights in Antebellum America." In *The Abolitionist Sisterhood: Women's Political Culture in Antebellum America*, edited by Jean Fagan Yellin and John C. Van Horne, 159–78. Ithaca, N.Y.: Cornell University Press, 1994.

Williams, David. *A People's History of the Civil War: Struggling for the Meaning of Freedom*. New York: New Press, 2005.

Williams, Raymond. *Keywords: A Vocabulary of Culture and Society*. New York: Oxford University Press, 1976.

Williams, Robert C. *Horace Greeley: Champion of American Freedom*. New York: New York University Press, 2006.

Wills, Garry. *"Negro President": Jefferson and the Slave Power*. Boston: Houghton Mifflin, 2003.

Wilson, Carol. "Active Vigilance Is the Price of Liberty: Black Self-Defense against Fugitive Slave Recapture and Kidnapping of Free Blacks." In *Antislavery Violence: Sectional, Racial, and Cultural Conflict in Antebellum America*, edited by John R. McKivigan and Stanley Harrold, 108–27. Knoxville: University of Tennessee Press, 1999.

Wilson, Major L. *Space, Time and Freedom: The Quest for Nationality and the Irrepressible Conflict, 1815–1861*. Westport, Conn.: Greenwood Press, 1974.

Winch, Julie. *A Gentleman of Color: The Life of James Forten*. New York: Oxford University Press, 2002.

Winders, Richard Bruce. *Crisis in the Southwest: The United States, Mexico, and the Struggle over Texas*. Wilmington, Del.: Scholarly Resources, 2002.

Wolf, Eva Sheppard. *Race and Liberty in the New Nation: Emancipation in Virginia from the Revolution to Nat Turner's Rebellion*. Baton Rouge: Louisiana State University Press, 2006.

Wyatt-Brown, Bertram. *Southern Honor: Ethics and Behavior in the Old South*. New York: Oxford University Press, 1982.

———. *Yankee Saints and Southern Sinners*. Baton Rouge: Louisiana State University Press, 1985.

Yacavone, Donald. "Abolitionists and the 'Language of Fraternal Love.'" In *Meanings for Manhood*, edited by Mark C. Carnes and Clyde Griffen, 85–95. Chicago: University of Chicago Press, 1990.

Yellin, Jean Fagan, and John C. Van Horne, eds. *The Abolitionist Sisterhood: Women's Political Culture in Antebellum America*. Ithaca, N.Y.: Cornell University Press, 1994.

Zaeske, Susan. *Signatures of Citizenship: Petitioning, Antislavery, and Women's Political Identity*. Chapel Hill: University of North Carolina Press, 2003.

Zelinsky, Wilbur. *Nation into State: The Shifting Symbolic Foundations of American Nationalism*. Chapel Hill: University of North Carolina Press, 1988.

Index

Abbott, L. S., 216–17

Abolitionists and abolitionism: economic context of, 3; and threats of disunion, 7, 8–9, 62, 105, 108, 152, 174, 181, 216, 221, 223, 228, 231, 238, 264, 275, 276–77, 301–2; and accusations of disunion, 9, 10, 15, 63, 102–3, 121, 181, 255, 290, 341, 344, 347; and racial egalitarianism, 9, 70, 84, 85, 96, 104, 115, 275, 345; and gender egalitarianism, 9, 70, 84, 96–97, 132, 135, 275; Calhoun on, 11; and blundering generation argument, 14; gradual emancipation distinguished from, 15, 61, 72, 352 (n. 22); and slavery as moral issue, 53, 61, 64, 70, 73, 85, 97, 105, 109–10, 118, 119, 124, 131, 144, 152, 153, 157, 163, 180, 195, 197, 202, 277; and North's complicity in slave system, 60, 235; and Garrison, 60–61, 66, 69, 70, 72; and free blacks, 61, 62–66, 69, 79, 85, 97–98, 102, 114–15, 236–39, 242–43, 264–65, 303–4; and white Southerners, 61, 66, 74; and white men, 61, 66–67, 73; and white women, 61, 73, 84, 130; in Britain, 61, 119, 132, 150, 161, 246, 262; and prophecies of disunion, 64, 67, 78, 342; and borderlands, 66–68; and Quakers, 71–72; Southern demonization of, 84–85; and Child, 95, 99; and constitutional issues, 95–96, 303; and coalitions, 96–102; and Frederick Douglass, 100–101; and sectional crisis of 1835, 102–5; and anti-abolitionism, 103–5, 107, 121, 133, 134, 144, 150, 338; and partisan politics, 105–7; and Protestant churches, 107, 108; and antislavery petitions to Congress, 109–10, 112, 113, 114, 116–17, 118; and Texas annexation, 128, 129, 165, 168, 174; and female authors, 137–38; schism over political action, 144, 163, 195–96, 204; and woman's rights, 144–45, 205; and *Amistad* case, 155, 157, 159, 161; and *Prigg* case, 159; and Latimer controversy, 162–64; and Mexican War, 181, 195–96; and Wilmot Proviso, 186, 190, 192, 194–97; gendered language concerning, 186–87, 190–91, 378 (n. 45); and Mexican Cession, 199; and election of 1848, 201; and Elizabeth Cady Stanton, 203–4, 205; and disunion petitions, 214, 216; and European radicalism, 215; and Webster, 217–18, 219; and Fugitive Slave Law, 241–43; disunion as retributive justice, 251, 256, 269; Seward on, 263; radical abolitionists, 265–66, 267, 278, 300, 319; and Lincoln, 280; and *Dred Scott* decision, 300–302, 303. *See also* Garrison, William Lloyd

Adams, James H., 294

Adams, John, 34–35

Adams, John Quincy: and National Republicans, 56, 57; and Whig Party, 106; and antislavery petitions, 111, 112, 114, 128, 130, 146, 157, 172–73, 213; and Haverhill petition, 150–52, 214, 301, 341, 345; and *Amistad* case, 155, 157, 158, 159, 160; and Texas annexation, 165, 166, 168, 169; and accusations of disunion, 209, 345; and threats of disunion, 320

African American Female Intelligence Society of Boston, 65

African American women, 65, 96–98, 132, 204–5, 242–43. *See also* Free blacks

African Female Benevolent Society of Troy, New York, 97

African Methodist Episcopal (AME) Church, 50, 51

African Methodist Episcopal Zion Church, 101

Albany Evening Journal, 270, 303

American and Foreign Anti-Slavery Society (AFASS), 144–45, 177–78

American Anti-Slavery Society (AASS), 60, 95–96, 98, 101, 102, 138, 145, 180, 238, 242, 303

American Bible Society, 179

American Colonization Society (ACS), 48, 49–50, 57, 62, 92, 101, 179, 359 (n. 33), 364 (n. 37)

American Party, 257–59, 261–62, 265, 269, 274, 275, 277, 287

American System, 56, 94, 143

American Whig Review, 224, 230

Amistad case, 141, 145, 154–55, 157–61

Anbinder, Tyler, 258

Andrew, James Osgood, 178

Antislavery movement: and accusations of disunion, 9–10, 15, 52, 102, 121–22; petition campaign of, 11, 109–14, 116–21, 127, 135, 145–46, 196, 245; and process of sectional alienation, 11–12, 116–21, 338; in Britain, 52; and Southern defiance, 58; and Upper South, 66–68; and mob violence, 133–35, 177; divisions within, 134–35, 144–45; and constitutional issues, 154; and *Amistad* case, 155; and Latimer controversy, 163; and Texas annexation, 164, 165, 190; and election of 1840, 201; and European revolutions, 215–16; and sectional differences, 221; and Fugitive Slave Law, 236; paternalism of, 239; and Boston Vigilance Committee, 241, 242; and Kansas-Nebraska Act, 251–52, 256–57; and Lincoln, 280; and Republican Party, 283–84, 285, 286, 302, 320; and *Dred Scott* decision, 297, 300–301, 303, 305; antislavers distinguished from abilitionism, 352 (n. 22). *See also* Gradual emancipation

"Appeal of the Independent Democrats," 253–54, 256

Arnold, Thomas Dickens, 150–51

Articles of Confederation, 25, 39, 40

Ashworth, John, 3, 47, 167, 190

Atchison, David Rice, 252, 260

Atkins, Jonathan M., 93

Atlantic Monthly, 14

Atlee, Edwin, 102–3

Baker, Jean H., 274, 287

Baptist churches, 178, 179

Barbour, James, 43, 47–48

Bayly, Thomas, 208–9

Beard, Charles A., 2

Beard, Mary R., 2

Beardsley, Samuel, 173

Beecher, Catharine, 132

Beecher, Lyman, 108

Bell, John, 313, 339

Bell, Philip A., 344

Benedict, Michael Les, 93–94

Bennett, James Gordon, 166, 190

Benton, Thomas Hart, 167, 175, 222, 252, 274, 285

Bill of Rights, 26, 154

Bingham, John, 305

Birney, James, 98, 128, 145, 147, 154, 155, 172

Black convention movement, 205, 278

Blair, Montgomery, 296

Blair, William, 290–91

Bledsoe, Albert T., 290–91, 293

Bluffton, S.C., 1844 meeting in, 171

Blundering generation argument, 3, 14

Bonaparte, Napoleon (president of France), 215

Boston, Uriah, 264, 265

Boston Atlas, 261

Boston Female Anti-Slavery Society, 133

Botts, John Minor, 151, 160, 166, 209, 340, 398 (n. 10)

Brattleboro Wyndham County Democrat, 203

Breckinridge, John Cabell, 339

Britain: and War of 1812, 37; antislavery movement in, 52; and tariffs, 57; abolitionism in, 61, 119, 133, 150, 161, 246, 262; and *Creole* case, 159–60; and Texas annexation, 166–67, 174; and Anglo-Saxonism, 183; and Oregon, 185; and Stowe, 246

Brodhead, Richard, 180, 181, 182

Brooklyn Daily Eagle, 185

Brooks, Preston, 268, 269, 270, 271, 283

Brown, Albert Gallatin, 321

Brown, Bedford, 146, 273

Brown, John: raid at Harpers Ferry, 6, 13, 326–33, 334, 335, 339; and radical abolitionists, 265, 267; and Pottawatomie massacre, 267–68, 326; and Provisional Constitution, 327–28, 329; as martyr, 329

Brown, Joseph E., 293–94

Brown, Milton H., 175

Brown, William Wells, 163–64, 208, 264

Brownlow, William G., 224, 343

Bryant, William Cullen, 190, 334–35

Buchanan, James: and accusations of disunion, 10; and election of 1856, 273, 275, 282, 286–87, 290; and filibusters, 286; Southerners' influence over, 291, 295, 301, 312, 320; and *Dred Scott* decision, 299–300; and popular sovereignty, 305–7; and Democratic Party, 308; and Jefferson Davis, 314; and Lincoln, 316; and economics, 320; and Brown's raid on Harpers Ferry, 328

Buel, Richard, Jr., 37, 39

Burin, Eric, 358–59 (n. 33)
Burns, Anthony, 240–41, 327
Burr, Aaron, 35, 37, 340, 341
Butler, Andrew, 236, 254, 268–69, 333

Calhoun, John C.: and process of sectional alienation, 11, 12, 118–19, 120, 216, 219; and nullification, 11, 57–58, 87, 89, 90, 91, 92, 171; and accusations of disunion, 38, 152; as vice president, 56; and gag rule, 110, 116–17, 118, 128, 146, 206; and Southern novelists, 136; and election of 1840, 141; and election of 1844, 149, 167–68, 171; and threats of disunion, 152, 153, 220–21, 276; and *Creole* case, 160; and Texas annexation, 167–68, 173; and states' rights, 179, 211, 216, 222, 225, 324, 331; and Mexican War, 181–82; and Wilmot Proviso, 189, 193, 194, 195; on slaveholder rights, 206, 208, 209; on emancipation, 206–7; and Taylor, 207–8; and European revolutions, 216; Webster's rebuttal of, 217–19; and Seward, 220–21
Canada, 238, 243
Carolina Centinel, 44
Cass, Lewis, 194, 199, 201, 269
Catholic Church, 248–49, 257, 258, 262
Channing, William Ellery, 108, 122–23
Chapman, Maria Weston, 60–61
Charleston Mercury, 149, 154, 169, 173–74, 230, 291, 308, 331
Charleston Standard, 324
Chase, Salmon P.: and Free-Soil Party, 210, 216–17; and rejection of disunionism, 221; on Missouri Compromise, 253–54, 256; and Republican Party, 262, 269; and constitutional issues, 263, 300; and election of 1856, 274, 278; and Lincoln, 317
Chicago Tribune, 267, 303
Child, Lydia Maria, 87, 91–92, 94–95, 99, 134–35
Christiana affair, 236, 238, 243
Cinqué (African rebel leader), 155
Citizenship: of free blacks, 60, 63–64, 114, 279, 297, 300, 391 (n. 42); Frederick Douglass on, 303
Civil War: causes of, 2–4, 14, 61; and Southern opposition to Confederacy, 343–44, 398 (n. 10)
Class: Northern middle class, 70, 161; and slave rebellion, 76, 77, 79; and democratization, 80; and cohesiveness of white ruling elite, 91–93, 366 (n. 9); in Southern society, 92, 99–100, 263, 283, 291, 293–94, 311–12, 338, 343, 398 (n. 10); and pro-Southern meetings in North, 102; and cult of honor, 104; and racism, 161; and Free-Soil Party, 202; and American Party, 258
Clay, Cassius, 176–77, 283, 312
Clay, Henry: and prophecies of disunion, 7, 90; oratorical style of, 7, 105; and Compromise Tariff, 8, 90; and process of sectional alienation, 12; and Missouri Compromise, 46–47, 90, 212; and diffusion argument, 48; and American System, 56, 94, 143, 176; David Walker on, 64; and Jackson, 93; and Whig Party, 106, 140, 143, 148, 149; and gag rule, 117, 146–47; on women's antislavery peti-

tions, 130; and *Creole* case, 160; and
Texas annexation, 169, 172, 175; and
election of 1844, 169, 176; and tariff of
1842, 170; and slavery in territories,
199–200; and Compromise of 1850,
212–13, 214, 219, 222–23, 224, 225;
and sectional differences, 219; and
Calhoun, 222

Cleveland Plain Dealer, 189

Clingman, Thomas Lanier, 211, 226

Clinton, Catherine, 77, 243

Cobb, Howell, 208, 210, 225, 228, 291

Cobb, Thomas, 42–43, 44, 52

Colcock, William F., 209–10

Colored American, 132, 134, 145, 152, 155

Columbus Republican Journal, 303

Compromise of 1833, 170, 171

Compromise of 1850: and Fugitive Slave
Law, 159, 212, 213, 214, 219, 222, 226–
27, 228, 229, 231; and Henry Clay,
212–13, 214, 219, 222–23, 224, 225;
and Douglas, 226–27, 252; and
threats of disunion, 227, 229, 231; and
rise of black militancy, 239; and election of 1852, 248, 249, 250–51; and
Missouri Compromise, 252; and Fillmore, 274

Confederate States of America, 13, 121,
223–24, 339, 343–44, 398 (n. 10)

Constitutional Convention, 22–27

Constitutional issues: and prophecies of
disunion, 6, 7; and Missouri debates,
41, 45, 48; and slavery debates, 49,
153–55, 157–64, 202, 220, 223, 238,
253, 263, 280, 300, 305; and political
compromise, 91; and nullification,
57–58, 93–94; and states' rights, 36–
37, 45, 57–58, 94, 179, 192–94; and

immediatism, 95–96, 124, 157, 163;
and abolitionists, 95–96, 303; and
women's anti-slavery petitions, 130;
and election of 1840, 143; and Fugitive Slave Law, 153, 158, 159, 163, 218,
220, 237; and Texas annexation, 165;
and Wilmot Proviso, 193–94, 195;
and secession, 227–30; and Missouri
Compromise, 252; and Republican
Party, 264; and radical abolitionists,
265–66; *Dred Scott* decision, 297

Cooper, William J., Jr., 36, 107, 223, 225,
249

Cornish, Samuel, 62, 69, 132, 146

Creole case, 159–61

Crittenden, John J., 313

Cuba, 158, 286, 322

Curtis, Benjamin, 297, 298–99, 300,
303

Cushing, Caleb, 332, 341

Cuthbert, Alfred, 110–11

Daily Madisonian, 166

Daily National Intelligencer, 44

Daly, John Patrick, 108, 178

Davis, Jefferson, 214, 227–28, 314, 321,
325, 343, 398 (n. 10)

Davis, William C., 171, 230

Dawes, Henry L., 333

De Bow, J. B., 291, 292–93, 324, 325

De Bow's Review, 292, 324, 340

Declaration of Independence, 20, 41,
50, 64, 153–55, 163, 254, 264, 300

Deep South: Upper South differentiated
from, 4; and slavery debates, 32; and
prophecy of disunion, 90; and conditions of slavery, 139; and election of
1844, 172; and Compromise of 1850,

227; and threats of disunion, 227, 230, 274–75; and Democratic Party, 228, 274; and cooperationists, 230–31; and Whig Party, 250; and Southern Commercial Convention, 314; and secessionism, 339, 341

Delany, Martin, 238–39, 327

Democratic Party: and election of 1856, 7, 273–75; and accusations of disunion, 10, 228, 250, 269, 275–76, 279, 310–11, 332, 340–41, 344–45; and Jackson, 56, 57, 92, 105; and nullification, 58; and states' rights, 94, 229–30, 274; and partisanship, 105; and gag rule, 110, 112, 146, 173; and Slave Power Conspiracy, 131; and anti-abolitionism, 133, 190–91, 221; and women's partisanship, 136; and election of 1840, 140, 141, 142, 144, 145, 147, 148–49; and Texas annexation, 149, 168, 170, 173–74, 175; and election of 1844, 167, 172; and Mexican War, 181–82; and Manifest Destiny, 184; and Wilmot Proviso, 184, 185, 186, 188–89, 190, 191, 192, 194; and sectional differences, 184–85, 191, 193, 228, 249, 273, 274, 321; and election of 1848, 199, 200–201, 206; and 1849 Speaker of the House debate, 208–9; and territorial expansion, 212; and Compromise of 1850, 213, 226, 227; and popular sovereignty, 224, 252–53, 277, 312; and Nashville Convention, 224–25; and Jefferson Davis, 228, 321; and election of 1852, 248–51; and immigrants, 249, 258; and Kansas-Nebraska Act, 256, 257; and Kansas Territory, 261,

268, 288, 305–8; as anti-black party, 279–80; and proslavery propaganda, 288; and wounded pride rhetoric, 291; congressional seats of, 320; and secessionism, 333

Democratic-Republican Party, 34, 35–37, 38, 39, 56

Democratic Review, 221, 275–77, 287–88, 332

Democratization: national trend toward, 56; and Herrenvolk democracy, 77, 81, 92; and voting rights, 80; and Protestant churches, 108; and Mexican War, 183

Dew, Thomas, 82–84, 109, 117, 120, 136, 178, 289

District of Columbia, 206, 209, 212, 213, 222, 226, 253

Disunion: meanings of, 1–2, 5, 6, 14; secession distinguished from, 5–6

—accusations of: and treason, 5, 34, 43, 90, 151, 152, 300, 332, 337–38, 341, 397 (n. 6); and abolitionists, 9, 10, 15, 63, 102–3, 121, 181, 255, 290, 341, 344, 347; and antislavery movement, 9–10, 15, 52, 102, 121–22; and Democratic Party, 10, 228, 250, 269, 275–76, 279, 310–11, 332, 340–41, 344–45; and Republican Party, 10–11, 263–64, 275–76, 281–82, 310–11, 332, 341, 345; and Democratic-Republican Party, 34, 35–36, 37, 38; and Federalists, 34, 35–36, 37–38, 44–45; and Missouri crisis of 1819-21, 40–43; and Hartford Convention, 44–45, 59, 277; and Vesey rebellion, 51; and nullification, 89–90; ubiquity of, 123; and female oratory, 132; and Texas annexation, 168; and Speaker of the House debate of 1849, 209; and American Party, 277

—as process of sectional alienation: and disunion rhetoric, 5, 11–12; and antislavery petitions, 11, 116–21, 338; and economics, 12, 33; and immediatists, 128, 338; and Southern solidarity, 152; and Garrison, 154; and Protestant churches, 179; and Wilmot Proviso, 190, 194; and territorial expansion, 211; and Compromise of 1850, 213; and Calhoun, 216, 219; and Webster, 219; and Stowe, 246; and Butler, 255. *See also* Sectional differences

—as program: and disunion rhetoric, 5, 13–14; and states rights, 210; and Clingman, 211; and Compromise of 1850, 213; and economics, 293–94. *See also* Secessionists and secessionism

—prophecies of: and biblical language, 5, 6–7; and Missouri controversy of 1819, 42–43; and free blacks, 49; and immediatism, 64; and abolitionists, 64, 67, 78, 154, 256, 269, 342; and gradual emancipation, 81, 82–83; and nullification, 59, 90; and Texas annexation, 169; and retributive justice, 251, 256, 269; and Kansas-Nebraska Act, 256; and secessionism, 342

—threats of: and federal compact, 5; and abolitionists, 7, 8–9, 62, 105, 108, 152–54, 174, 181, 194–95, 216, 221, 223, 228–29, 231, 238, 252, 254, 264, 271, 275, 276–77, 301–2, 320; and cult

of honor, 7–8; and slavery debates, 7–9, 32, 36, 43, 82, 122; and fear, 8, 10, 15–16, 32, 33, 221, 228; and tyranny, 15–16, 230; and states' rights, 8, 11, 36, 58, 117–18, 153, 173, 179, 221–22, 228, 230, 308–9, 319; and sectional differences, 153, 209–10; and Texas annexation, 165, 168–69; and Wilmot Proviso, 189–90, 194; and territorial expansion, 207, 211; and Speaker of the House debate, 209; and Compromise of 1850, 227, 229, 231; and election of 1852, 251; and Kansas Territory, 265, 308

Dixon, James, 186, 189–90, 196

Douglas, Stephen: and Young America movement, 184; and popular sovereignty, 222, 226, 306, 307, 312; and Compromise of 1850, 226–27, 252; on Missouri Compromise, 252–53, 254; and Kansas-Nebraska Act, 256; and Sumner, 269; and election of 1856, 274; and Lincoln, 281, 315–17, 320, 321, 333, 339, 393 (n. 23); and Democratic Party, 307–8, 312, 315; and accusations of disunion, 315–17; and election of 1858, 320; and election of 1860, 320; and secessionists, 325; and Freeport Doctrine, 393 (n. 23)

Douglass, Frederick: and right side/wrong side of Civil War, 15; on slavery as cause of sectional differences, 16; and slave narrative, 100–101; on corruption of American Christianity, 179–80; on election of 1848, 201; and Elizabeth Cady Stanton, 204; and Negro Convention movement, 205;

and violent resistance, 238; on emigration, 239; on Stowe, 245; on election of 1852, 250, 251; and Kansas-Nebraska Act, 256, 278; on disunionism, 16, 264–65; and Republican Party, 278, 279, 286; and constitutional issues, 300, 303; on *Dred Scott* decision, 303–4; and Lincoln, 317; and John Brown, 327, 328, 329, 335, 339; on secessionism, 342; on purpose of Civil War, 344; on voting rights, 345

Douglass, Sarah Mapps, 97, 98

Dred Scott v. Sandford (1857), 295–304, 305, 306, 317, 325, 391 (n. 42)

Du Bois, W. E. B., 3

Duer, William, 208–9, 210

Eastman, Mary, 246–47

Economics: and Civil War origins, 2, 3; and process of sectional alienation, 12, 33; and industrial slavery, 12, 239–41; and patterns of slavery, 17, 19; and Hamilton, 33; diffusion argument, 42; and Clay's American System, 56, 94, 143, 176; and modernization of North, 70; and gradual emancipation, 83; and ruling white elite, 92; and tariffs, 92; and Jackson, 95; and Whig Party, 106, 149, 157; and expansion of slavery, 129; and election of 1840, 140–43, 147; and slavery debates, 177, 311; and commerce-disrupting disunion, 219; and free labor ideology, 257; and De Bow, 292–93; and Southern independence, 293–94, 308, 325; and Buchanan, 320

Edgefield Advertiser, 270

Education: of free blacks, 103, 116, 202; and American Party, 258; in South, 293, 294

Elliot, John, 41–42

Emancipation Proclamation, 346

Emancipator, 121, 122

English Bill, 313–14, 321

English common law, 18

Enlightenment, 15

Etcheson, Nicole, 260, 261, 306

Europe, failed revolutions in, 215–16

European intervention, fears of, 52, 90, 133, 166

Evangelical religion: and prophecy of disunion, 49; revolutionary evangelicalism, 63, 64, 67, 70; and slavery as moral issue, 73, 83, 109; and abolitionism, 119, 157, 178; and domestic fiction, 137; and antislavery movement, 145; and Texas annexation, 172; and sectional differences, 178

Everett, Edward, 5, 256

Federalists, 24–27, 33, 34, 35–39, 40, 43, 44–45, 56

Fehrenbacher, Donald E., 159, 319

Fifth Amendment, 154, 253, 298

Filibusters, 37, 286

Fillmore, Millard, 226, 236, 259, 274, 287, 298

Fitzhugh, George, 288–91

Floyd, John, 79, 84, 108

Foner, Eric, 3, 55, 263, 279, 319

Foote, Henry S., 222, 324–25

Forten, James, 49, 50, 63, 69, 73, 74, 97

Founders: Everett on, 5; and disunion rhetoric, 14; and New England vs. Virginia claims, 37; on slavery, 39, 41,

154, 220, 253–54, 255, 280, 298, 315–17, 318, 333, 337; and Wilmot Proviso, 185; and compromise, 191; ideals of, 215, 230, 351 (n. 7); and fragility of republic, 221, 337; and strength of electoral process, 221; and citizenship, 297, 303; and example of harmony, 313

France, 34, 35, 40–41, 215

Franklin, Benjamin, 20, 32

Franklin, John Hope, 68

Frederick Douglass' Paper, 264

Free American, 147

Free blacks: and emancipation arguments, 20–21; and Israel Hill community, 22; and congressional representation, 23; and colonization movement, 48, 49–50, 57, 62, 63, 79–81, 92, 101, 114–16, 143–44, 146, 155, 238, 279, 280, 358–59 (n. 33); and republicanism, 49; and vision of Union, 49–50, 63–64, 97–98; and Fugitive Slave Law, 49, 237, 238–39; and white supremacy doctrine, 60, 103–5; citizenship of, 60, 63–64, 114, 279, 297, 300, 391 (n. 42); and abolitionism, 61, 62–66, 69, 79, 85, 115, 237, 238, 264; on Missouri Compromise, 62, 64; and disunion, 62–63, 264; and Garrison, 69, 73; and Quakers, 72, 363 (n. 35); prohibitions on preaching of, 79; relationship with slaves, 97–98; education of, 103, 116; and gag rule, 114; petitions of, 114–16; and Webster, 220; and Compromise of 1850, 231; violence against, 65, 236; and armed resistance, 237–38; and emigration, 238–39; rise of black

militancy, 237–39; and Republican Party, 278, 279; deterioration in status of, 279; second compromise on Missouri admission, 358 (n. 27); population of, 361 (n. 11)

Freedom's Journal, 62, 63, 74, 362 (n. 16)

Freehling, William W., 3, 47, 83, 84, 91, 117, 168, 226, 306; and prophecy of disunion, 7; ideology: of Republican Party, 3, 263, 284, 304; Lincoln on, 3, 316; and process of sectional alienation, 11; and abolitionism, 61; and spiritual perfectionism, 70; and democratization, 80; and West, 185, 203; and Kansas-Nebraska Act, 255, 256; and Kansas Territory, 260; and Frémont, 284; and proslavery propaganda, 288–89; and Seward, 309–10, 318–19

Free-Soil Party: and accusations of disunion, 10; and process of sectional alienation, 12, 190; abolitionism distinguished from, 15, 352 (n. 22); and Wilmot Proviso, 184, 189–90, 192, 196, 202–3, 263–64; and agrarian ideal, 188; and election of 1848, 201–2, 206; and Stanton, 204; and Calhoun, 207; and Speaker of the House debate, 208–9; and Chase, 210, 216–17; and Taylor, 211; Southern attitudes toward, 223; and election of 1852, 248; and Pierce, 249; and Kansas-Nebraska Act, 253; and Kansas Territory, 260–61, 266, 268, 311, 313; and Frederick Douglass, 278

Free speech issues: and gag rule, 111–13, 114, 146, 150, 152, 173, 175–76; and John Quincy Adams, 114, 214; Garrison on, 124; Southern suppression of, 176–77, 271, 283; and Mann, 250–51; Seward on, 262–63; and Kansas Territory, 266; Lincoln on, 283

Frémont, Jessie Benton, 274, 283–84, 285, 286

Frémont, John C., 274–75, 277, 283–86, 287

Friends' Intelligencer, 215–16, 295

Fugitive Slave Act (1793), 49, 61, 68

Fugitive Slave Act (1850): and process of sectional alienation, 12; and constitutional issues, 153, 158, 159, 163, 218, 220, 237; and Compromise of 1850, 159, 212, 213, 214, 219, 222, 226–27, 228, 229, 231; and Webster, 218, 219, 220; and Seward, 220; measures of, 235–36; resistance to, 236–37, 241–42, 304; and emigration of free blacks, 238–39; petitions for repeal of, 241; and Stowe, 243–44; and election of 1852, 248; and Pierce, 249; and threats of disunion, 264; and Curtis, 298–99

Fugitive slaves: and runaway advertisements, 18, 139, 162; and slave patrollers, 18–19, 67, 242; free blacks arrested as, 114, 158, 220, 237–38; and *Prigg* case, 158–59; and Latimer controversy, 161, 162–63; and Texas annexation, 167; and sectional differences, 212, 218; increase in, 240; and Burns case, 240–41; and Underground Railroad, 242–43

Furman, Richard, 51–52

Gabriel's Rebellion, 35, 45, 63

Gag rule: and antislavery petitions, 109–14, 116, 117, 119, 120, 121, 128, 130, 145–47, 150; and threats of disunion, 122; rescinding of, 172, 192

Garnett, Muscoe R. H., 229–30

Garrison, William Lloyd: and threats of disunion, 8–9, 152–54, 194–95, 229, 252, 254, 271, 320; and immediatism, 15, 60–61, 66, 69, 70, 74, 95, 118; and Forten, 68–69; and biracial abolition network, 69, 73–74; early life of, 69–70; and Quakers, 72–73, 363–64 (n. 37); on Turner, 78, 81; and prophecies of disunion, 78, 154, 256, 269, 342; and Child, 91; and Frederick Douglass, 101, 238, 265; and anti-abolitionists, 103, 105, 107, 144; on Southern antislavery support, 123; on reality of disunion, 123–24; and election of 1840, 144, 147, 148; and human rights, 145; and *Amistad* case, 155, 157; and *Prigg* case, 158, 159; and Latimer controversy, 162, 163; and Texas annexation, 164, 174; and Cassius Clay, 176; and Wilmot Proviso, 194–95; on Sumner, 271; and Republican Party, 277–78, 286; and *Dred Scott* decision, 302, 304; on John Brown, 329; and emancipation as justification for war, 342. *See also* Abolitionists and abolitionism

Gates, Henry Louis, 364 (n. 39)

Geffert, Hannah, 326–27

Gender egalitarianism: of abolitionists, 9, 70, 84, 96–97, 132, 135, 275; and Garrison, 73, 145; and Sarah Grimké, 132; and Stowe, 246

Genius of Universal Emancipation, 70, 73

Genovese, Eugene, 76
Giddings, Joshua: and Whig Party, 157, 201; and *Creole* case, 160–61; and Texas annexation, 165; and Wilmot Proviso, 186; and Southern attacks on, 191; and slave trade in District of Columbia, 209; and antislavery petitions, 214–15; and accusations of disunion, 221, 345; on Stowe, 245; on election of 1852, 250, 251; and "Appeal of the Independent Democrats," 253; on American Party, 259; and Lincoln, 280, 317; and Helper, 312
Gienapp, William E., 3, 279, 319
Gilman, Caroline, 136, 137
Goodell, William, 145, 154
Goodwin, Doris Kearns, 319, 341
Goulden, William B., 294–95
Gradual emancipation: abolitionism distinguished from, 15, 61, 72, 352 (n. 22); and authority of U.S. Congress, 33; and Missouri debates, 41–42; and colonization of freed slaves, 48, 57, 79–80, 81, 359 (n. 33); and Janney, 72; Thomas Jefferson Randolph's proposal for, 79, 80–81; Dew on, 82–84; and racial caste system, 85; South Carolina's opposition to, 92; and Protestant churches, 108; and female oratory, 132; and Texas annexation, 168, 174; and Cassius Clay, 176–77; Webster on, 217; and Seward, 221; and nonextensionism, 263; and Republican Party, 263; and Upper South, 280; and Lincoln, 281, 318, 334
Greeley, Horace, 149, 165–66, 176, 263, 265, 283, 299, 303, 311, 329, 341

Grimké, Angelina. *See* Weld, Angelina Grimké
Grimké, Sarah, 98, 124, 130–33, 134, 138–40, 144
Grimké, Thomas S., 59–60, 98
Grimsted, David, 102, 103

Hale, John Parker, 209, 210, 213–15, 221, 345
Hamilton, Alexander, 25, 26, 31, 33, 34
Hamilton, James, Jr., 52, 79, 84, 89, 92, 171
Hamilton, Richard, 21
Hammond, James Henry: and nullification, 89, 117; on abolitionists, 103; and gag rule, 110, 128; and threats of disunion, 117–18, 153, 308–9; and process of sectional alienation, 119, 121; and proslavery ideology, 136; and Protestant schisms, 179; and Nashville Convention, 223; and right of secession, 223; mudsill speech of, 308–9, 310; and Crittenden, 313; and Democratic Party, 314; on Seward, 321; "Cotton is King" speech, 325
Harper, Frances Ellen Watkins, 242–43
Harrison, William Henry, 106, 141–44, 148–49, 157, 167
Hartford Convention of 1814, 5, 38–39, 44–45, 59, 224, 277, 340, 341, 345
Hartford Courant, 279
Hatcher, Jordan, 240
Haverhill petition, 150–51
Hayne, Robert Y., 52, 58, 90
Hedrick, Joan D., 244–45
Helper, Hinton Rowan, 311–12, 331
Henry, Patrick, 26, 101, 155
Herrenvolk democracy, 77, 81, 92, 294

Hicksite Quakers, 203, 295, 364 (n. 37)
Higginson, Thomas Wentworth, 327, 330
Hilliard, George S., 270
Hilliard, Henry, 194, 210
Hodges, Willis A., 108, 327
Holmes, G. W., 246
Holmes, Isaac Edward, 174
Holt, Michael F., 3, 94, 129, 185, 193, 194, 200, 210, 213, 226, 256, 259
Holzer, Harold, 315–16, 333, 334
Honor, cult of: in South, 3, 104; and threats of disunion, 7–8, 33; and slanders of North, 43; and anti-abolitionists, 104; and partisanship, 105; and gender aspersions, 191, 264, 266–67, 270; and gender discrimination, 205; and Taylor, 206; and Compromise of 1850, 228; and Brooks, 268, 270; and Rhett, 291–92; and Christian duty, 340
Horsman, Reginald, 183
Houston, Sam, 167, 323
Howe, Daniel Walker, 280
Howe, Samuel Gridley, 327
Hunt, Washington, 187

Illinois State Register, 332
Immediatism. *See* Abolitionists and abolitionism
Immigrants, 129, 161, 172, 248–49, 257–59, 262
Ingersoll, Charles J., 174, 187
Iverson, Alfred, 322–23, 324

Jackson, Andrew: and Democratic Party, 56, 57, 92, 105; and nullification, 58, 87, 89–90, 92–95, 106, 120, 224; Northern support for, 60; on slavery, 60; and Van Buren, 93, 105, 106; and banking, 94, 106, 253; hard money philosophy of, 141; and executive tyranny, 143; and veto power, 149; and Frémont, 284
Jackson, James, 32
Jackson, Thomas, 183
Jacobs, Harriet, 76
Janney, Samuel, 72, 84
Jay, John, 33
Jefferson, Thomas: on slavery, 20, 21, 41, 42, 357 (n. 19), 362 (n. 20); on Revolutionary War debts of states, 32; and accusations of disunion, 34, 37; Kentucky resolution of, 34, 230; and election of 1800, 35–36; on emancipation, 45; and Missouri controversy of 1819, 48; and fears of disunion, 48–49; agrarian principles of, 56, 94, 168; and states' rights, 58; legacy of, 94, 362 (n. 20); and *Amistad* case, 155; Lincoln on, 281; on Wheatley, 364 (n. 39)
Johnson, William Cost, 145–46, 150
Judson, Andrew T., 103, 155, 157
Julian, George W., 226–27

Kansas-Nebraska Act of 1854, 251–59, 274, 278, 280, 304, 315, 317
Kansas Territory: and process of sectional alienation, 12; and popular sovereignty, 259, 261, 305–6; and pro-slavery Missourians, 260–61; and Free-Soil Party, 260–61, 266, 268, 311, 313; and Republican Party, 261, 267, 269, 307, 314, 316; and Democratic Party, 261, 268, 288, 305–8;

Seward on, 262–63; and Pike, 265;
and threats of disunion, 265, 308;
Frederick Douglass on, 266; violence
in, 266–68, 273, 277, 314; Sumner on,
268–69; and Frémont, 274; and
Lecompton constitution, 305–14

Keitt, Lawrence M., 291, 292, 307, 308,
333

Kelley, Abby, 96, 133, 145

Kendall, Amos, 102, 107

Kennedy, John Pendleton, 136

Kentucky resolution (1798), 34, 36, 57–
58, 230, 299

Kersh, Rogan, 26–27, 62–63, 115

Know-Nothing Party. *See* American
Party

Knoxville Whig, 224

Lamar, L. Q. C., 307, 308

Latimer controversy, 161, 162–64

League of United Southerners, 322, 324

Leavitt, Joshua, 121–22, 145

Lecompte, Samuel, Jr., 266

Lee, Robert E., 183, 328

Libby, Jean, 326–27

Liberator: founding of, 60, 68–69; and
public opinion, 69; and free labor
ideology, 70; on Northerners, 70–71;
and Quakers, 72–73; and free blacks,
73–74; and Turner's rebellion, 76, 78;
and Sarah Mapps Douglass, 97; and
Roper, 100; and Sarah Grimké, 132;
and electoral politics, 144; and racial
and gender egalitarianism, 145; and
Prigg case, 159; and Philadelphia race
riot, 161; and Texas annexation, 174;
and Wilmot Proviso, 195, 197; and
Webster, 219–20; on Sumner, 271;

and election of 1856, 277; and threats
of disunion, 302

Liberty Party: and accusations of disunion, 10; and abolitionist schism,
144, 145; and election of 1840, 147–
48; and constitutional issues, 154,
263; and Latimer controversy, 163;
and election of 1844, 172, 206; and
Whig Party, 173, 175; and Mexican
War, 182; and Wilmot Proviso, 185,
190; and election of 1848, 201; and
Stanton, 204; and Frederick Douglass, 278

Lincoln, Abraham: and free labor ideology, 3, 316; on secession, 13–14; and
Amistad case, 158; and Republican
Party, 259, 279, 280, 281–82, 285,
287, 316, 321, 334–35; on colonization, 280, 281; on slavery, 280–82;
and Douglas, 281, 315–17, 320, 321,
333, 339, 393 (n. 23); on proslavery
propaganda, 289–90; "House
Divided" speech of, 315, 316, 317,
332; on Harpers Ferry raid, 332–33,
334, 335; Cooper Union speech of,
333–35; election as president, 339;
reelection of, 345

Lincoln, Mary Todd, 280

Link, William, 239–40

Livermore, Arthur, 41, 46

Longstreet, Augustus Baldwin, 178, 194

Louisiana Purchase, 37, 40–41, 47, 129,
252, 255

Louisville (Ky.) Journal, 123

Lovejoy, Elijah, 134–35

Lowell, James Russell, 196

Lowell, John, Jr., 37–38

Lundy, Benjamin, 70, 72–73, 128

Macon, Nathaniel, 36, 42, 43, 45, 52

Madison, James, 22, 25, 26–27, 32–33, 34, 230

Manifest Destiny, 183–84

Mann, Horace, 250–51, 256, 269

Manumission, 48, 81, 114, 358–59 (n. 33)

Marshall, Thomas, 80, 151, 176

Martial manhood, 92, 110, 168, 378 (n. 45)

Mason, George, 24, 25–26, 27

Mason, James, 213, 216, 236, 237, 269–70, 307, 333

Mason, Matthew, 32, 40

Massachusetts Anti-Slavery Society, 180

Massachusetts General Colored Association, 63, 65

Mayer, Henry, 70, 71, 73, 152, 155, 157, 163, 266

McClellan, George B., 183, 345

McKivigan, John R., 107–8

McLean, John, 297, 299, 300

McPherson, Edward, 333

McPherson, James M., 3, 262

Meade, Richard K., 209, 210, 229

Melville, Herman, 329, 385 (n. 23)

Methodist Church, 177–78, 179, 203

Mexican Cession, 199–200, 212, 220, 222, 254

Mexican War, 1, 10, 180–83, 195–97, 201, 205–6, 224, 249

Mexico, 127, 166, 168, 169, 174, 180–81, 185

Milledgeville Federal Union, 300

Miller, William Lee, 110, 146

Missouri Crisis (1819–21), 39–51, 358 (n. 27); and Henry Clay, 46–47, 90, 212; and Jefferson, 48; and Vesey, 52;

and complicity of North in slave system, 60; free blacks on, 62, 64; and Thomas Rankin, 67–68; and Texas annexation, 129, 175; and territorial expansion, 193, 225; Douglas on, 252–53, 254; Chase on, 253–54, 256; and antislavery movement, 255; and Frémont, 274; Lincoln on, 281; and *Dred Scott* decision, 295, 297–98, 300

Mitchell, Betty L., 223–24

Mobile Register, 308

Monroe, James, 35, 47, 48, 106

Morone, James A., 49

Morril, David L., 41, 42

Morris, Thomas, 113, 131

Morrison, Michael A., 168, 215, 351 (n. 7)

Mott, Lucretia, 97, 98, 133–34, 203–4, 242

Napoleon I (emperor of France), 37

Nashville Convention of 1850, 5, 223–25, 227, 229, 230

National Era, 207, 229, 256, 312, 321, 322

National Intelligencer, 78, 169

Nationalist ideology: and definition of Union, 5, 27; and Constitution, 27; and Mexican War, 183; and Southern nationalism, 223–24, 228, 248, 291, 293, 344, 345; and Republican Party, 282, 285–86

National Republicans, 56, 57, 58, 93, 94, 106

Native Americans, 56, 95, 178, 326

Nativism, 4, 248–49, 257–58, 259, 262, 274, 277

Negro Seaman's Act, 52

New England Emigrant Aid Company, 260, 261

New Orleans Crescent, 292

New Orleans Daily Picayune, 246

New Orleans Delta, 308

New Orleans Picayune, 127, 300

New York Anti-Slavery Society, 103

New York Commercial Advertiser, 104

New York Evening Post, 302–3

New York Herald, 155, 166, 206, 212–13, 300

New York Independent, 247

New York Observer, 325–26

New York Post, 334–35

New York Times, 283, 284, 303, 321–22

New York Tribune, 149, 151, 165–66, 256, 263, 265, 267, 303, 329, 341

New York World, 143

Niles' Weekly Register, 44

Norfolk and Portsmouth Herald, 104

North: economic interests of, 2, 3, 70; backlash against abolitionism, 9, 133; and New England's threats of disunion, 37–39, 40, 56, 59; demographics of, 40, 129, 257; and Missouri Compromise, 47, 48; racist legislation of, 49; balance of power with South, 53; and slave system, 69, 70–71; and Democratic Party, 92, 106; racism in, 98, 114, 279, 280; European immigrant population, 129, 172; ties to South, 133; and plantation fiction, 137. *See also* Sectional differences

North American Review, 59

North Star, 201

Northwest Ordinance, 39, 40, 41, 185, 281

Norvell, John, 130

Nullification crisis: and threats of disunion, 5, 8, 11, 58, 87, 89, 209–10, 341; and Calhoun, 11, 57–58, 87–89; and Southern Unionism, 59; Webster on, 59; and accusations of disunion, 89–90; and Nullification Convention, 87; and ruling elite, 91–93, 366 (n. 9); and constitutional issues, 93–94; and antislavery nullification doctrine, 95; Roper on, 99–100; and threats of disunion, 209–10, 341

Oakes, James, 267, 279

O'Brien, Michael, 137, 289, 290

Olsen, Christopher J., 228

Onuf, Peter, 48–49

Oregon Treaty of 1846, 200

Otis, Harrison Gray, 37–38

Palfrey, John G., 189, 209

Palladium of Liberty, 169

Palmer, B. M., 340

Panic of 1857, 320

Parker, John, 66, 68, 242

Parker, Theodore, 241, 277–78, 312, 327

Parker, William T., 236, 237–38

Partisanship: Washington on, 33–34; and War of 1812, 37; and Missouri controversy of 1819, 43; divisiveness of, 53; and slavery debates, 105–7; and gag rule, 111–12, 146, 150; and women's public identities, 136. *See also* Presidential elections

Patriotism, 5, 181, 184

Pennington, James W. C., 162, 163, 244

Pennsylvania Abolition Society (PAS), 32, 72, 73, 79, 102–3, 242, 363 (n. 35), 364 (n. 37)

Pennsylvania Anti-Slavery Society, 264, 277

Pennsylvania Freeman, 123, 146, 236

Pennsylvania Hall, burning of, 134, 161

Personal liberty laws, 158, 159, 163, 218, 237

Phelps, Amos, 134–35, 145

Philadelphia Evening Bulletin, 202

Philadelphia Female Anti-Slavery Society, 98, 124, 342

Philadelphia North American, 1

Philadelphia Public Ledger, 215, 300

Philadelphia race riot of 1842, 161

Phillips, Wendell, 134–35, 162, 219, 301–2, 342

Pierce, Franklin, 249, 252, 257, 266, 269, 274, 316

Pierson, Michael D., 147, 285

Pike, James S., 265–66

Pinckney, Charles Cotesworth, 23–24

Pinckney, Henry L., 110

Pittsburgh Saturday Visitor, 203

Plantation fiction, 136–37, 138

Pleasants, John Hampden, 104–5

Polk, James K.: and election of 1844, 149, 167, 171–73; and Texas annexation, 175, 184–85, 208; and Mexican War, 180–81, 182, 184; and Wilmot Proviso, 182, 185, 190, 193; and Oregon, 200

Popular sovereignty: and territorial expansion, 199; and Taylor, 208, 211, 212; and Douglas, 222, 226, 306, 307, 312; and Democratic Party, 224, 252–53, 277, 312; and Whig Party, 227; and Kansas-Nebraska Act, 252–53; and Kansas Territory, 259, 261, 305–6; and *Dred Scott* decision, 298, 299

Potter, David M., 3, 47, 331

Presidential elections: of 1800, 35; of 1824, 56; of 1828, 56–57; of 1832, 93–94; of 1836, 105–6; of 1840, 142–44, 157; of 1844, 167–68; of 1848, 200–203, 206; of 1852, 248–50; of 1856, 273–77, 281–87; of 1860, 333–35, 339–41

Press: on secessionism, 14, 325–26; and prophecies of disunion, 44, 59; and states' rights, 45; and antislavery movement, 72; on Garrison, 78; and partisanship, 105; and anti-abolitionism, 107, 121, 133, 134; religious press, 108; and gag rule, 111; and anti-nullification opinion, 123; on Fanny Wright, 131; and conditions of slavery, 139; and election of 1840, 143, 148–49; and *Amistad* case, 154–55, 157; and Texas annexation, 165–66, 171–74; and nullification, 171; and Mexican War, 183; and Wilmot Proviso, 189; and election of 1848, 202, 206; and Free-Soil women, 203; and woman's rights, 205; and accusations of disunion, 209, 341, 345; and Taylor, 212; and disunion petitions, 214–15; and European revolutions, 215–16; and Webster, 219; and Seward, 221; and Fugitive Slave Law, 236, 237; and Stowe, 246; and Eastman, 247; and American Party, 261; on John Brown, 267, 329, 330, 332; on Brooks, 270; and election of 1856, 275–77, 284, 287; and threats of disunion, 287–88; and Republican Party, 292, 332; and *Dred Scott* decision, 300, 302–3; and Kansas Territory, 307; and Lincoln-Douglas debates, 315; on Jefferson Davis, 321–22; and Lincoln's Cooper Union speech, 334–35

Preston, William C., 110, 119–20, 128–29, 150, 160

Prigg, Edward, 158, 159

Prigg v. Pennsylvania (1842), 158–59, 161, 163

Protestant churches, 107, 108, 177–80, 216, 248–49, 256, 258

Pryor, Roger, 314–15, 331–32

Public opinion: and *Liberator*, 69; and gag rule, 113; and process of sectional alienation, 118; and Wilmot Proviso, 190; Lincoln on, 282–83; and abolitionists, 301; and secessionism, 325, 340; and Brown's raid on Harpers Ferry, 329–30

Purvis, Robert, 85, 161–62, 242, 264, 302

Quakers, 20, 32, 71–73, 79, 203, 242, 363–64 (n. 37)

Quitman, John A., 227, 286, 291, 324

Racial egalitarianism: of abolitionists, 9, 70, 84, 85, 96, 104, 115, 275, 345; and Garrison, 73–74; and sectional differences, 84, 117; and female abolitionist societies, 133–34; Lincoln's disavowing of, 281; Frederick Douglass on, 346

Racism: and slave codes, 18–19; and colonization, 49; and immediatism, 62–66, 97; and proslavery propaganda, 73, 288, 290; and reprisals for slave rebellions, 77; in North, 98, 114,

279; and anti-abolitionism, 103; and miscegenation as social taboo, 104, 117; and class issues, 161; and Texas annexation, 168, 174; and Mexican War, 181; and Wilmot Proviso, 185, 189; and Mexican Cession, 200; and American Party, 258; and Republican Party, 279–80; Lincoln's concessions to, 280, 281; and *Dred Scott* decision, 297, 300, 391 (n. 42); and Helper, 311

Radical abolitionists, 265–66, 267, 278, 300, 319

Rael, Patrick, 239, 320

Raleigh Register, 330

Randolph, John, 36–37, 39, 45

Randolph, Martha Jefferson, 79

Randolph, Richard, 21–22

Randolph, Thomas Jefferson, 79–80, 81, 82

Rankin, Christopher, 45

Rankin, John, 66–68, 69, 84, 139

Rankin, Thomas, 66–67

Raymond, Henry J., 397 (n. 6)

Reconstruction, 345

Religion: First Great Awakening, 20; Second Great Awakening, 61; and spiritual perfectionism, 61, 70, 144; religious revivalism, 70. *See also* Catholic Church; Evangelical religion; Protestant churches

Remond, Charles Lenox, 238, 302

Republicanism: and slavery debates, 41, 42, 45, 49, 83; abolitionism, 119; and absolute power, 140; and constitutional issues, 154; and Mexican War, 183; in France, 215; and free speech, 283; Frederick Douglass on, 346

Republican Party: free labor ideology of, 3, 263, 284, 304; and territorial expansion, 10; and accusations of disunion, 10–11, 263–64, 275–76, 281–82, 310–11, 332, 341, 345; critique of South, 13, 291–92; and Kansas-Nebraska Act, 256–57; and American Party, 259, 262, 278; and Kansas Territory, 261, 267, 269, 307, 314, 316; and nonextensionism, 263, 271, 274, 278, 279, 280, 284, 285, 304; as moderates, 265; and election of 1856, 273–75, 278–87, 291; and threats of disunion, 276–77; and racial issues, 279–80; and sectional differences, 281; and women's activism, 285–86; and filibustering, 286; and election of 1860, 287, 292, 322, 330–31, 332, 333, 339; on proslavery propaganda, 289–90; and *Dred Scott* decision, 299, 300–301, 303, 304; and congressional seats of, 320, 321; and Harpers Ferry raid, 332–33, 335

Revolutionary War, 20–21, 31

Reynolds, David S., 326, 327, 328, 378 (n. 36)

Rhett, Robert Barnwell: and threats of disunion, 8, 11, 58, 117, 171–73, 222, 230, 319; and disunion as program, 13, 230, 291; and Southern nationalism, 13, 224, 225, 228, 229; and nullification, 89, 151, 171; and gag rule, 113; and states' rights, 149, 192–93; and accusations of disunion, 151, 173, 174, 209; and election of 1844, 167; and Texas annexation, 170, 174; and Henry Clay, 170–71; and process of sectional alienation, 173, 338; and

Wilmot Proviso, 192–93; and Fugitive Slave Law, 237; Pike compared to, 265; and Democratic Party, 291; and honor, 291–92

Rhode Island Anti-Slavery Society, 113

Richmond Daily Dispatch, 345

Richmond Enquirer: and states' rights, 45, 171; on Garrison, 78; on Tyler, 148–49; on Haverhill petition, 150; and *Amistad* case, 154–55; and Texas annexation, 169; and Ruffin, 223; on Stowe, 248; and accusations of disunion, 255; on Sumner, 270; and election of 1856, 275; and Republican Party, 292; on *Dred Scott* decision, 300; on Brown's raid on Harpers Ferry, 329

Richmond Republican, 219

Richmond Whig, 104, 151, 207, 270

Rives, William Cabell, 117, 118

Roberts, Robert W., 186, 192

Rogin, Michael Paul, 385 (n. 23)

Roper, Moses, 99–100

Ruffin, Edmund, 223, 291, 292, 322

St. Domingo (Haiti), 45

Sandusky Democratic Mirror, 189

Scott, Dred, 295–97, 317

Scott, Winfield, 248, 249

Secession: disunion distinguished from, 5–6; Lincoln on, 13–14; right of, 36; and nullification, 57–58, 89; first secession crisis, 223–31, 324; and constitutional issues, 227, 230; crisis of 1859–61, 339–40

Secessionists and secessionism: and Nashville Convention, 5, 223–24; and Calhoun, 11, 216, 219; and disunion

as program, 13, 230, 291, 337; and
blundering generation argument, 14;
and Jefferson's and Madison's resolutions, 34; and states' rights, 36, 179;
and tariffs, 87; and Rhett, 171, 230,
291; Webster on, 218–19; and Deep
South Unionists, 228–29; and threats
of disunion, 292, 339; and Iverson,
322–23; Houston on, 323; organizations of, 324; and slaveholders' rights,
325; generational component to, 325–
26; and Brown's raid on Harpers
Ferry, 329–30, 332, 339; and Democratic Party, 333; Lincoln on, 334;
debates over, 340; Southern opposition to, 343

Second African Presbyterian Church,
161

Sectional differences: slavery as cause
of, 16, 24, 31–33, 121–22; and Constitutional Convention, 22–27; and Revolutionary War debts of states, 31–32;
and tariffs, 57, 58–59; and abolitionism, 61, 102; and slave rebellion, 78;
and democratization, 80; Child on,
91; and crisis of 1835, 102–5; and partisanship, 105–6; and Protestant
churches, 109, 177–80; and gag rule,
109–14, 116, 150; and Whig Party,
111–12, 117, 191, 193, 199–200, 211,
212, 228, 248; and free blacks' petitions, 114–16; and election of 1840,
148; and threats of disunion, 153,
209–10; and Texas annexation, 166,
167–68; and Democratic Party, 184–
85, 191, 193, 228, 249, 273, 274, 321;
and Wilmot Proviso, 184–85, 191–94,
208, 215; and crisis of 1846–47, 186;

and election of 1848, 201; and Calhoun, 207, 219; and accusations of
disunion, 209; and Compromise of
1850, 212–13; and disunion petitions,
213–15; and Revolution's legacy, 215;
and Webster, 219; and Seward, 220–
21; and election of 1852, 248; and
American Party, 259; and election of
1856, 273; and Rhett, 291

Seddon, James, 191, 192, 229

Sedition Act, 34, 277

Seneca Falls convention, 203–5, 254

Sentimental fiction, 187, 244, 289

Seward, Frances, 310, 341–42

Seward, William Henry: irrepressible
conflict speech, 12, 13, 317–23, 330–
31, 332, 335; and process of disunion,
12, 13, 320; and territorial expansion,
201, 210, 220–22; higher law argument
of, 221, 327; and Whig Party, 249, 259;
and Republican Party, 259, 262–64,
269, 274, 278, 309, 318, 321; on Southern disunionism, 265; and constitutional issues, 300; and free labor ideology, 309–10, 318–19; and Helper,
311, 312; and military conquest imagery, 316, 318, 321, 322; and Lincoln,
317, 333, 335; on aggression of South,
324; on Harpers Ferry raid, 332–33;
procompromise speech of, 341–42;
and accusations of disunion, 345

Sewell, Richard H., 202–3, 279

Shays' Rebellion of 1786, 25

Signal of Liberty, 147

Silbey, Joel H., 3, 207

Simms, William Gilmore, 136

Sinha, Manisha, 52, 308

Sklar, Kathryn Kish, 203, 204–5

Slade, William, 112–13, 151, 165

Slave narratives, 99–101, 244

Slave Power Conspiracy: and accusation of disunion, 10; and process of disunion, 12, 128; and Democratic Party, 131; and Liberty Party, 147; and Latimer controversy, 162, 164; and Polk, 182, 185; North's alienation from, 190, 202; and Mexican War, 196; and Bailey, 207; and Chase, 217; and Seward, 220, 318; and popular sovereignty, 226; Frederick Douglass on, 238, 303–4; and threats of disunion, 253, 301, 302, 338; and Missouri Compromise, 255; political dominance of, 257, 316; and American Party, 258; and Kansas Territory, 260, 305; and Republican Party, 262–63, 267, 304, 319, 338, 339; free blacks on, 264; and radical abolitionists, 266; and Sumner, 271; and free speech, 283; and filibusters, 286; and *Dred Scott* decision, 295, 300–304, 305; Helper on, 312

Slave rebellion: and abolitionism, 9, 74, 78–79, 84, 85, 102, 168; fears of, 45–46, 51, 52, 53, 91, 102, 110; and Vesey, 50–52, 78; and revolutionary evangelicalism, 63, 64, 67; John Rankin on, 67; and Turner, 74–79, 80, 83, 84, 92, 110, 178; punishing of, 76–77; causes of, 85

Slave resistance: culture of, 63; and David Walker, 74; forms of, 77; and rise of black militancy, 239–40; and disunion as retributive justice, 251; and John Brown, 326. *See also* Slave rebellion

Slavery debates: and Mexican War, 1, 10, 181; and prophecy of disunion, 6; and threats of disunion, 7–9, 32, 36, 43, 82, 122; and accusations of disunion, 9–11; "positive good" defense of slavery, 15, 42, 46, 51–52, 82, 83–84, 117, 118, 167, 203, 217, 290, 297; and Garrison, 15, 74; and moral issues, 16, 32, 39, 42, 43, 46, 48, 53, 64, 70, 73, 110, 118, 124; and compromise on slavery, 39, 188, 189, 191, 193–94; and admission of new states, 39–41; and republicanism, 41, 42, 45, 49, 83; and diffusion argument, 41–42, 46, 48, 74, 115, 168, 174, 181, 185, 306; and colonization, 48–50, 57, 62, 79–80, 81, 92, 101, 115, 143–44, 146, 155, 238, 358–59 (n. 33), 364 (n. 37); and constitutional issues, 49, 154–55, 157–64, 202, 220, 223, 238, 253, 263, 280, 300, 305; and national security, 53; and balance between agrarian and manufacturing interests, 57, 60; "necessary evil" defense of slavery, 72, 82, 84, 117, 217, 288; and partisanship, 105–7; and gag rule, 110; comparative defense of slavery, 117, 288; and election of 1840, 143–44, 147–48; and *Creole* case, 159–60; and Texas annexation, 165–68, 174; and economics, 177, 311; and Protestant churches, 177–80, 216; and territorial expansion, 199–202, 206, 207, 210, 211–12, 225, 297–300, 309, 334; and Lincoln-Douglas debates, 315–17

Slave system: conditions of, 17–18, 66–67, 76, 81, 83, 99–100, 117, 138–39, 203, 240, 246, 280, 288–89, 290;

origins of, 18, 19–20; complicity of North in, 60, 69, 70–71, 78, 103, 128, 133, 139, 153, 235, 266, 282; security of, 68, 77, 80, 119; inferiority of blacks as premise of, 73, 290, 364 (n. 39); South's economic investment in, 82; and paternalism, 100, 240, 244; scriptural support for, 109, 178–79, 290; gendered language concerning, 187–88; and moral issues, 245, 246, 290

Slave trade: and Constitutional Convention, 23–24; U.S. Congressional debates on, 32; and threats of disunion, 36; Virginia's support for, 48; and free blacks, 49, 72; and abolitionism, 96; and constitutional issues, 153; and *Amistad* case, 159; in District of Columbia, 206, 209, 212, 222, 226; and sectional differences, 212; and Stowe, 244; campaign to reopen, 294–95, 314, 318, 324, 325

Smith, Alfred A., 325

Smith, Gerrit, 96, 145, 147, 148, 253, 263, 265, 278, 327

Smith, James McCune, 265

Smith, Perry, 146–47

Smith, William A., 290, 293

Smith, William Loughton, 32, 42, 43, 46, 52, 178

South: economic interests of, 2, 3, 82, 257, 263; political leadership tied to slavery, 17, 39, 40; agrarian independence of, 36; and Missouri Compromise, 47; divisions within, 47, 82; balance of power with North, 53; Unionists of, 123, 339–40, 343, 344, 398 (n. 10); gendered language concerning, 187–88; and woman's rights, 205. *See also* Deep South; Secessionists and secessionism; Sectional differences; Slavery debates; Slave system; States' rights; Upper South

South, The (Richmond), 308

Southern Baptist Convention, 178

Southern Commercial Convention, 314

Southern Literary Messenger, 246

Southern Quarterly Review, 246, 385 (n. 23)

Southwest, 37, 39

Spratt, Leonidas W., 294, 324

Stampp, Kenneth, 3, 279–80, 301

Stanly, Edward, 224

Stanton, Edwin, 210

Stanton, Elizabeth Cady, 203–5

Stanton, Frederick P., 307, 312

Stanton, Henry, 204

States' rights: South's preoccupation with, 3; Jefferson on, 34, 58; Madison on, 34, 58; and threats of disunion, 36, 58, 153, 179, 221–22, 228, 230; and Missouri crisis, 45, 46, 47; and tariffs, 57, 87, 93; and doctrine of state interposition, 57–58, 87, 89; Webster on, 59; and constitutional issues, 94, 179, 192; and Democratic Party, 94, 229–30, 274; and Whig Party, 106, 143; and Tyler, 148; and national expansion, 184; and disunion as program, 210; and Nashville Convention, 223; and Fugitive Slave Law, 237; and Pierce, 249; and secessionism, 325

States' Rights Party (Mississippi), 314

State v. Mann (1830), 139

Staunton Spectator, 346

Staunton Vindicator, 337

Stearns, George L., 327

Stephens, Alexander, 209, 211, 225, 228, 248

Stewart, Alvan, 145, 154

Stewart, James A., 398 (n. 10)

Stewart, James Brewer, 70, 157

Stewart, Maria, 65, 69

Still, William, 236, 242–43

Story, Joseph, 157–59, 162, 163

Stowe, Harriet Beecher, 137, 140, 243–48, 251, 254, 280, 384–85 (n. 23)

Strader v. Graham (1851), 297

Streichler, Stuart, 298, 299

Sumner, Charles, 195, 237, 253, 255, 263, 268–71, 278, 301

Swisshelm, Jane Grey, 203, 205

Tallmadge, James, Jr., 39, 40, 41, 43–46, 121, 146

Taney, Roger Brooke, 158, 296–300, 302, 304, 316, 317, 391 (n. 42)

Tappan, Lewis, 61, 96, 144–45, 155, 177–78, 207

Tariffs: and nullification controversy, 52, 87, 91, 92; and National Republicans, 56, 57; and sectional differences, 57, 58–59; and Jackson, 58, 92–93, 95; and Compromise Tariff, 90, 170; and constitutional issues, 94; and Texas annexation, 170; and Polk, 185; and Buchanan, 320

Taylor, John (of Virginia), 36, 45, 223

Taylor, John W. (of New York), 40

Taylor, Susie King, 347

Taylor, William R., 137

Taylor, Zachary: and Mexican War, 181, 183; and election of 1848, 200–201,

206, 248; and Calhoun, 207–8; and territorial expansion, 210–12; and Compromise of 1850, 225; death of, 225–26

Temperance, 203, 258

Tenth Amendment, 26, 36

Territorial expansion: and accusations of disunion, 10; and slavery debates, 199–202, 206, 207, 210, 211–12, 225, 297–300, 309, 334; and Taylor, 208, 210, 212; and Compromise of 1850, 212–13, 222; and Yancey, 224; and Kansas-Nebraska Act, 251–59

Tertium Quids, 36–37, 45, 58, 223

Texas, Republic of, slavery in, 127–28

Texas annexation: and antislavery petitions, 127, 128–30, 150; and Tyler, 129, 149, 166, 167–70, 173–74, 175; and antislavery movement, 164, 165, 190; and U.S. Congress, 172–77; and Polk, 175, 184–85, 208; and Mexican War, 180–81

Texas State Gazette, 308

Thacher, George, 251

Thayer, Eli, 310

Thirteenth Amendment, 345–46

Thomas, Jesse B., 46, 47, 48

Thoreau, Henry David, 196–97, 329

Three-fifths compromise, 23, 37, 39, 40, 147, 153

Toombs, Robert, 209, 211, 225, 228, 248, 286, 307, 308, 313, 333

Treason: and accusations of disunion, 5, 34, 43, 90, 151, 152, 300, 332, 337–38, 341, 397 (n. 6); abolition associated with, 9, 78, 103; and threats of disunion, 15–16, 230; nullification as, 59; and Wilmot Proviso opposition, 189;

and disunion petitions, 215; and Fugitive Slave Law, 236, 241; and Free-Soil Party, 266; and John Brown, 329, 333

Treaty of Guadalupe Hidalgo, 200–201

True American, 176

Trumbull, Lyman, 279, 323

Truth, Sojourner, 205

Tubman, Harriet, 77, 242, 243

Tucker, Nathaniel Beverly, 120–21, 136, 223, 228, 229

Turnbull, Robert J., 52

Turner, Nat, 74–79, 80, 83, 84, 92, 110, 178

Tyler, John: and Texas annexation, 129, 149, 166, 167–70, 173–74, 175; and election of 1840, 143, 144, 145, 148, 157; and veto power, 149; and *Amistad* case, 158; and *Creole* case, 160; and tariff of 1842, 170–71

Tyranny: and threat of disunion, 15–16, 74; and Revolutionary rhetoric, 20; of slaveholders, 140; and Jackson, 143; and Mexican War, 183; and national expansion, 184; and slave system, 190; and Wilmot Proviso, 191; and states' rights, 211; and Calhoun, 216; and Seward, 263, 309; and *Dred Scott* decision, 303

Underground Railroad, 66, 67, 72, 77, 148, 236, 241–43, 326

Underwood, John, 283

Union (newspaper), 44

Union Party, 228

U.S. Army, 183, 195, 268

U.S. Congress: and Revolutionary War debts of states, 31; and location of

U.S. capital, 31, 32; and Hartford Convention, 39; and 1819-21 Missouri crisis, 39–44, 46–47; and North's demographic advantage, 40, 129; and tariff debates, 58; and antislavery petitions, 109–14, 116–21, 127, 128, 130, 145–46; and Texas annexation, 172–77; and Wilmot Proviso, 186–91, 197; and Speaker of the House debate, 208–10; and Taylor, 210–11; and disunion petitions, 213–14; and Compromise of 1850, 226; and Kansas-Nebraska Act, 254–56; legislative discretion in territories, 298–99

U.S. Supreme Court, 95, 154, 155, 157–60, 295–304, 317

Upper South: Deep South differentiated from, 4; manumission in post-Revolutionary era, 22, 66, 354 (n. 11); and antislavery movement, 66–68; anti-nullification opinion in, 123; and conditions of slavery, 139; and threats of disunion, 211; and gradual emancipation, 280; and Southern Commercial Conventions, 314; and secessionism, 339; Unionists of, 340

Upshur, Abel P., 151, 166, 167, 209

Van Buren, Martin: and Democratic Party, 56, 57, 140, 184–85; and Jackson, 93, 105, 106; and election of 1836, 106, 107; and gag rule, 110; propaganda against, 120; and Texas annexation, 129–30; and election of 1840, 141, 142, 143, 148; and *Amistad* case, 141, 145, 154, 155, 157; and election of 1844, 149, 167, 173; and election of 1848, 201–2, 206

Vanderpoel, Aaron, 122

Van Dyke, Henry J., 340–41

Van Lew, Elizabeth, 330, 398 (n. 10)

Van Rensellear, Thomas, 195

Vesey, Denmark, 50–52, 63, 78

Virginia resolution (1798), 34, 36, 57–58, 230, 299

Voting rights, 56, 77, 80, 105, 204, 279, 345

Wage labor. *See* Free labor ideology

Waldstreicher, David, 20

Walker, David, 63–65, 67, 69, 74, 75, 79, 84, 251, 269, 362 (n. 20)

Walker, Freeman, 43, 52

Walker, Robert J., 90, 168, 174, 181, 305–6

Walker, William, 286, 314

Walther, Eric, 321

Ward, Samuel Ringgold, 108, 220

War of 1812, 37, 40, 56, 115, 116, 129

Washburn, Israel, Jr., 256, 323

Washburne, Elihu B., 255

Washington, George, 21, 24, 33–34, 183, 284

Washington Daily Union, 214, 219, 300

Webster, Daniel: and prophecies of disunion, 7, 59; oratorical style of, 7, 105; and compromises, 8; and process of sectional alienation, 12; and Hayne, 58–59, 90; and banking, 94; as Whig candidate, 106; and Southern Unionists, 123; and election of 1840, 143; and *Creole* case, 160; and Texas annexation, 166; and Calhoun, 217–19, 222, 228; and Fillmore, 226; and Texas boundary, 226

Weekly Advocate, 114

Weld, Angelina Grimké, 98, 124, 130–32, 134, 138–40, 144, 187

Weld, Theodore, 61, 96, 133, 138–40, 187

West: and slavery debates, 10, 46, 181, 191, 194, 306; regional interests of, 37; and Jackson, 56, 92; and martial manhood, 168; and Texas annexation, 168, 171, 306; and free labor ideology, 185, 203; racism in, 280

Wheatley, Phillis, 20, 364 (n. 39)

Whig Party: emergence of, 105, 106; and gag rule, 111–12, 113, 117, 146; and sectional differences, 111–12, 117, 191, 193, 199–200, 211, 212, 228, 248; and Texas annexation, 129, 165–66, 168–72, 174–75; and anti-abolitionism, 133; and women's partisanship, 136; and election of 1840, 140, 141–44, 145, 146–47, 148, 200; and abolitionism, 157, 184; and election of 1844, 169, 171–72; and antislavery movement, 176; and Mexican War, 182, 183; and Wilmot Proviso, 184, 186, 188, 190, 191, 193, 222; and territorial expansion, 193, 199–200, 212; and election of 1848, 200–201; and Speaker of the House debate, 208–9; and process of disunion, 211; and threats of disunion, 211; and Compromise of 1850, 224, 227; and Texas boundary, 226; and election of 1852, 248–51; and Kansas-Nebraska Act, 253; and Republican Party, 257, 278; and American Party, 258, 259, 274; and election of 1856, 274–75; and Lincoln, 279

White supremacy, 60, 183, 279. *See also* Racism

White women: Southern ban on interracial liaisons, 18; planters' supremacy over, 19; and immediatism, 61, 84, 96; and gradualism, 79, 80, 81, 83, 84; and separate spheres, 96–97, 130, 131, 132, 135, 187, 204, 205, 245, 254; and anti-slavery petitions, 110, 130–31; and female oratory, 131–35, 136; and accusations of disunion, 132; and plantation fiction, 136–37; and pro-slavery ideology, 136–38; and Northern domestic fiction, 137; and sentimental fiction, 187; and disunion petitions, 214; as Stowe's audience, 244, 245; and Republican Party, 285–86

Whiting, Anne, 284

Whitman, Walt, 185, 189, 329, 378 (n. 36)

Whittier, John Greanleaf, 329

Wicks, Elizabeth, 97

Wigfall, Louis T., 291

Wilberforce, William, 119, 150

Wilentz, Sean, 3, 33, 210, 219, 296

Wilmot, David, 10, 12, 182, 184–88, 190, 191–92, 208, 279

Wilmot Proviso: and slavery debates, 10, 182, 184–86; and Free-Soil Party, 184, 189–90, 192, 196, 202–3, 263–64; and sectional differences, 184–85, 191–94, 208, 215; and abolitionists, 186, 190, 192, 194–97; gendered language concerning, 186–88, 189, 190–91, 196; and U.S. Congress, 186–91, 197; and enslavement metaphor, 188; and threats of disunion, 189–90, 194; Southern reactions to, 191–94, 195, 197; and process of disunion, 194;

and Taylor, 201, 208, 212; and Compromise of 1850, 213; and Seward, 220; and Foote, 222; and disunion as retributive justice, 251; and Revolutionary ideals, 351 (n. 7)

Wilson, Henry, 310, 311, 323, 333

Winthrop, James, 25

Winthrop, Robert C., 174, 208

Wise, Henry A., 113, 150–51, 165, 261–62, 307, 308, 312

Wolf, Eva Sheppard, 45, 80, 354 (n. 11)

Woman's rights: disunionism associated with, 9, 132; and abolitionists, 144–45, 205; and Liberty Party, 147; and Free-Soil Party, 203; and African American women, 204–5; and European radicalism, 215; Frances Harper, 242–43; and Stowe, 245, 246; Butler on, 254; and Republican Party, 276

Women. *See* African American women; Gender egalitarianism; White women; Woman's rights

World Antislavery Convention, 145, 150, 203

Wright, Fanny, 131, 132, 205

Wright, Hendrick B., 253

Wright, Henry C., 161–62, 302, 304

Wright, Silas, Jr., 167

Wyatt-Brown, Bertram, 3, 190

Yancey, William Lowndes, 223, 224, 291, 314–15, 322, 324, 325, 397 (n. 6)

York Democratic Press, 275

Young America movement, 184

Young Men's Anti-Slavery Society of New York, 122

Zaeske, Susan, 110